"In Nature's infinite book of secrecy, a little I can read."

—William Shakespeare

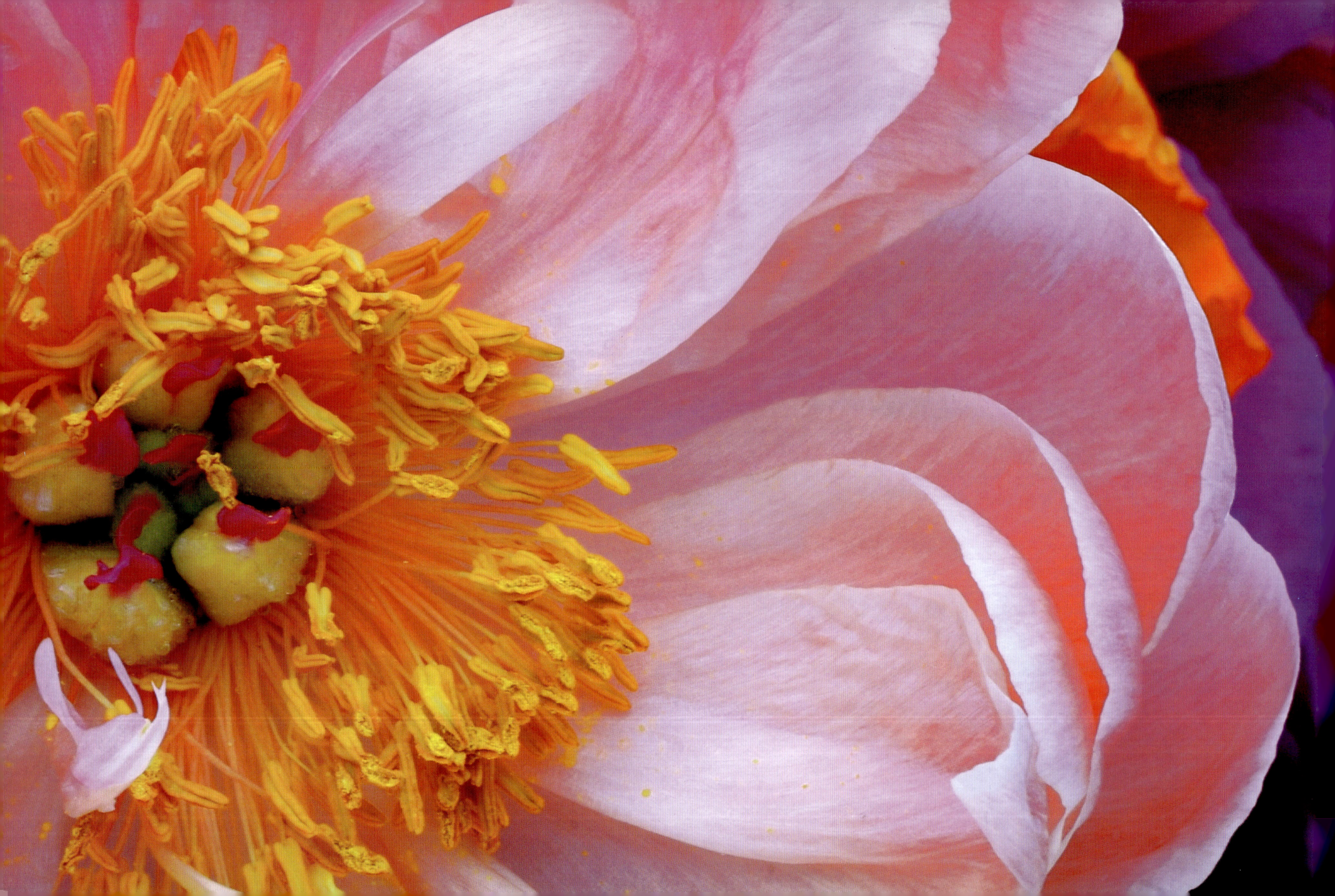

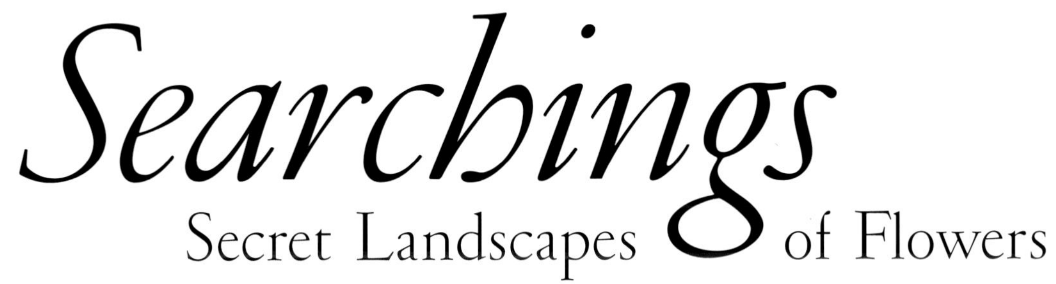

Barbara Bordnick

WELCOME BOOKS
NEW YORK & SAN FRANCISCO

PLATE 1: *Paeonia* (preceding spread)
PLATE 2: *Tulipa* (following spread)

For Rose and Morris.
And, for Phyllis, perhaps the most beautiful flower of them all.

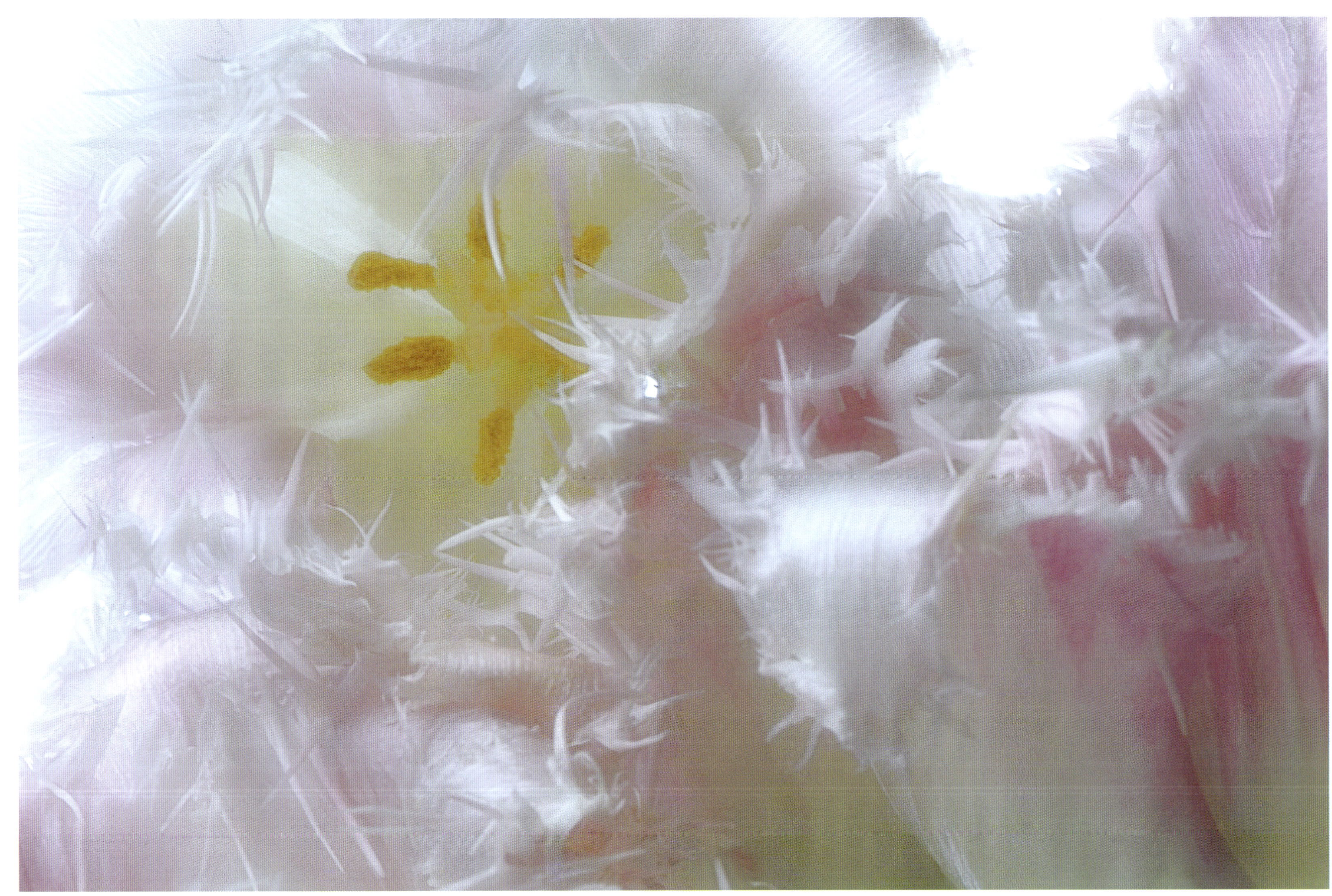

THERE WAS A LITTLE GIRL who, when she needed a quiet empty space where the images in her head could come to life, would run to bed and pull the covers over her head. In the darkness, safe from the demands of the adult world, images would tumble out every which way, taking on their own life until she was surrounded. There, for a time before sleep, she would watch as they rythmically changed sizes, textures, shapes, and colors, continually forming new worlds.

By morning her imaginings would have have filled volumes.

This book is the most recent manifestation of those imaginative adventures . . . *searchings*.

—Barbara Bordnick, New York City, July 2002

I

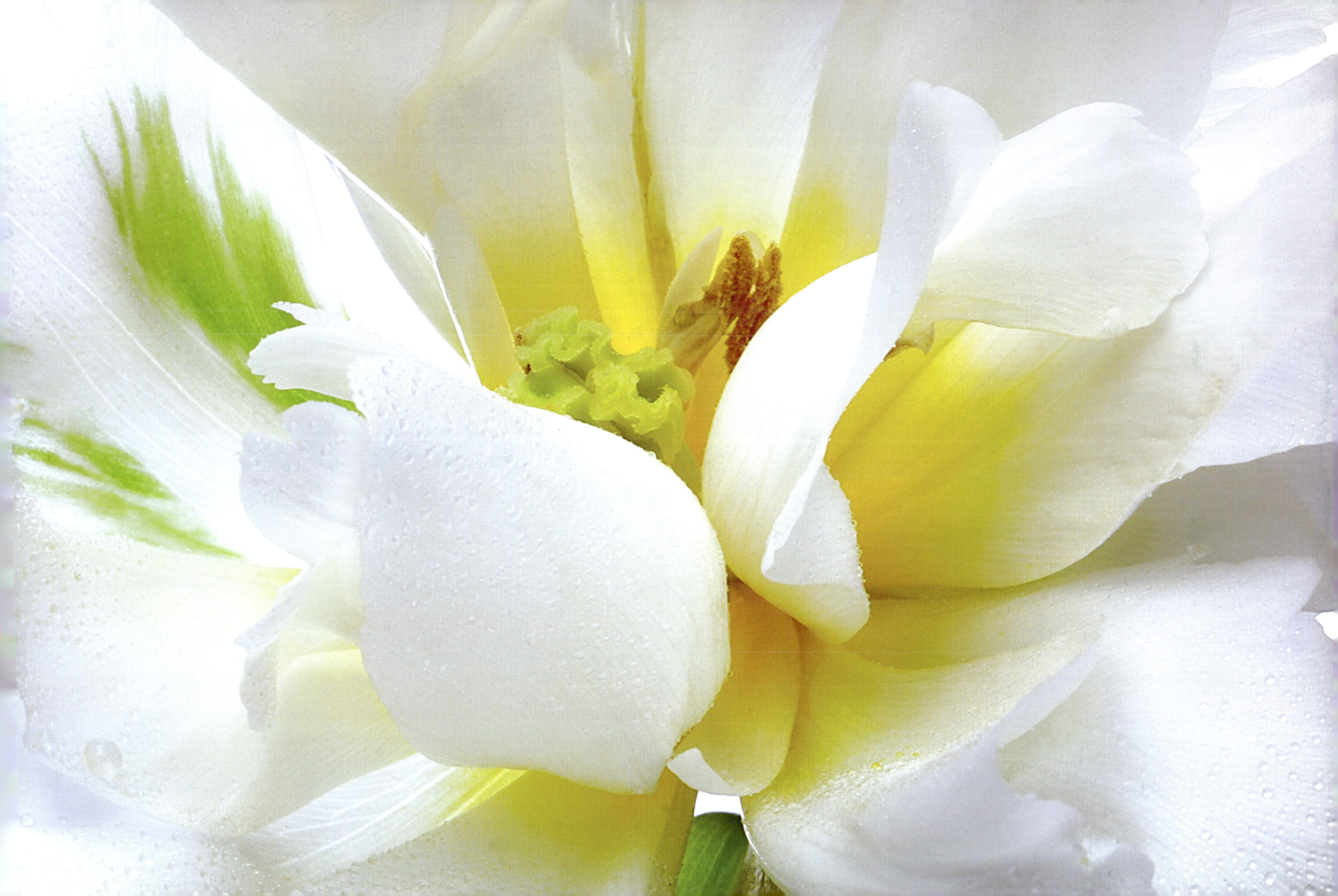

PLATE 3: *Tulipa* (preceding page)

PLATE 4: *Phalaenopsis*

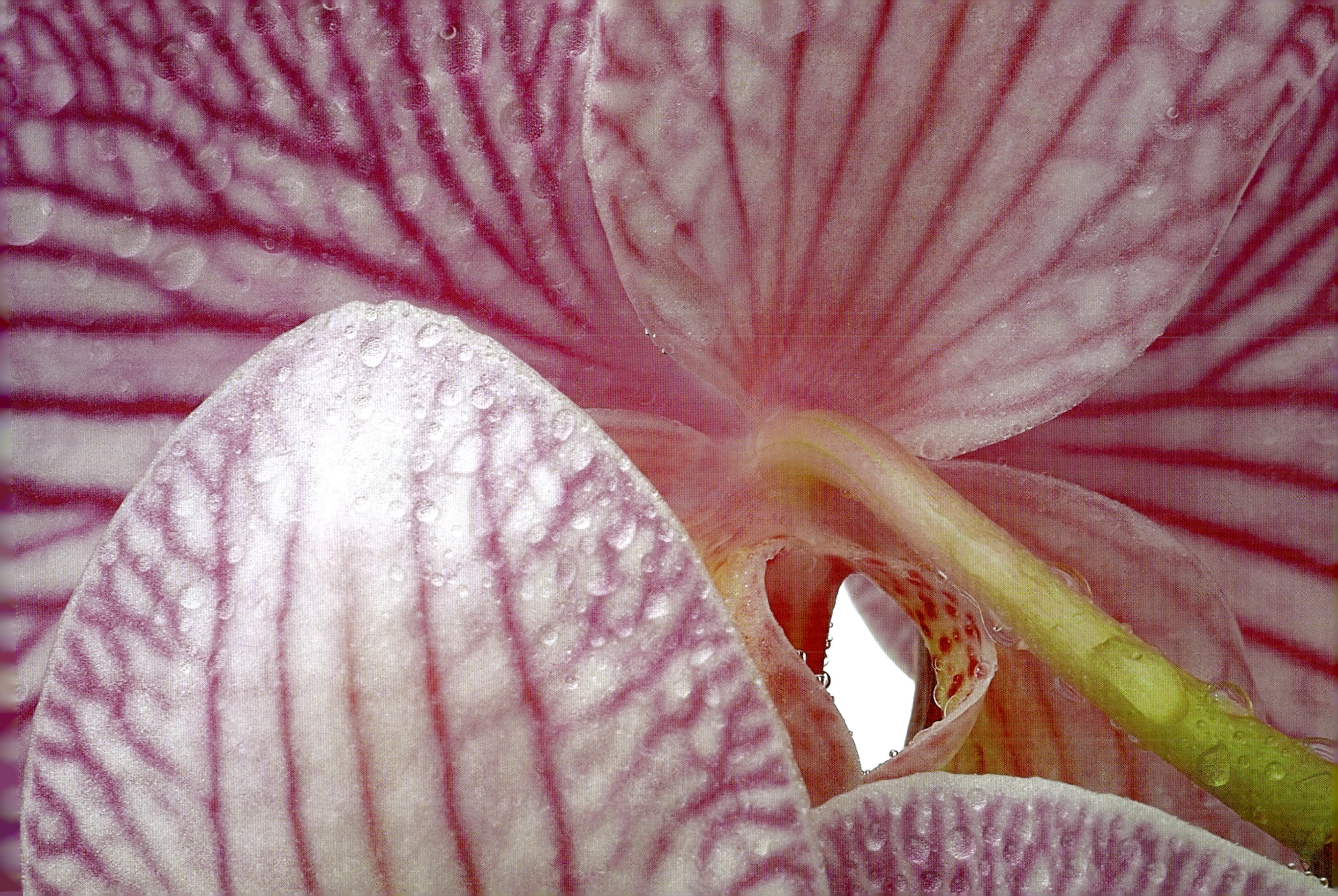

PLATE 5: *Phalaenopsis*

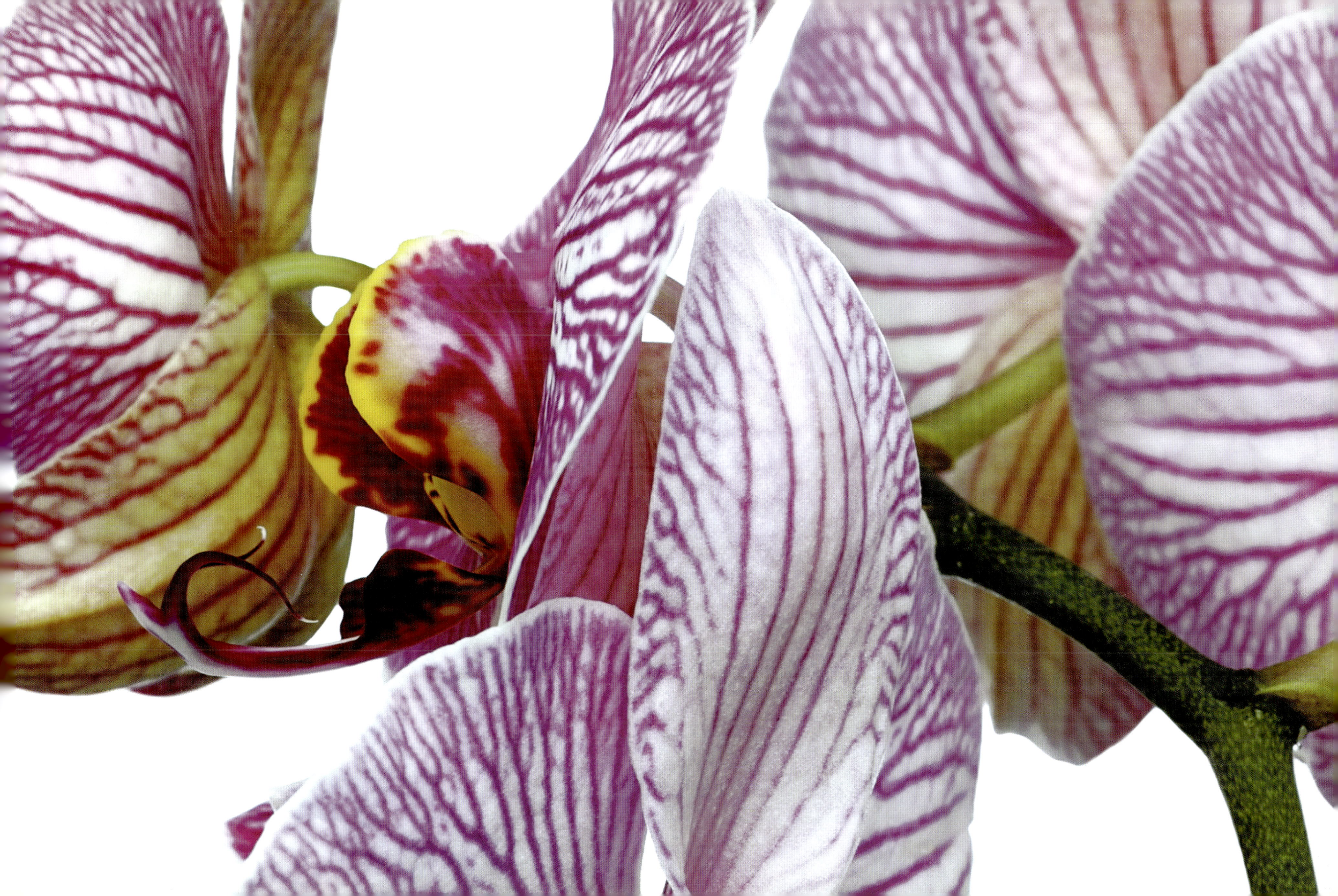

PLATE 6 : *Hyacinthus orientalis*

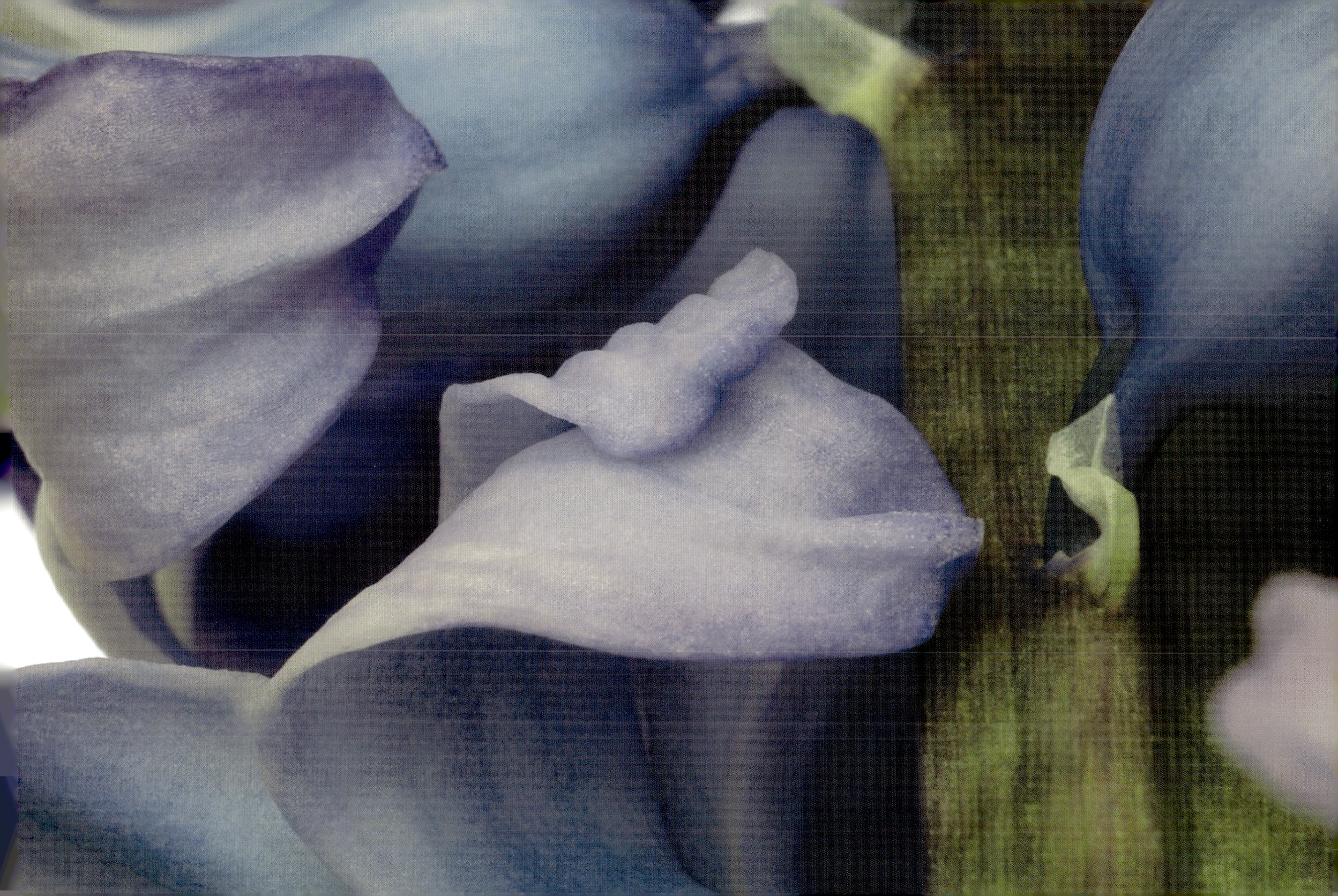

PLATE 7: *Phalaenopsis*

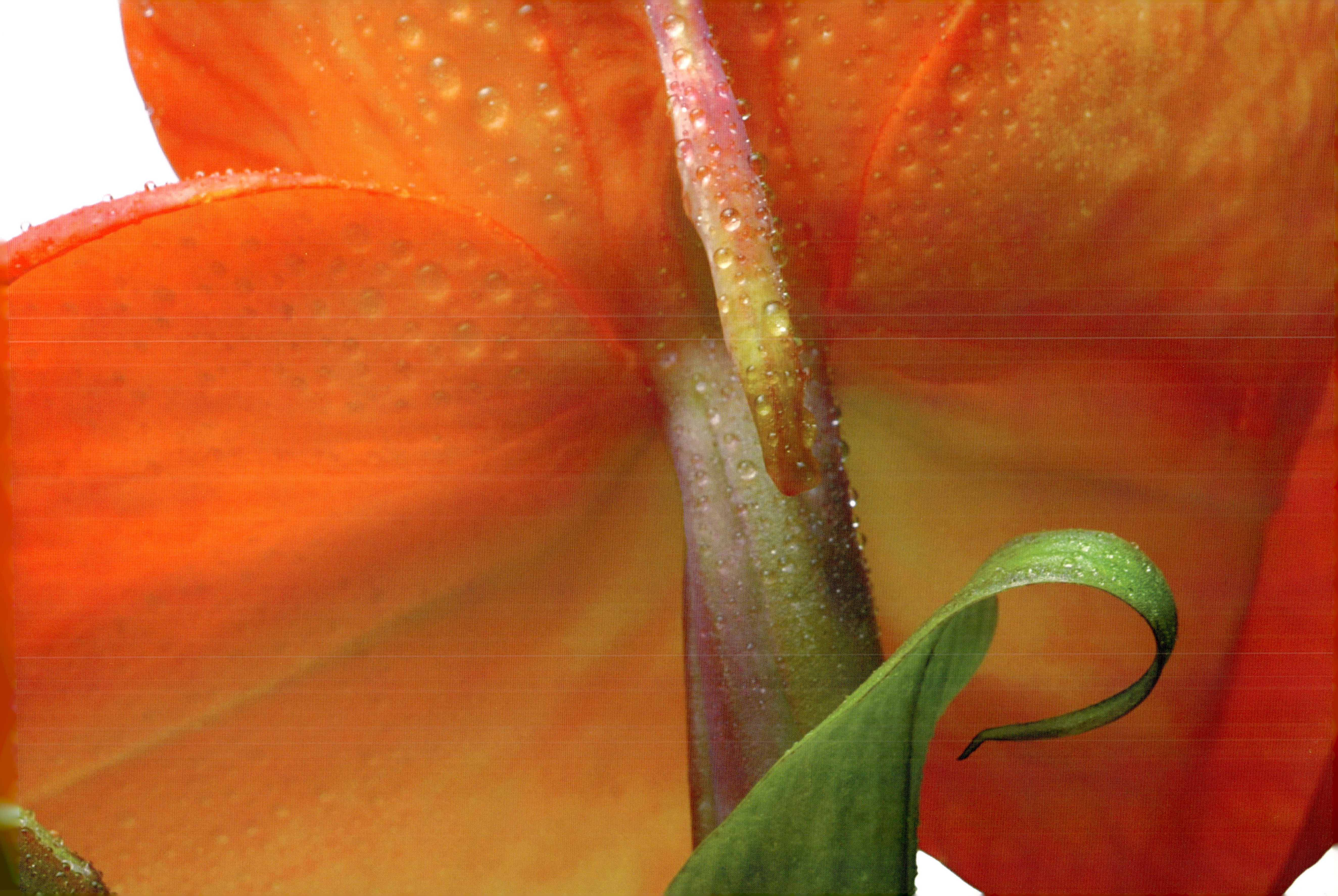

PLATE 8: *Dahlia*

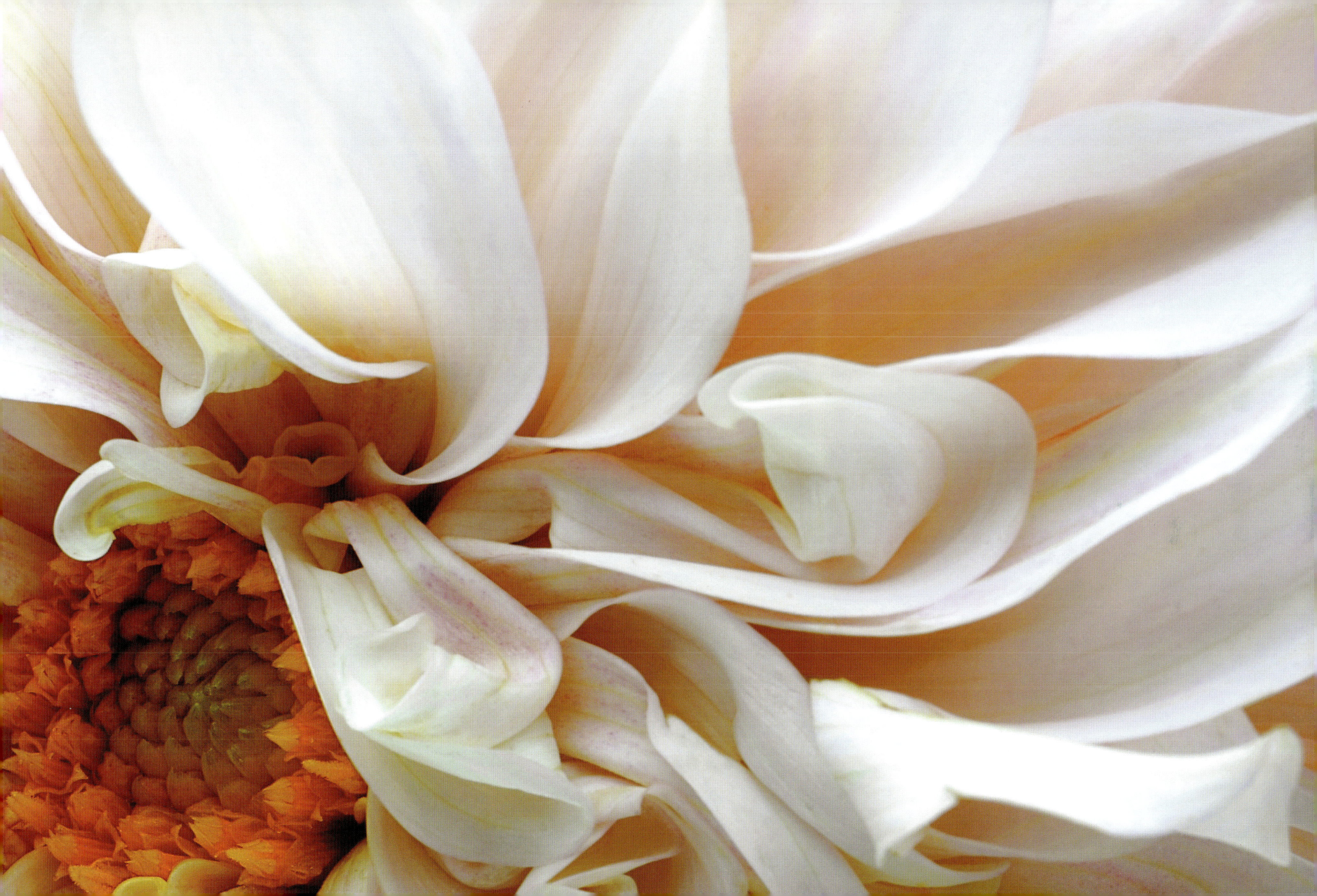

PLATES 9, 10, & 11: *Helleborus* x *hybridus* (opposite and following pages)

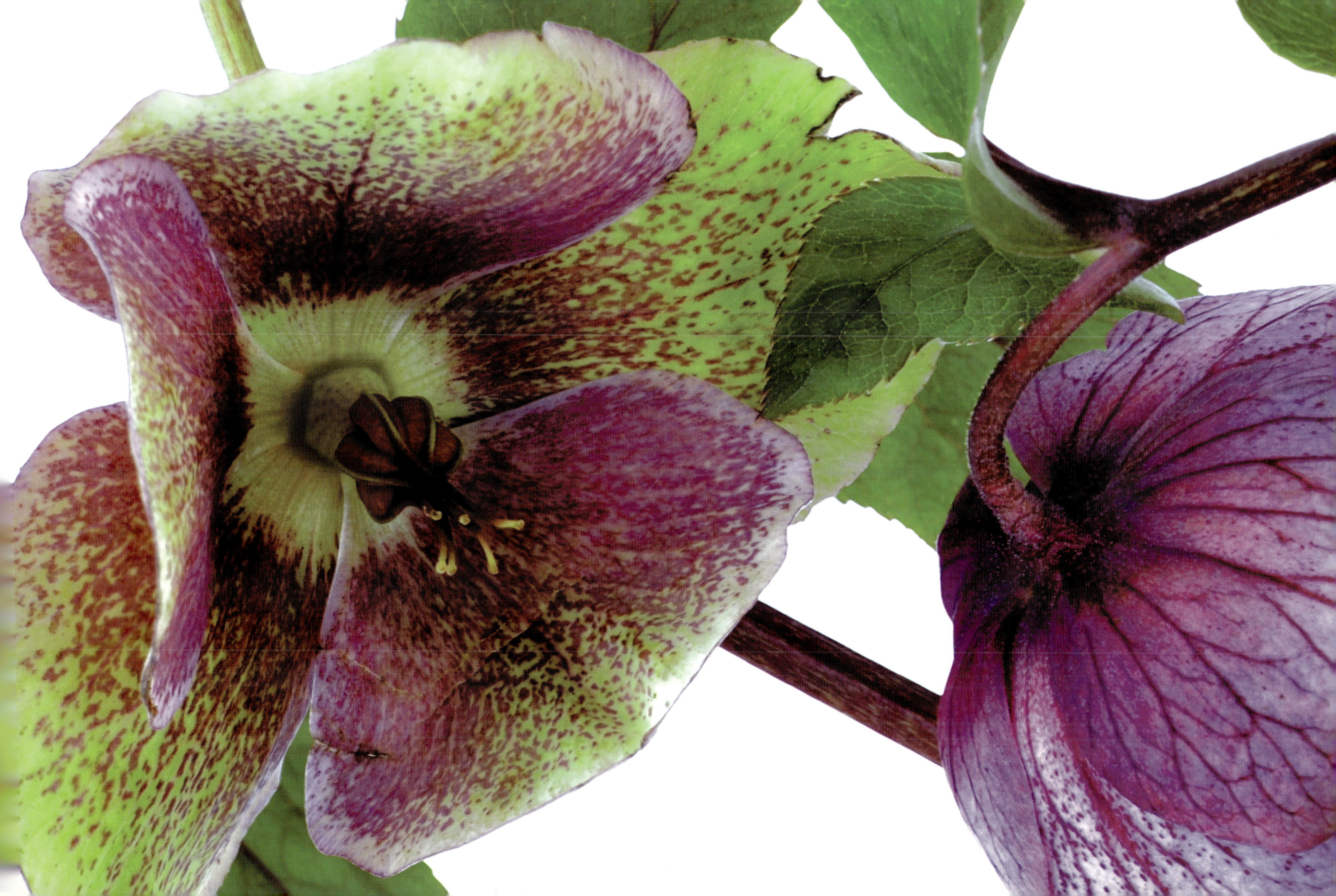

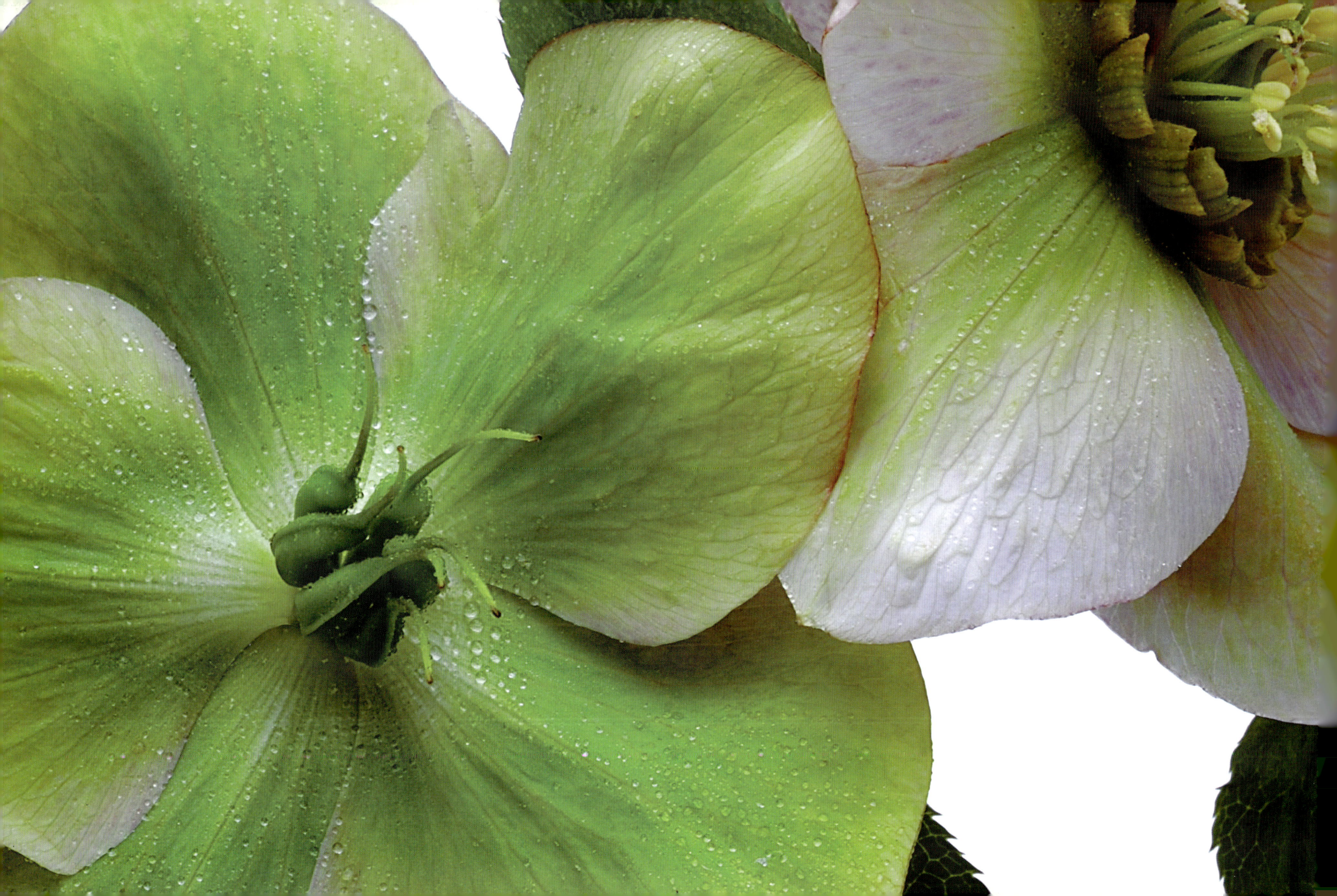

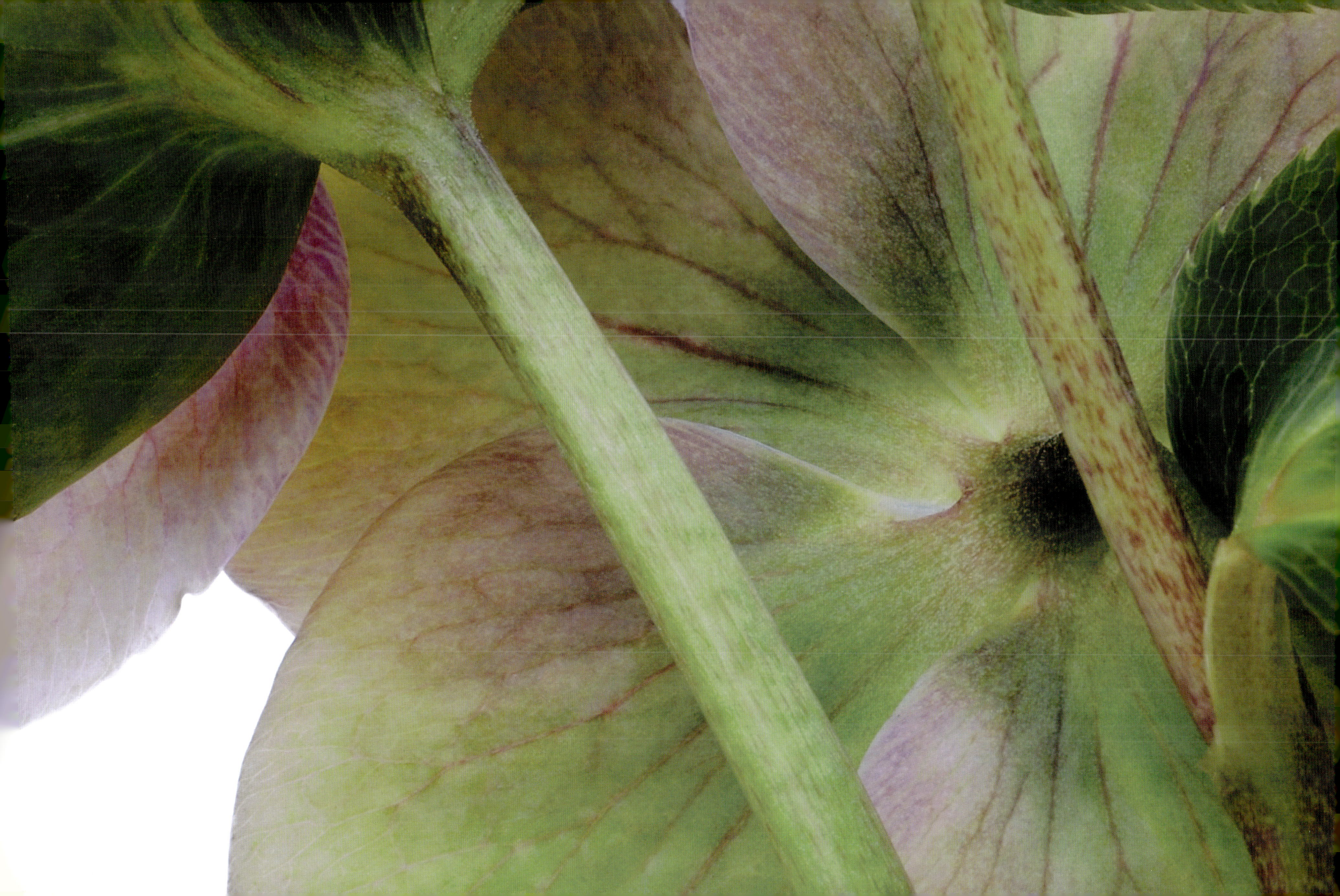

PLATE 12 : *Hyacinthus orientalis*

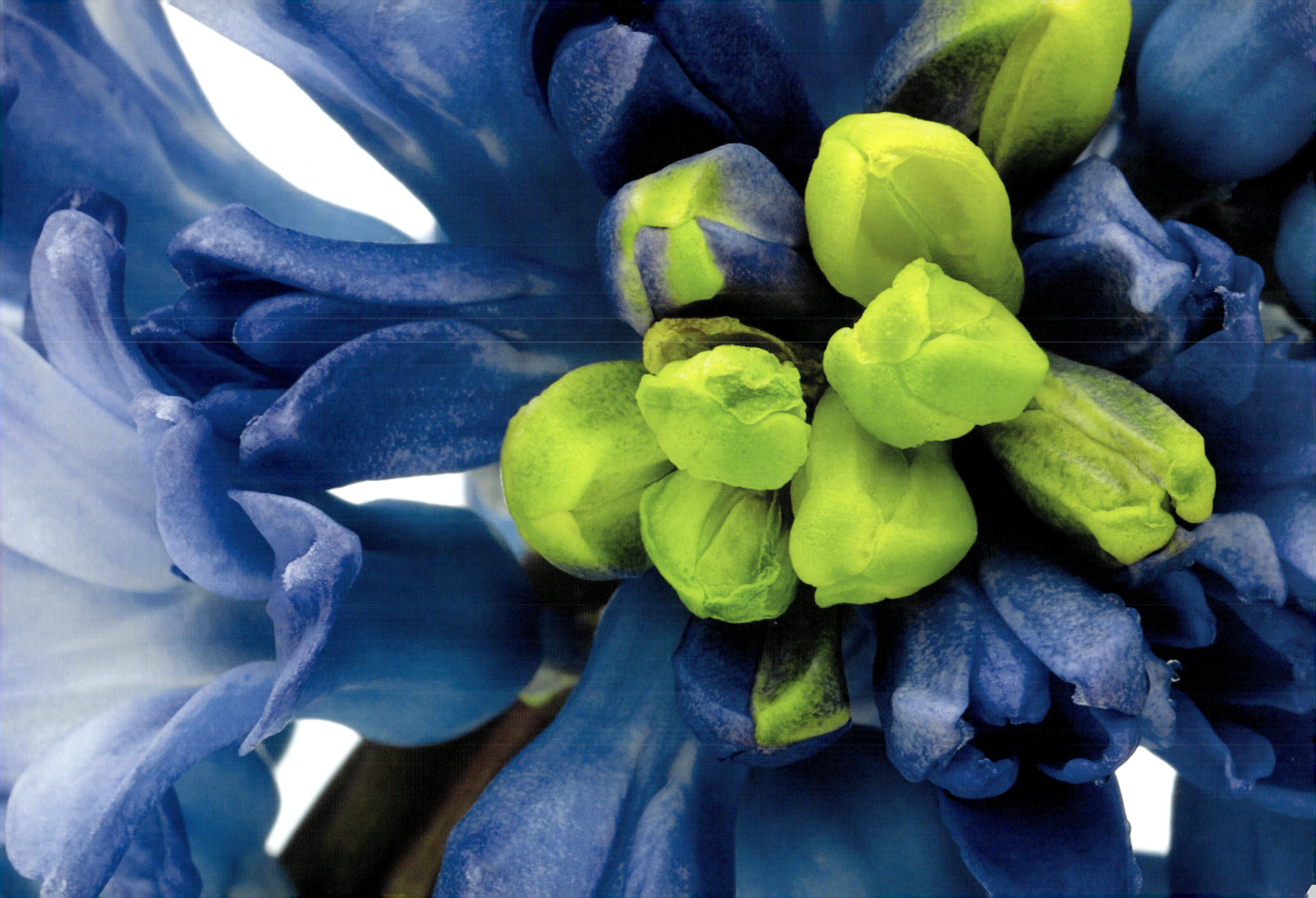

PLATE 13: *Tulipa*

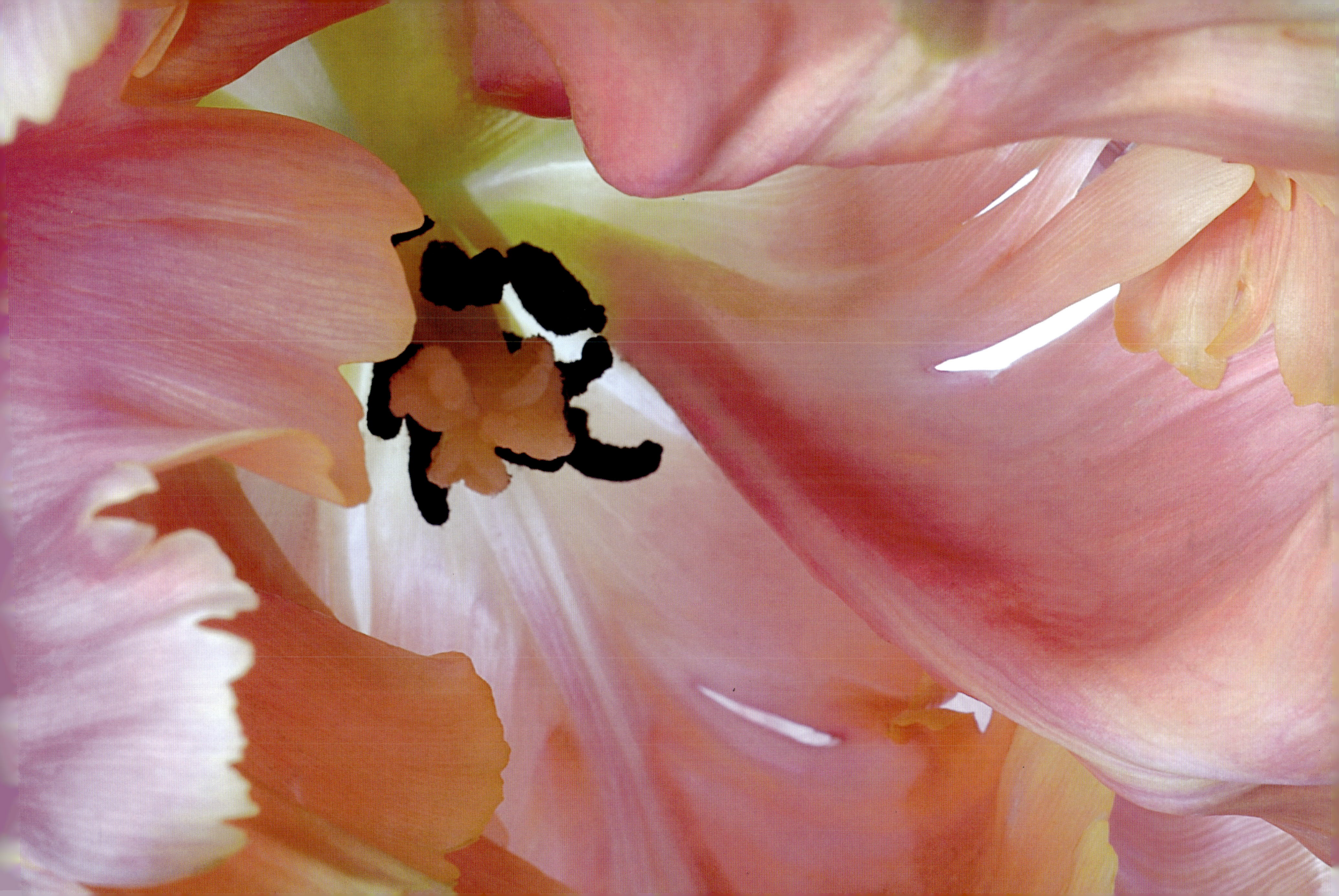

PLATE 14 : *Ranunculus*

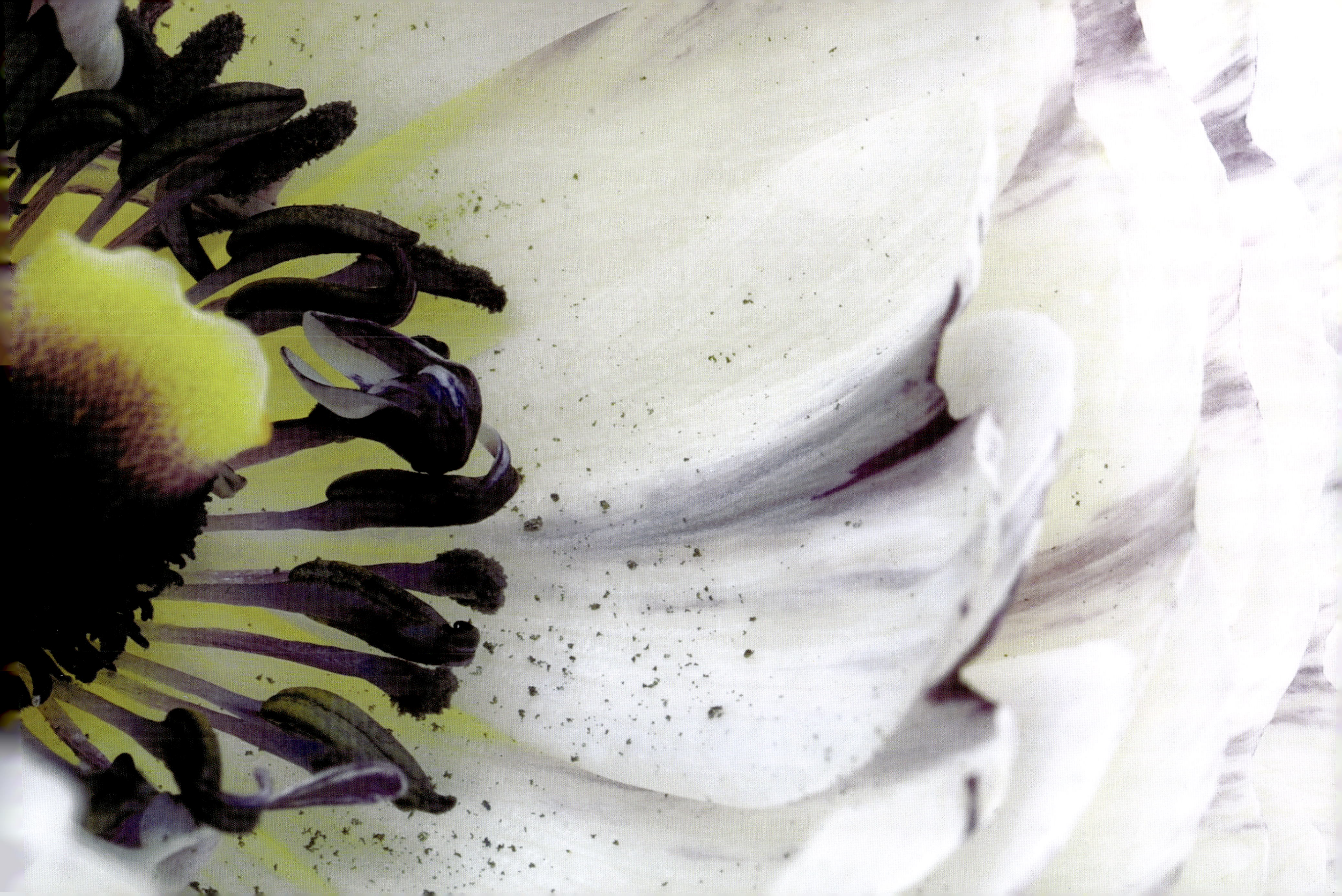

PLATE 15: *Paeonia*

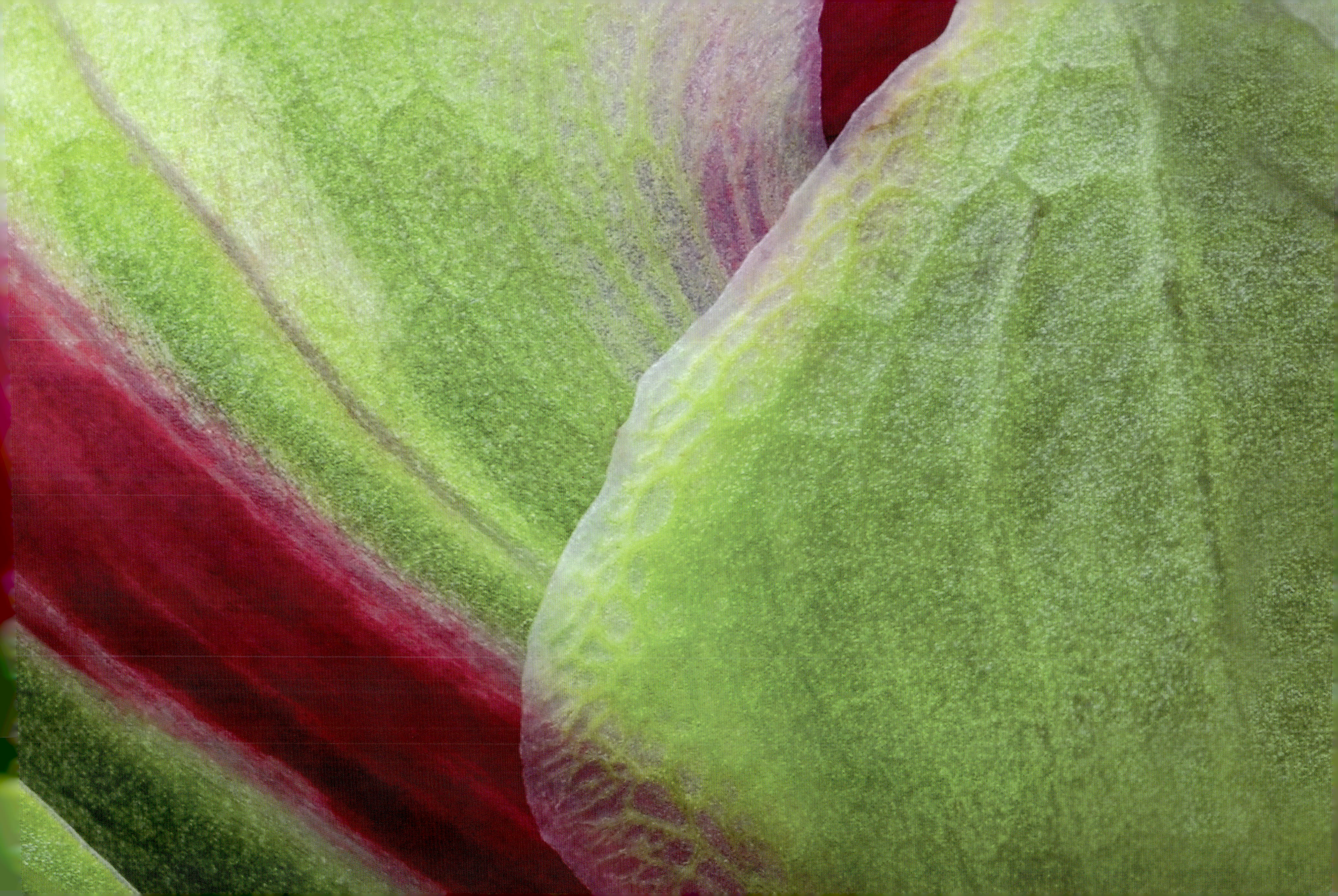

PLATE 16 : *Hydrangea macrophylla*

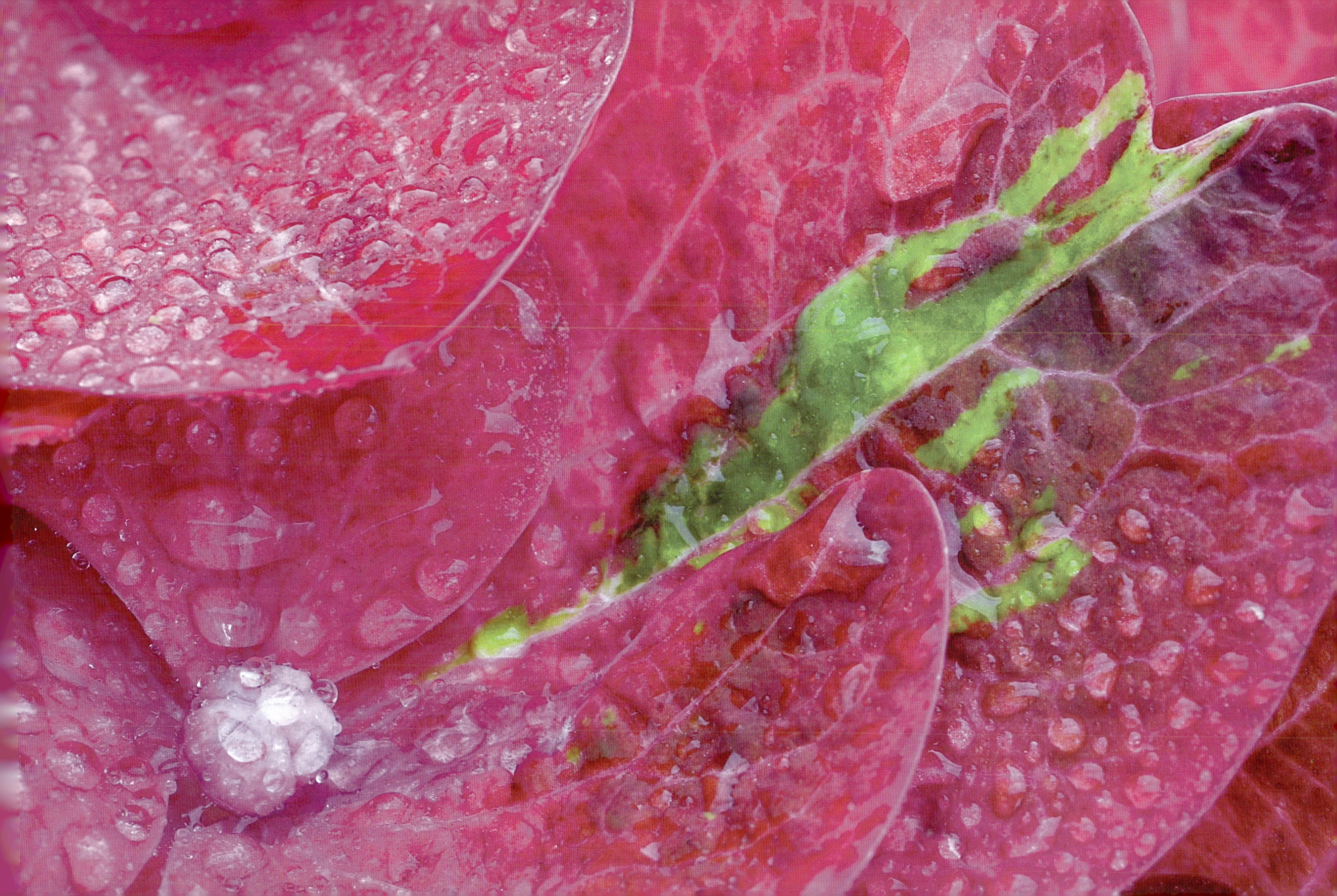

PLATE 17 : *Ranunculus*

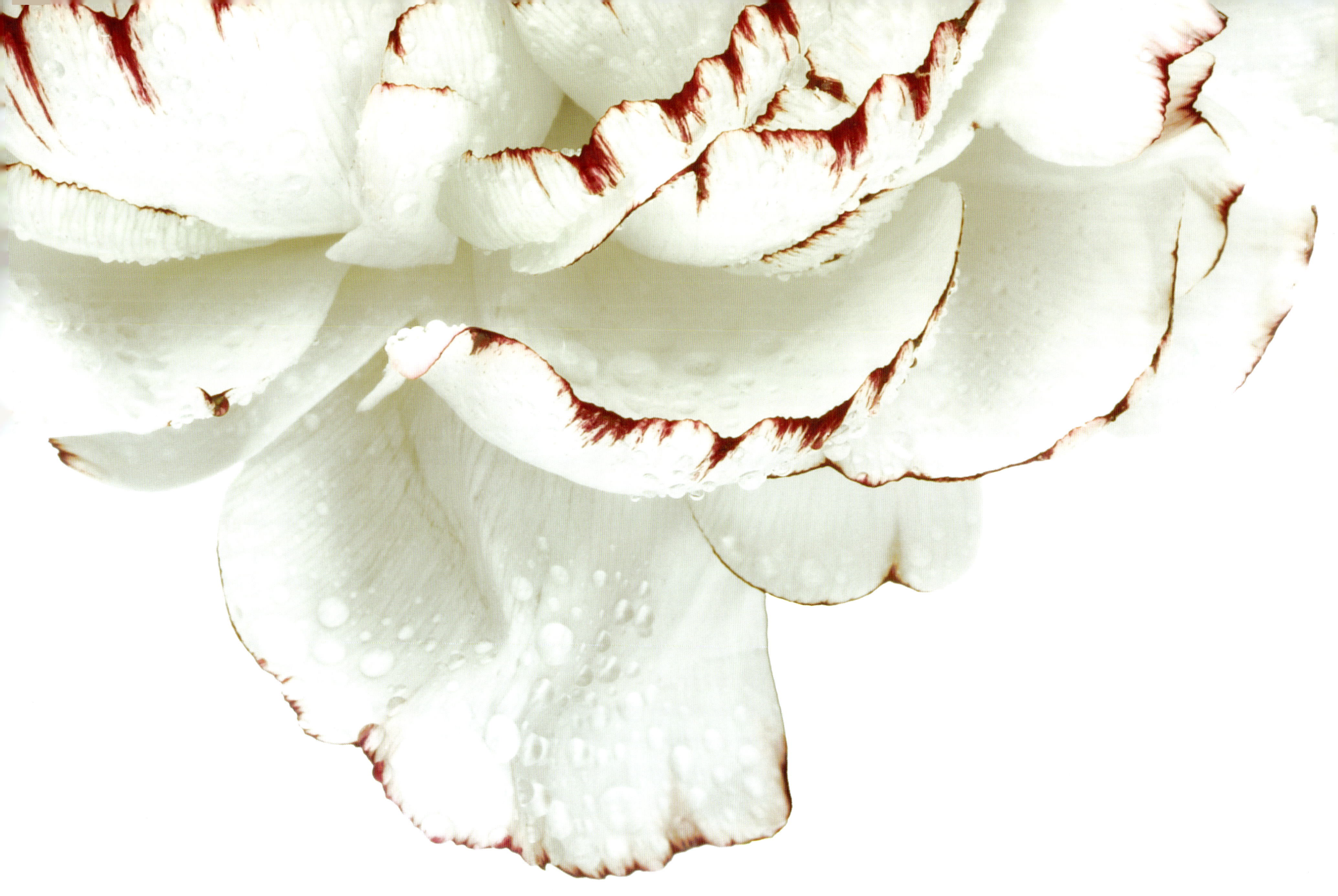

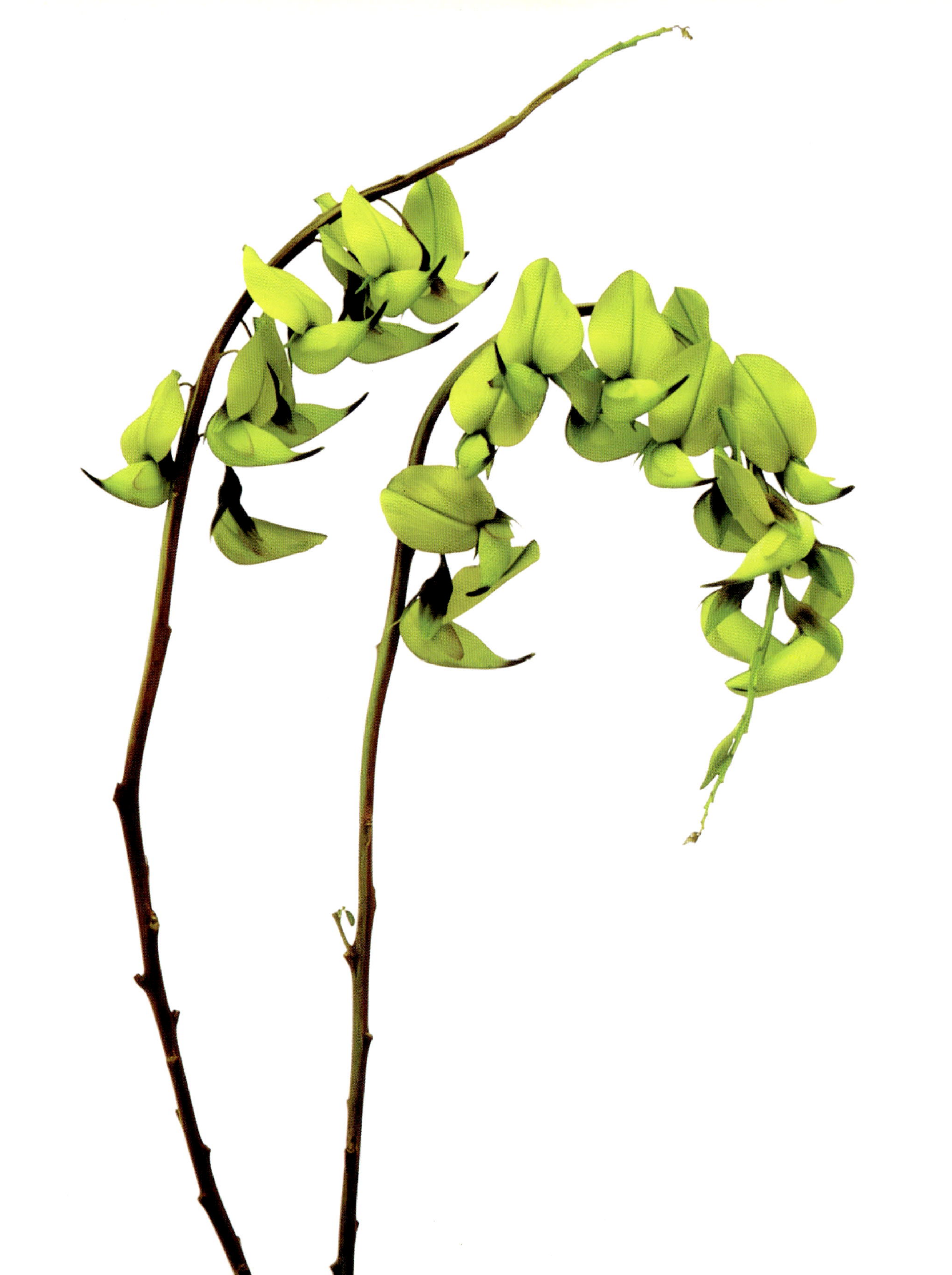

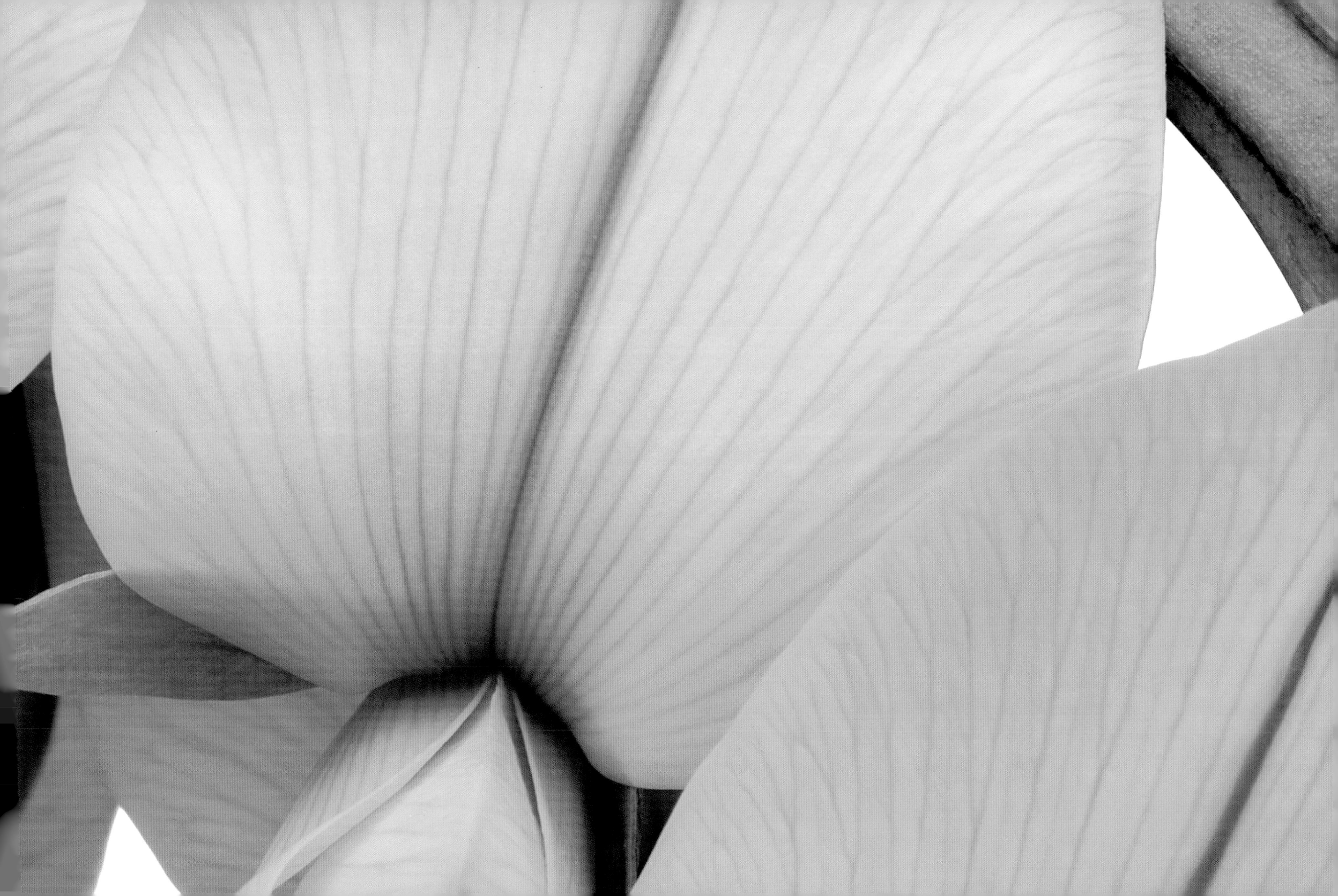

PLATES 18 & 19 : *Crotalaria* (preceding pages)

PLATE 20 : *Ranunculus*

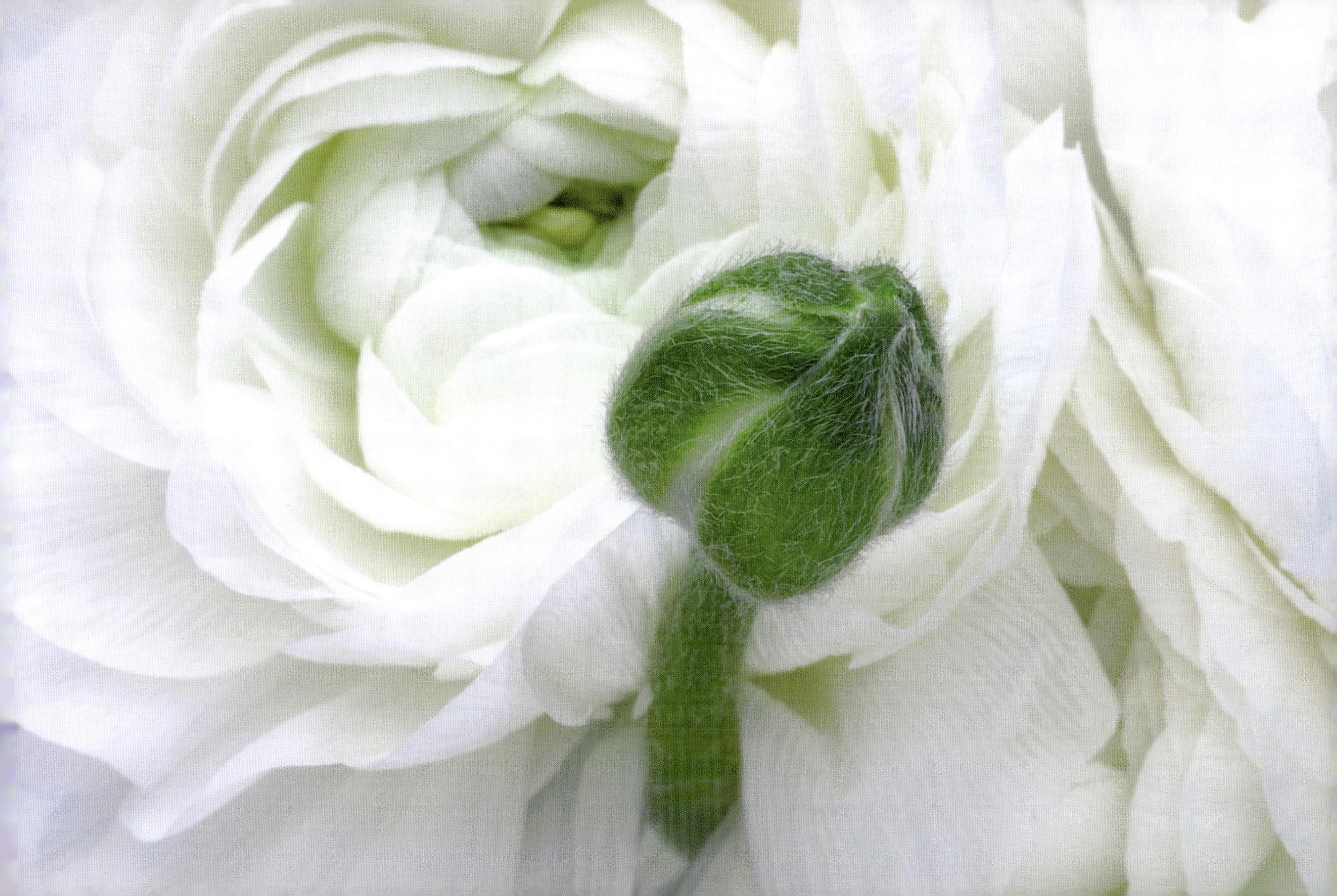

PLATE 21: *Tulipa*

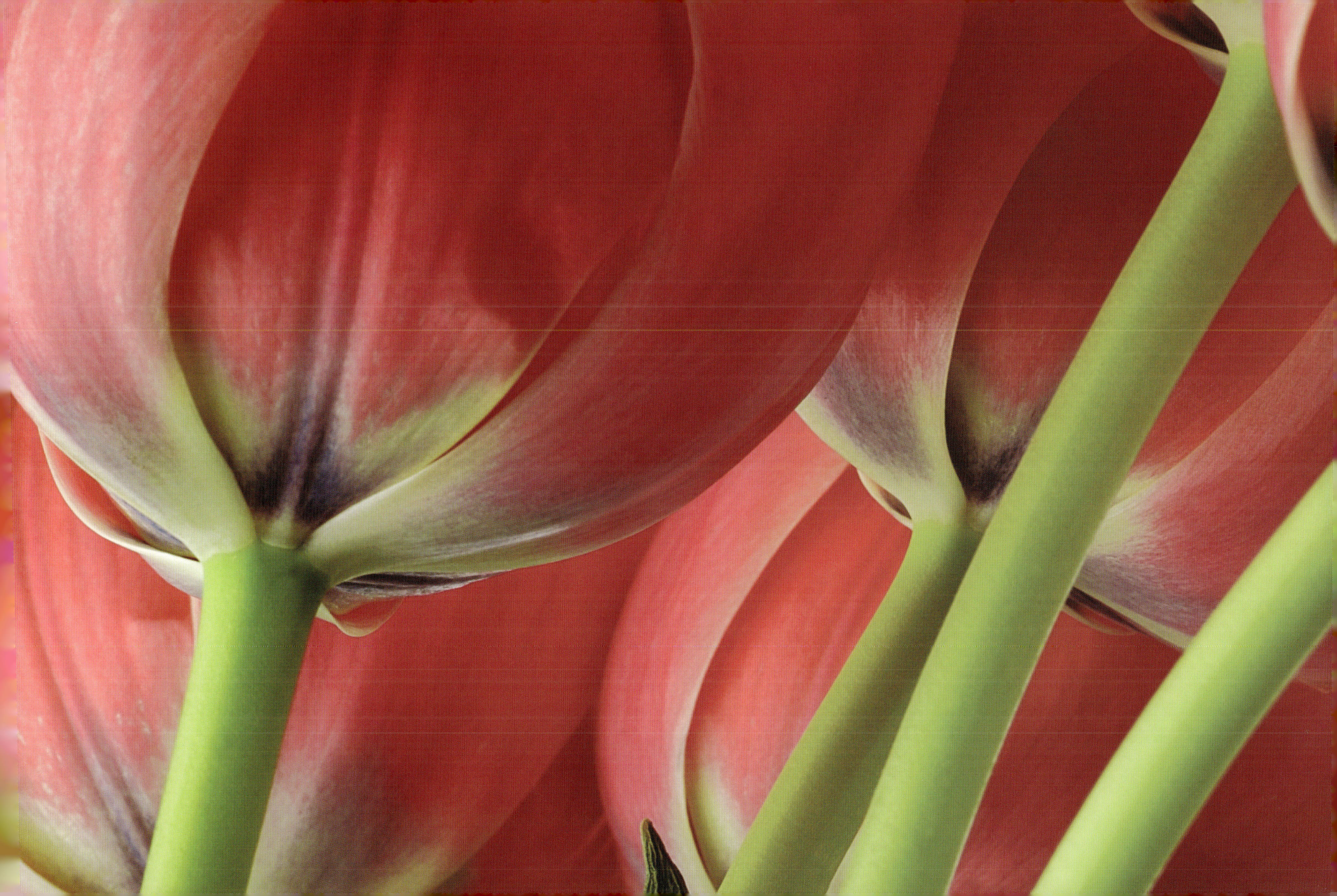

PLATE 22 : *Ranunculus*

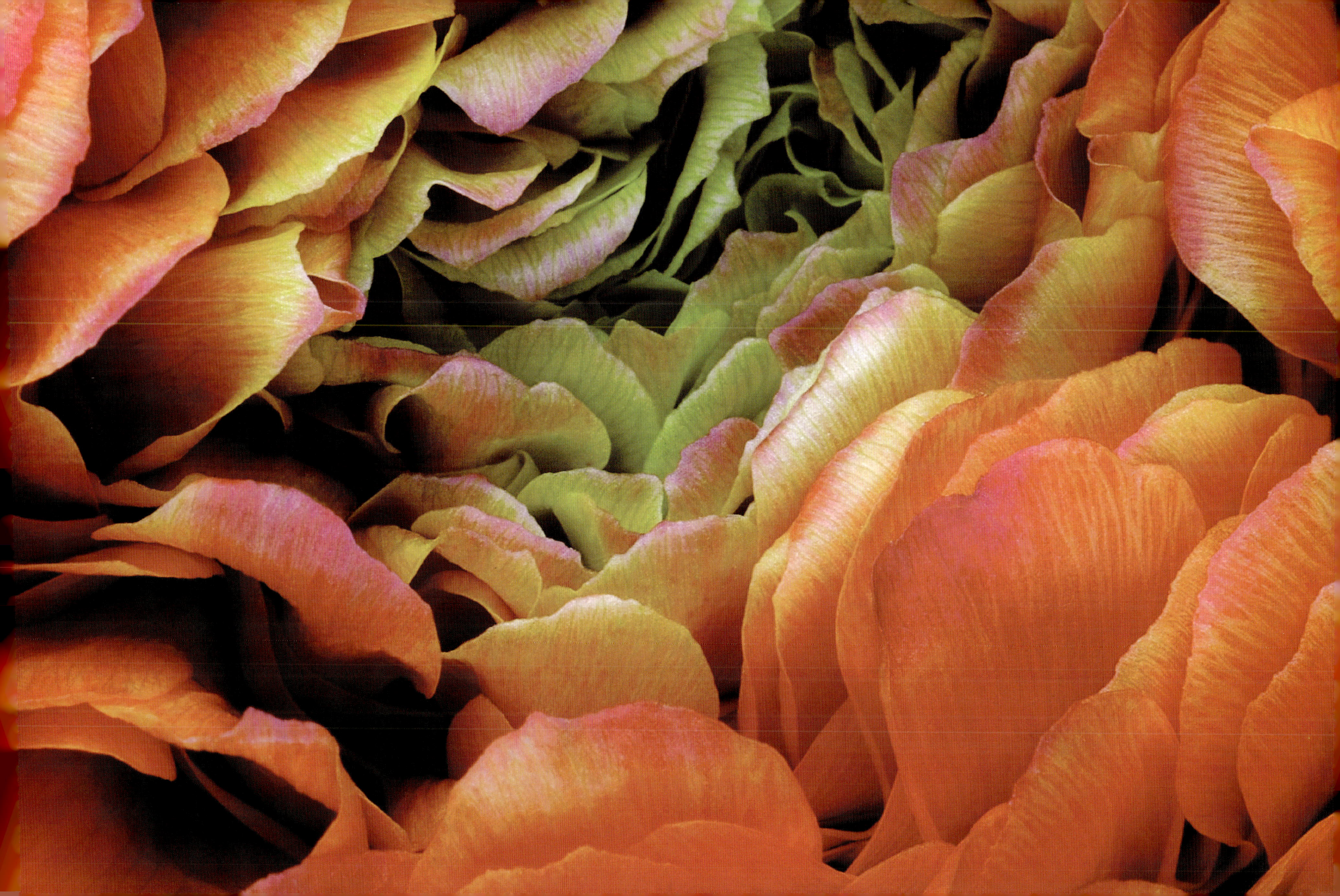

II

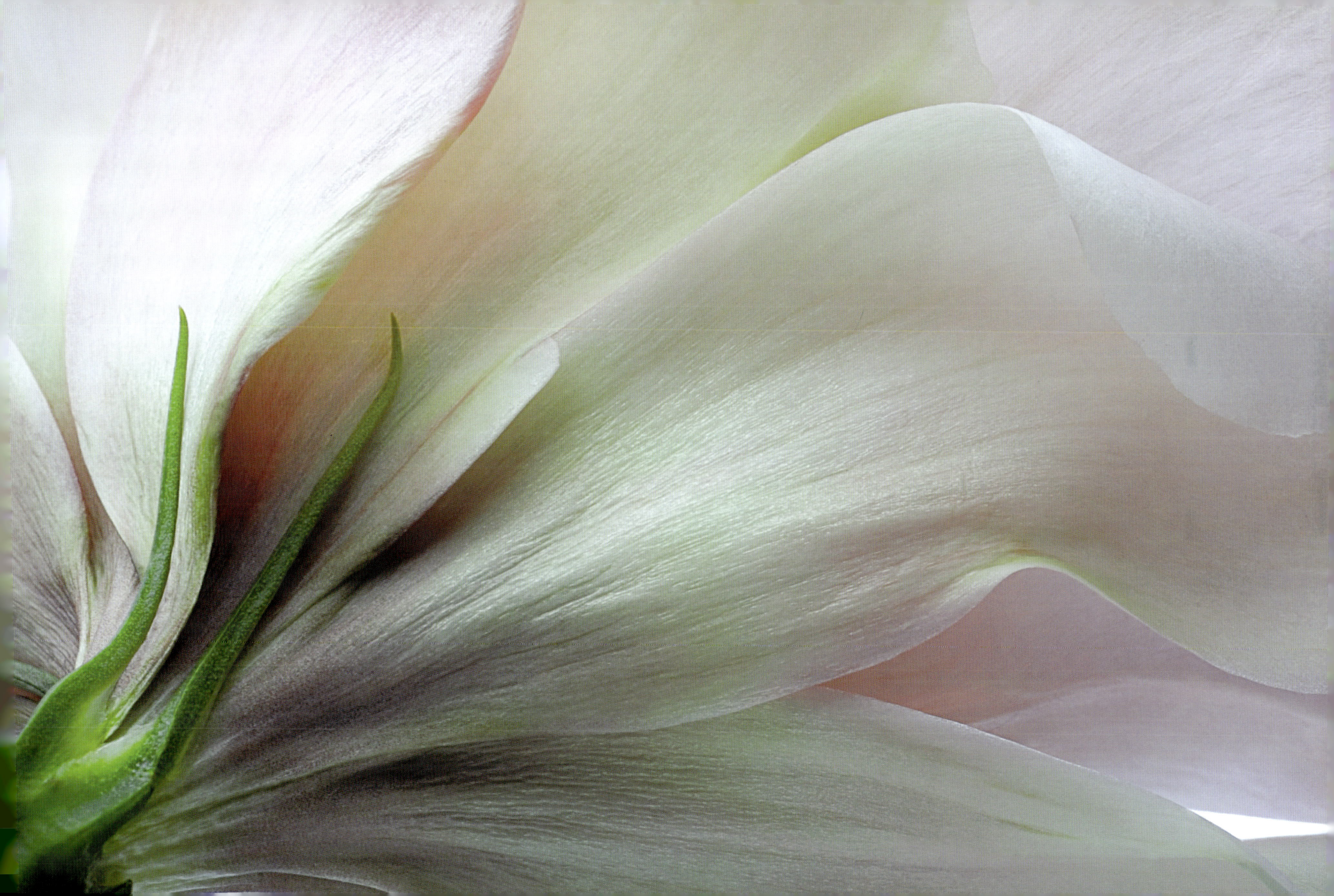

PLATE 23: *Eustoma* (preceding page)
PLATE 24: *Eustoma*

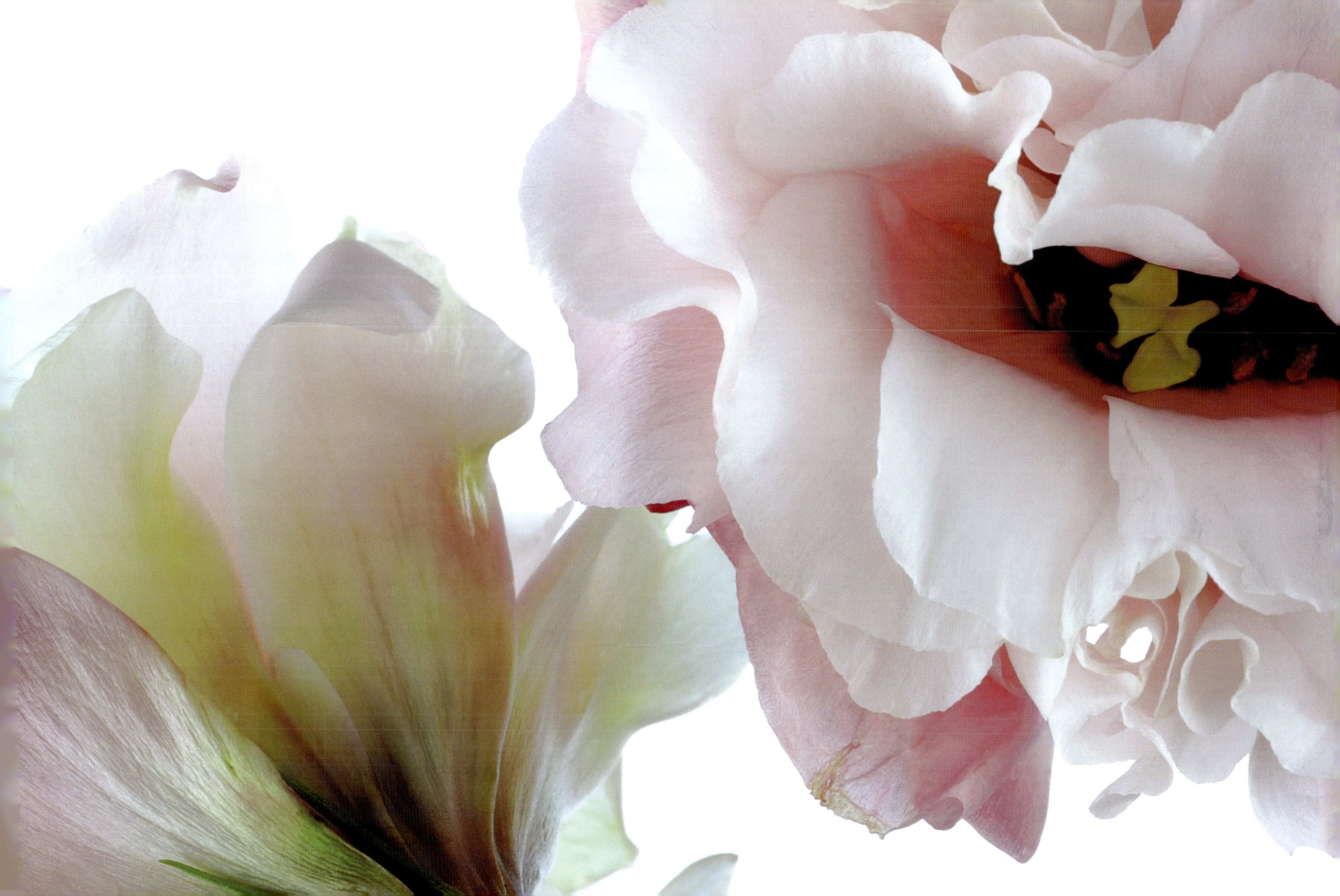

PLATE 25: *Scabiosa*

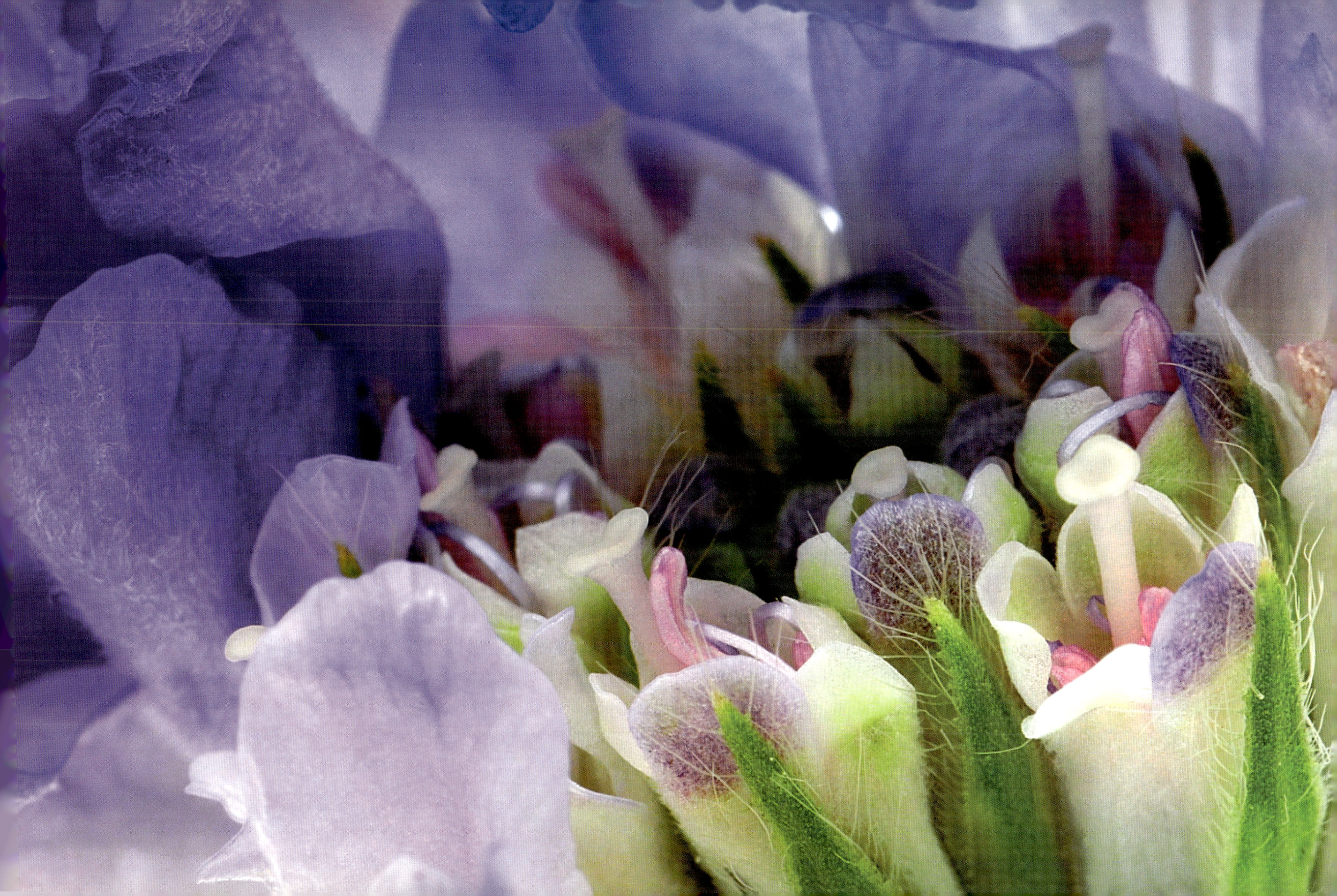

PLATE 26 : *Ranunculus*

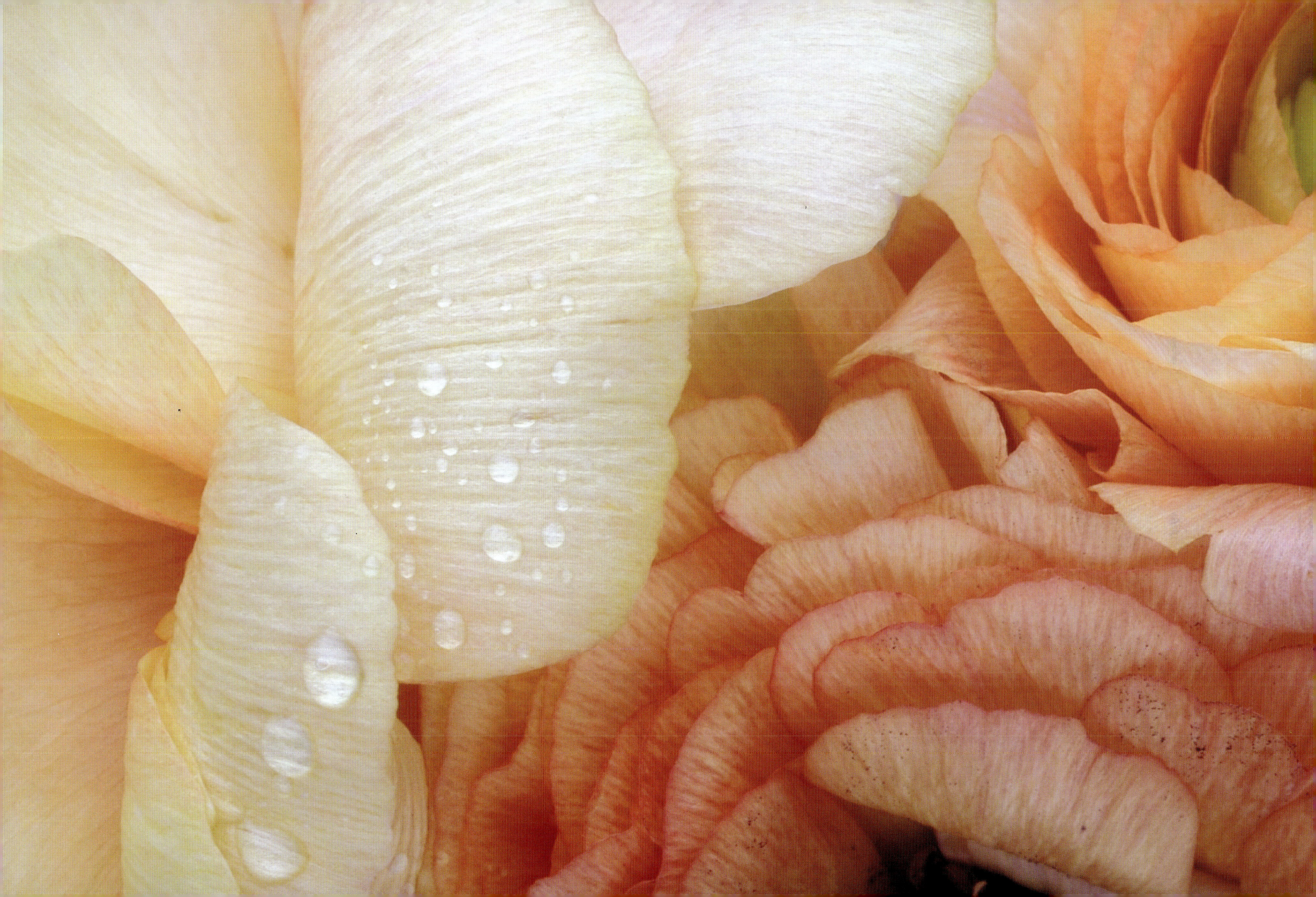

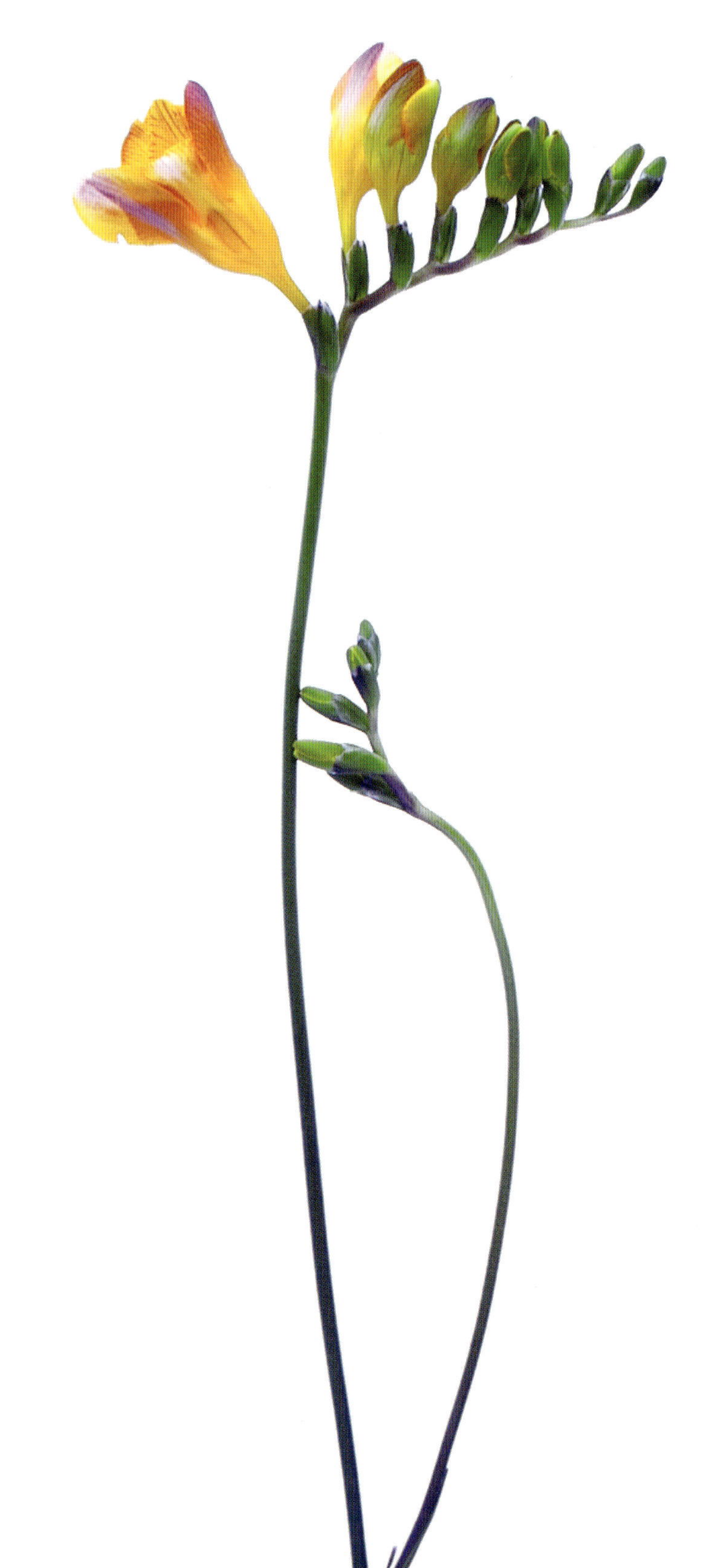

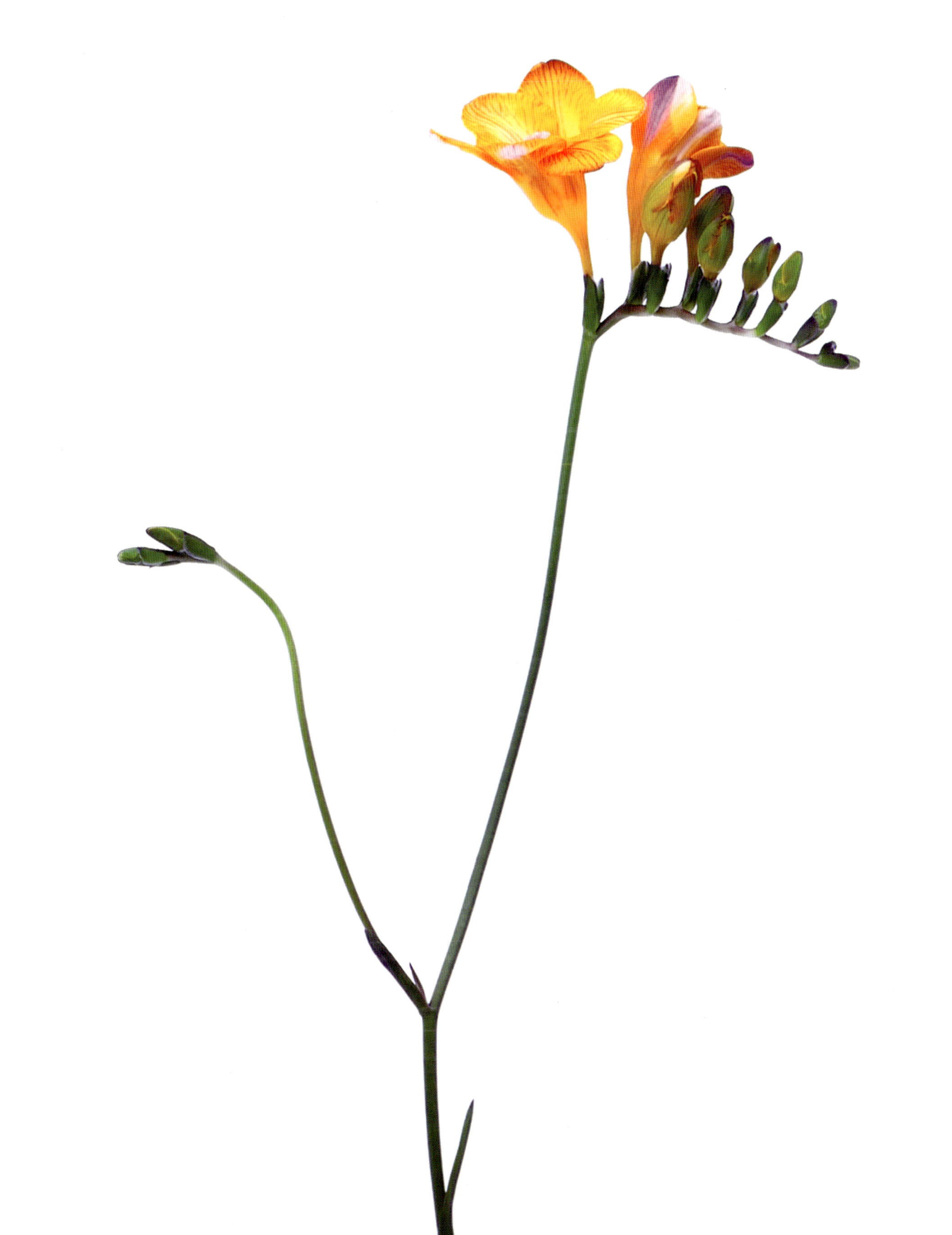

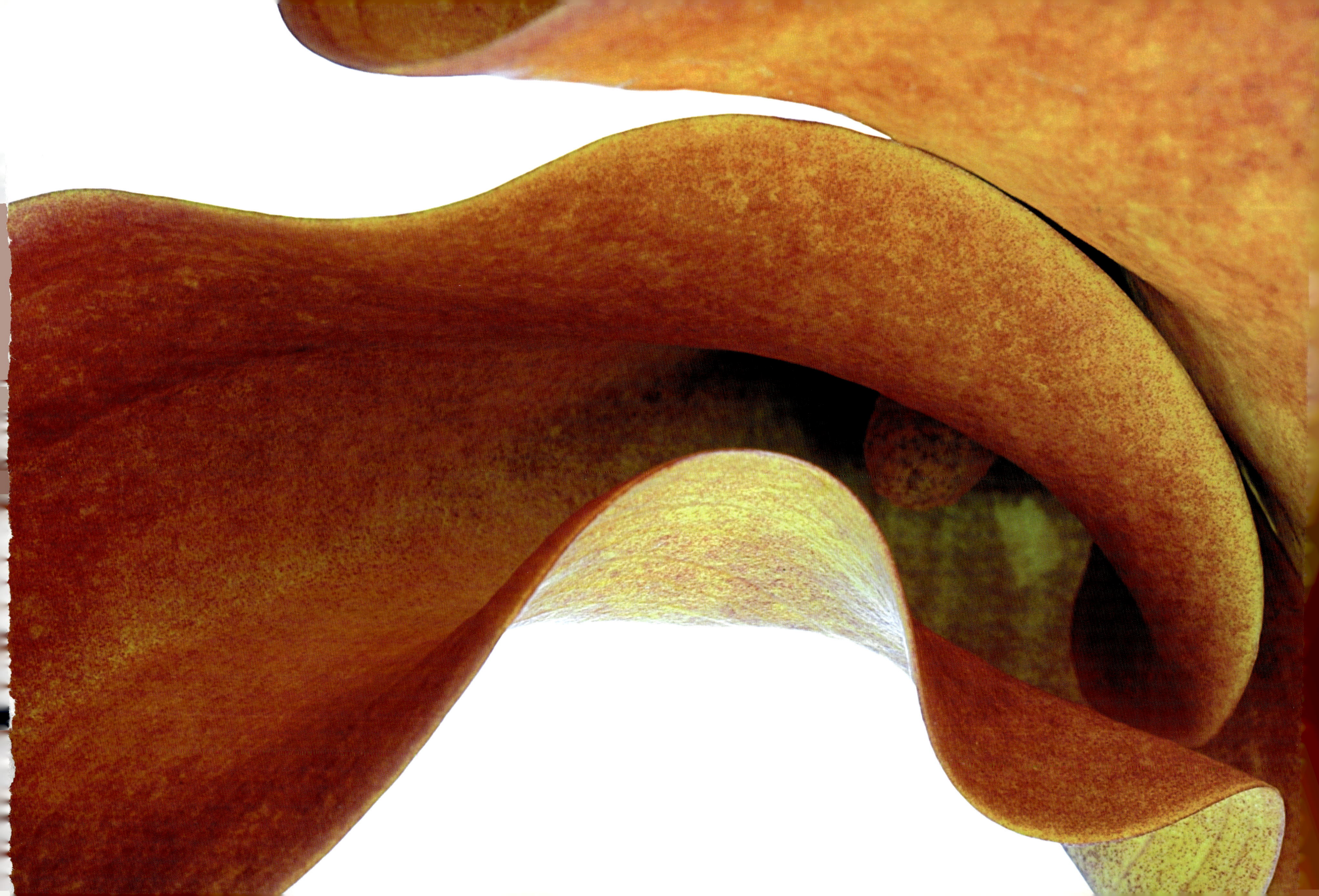

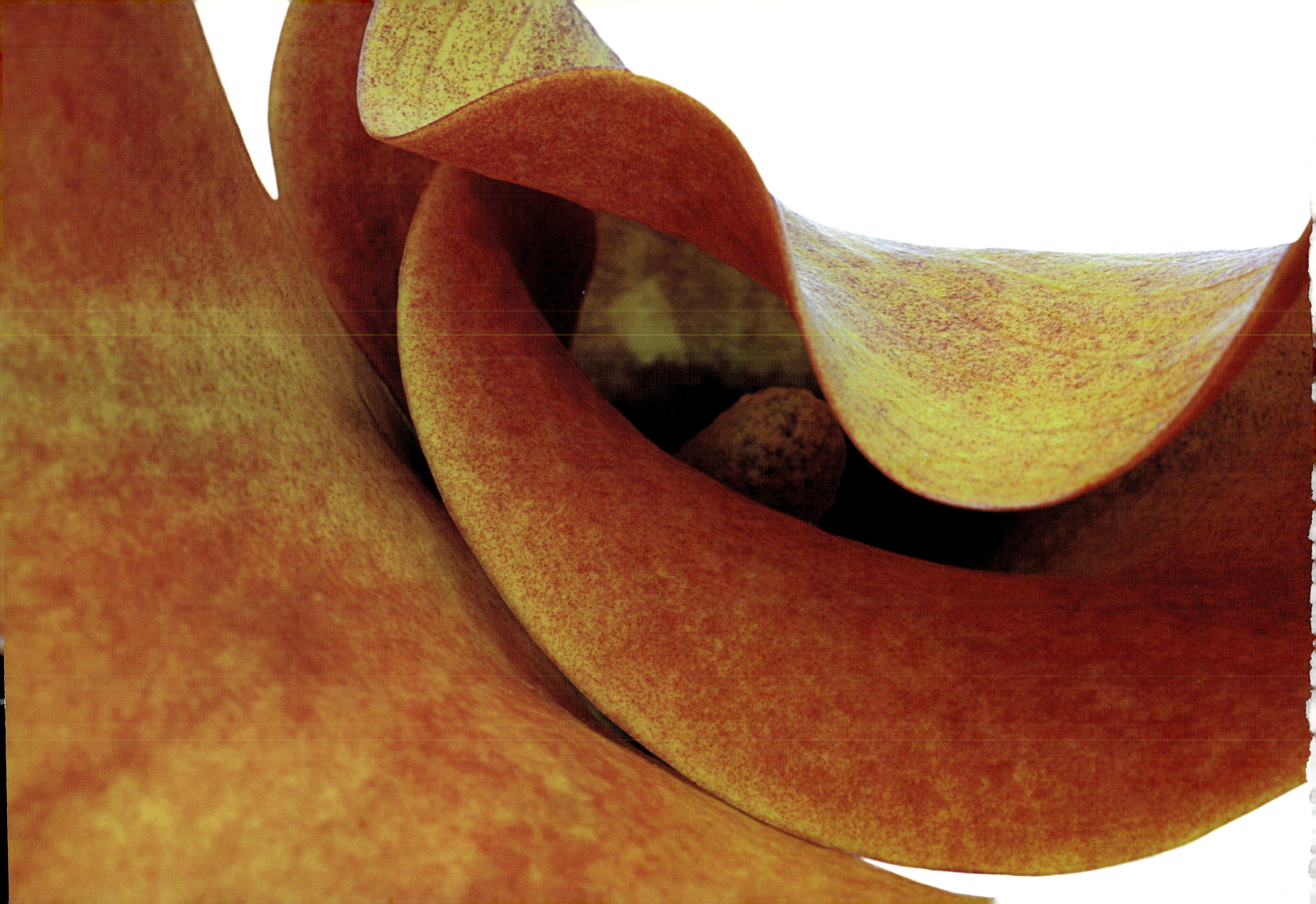

PLATES 27 & 28 : *Freesia* (preceding pages)
PLATES 29, 30, & 31 : *Zantedeschia* (gatefold)

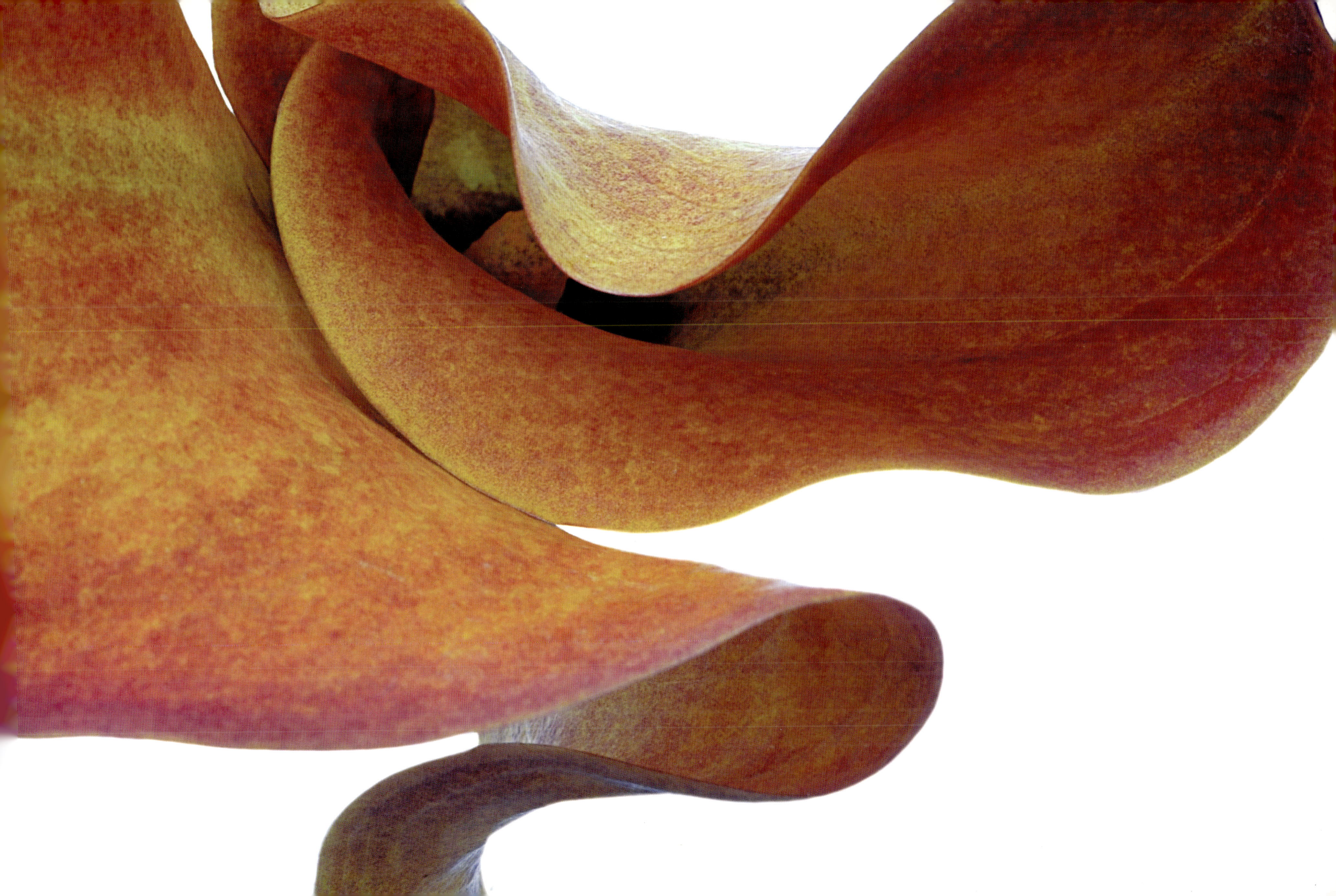

PLATE 32: *Tulipa*

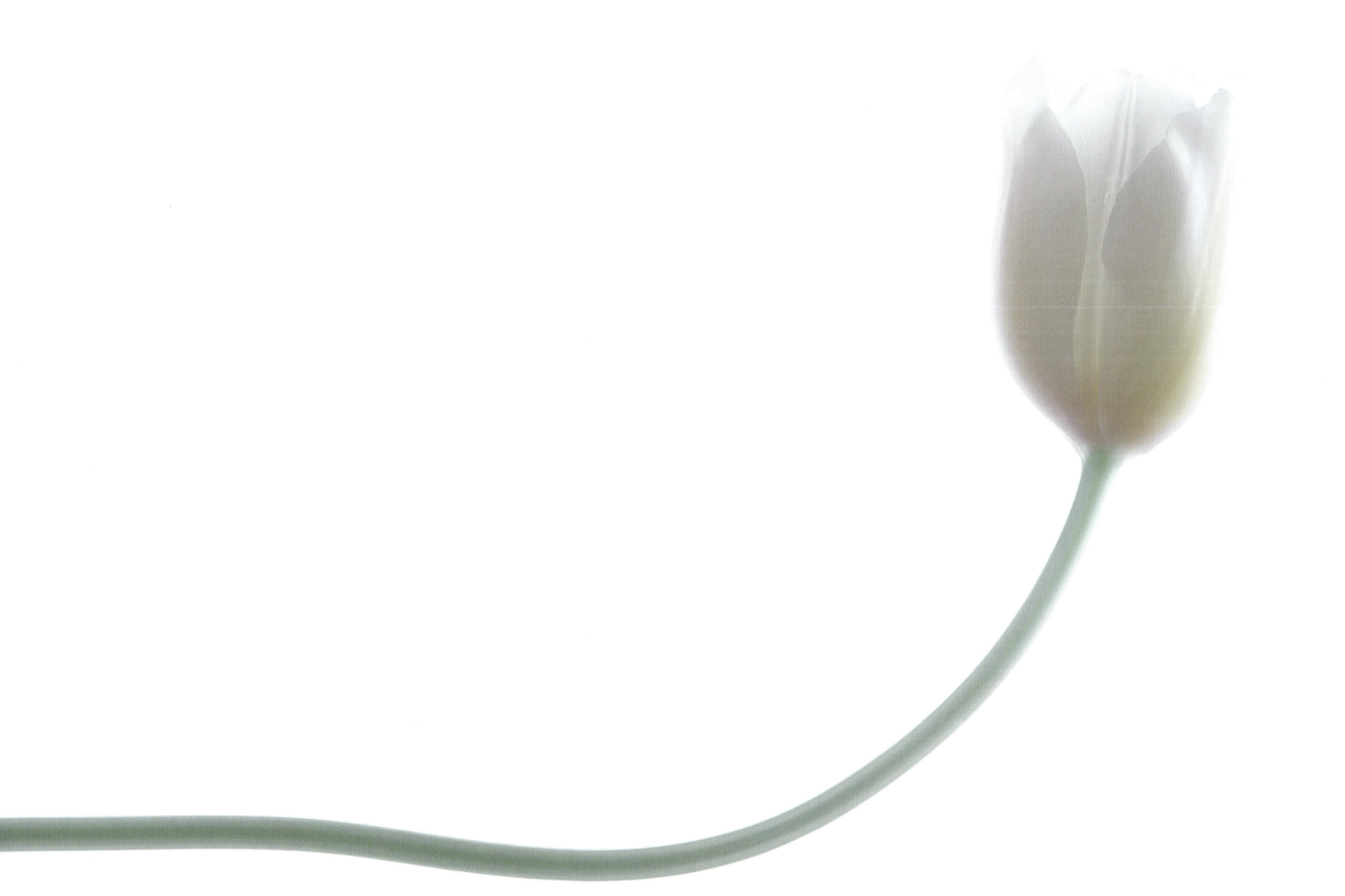

PLATE 33: *Magnolia* x *soulangeana*

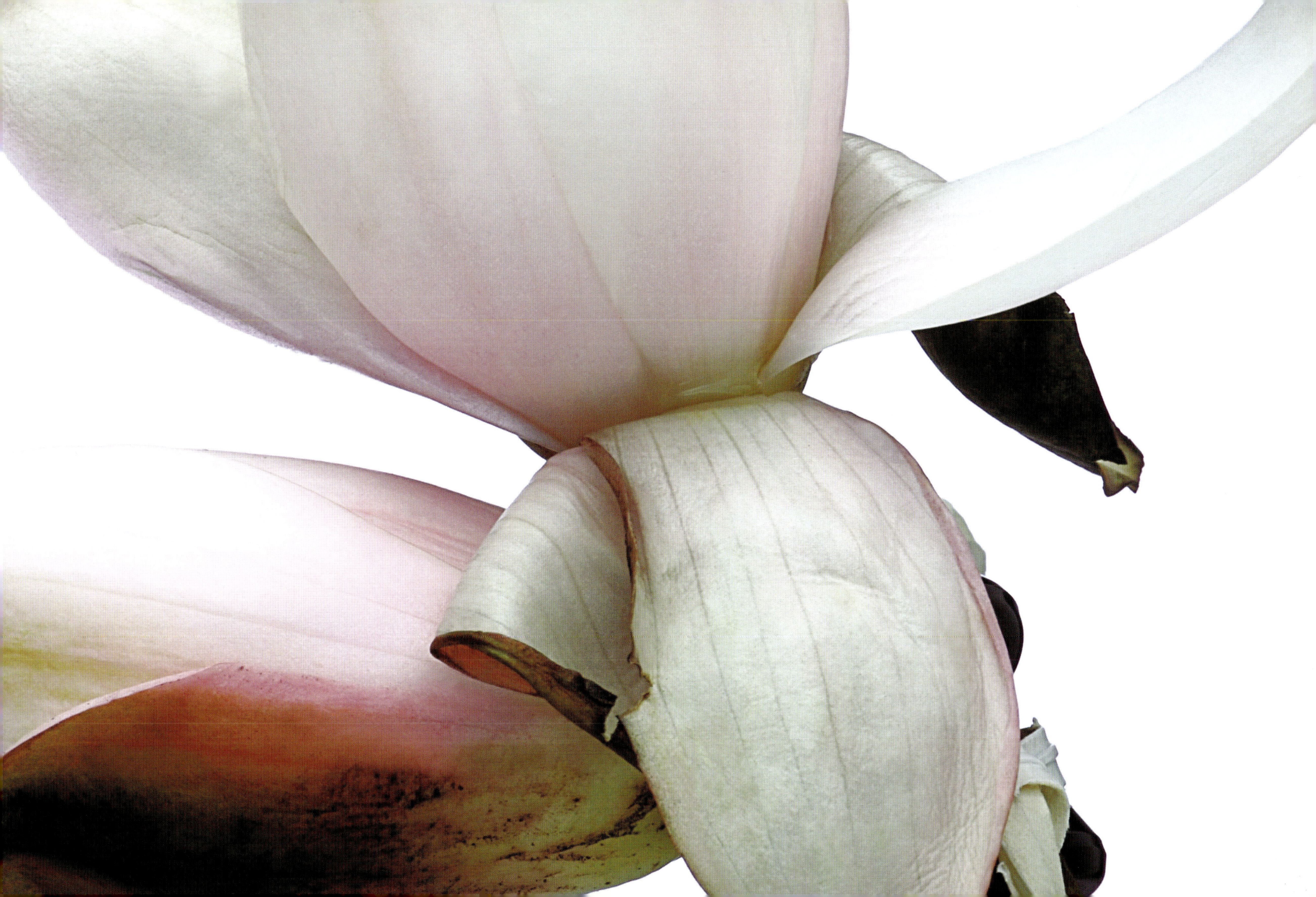

PLATE 34 : *Hydrangea macrophylla*

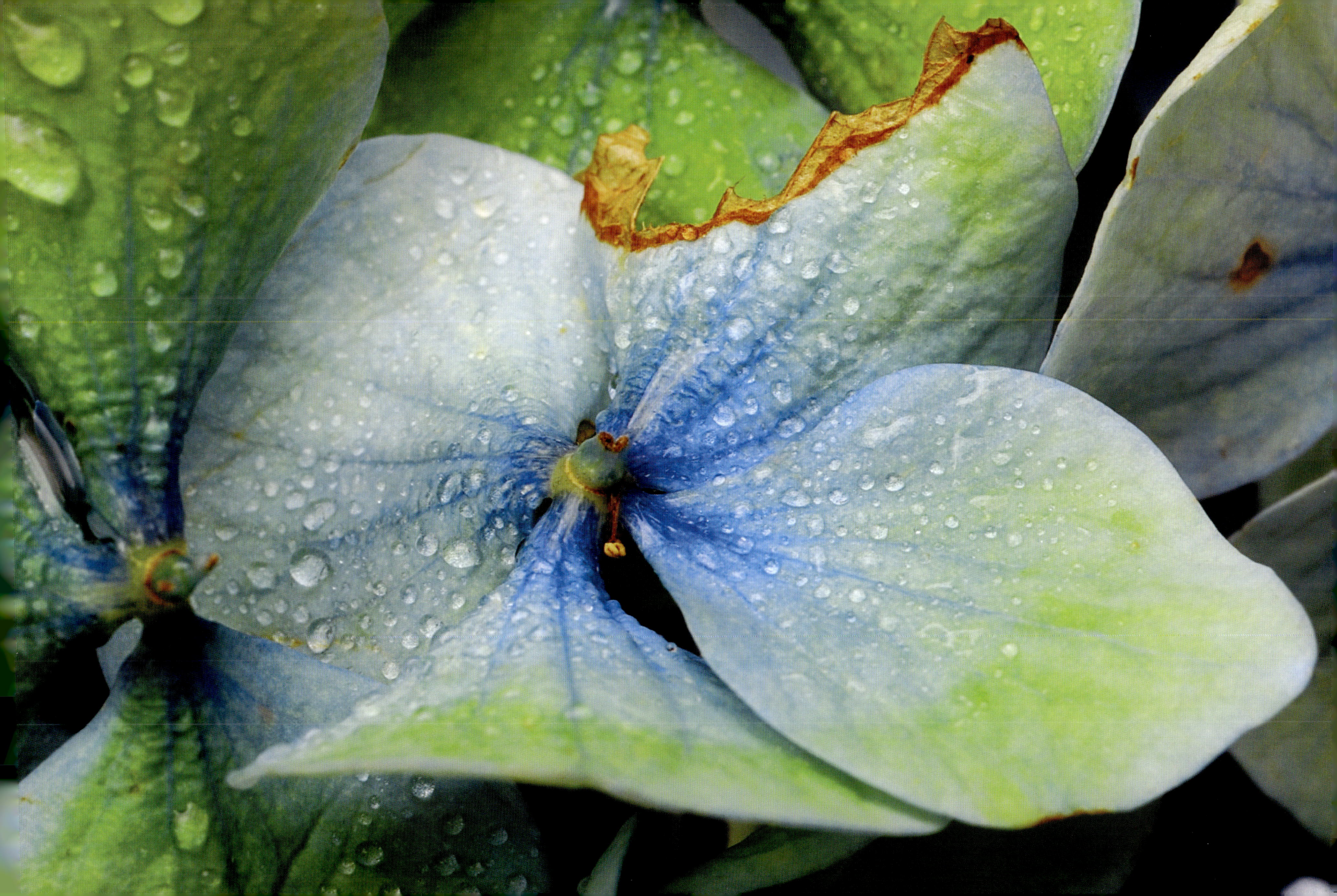

PLATE 35: *Tulipa*

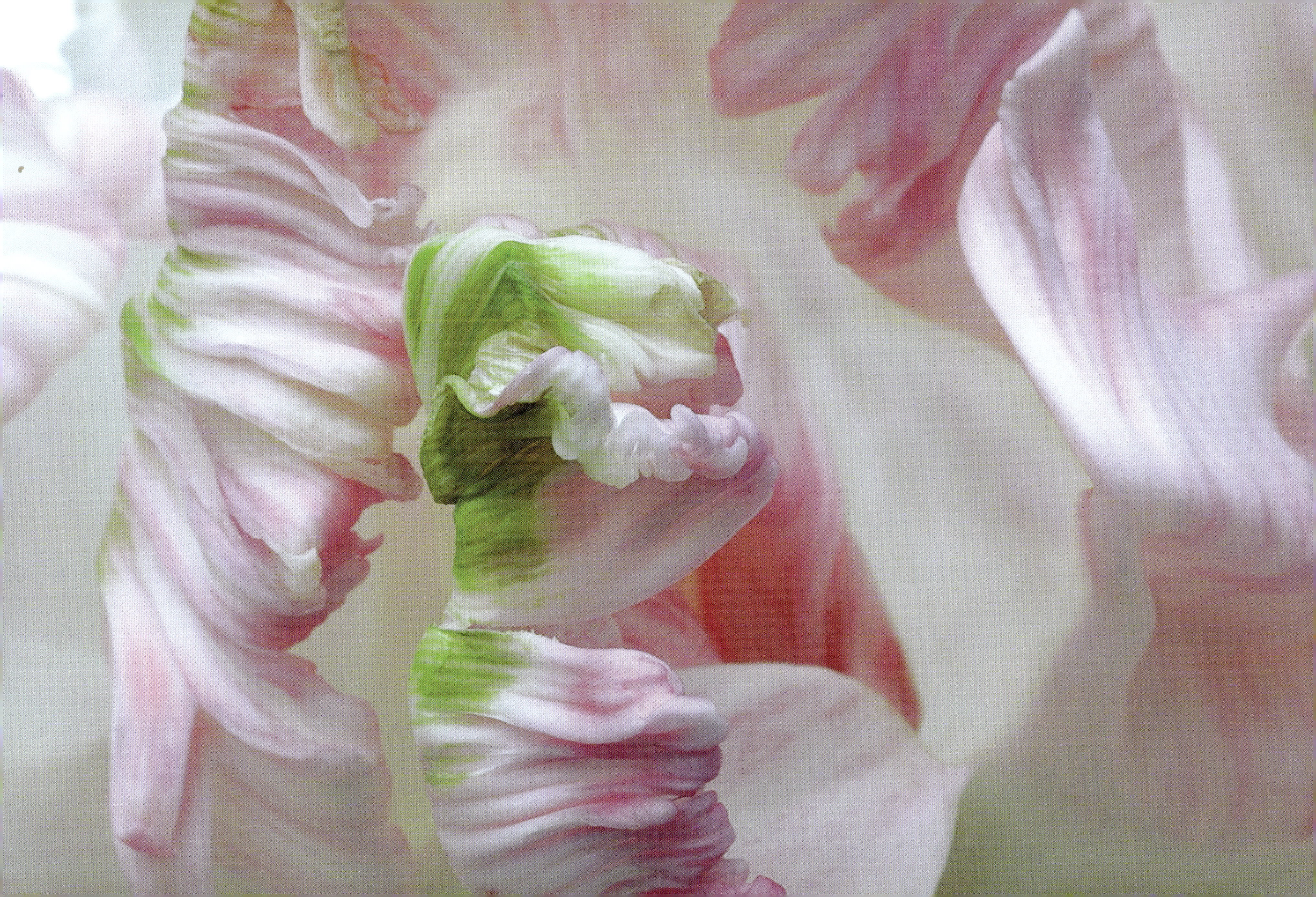

PLATE 36 : *Tulipa*

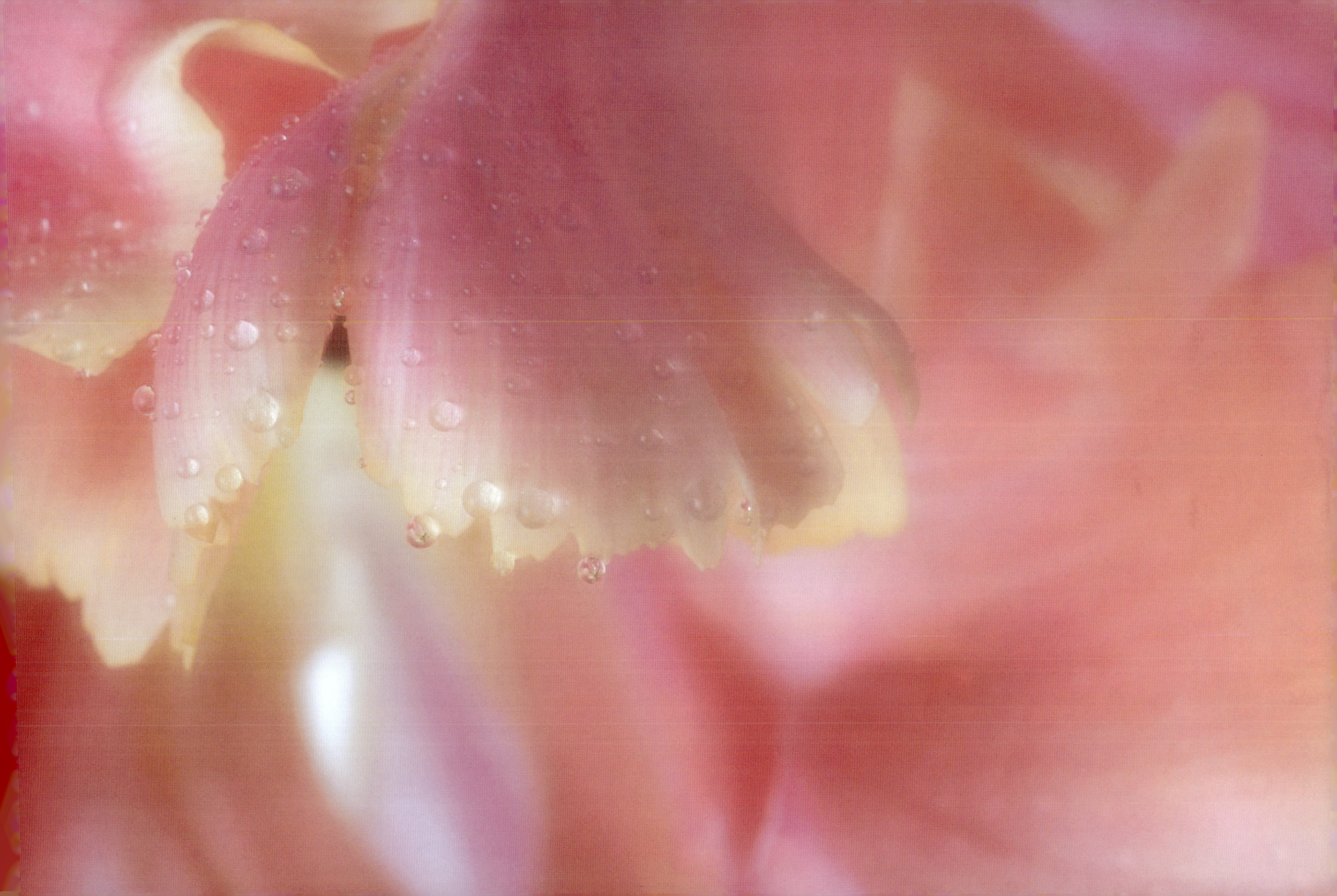

PLATE 37 : *Lilium*

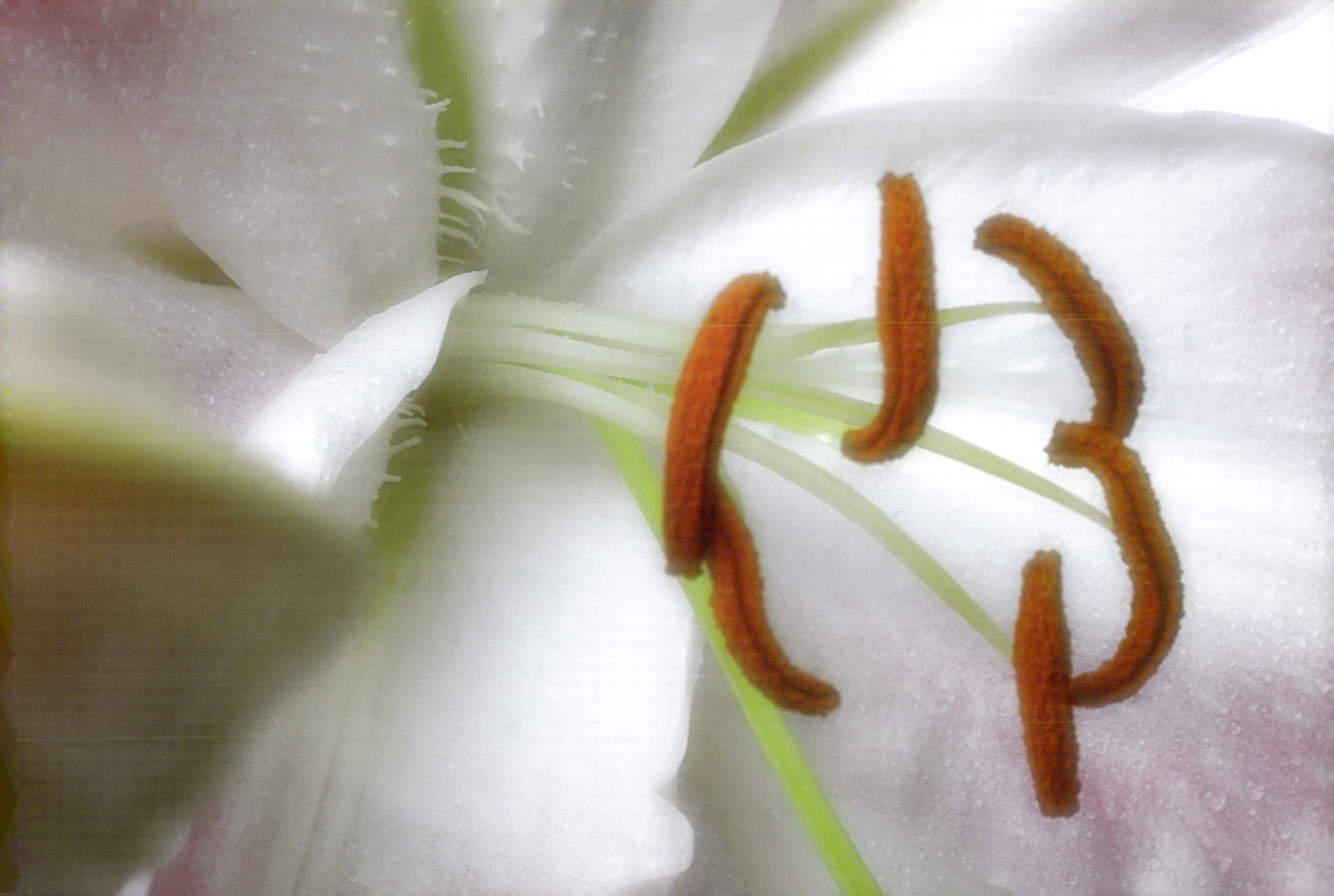

PLATE 38 : *Lilium*

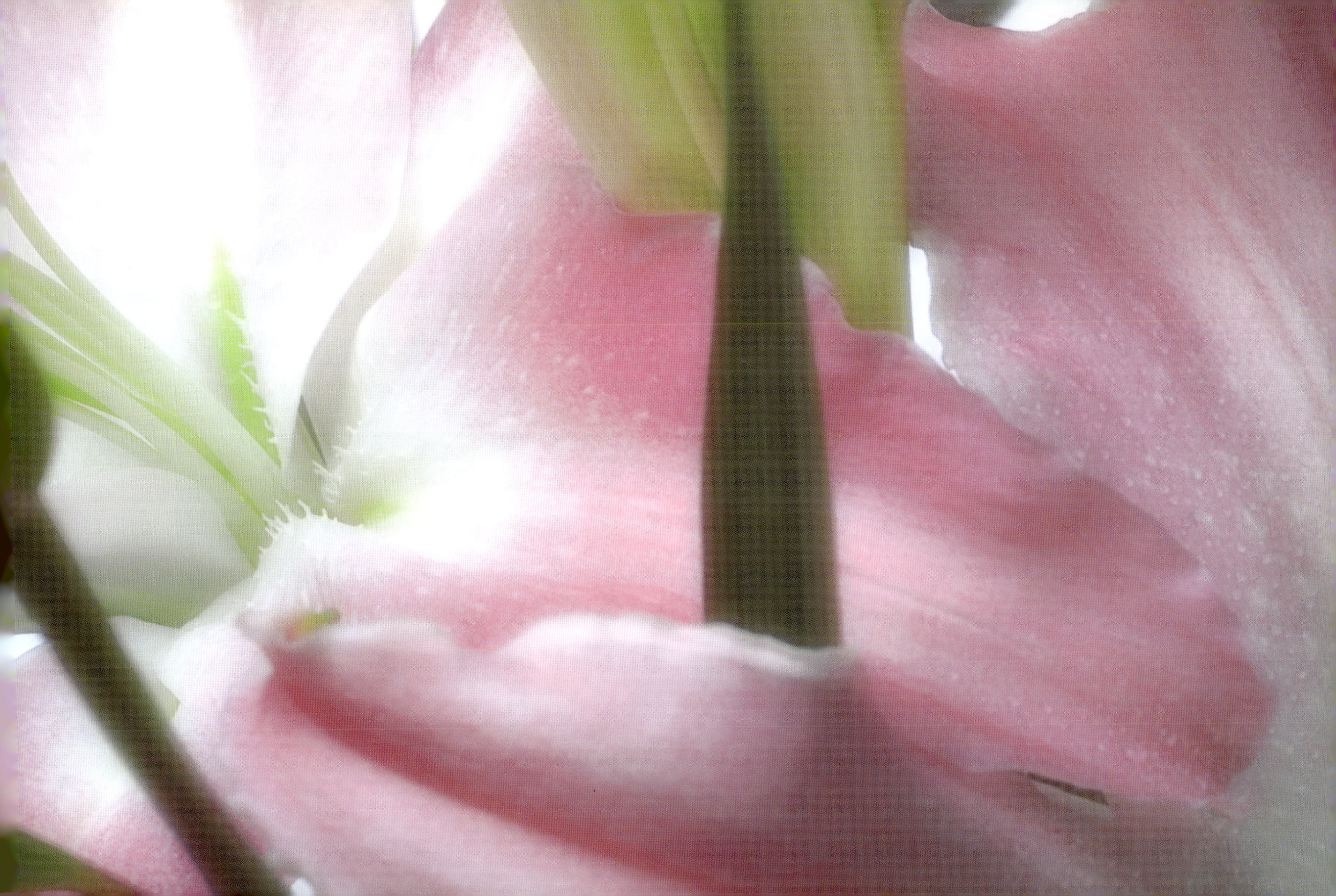

PLATE 39: *Leucadendron* 'Safari Sunset'

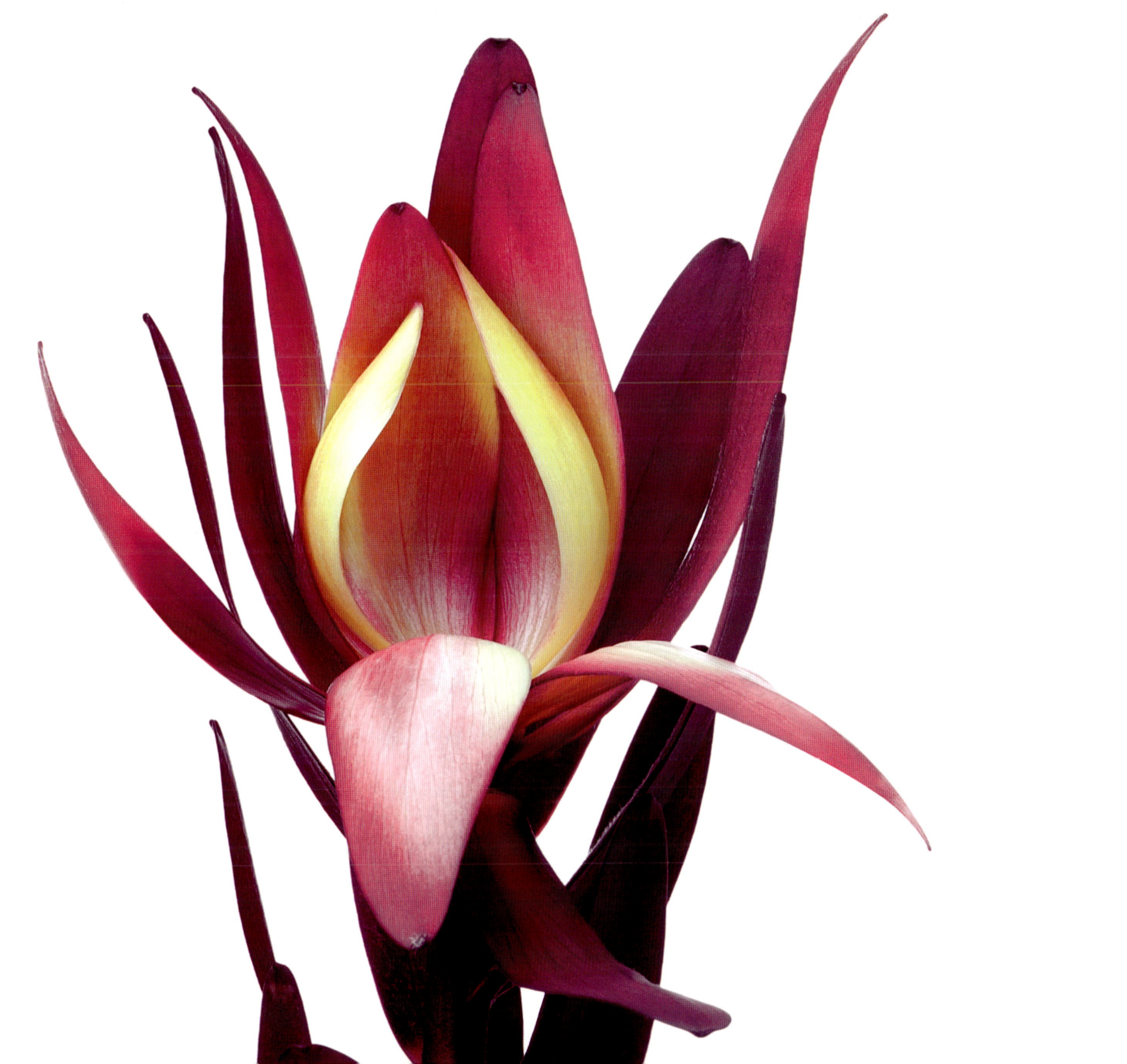

PLATE 40 : *Paeonia*

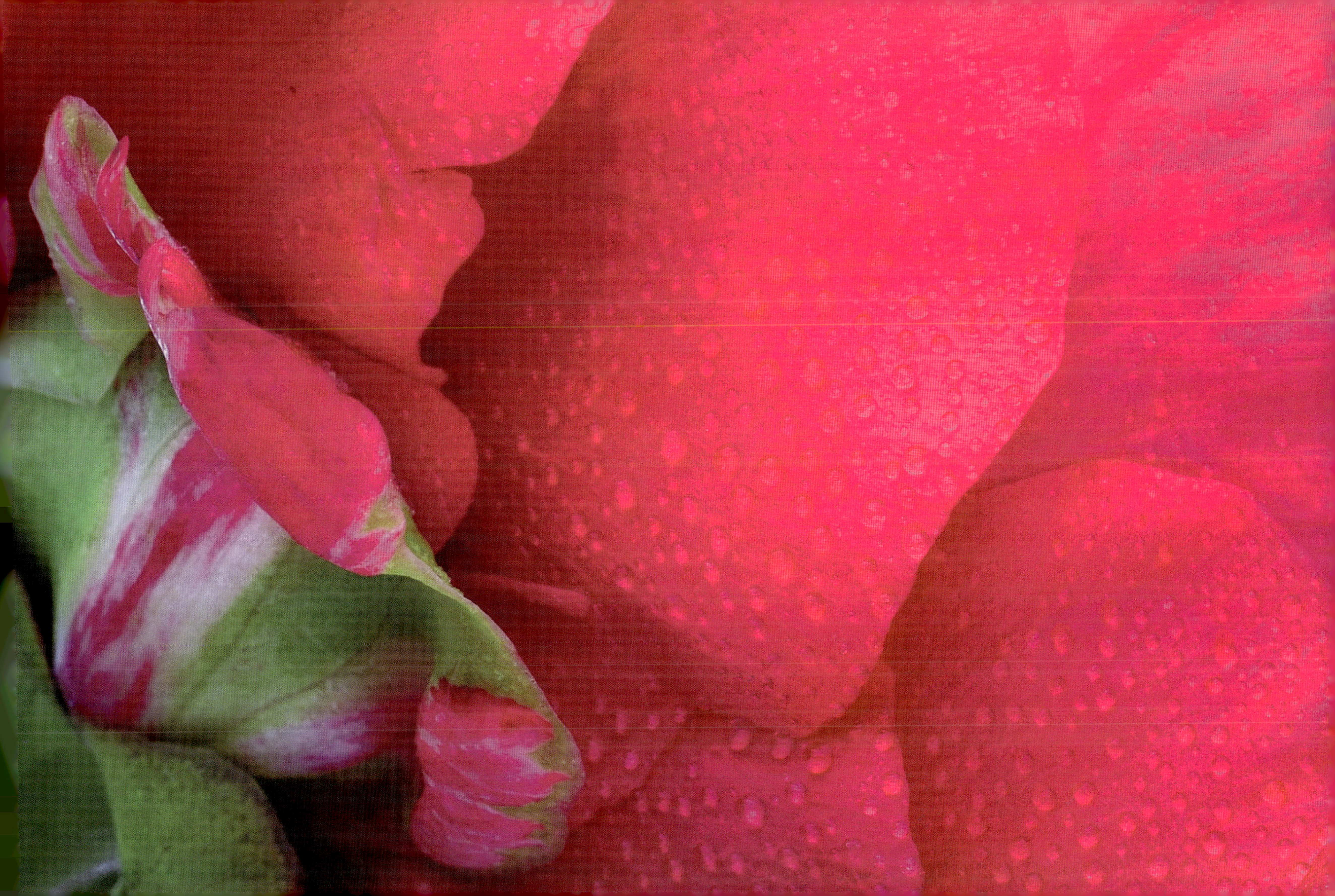

PLATE 41: *Phalaenopsis*

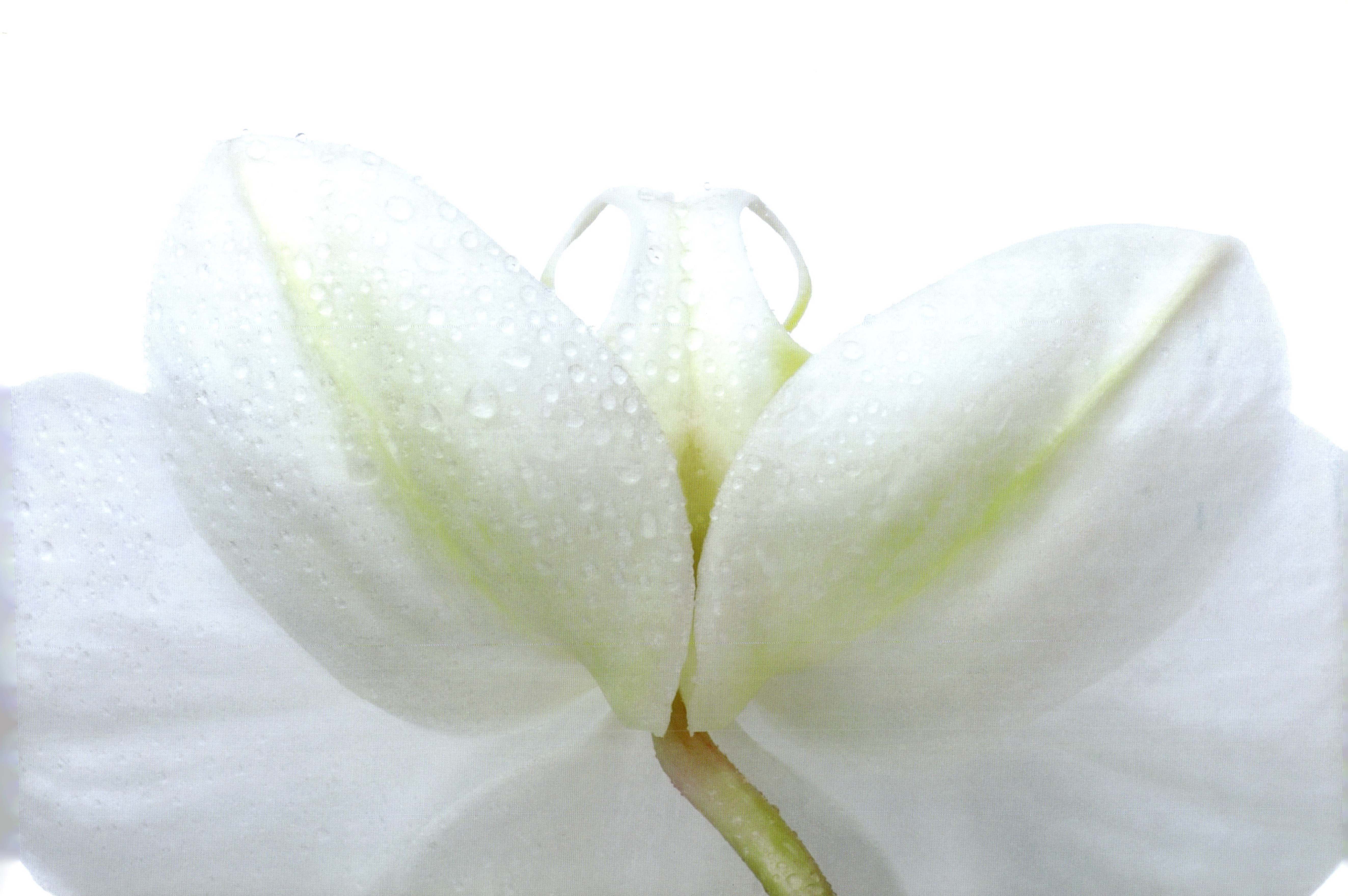

PLATE 42: *Phalaenopsis*

PLATE 43: *Phalaenopsis*

PLATE 44 : *Paeonia* 'Festiva Maxima'

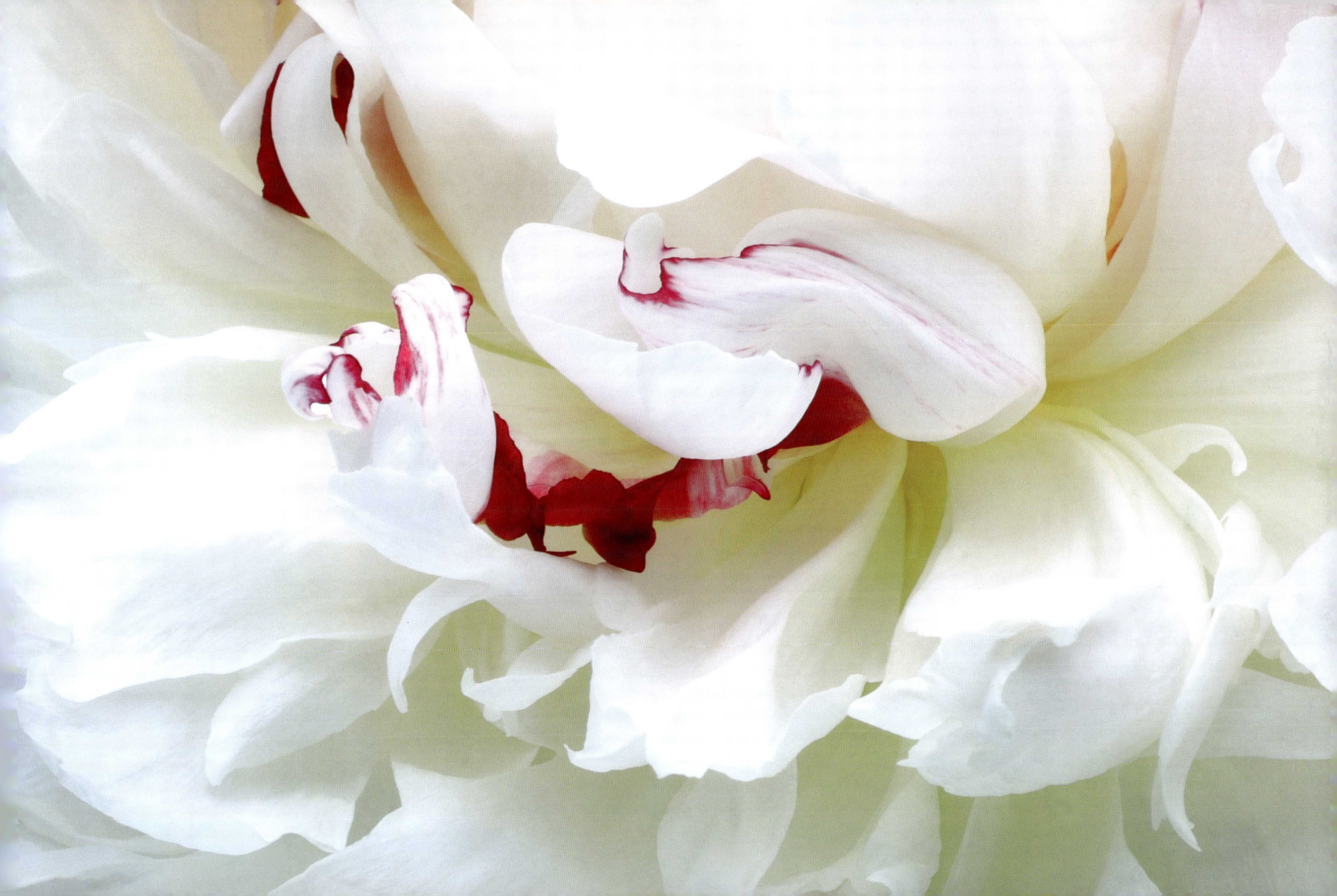

III

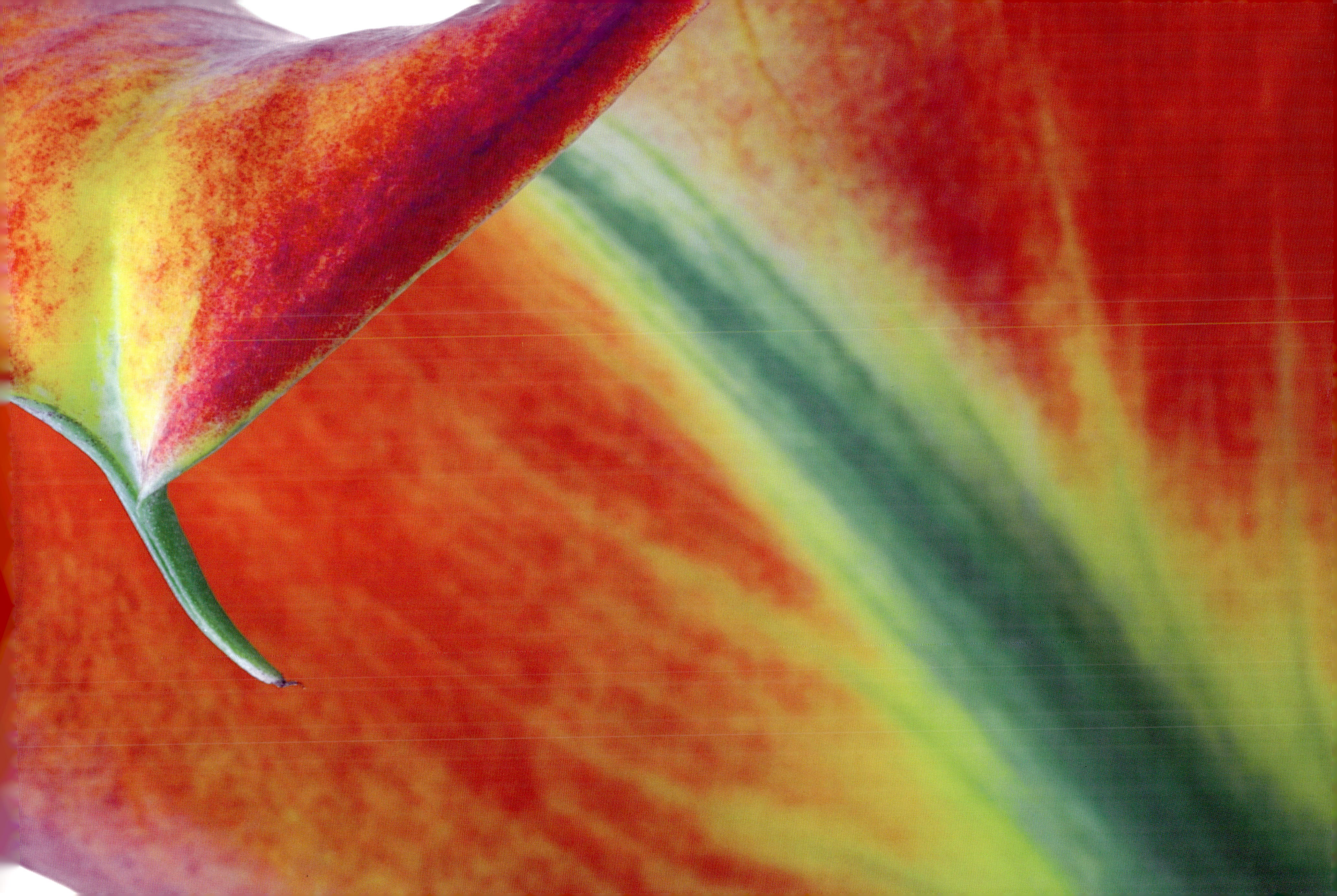

PLATE 45: *Zantedeschia* (preceding page)
PLATE 46: *Aconitum*

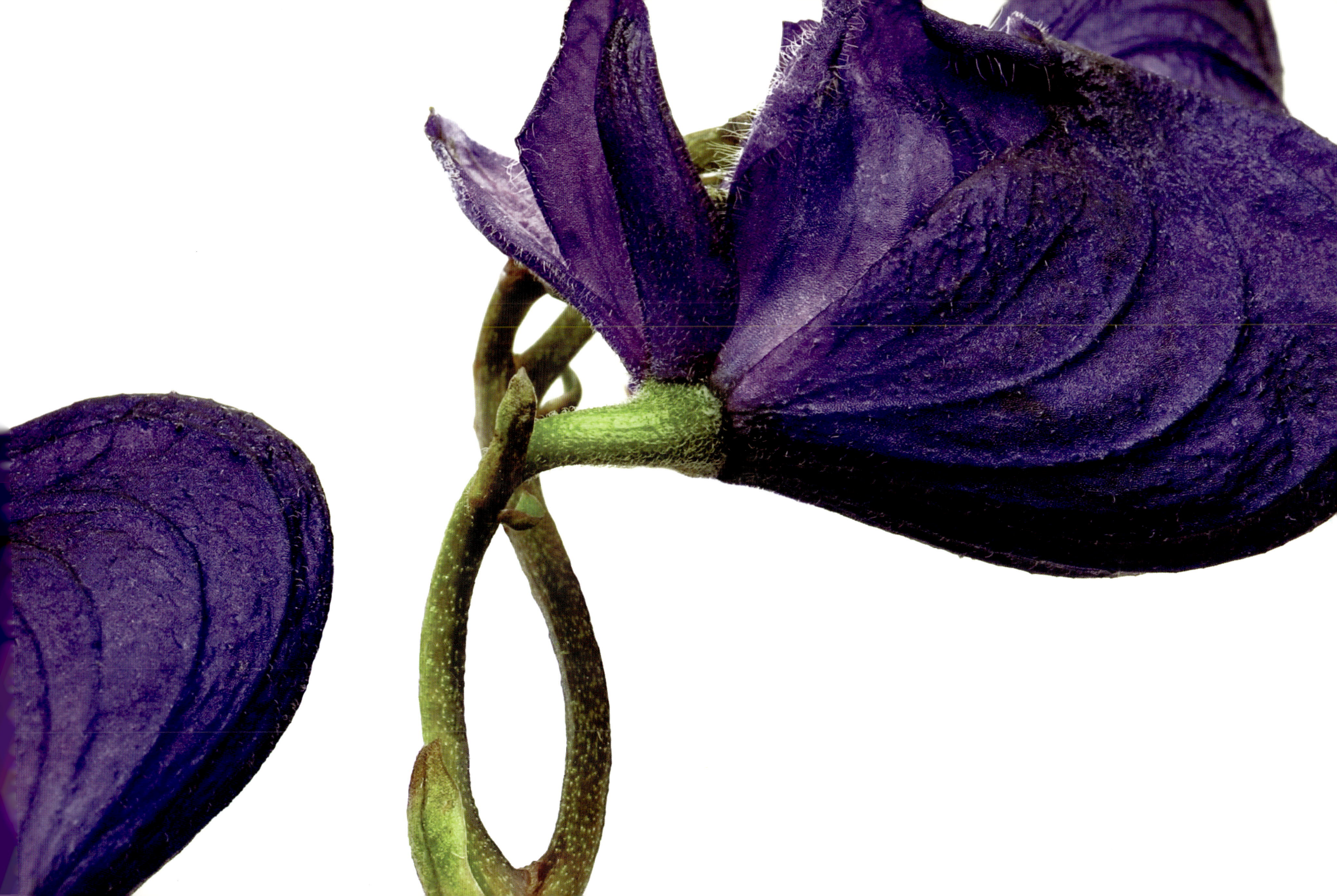

PLATES 47, 48, & 49 : *Papaver* (opposite and following pages)

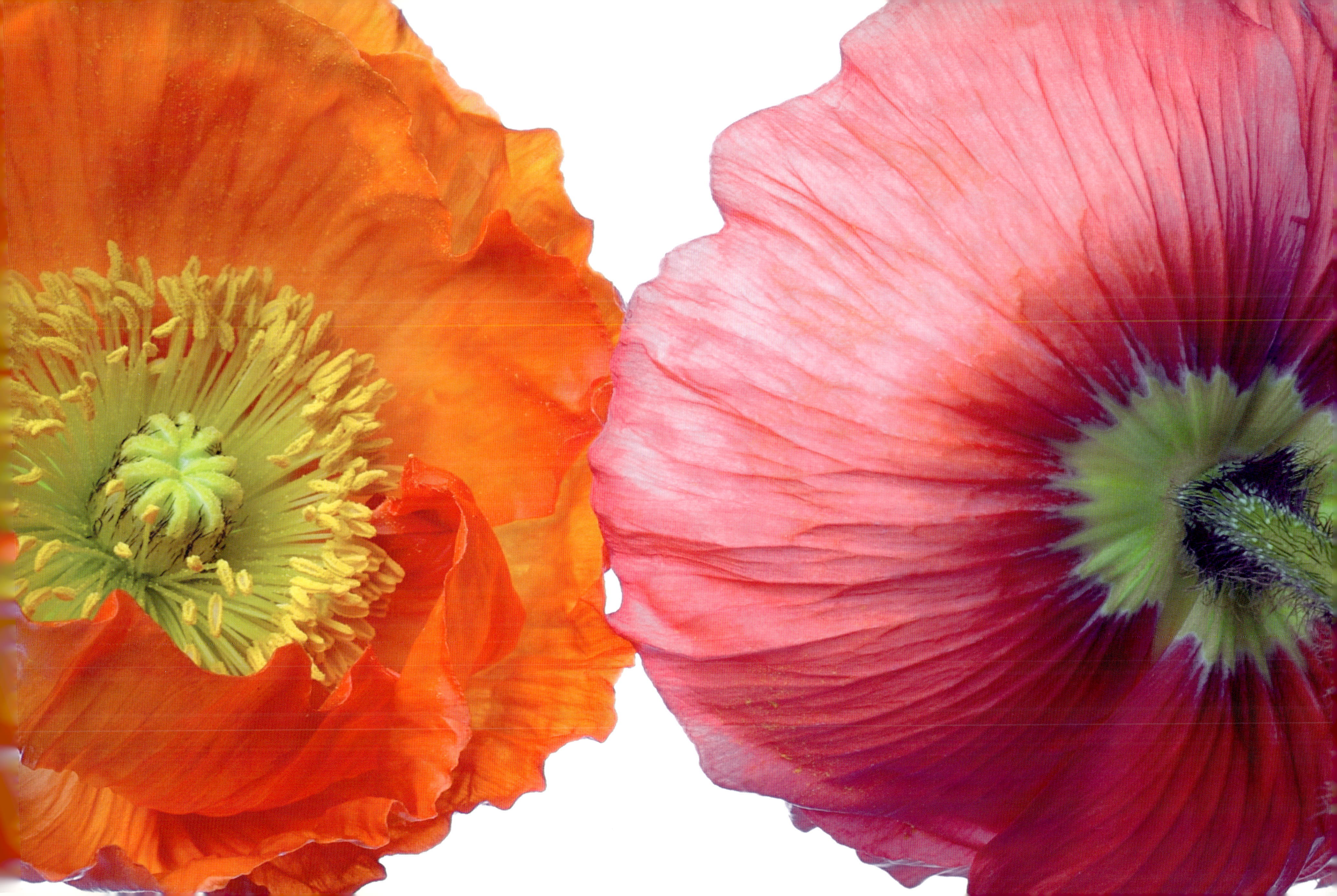

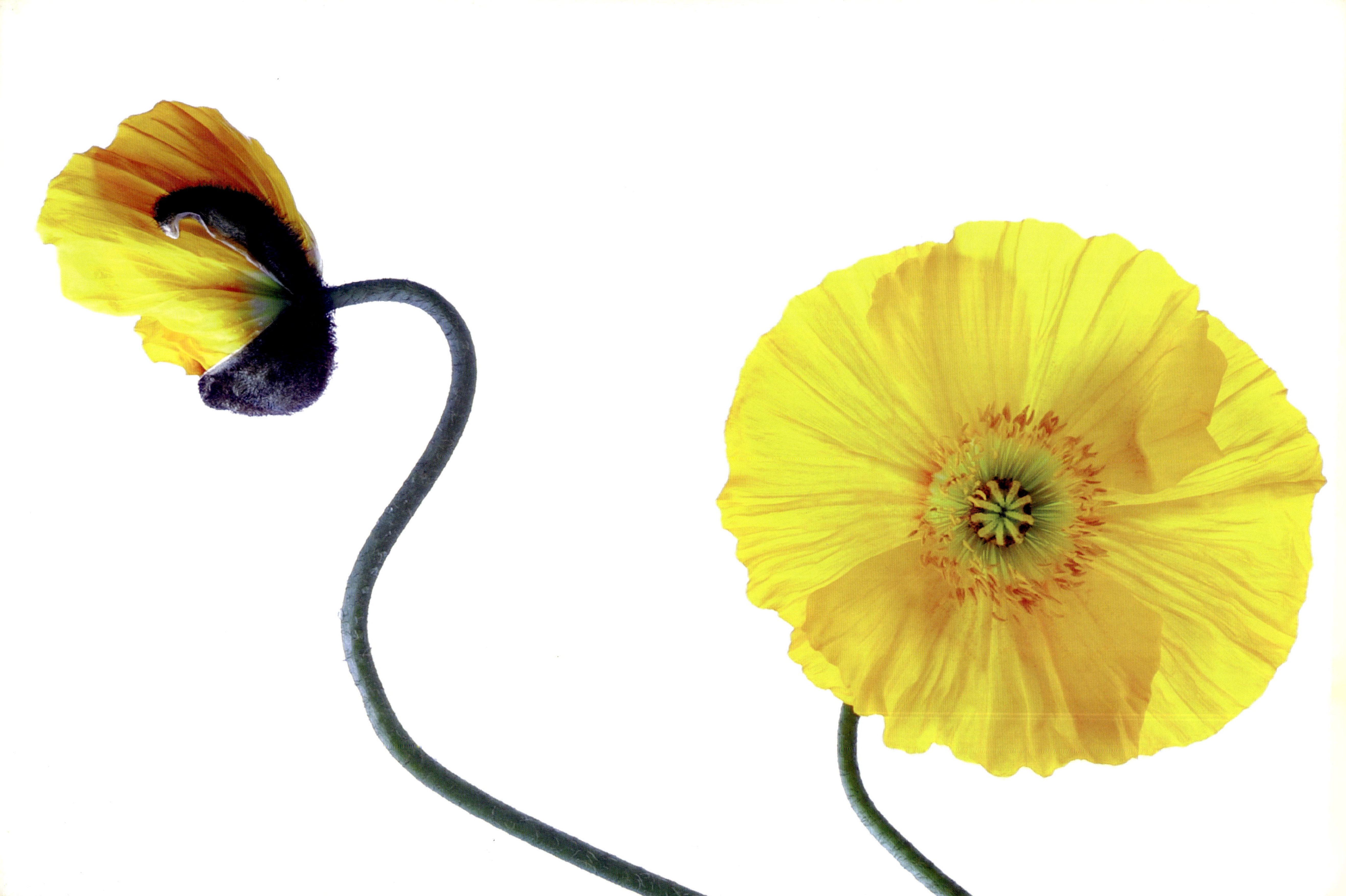

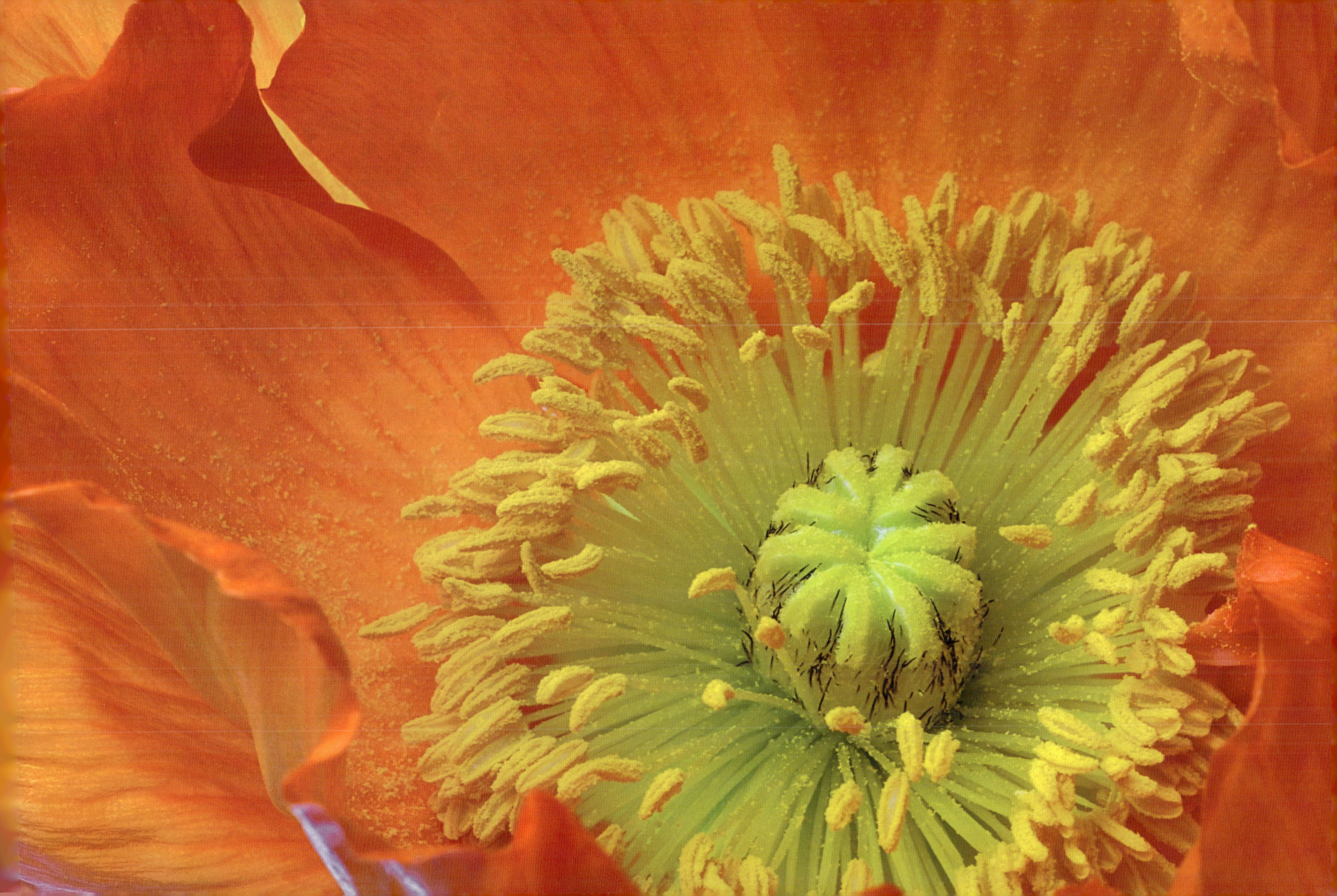

PLATE 50: *Gerbera*

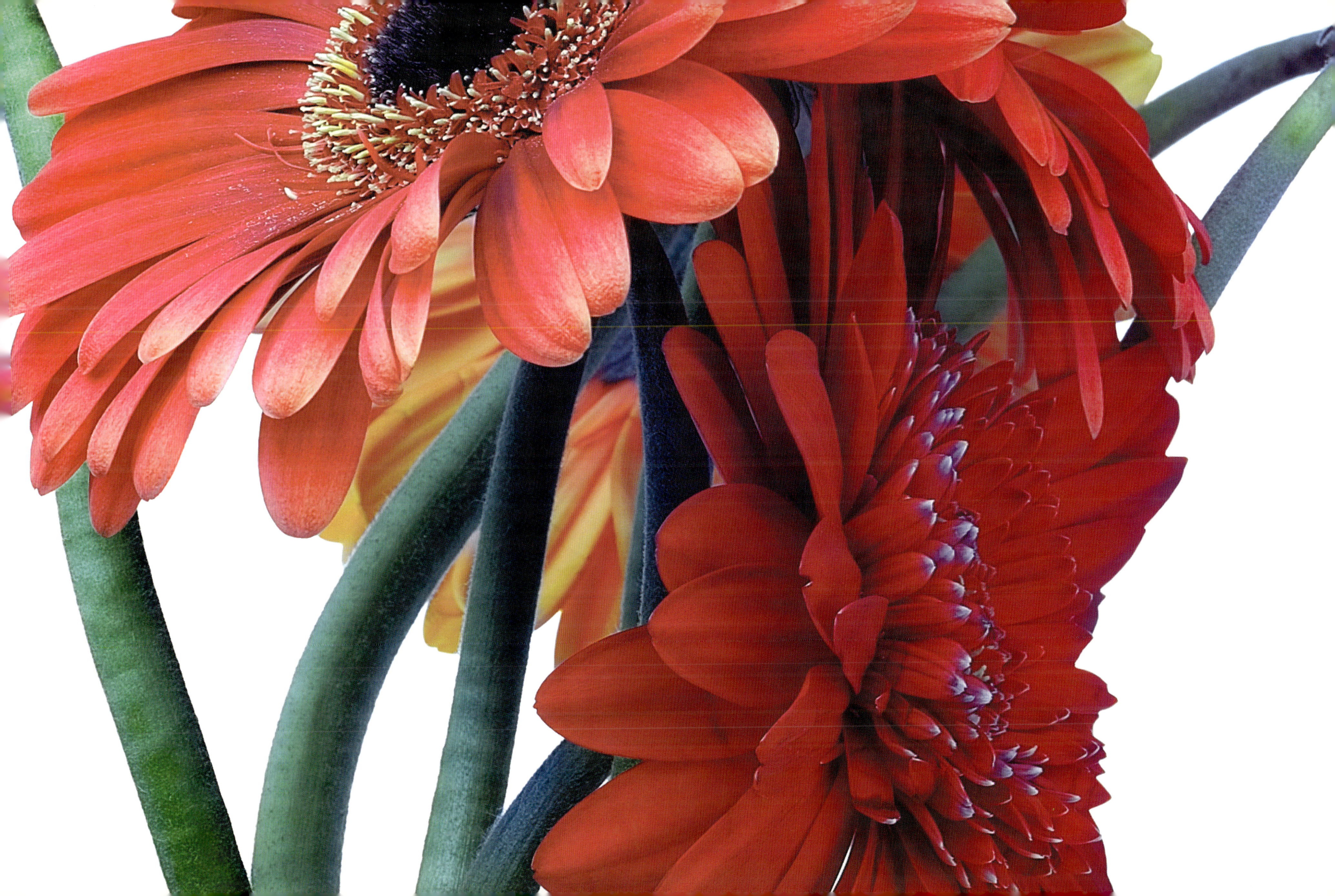

PLATE 51: *Cornus Florida*

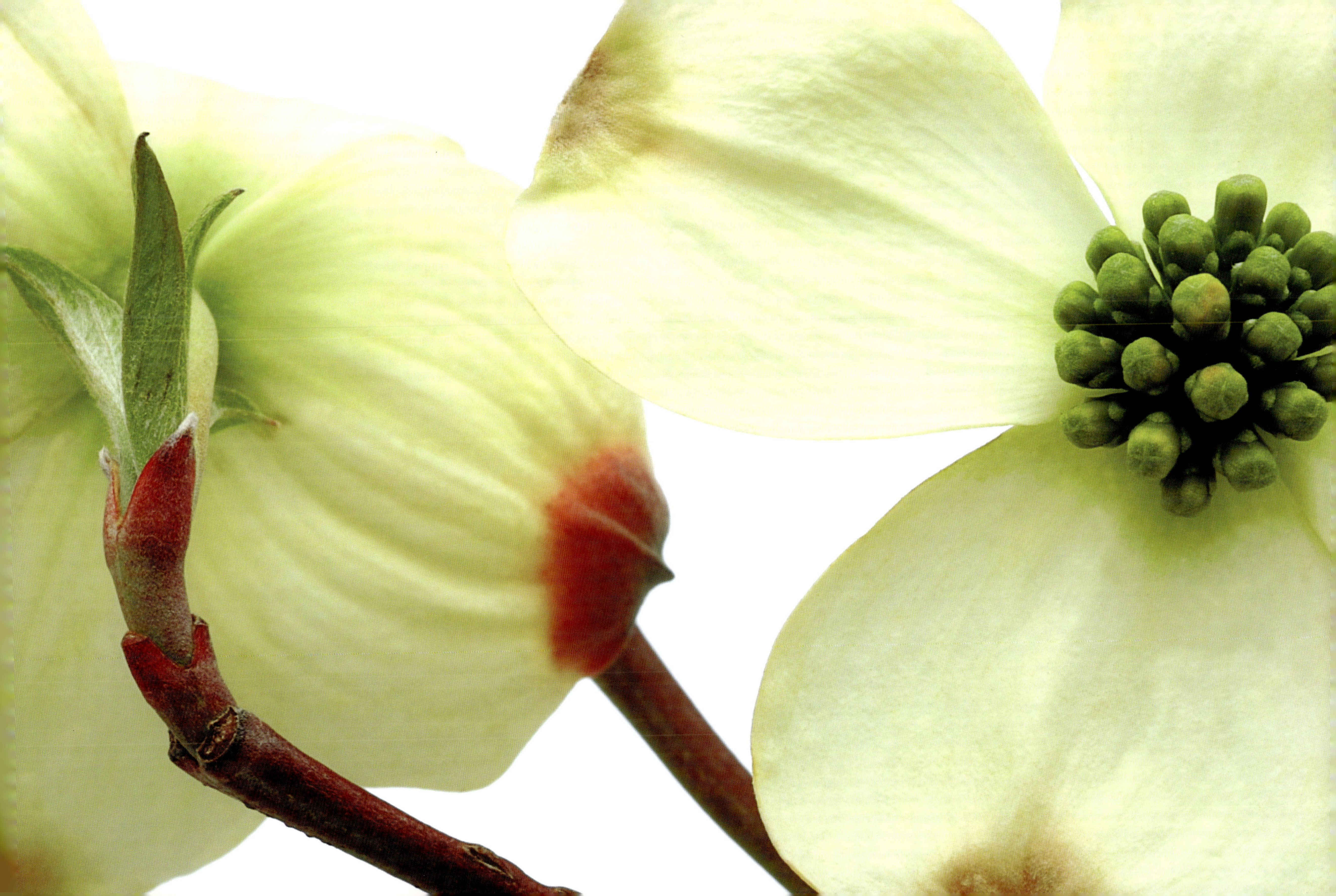

PLATE 52: *Muscari*

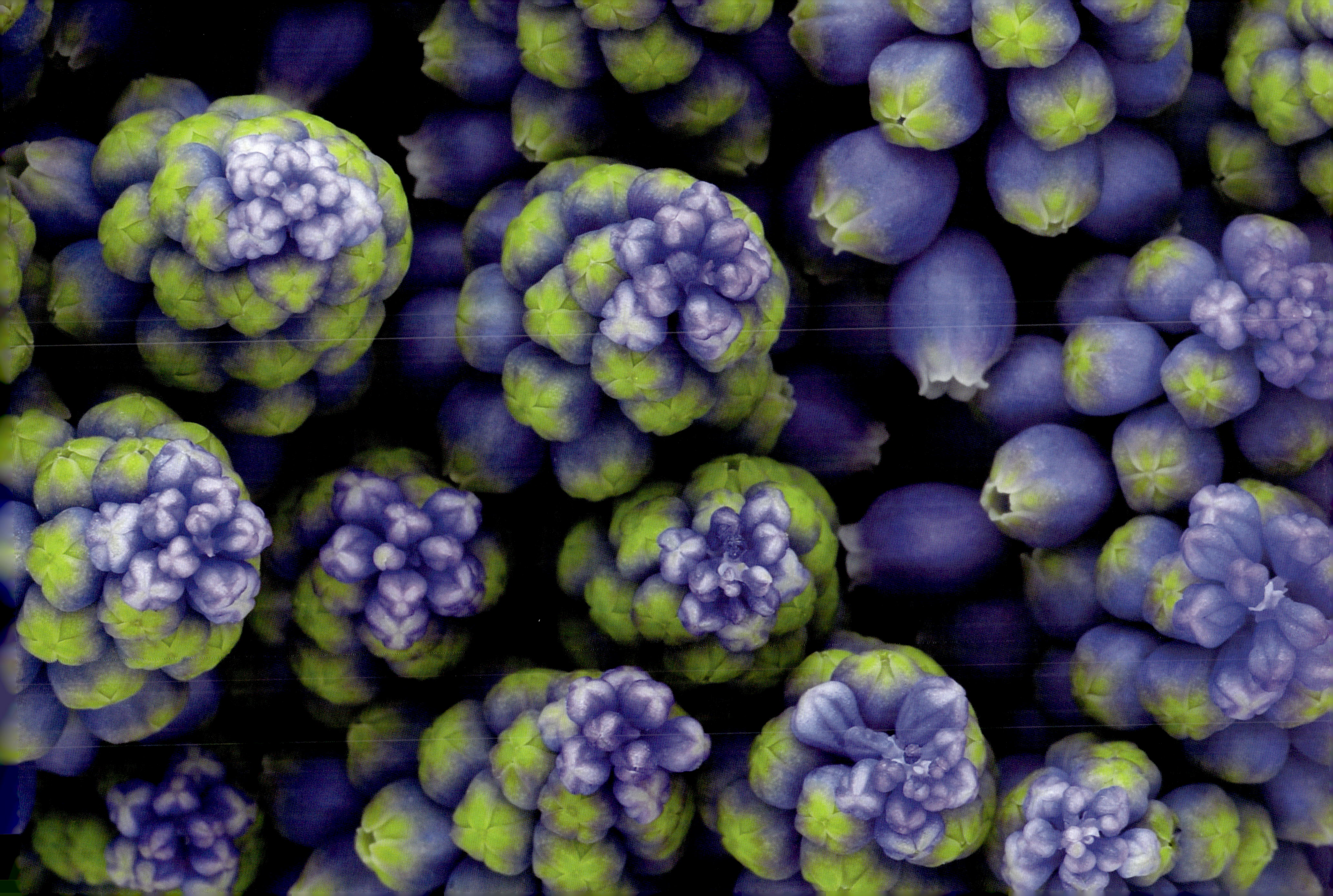

PLATE 53: *Rosa* 'Hocus-Pocus'

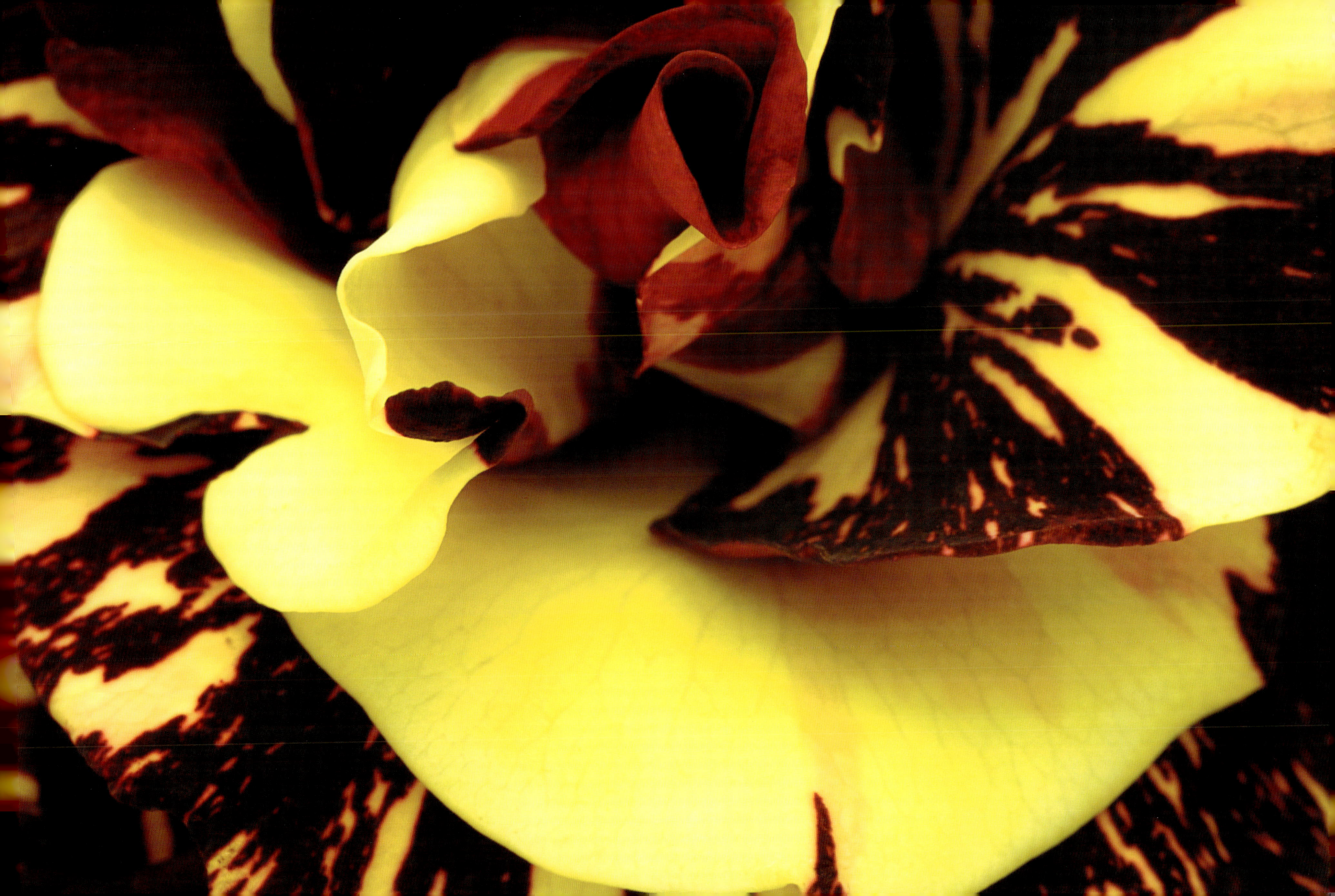

PLATE 54: *Zantedeschia*

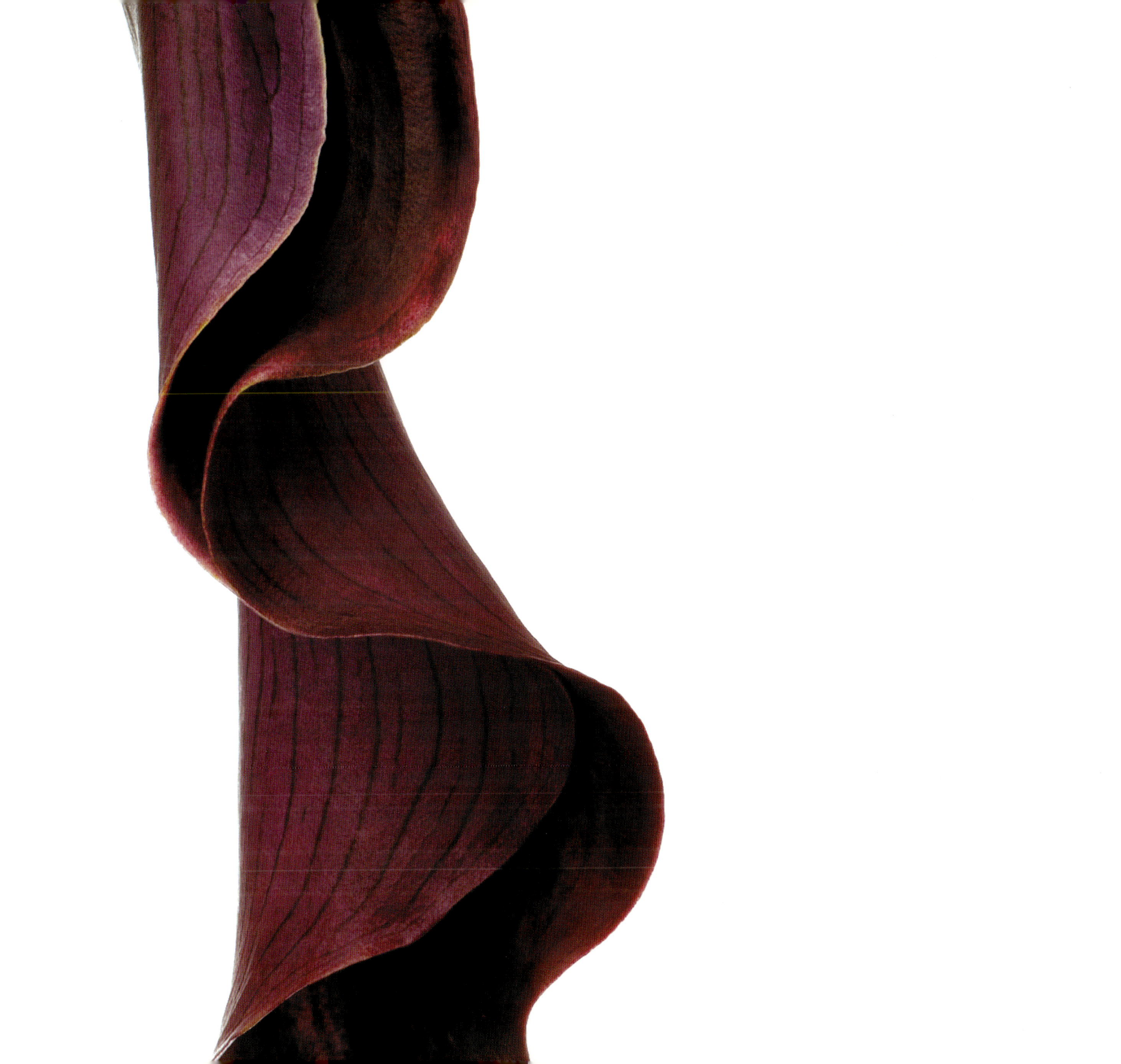

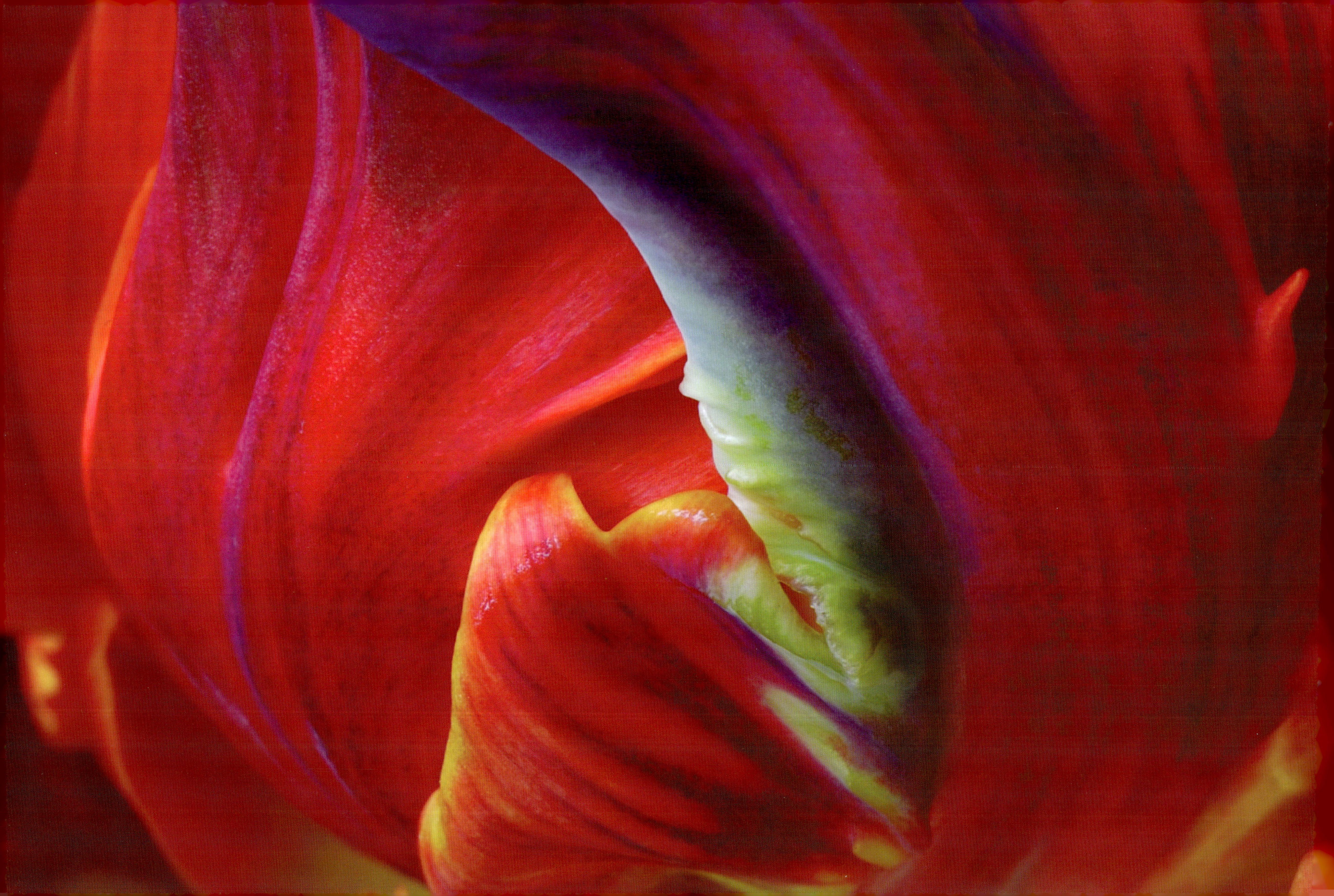

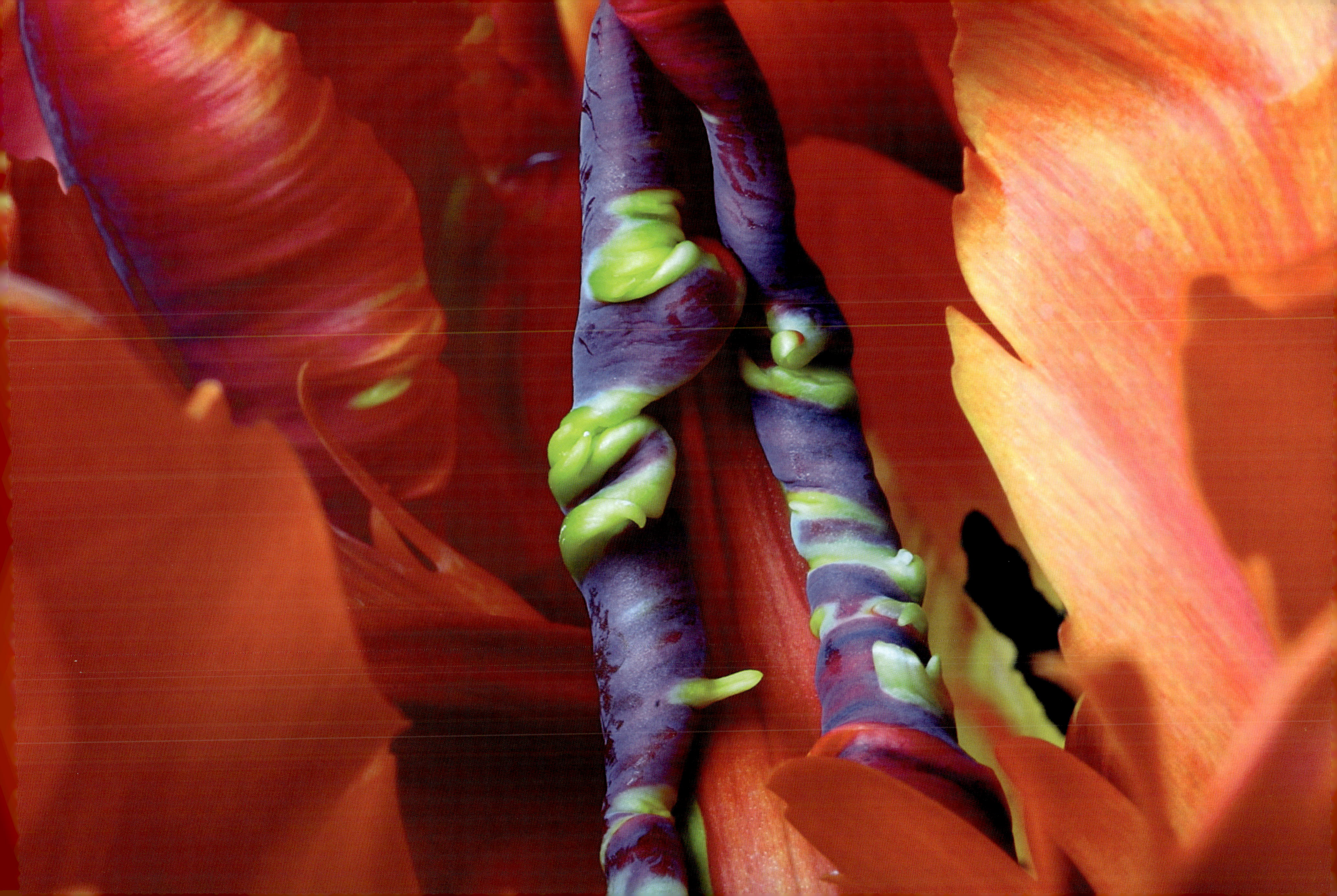

PLATES 55, 56, & 57 : *Tulipa* (preceding pages and opposite)

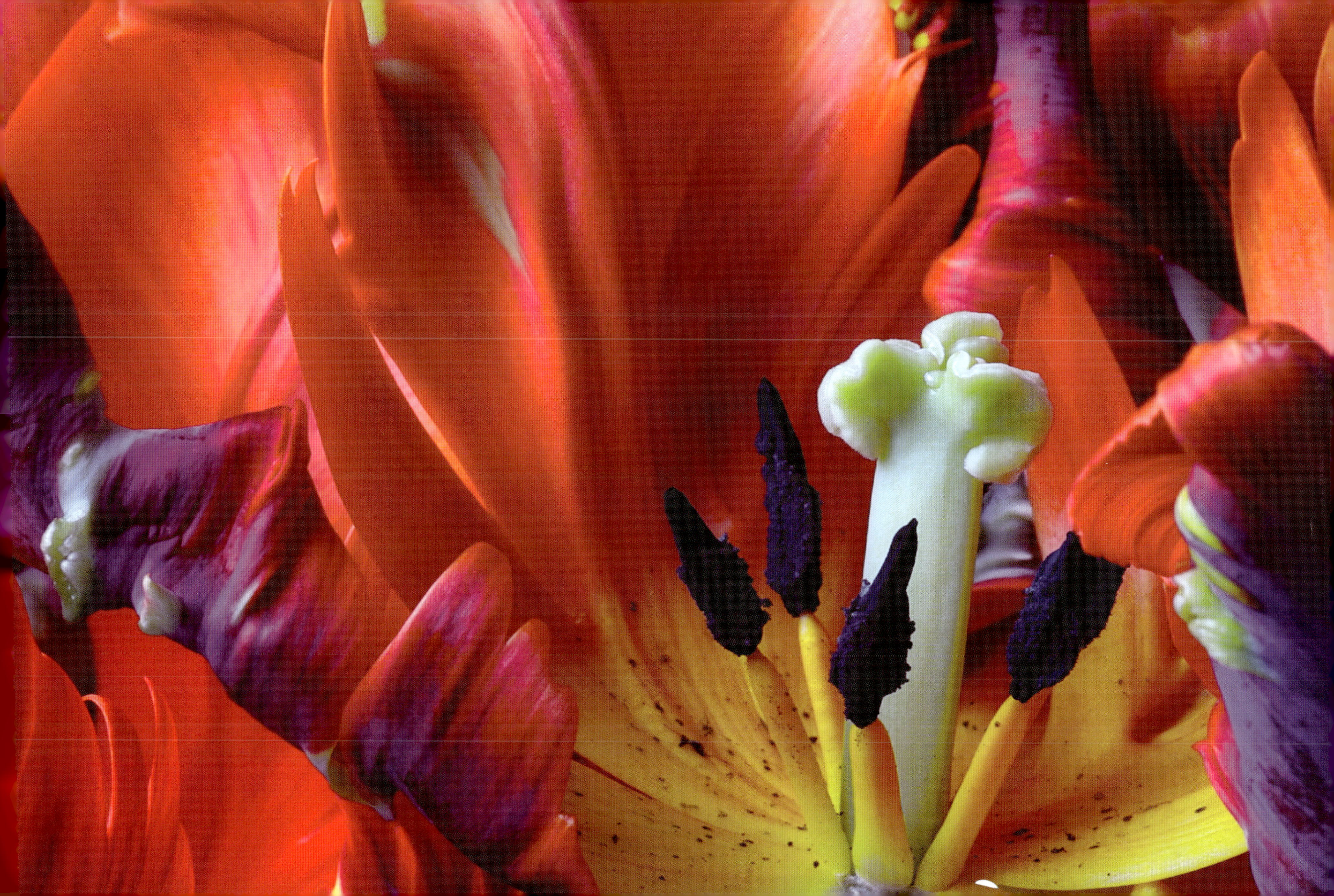

PLATE 58: *Fritillaria imperialis* 'Rubra Maxima'

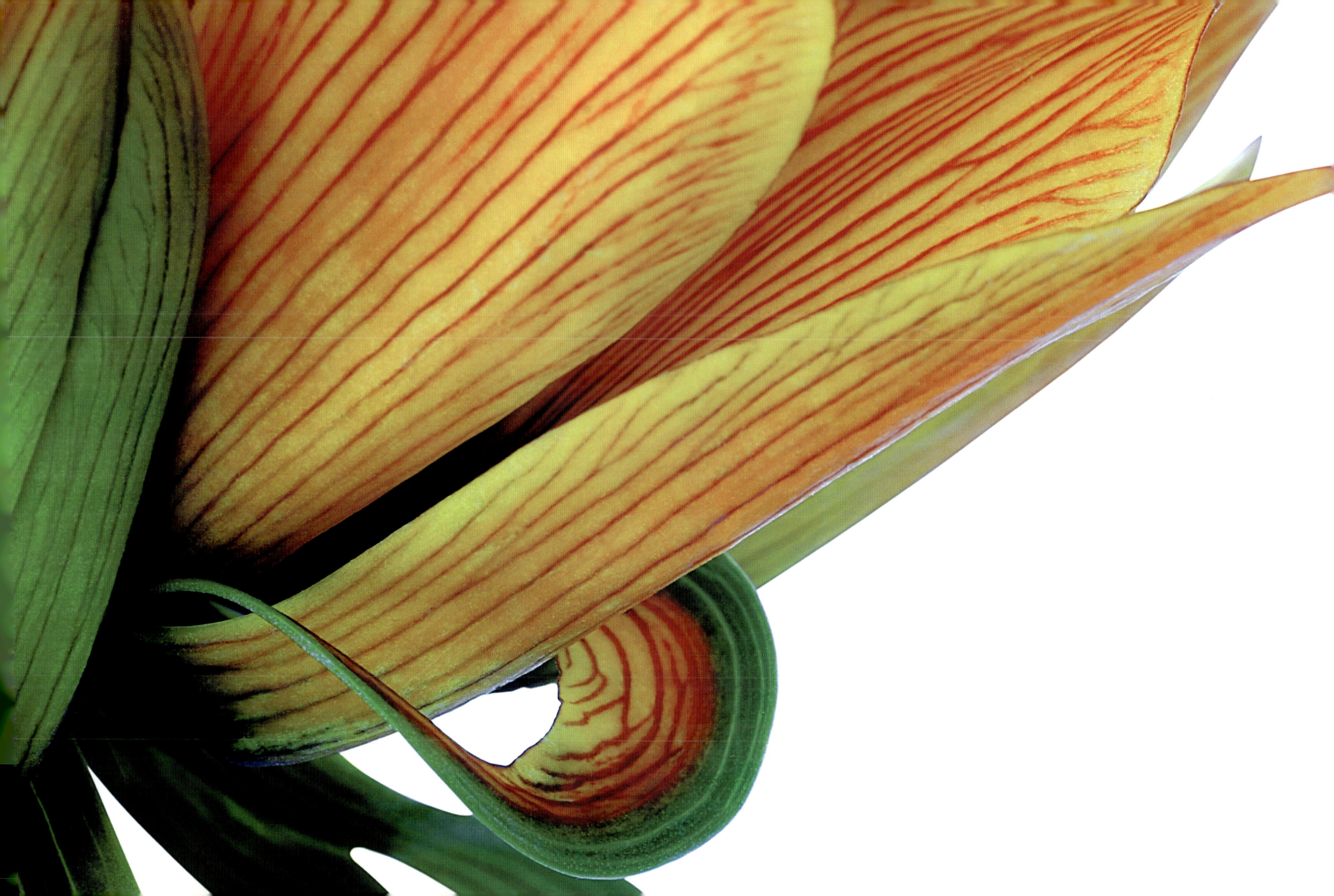

PLATE 59: *Fritillaria imperialis* 'Rubra Maxima'

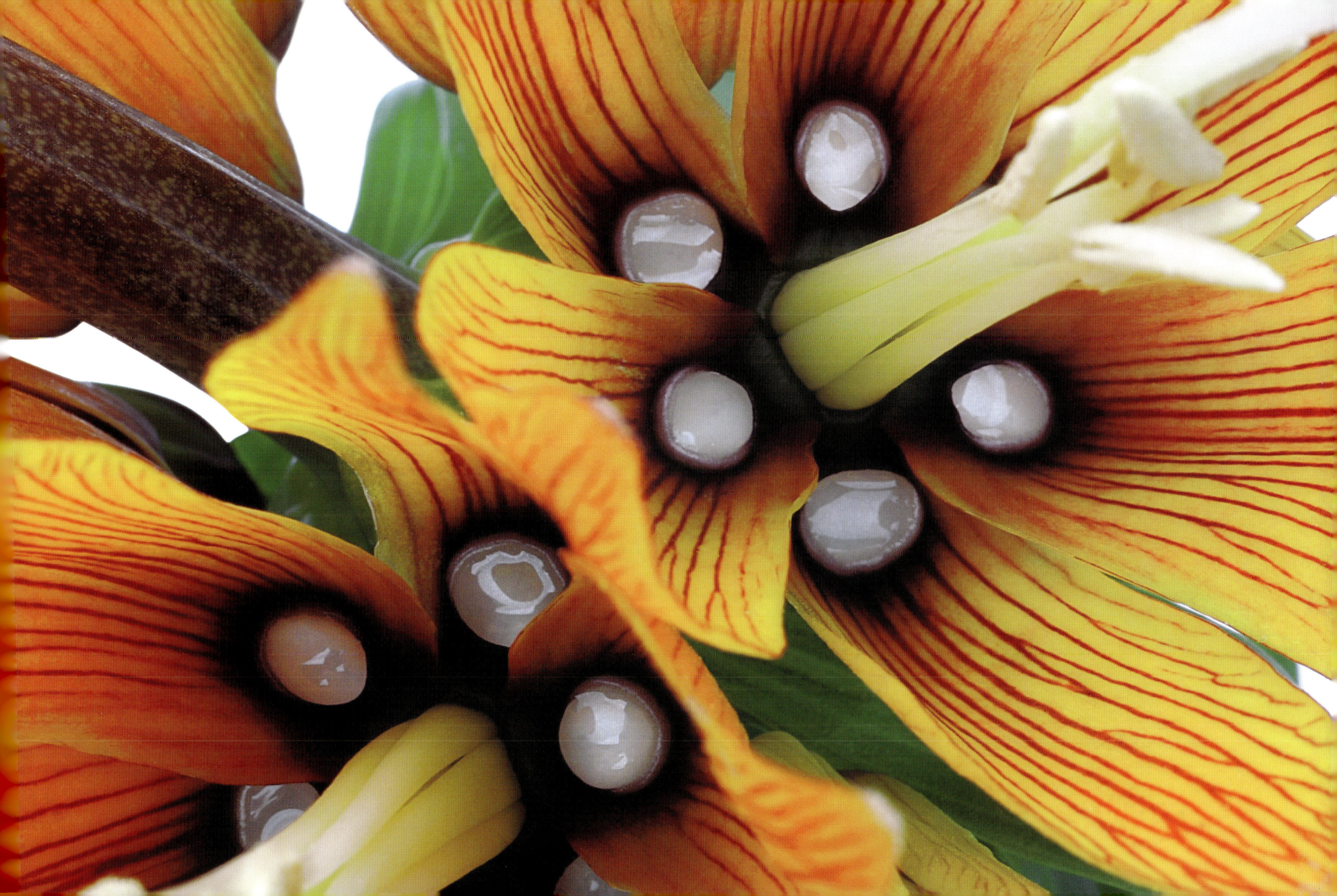

PLATE 60: *Hydrangea macrophylla*

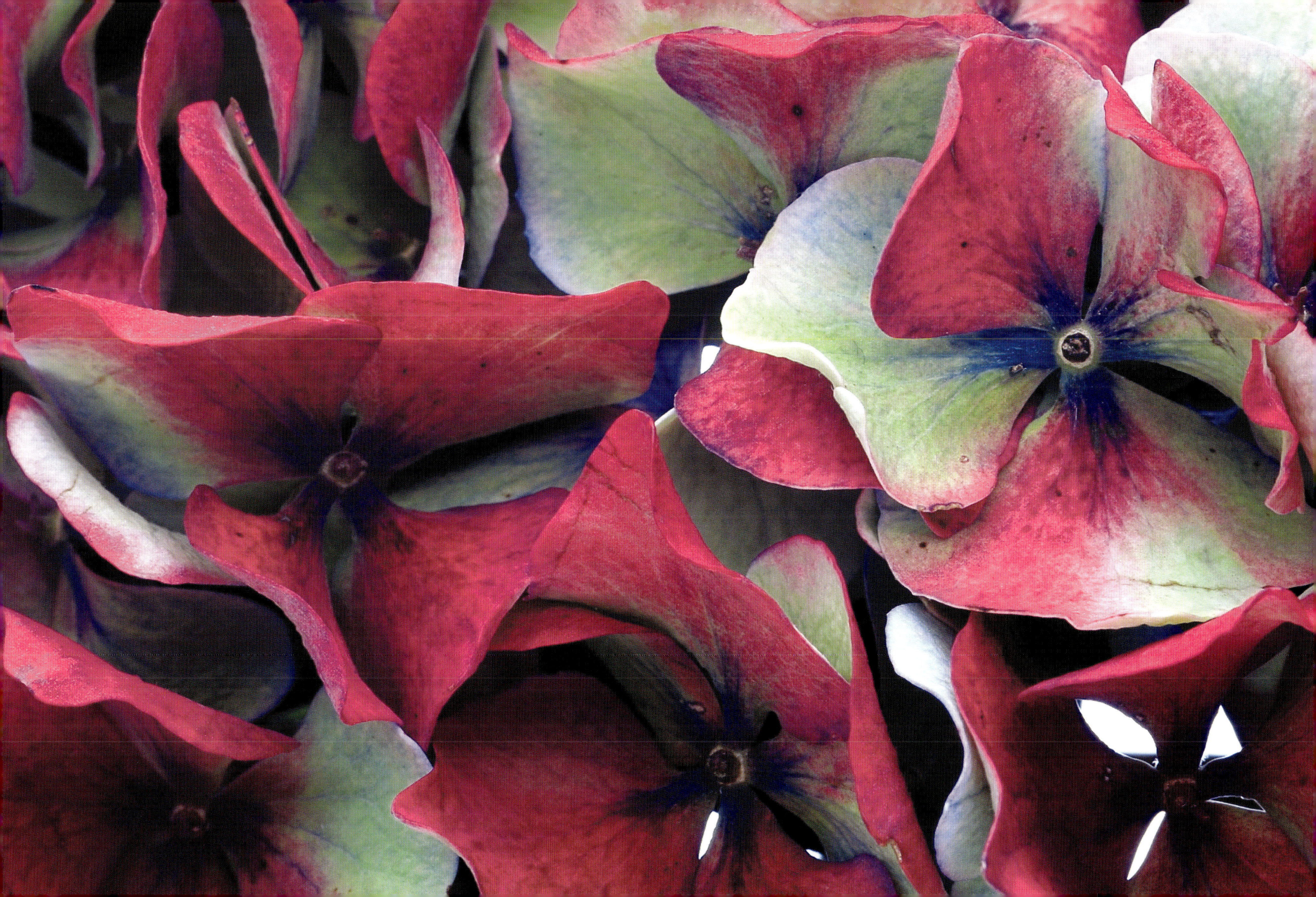

PLATE 61: *Hippeastrum*

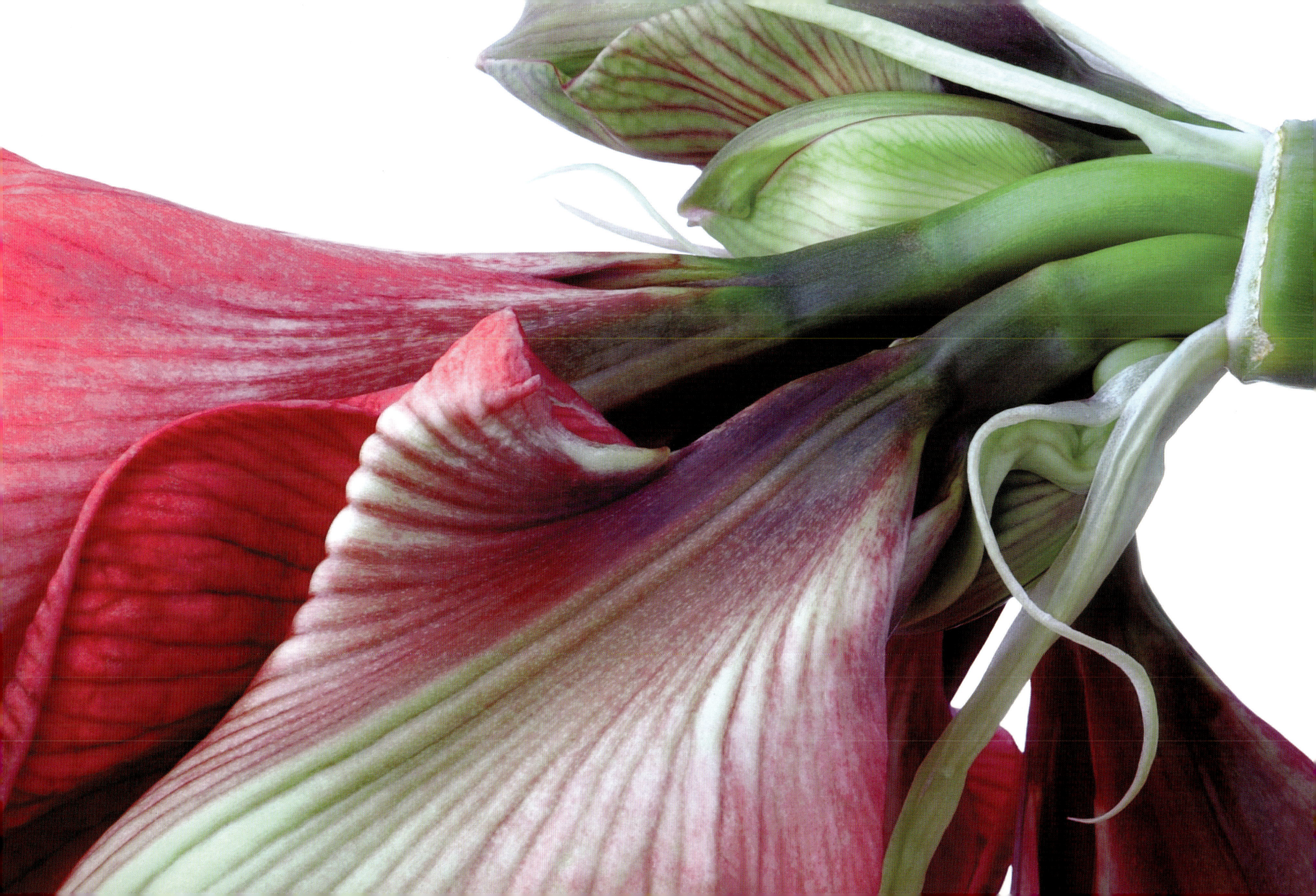

PLATE 62: *Hyacinthus orientalis*

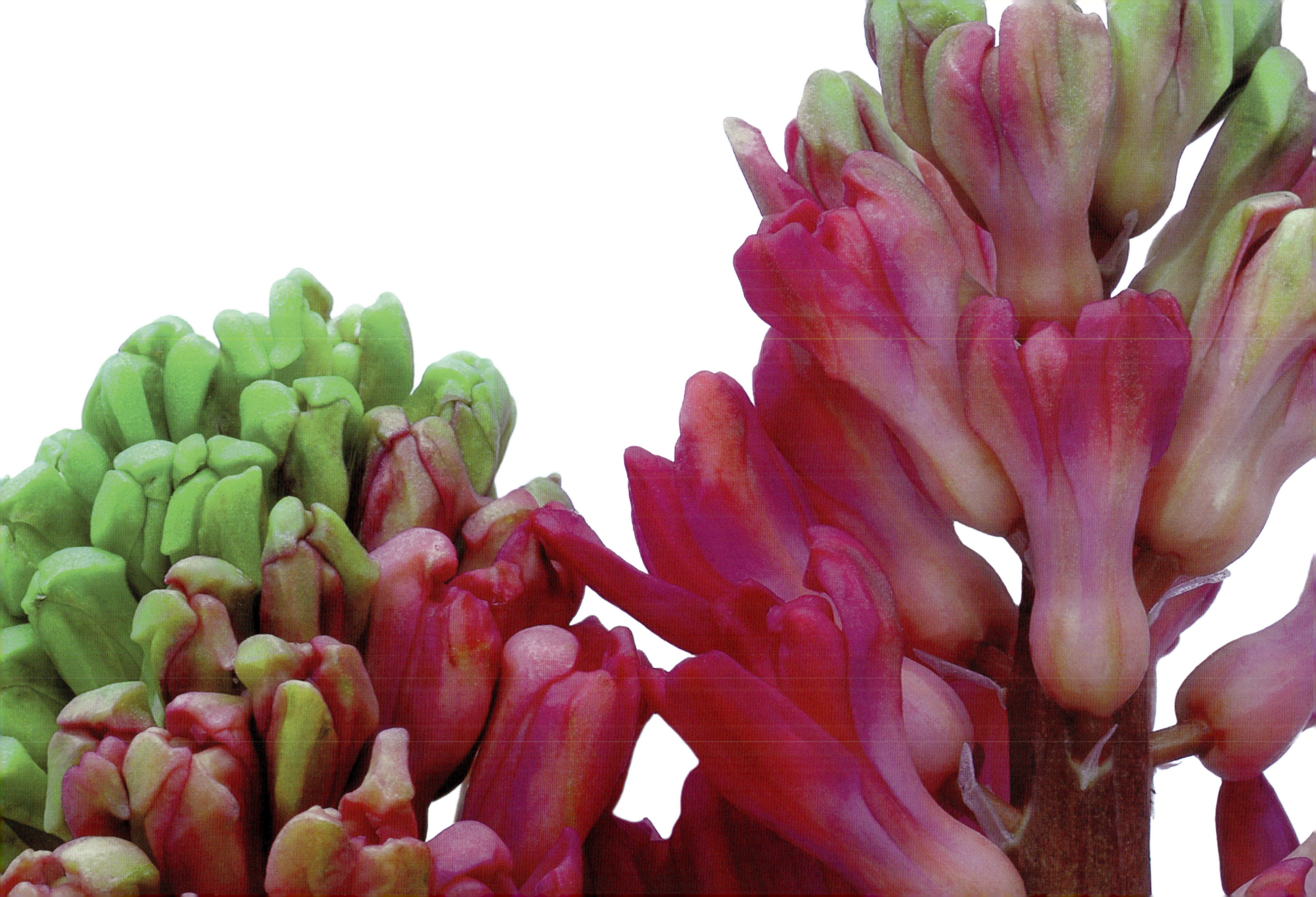

PLATE 63: *Paeonia*

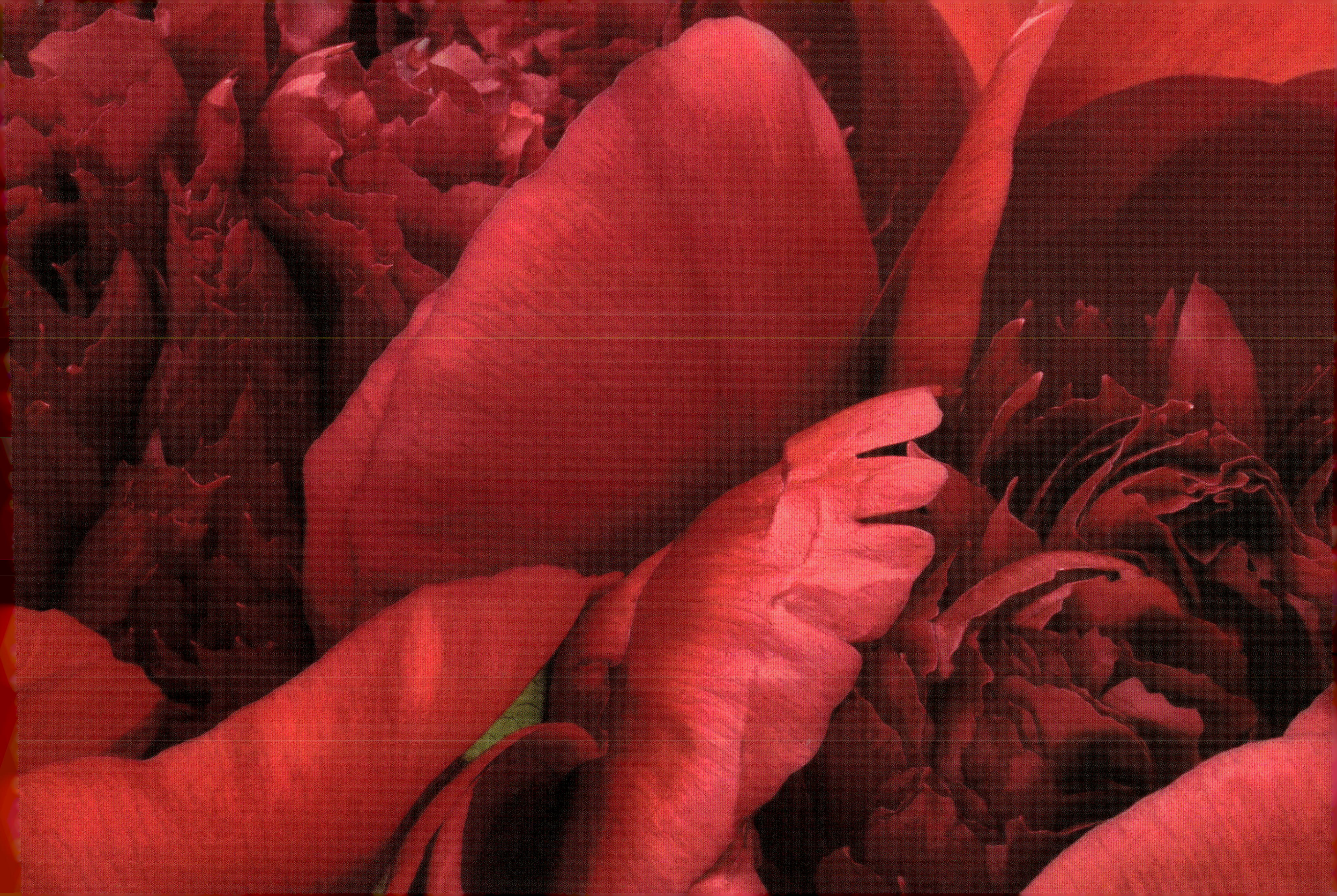

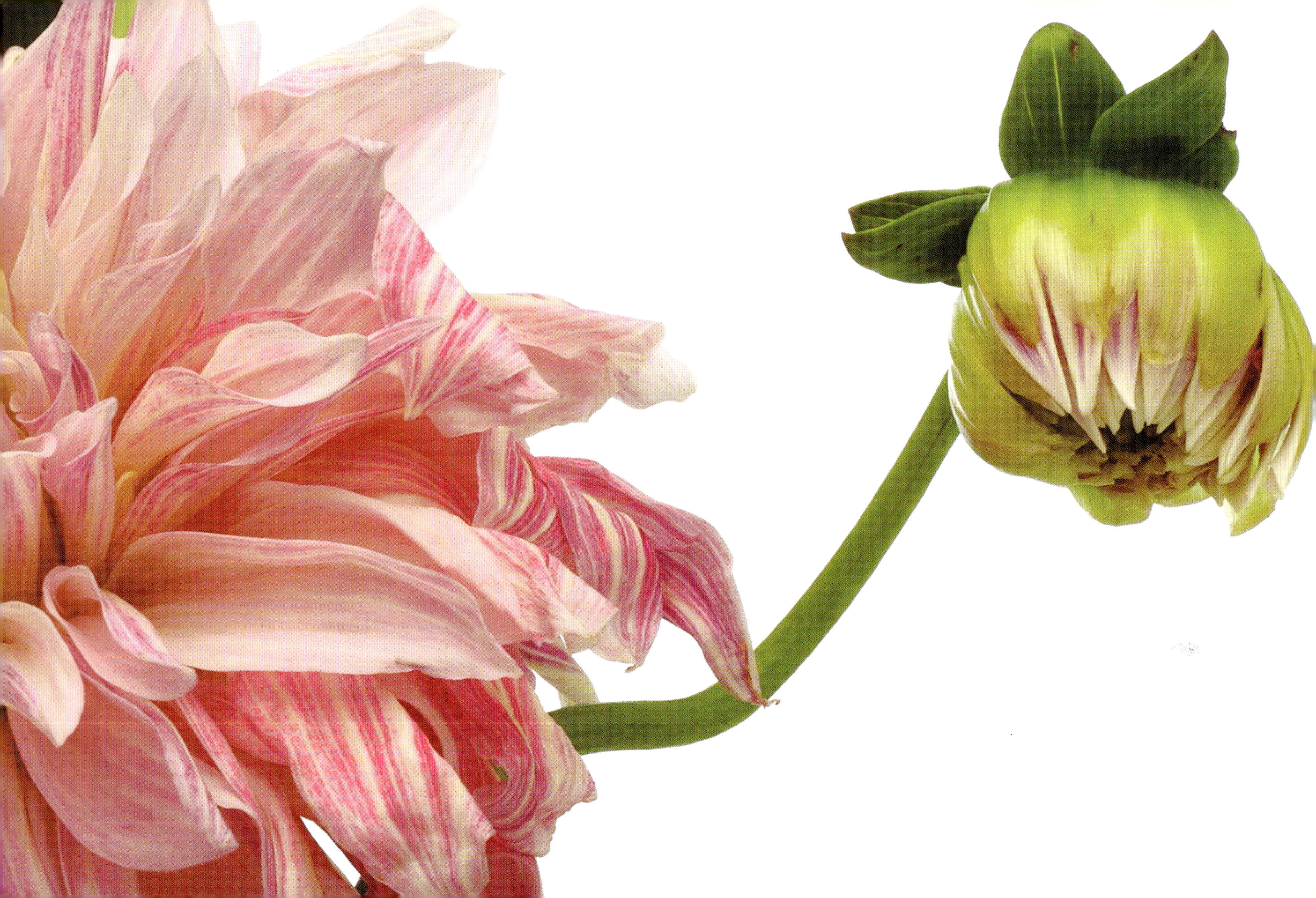

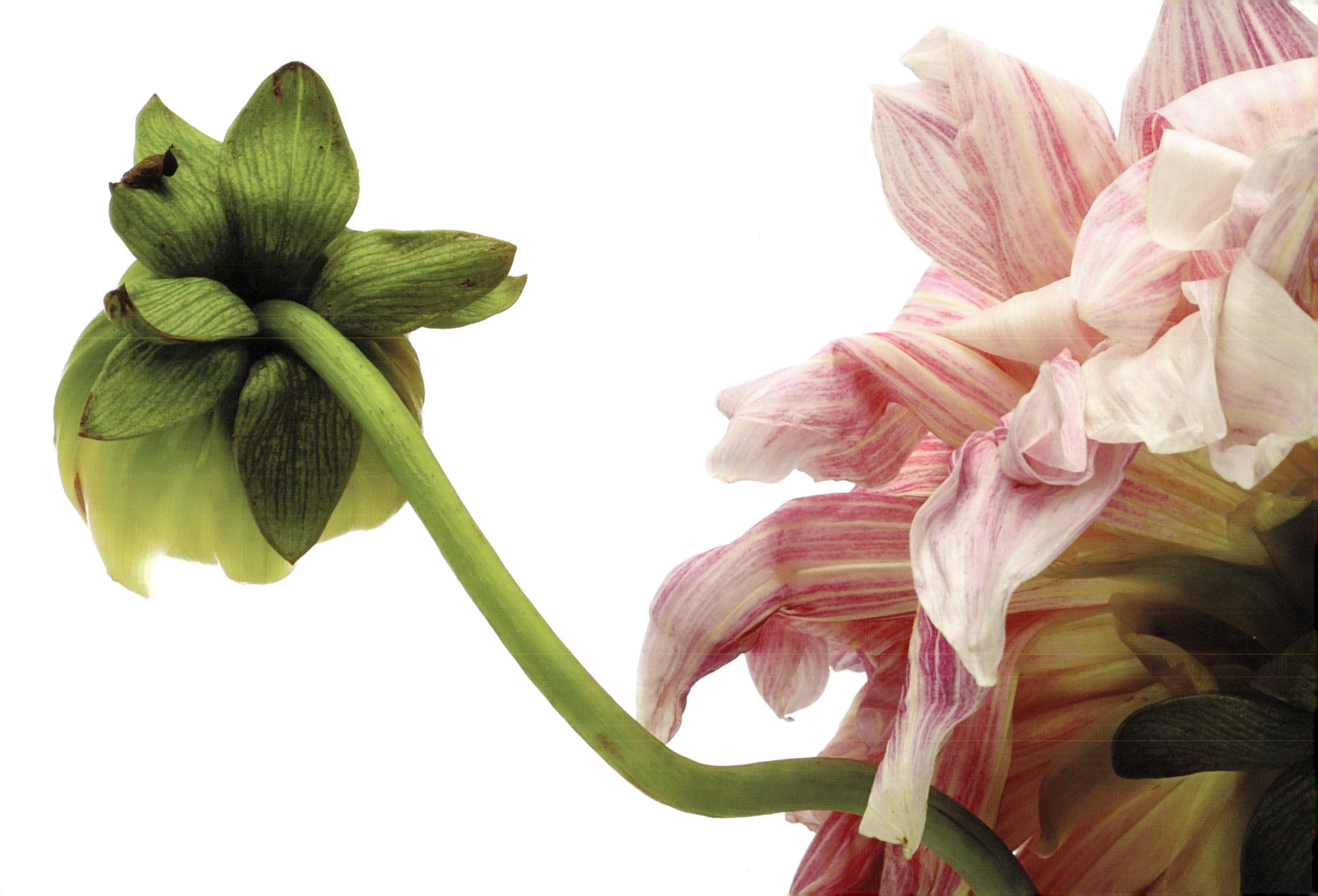

PLATES 64 & 65 : *Dahlia* (preceding pages)
PLATE 66 : *Centaurea cyanus*

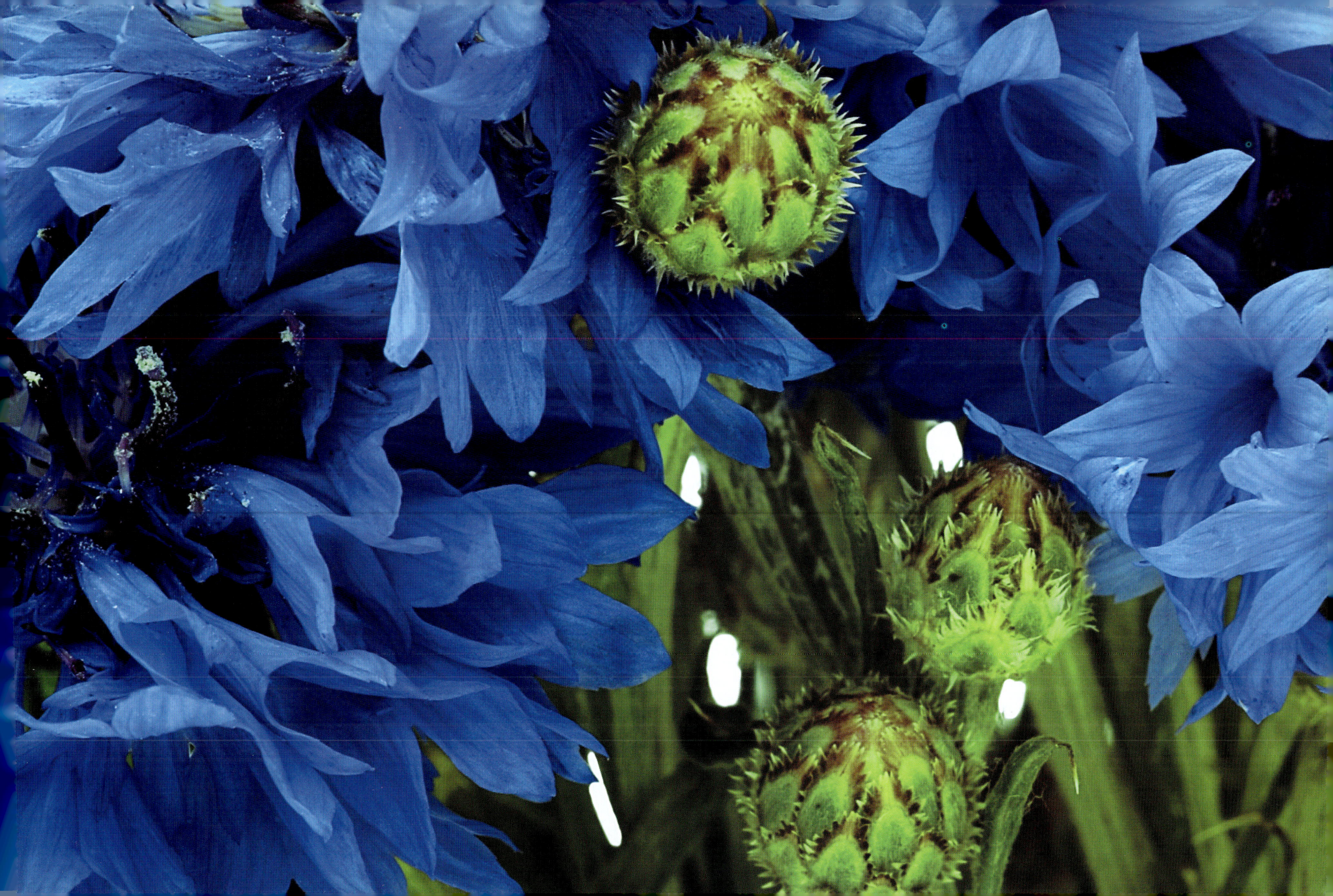

PLATE 67 : *Lilium*

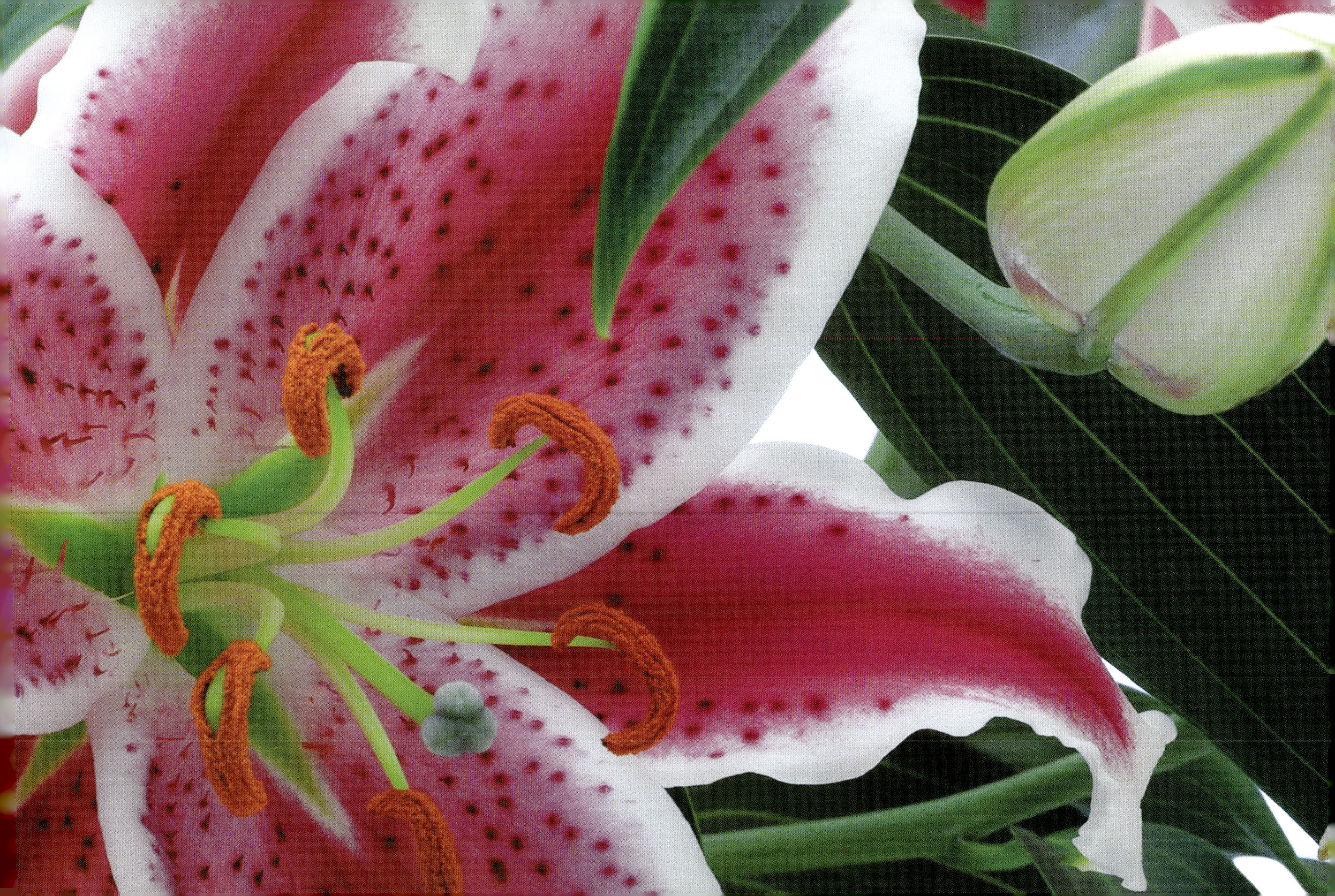

PLATE 68 : *Magnolia* x *soulangeana*

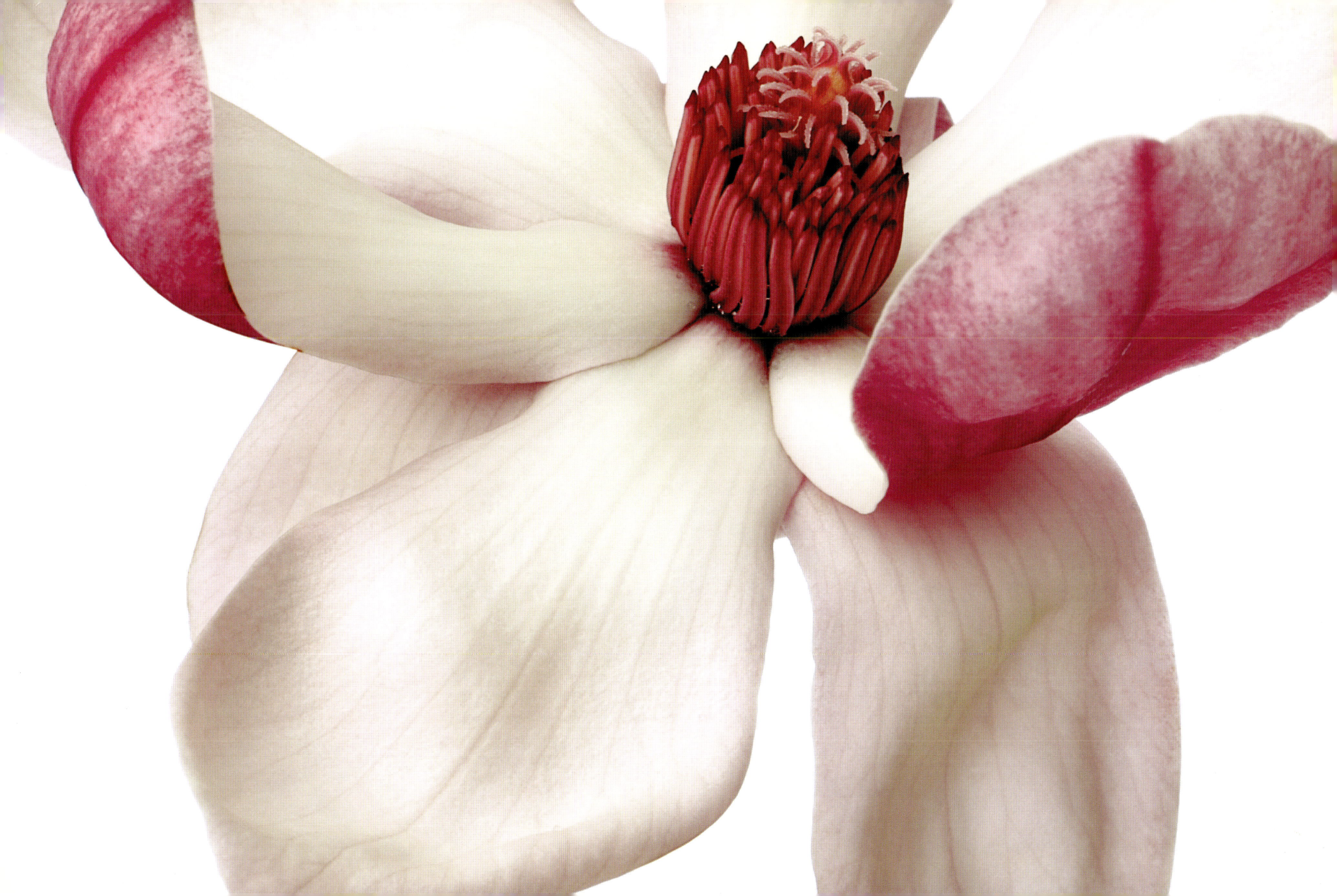

Acknowledgments

There are those people without whom I could never have done this book and to whom I am exceedingly grateful:

Christa Huffman—my wonderful assistant, for being by my side through it all
Sarah Moon—for helping me in the "Search"
Donna Mitchell—for somehow always knowing
Triana Sinclair—for gathering the most beautiful flowers
Phillip Weiner—for being my "angel"
Jason Gallacher—for his technical assistance, patience and tolerance
Michael Newler & Canon USA—for outstanding support of photographers and photography

Clark Wakabayashi—for giving such caring and diligent attention from the very beginning
Gregory Wakabayashi—for designing the book with love for the work
Lena Tabori—for sharing the vision and publishing it

For their extraordinary help and support:

Linda Lewis, Mel and *Phyllis Litoff*
China Machado, Ed Agostini, Barbara Bowen, Duane Michals, Sandro Santioli, John Stark, and *Mary Wells Lawrence*

Ossie—for keeping me company well into all those nights working

I would also like to note the generosity of the following persons and organizations:
The staff at Welcome Books, *Dan Steinhardt, David Metz,* Apple Computers, Inc., and The New York Botanical Gardens

And, above all, *Mother Nature* for her endless inspirations

The photographs in *Searchings* were all created using Canon's EOS digital cameras (D30 and D60).

PLATE 69 : *Hippeastrum*
"September 11, 2001"
Two days after September 11, these flowers seemed to reflect what I had witnessed on that day.

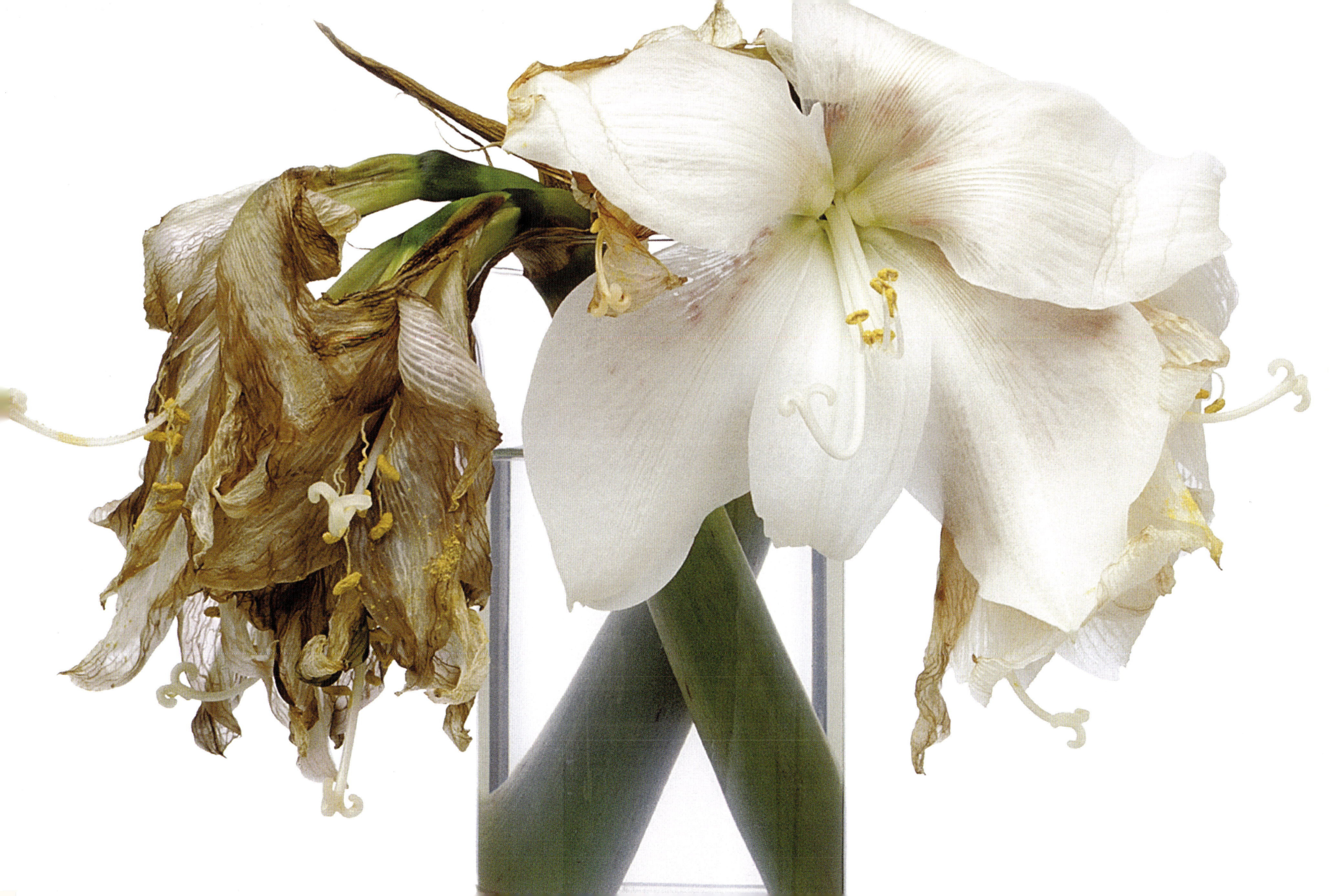

Published in 2002 by Welcome Books,
An imprint of Welcome Enterprises, Inc.
6 West 18th Street, New York, NY, 10011
(212) 989-3200; Fax (212) 989-3205
email: info@welcomebooks.biz
www.welcomebooks.biz

Publisher: Lena Tabori
Project Director: H. Clark Wakabayashi

Designed by Gregory Wakabayashi and Barbara Bordnick
Botanical identification by Margaret Falk

Distributed to the trade in the U.S. and Canada by
Andrews McMeel Distribution Services
Order Department and Customer Service: (800) 223-2336
Orders Only Fax: (800) 943-9831

For information regarding the purchase of original limited edition prints please contact:
info@searchings.us

Library of Congress Cataloging-in-Publication Data

Bordnick, Barbara.
Searchings : secret landscapes of flowers / Barbara Bordnick.
p. cm.
ISBN 0-941807-74-6 (hardcover)
1. Flowers--Pictorial works. 2. Photography of plants. I. Title.

SB408 .B67 2002
635.9'022'2--dc21

Printed in China

First Edition
1 3 5 7 9 10 8 6 4 2

WILD&SCENIC

ILLINOIS

Photography by Willard Clay
Text by Robert Hutchinson

Illinois is more than corn fields,
Willard Clay

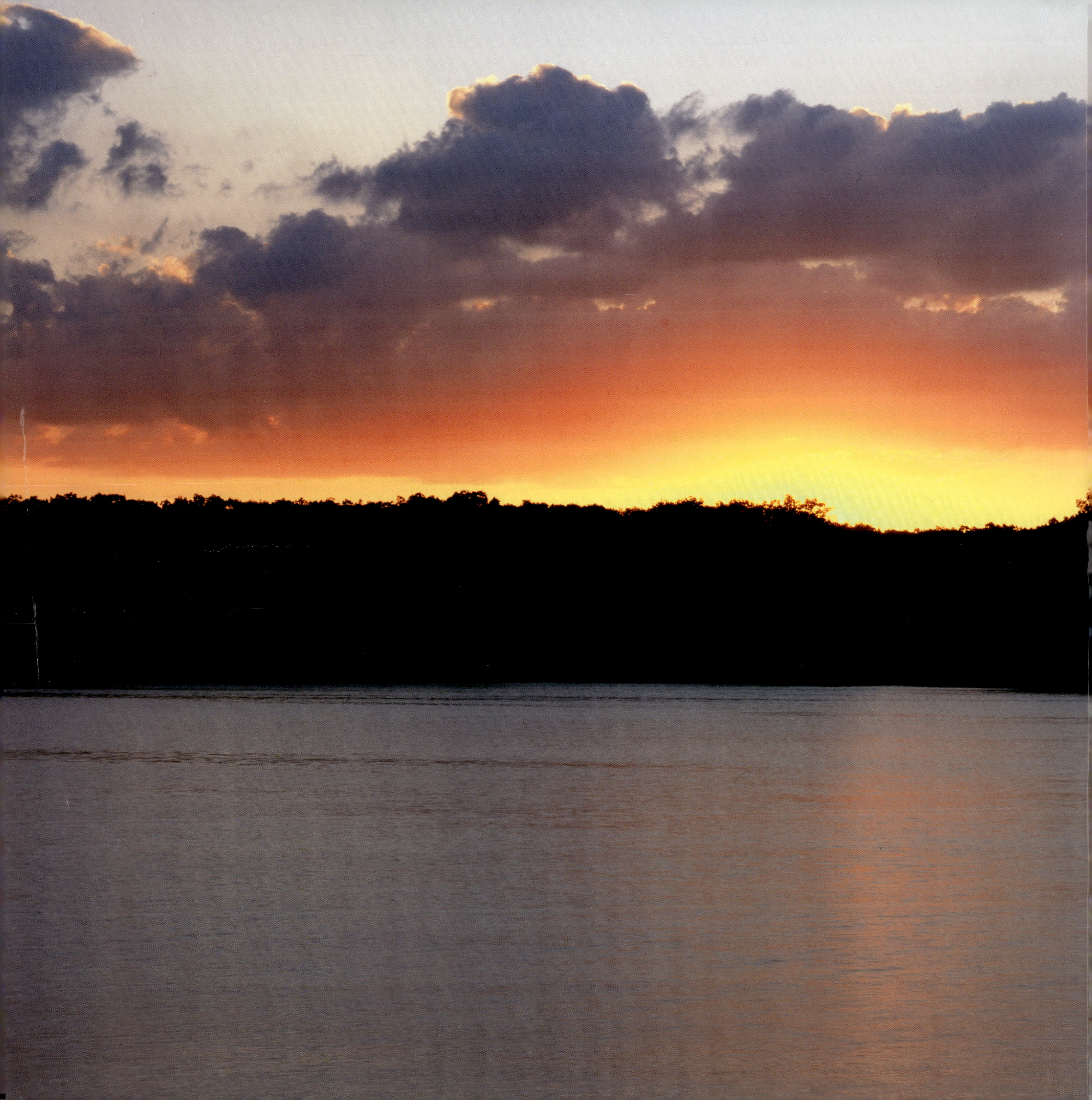

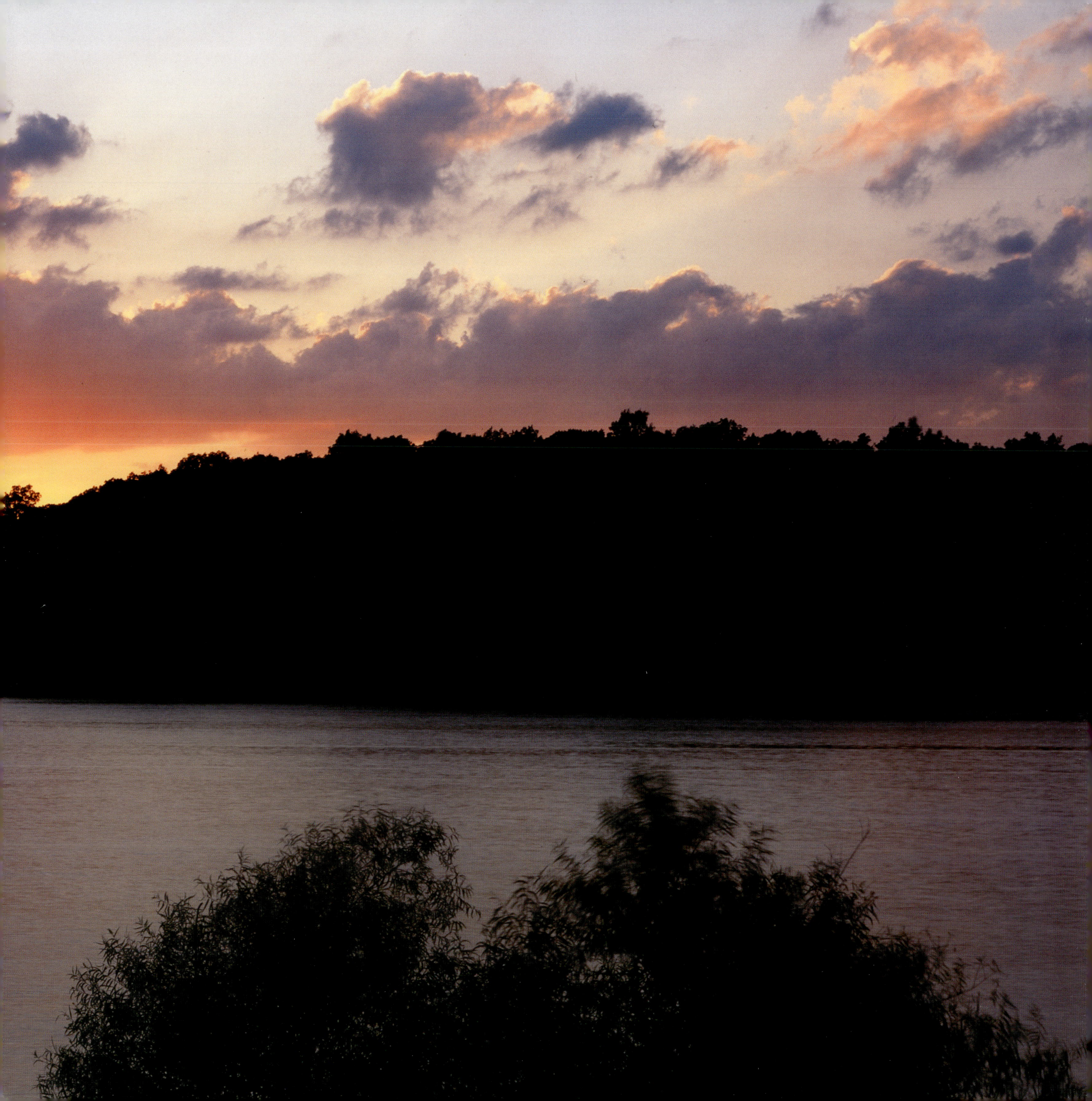

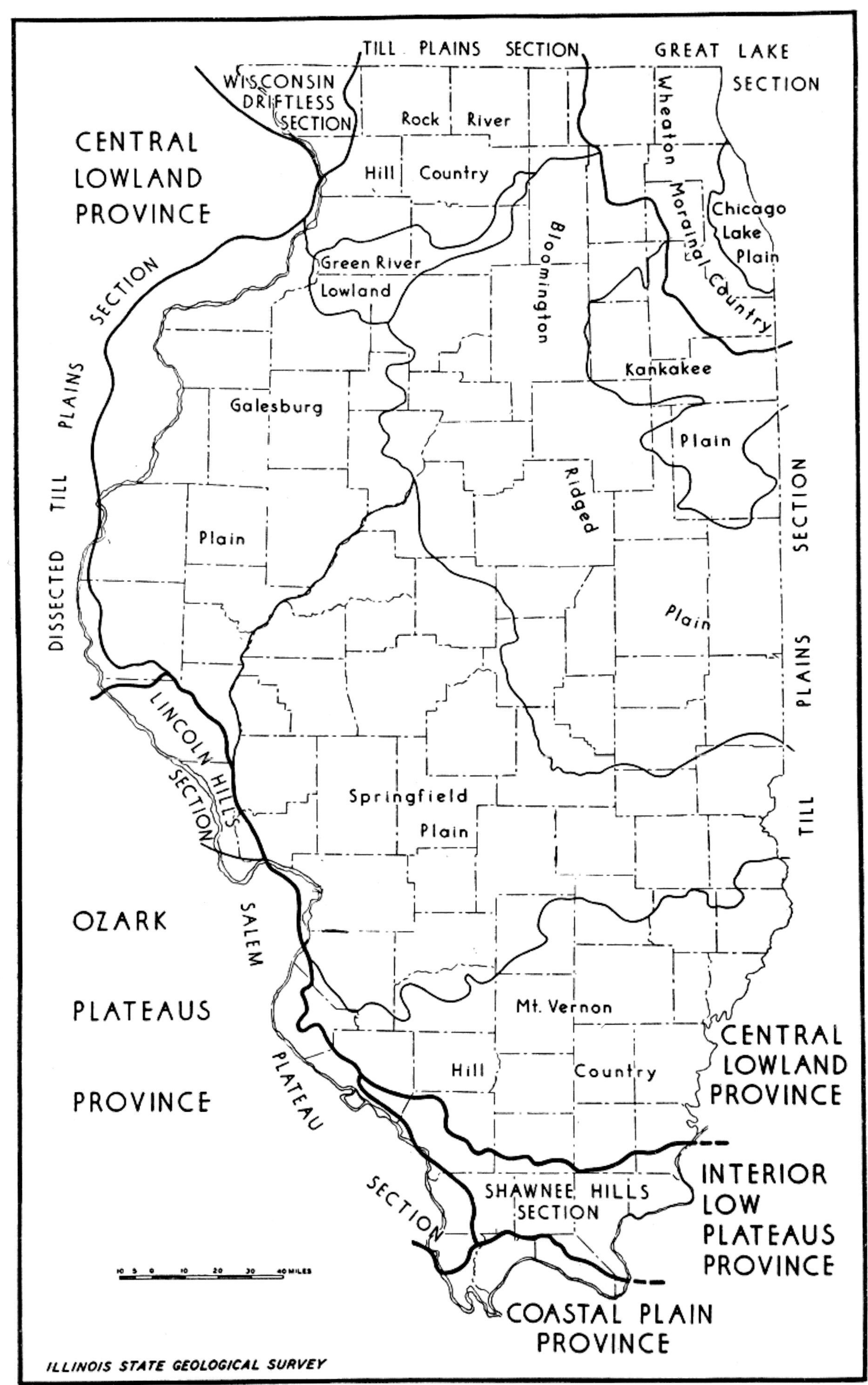

FIG. 1.—Physiographic divisions of Illinois, by Leighton, Ekblaw, and Horberg

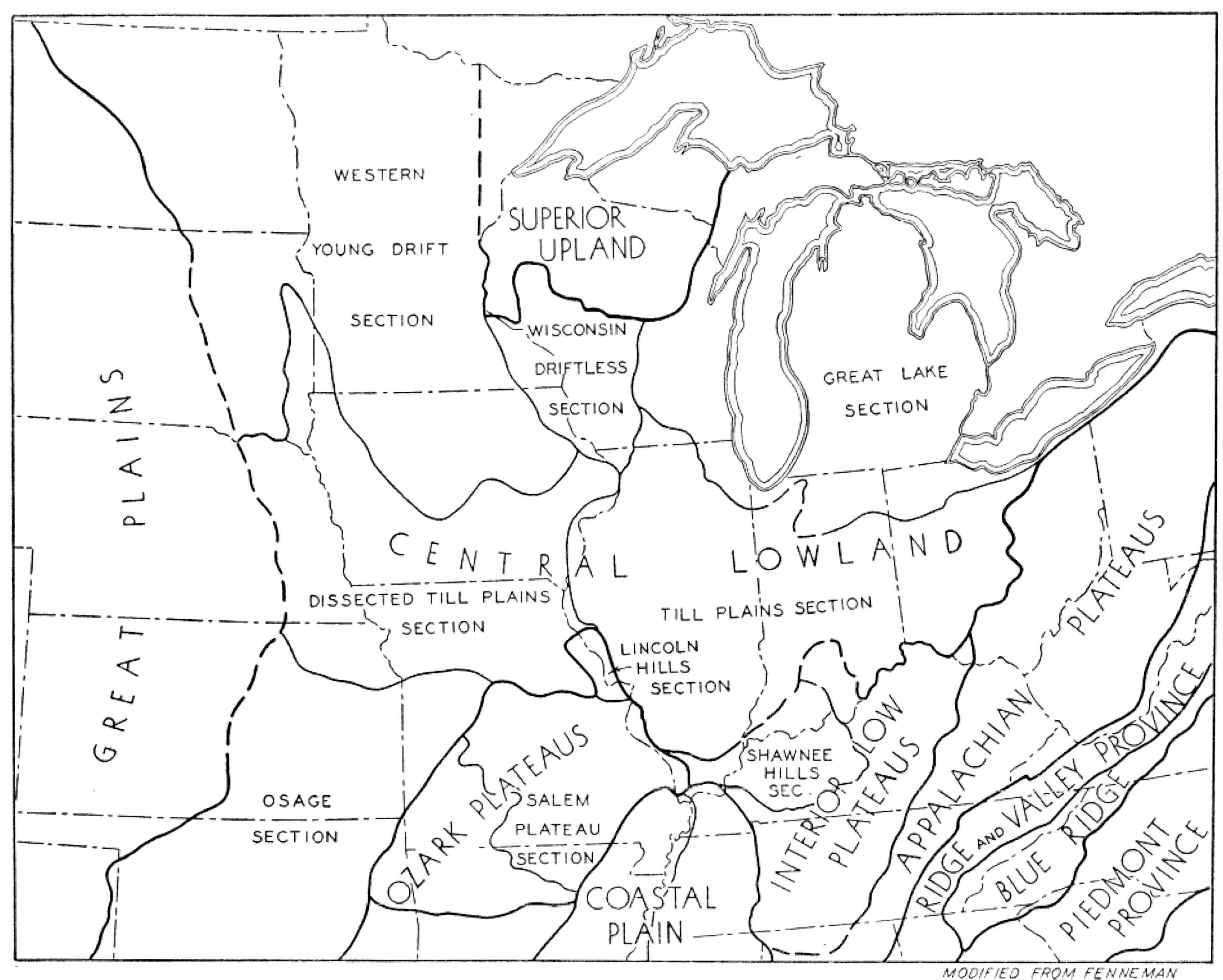

FIG. 2.—Major physiographic divisions in central United States (after Fenneman)

Wild & Scenic Illinois
Photography by Willard Clay
Text by Robert Hutchinson

Library of Congress Cataloging-in-Publication Data

Clay, Will, 1941 –
Wild & scenic Illinois / photography by Willard Clay;
text by Robert Hutchinson
p. cm
ISBN (cloth): 1-56313-942-1 (alk. paper)
1. Illinois—Pictorial works. 2. Illinois—Description and travel. 3. Natural history—Illinois—Pictorial works. 4. Landscape—Illinois—Pictorial works. 5. Landscape photography—Illinois. I. Title: Wild and scenic Illinois. II. Hutchinson, Robert, 1951- III. Title.
F542.C58 2004
977.3'0022'2—dc22
2004006127

Pages 2-3: Sunset on Lake Dawson, Moraine View State Recreation Area, McLean County.

10 9 8 7 6 5 4 3 2 1

Published by BrownTrout Publishers, Inc.,
P.O. Box 280070, San Francisco, CA 94128-0070 U.S.A.
800-777-7812
www.browntrout.com

Printed and bound by Pac-Com, Korea

PHOTOGRAPHER'S ACKNOWLEDGMENTS

The state of Illinois has a land area of 55,593 square miles and a population of 12,600,620, for a population density (2002) of 227 people per square mile. Among the fifty states, Illinois ranks twenty-sixth in land area; fifth in population; and eleventh in population density. Of Illinois's land cover, 76 percent is agricultural; 12 percent, forest; 6 percent, urban (accounting for 88 percent of the population); 4 percent, wetland; and 2 percent, other.

When the French explorers Louis Joliet and Father Jacques Marquette paddled down the Mississippi and up the Illinois Rivers in 1673, the country corresponding to the modern state of Illinois had a population of less than 20,000—mostly Illinois (including the Cahokia, Kaskaskia, Michigamea, Peoria, and Tamaroa tribes) and some Miami—for a population density of about one-third of a person per square mile. Illinois's landscape was a mosaic of prairies, forests, marshes, and swamps. Of Illinois's land cover at that time, 55 percent was prairie and 39 percent was forest.

In the intervening 330 years, the original prairies have been transformed into monocultural fields of corn, soybeans, and wheat; the forests have been logged; and the marshes and swamps have been drained. What precious little remains of the pre-contact landscape are several hundred preserves—some pristine but most restored; ranging in size from a national forest of 277 thousand acres to a vest-pocket wetland of less than half-an-acre—which have been set aside over the last eighty years under the stewardship of government agencies and public conservancies.

As of 2002, Illinois has 1,064 square miles of natural open space protected in 1 national forest, 62 state parks, 28 conservation areas, 32 fish and wildlife areas, 34 natural areas, 96 nature preserves, 7 state forests, 13 greenways and state trails, and 1 state recreation area—altogether accounting for only one-and-a-half percent of the state's area. Despite being the fifth most populous state in the Union, Illinois ranks but forty-eighth in amount of public land set aside!

To make this book, I have, in each one of the last seventeen years, added more and more of Illinois's numerous, but often sequestered and not widely known, natural sanctuaries to my photographic portfolio. I only regret that all of Illinois's hundreds of preservation entities could not be represented in this book. Every one of them has its distinct character and charm and it was a painful duty having to leave out so many worthy sites in order to accommodate the physical constraints of an exhibit-format photographic book. I have tried my hardest to ameliorate this selective exigency by systematically plotting my photographic coverage of the state to ensure that every physiographic section in the state and as many of its counties as possible are represented in this book.

I would like to acknowledge the countless organizations and people who have assisted me over the last seventeen years in tracking down the locations that would best depict Illinois's natural beauty in all its variety. First and foremost, I wish to thank the many dedicated employees of the Illinois Department of Natural Resources, whose friendly assistance has been invaluable to this project.

Scarcely less important to my work have been the contributions of the personnel of a bright array of governmental and non-governmental organizations: various of our state's 102 county park departments (especially those of Du Page County, with its many preserves), Chicago Wilderness, the Illinois Department of Tourism, Illinois Now!, the Illinois Nature Conservancy, Morton Arboretum, Natural Area Guardians, Save The Prairie Society, and many others. Special thanks go to the U.S. Forest Service for their efforts to preserve the natural integrity of the Shawnee National Forest: enchanted spots like Bell Smith Springs are too precious a public asset to lose to logging or other private commercial operations.

A general blessing must be bestowed on the army of citizen volunteers and contributors who expend their time, labor, and treasure on the preservation and restoration of Illinois's natural heritage, expecting in exchange only beauty, biodiversity, and the satisfaction of performing public good. And lastly, credit must be given to my Illinoian nature photography colleagues—especially Joseph Kayne, Doug Sherman, and Hank Erdmann—for freely sharing with me their favorite "secret" locations.

I would like to dedicate this book to Debra Alsvig-Clay for her unending support; to her sons, Curtiss and David; to the Helffrich family: Austin, Therese, Tim, Jayme, and Lindsay; and to my dear friend, Aunnie "Dog" —ever a friend even when it could not have been easy to be so. A general dedication also goes to all the people of Illinois who appreciate the natural beauty of our state and do not take it for granted.

ABOUT THE PHOTOGRAPHY

Having grown up in Arizona and photographed extensively in the Rocky Mountains, I came naturally by a style of photography that conjures with expansive views of pristine landscape horizontally stiffened by clean skyline and bare rock, like a vast stave upon which I could write my visual music. When asked to do my first book on Illinois in 1988, I was confronted with the necessity of completely rethinking of my photographic style.

Diligent search yielded few spots in Illinois with an uncluttered horizon on which I might hang a composition in the wide Western manner to which I was accustomed. Everywhere I looked, power lines, poles, highways, and buildings poked the sky and slashed the land. Apart from a handful of natural locations such as Illinois Beach State Park and the Garden of the Gods, Illinois's big vistas are ineluctably urban or agricultural in character.

To portray the unspoiled remnants of the natural face of Illinois, I was compelled to foreshorten and miniaturize my photographic vision. I applied many of the technical lessons implicit in Eliot Porter's classic portfolio of "intimate landscapes" to my close-up studies of hardwood forests and prairies, the predominant natural ecosystems of Illinois.

I took all the photographs in this book with a large-format 4x5 Cambo view camera on Gitzo and Bogen tripods. My assortment of lenses included 90mm Rodenstock, 120mm Nikkor, 150mm Rodenstock, 180mm Nikkor, 240mm Nikkor, 360mm Rodenstock, 450mm Nikkor, and 600mm Fujinon. Early in the project, I used Kodak- Ektachrome film; during the middle years, Fuji 50 and 100; during the last years, Fuji Velvia and Provia. I metered all scenes with a Pentax digital Spot Meter.

PHOTOGRAPHER'S PREFACE

When it came time to find, explore, and photograph nature in our home state of Illinois, the prospect seemed daunting. Was there actually any pristine, unspoiled nature remaining in the state of Illinois? We put this question, which we feared was oxymoronic, to the experts at the non-profit Illinois Nature Conservancy and at the Illinois Department of Natural Resources, the agency charged with managing the Illinois State Park system. We gave pundits at both organizations a detailed map of the state of Illinois and asked them to circle any areas "worthy of being photographed" for an exhibit-format book. The results were totally unexpected. Our map was a dense honeycomb of little circles. "Really, there are that many locations worthy of exploration by a landscape photographer?"

Illinois contains countless state parks, fish and wildlife areas, designated conservation areas, rivers, lakes—most impressively, of course, the shore of Lake Michigan. "This looks like it could take a while!" And indeed it did.

As we crisscrossed our densely populated state, island-hopping from one nature location to the next, our imaginations were often kindled to try to picture what Illinois must have looked like to the Native Americans and first European pioneers when the whole territory was just one continuous nature location. The remnants of Illinois's once vast prairies—the extensive Goose Lake Prairie, the Gensburg-Markham Prairie with its burst of rainbow hues in a good bloom year, the rolling hills of the Nature Conservancy-owned Nachusa Grassland—might have dropped straight out of a Willa Cather novel.

Which of all the nature locations in Illinois qualify as the brightest of the state's "natural jewels" is, to some extent, a question of taste. As for our judgment, let us just say that each time we return from our travels around the United States photographing its many national parks, we look with renewed wonder and respect at an area that would easily have qualified for National Monument or National Park status if it had been located farther West. This area—consisting of Starved Rock and Matthiessen State Parks, together with a significant portion of the Illinois River corridor and a million or so acres of surrounding native prairie—ranks as one of our favorites in the nation to visit and photograph.

The deep canyons and plunging streams that dissect Starved Rock, Matthiessen, and Giant City State Parks all belie the careless sneer that Illinois's landscape is just an endless flatness punctuated by silos, smokestacks, and skyscrapers. Sprawling across the southern section of the state lies Illinois's only National Forest, the Shawnee National Forest: a varied wonderland of canyons, streams, and rivers; hardwood trees that blaze color in the fall; rock formations so bizarre that they deserve to be called the "Garden of the Gods"; enchanted cypress swamps, such as those in Horseshoe Lake Conservation Area. So this is the state that's just one big cornfield? Hardly.

Northern Illinois also has its scenic attractions worthy of exploration. Setting up a camera in Illinois Beach State Park on the grass-covered dunes along the shore of Lake Michigan or capturing the sun rising over the lake is well worth the effort. Imagine evening light skimming over a lily pad-covered lake at Moraine Hills State Park, especially when one has the fortunate experience of photographing the scene in solitude. Oh the picturesque rolling hillsides with expansive views of the Galena area so reminiscent of New England! One of the sideline pleasures of shooting the Galena hillsides is eating in one of the many excellent restaurants in the town when the work is done for the day!

Whether in northern Illinois and southern Illinois, there is definitely beauty and attractiveness there for those photographers searching for photographs in this state. In order to do a complete photographic representation of this state however, one must visit the central region, roughly circumscribed by I-74 to the south and I-64 to the north. Much to our surprise, we found a photographic fishermen's paradise.

What is there to photograph in this flattest of agricultural flat land? The most obvious feature of central Illinois is water and plenty of it. With all that water, there is fishing, boating, and waterfowl in profusion. I grew up hearing about the beautiful lakes and great fishing from my relatives. They did not exaggerate. There are many lakes in the region, but the most attractive from a photographic perspective are Carlyle Lake, Clinton Lake, Lake Shelbyville, Moraine View, Sangchris Lake, and the picturesque lake at Weldon Spring State Park. The best-kept secret in central Illinois is the emerald-watered Middle Fork River County Forest Preserve in Champaign County, a location we would never have found without the assistance of a naturalist familiar with the area.

Central Illinois has also been blessed with an abundance of birds because of the extensive water. For those interested in Canada geese, Chautauqua National Wildlife Refuge south of Peoria offers plentiful viewing opportunities. An image that will remain with us is photographing an orange sunset at Chain Lake in Sanganois State Wildlife Area in Mason County while sharing the lake with more Great Blue Herons than we had ever seen in one location. Though technically in southern Illinois, Crab Orchard National Refuge near Carbondale is another waterfowl jewel in the state.

The two great rivers that form the east and west borders of Illinois make a noble frame for a state full of so much beauty. A memorable scene is to capture the sunrise color on the warm cliff faces at Tower Rock in the Shawnee National Forest overlooking the Ohio River on the eastern border. The Mississippi River on the western border can be seen from high vantage points at Mississippi Palisades State Park near Galena or the Illinois/Mississippi Rivers from Pere Marquette State Park near St. Louis. For those seeking a more intimate rapport with the Mississippi River, it can be savored close up at the lightly-visited Delabar State Park west of Galesburg. Photographing sunsets over the Mississippi River from Delabar is as good as it gets.

The same black soil that has made Illinois renowned for its bumper crops of corn and soybeans also engenders wildflowers in profusion. The bluebells that carpet the canyon floors in Starved Rock State Park; the blazing stars in Gensburg-Markham Prairie and Nachusa Grassland; and the prairie phlox at the West Chicago Prairie Natural Preserve are all spectacular examples. But the crowning jewel of Illinois's natural gardens is surely Messenger Woods, in Will County. Once threatened by developers, Messenger Woods supports some of the most extensive populations of blue-eyed Marys and white trilliums found anywhere in this country.

Author Henry David Thoreau once mused, " I have known no companion as companionable as solitude." More than most other kinds of artists, nature photographers, draw inspiration from engagement with nature in solitude. In contrast to the physically grand but humanly congested national parks such as Grand Teton, Yellowstone, Acadia, Grand Canyon, and Great Smoky Mountains National Parks, Illinois's parks and preserves offer less physical razzmatazz but, paradoxically, more human solitude in which to work. These oases of solitude in such a densely populated state must be preserved for the sake of the human population's mental health as well as the natural populations' physical health. We welcome this opportunity to thank and applaud all the dedicated folks we have met who are working toward this goal in such organizations as the Illinois Department of Natural Resources, the U.S. Forest Service, the Illinois chapters of the Sierra Club, The Audubon

Society, The Nature Conservancy, and The Natural Area Guardians.

We cannot encourage strongly enough all residents of Illinois to support these and other environmental organizations with their treasure and talent. As Will Rogers once said about our land, "They ain't makin' any more of it!"—to which may be added, "Once it's gone, it's gone forever!" We hope that you will enjoy looking at this panorama of our beloved state as much as we have enjoyed making it. And we especially hope that it will prompt you to embark on your own voyages of discovery of the myriad hidden beauties of *Wild and Scenic Illinois*.

Willard Clay and Debra Alsvig-Clay

CONTENTS

Introduction — CORN STATE, PRAIRIE STATE, STATE OF HIDDEN DELIGHTS · 13 ·

1 CENTRAL LOWLAND Province

Great Lake Section

Chicago Lake Plain · 19 ·

Wheaton Morainal Country · 23 ·

Till Plains Section

Kankakee Plain · 35 ·

Bloomington Ridged Plain · 41 ·

Rock River Hill Country · 95 ·

Green River Lowland · 111 ·

Galesburg Plain · 113 ·

Springfield Plain · 121 ·

Mount Vernon Hill Country · 135 ·

Wisconsin Driftless Section · 137 ·

2 OZARK PLATEAUS Province

Lincoln Hills Section · 143 ·

3 INTERIOR LOW PLATEAUS Province

Shawnee Hills Section · 147 ·

4 COASTAL PLAIN Province · 165 ·

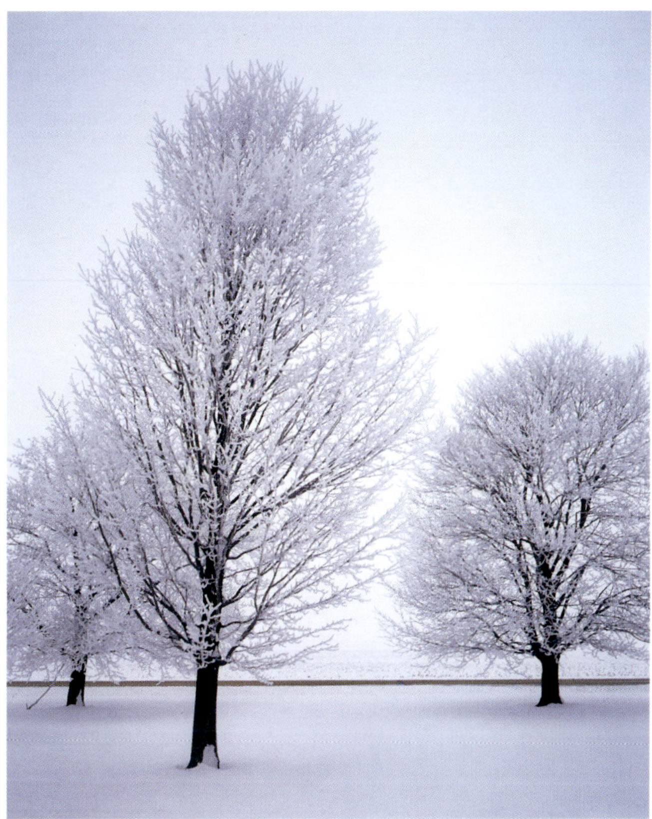

INTRODUCTION:
CORN STATE, PRAIRIE STATE, STATE OF HIDDEN DELIGHTS

Illinois is the Prairie State. It will come as no surprise that the Prairie State is, to a large extent, a prairie plain—smooth, gently undulating country with sufficient rainfall to support tall grass.

Except for a southern fringe accounting for less than one-tenth of the area of the state, Illinois lies entirely within the huge Central Lowland province of North America. From Illinois, the Central Lowland province stretches away northward to Saskatchewan, westward to Nebraska, southward to Texas, and eastward to New York, covering in whole or in part sixteen states. The Central Lowland province ranks as the largest physiographic province in the conterminous United States, accounting for a fifth of the area of the lower forty-eight states.

Physiography, also called *geomorphology*, is the study of the natural physical features of the earth's surface, also called *landforms*, and their arrangement in relation to one another. *Physiographic provinces* are the primary natural units of study, corresponding to such large-scale landforms as plains, plateaus, and mountain systems. To the earth scientist, landforms are the end of the story. To the geographer, landforms are the beginning of the story. To the people who live on them and to the landscape photographer who roams on them, landforms are the stage for their own stories.

The Central Lowland is vast in extent but remarkably subdued in relief, reflecting the nearly flat-lying, essentially undisturbed attitude of the sedimentary strata that everywhere make up the province's bedrock. What little sharp relief is scratched on the face of the province tends to be found where rivers have, here and there, cut down into resistant, bluff-forming bedrock.

Local relief is slight throughout the Central Lowland province but especially so in Illinois. The difference in elevation between the highest and lowest points in most counties of Illinois is less than 300 feet. The total relief across the whole state—namely, the difference between the top of Charles Mound (1,235 feet above sea level) in the northwest corner of the state and the Mississippi River at southwest corner of the state (279 feet)—is less than a thousand feet. Only a handful of coastal states such as Delaware and Mississippi have lower total relief than Illinois.

Local relief is greatest at the northern and southern ends of the state. Pope County in the extreme south has a relief of 680 feet owing to the ruggedness of the never-glaciated Shawnee Hills. Jo Daviess County in the extreme north has a relief of 645 feet owing its being in the Wisconsin Driftless section, an interlobate upland also spared the effects of glacial smoothing (because located between adjacent glacial *lobes*, the great tongue-like protrusions of the margin of the continental ice sheet). Between these driftless uplands at opposite ends of the state lies the central basin, encompassing most of the state's area.

Here in the broad Illinois basin, local relief is least, going down to under 100 feet in Douglas County, where superposition of successive glacial tills has resulted in a nearly featureless ground-moraine plain. *Ground moraine* is the material that has been extensively deposited from a glacier on the ground surface over which the glacier moves; as distinguished from raised *moraines*—including both *lateral moraines* and *end* or *terminal moraines*—which are deposited as ridges enclosing ground-moraine districts. Unsorted sediment that has been carried and deposited by a glacier is called *till. Drift* is a more inclusive term, including both till and sediment that has been transported and deposited by the action of glacial meltwater.

The lowness of the Central Lowland province is not uniformly low. The term *lowland* is here to be understood in a sense relative to the superior elevation of the surrounding provinces—and not in the sense that all portions of the Central Lowland hug that province's base level. Dominant slopes within the Central Lowland province are locally imperceptible but regionally significant. The dominant slopes within the Central Lowland province—and therefore within the state of Illinois—are toward the Mississippi and Ohio Rivers, which are Illinois's western and southern borders, respectively. The overall surface of Illinois, then, may be notionally interpreted as an inclined plane dipping subtly southward.

With a mean elevation of 600 feet above sea level, Illinois is looked down upon by all its neighboring states. Illinois is the lowest of the Midwestern states, situated as it is athwart the confluence of the major lines of drainage in the central part of the Central Lowland. Across the Wabash River to the east, Indiana has a mean elevation of 700 feet. Across the Ohio River to the south, Kentucky has a mean elevation of 750 feet. Across the Mississippi River to the west, Missouri has a mean elevation of 800 feet and Iowa has a mean elevation of 1,100 feet. Across the line of latitude 42° 30′ North, Wisconsin has a mean elevation of 1,050 feet.

Along most of its length, the province boundary of the Central Lowland is marked by a visible contrast in topography, which in many places takes the form of an escarpment ramping up to a higher (and older) plateau. Outside Illinois, such escarpments characterize the boundary of the Central Lowland province with the Superior Upland province to the north, with the Appalachian Plateaus province to the east, and with the Great Plains province to the west. Within Illinois, such escarpments ramping up to higher (and older) plateaus characterize the boundary of the Central Lowland province with the Interior Low Plateaus province to the south and the Ozark Plateaus province to the southwest.

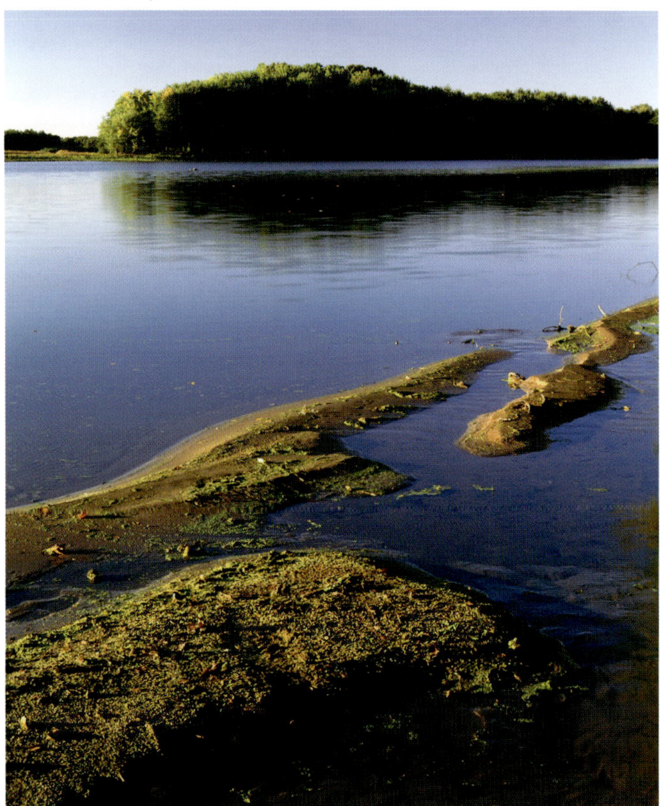

THIS PAGE: Mississippi River bank in evening, Delabar State park, Henderson County.

PAGE 11: Hoarfrosted trees in morning fog, La Salle County.

The boundary in southern Illinois between the Central Lowland and Interior Low Plateaus provinces extends from the junction of the Wabash and Mississippi Rivers (where Illinois, Indiana, and Kentucky trisect) westward to the Kaskaskia River in Randolph County. This province boundary is marked by the northernmost escarpment of the Shawnee Hills.

The boundary in southwestern Illinois between the Central Lowland and Ozark Plateaus provinces runs northwestward from the Kaskaskia River in twining parallelism to the Mississippi River, which it crosses at three places before setting off across the state of Missouri at Hannibal. This province boundary is marked by the escarpments of the Salem Plateau and Lincoln Hills. The nine-tenths of Illinois to the north of the Shawnee-Salem-Lincoln line of escarpments, sweeping an arc from the Wabash-Ohio confluence round to East Hannibal on the Mississippi, lies entirely within the Central Lowland province.

To a fairly close approximation, the boundary between the Central Lowland province to the north and the Interior Low Plateaus and Ozark Plateaus provinces to the south coincides with the southward limit of the Illinoian advance of the Laurentide continental ice sheet (so-called because it radiated from the Laurentian Uplands of Canada), reached some 150 thousand years ago. Most of the nine-tenths of Illinois within the Central Lowland province, with the notable exception of the Wisconsin Driftless section in Jo Daviess and Carroll Counties, has been glaciated at least once. Conversely, most of that one-tenth of Illinois that is outside the Central Lowland province has never been glaciated.

The unglaciated tenth of the state includes Illinois's meager portion of the Coastal Plain province. This province extends all the way from Cape Cod to the Yucatan and is scarcely less extensive than the Central Lowland province. Yet only the very northernmost extremity of the Mississippi embayment of the Coastal Plain province grazes Illinois. The smallest and lowest of the four physiographic provinces impinging on Illinois, the Coastal Plain province is confined to Illinois's southernmost tier of counties: Alexander, Pulaski, Massac, and the toe of Pope.

The glaciated nine-tenths of the state is covered with variable thicknesses and ages of glacial till, consisting of the loads of unconsolidated sand, clay, gravel, and boulders that have been picked up, carried, and deposited by continental glaciers as they advanced, merged, and retreated. This ill-sorted rocky rubbish was deposited by the mobile lobes of the southern margin of the Laurentide continental ice sheet as it has repeatedly invaded and retreated from Illinois over the past million years.

A given locality in the glaciated portion of Illinois might bear the burden of the glacial drift (which term includes glacial outwash deposits as well as glacial till) of as many as four, or as few as one, major glacial episodes. Because older glacial episodes acted to fill in the low spots of pre-glacial topography, Illinois's smoothest and most featureless plains are found in those portions of the central Illinois basin that have been blanketed by the drift of all four Pleistocene glacial stages.

The oldest Pleistocene glacial stages in Illinois are the pre-Illinoian Kansan and Nebraskan stages, ranging in age between one million and 600,000 years ago. The most extensive Pleistocene glacial stage in Illinois is the Illinoian, ranging in area as far south as the northernmost escarpment of the Shawnee Hills, and in age from 300,000 to 140,000 years ago. The youngest and least extensive of the four Pleistocene glacial stages is the Wisconsinan, whose relatively fresh sediments are piled thick in the northeast quadrant of the state in four substages, ranging in age from 50,000 to 14,000 years ago.

Beneath its veneer of glacial deposits, most of the Central Lowland province in Illinois is underlain by sedimentary rocks (shale, sandstone, siltstone, limestone, and coal) laid down in the Illinois basin during the Pennsylvanian period between 323 and 290 million years ago. These rocks, deposited in marine, deltaic, and continental-cyclic settings, are relatively weak and easily eroded. Although these rocks are exposed in few places today, they previously—for long ages prior to the onset of continental glaciation a million years ago—underwent deep erosion to form an extensive basin.

Enclosing the Illinois basin on the north, west, and south are uplands that were developed, for the most part, on older and more resistant limestones and dolomites laid down during the periods from the Cambrian through the Mississippian, between 540 and 323 million years ago. The uplands of northwestern Illinois (underlain by limestones and dolomites mostly of Ordovician age, 490 to 443 million years ago) and of southern Illinois (underlain by limestones and sandstones mostly of Mississippian age, 354 to 323 million years ago) both blocked the advance of the Illinoian glacial lobe. Across these lowland-upland borders, in result, the controlling topographic transition is accentuated by the contrast between glaciated and non-glaciated land surfaces.

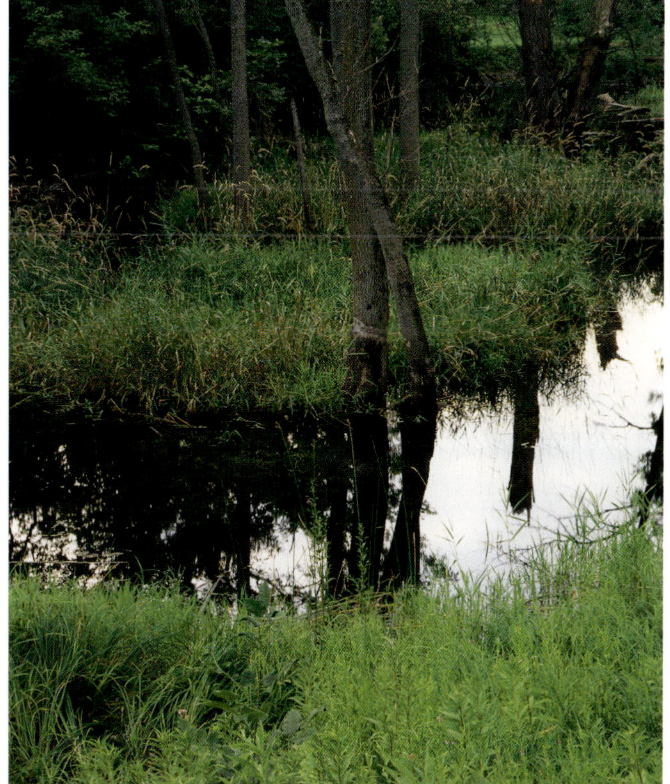

Bluff Spring Fen, Cook county.

Physiographic provinces—such as the Central Lowland, Interior Low Plateaus, Ozark Plateaus, and Coastal Plain provinces, among which the lands of Illinois are allotted in unequal shares—are, as noted above, the primary units into which physical geographers divide up the terrestrial surface, within each of which the landscape style is fundamentally uniform. Similarity of appearance is grounded in the physical character of the material being shaped—ultimately, the underlying rock—and in the panoply of physical forces brought to bear upon that parcel of material: whether recent forces, such as rivers, acting into the present; or ancient forces, such as glaciers, whose effects are fortuitously preserved in the present material. These geomorphic ("earth-shaping") forces vary as a dauntingly complex function of climate, altitude, hydrologic and glacial regimes, marine fluctuations, tectonic events, organic processes, anthropogenic modifications, extraterrestrial impacts, and so on.

The classic text on the physiography of the United States is in two volumes by Nevin M. Fenneman (1931, 1938). Fenneman parses the whole of the conterminous United States into twenty-five physiographic provinces. These twenty-five provinces he gathers into eight higher-order divisions and subdivides into eighty-six lower-order sections. It is a testament to the unexpected variety of Illinois's terrain and scenery that fifteen percent of Fenneman's twenty-five physiographic provinces impinge on Illinois—even though Illinois accounts for less than two percent of the area of the conterminous United States.

Even more surprisingly for a middling Midwestern state with a reputation for an unsurprising plain landscape, Illinois contains portions of nearly forty percent of the eight physiographic divisions of the conterminous United States: namely, the Interior Plain division (which includes the Central Lowland and Interior Low Plateaus provinces), the Interior Highlands division (which includes the Ozarks Plateaus province), and the Atlantic Plain division (which includes the Coastal Plain province).

Finally, despite its relatively small area, Illinois contains portions of eight percent of the eighty-six physiographic sections into which Fenner divides the conterminous United States: three sections (the Till Plains, Great Lake, and Wisconsin Driftless sections) of the Central Lowland province; one section (the Shawnee Hills section) of the Interior Low Plateaus province; two sections (the East Gulf Coastal Plain and Mississippi Alluvial Plains sections) of the Coastal Plain province; and one section (the Springfield-Salem Plateaus section) of the Ozark Plateaus province.

The Illinois Geological Survey refined Fenneman's classification as applied to Illinois in a landmark paper by Survey Chief M.M. Leighton, George E. Ekblaw, and Leland Horberg (1948), whose map of the physiographic divisions of Illinois is reproduced on page 4 of this book. By the classification of Leighton et al., the Great Lake section is subdivided into two subsections (the Chicago Lake Plain and Wheaton Morainal Country); the Till Plains section is subdivided into seven subsections (the Kankakee Plain, Bloomington Ridged Plain, Rock River Hill Country, Green River Lowland, Galesburg Plain, Springfield Plain, and Mount Vernon Hill Country); the Ozark Plateaus section is subdivided into the Lincoln Hills and Salem Plateau sections; and the Coastal Plain province within Illinois is not regarded as separable into sections at all. In total, then, Leighton et al. divide the state of Illinois into fourteen discrete physiographic sections.

The subsections whose surfaces are covered by the Wisconsinan drift-sheet are the Chicago Lake Plain, Wheaton Morainal Country, Kankakee Plain, and Bloomington Ridged Plain. The subsections whose surfaces are covered by the Illinoian drift-sheet are the Rock River Hill Country, Green River Lowland, Galesburg Plain, Springfield Plain, and Mount Vernon Hill Country. The sections whose surfaces are partially and patchily covered by pre-Illinoian drift are the Dissected Till Plains and Lincoln Hills sections bordering the Mississippi River. The surfaces of the other peripheral sections of the state—the Wisconsin Driftless, the Shawnee Hills, and the Coastal Plain—are driftless.

The classification of Leighton et al. is followed in the organization of the photographs in this book, in which thirteen of Leighton's sections are represented. Since physiographic sections correspond closely with landscape styles, the photographs in any given section of this book can be expected to show a degree of stylistic affinity. A précis of Leighton et al.'s characterization of the thirteen physiographic sections of Illinois follows. It should be read in tandem with the corresponding thirteen photographic sections of this book and with reference to page 4.

CHICAGO LAKE PLAIN
(Great Lake Section, Central Lowland Province)

The Great Lake section of the Central Lowland province is divided in Illinois into the Chicago Lake Plain and the Wheaton Morainal Country, with the boundary between them marked by the highest shoreline of glacial Lake Chicago. This glacial lake began to form at the southern end of the Lake Michigan basin 14,000 years ago as the Michigan lobe of the Laurentide continental ice sheet began rapidly to recede and proglacial (located in front of the ice margin) meltwaters became impounded between the lobe margin and the Tinley and Lake Border moraines, which define the lakeward border of the Wheaton Morainal Country. The Chicago Lake Plain is a prairie plain, underlain by glacial till of late Wisconsinan age, which slopes gently toward Lake Michigan and whose essential flatness is interrupted by low relict beach ridges, morainal headlands, and islands and by the successors of two large glacial Lake Chicago drainage outlets, the Des Plaines River and Calumet-Sag Channel. The ancient beach ridges include spits and bars of glacial Lake Chicago, which parallel the modern lakefront of Chicago and funnel toward the outlet channel occupied by the Des Plaines River. Before European settlement, the Chicago Lake Plain was swampy and poorly drained. The Chicago Lake Plain's three rivers—the Des Plaines, Calumet, and Chicago—lack true valleys, their courses within this section being controlled by relict beach ridges.

WHEATON MORAINAL COUNTRY
(Great Lake Section, Central Lowland Province)

The topography of this section is determined by a series of broad parallel morainal ridges encircling Lake Michigan and composed of thick drift deposited during the Tazewell and Cary substages (the last constructive episodes of the Wisconsinan glaciation in Illinois) between 20,00 and 14,00 years ago by the Michigan lobe of the Laurentide continental ice sheet. The youngest, easternmost ridge series includes the Valparaiso moraine (which stretches continuously from Wisconsin to Indiana), the Tinley moraine, and the Lake Border moraine. In most of this section, the drift of previous glacial advances was removed prior to the deposition of the Wisconsinan drift. Postglacial erosion has been slight, except in youthful valleys cut by the glacial outlet precursors of the Fox and Des Plaines Rivers. During glacial recession, large blocks of ice became buried and, upon melting, left the basins now occupied by Fox Lake and other lakes in this section.

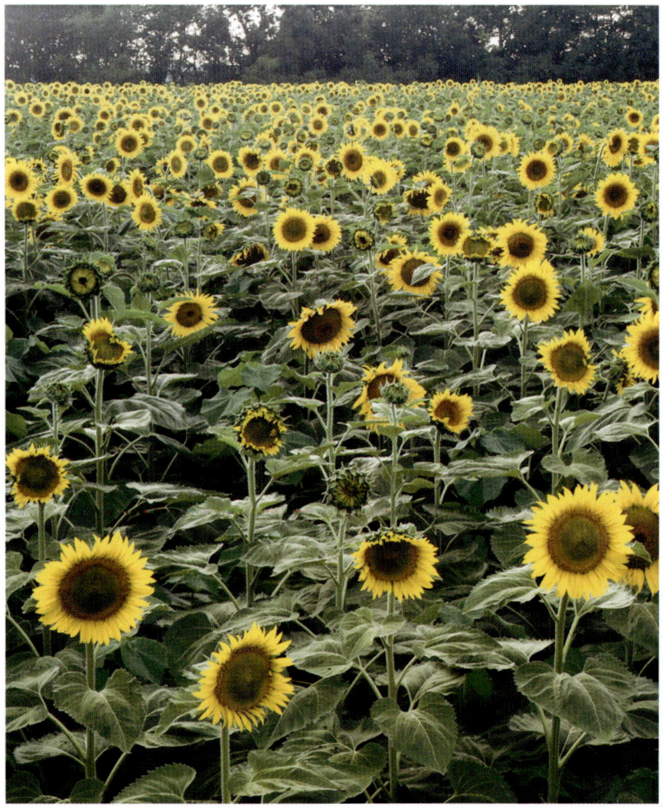

Sunflower sunset, Bureau County.

KANKAKEE PLAIN
(Till Plains Section, Central Lowland Province)

The Till Plains section, covering four-fifths of Illinois, is divided into seven subsections: the Kankakee Plain, Bloomington Ridged Plain, Rock River Hill Country, Green River Lowland, Galesburg Plain, Springfield Plain, and Mount Vernon Hill Country. The outer boundary of the Till Plains section coincides with the margin of Illinoian drift, deposited between 300,000 and 140,000 years ago. The Kankakee Plain is a level to gently undulating plain relieved by low relict morainal islands, glacial terraces, bars, and dunes. The Kankakee Plain is essentially an intermorainal basin floored by late Wisconsinan ground moraine of variable thickness and enclosed on the north and east by moraines of Cary age (14,000 years old) and on the south and west by moraines of Tazewell age (15,000 to 20,000 years old). The Kankakee Plain is poorly drained except by its two major streams—the Kankakee and Des Plaines—which occupy glacial sluiceways locally entrenched in Silurian dolomite bedrock.

BLOOMINGTON RIDGED PLAIN
(Till Plains Section, Central Lowland Province)

The Bloomington Ridged Plain, containing most of Illinois's moraines of Tazewell age (20,000 to 15,000 years old), is festooned by a concentrically nested series of thirteen broad low morainal ridges separated by wide intervals of flat or gently undulating ground moraine. At the time of initial European settlement, the Bloomington Ridged Plain was exemplary of the dominant style of Illinois country: rolling tallgrass prairie interspersed with swamps. The outer boundary of the Bloomington Ridged Plain follows the Shelbyville moraine along a ten-county arc from the Indiana Border to Peoria, and the Bloomington moraine along a seven-county arc from Peoria to northwest corner of Kane County. The glacial deposits, composed of pre-Illinoian and Illinoian drift stacked undeneath the Wisconsinan surface drift, are thick throughout the Bloomington Ridged Plain and almost everywhere conceal the bedrock. The Illinois River is the master stream of the Bloomington Ridged Plain. It has a broad, flat-bottomed valley with steep walls. Between the "Big Bend" and Peoria, the Illinois River valley occupies the wider and more mature valley of the pre-Wisconsinan Mississippi River.

ROCK RIVER HILL COUNTRY
(Till Plains Section, Central Lowland Province)

The Rock River Hill Country is characterized by subdued rolling hills in a late youthful stage of erosion. It includes an extensive eroded Illinoian drift-plain touching seven counties centered on Ogla County and a lesser fringe of early Wisconsinan drift centered in Boone County. The Illinoian drift (between 300,000 and 140,000 years old) is thin and not underlain by pre-Illinoian drift. As a result, the topography of the Rock River Hill Country is mainly controlled by the bedrock topography. In the west part of the Rock River Hill Country, bordering the Mississippi Valley, thick deposits of loess (wind-deposited dust and silt) and fine sand cover the Illinoian till plain. The major streams flow radially from a central upland into the Mississippi River on the west and the Rock River on the west and south. River valleys are steep-walled and in many places have cut gorges into the upland bedrock.

GREEN RIVER LOWLAND
(Till Plains Section, Central Lowland Province)

The Green River Lowland is a low, poorly drained plain relieved by prominent sand ridges and dunes. The Green River Lowland is bounded on the north and south by the moraine of the Green River glacial lobe and on the east by the Bloomington moraine, both of Tazewell age (20,000 to 15,000 years old). Most of the Green River Lowland is a late Wisconsinan outwash plain associated with the deposition of the Bloomington moraine. The Green River Lowland coincides in large part with a bedrock lowland occupied by the Mississippi River up until the Wisconsinan glaciation.

GALESBURG PLAIN
(Till Plains Section, Central Lowland Province)

The Galesburg Plain is a level to undulating plain of thick Illinoian till underlain by pre-Illinoian tills. The pre-Illinoian tills infill lows in the preglacial topography and conduce to level the surface of the Illinoian till. The Galesburg Plain is in a late youthful stage of erosion and is traversed by four subdued morainal ridges. The Galesburg Plain is bounded on the northeast by the western margin of the Wisconsinan till, on the southeast by the Illinois River Valley, on the southwest by the western margin of the Illinoian till, and on the northwest by the Mississippi River. The Galesburg Plain is drained by streams that flow from a central upland down deep, steep-walled valleys westward into the Mississsippi River and eastward and southward into the Illinois River.

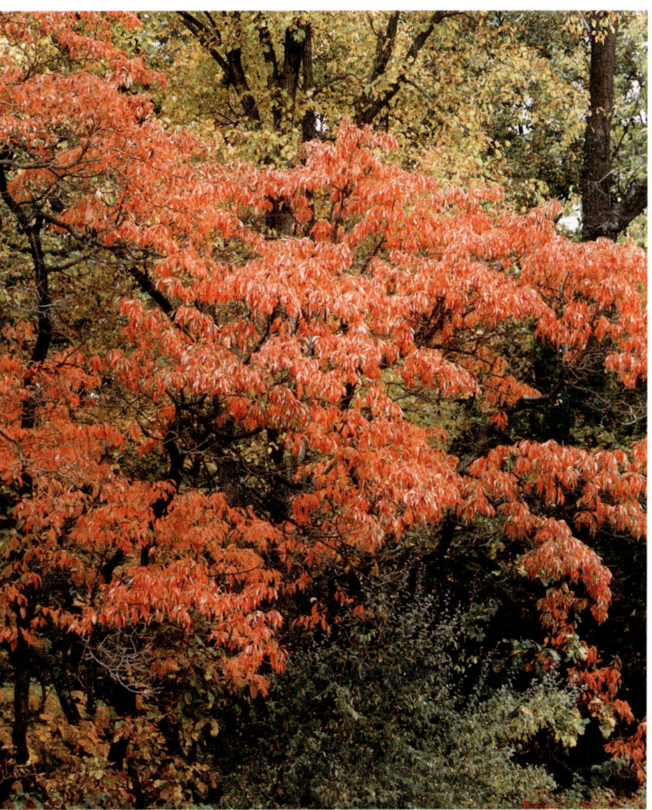

Sassafras tree (Sassafras albidum), Siloam Springs State Park, Adams County.

SPRINGFIELD PLAIN
(Till Plains Section, Central Lowland Province)

The Springfield Plain is a level plain of moderately thick Illinoian till underlain by pre-Illinoian tills. The pre-Illinoian tills infill lows in the preglacial topography and conduce to level the surface of the Illinoian till. The Springfield Plain is in a late youthful stage of erosion. Although the Springfield Plain is predominantly flat, its western portion is traversed by conspicuous morainal ridges associated with prominent kame terraces (glacial sand and gravel terraces deposited between a stagnant valley ice lobe and the bounding valley slope). The Springfield Plain is bounded on the east by the western margin of the Wisconsinan till, on the northwest by the Illinois River Valley, on the southwest by the western margin of the Illinoian till, and on the southeast by a line beyond which the Illinoian drift thins over the Mount Vernon Hill Country. The Springfield Plain is drained by low-gradient streams that flow from low uplands down shallow valleys. Along the Illinois River Valley lies a belt of thick loess.

MOUNT VERNON HILL COUNTRY
(Till Plains Section, Central Lowland Province)

The Mount Vernon Hill Country is a district of mature topography of low relief patchily covered with Illinoian drift too thin to embody glacial landforms. The surface of the Mount Vernon Hill Country is primarily a Pennsylvanian bedrock surface, only slightly modified and subdued by a thin and discontinuous drape of Illinoian drift not underlain by pre-Illinoian drift. The Mount Vernon Hill Country is bounded on the south by the limit of Illinoian glaciation and on the north by the thick and continuous Illinoian drift of the Springfield Plain.

WISCONSIN DRIFTLESS SECTION
(Central Lowland Province)

The Wisconsin Driftless section is a maturely dissected plateau underlain by dolomites and shales, mostly of Ordovician age (490 to 443 million years ago). The Wisconsin Driftless section, which extends northward from the northwest corner of Illinois to cover the southwestern third of the state of Wisconsin, is bounded on the east by the western margin of Illinoian drift and on the west by the Mississippi River Valley. The Mississippi River Valley in this section has broad terraced bottom lands, composed largely of glacial outwash, and steep bluffs, composed largely of loess. This section accounts for about two percent of the area of Illinois.

LINCOLN HILLS SECTION
(Ozark Plateaus Province)

The Lincoln Hills section of Illinois is a maturely dissected watershed plateau wedged between the convergence of the Mississippi and Illinois Rivers. The rest of the plateau lies on the other side of the Mississippi River Valley in the state of Missouri. Patches of Kansan drift cover parts of the northern portion of the Lincoln Hills section, whose eastern boundary is the western margin of Illinoian drift. The Lincoln Hills plateau is the surface expression of the Lincoln fold, which is a subsidiary structure of the Ozark dome, centered in southern Missouri and northern Arkansas. The pre-Pennsylvanian limestone and dolomite cuestas that crop out in the Lincoln Hills are a characteristic feature of the Ozark dome. A *cuesta* is a sloping plain that is terminated on the higher side by a continuous escarpment. The Lincoln Hills plateau surface is rugged and broken by closely spaced valleys and ridges. This section accounts for about two percent of the area of Illinois.

SHAWNEE HILLS SECTION
(Interior Low Plateaus Province)

The Shawnee Hills section, popularly known as the "Illinois Ozarks," is a maturely dissected upland, underlain by Mississippian and Pennsylvanian rocks complicated by folding and faulting, located on the southern rim of the Illinois basin. The Shawnee Hills section is bounded on the north by a Pennsylvanian-age sandstone cuesta, with gentle slope to the north and steep slope to the south, that extends completely across the state and coincides with the southern limit of Illinoian glacial drift. The Shawnee Hills section is bounded on the south by the northern edge of the overlapping Coastal Plain sediments. This section accounts for less than three percent of the area of Illinois.

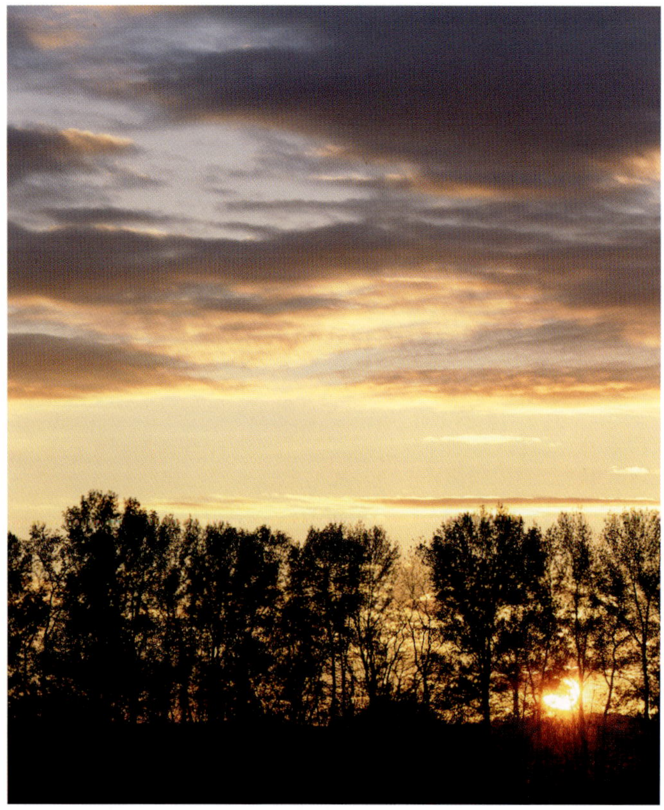

Sunset, Shawnee National Forest, Pope County.

COASTAL PLAIN PROVINCE

The Coastal Plain at the southern tip of Illinois is underlain by unconsolidated Cretaceous and Tertiary sediments, which overlap the Mississippian limestones and sandstones of the Shawnee Hills on the north. The Coastal Plain section consists of the *alluvial plain* (a flood plain or bottomland that is produced by the filling of valley bottoms with mud, sand, and clay deposited by modern rivers) at the nexus of the Mississippi, Cache, and Ohio River Valleys; together with the maturely eroded Cretaceous Hills wedged between the convergence of the Mississippi and Cache Rivers. Prior to glaciation, the Cache River Valley was occupied by the Ohio River, which did not assume its present course until valley *aggradation* (buildup of the valley surface by deposition) by glacial outwash brought the Ohio River channel up to the level of the divide at Bay City in southern Pope County. This province accounts for less than two percent of the area of Illinois.

1

CENTRAL LOWLAND PROVINCE
GREAT LAKE SECTION
CHICAGO LAKE PLAIN

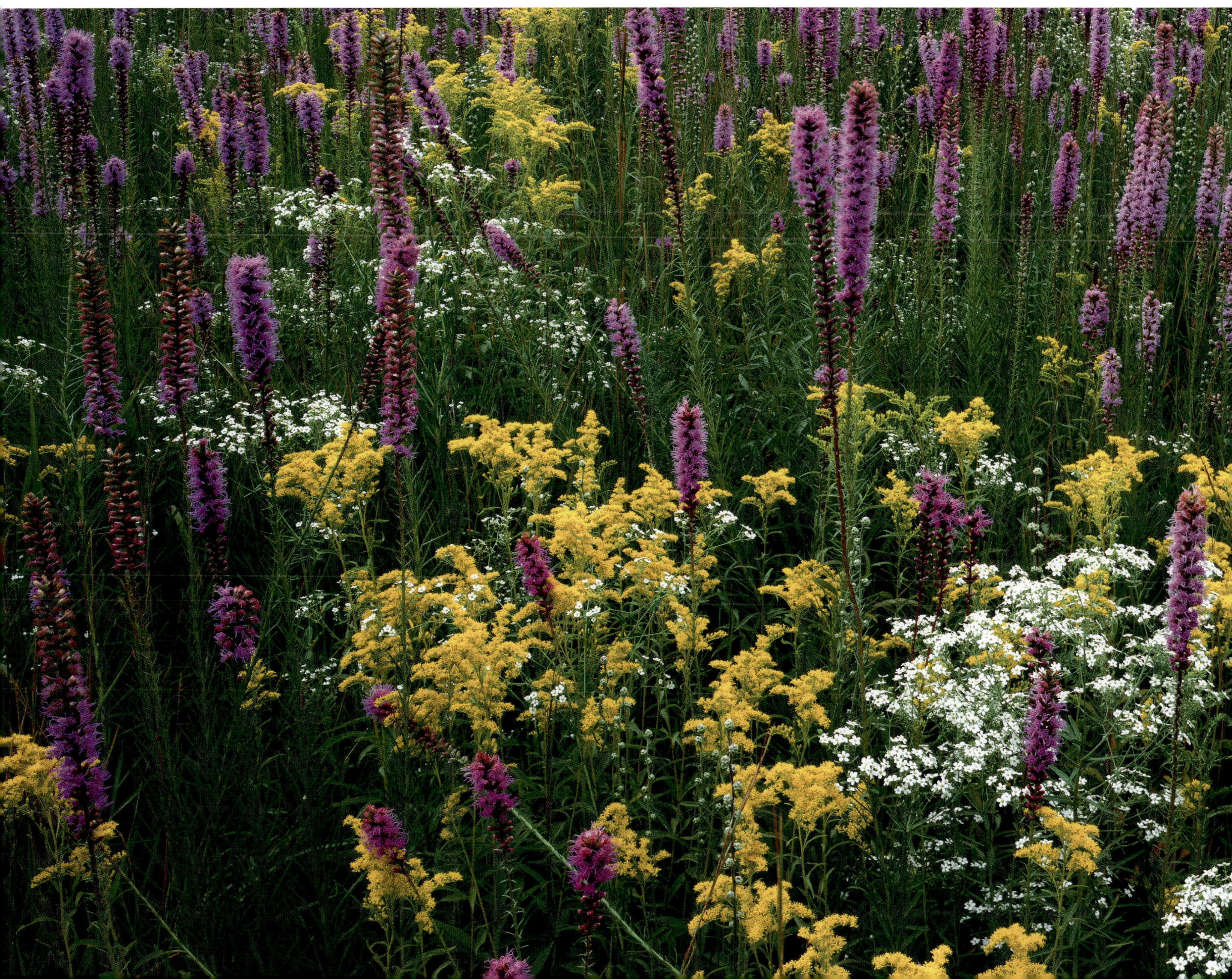

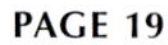

PAGE 19:

Blazing star ***(Liatris pycnostachya)*****, goldenrod** ***(Solidago juncea)*****, and flat-topped spurge** ***(Euphorbia corollata)*****:** Gensburg-Markham Prairie, Markham, Cook County *(Chicago Lake Plain, Great Lake Section, Central Lowland Province)* Over one hundred acres of restored prairie grow on the sandy strand of ancient Lake Chicago that underlies the suburban town of Markham, south of Chicago. The discoverer and savior of this high-quality prairie community was Northeastern Illinois University biochemist Dr. Robert Betz, an avid hunter of the small remnants of Illinois's native grassland communities in country cemeteries. In the 1960s, Dr. Betz stumbled on what he recognized as large patch of original prairie threatened by trees, shrubs, and development. In 1971 the Gensburg family donated the 60-acre core of this remnant prairie to the Nature Conservancy. Gensburg-Markham is now a National Natural Landmark, owned and administered by Northeastern Illinois University, the Natural Land Institute, and the Nature Conservancy. After years of prescribed burning and restorative seeding, first prairie betony and then pink phlox plants, white prairie clover, and wild quinine have spread out from the core area to the degraded periphery. *July 1998*

THIS PAGE:

Wild Hyacinth ***(Camassia scilliodes)*****:** Wolf Road Prairie Nature Preserve, Cook County *(Chicago Lake Plain, Great Lake Section, Central Lowland Province)* Wolf Road Prairie Nature Preserve is an excellent example of Illinois's classic tallgrass prairie and is the largest vestige of this type of prairie in the Chicago area. Its 44 acres were set aside in 1988, thanks largely to the efforts of the Save the Prairie Society. The prairie is dominated by big bluestem, little bluestem, prairie dropseed, and Indian grass. A marsh dominated by bulrush and cattail and a small savanna remnant also occur here. The savanna is dominated by bur oak with wild hyacinth, seen in this photograph. Western chorus frog, fox snake, woodchuck, common snipe, and swamp sparrow flourish in this preserve just west of Chicago. *May 1995*

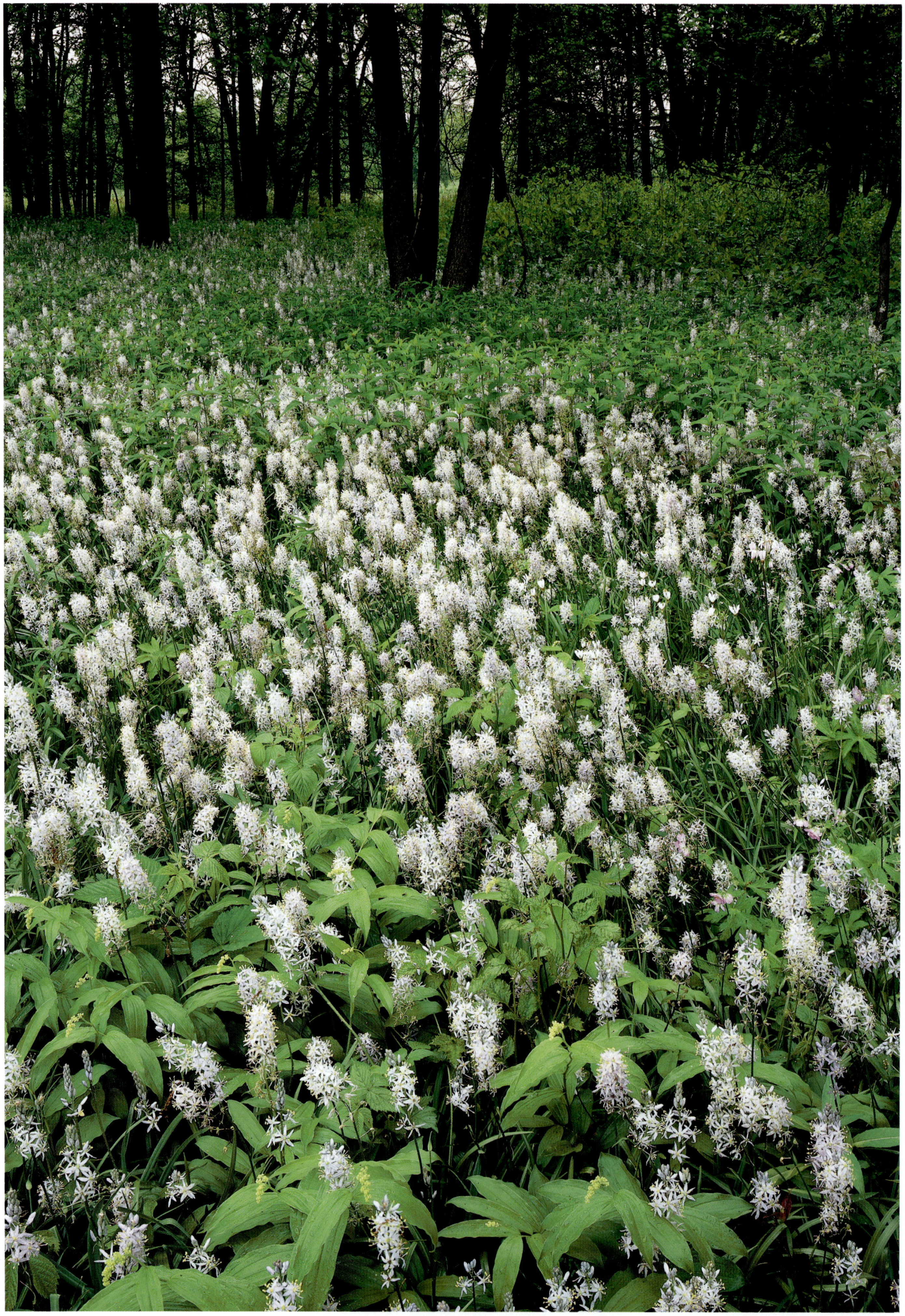

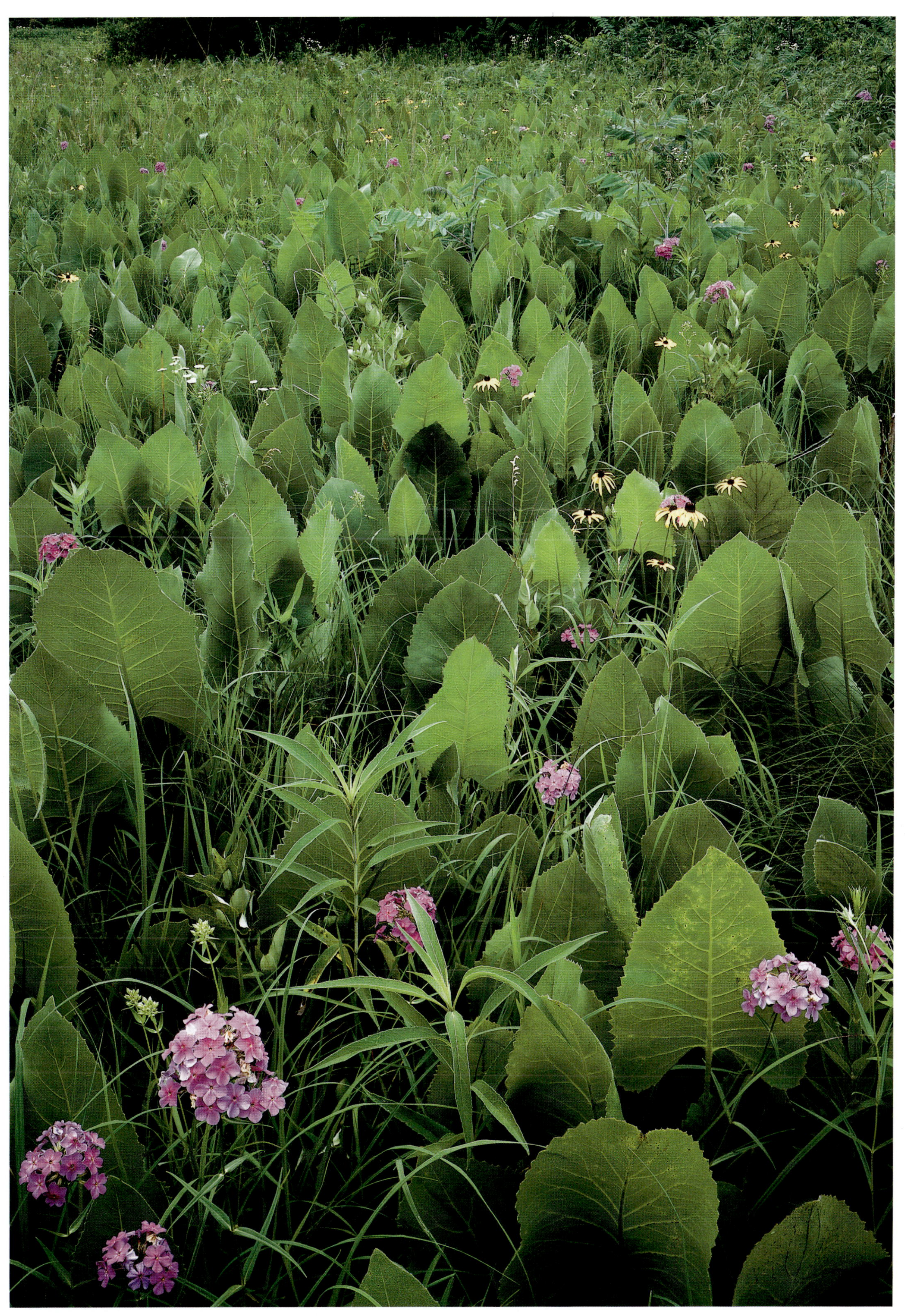

Prairie phlox *(Phlox pilosa)* in a stand of prairie dock *(Silphium terebinthinaceum)*: West Chicago Prairie Forest Preserve, West Chicago, Du Page County *(Chicago Lake Plain, Great Lake Section, Central Lowland Province)*

The 305 acres of West Chicago Prairie feature nearly every type of natural landscape found in northern Illinois: prairies (both wet and mesic), sedge meadows, a bur oak savanna, woodlands, ponds, and postglacial swamp. The five hundred native plant species and 170 species of birds recorded in these habitats make West Chicago Prairie the richest preserve in Illinois. In the wet-mesic prairie habitat, shooting star and hoary puccoon bloom in spring and early summer, while sky-blue aster and prairie dock dominate in late summer and fall. The core of the preserve, from 1850 to 1960 the site of a railroad stockyard, is 150 acres of high-quality land bought in 1979 by the Du Page County Forest Preserve District and the City of West Chicago from a developer whose plans were frustrated by the wetness of the property. Another 155 acres have since been added as a buffer. *June 1999*

OPPOSITE PAGE LEFT:

Wild bergamot *(Monarda fistulosa)* and drooping coneflower *(Ratibida pinnata)*: Bluff Spring Fen Nature Preserve, near Elgin, Cook County *(Wheaton Morainal Country, Great Lake Section, Central Lowland Province)*

Bluff Spring Fen Nature Preserve contains on its ninety acres an astonishing variety of relict habitats that conjure the Fox River Valley as it was prior to European settlement. Habitats represented include not only the fen itself but also dry gravel prairie on kames, mesic black soil prairie, sedge meadow, bur oak-hickory savanna, and marsh. The fen is a poorly drained wetland with alkaline water and soil which support a rich community of specially adapted plants. A majority of the preserve's four hundred plant species grow in the fen. Among the fifty species of butterfly found at Bluff Spring Fen are two rare fen species, the mulberrywing skipper and the Baltimore checkerspot. Several species of dragonfly also inhabit the site, including the ebony jewel wing and the green darner. The clear meandering streams in the sedge meadow are home to the mottled sculpin, a bullheaded bottom-feeder. The joint owners of Bluff Spring Fen—the Metropolitan Water Reclamation District of Greater Chicago and the City of Elgin—consented to its dedication in 1987 as an Illinois State Nature Preserve. The Nature Conservancy and the Friends of the Fen are responsible for the preserve's restoration and stewardship. *July 1995*

OPPOSITE PAGE RIGHT:

Butterfly weed and pale prairie coneflower: Belmont Prairie Nature Preserve (Downers Grove), Du Page County *(Wheaton Morainal Country, Great Lake Section, Central Lowland Province)*

Nestled among the housing developments of Downers Grove, ten-acre Belmont Prairie Nature Preserve is a dry-mesic prairie sloping down to prairie wetland, protected since 1979 as the first nature preserve in Du Page County. The prairie remnant, lying on the Valparaiso

CONTINUED ON PAGE 25

WHEATON MORAINAL COUNTRY

GREAT LAKE SECTION OF CENTRAL LOWLAND PROVINCE

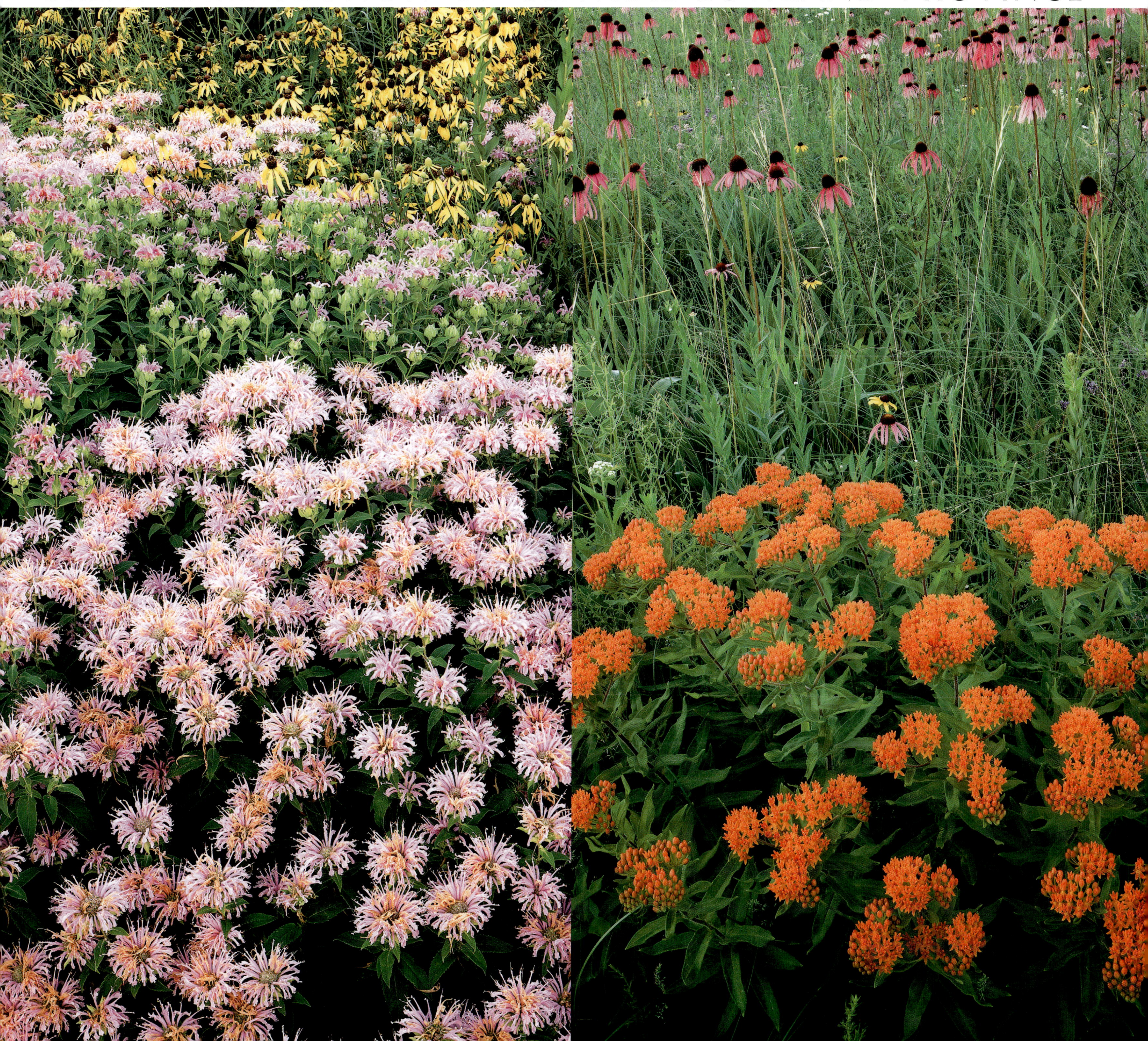

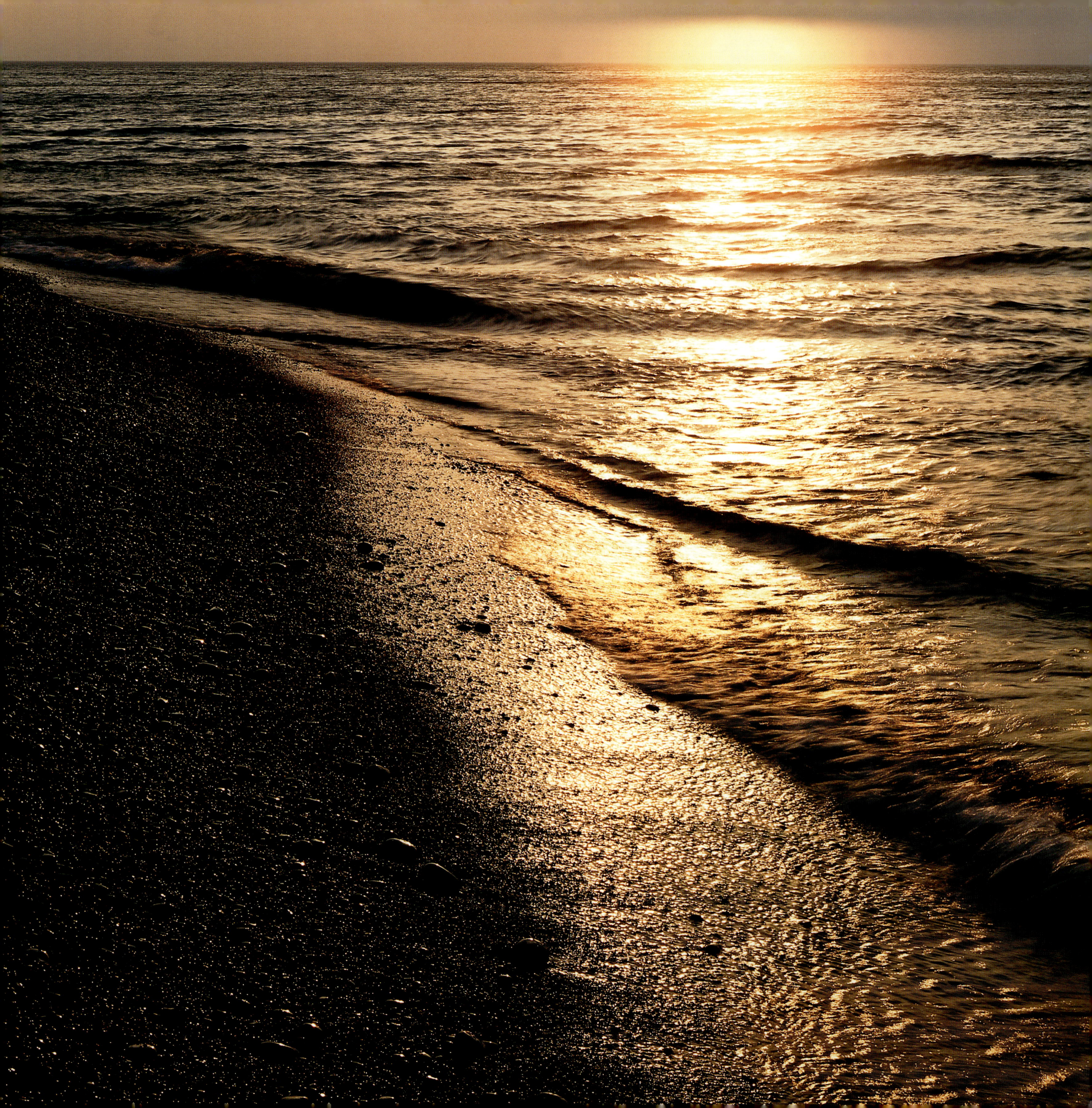

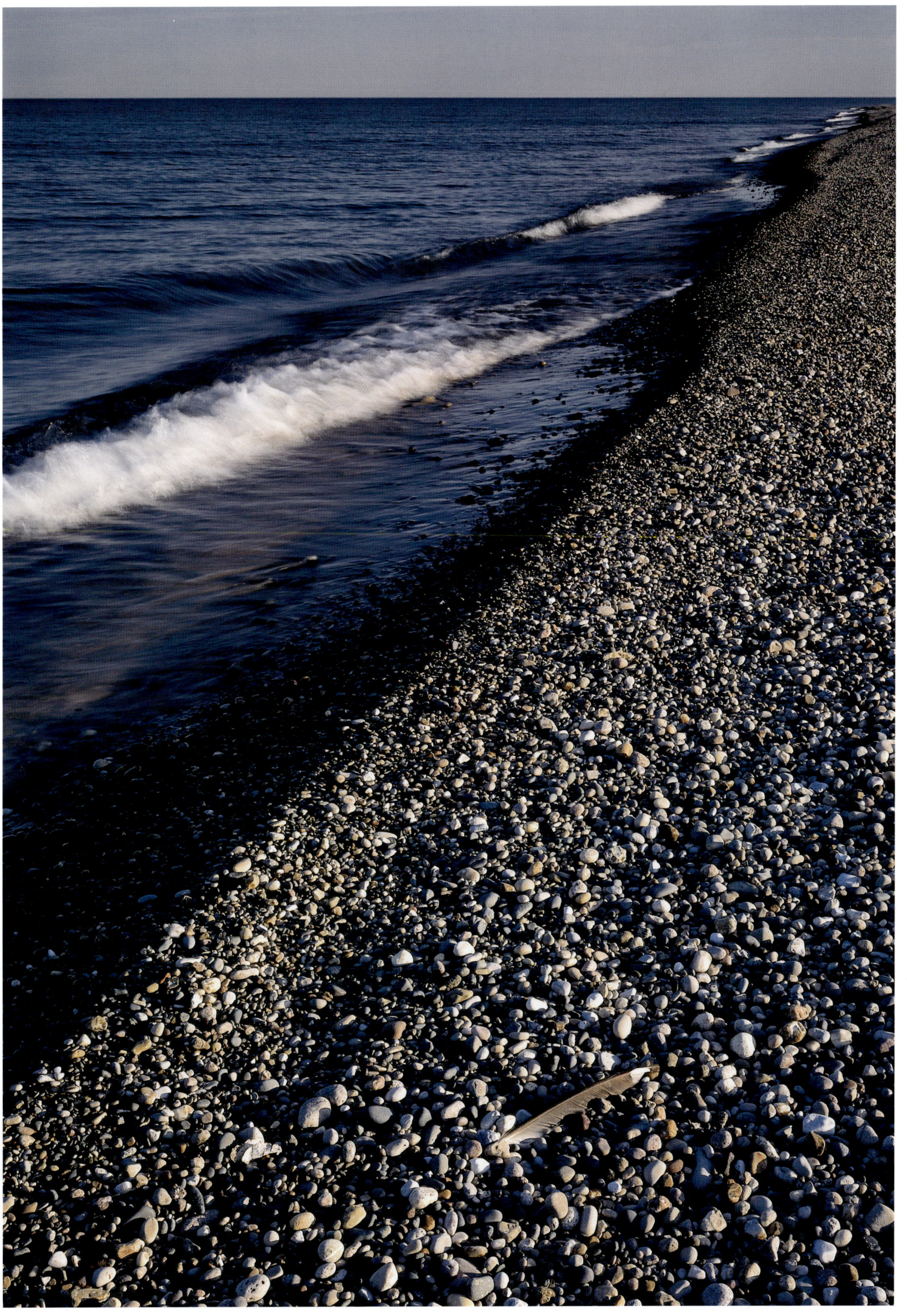

CONTINUED FROM PAGE 22

moraine, has well-drained dry-mesic prairie soil at the top, dominated by porcupine grass, and marshy wet-prairie soil at the bottom, dominated by blue-joint grass. Belmont Prairie supports 150 plant species, including butterfly weed *(Asclepias tuberose)* and pale prairie coneflower *(Echinacea pallida)*. *July 1999 (Photograph © Joseph Kayne)*

OPPOSITE PAGE:

Sunrise on Lake Michigan cobble beach: Illinois Beach State Park, Lake County *(Wheaton Morainal Country, Great Lake Section, Central Lowland Province)*
The 4,160-acre Illinois Beach State Park stretches for 6.5 miles along the shore of Lake Michigan, terminating at the Wisconsin border. The park, which features the last remaining beach ridge shoreline in the state, is split into a southern and a northern unit by a mile-long corridor of lakefront occupied by Commonwealth Edison's Zion Nuclear Power Plant, which was decommissioned 1998 but still holds 1,100 tons of radioactive spent fuel from its twenty-five years of service. The northern unit, acquired by the State between 1971 and 1982, contains protected historical remnants of Camp Logan, which served as an Illinois National Guard training facility from 1892 to 1971. Although the National Guard leveled the dunes, they left much of the original prairie and savanna intact. During the same time, commercial sand mining of the dunes advancing from the south, threatening what is now the southern unit of Illinois Beach State Park. To preserve Illinois's last remaining beach ridge shoreline, the state acquired in 1948 the first parcels of what would become the southern unit of the state park. In 1964, this portion was dedicated as the first Illinois Nature Preserve; in 1980, it was also declared a National Natural Landmark. *September 1995*

THIS PAGE:

Sunset on Lake Michigan pebble beach: Illinois Beach State Park, Lake County *(Wheaton Morainal Country, Great Lake Section, Central Lowland Province)*
The dunes and ridges that cut across Illinois Beach State Park are part of a narrow beach-dune system that developed about 3500 years ago between Waukegan, Illinois, and Kenosha, Wisconsin. The system resulted from the complex interaction of receding lake levels and rising land levels. Each sandy ridge represents an ancient beach that formed, along with the dunes behind it, during a stillstand of the lake in relation to the land. The swampy swales between the ridges represent periods of time when the relative recession of the lake was too fast for beach formation. *September 1995*

PAGE 26:

Dune grasses, Lake Michigan shore, evening: Illinois Beach State Park, Lake County *(Wheaton Morainal Country, Great Lake Section, Central Lowland Province)*
Carl Sandburg wrote: "The dunes are to the Midwest what the Grand Canyon is to Arizona. They constitute a signature of time and eternity." Illinois dunes, rarely growing to more than ten feet in height, are smaller than their counterparts in Indiana because the prevailing winds on the Illinois shore blow lakeward. Since the beach-dunes mature in age landward from the modern beach, the more landward a dune is, the more colonized it is by plants. On the modern beach and

CONTINUED ON PAGE 26

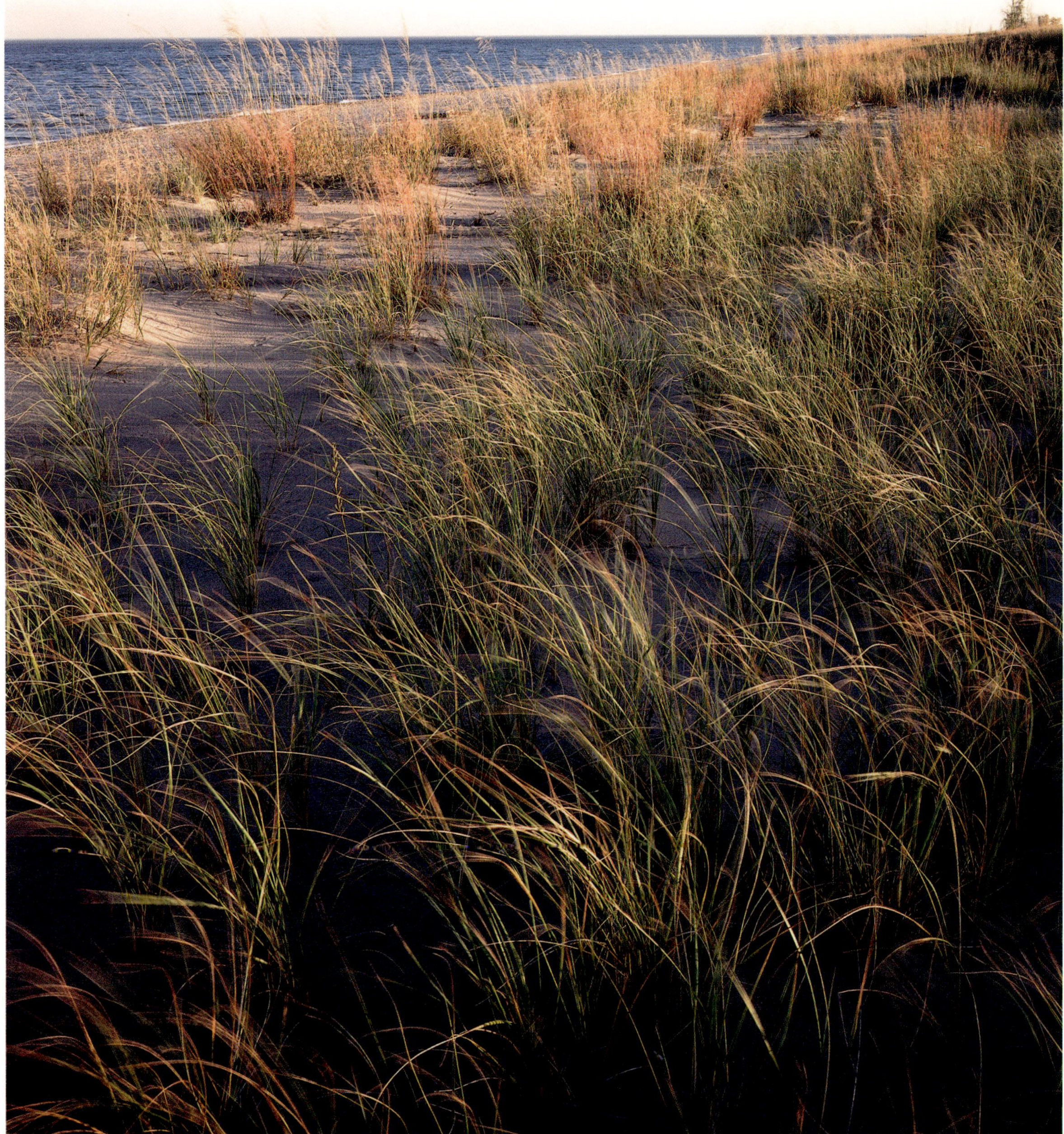

CONTINUED FROM PAGE 25

foredunes, the harsh wind and mobile sand limit plant life to the hardiest species such as marram grass, sea rocket, bearberry, and prostrate Waukegan juniper. Inland of the modern dunes is the dry sand prairie on older stabilized dunes and ridges, supporting Indian grass, little bluestem, switch grass, sand reed grass, and large patches of prickly pear cactus. Inland again are the wet prairies, carpeted with a wide variety of grasses and sedges. Farther inland still are the black-oak sand savannas. The wetlands (fens, panes, marshes, and pons) in the intervening swales host cattail, bluejoint grass, prairie cordgrass, reed grass, big bluestem, sedges, Kalm's St. Johnswort, sundew, and a variety of orchids. More than 650 species of plants have been recorded in these five ecological niches of the beach-dune system in Illinois Beach State Park. *October 1995*

OPPOSITE PAGE:

Dead River, lily pads, sunrise: Illinois Beach State Park, Lake County *(Wheaton Morainal Country, Great Lake Section, Central Lowland Province)* The Dead River, which drains an 18 square-mile urban watershed before traversing the southern unit of Illinois Beach State Park, is the only river left in Illinois that still flows into Lake Michigan. Actually, "flows" sometimes overstates the case. Within Illinois Beach State Park, the Dead River is a complex of small lakes, wetlands, and sluggish channels. For much of the year, the river's mouth is plugged by sand and gravel delivered by Lake Michigan's surf and longshore current. At such times, the Dead River is truly dead: a long, stagnant pond surrounded by marshes. After heavy rains or snowmelt, when the impounded river rises high enough to top its natural dam, the Dead River comes to life, avulses the sandbar, and drains the

CONTINUED ON PAGE 28

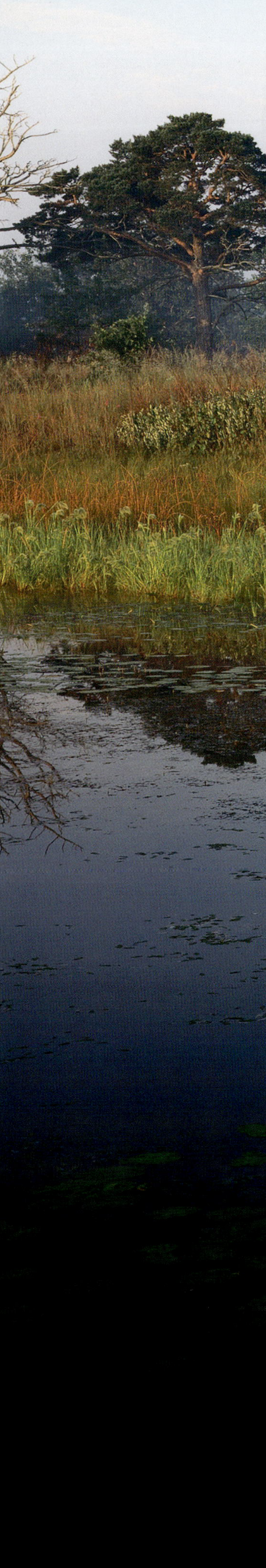

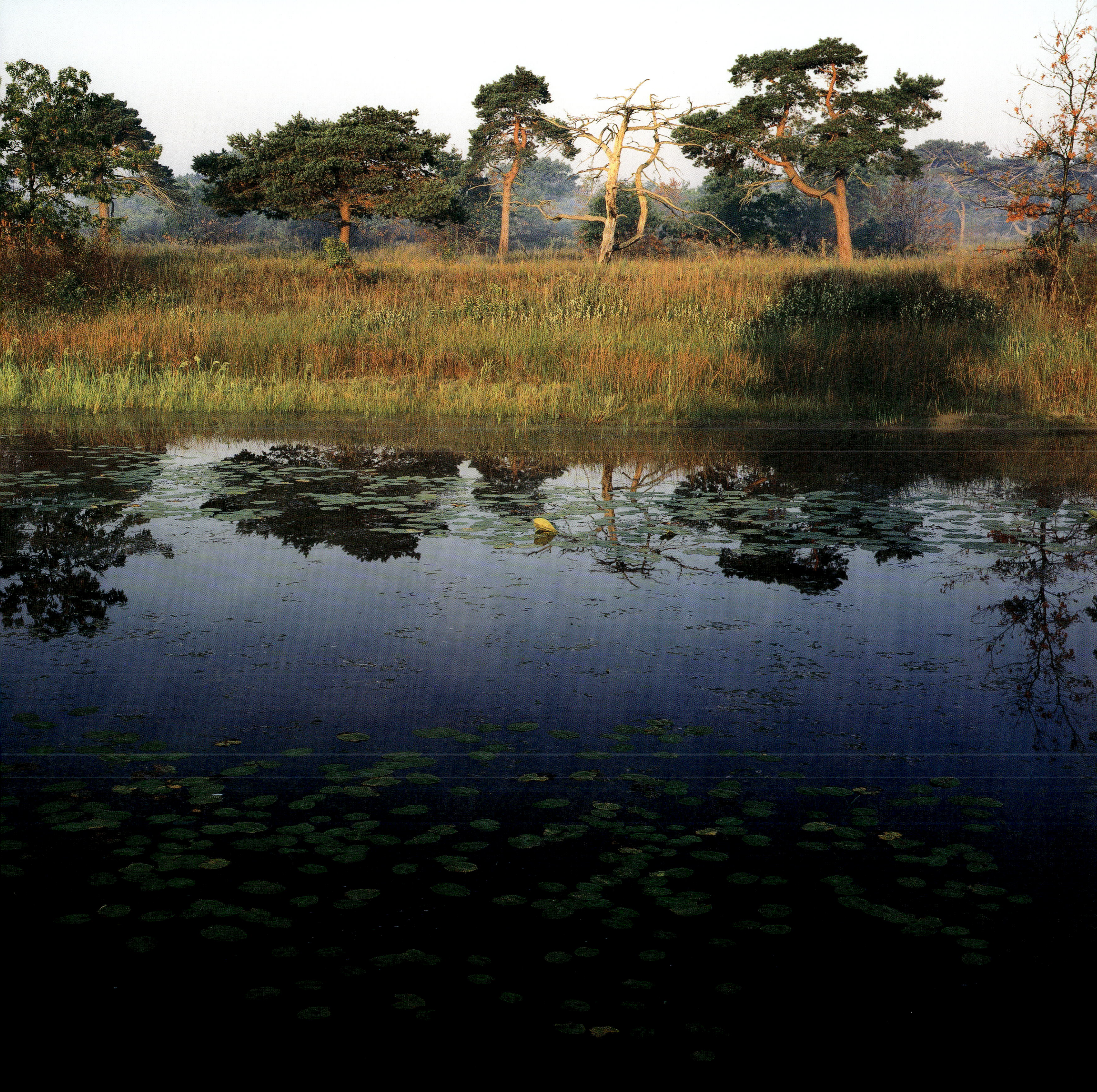

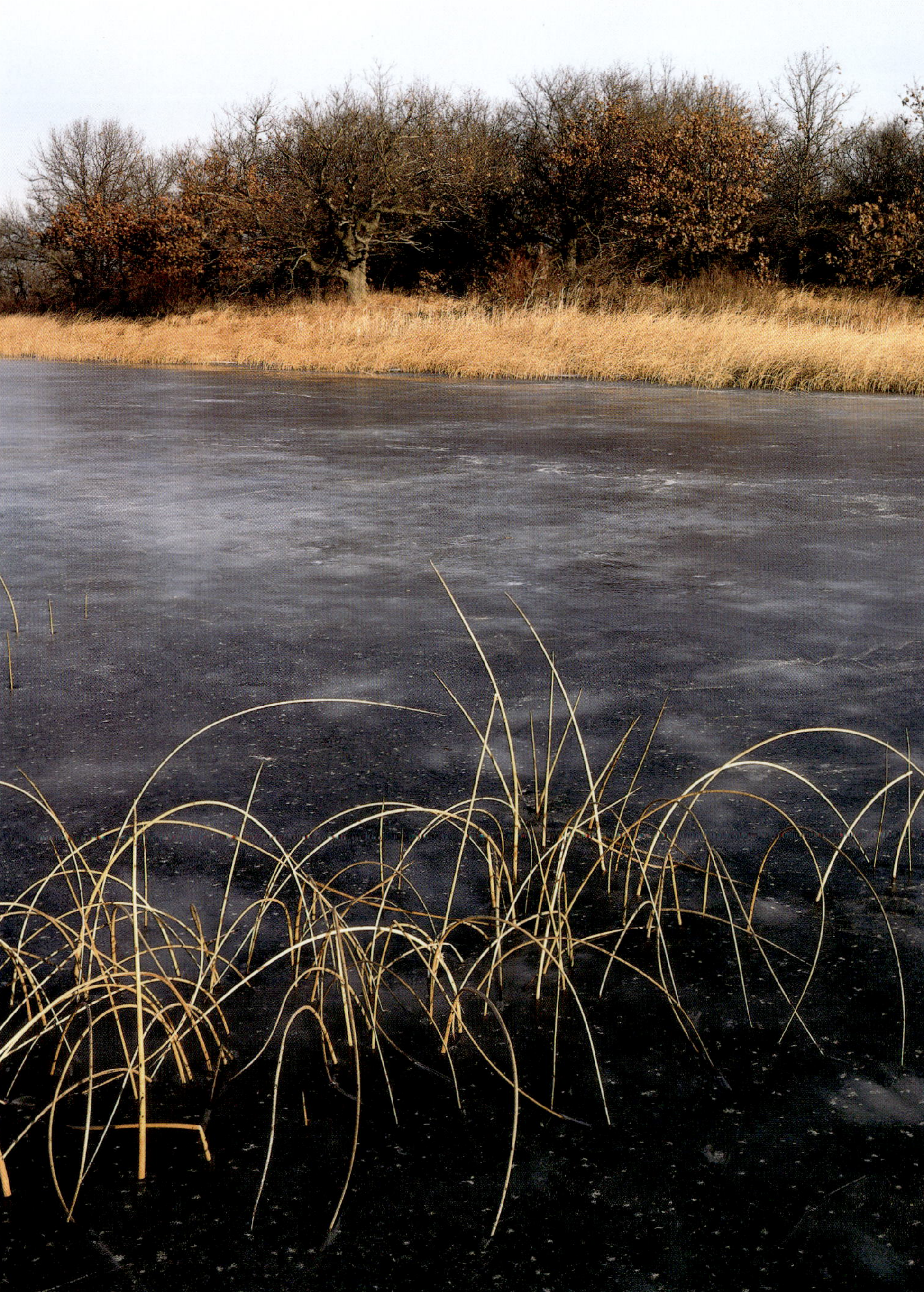

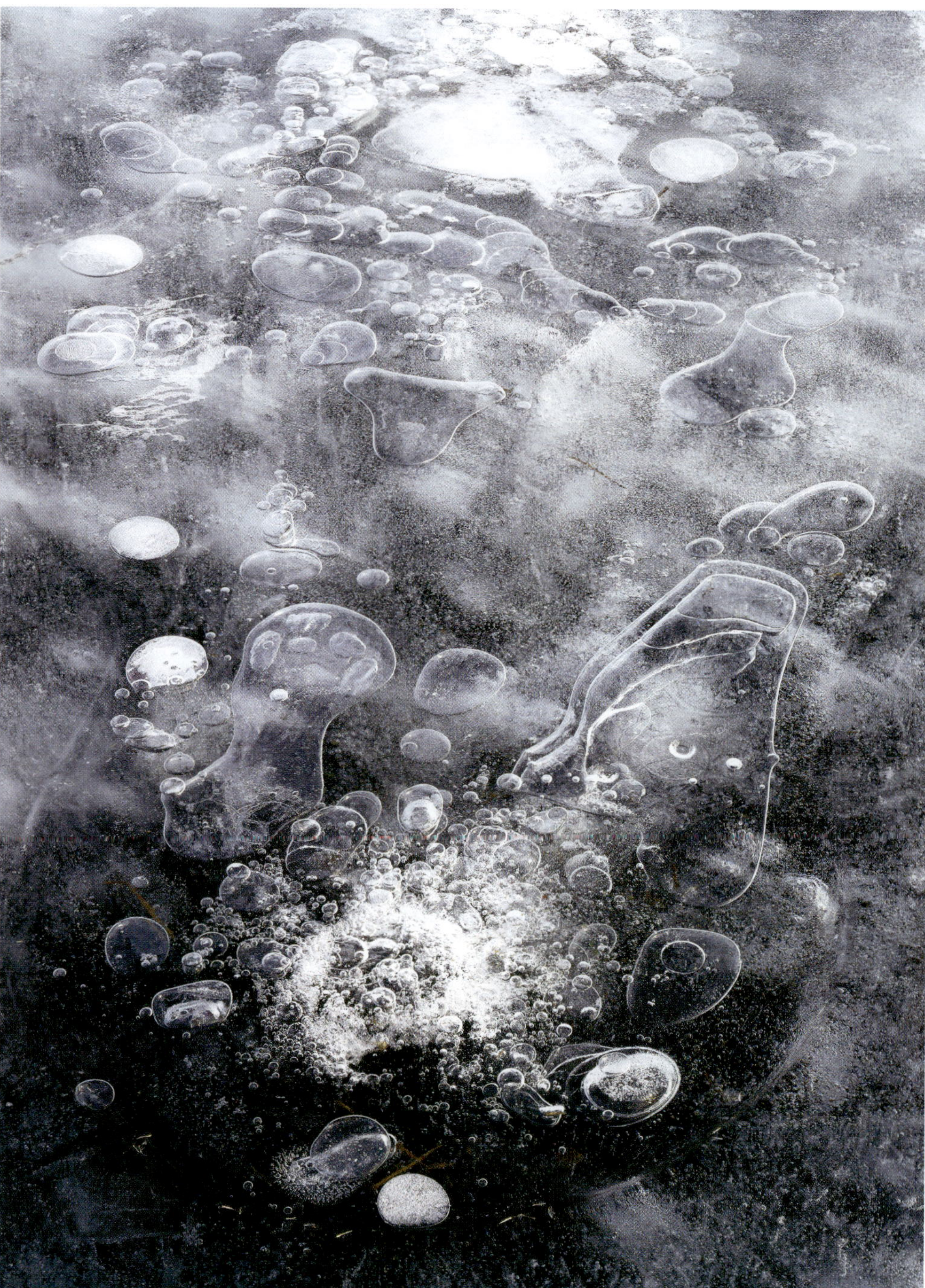

CONTINUED FROM PAGE 26
marshes. The Dead River is a good model of what the Chicago River used to look like and how it used to behave before the City of Chicago did all those kinky things to it. *September 1999*

THIS PAGE LEFT:

Dead River, frozen, reeds and ice patterns: Illinois Beach State Park, Lake County *(Wheaton Morainal Country, Great Lake Section, Central Lowland Province)*
This photograph was taken at sunrise on the first morning of the new millennium. *January 2000*

THIS PAGE RIGHT:

Dead River, frozen, bubbles and ice patterns: Illinois Beach State Park, Lake County *(Wheaton Morainal Country, Great Lake Section, Central Lowland Province)*
This photograph was taken at sunrise on the first morning of the last year of the old millennium. *January 2000*

OPPOSITE PAGE:

Sugar Maple in fall color: Ryerson Woods, Lake County *(Wheaton Morainal Country, Great Lake Section, Central Lowland Province)*
Ryerson Woods, situated on the east bank of the Des Plaines River near Deerfield, represents some of the finest hardwood forest in the Chicagoland area. Also known as the Edward L. Ryerson Conservation Area, half of the 552 acres of Ryerson Woods have been designated an Illinois Nature Preserve. Managed by the Lake County Forest Preserve District and supported

CONTINUED ON PAGE 31

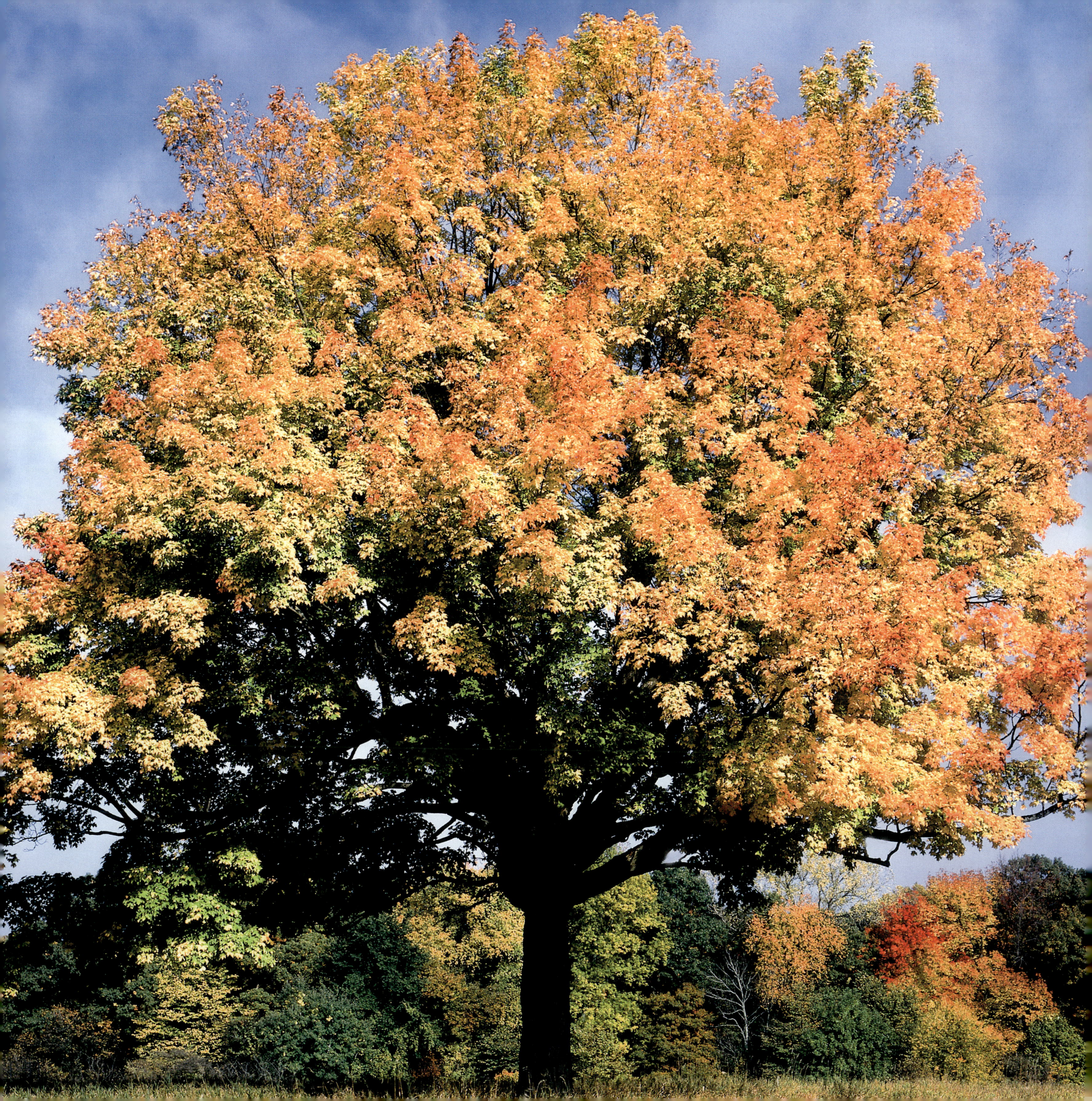

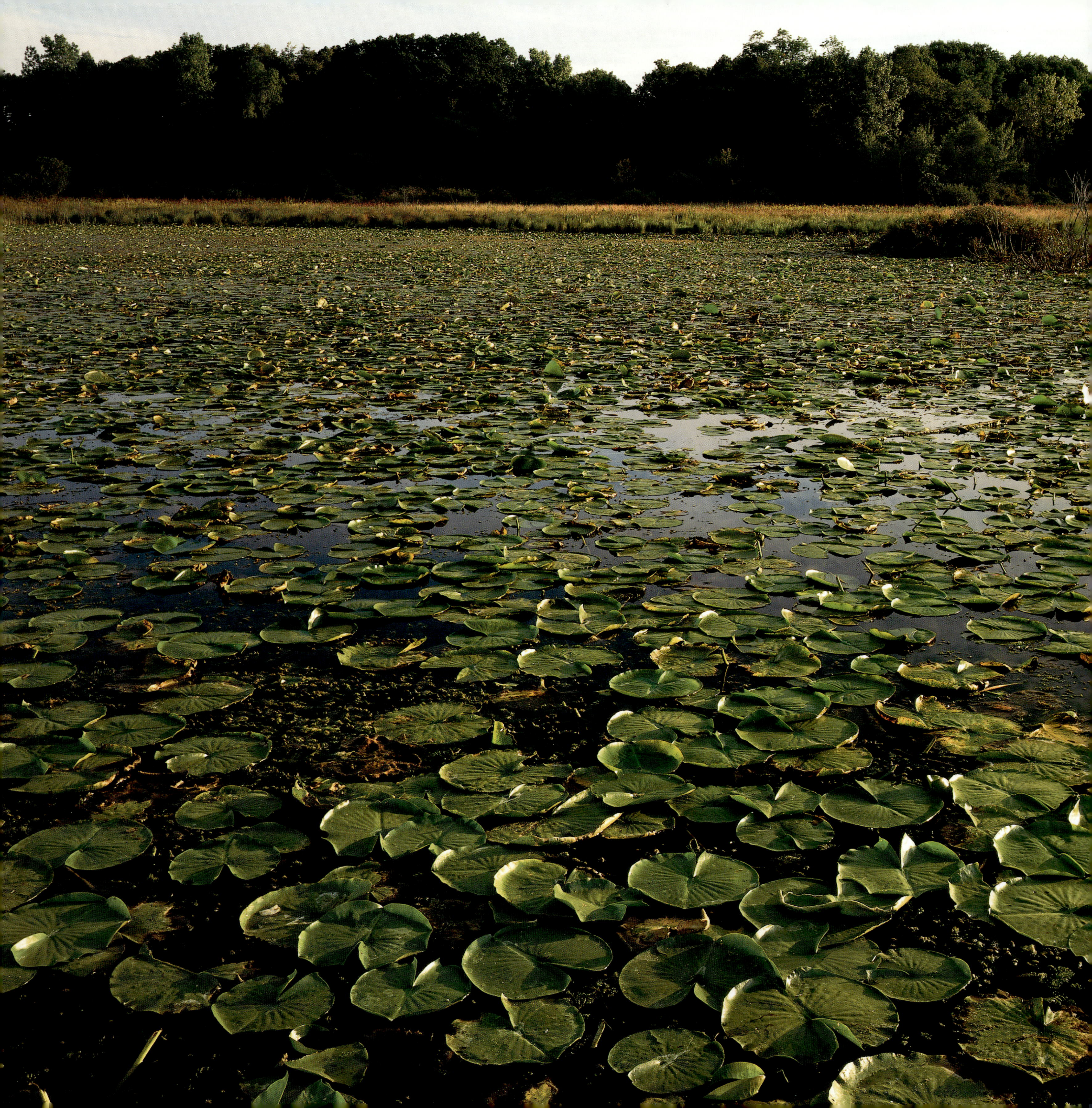

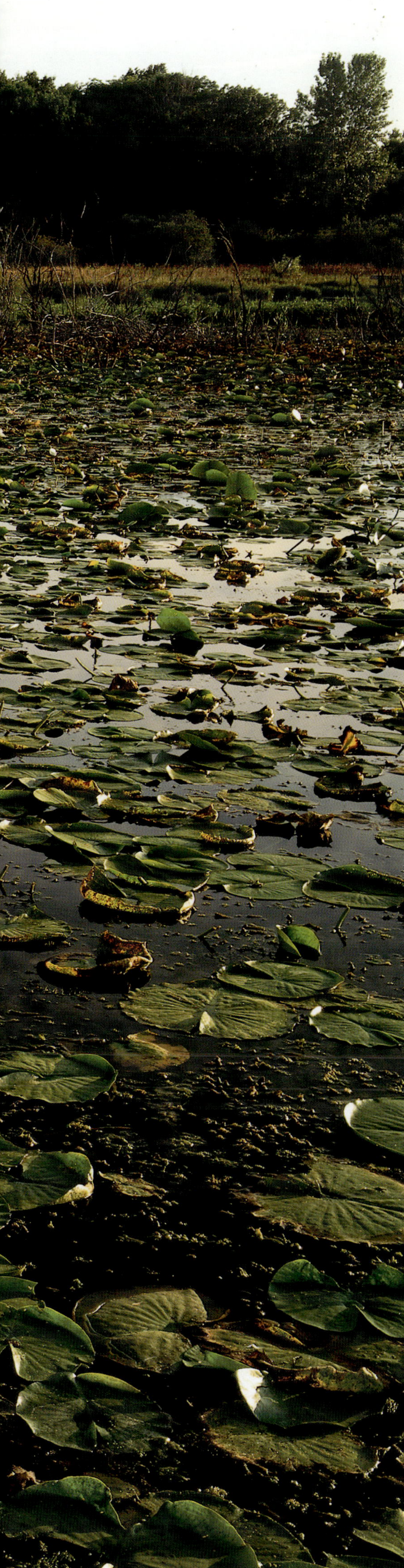

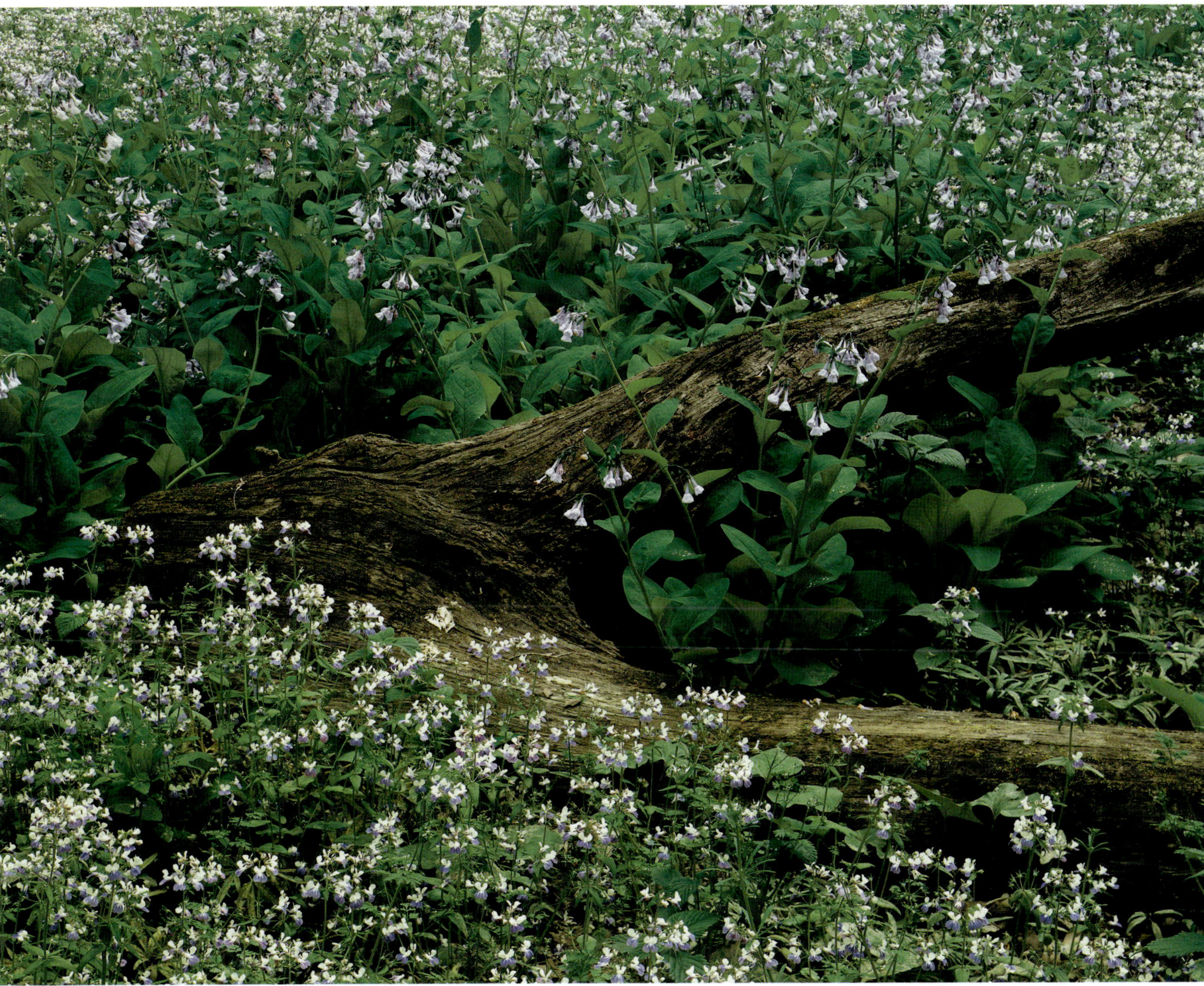

CONTINUED FROM PAGE 28

by Friends of Ryerson Woods, this mesic sugar maple forest is a haven for nearly five hundred species of flowering plants (including the purple fringed orchid) and many rare animal species (including the blue-spotted salamander, wood frog, eastern massasauga rattlesnake, red-shouldered hawk, and veery). *October 2002 (Photograph © Joseph Kayne)*

OPPOSITE PAGE:

Lily pads on Lake Defiance: Moraine Hills State Park, McHenry County *(Wheaton Morainal Country, Great Lake Section, Central Lowland Province)*

Lake Defiance, a 48-acre kettle lake at the center of 1,700-acre Moraine Hills State Park, was formed by the melting of a chunk of ice buried in the late Wisconsinan moraine, whose porous soil today favors oak-hickory forest. Lake Defiance, gradually filling in with peat, is one of the few glacial lakes in Illinois that has remained largely undeveloped. A nearby kettle, Pike Marsh, has filled in almost completely. *August 1999*

THIS PAGE:

Blue-eyed Marys *(Collinsia verna)*: Messenger Woods Nature Preserve, Lockport, Will County *(Wheaton Morainal Country, Great Lake Section, Central Lowland Province)*

Messenger Woods Nature Preserve, owned by the Forest Preserve District of Will County and purchased in a series of tracts beginning in 1930, today totals 946 acres of rolling glacial hill terrain. Messenger Woods was designated an Illinois Nature Preserve in 1994 in recognition that it is the best example of undisturbed, old grove, dry mesic and mesic upland oak forests surviving south of the Chicago Lake Plain. Other plant communities present within the preserve include shrub swamp, wet prairie, and maple-basswood-ash-elm bottomlands. At least 146 native plant species have been recorded from the preserve, including the endangered rock elm and heart-leaved plantain. Messenger Woods is known throughout the region for the abundance of spring wildflowers that carpet its forest floors, as well as for the abundance of nature photographers who perch over their cameras to capture the lavish blooms of blue-eyed Marys, Virginia bluebells, red trillium, white trillium grandiflorum, and hepatica. There are now more than three hundred nature preserves in the Illinois Nature Preserves System, protecting fewer than half of the 635 high-quality undisturbed communities left in Illinois and together representing one-tenth of one percent of Illinois's area. Over one-quarter of the population of threatened plant and animal species in Illinois live in these nature preserves. *May 1983*

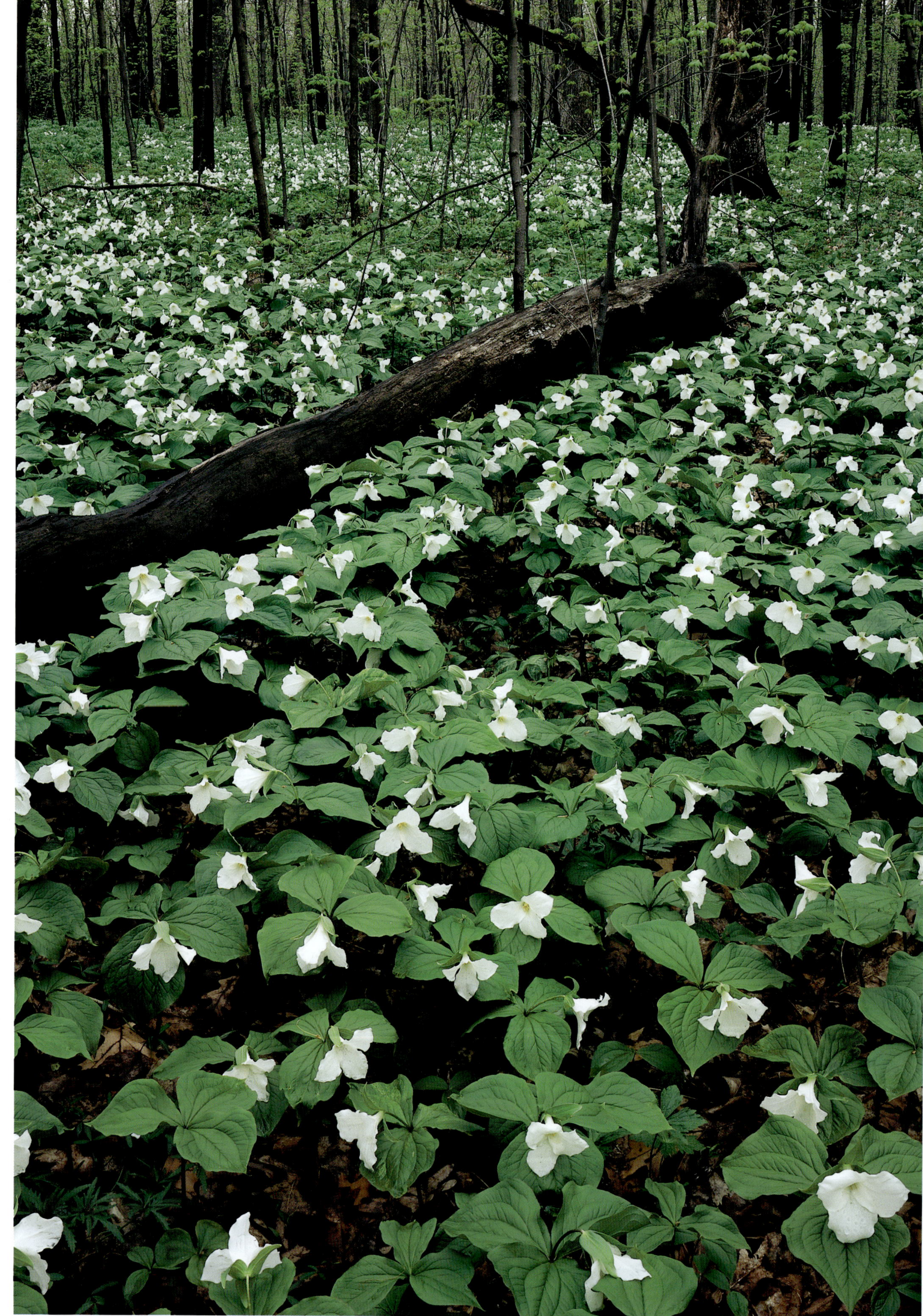

White Trilliums ***(Trillium grandiflorum)*****:** Messenger Woods Nature Preserve, Lockport, Will County *(Wheaton Morainal Country, Great Lake Section, Central Lowland Province)*

"Trillium" is a neologism coined by the botanist Linnaeus as an adaptation of the Swedish word trilling, meaning "triplet". And the trillium is indeed a three-petitous plant: three sepals, three leaves, and three petals. Flowering first in early spring and in profusion in the month of May, large-flowered white trilliums grow in rich soils of undisturbed forest floors from Quebec to Georgia. Messenger Woods Nature Preserve is noted for having some of the finest stands of white trillium to be found anywhere in this range. Unfortunately, overgrazing by the unchecked white-tailed deer population has recently been decimating the famous white trillium stands of Messenger Woods. *May 1995*

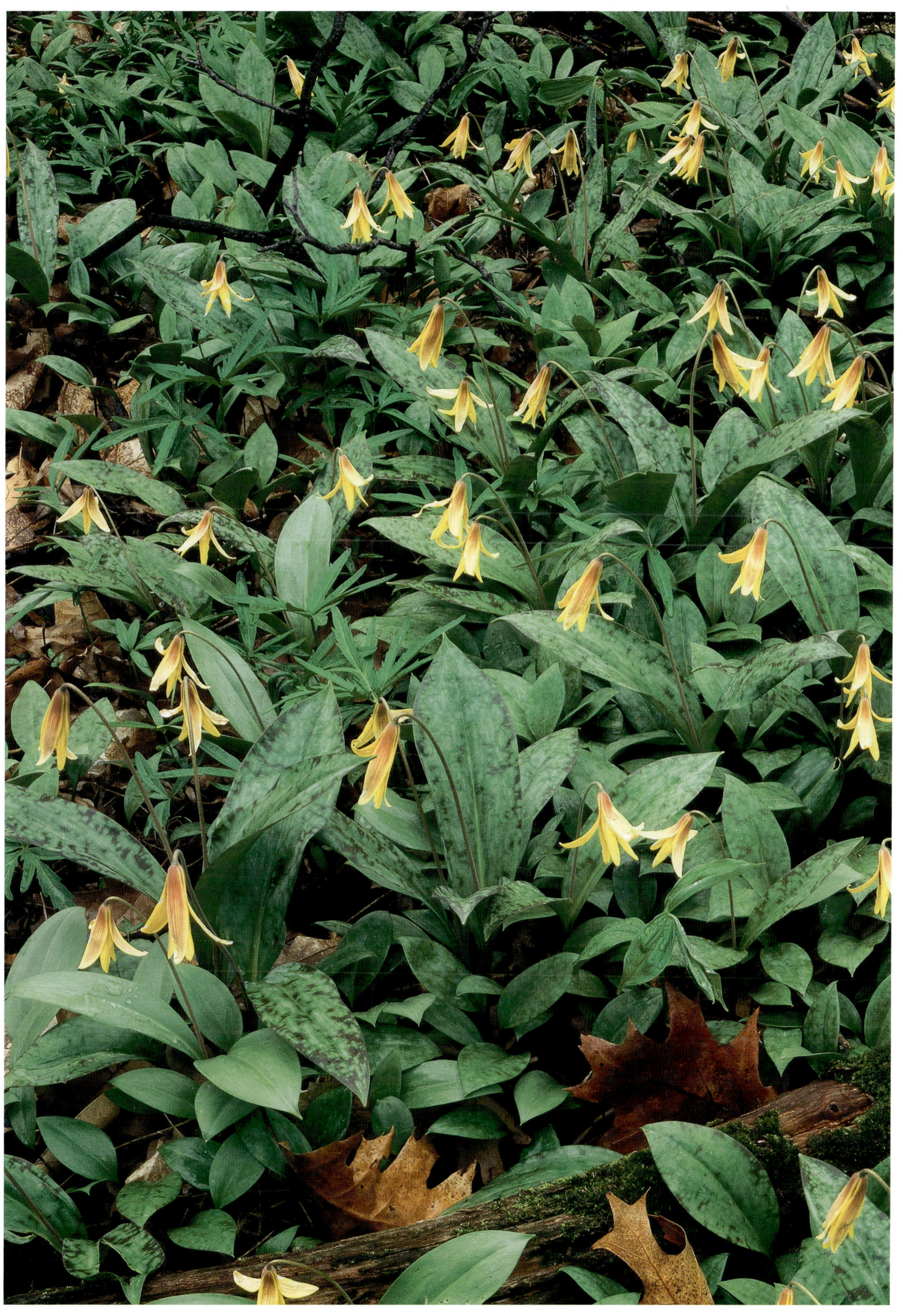

Trout lilies ***(Erythronium americanum)*****:** Higinbotham Woods, Joliet, Will County *(Wheaton Morainal Country, Great Lake Section, Central Lowland Province)*

Higinbotham Woods, a 238-acre preserve donated to the Joliet Park District in 1915 by the Joliet Rotary Club, contains near Hickory Creek the Higinbotham Woods Earthwork, probably a vestige of Hopewellian culture in the Illinois River Valley. Low rich woods along streams and on wooded slopes are the habitat for yellow trout lilies, whose brilliant yellow nodding flowers stand out against the leaf litter of the woods from March till May.

May 1995

OPPOSITE PAGE:

Sunset over residual pond along the Marsh Loop Trail: Goose Lake Prairie State Natural Area, Grundy County *(Kankakee Plain, Till Plains Section, Central Lowland Province)*
Goose Lake Prairie State Natural Area, located fifty miles southwest of Chicago and a mile southwest of the confluence of the Kankakee and Des Plaines Rivers at the Illinois River, is the largest tallgrass prairie remnant in Illinois. The 2,537 acres of Goose Lake Prairie, once a tract in the rolling grasslands that stretched continuously from Indiana to the Rockies, include varied prairie and marsh communities. The flat landscape of Goose Lake Prairie's clay-based soils was formed by the passage of the Late Wisconsinan glacial sheet, whose retreating edge melted 14,000 years ago to fill the precursor of Goose Lake. In 1890, local farmers drained the thousand-acre lake, leaving behind today's residual marshes and ponds, such as the one in the photograph. Mining for firebrick clay and coal stripped much of Goose Lake Prairie through the nineteenth and twentieth centuries. It is presently proposed that Goose Lake Prairie State Natural Area be administratively merged with neighboring prairies such as Grant Creek Prairie and Midewin National Tallgrass Prairie to form the Grand Prairie Parklands, which would total 60,000 acres. *May 1995*

PAGES 36-37

Rock Creek: Kankakee River State Park, Kankakee County *(Kankakee Plain, Till Plains Section, Central Lowland Province)*
The four thousand acres of Kankakee River State Park spread away on both sides of an eleven-mile stretch of the Kankakee River, beginning 6 miles northwest of Kankakee. The historic river is naturally channeled and listed on the Federal Clean Streams Register. Smallmouth bass, channel catfish, walleye, and northern pike abound in both the Kankakee and its tributary, Rock Creek. A three-mile nature trail descends the limestone canyon of Rock Creek. *June 1995*

TILL PLAINS SECTION

KANKAKEE PLAIN

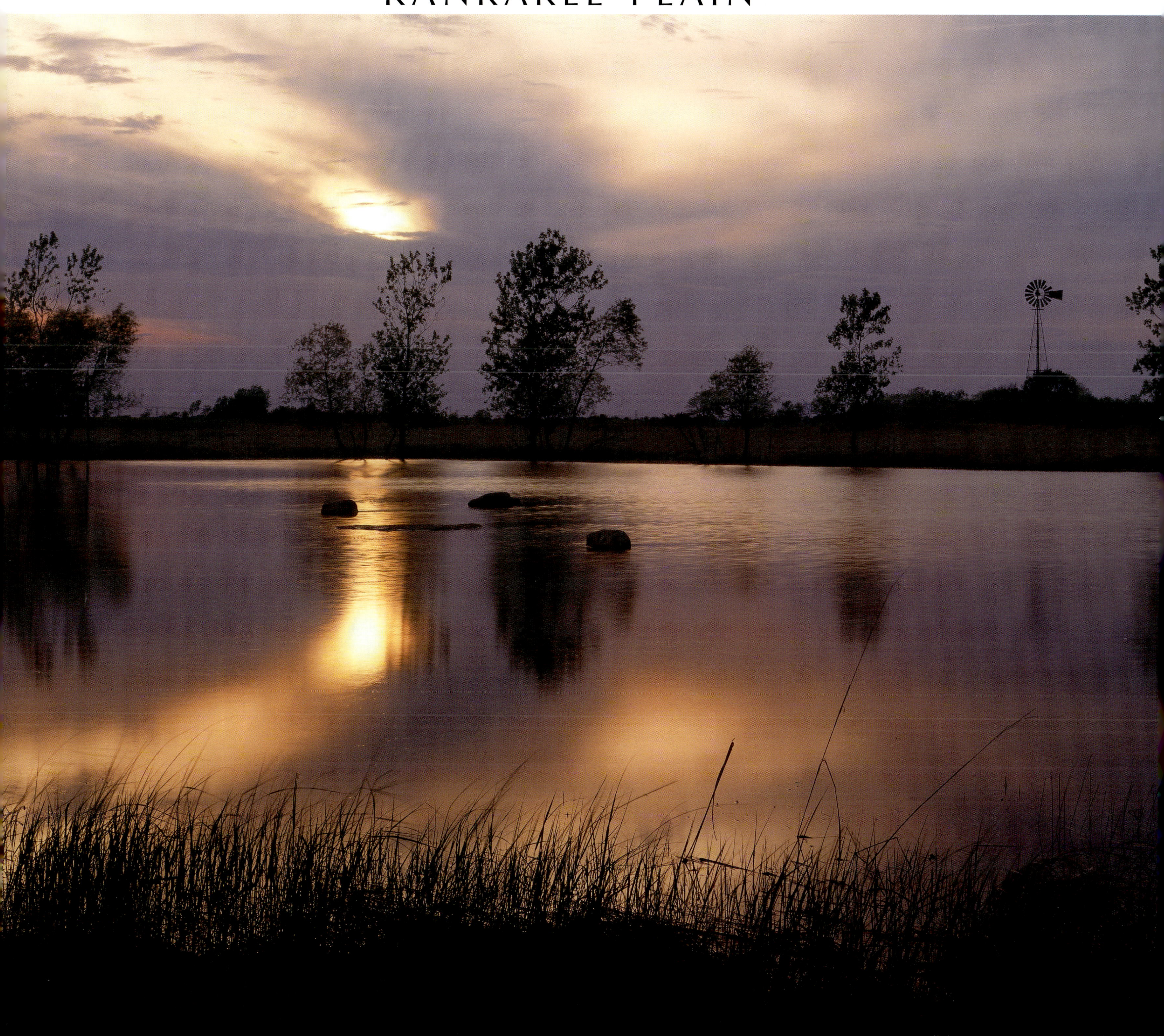

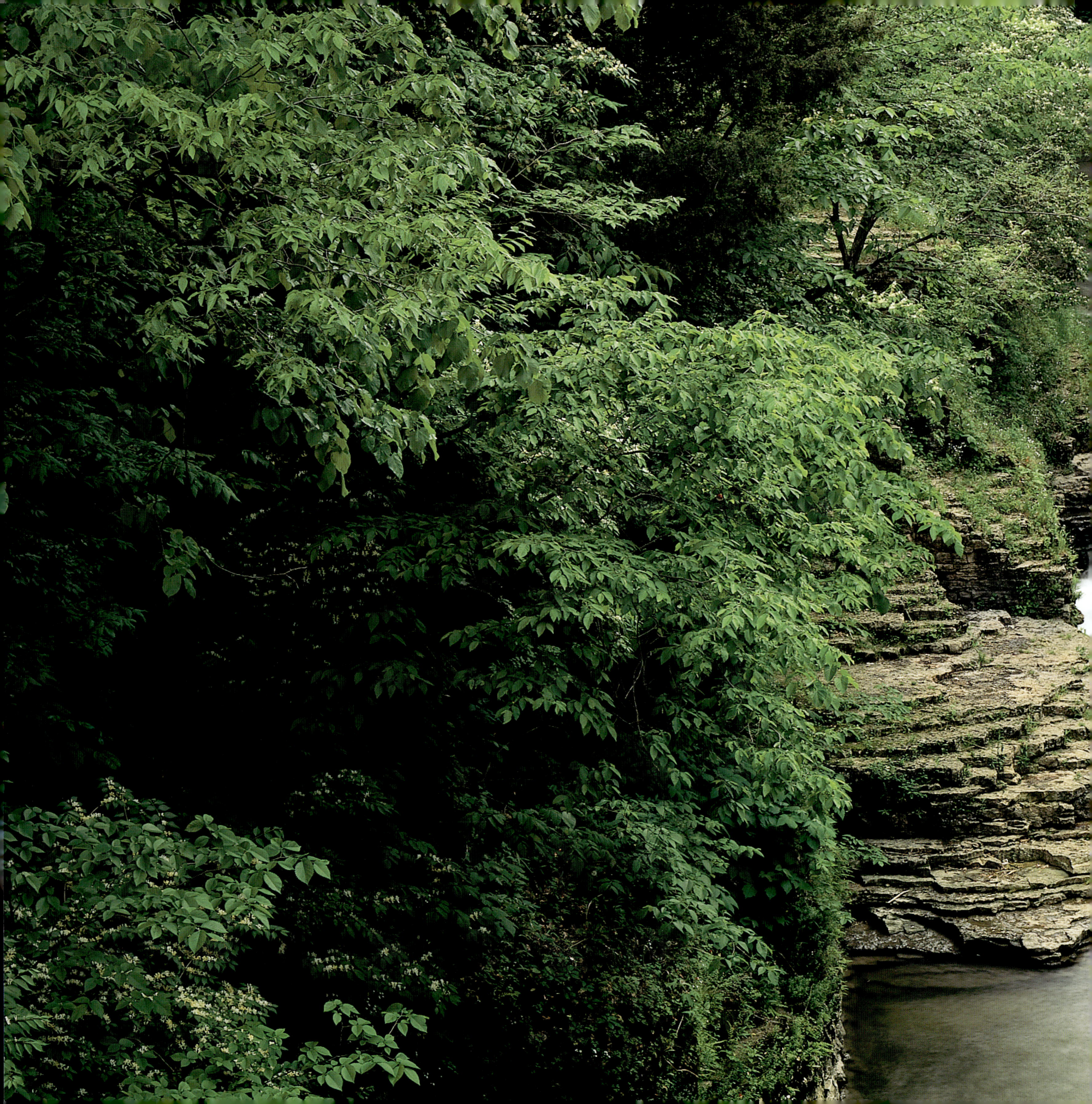

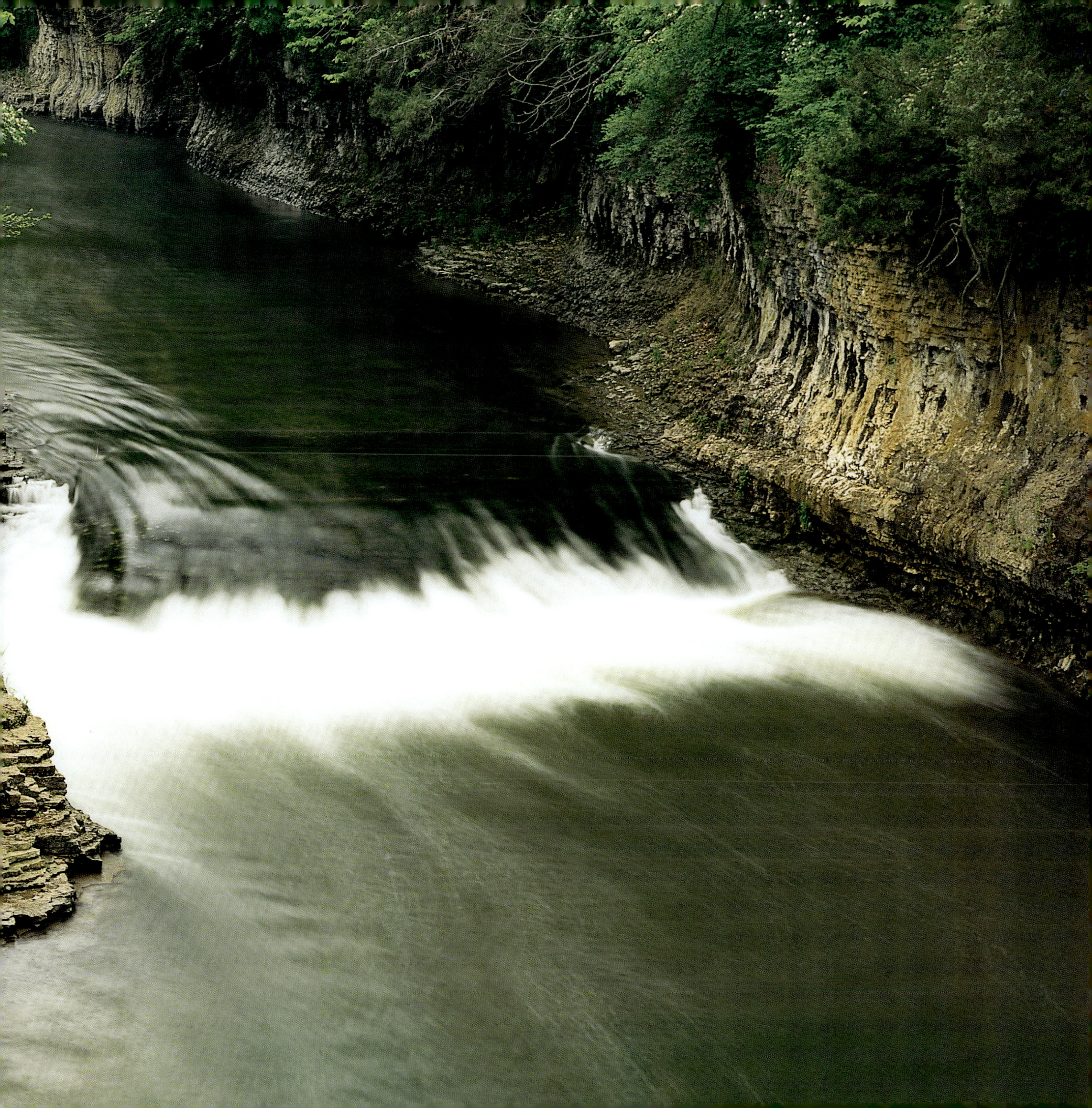

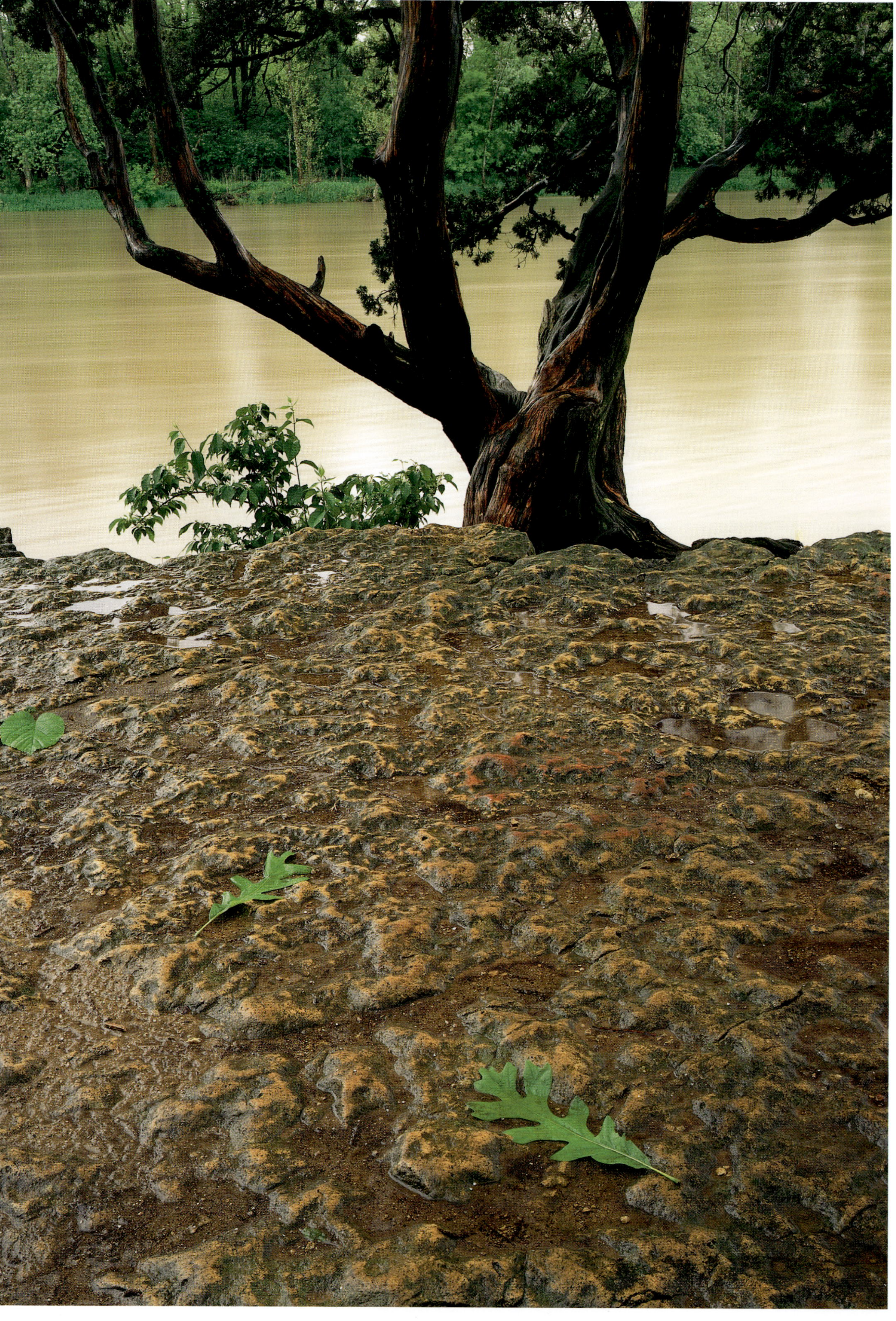

THIS PAGE:

Rock Creek: Kankakee River State Park, Kankakee County *(Kankakee Plain, Till Plains Section, Central Lowland Province)*

In the 1770s, the area now occupied by Kankakee River State Park came to be dominated by the Potawatomi, Ottawa, and Chippewa nations—"The Three Fires"—whose biggest village was sited near the mouth of Rock Creek. In 1830, Rock Village hosted the last Great Council of the Potawatomi. By treaty with the United States in 1832 after the Black Hawk War, the Potawatomi ceded and evacuated all of their land along the Kankakee and Illinois rivers. The grave of Chief Shaw-waw-nas-see is marked by a boulder along the nature trail at Rock Creek. *May 1995*

OPPOSITE PAGE:

Drooping coneflower *(Ratibida pinnata)*: Grant Creek Prairie Nature Preserve, Will County *(Kankakee Plain, Till Plains Section, Central Lowland Province)*

Grant Creek Prairie Nature Preserve is a 78-acre site of high-quality dolomite to wet/mesic prairie, rooted in 2-3 feet of black topsoil and glacial loess. Wisconsinan glaciers scraped down to the dolomite bedrock, on which organic-rich black earth has since formed. The glaciers also deposited many erratics—boulders imported by the glaciers from as far away as Canada—which had the later effect of keeping this prairie from being plowed under. Great blue herons and egrets frequently fly over Grant Creek Prairie on their way to the Kankakee River, a mile to the south. *July 1995*

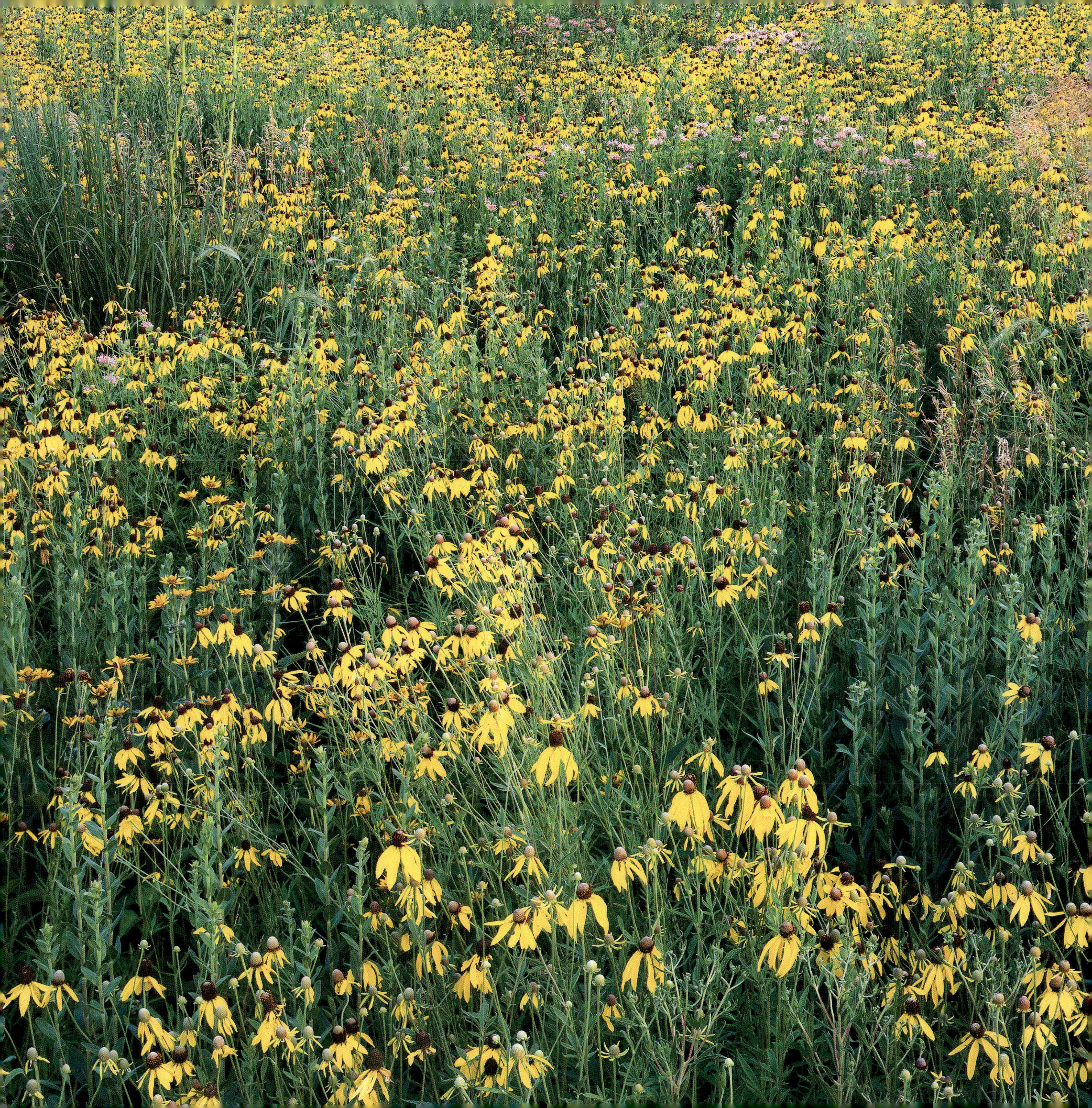

OPPOSITE PAGE:

Lake of the Woods Covered Bridge: Lake of the Woods County Park, Champaign County *(Bloomington Ridged Plain, Till Plains Section, Central Lowland Province)* Lake of the Woods County Park is a popular 900-acre park in the Sangamon River corridor, near Mahomet. Visitors to the park enjoy its rolling woodlands, the Early American Museum, the Mabery Gelvin Botanical Gardens, and this covered bridge. *September 2001*

PAGES 42-43:

Middle Fork of the Vermilion River: Middle Fork River County Forest Preserve, Champaign County *(Bloomington Ridged Plain, Till Plains Section, Central Lowland Province)* Deemed one of the most pristine rivers in Illinois, the Middle Fork of the Vermilion River has been designated a National Wild and Scenic River. This 1,530-acre county preserve through which the river passes affords a variety of habitats, including old hardwood forest, grassy meadows, and wetlands that attract large populations of waterfowl. *September 2001*

BLOOMINGTON RIDGED PLAIN

TILL PLAINS SECTION OF CENTRAL LOWLAND PROVINCE

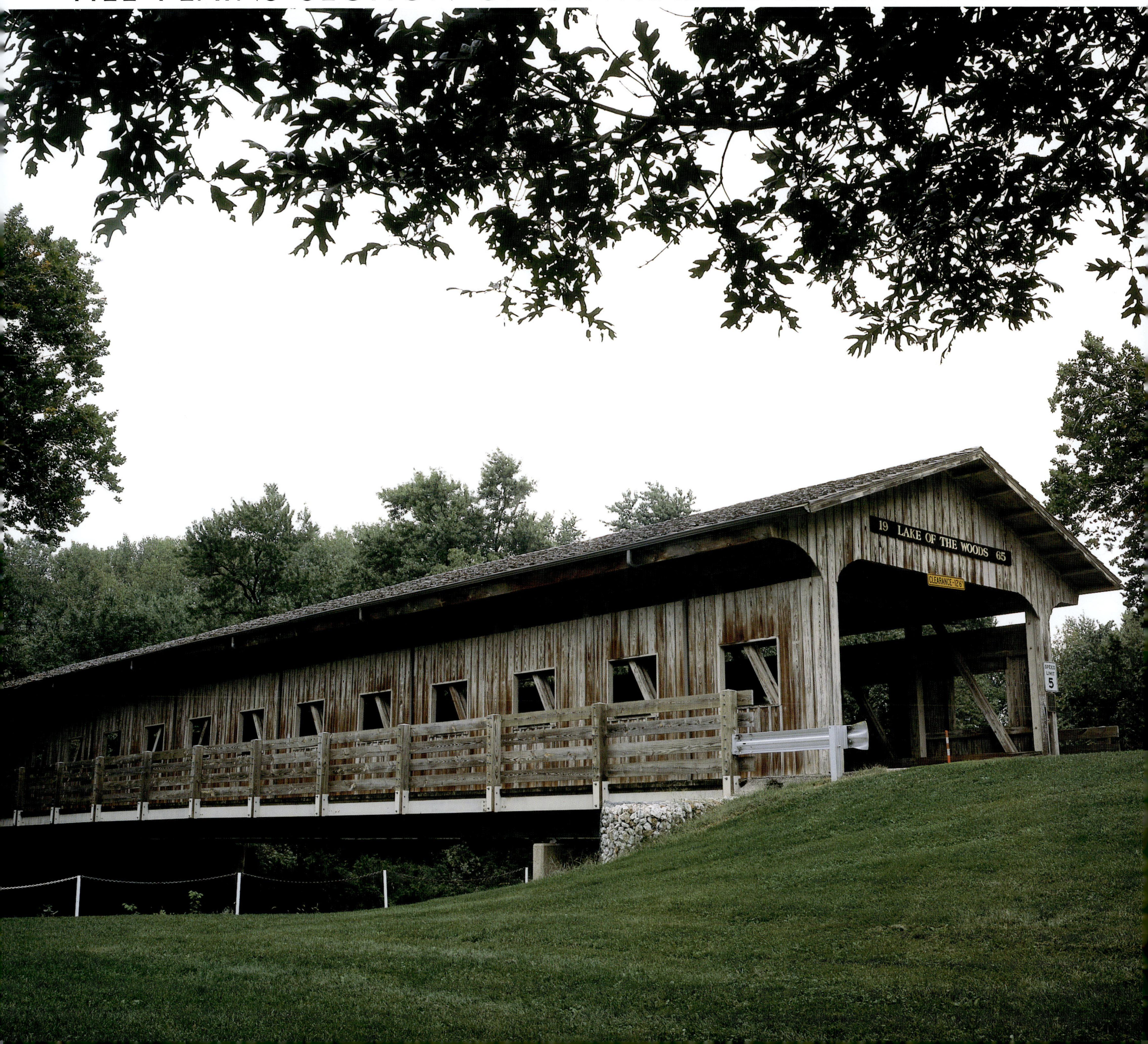

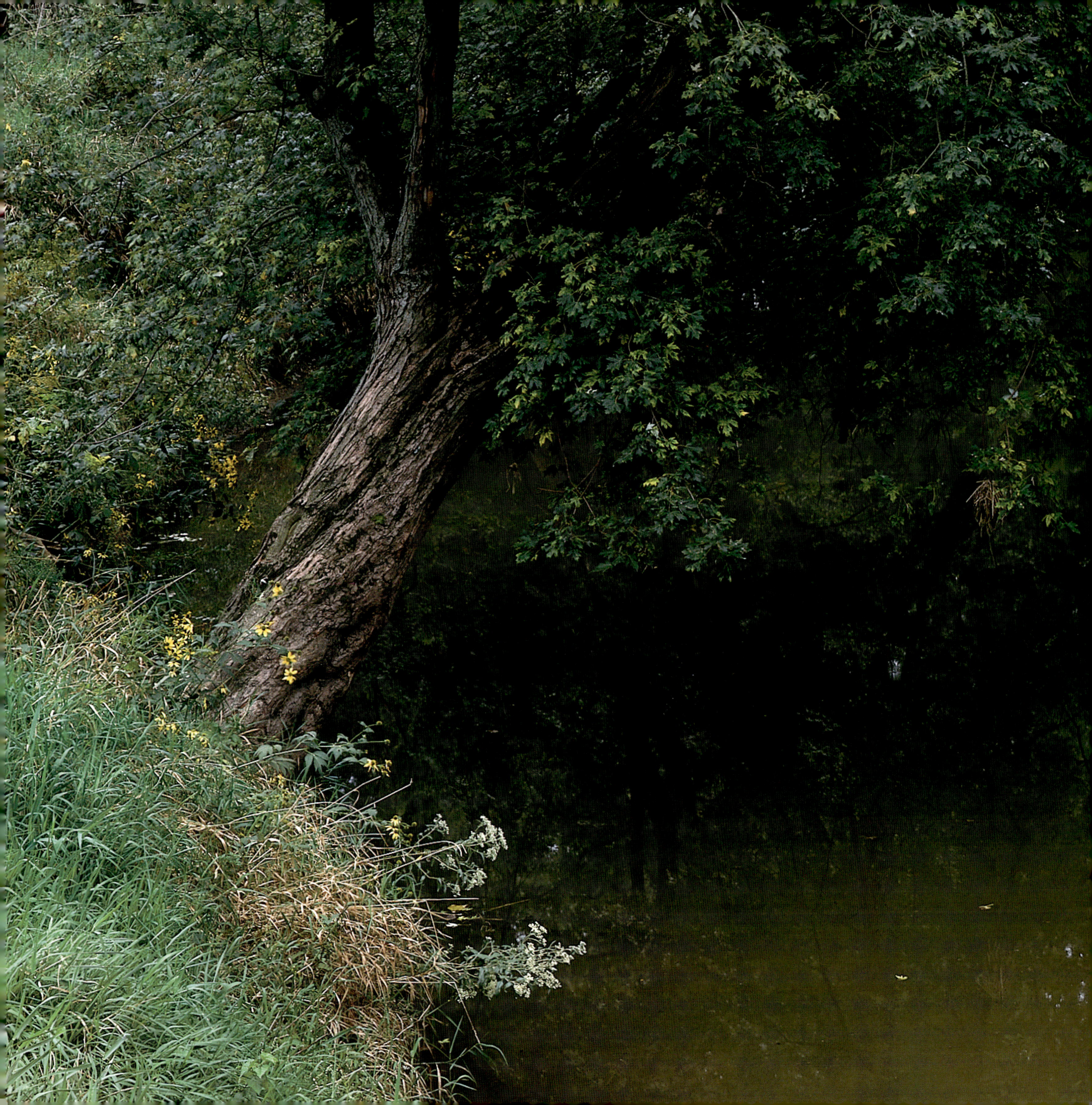

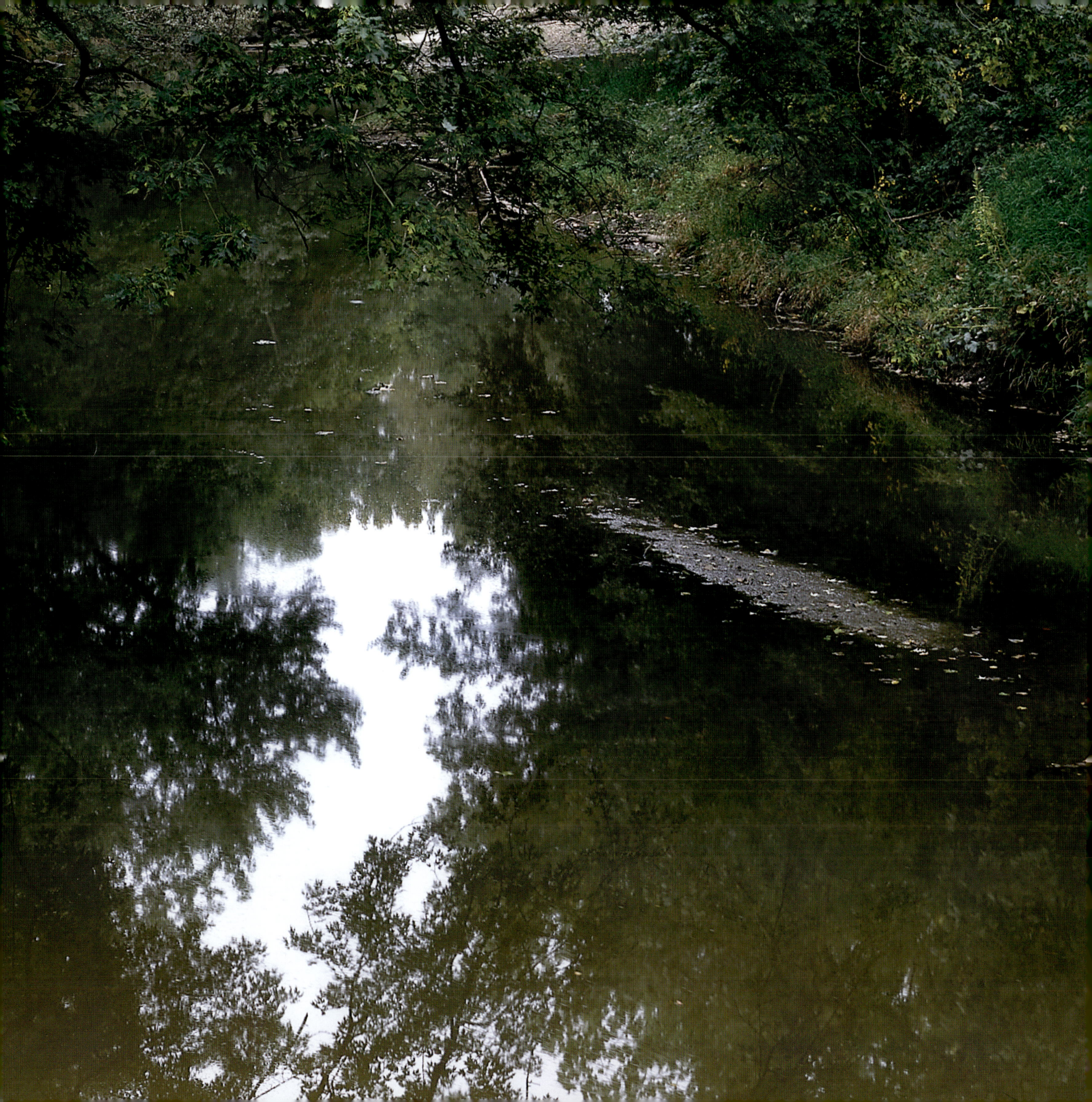

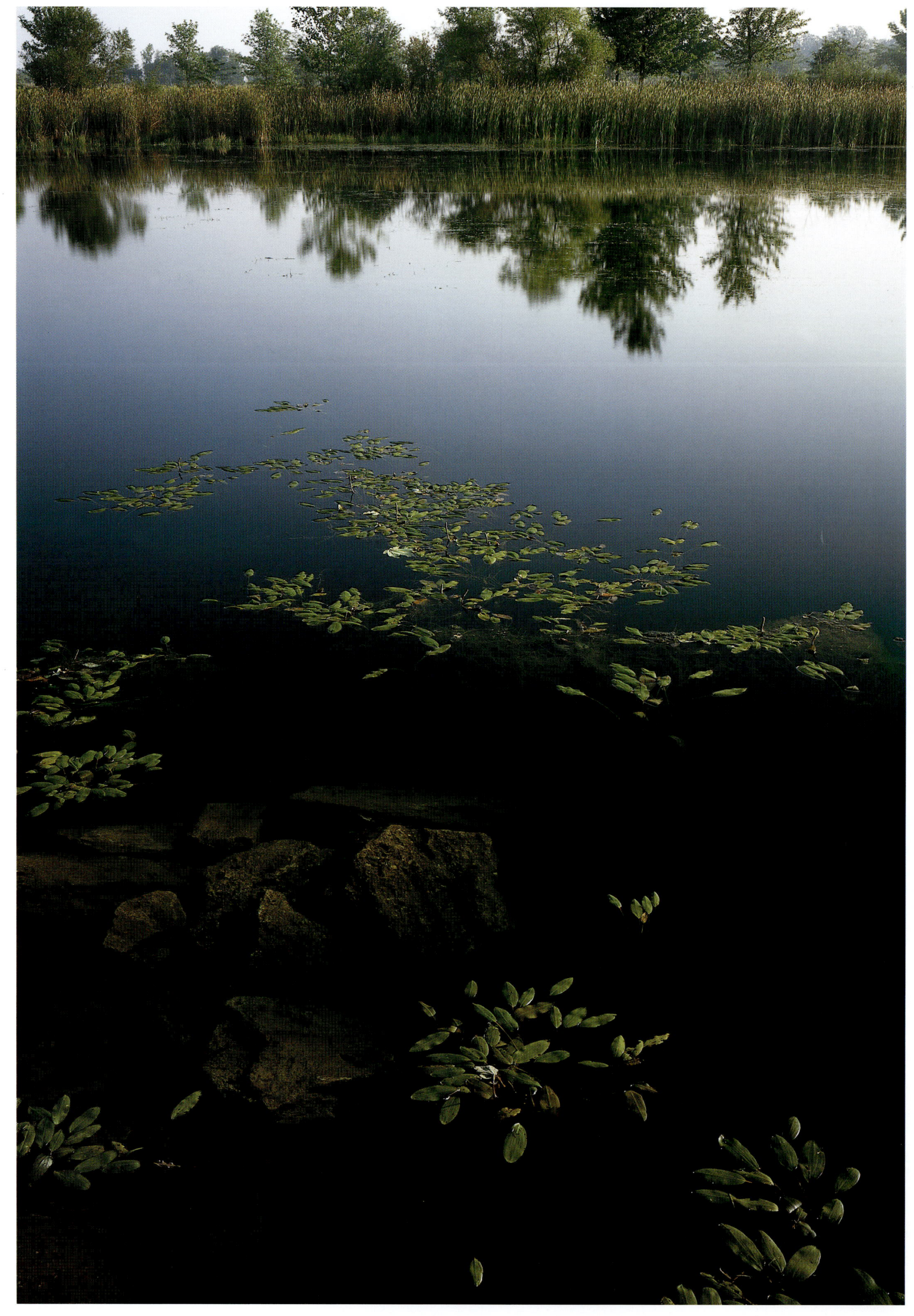

Emerald Pond: Middle Fork River County Forest Preserve, Champaign County *(Bloomington Ridged Plain, Till Plains Section, Central Lowland Province)*
The Middle Fork River County Forest Preserve contains three picturesque ponds: Willow, Cypress, and Emerald.
September 2001

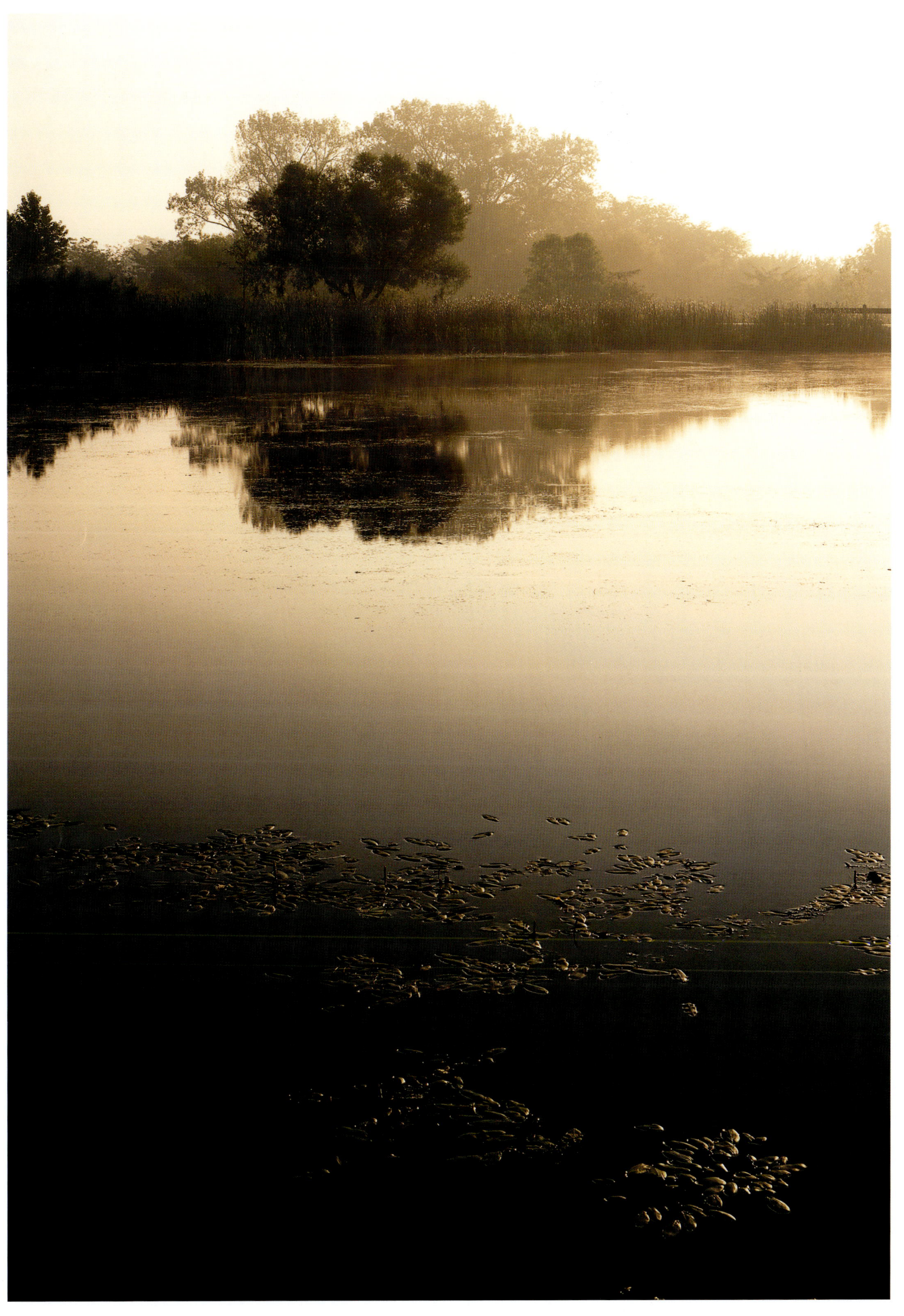

Emerald Pond: Middle Fork River County Forest Preserve, Champaign County *(Bloomington Ridged Plain, Till Plains Section, Central Lowland Province)* The Middle Fork River County Forest Preserve has the dual distinction of having one of the finest camping areas in Illinois, the Harry L. Swartz Campground, and of being the only place in Illinois where the silvery salamander can be found. *September 2001*

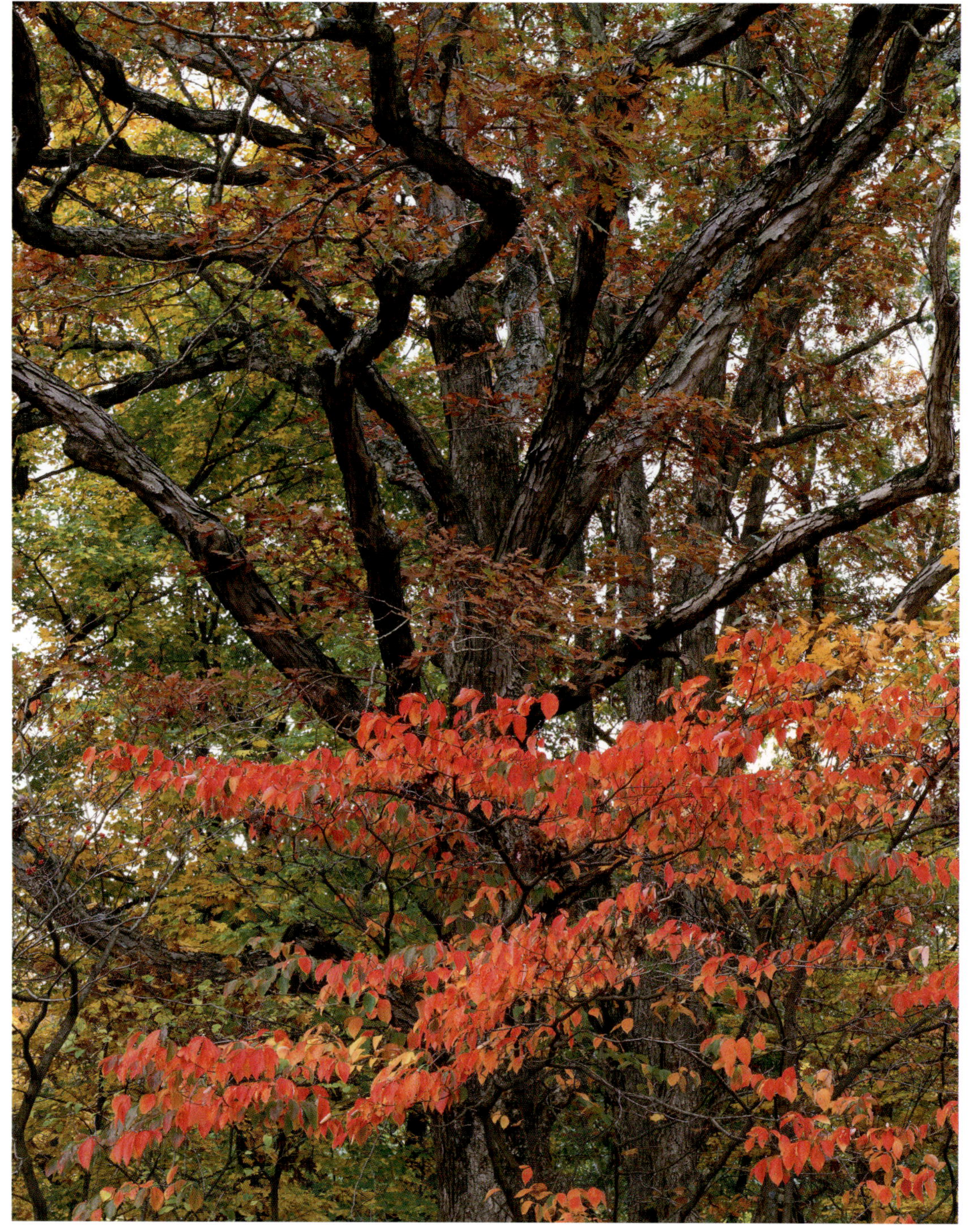

THIS PAGE ABOVE:

Dogwood and oak in fall foliage: Fox Ridge State Park, Coles County *(Bloomington Ridged Plain, Till Plains Section, Central Lowland Province)*
The steep, thickly wooded ridges of Fox Ridge State Park, near Charleston, burst into color in the fall. The seasonal show may be appreciated from the extensive the extensive trail system through the park's 1,632 acres. *October 2001*

OPPOSITE PAGE:

Goldenrod and Queen Anne's lace: Fox Ridge State Park, Coles County *(Bloomington Ridged Plain, Till Plains Section, Central Lowland Province)*
In the troughs between the wooded ridges of Fox Ridge State Park are set Ridge Lake, the Embarras River, and lush valleys with prairie vegetation such as goldenrod and Queen Anne's lace. *September 2001*

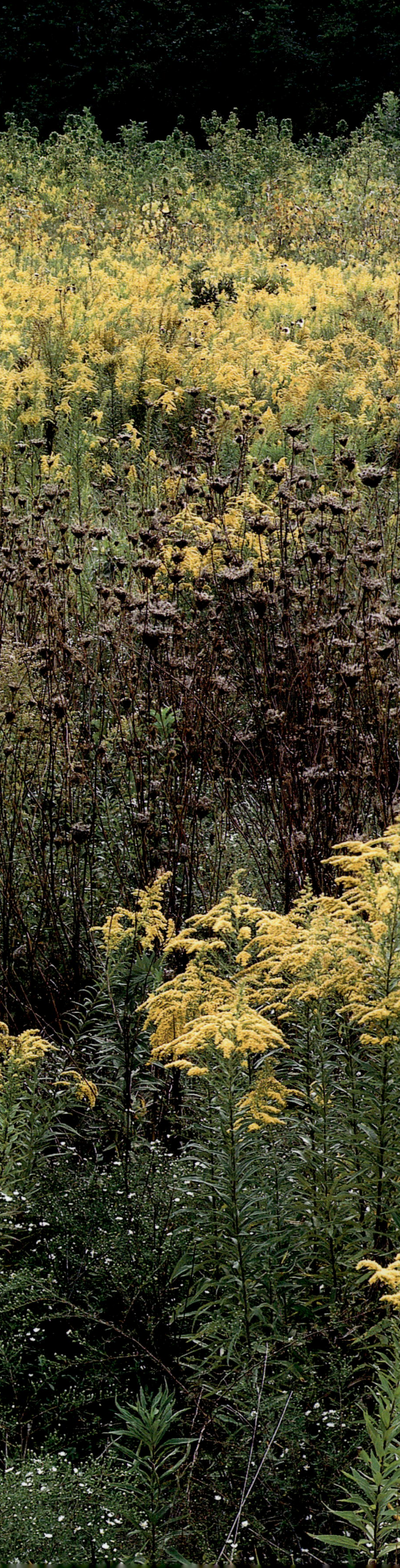

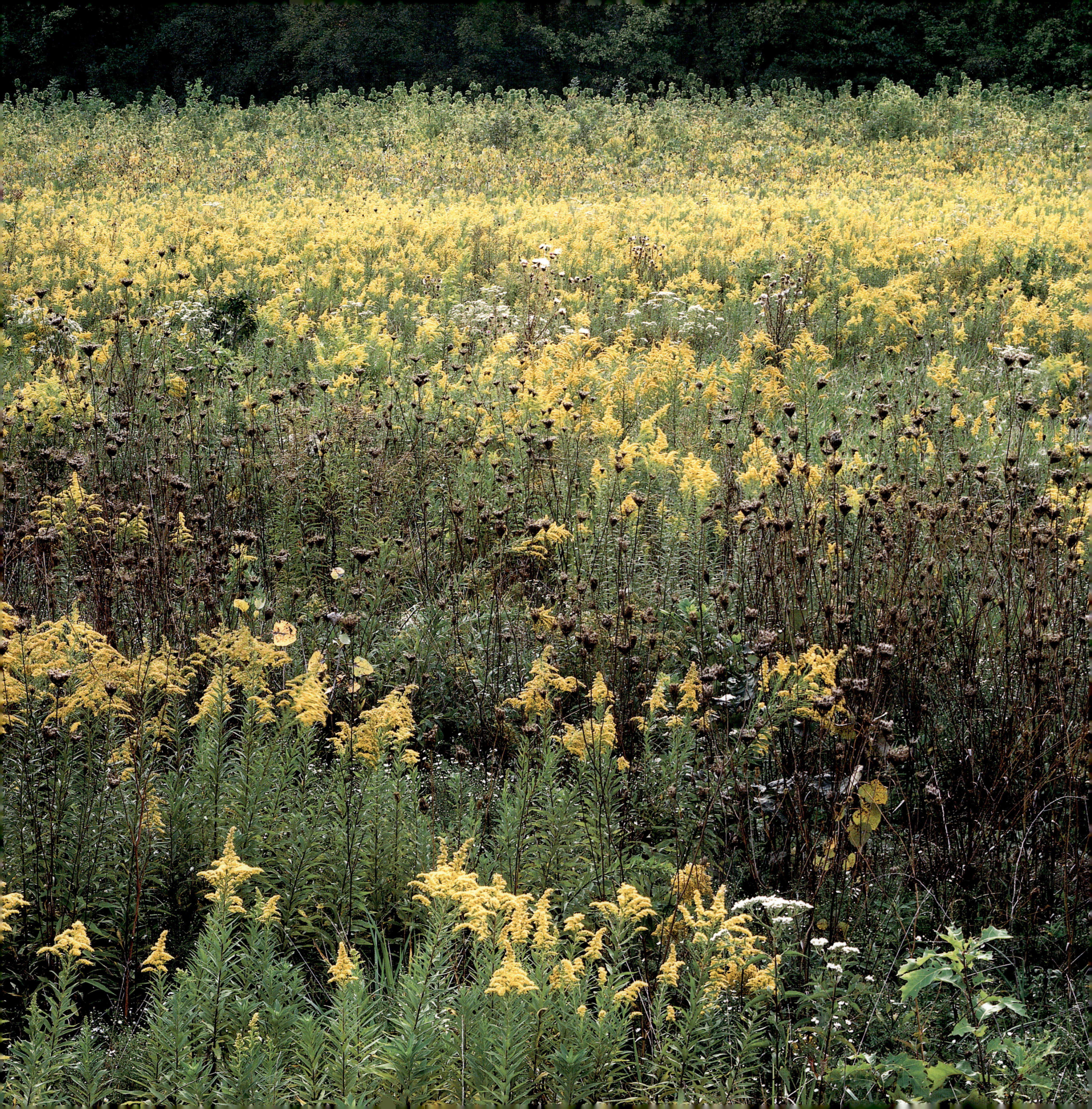

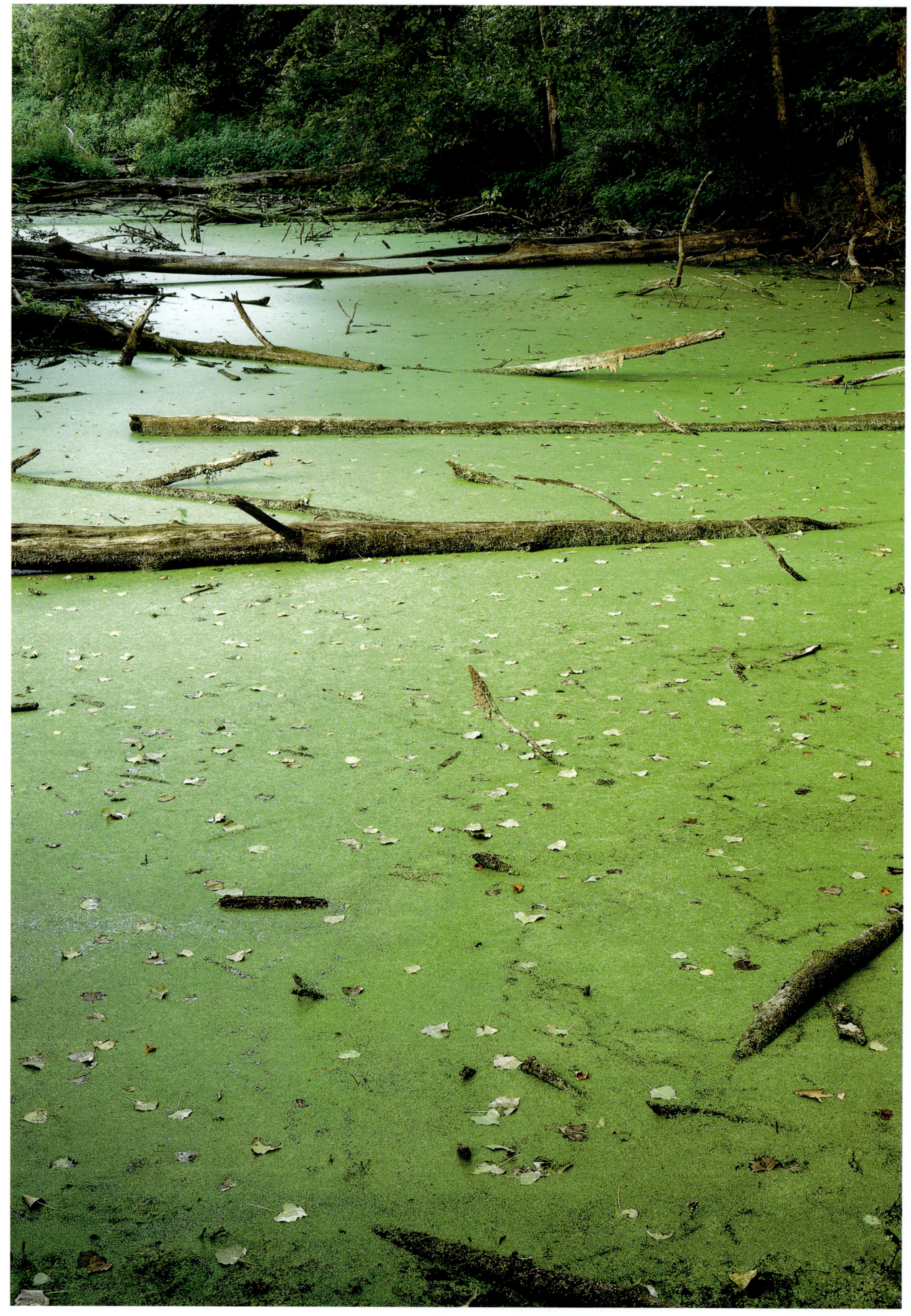

Hidden Pond, covered with Duckweed: Weldon Springs State Recreation Area, De Witt County *(Bloomington Ridged Plain, Till Plains Section, Central Lowland Province)*
Weldon Springs State Recreation Area, southeast of Clinton, is a 443-acre park containing Weldon Springs Lake and Hidden Pond. *August 2001*

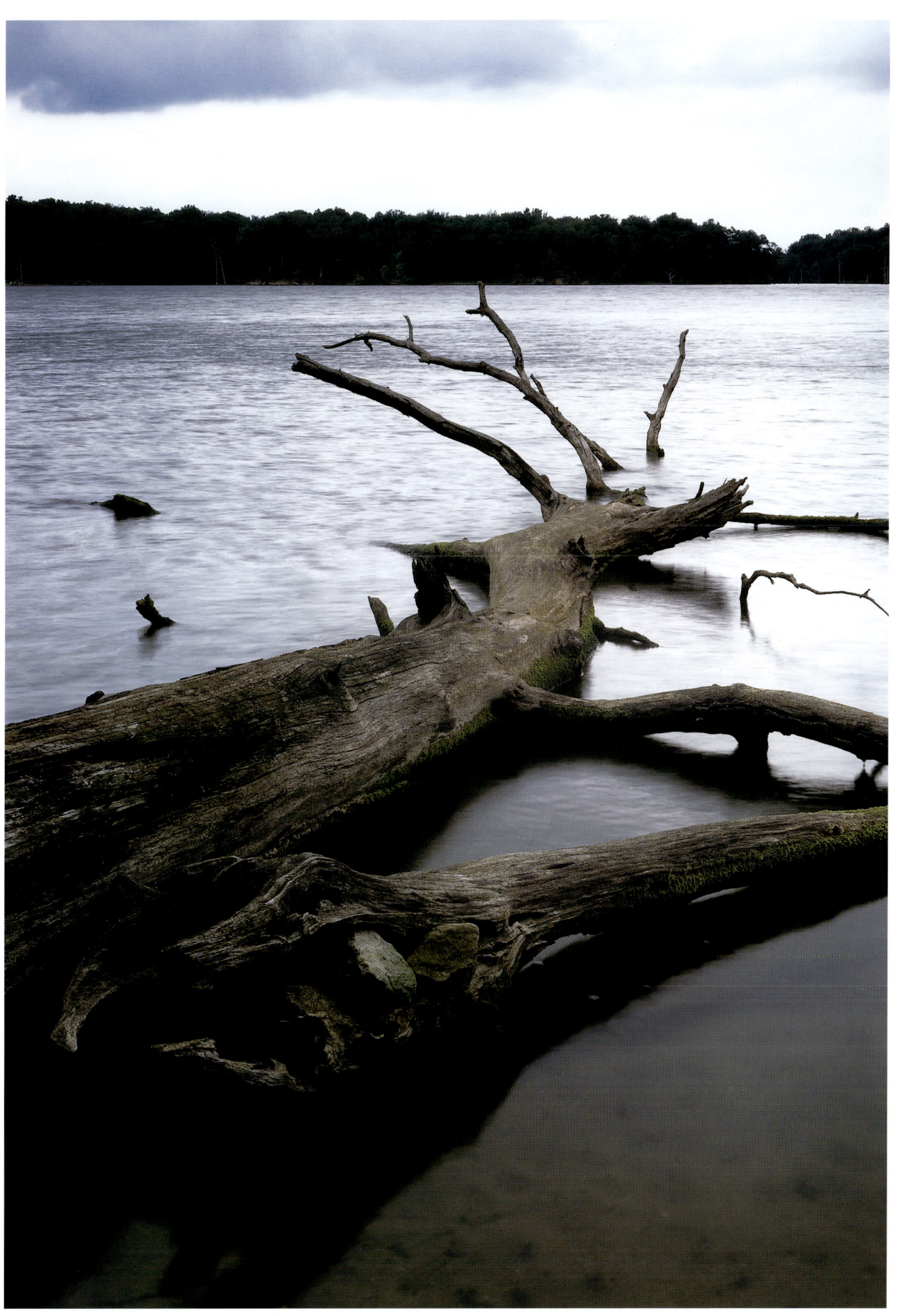

Beached logs in Peninsula Bay, Clinton Lake: Clinton Lake State Recreation Area, DeWitt County *(Bloomington Ridged Plain, Till Plains Section, Central Lowland Province)*
Over half of the 9,300 acres of Clinton Lake State Recreation Area is occupied by Clinton Lake, which was created in the 1970s as a cooling reservoir for a nuclear power plant. The plant's owner, AmerGen, leases the recreational area to the state. *August 2001*

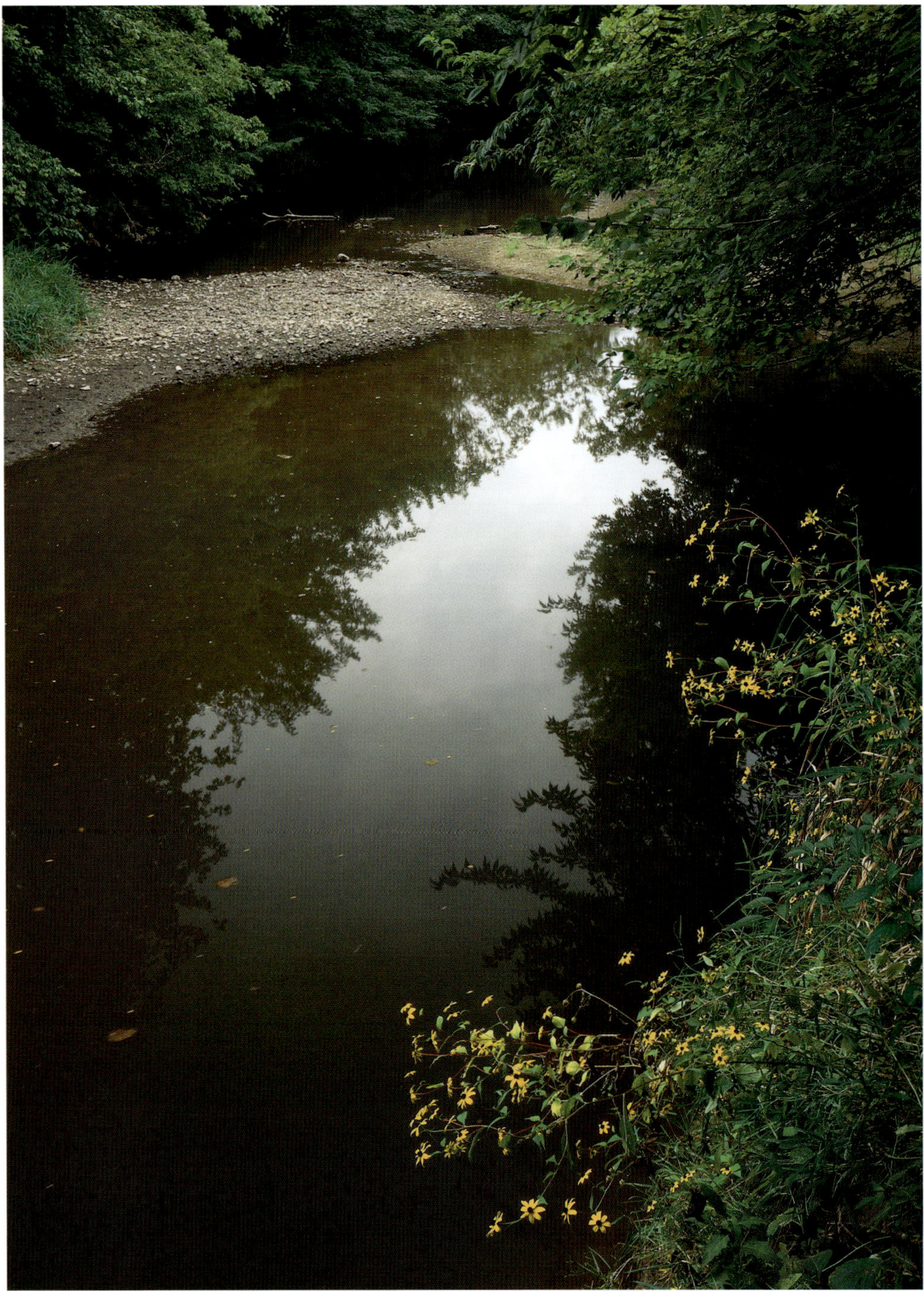

THIS PAGE LEFT:

Black-eyed Susans along Salt Creek, viewed from Toad Hill: Clinton Lake State Recreation Area, De Witt County *(Bloomington Ridged Plain, Till Plains Section, Central Lowland Province)*

Like Clinton Lake, Salt Creek offers good fishing. *August 2001*

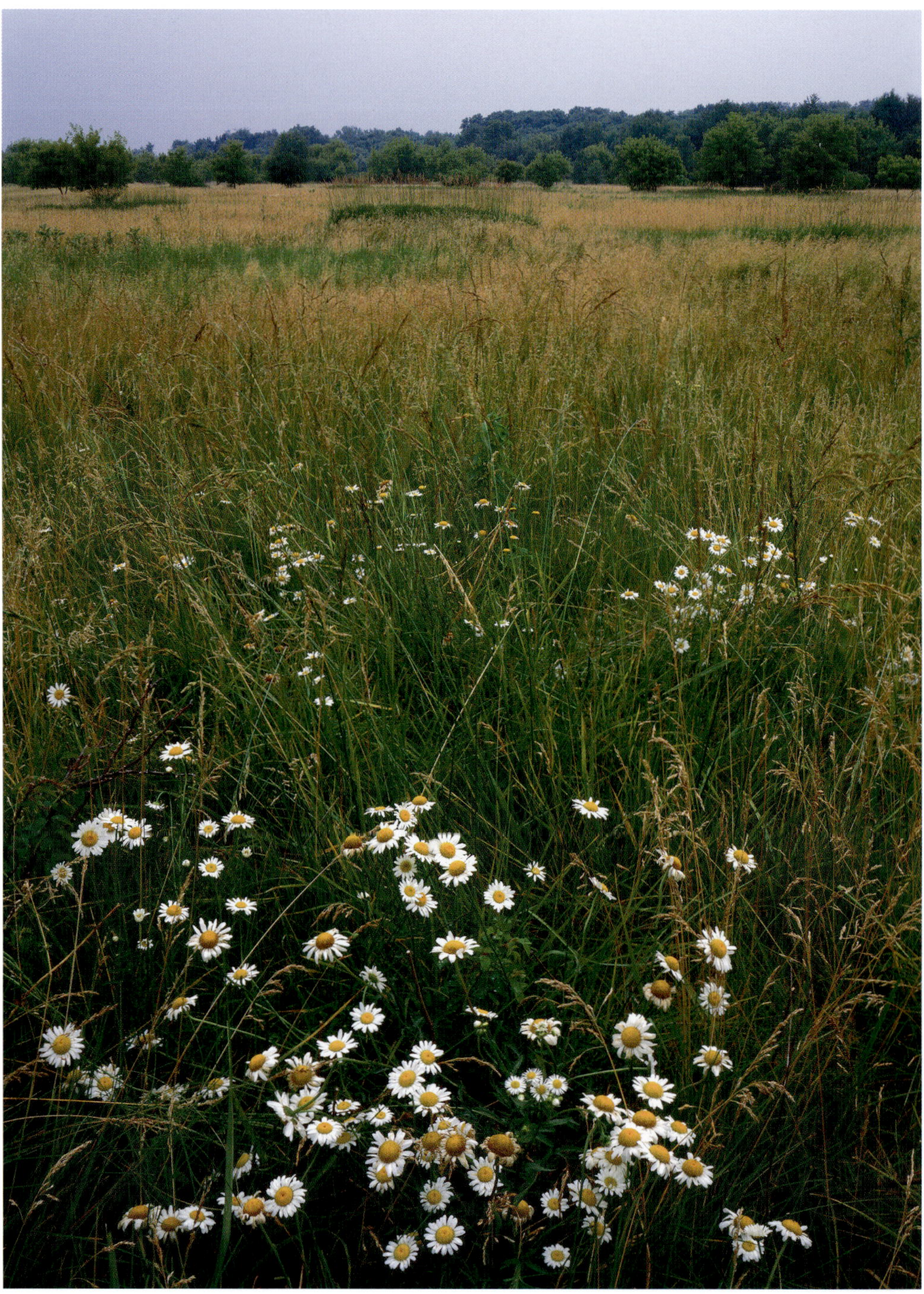

THIS PAGE RIGHT:

Daisies on savanna: McDowell Grove Forest Preserve, Du Page County *(Bloomington Ridged Plain, Till Plains Section, Central Lowland Province)*

The McDowell Grove Forest Preserve, which encloses the West Branch of the Du Page River near Naperville, is one of many forest preserves set aside in Du Page County. *June 2001*

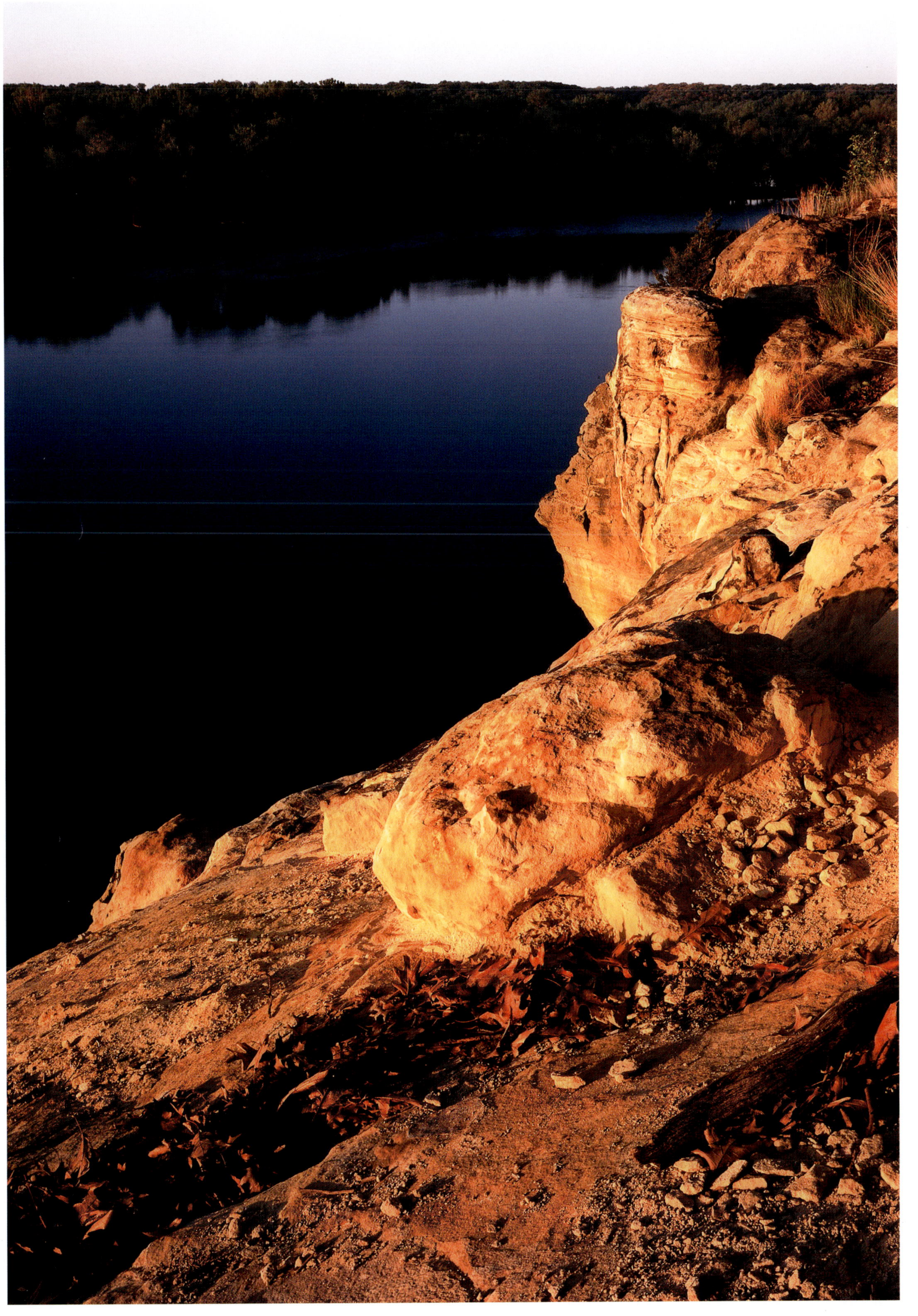

Sunrise from bluff overlooking the Illinois River: Buffalo Rock State Park, La Salle County *(Bloomington Ridged Plain, Till Plains Section, Central Lowland Province)*
Buffalo Rock State Park is perched on a bluff that was once an island in the Illinois River and now provides sweeping views from an excellent trail system through its 298 acres. *May 1994*

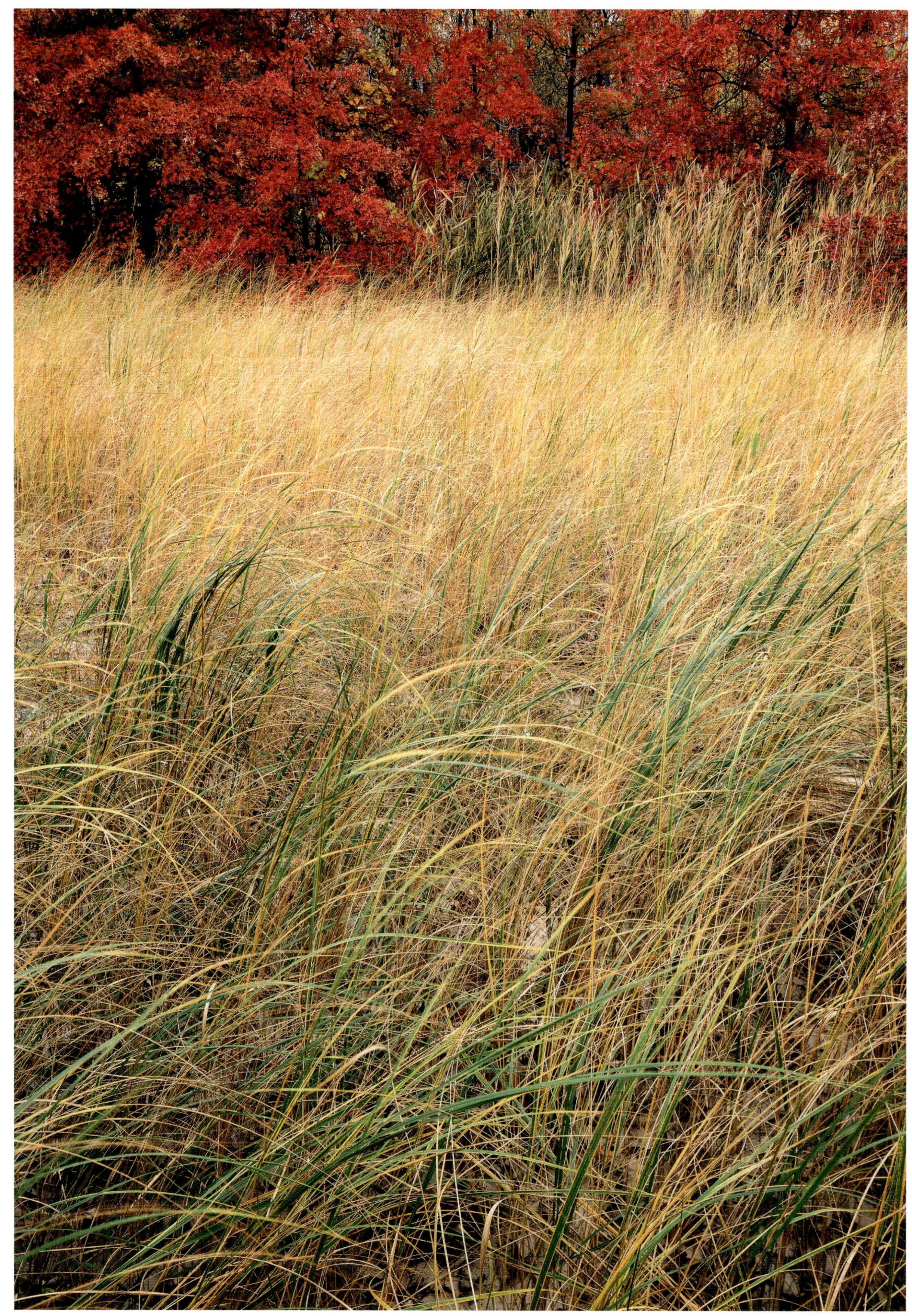

Grasses and oaks in fall foliage along the Illinois & Michigan Canal: Buffalo Rock State Park, La Salle County *(Bloomington Ridged Plain, Till Plains Section, Central Lowland Province)*
Buffalo Rock State Park provides access to the Illinois & Michigan Canal State Trail, a 61-mile historic trail beautifully maintained for hiking, bicycling, and snowmobiling. In fall, grasses and oaks lining the **I** & **M** Canal Trail often turn gold and red. *October 1995*

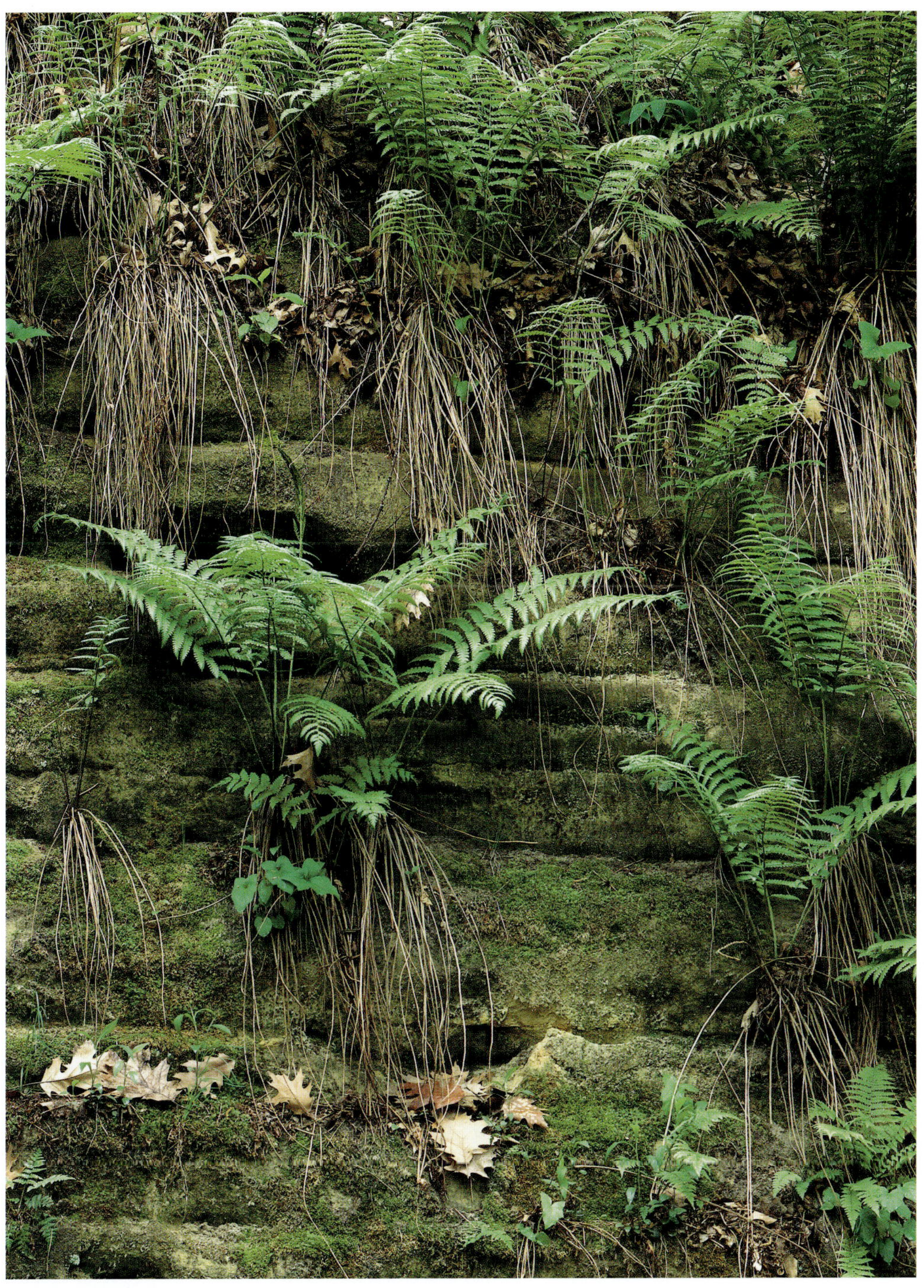

THIS PAGE LEFT:

Ferns on mossy ledge of sandstone cliff: Buffalo Rock State Park, La Salle County *(Bloomington Ridged Plain, Till Plains Section, Central Lowland Province)* The Woodland Trail in Buffalo Rock State Park wends through the interior of the park, affording many intimate studies, such as this one. *May 1992*

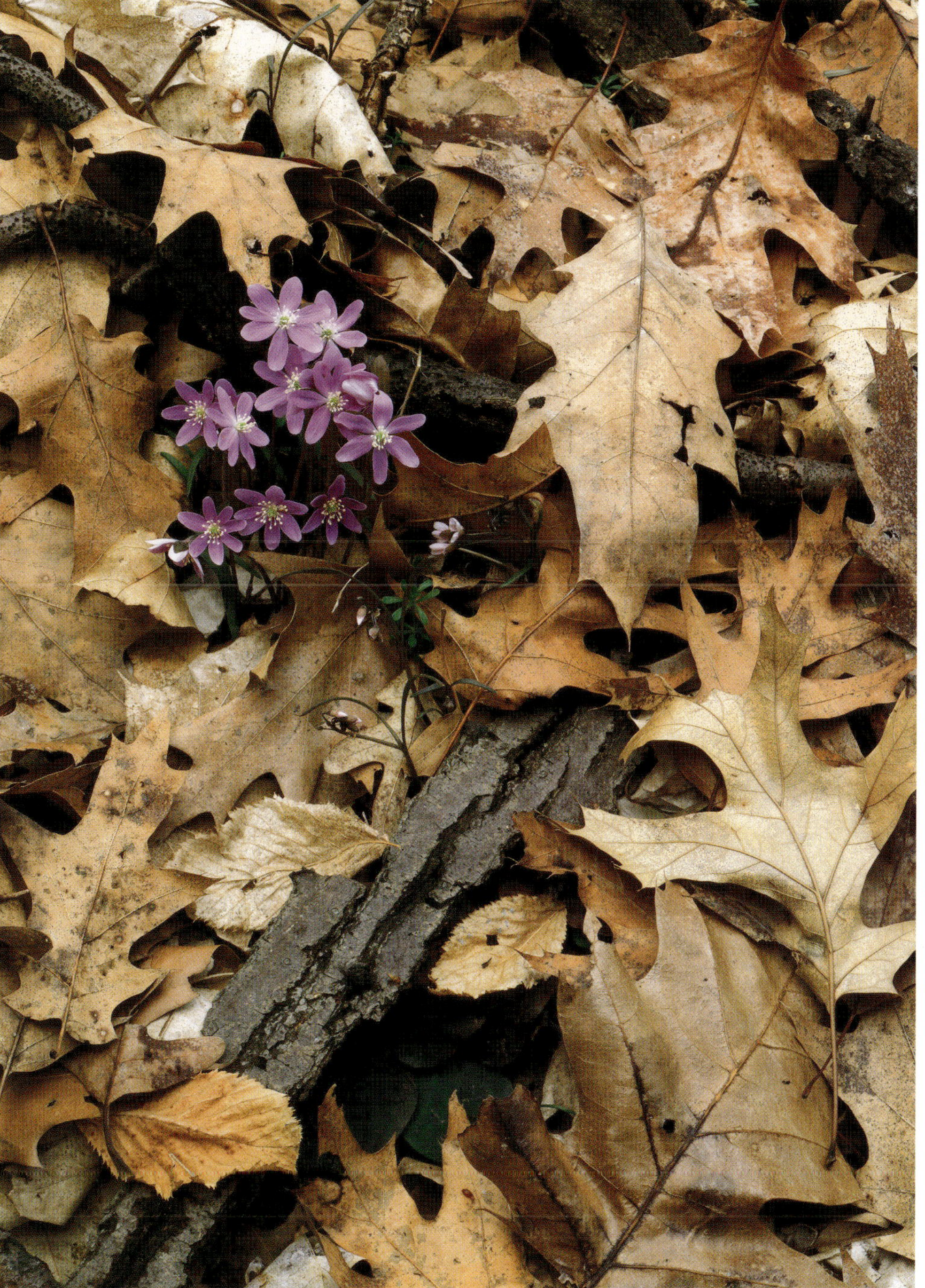

THIS PAGE RIGHT:

Sharp-lobed hepaticas: Margery C. Carlson Nature Preserve, La Salle County *(Bloomington Ridged Plain, Till Plains Section, Central Lowland Province)* Among the first plants to bloom in early spring are sharp-lobed hepaticas, also known as liver leaf *(Hepatica nobilis)*, which grows in the leaf litter of forest floors. *April 1988*

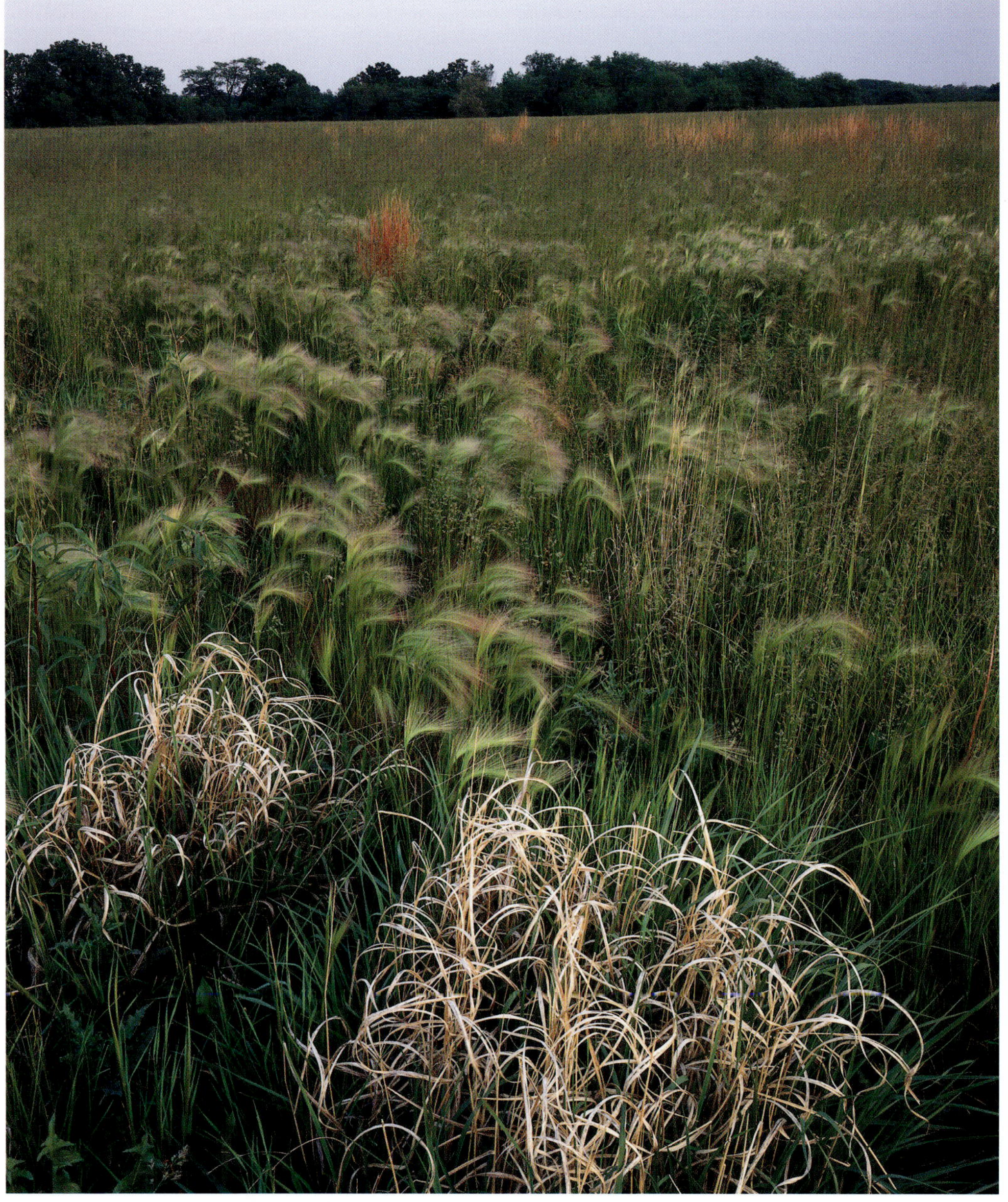

THIS PAGE ABOVE:

Prairie grasses and flowers:
Matthiessen State Park, La Salle County
(Bloomington Ridged Plain, Till Plains Section, Central Lowland Province)
Matthiessen State Park, with nearly 2,000 diverse acres of canyons, streams, waterfalls, prairies, and forests, contains a segment of the Vermilion River that passes through restored prairies of the Vermilion River Area. *June 1995*

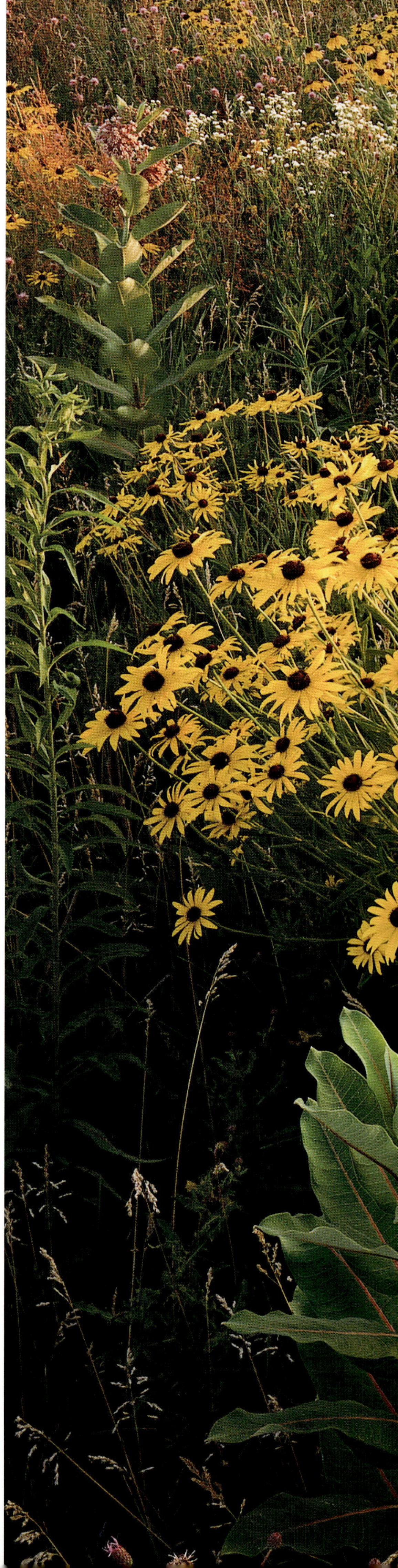

OPPOSITE PAGE:

Prairie grasses and flowers:
Matthiessen State Park, La Salle County
(Bloomington Ridged Plain, Till Plains Section, Central Lowland Province)
This stand of prairie plants was destroyed not long after this photograph was taken, in response to fears that the prairie plants would seed in nearby agricultural fields. *June 1987*

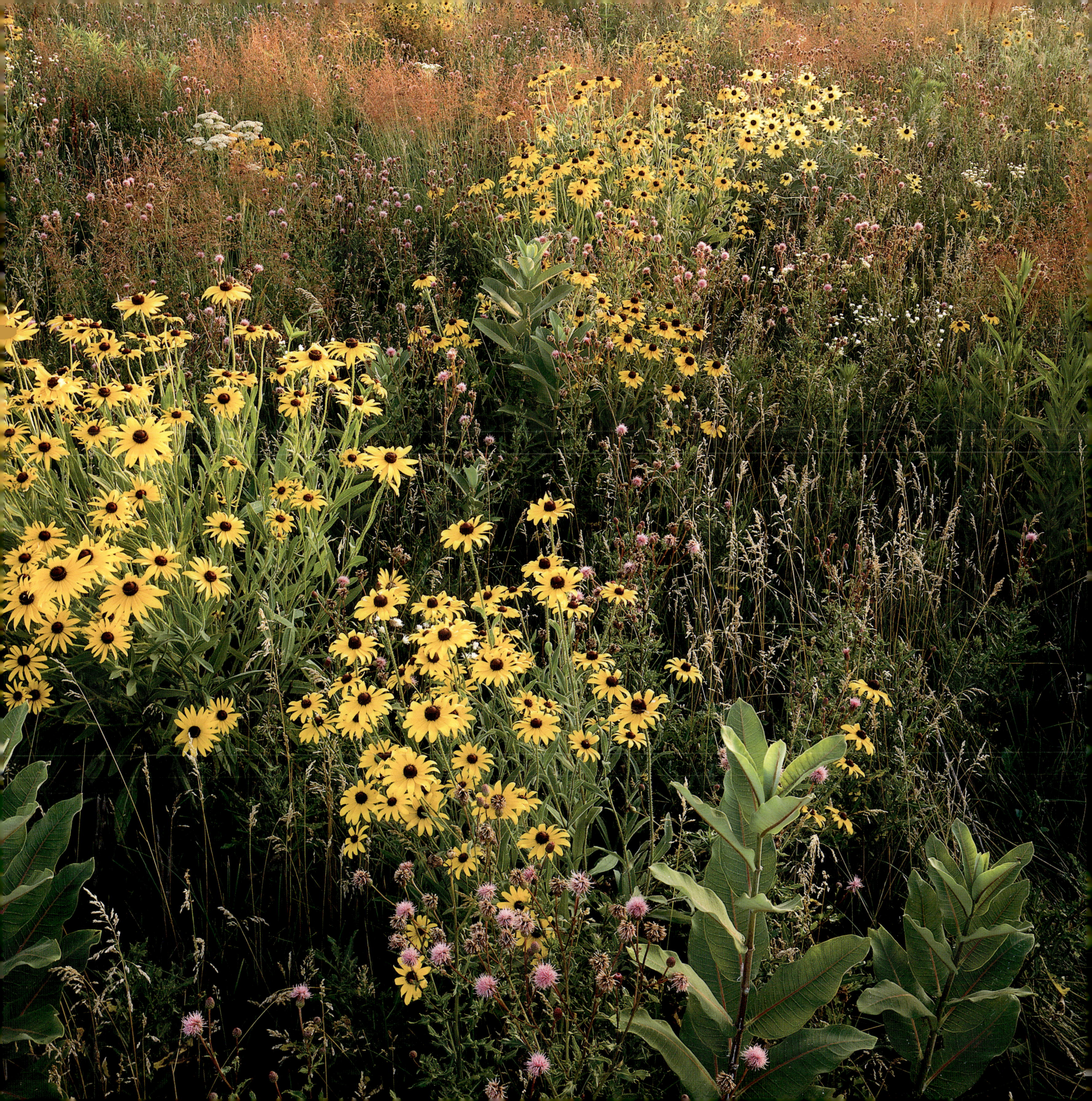

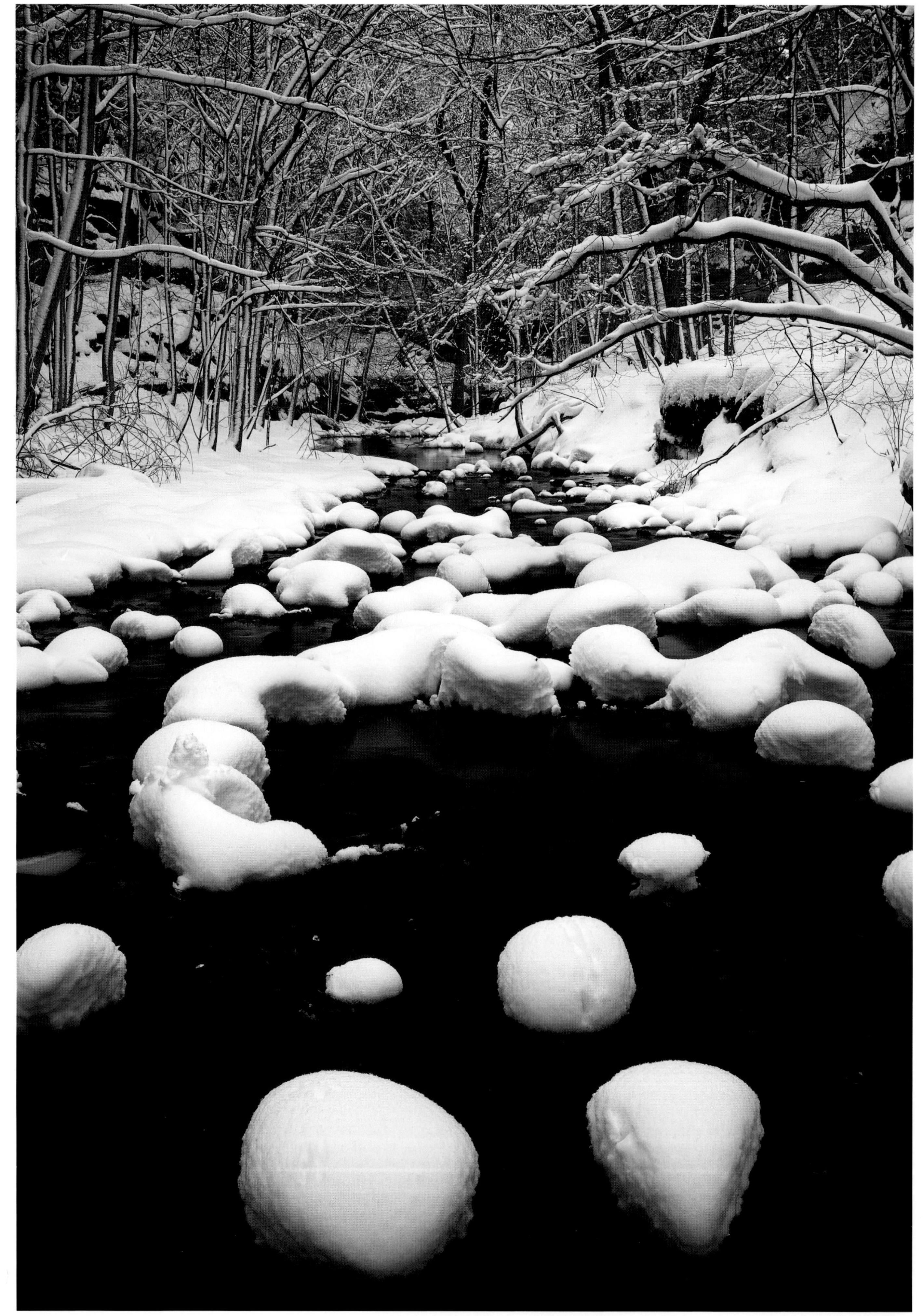

Stream of the main canyon of the Upper Dells, just below Deer Park Lake: Matthiessen State Park, La Salle County *(Bloomington Ridged Plain, Till Plains Section, Central Lowland Province)*
Because the steep sandstone canyons of the Upper Dells are shielded from the winds prevalent in Illinois, snow falling in them can accumulate on vegetation and rocks to produce picturesque scenes. *March 1999*

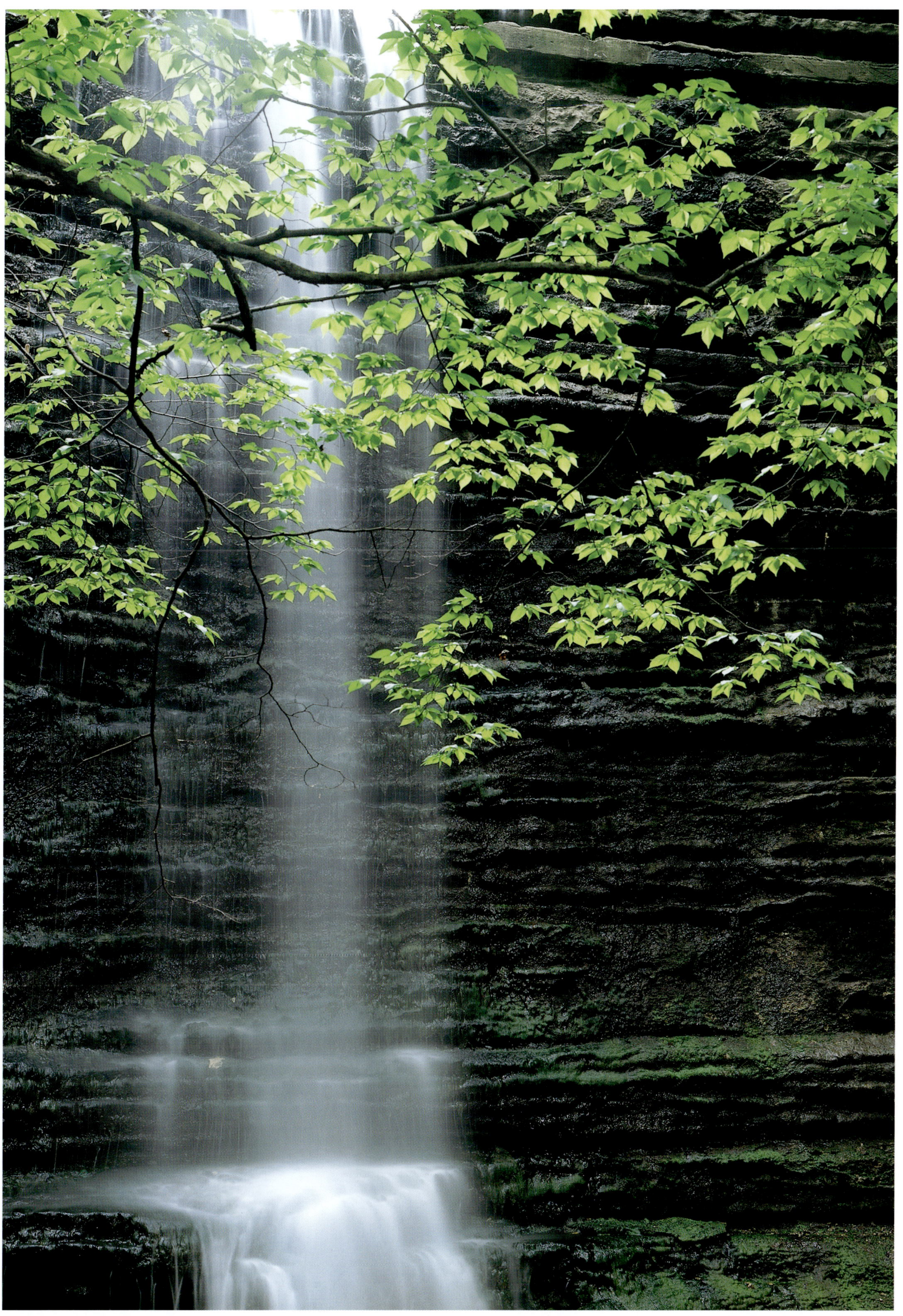

THIS PAGE:

Upper Falls of the Upper Dells: Matthiessen State Park, La Salle County *(Bloomington Ridged Plain, Till Plains Section, Central Lowland Province)* The long narrow main canyon of the Upper Dells contains a stream that flows a mile from Deer Park Lake to the Vermilion River. The Upper Falls, framed by trees, is at the head of the Upper Dells just below Deer Park Lake. *May 1992*

PAGES 58-59:

Gyre of dead leaves in Upper Dells: Matthiessen State Park, La Salle County *(Bloomington Ridged Plain, Till Plains Section, Central Lowland Province)* *October 1996*

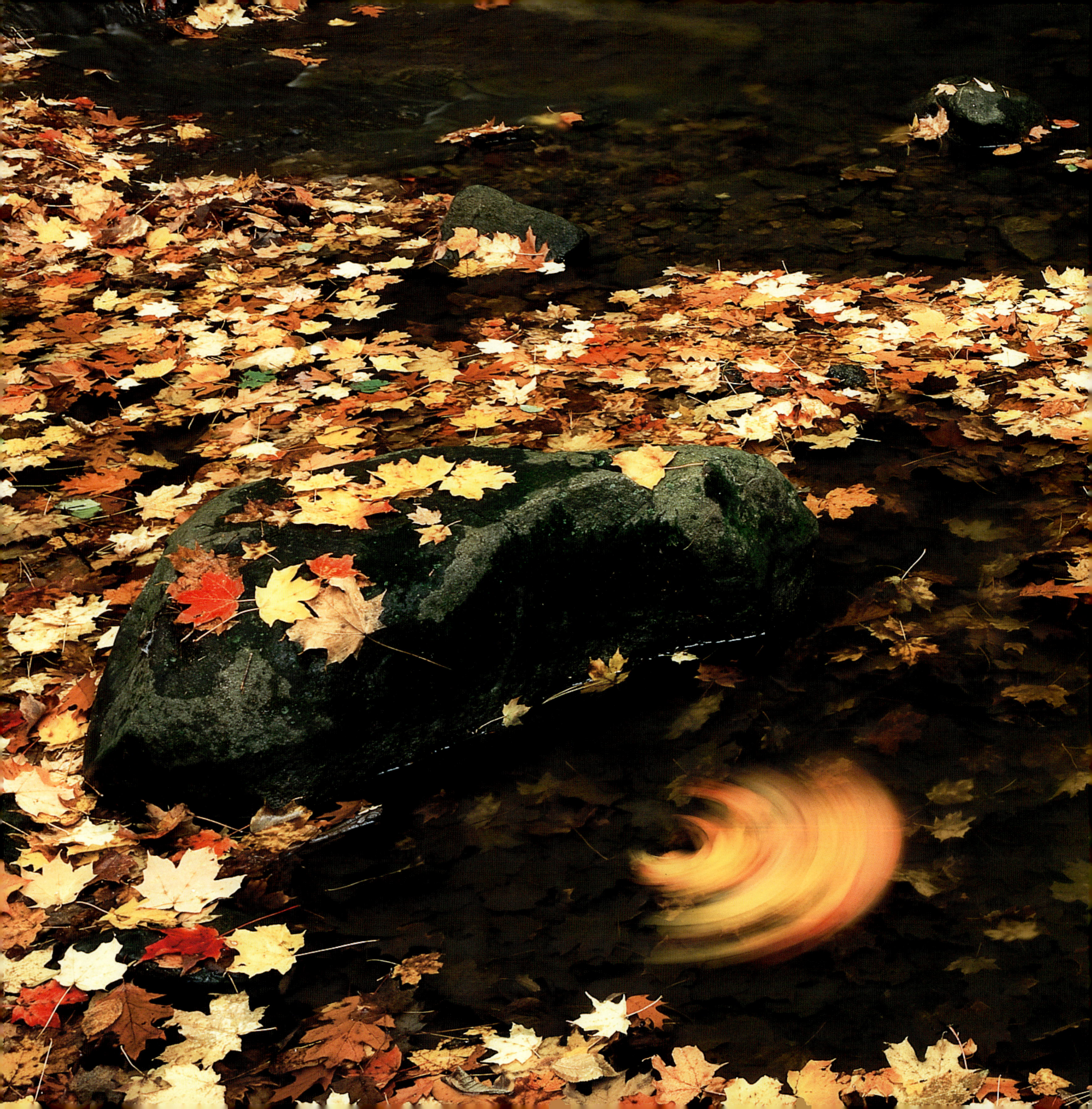

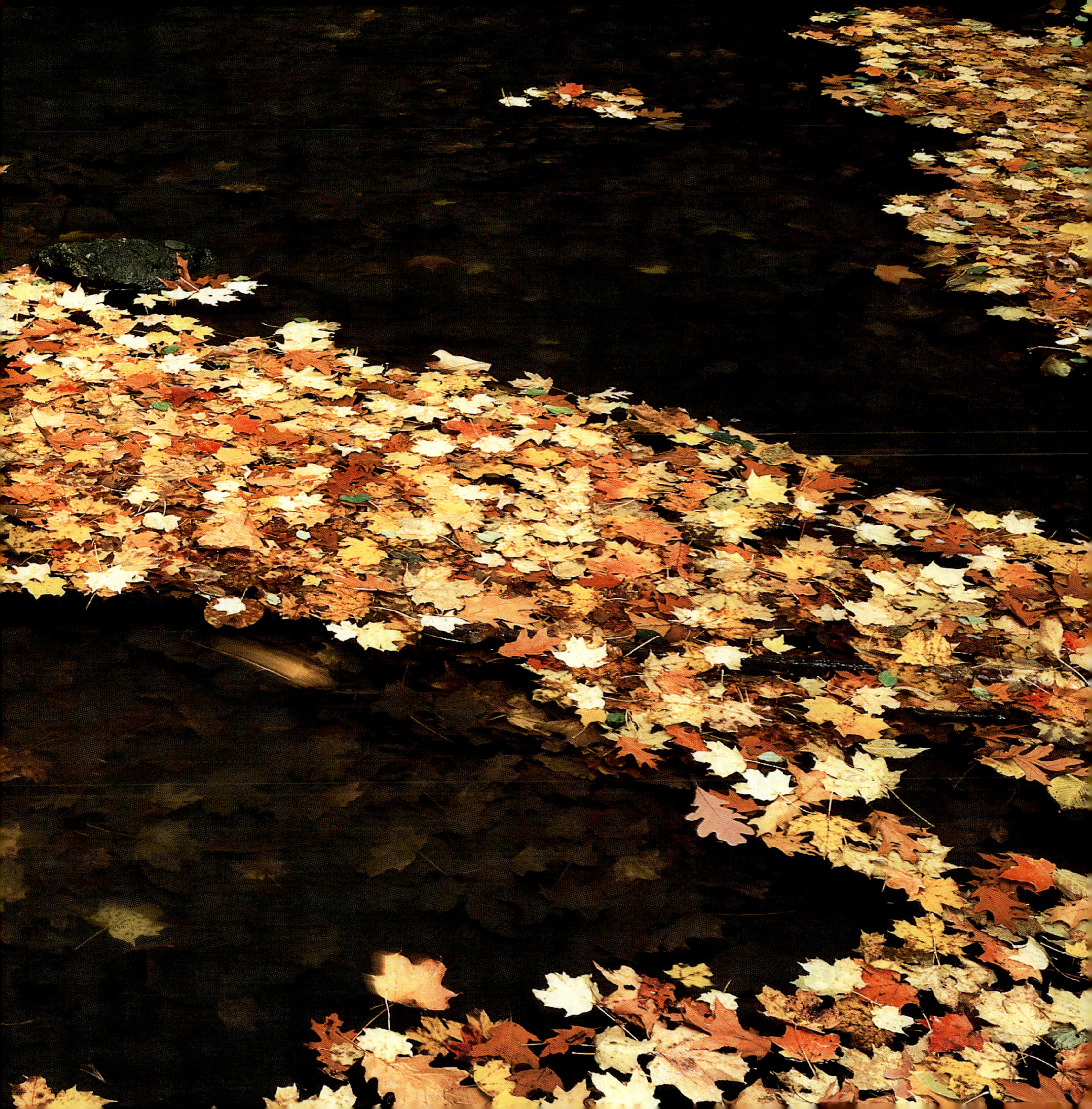

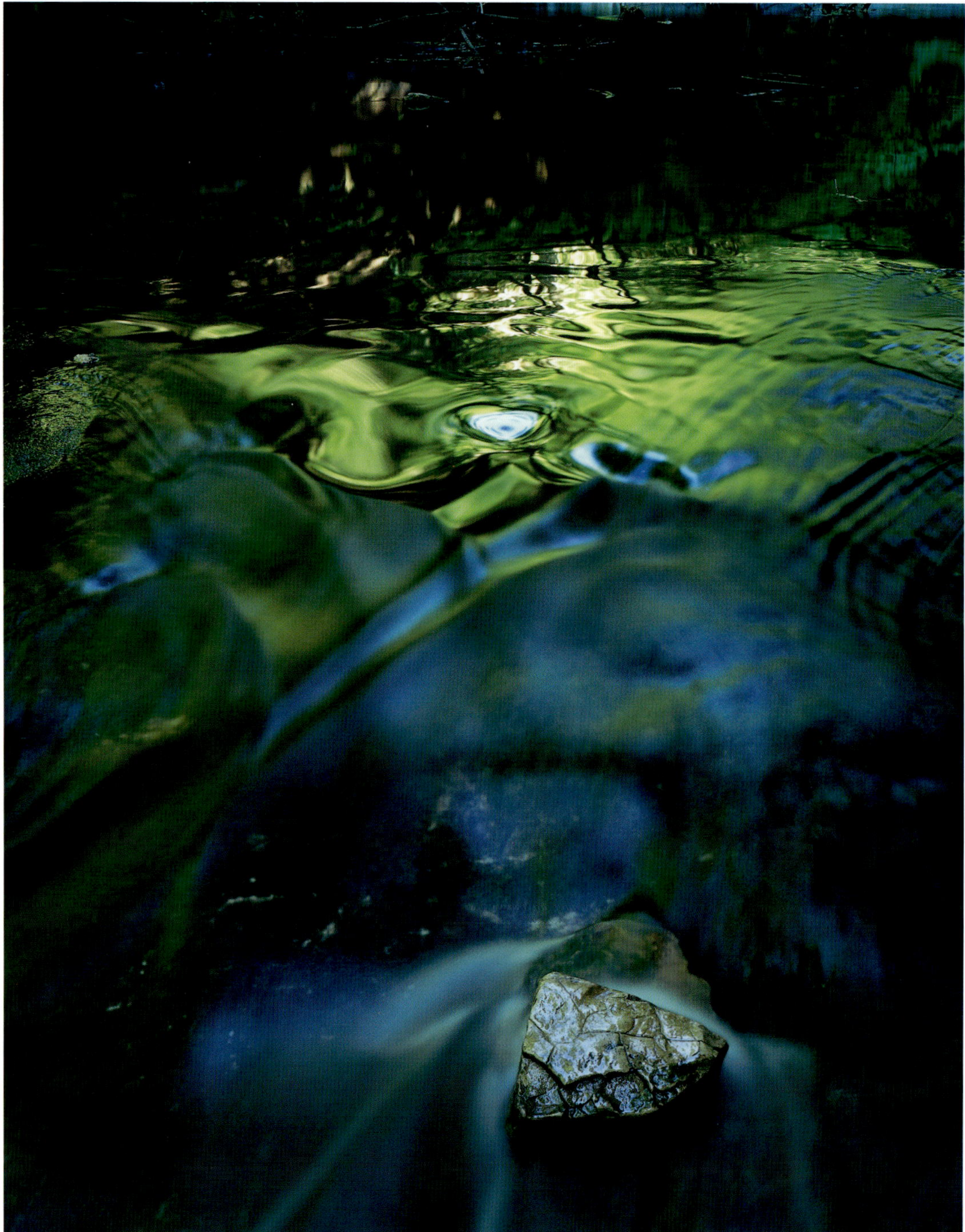

THIS PAGE ABOVE:

Ripples in Upper Dells: Matthiessen State Park, La Salle County *(Bloomington Ridged Plain, Till Plains Section, Central Lowland Province)*
May 1998

OPPOSITE PAGE:

Armstrong Creek, Illinois Canyon: Starved Rock State Park, La Salle County *(Bloomington Ridged Plain, Till Plains Section, Central Lowland Province)*
Eroded by glacial meltwater and streams across the 2,630 acres of Starved Rock State Park are eighteen canyons that slice through the sandstone bluffs along a four-mile stretch of the southern bank of the Illinois River, midway between the cities of LaSalle-Peru and Ottawa. *January 1987*

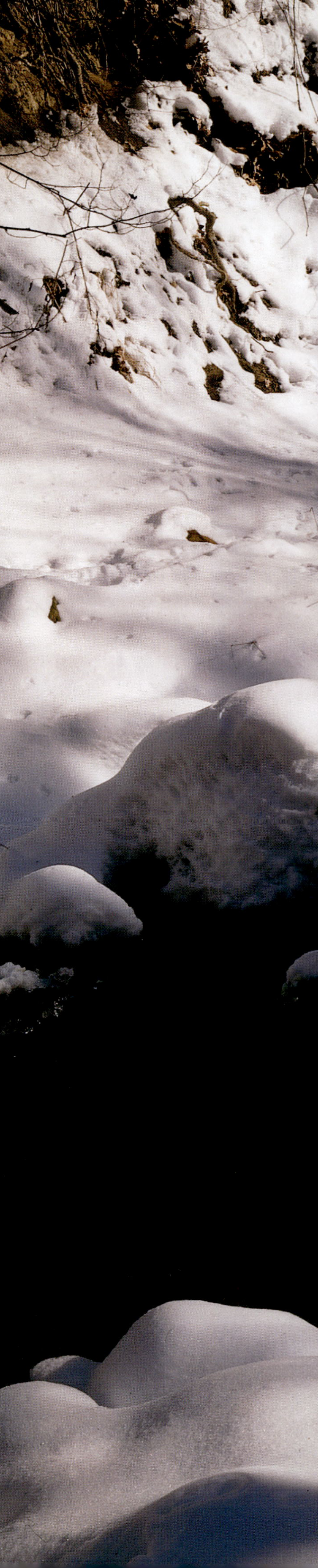

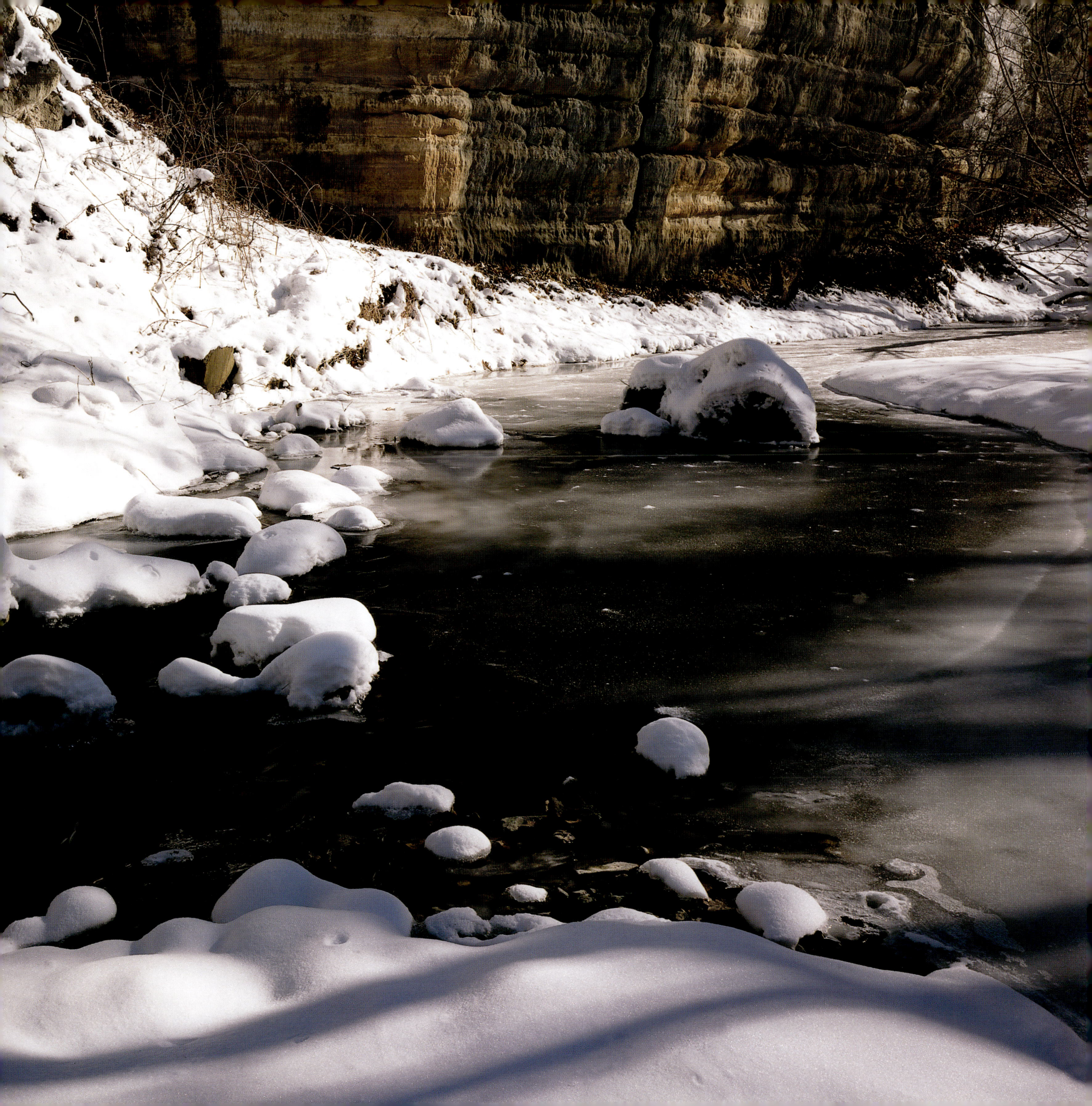

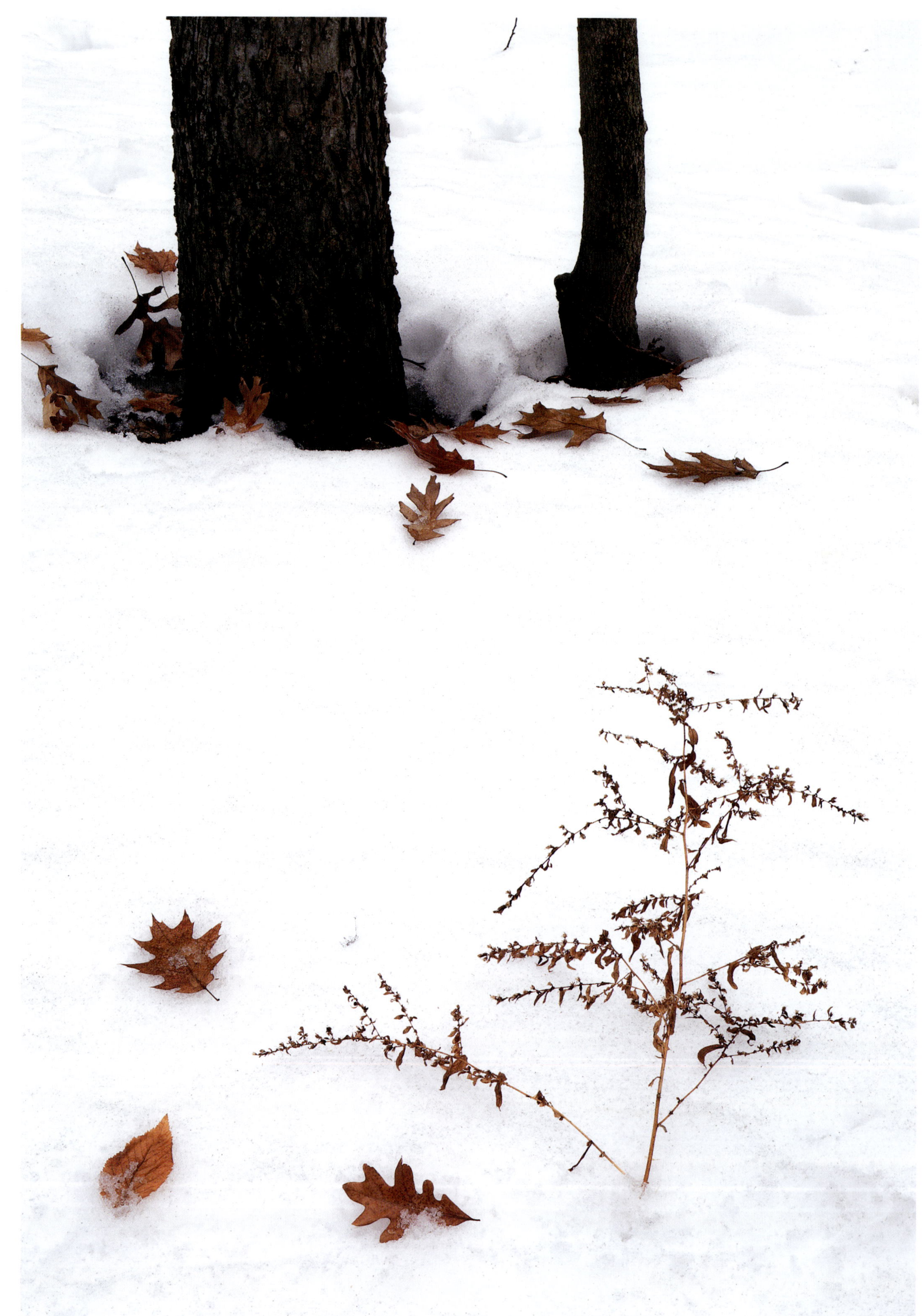

Illinois Canyon: Starved Rock State Park, La Salle County *(Bloomington Ridged Plain, Till Plains Section, Central Lowland Province)*
After a heavy snowfall in Starved Rock State Park, oak leaves and a protruding plant in Illinois Canyon resist being buried by the heavy snow. *January 1999*

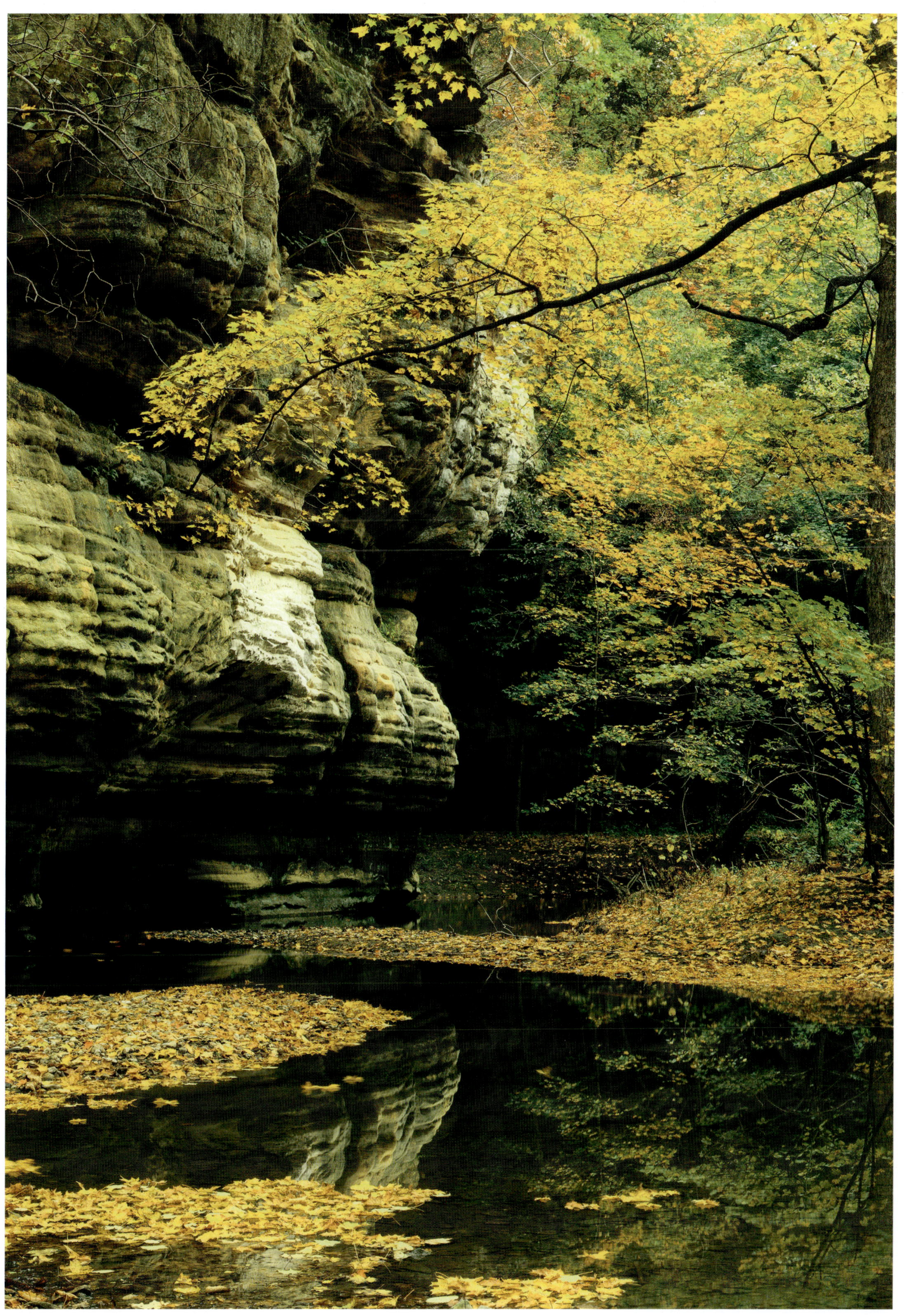

THIS PAGE:

Maple tree against reflected canyon wall of Illinois Canyon: Starved Rock State Park, La Salle County *(Bloomington Ridged Plain, Till Plains Section, Central Lowland Province)*

The canyons of Starved Rock State Park in LaSalle County are incised into St. Peter Sandstone, laid down in an inland sea 460 million years ago. *October 1986*

PAGES 64-65:

Flowering redbud tree against canyon wall of Illinois Canyon: Starved Rock State Park, La Salle County *(Bloomington Ridged Plain, Till Plains Section, Central Lowland Province)*

Starved Rock State Park is near the northern limit of the range of the redbud. *May 1988*

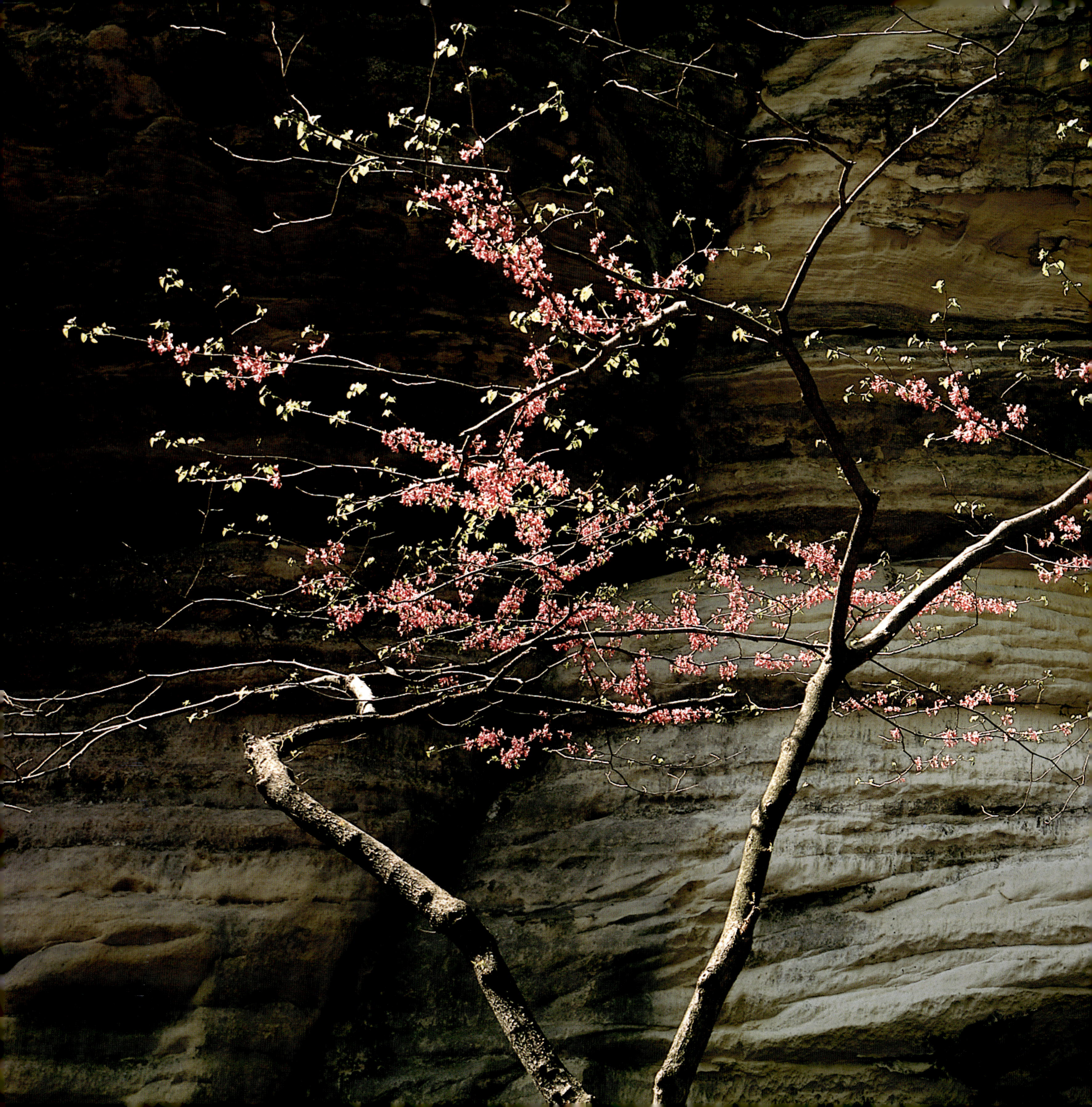

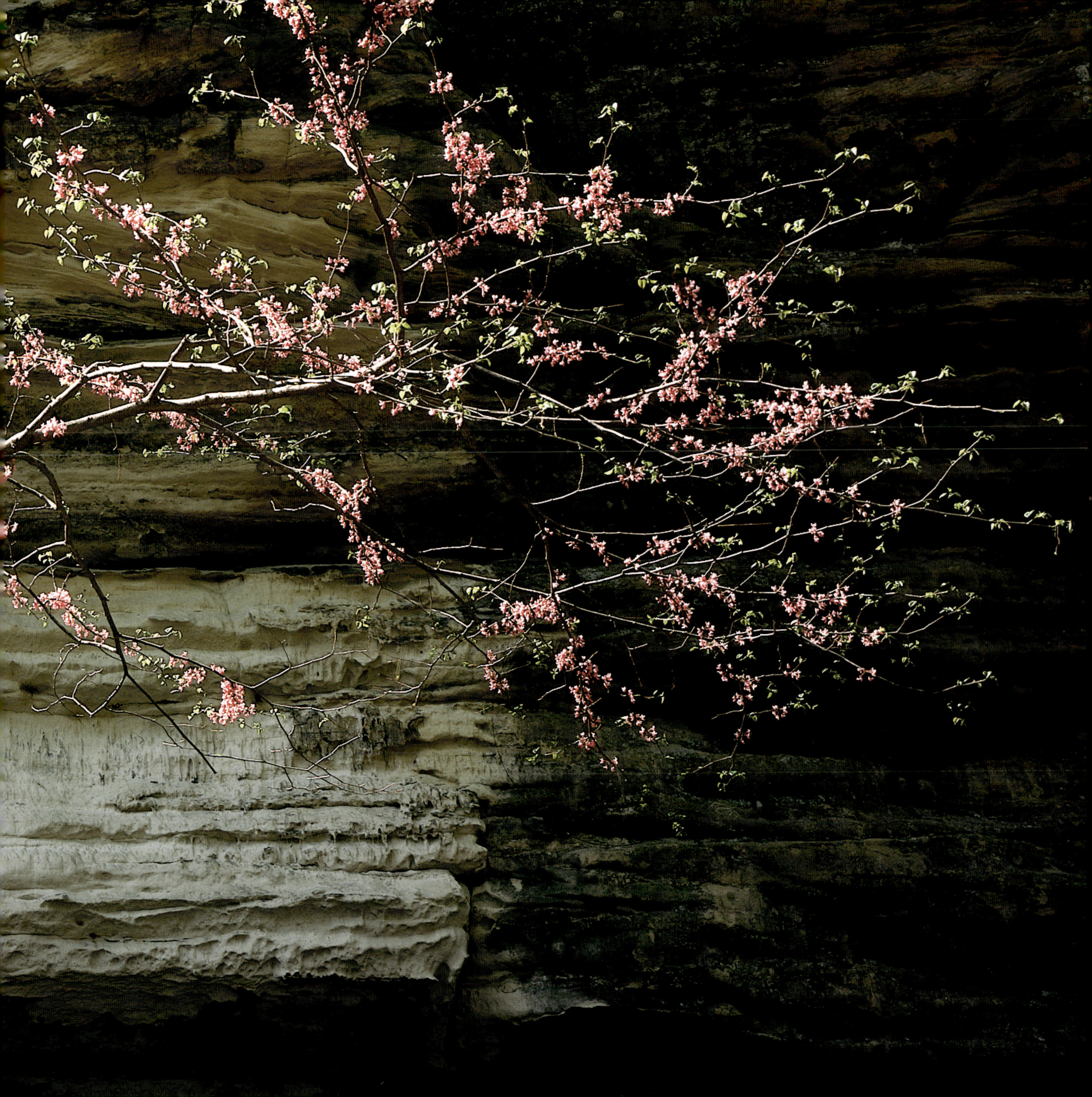

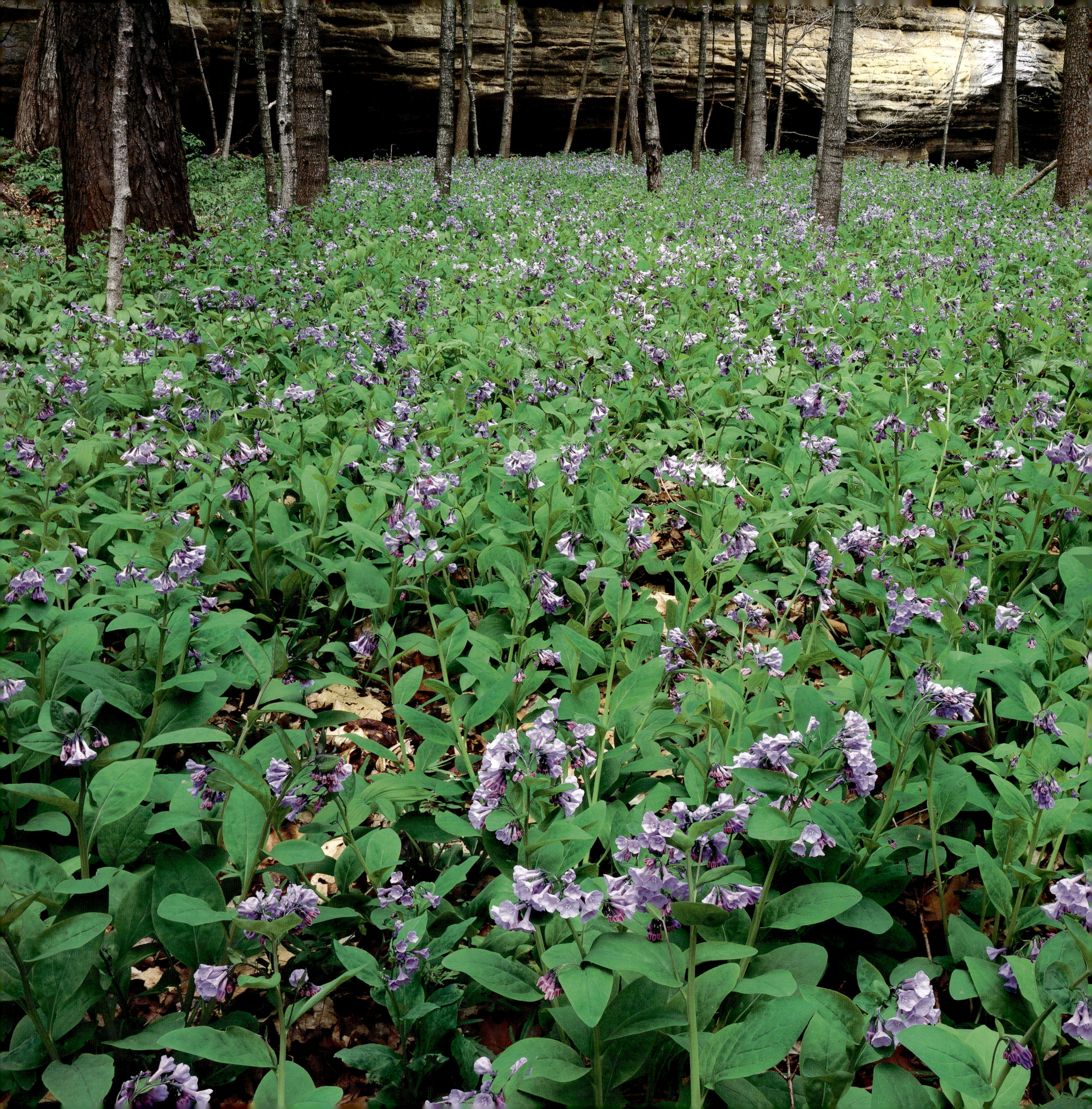

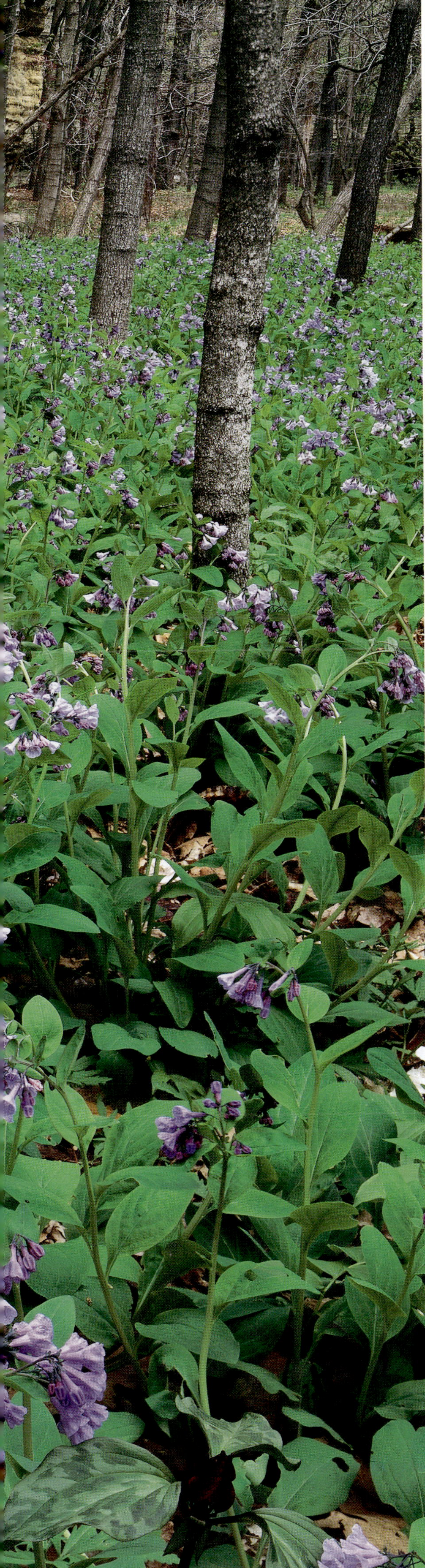

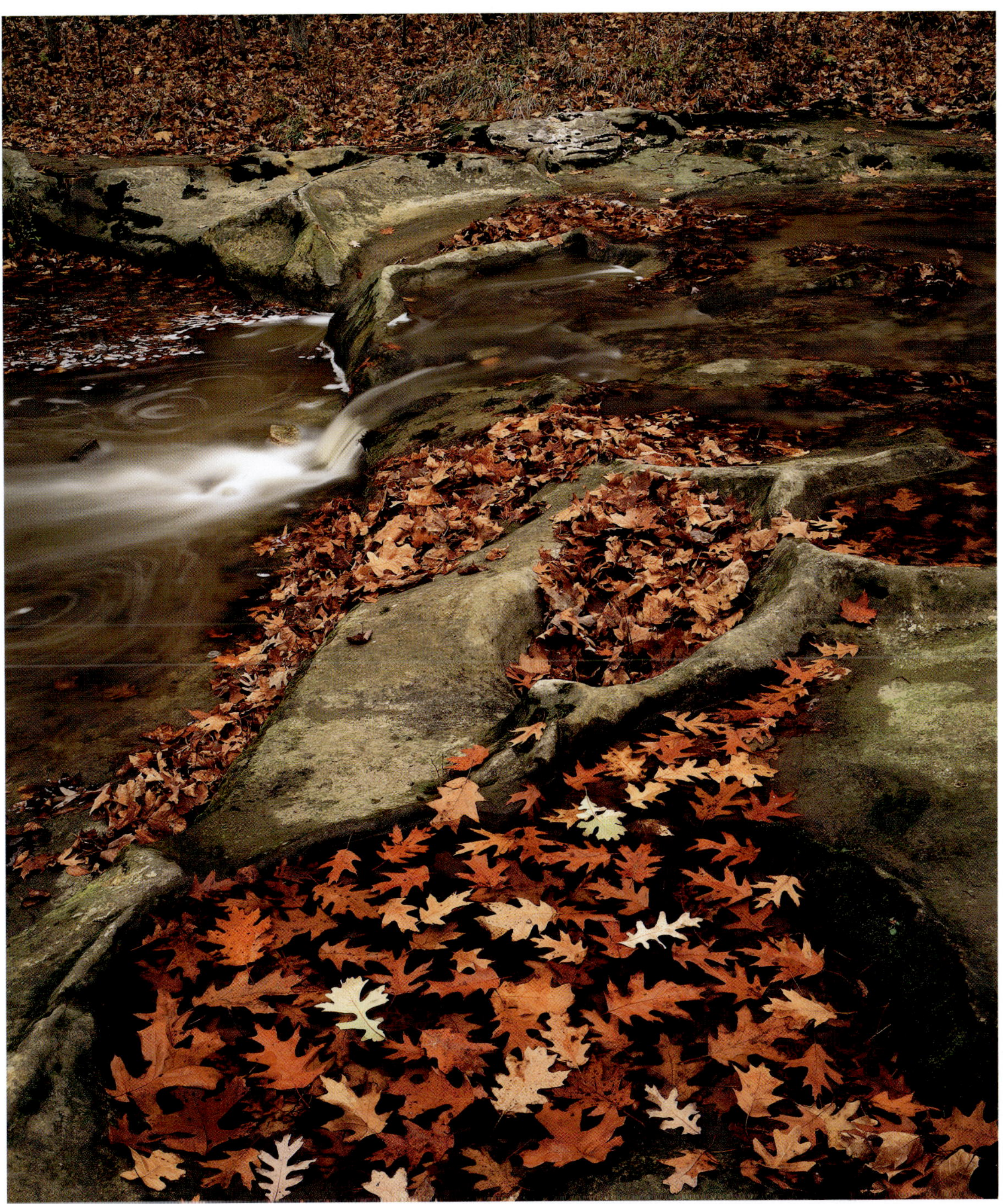

THIS PAGE ABOVE:

Armstrong Creek, Illinois Canyon: Starved Rock State Park, La Salle County *(Bloomington Ridged Plain, Till Plains Section, Central Lowland Province)* *November 1996*

OPPOSITE PAGE:

Virginia bluebells *(Mertensia virginica)* in Illinois Canyon: Starved Rock State Park, La Salle County *(Bloomington Ridged Plain, Till Plains Section, Central Lowland Province)* Each May, Starved Rock State Park holds its Annual Wildflower Pilgrimage, which includes Illinois Canyon, where dense stands of Virginia bluebells grow. *May 1995*

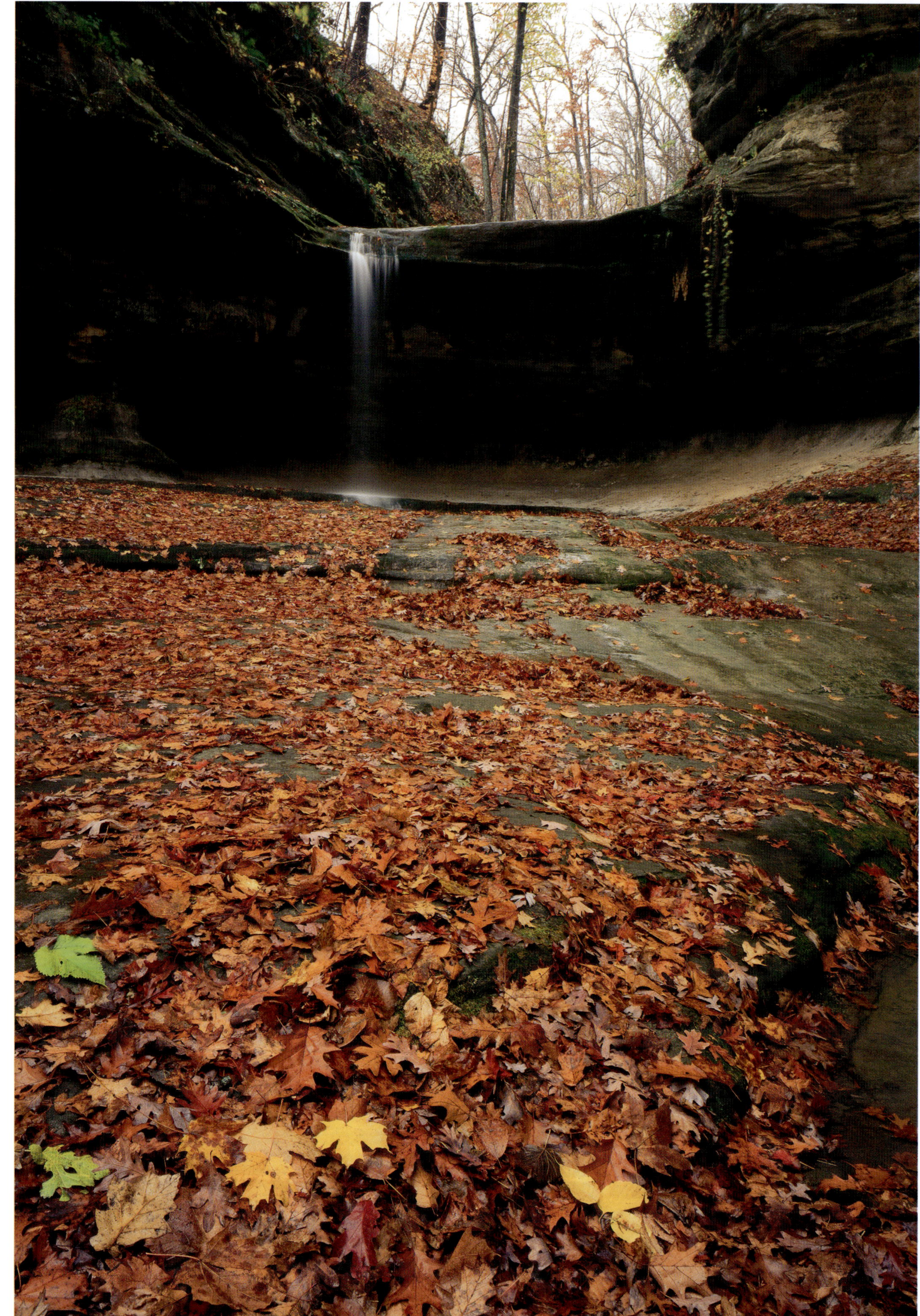

THIS PAGE:

La Salle Canyon: Starved Rock State Park, La Salle County *(Bloomington Ridged Plain, Till Plains Section, Central Lowland Province)*
During early spring, ephemeral waterfalls appear at the heads of all eighteen canyons in Starved Rock State Park. Some of the longer-lasting waterfalls are those of French, La Salle and St. Louis Canyons. The waterfall in La Salle Canyon is overhung, allowing hikers to walk behind it. *November 1995*

OPPOSITE PAGE:

La Salle Canyon: Starved Rock State Park, La Salle County *(Bloomington Ridged Plain, Till Plains Section, Central Lowland Province)*
The canyons in Starved Rock State Park support oak, cedar, hickory, maple, and white pine. *November 1995*

PAGES 70-71:

Hennepin Canyon: Starved Rock State Park, La Salle County *(Bloomington Ridged Plain, Till Plains Section, Central Lowland Province)*
October 1996

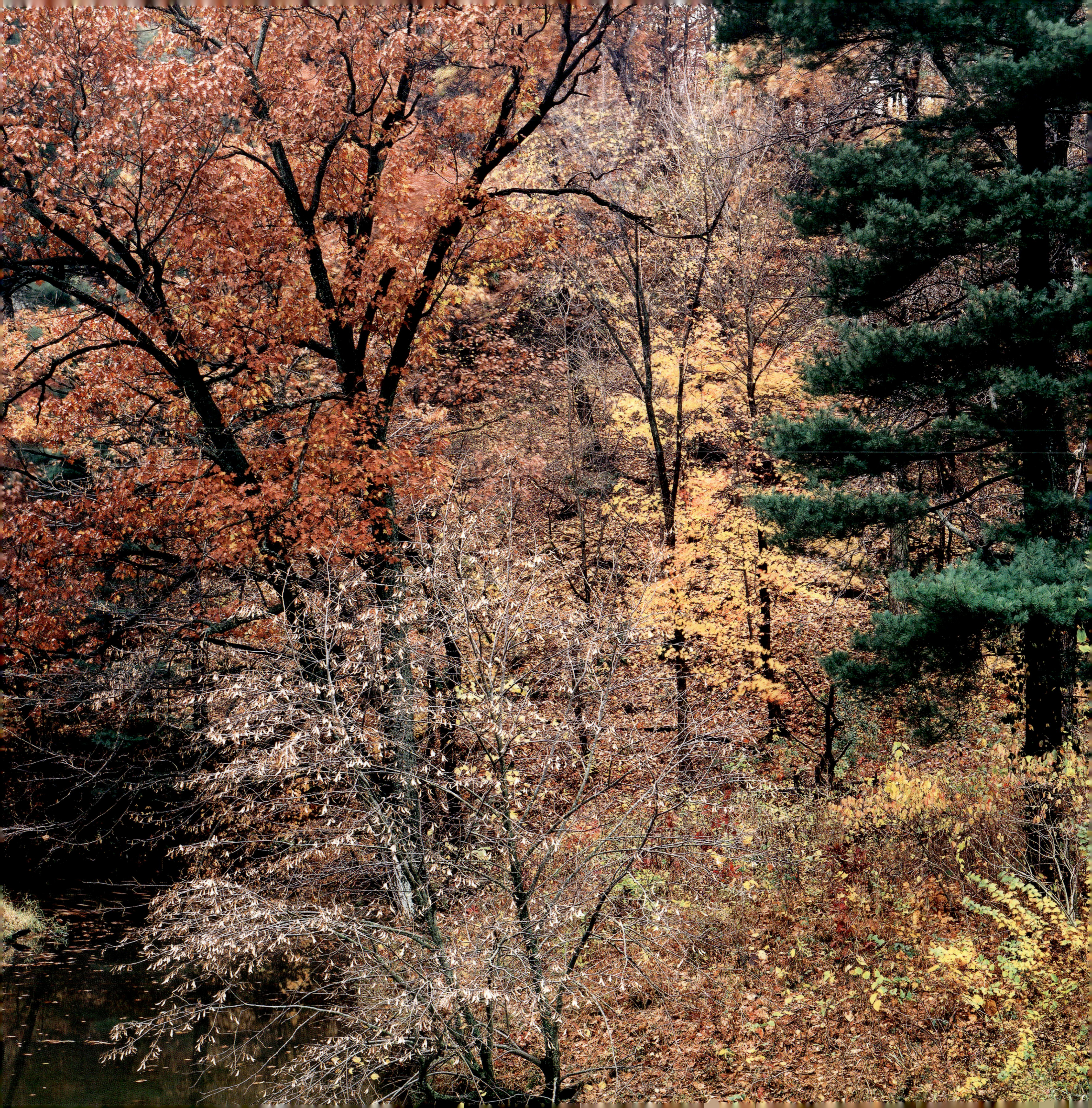

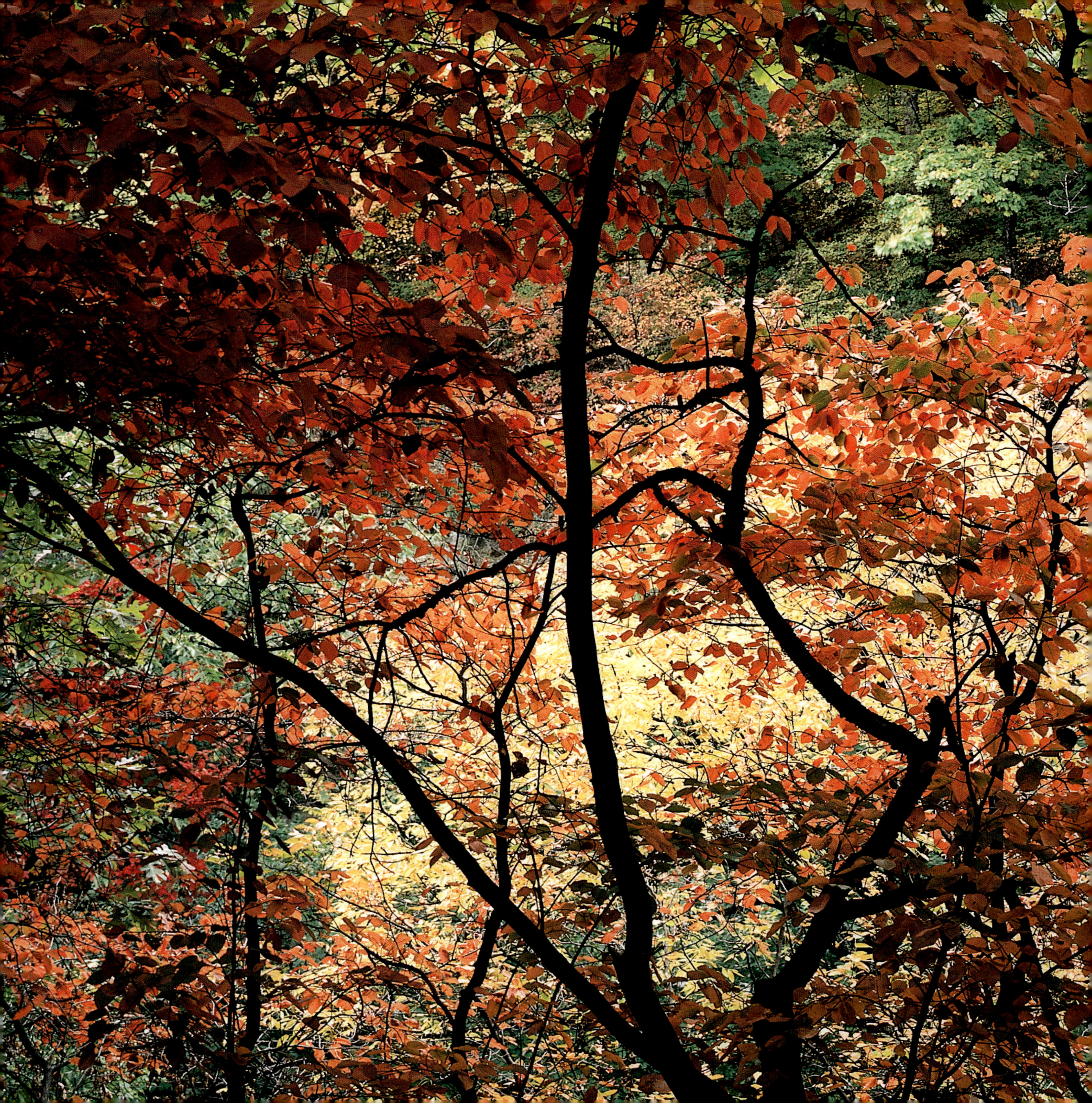

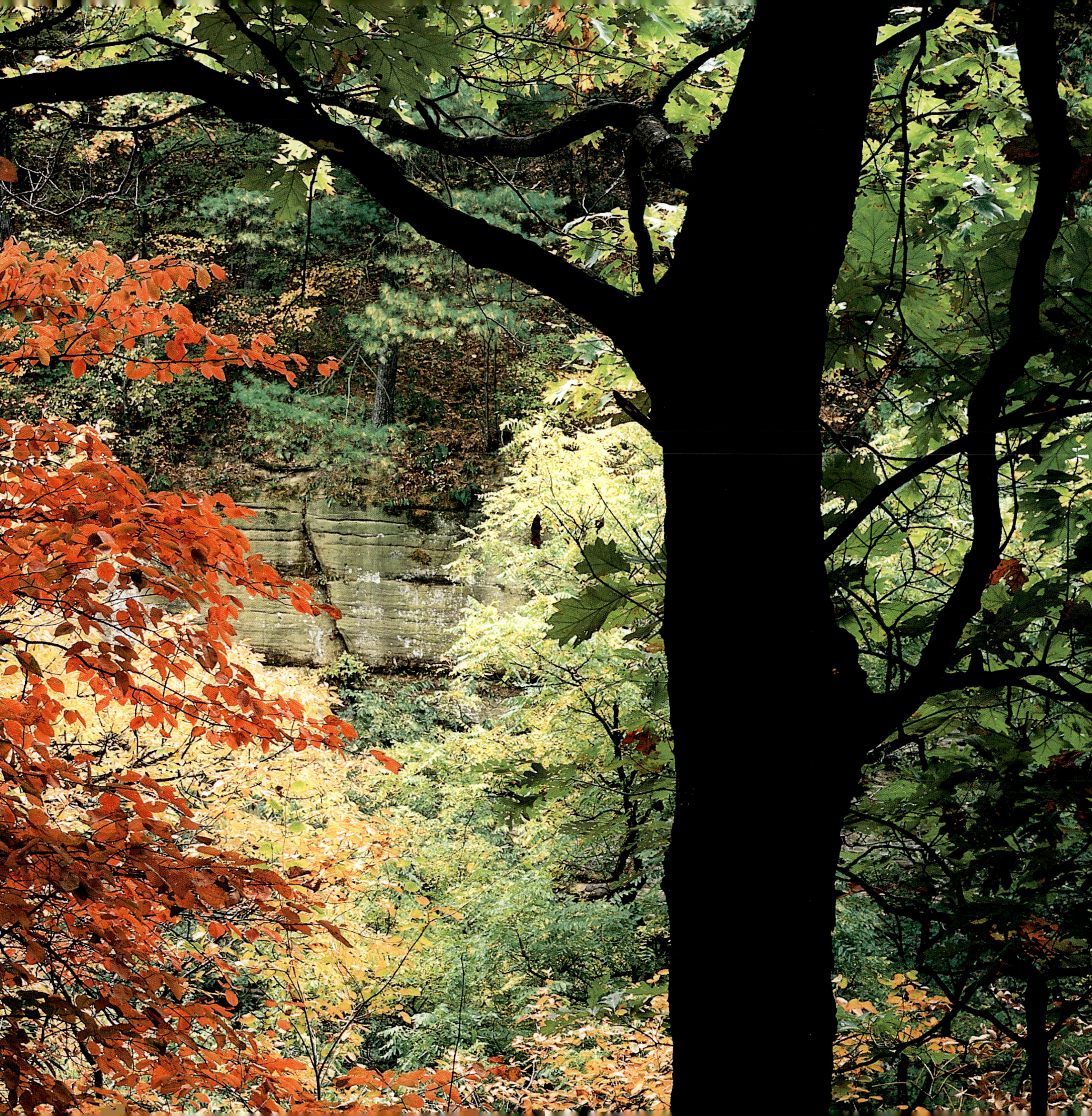

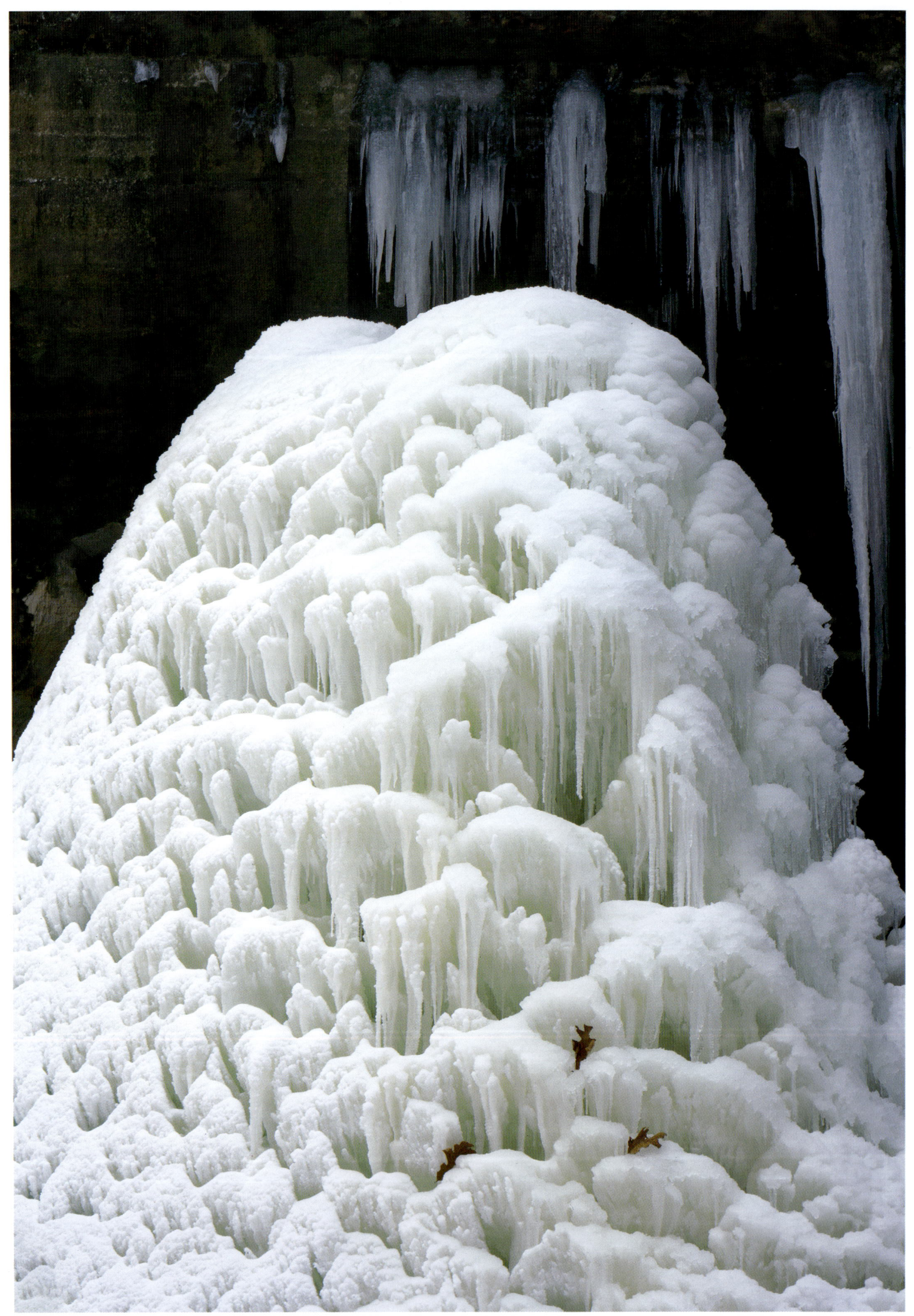

Frozen waterfall in Tonti Canyon: Starved Rock State Park, La Salle County *(Bloomington Ridged Plain, Till Plains Section, Central Lowland Province)* One of the many winter activities available in Starved Rock State Park is ice-climbing its frozen waterfalls. This photograph was made despite waterfall drops that splashed and froze on the camera lens. *January 1987*

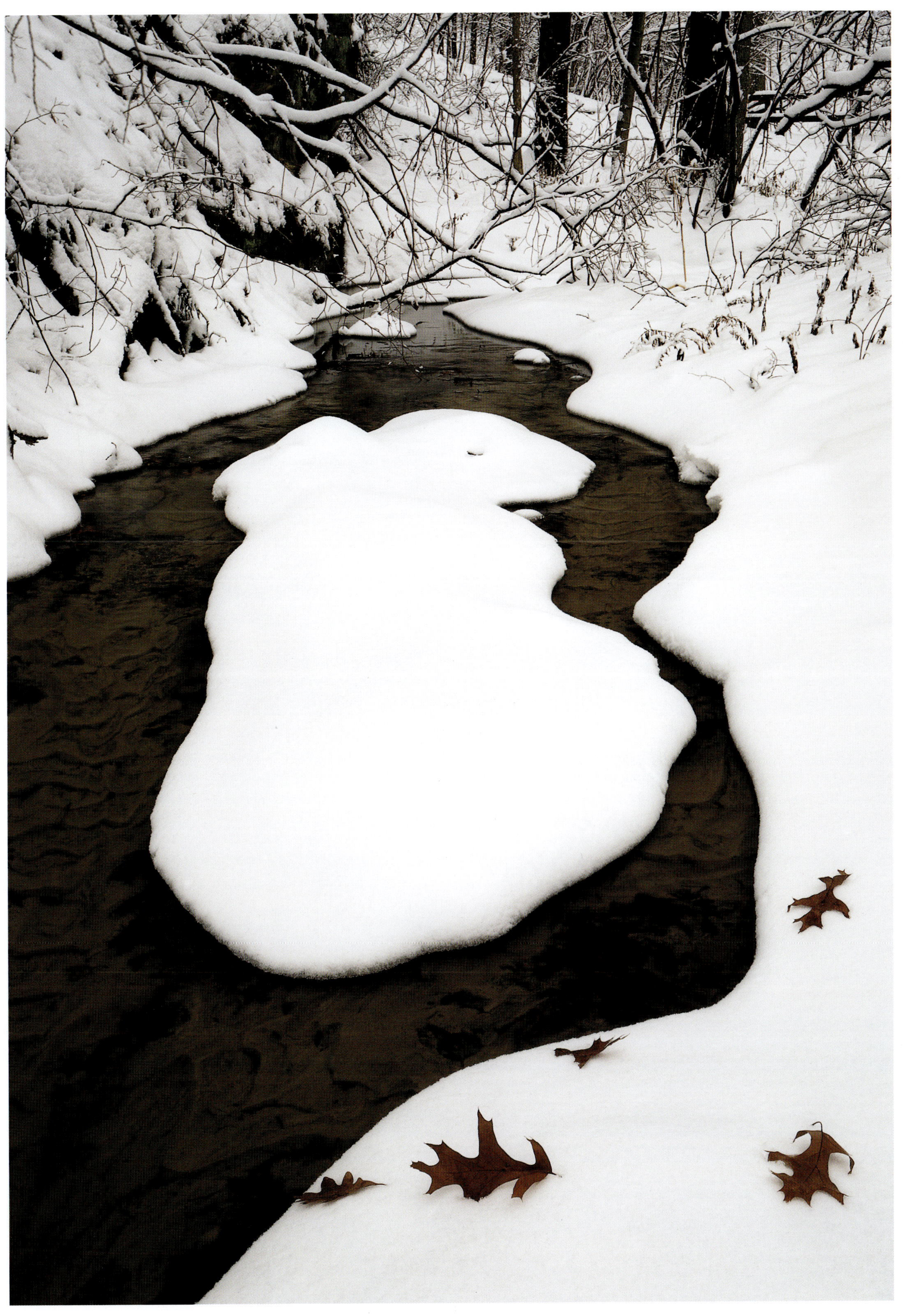

St. Louis Canyon: Starved Rock State Park, La Salle County *(Bloomington Ridged Plain, Till Plains Section, Central Lowland Province)*
December 1992

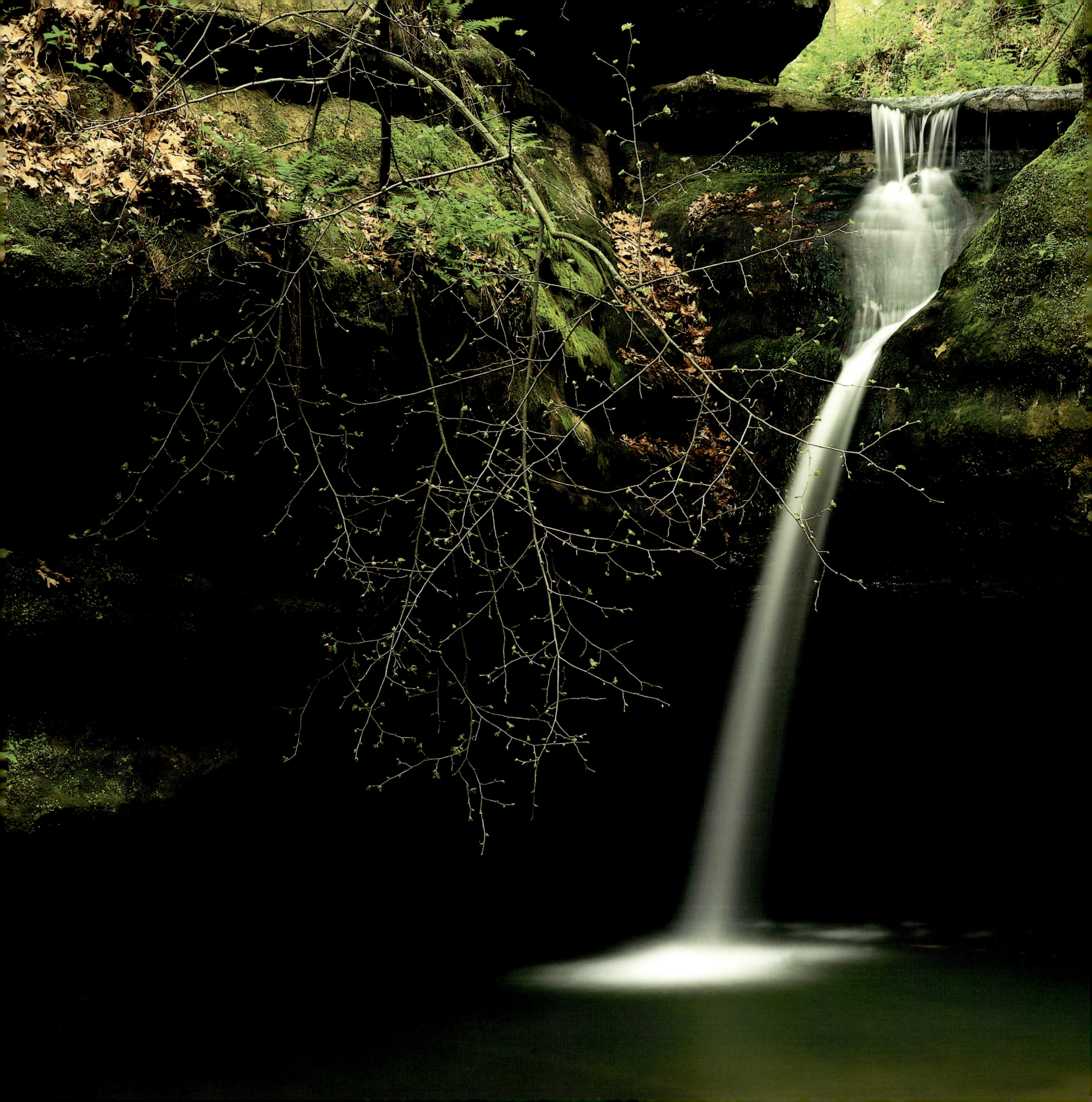

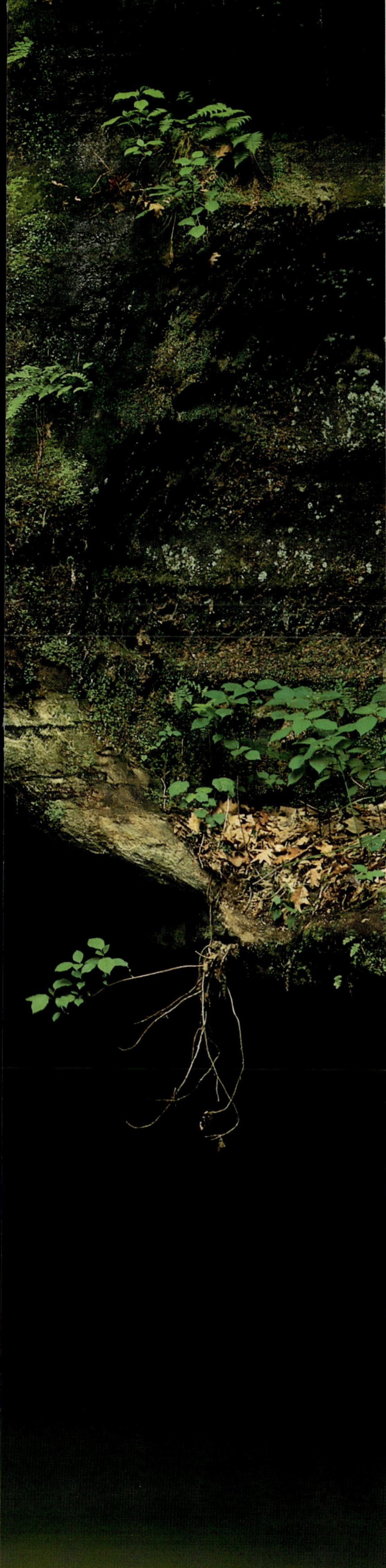

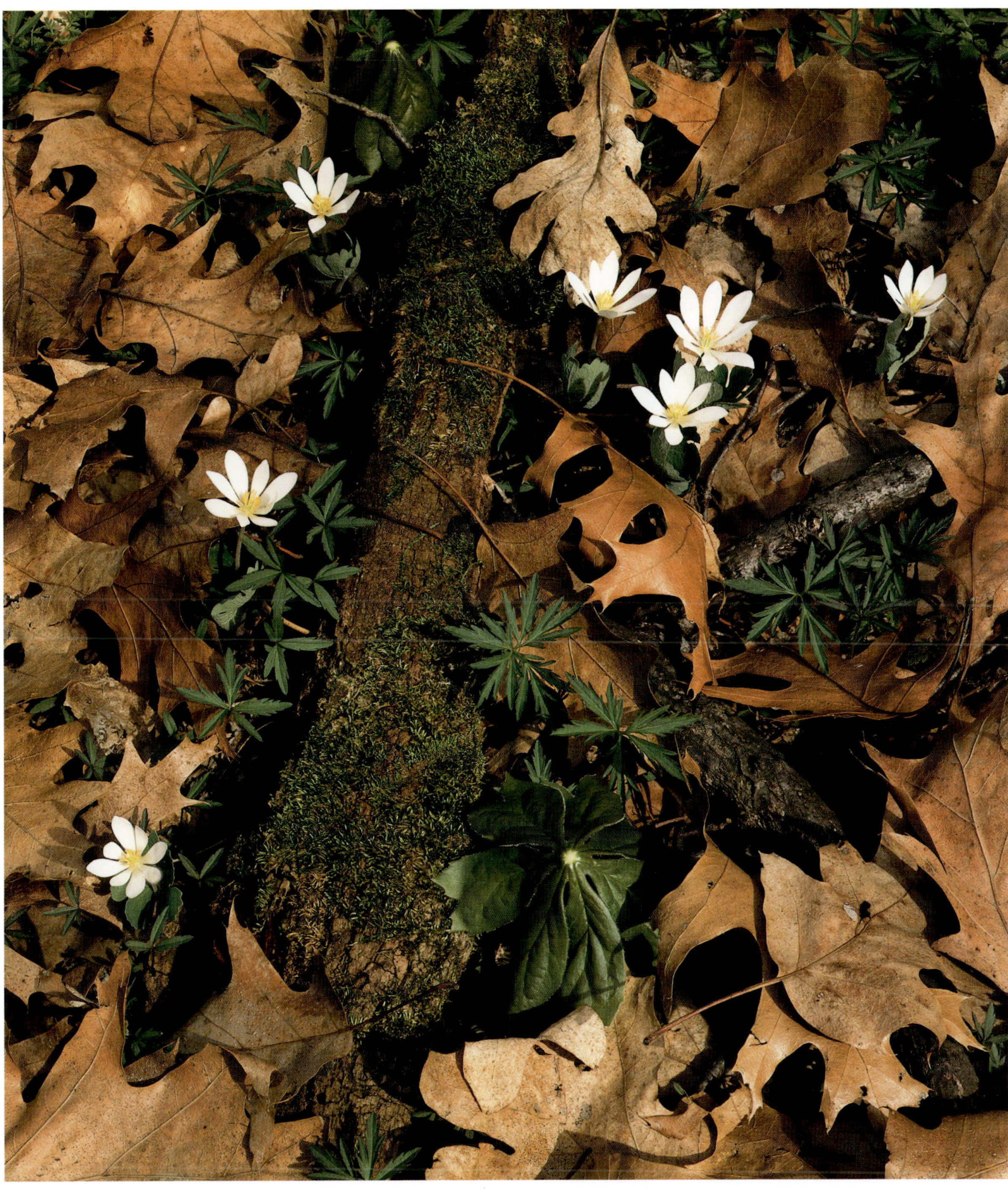

THIS PAGE ABOVE:

Bloodroot *(Sanguinaria canadensis)*: Starved Rock Nature Preserve, La Salle County *(Bloomington Ridged Plain, Till Plains Section, Central Lowland Province)*

Bloodroot is one of the first woodland wildflowers to bloom in the spring. It is found in moist rich woods, such as those in parts of the 582-acre Starved Rock Nature Preserve on the other side of the Vermilion River from Oglesby. Bloodroot's rhizome has medicinal properties and its red sap was used by Indian warriors as war paint. *April 1988*

OPPOSITE PAGE:

Waterfall in Kaskaskia Canyon: Starved Rock State Park, La Salle County *(Bloomington Ridged Plain, Till Plains Section, Central Lowland Province)*
May 1998

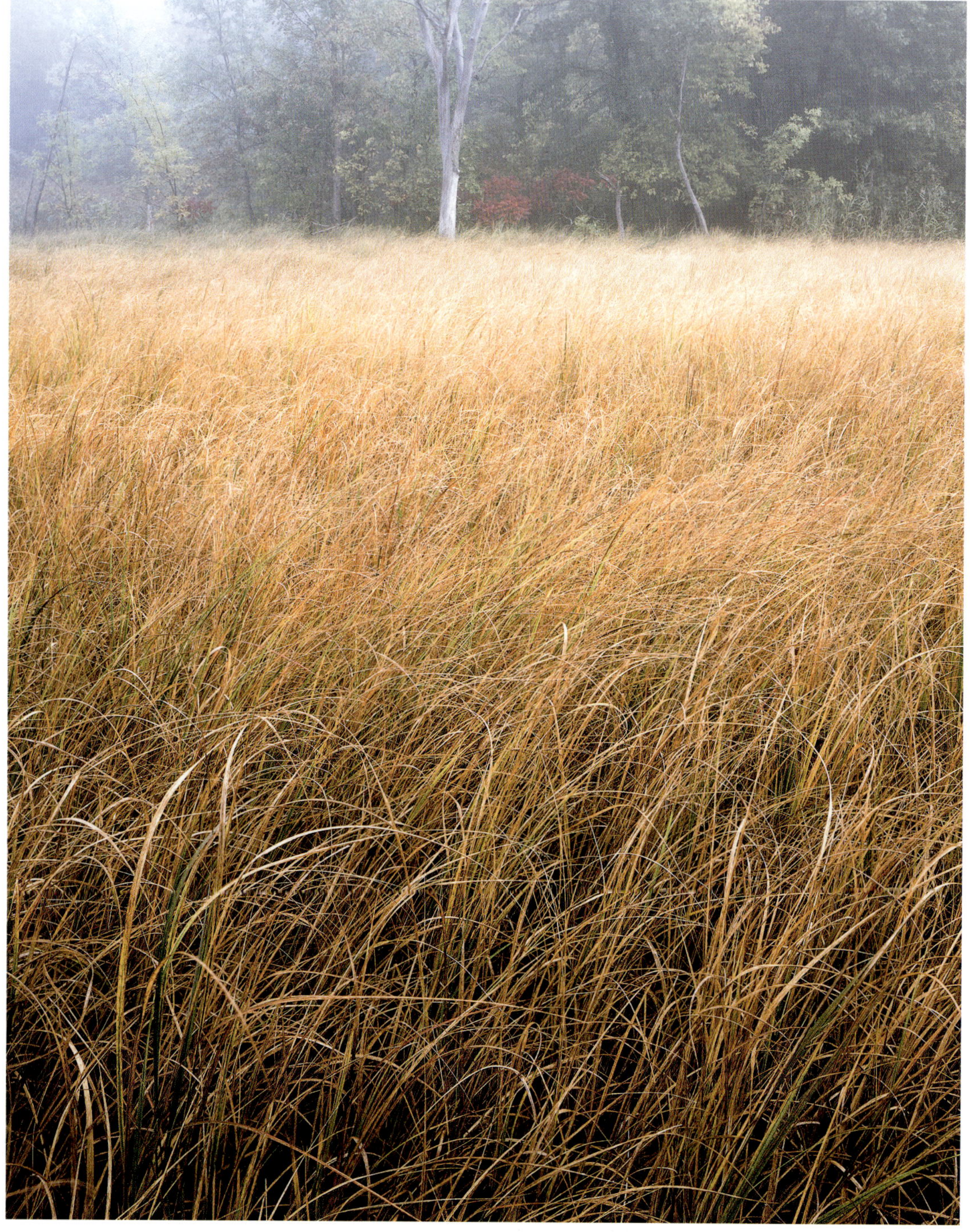

THIS PAGE ABOVE:

Meadow along the Illinois & Michigan Canal: Illinois & Michigan Canal State Trail, La Salle County *(Bloomington Ridged Plain, Till Plains Section, Central Lowland Province)*

The 61-mile route of the Illinois & Michigan Canal State Trail stretches from Brandon Road in Rockdale, Will County, west to LaSalle/Peru, LaSalle County. The well-built trail passes connections to many historic sites as well as beautiful meadows. *September 2001*

OPPOSITE PAGE:

Frozen pond at sunset along Illinois & Michigan Canal, near Utica: Illinois & Michigan Canal State Trail, La Salle County *(Bloomington Ridged Plain, Till Plains Section, Central Lowland Province)*

The Illinois & Michigan Canal State Trail is in use year round. In winter, the Trail is open for hiking, skiing, or snowmobiling. *February 2002*

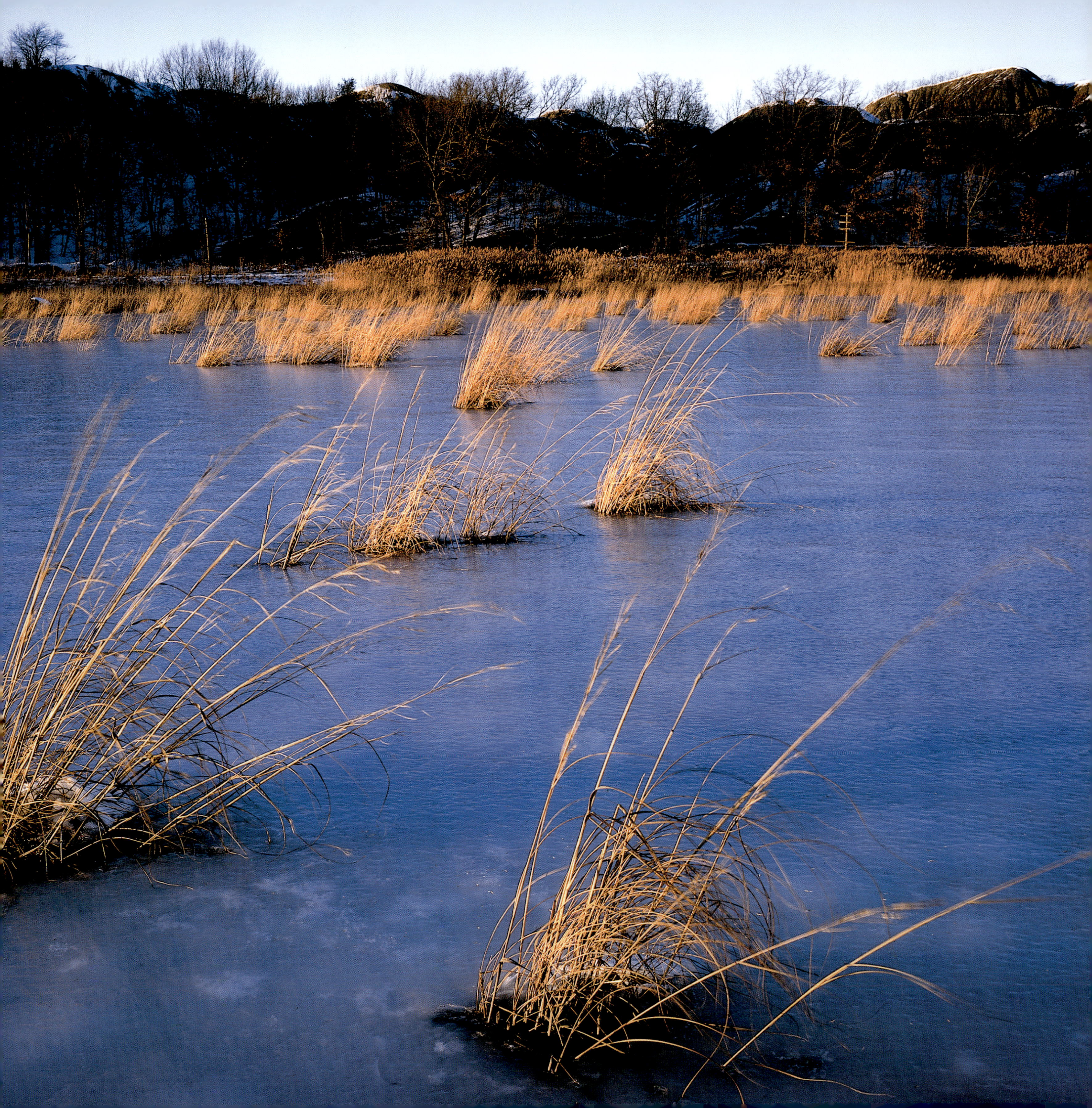

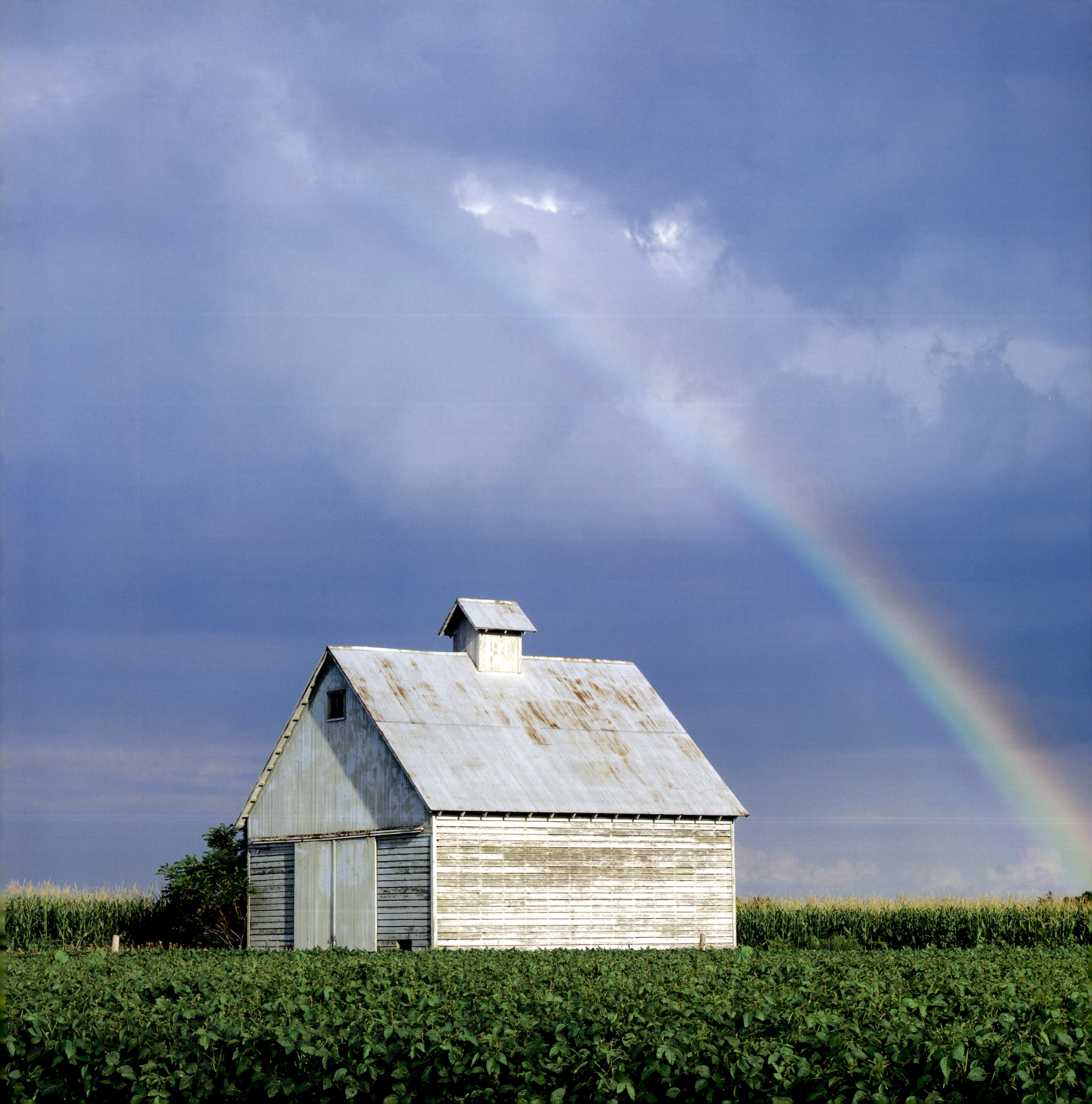

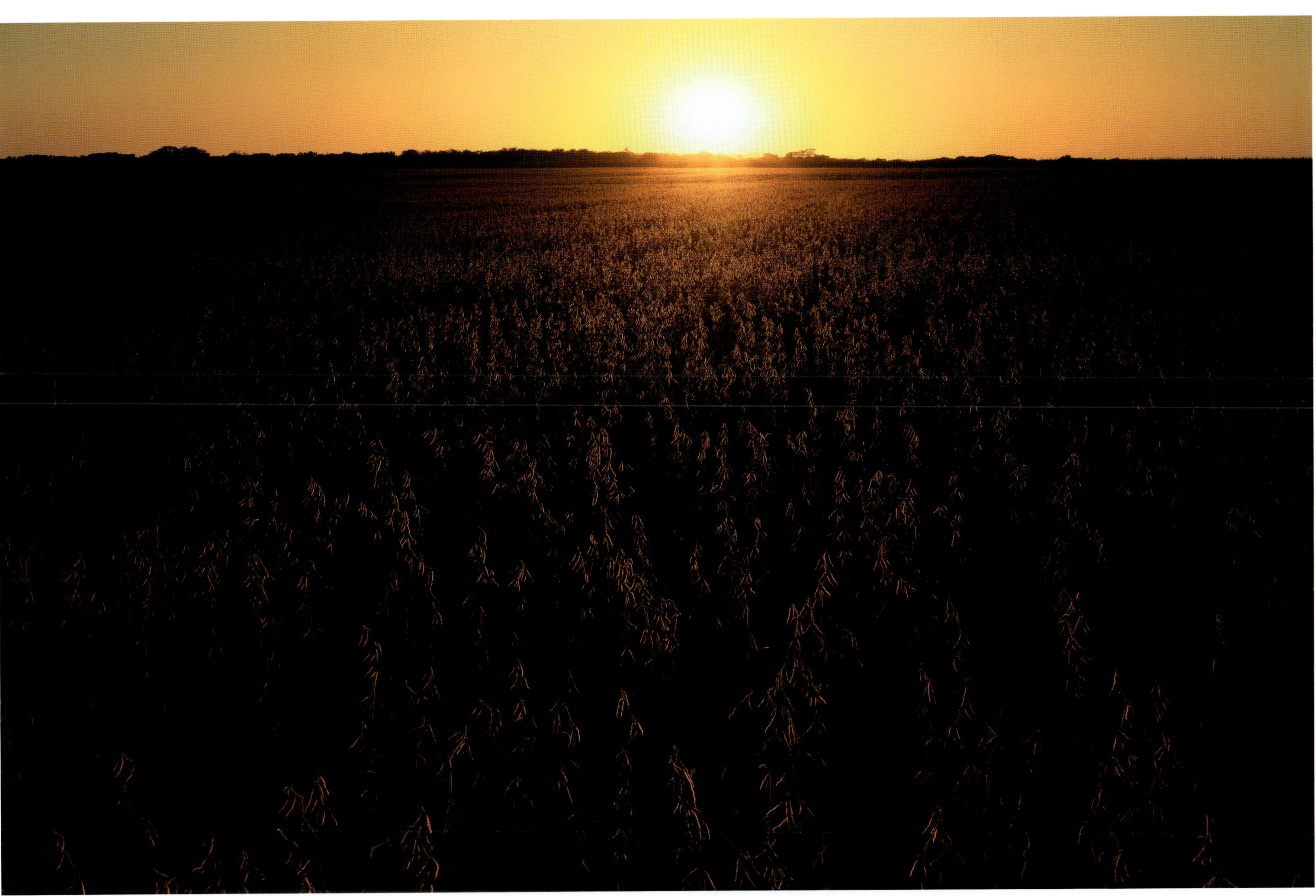

THIS PAGE ABOVE:

Field of soybeans at sunset: La Salle County *(Bloomington Ridged Plain, Till Plains Section, Central Lowland Province)*

The soybean, a plant probably native to eastern Asia, was first cultivated in Illinois around 1900. Illinois is among the leading producers in the United States, growing soybeans on 9.5 million acres with an average yield of almost 60 bushels per acre. *October 1995*

PAGES 80-81:

Soybean field: La Salle County *(Bloomington Ridged Plain, Till Plains Section, Central Lowland Province)*

The rising sun lights up a field of soybean plants that are "turning" as they mature in early fall. When the leaves dry and fall from the plants later in the fall, the combines begin harvesting. *September 1991*

OPPOSITE PAGE:

Corncrib and fields of soybeans and corn: La Salle County *(Bloomington Ridged Plain, Till Plains Section, Central Lowland Province)*
August 1992

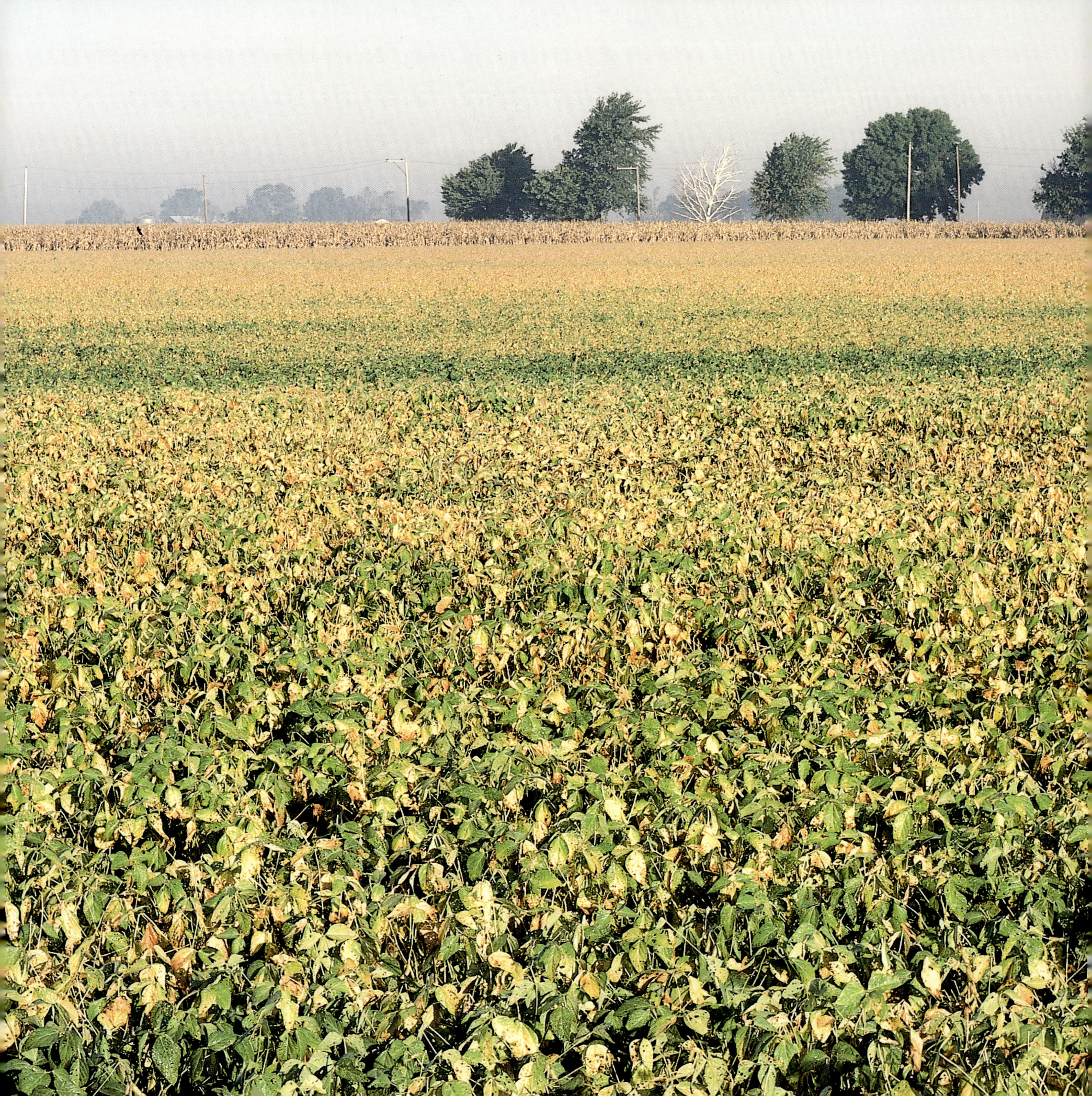

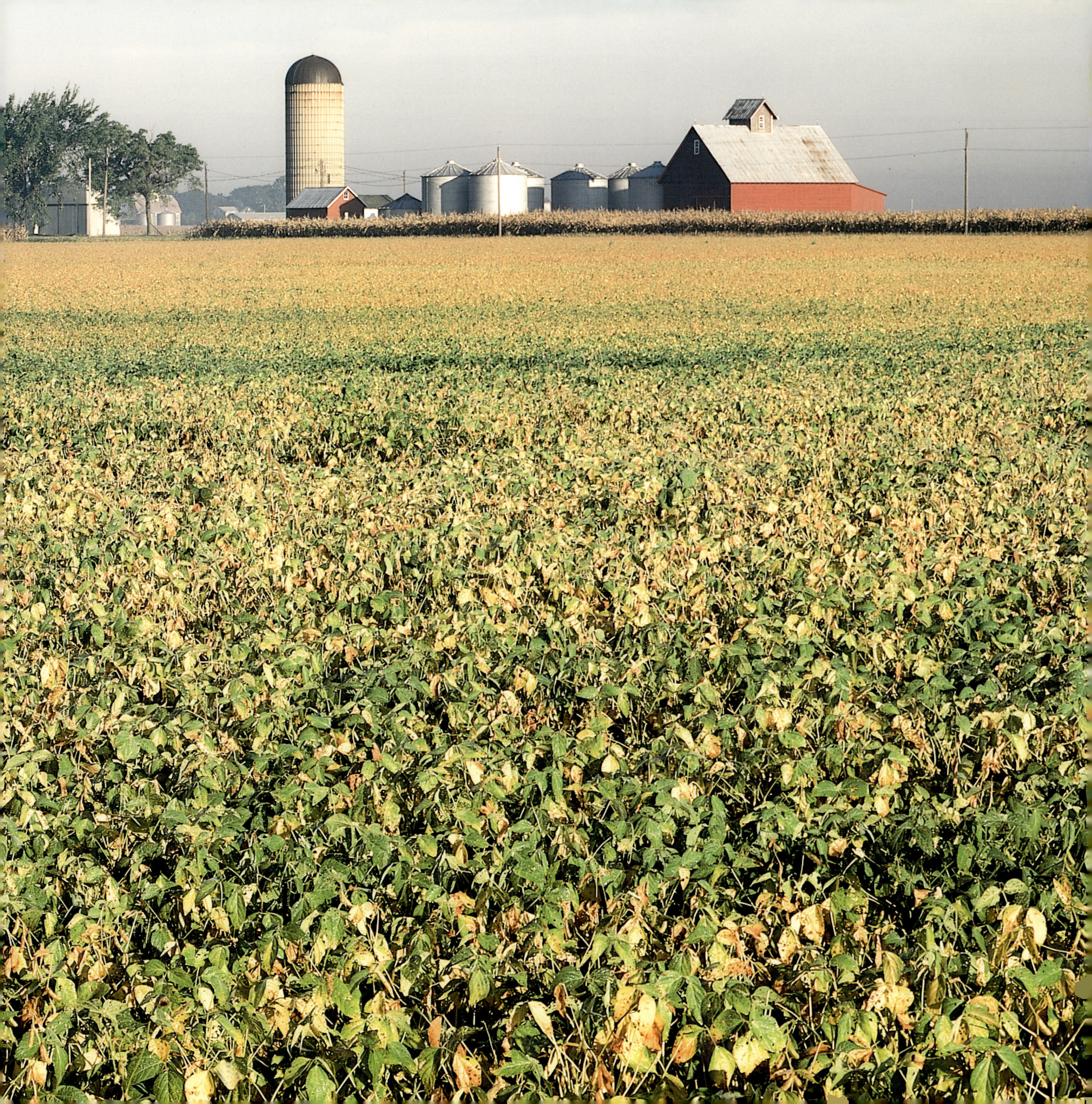

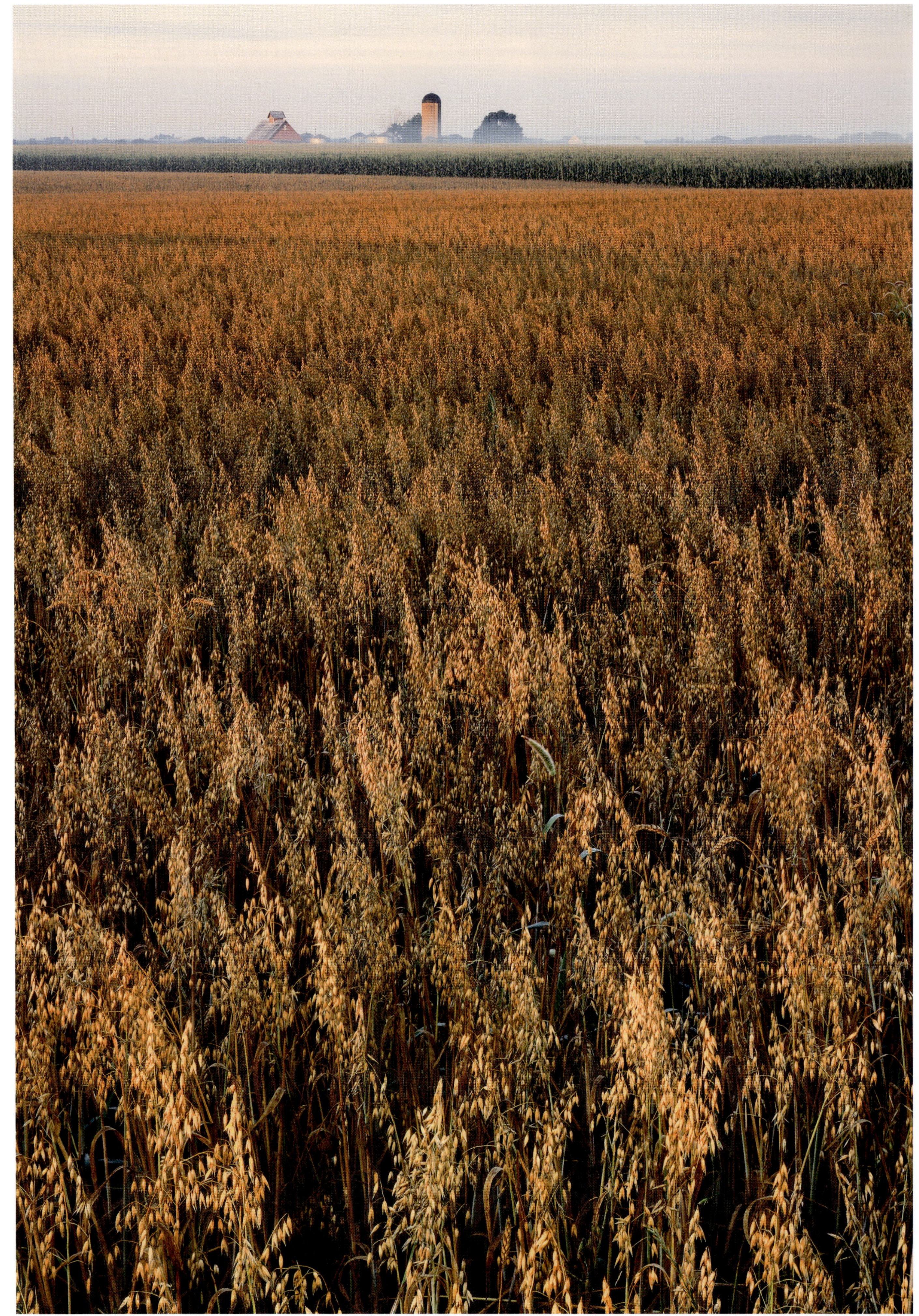

THIS PAGE:

Oat field at sunrise: La Salle County
(Bloomington Ridged Plain, Till Plains Section, Central Lowland Province)
Though trivial in agricultural importance compared to corn and soybeans in Illinois, oats have a high yield of 70 bushels per acre on the 75,000 acres that planted with oats in the state. *July 1995*

OPPOSITE PAGE:

Immature cornfield at sunrise: La Salle County
(Bloomington Ridged Plain, Till Plains Section, Central Lowland Province)
Corn is Illinois's leading cash crop, with over 11 million acres producing 1.5 billion bushels annually. *July 1995*

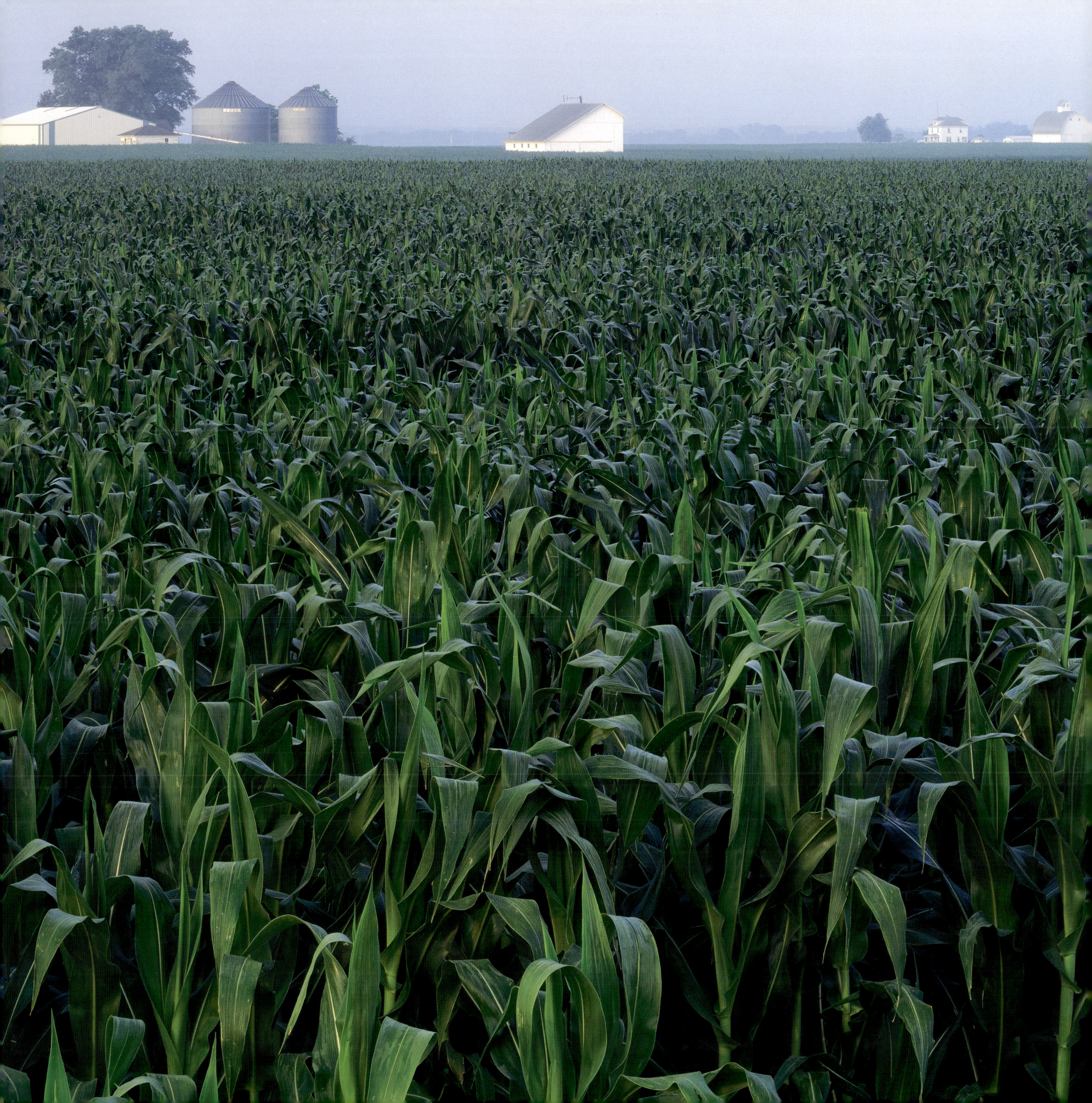
BROCK

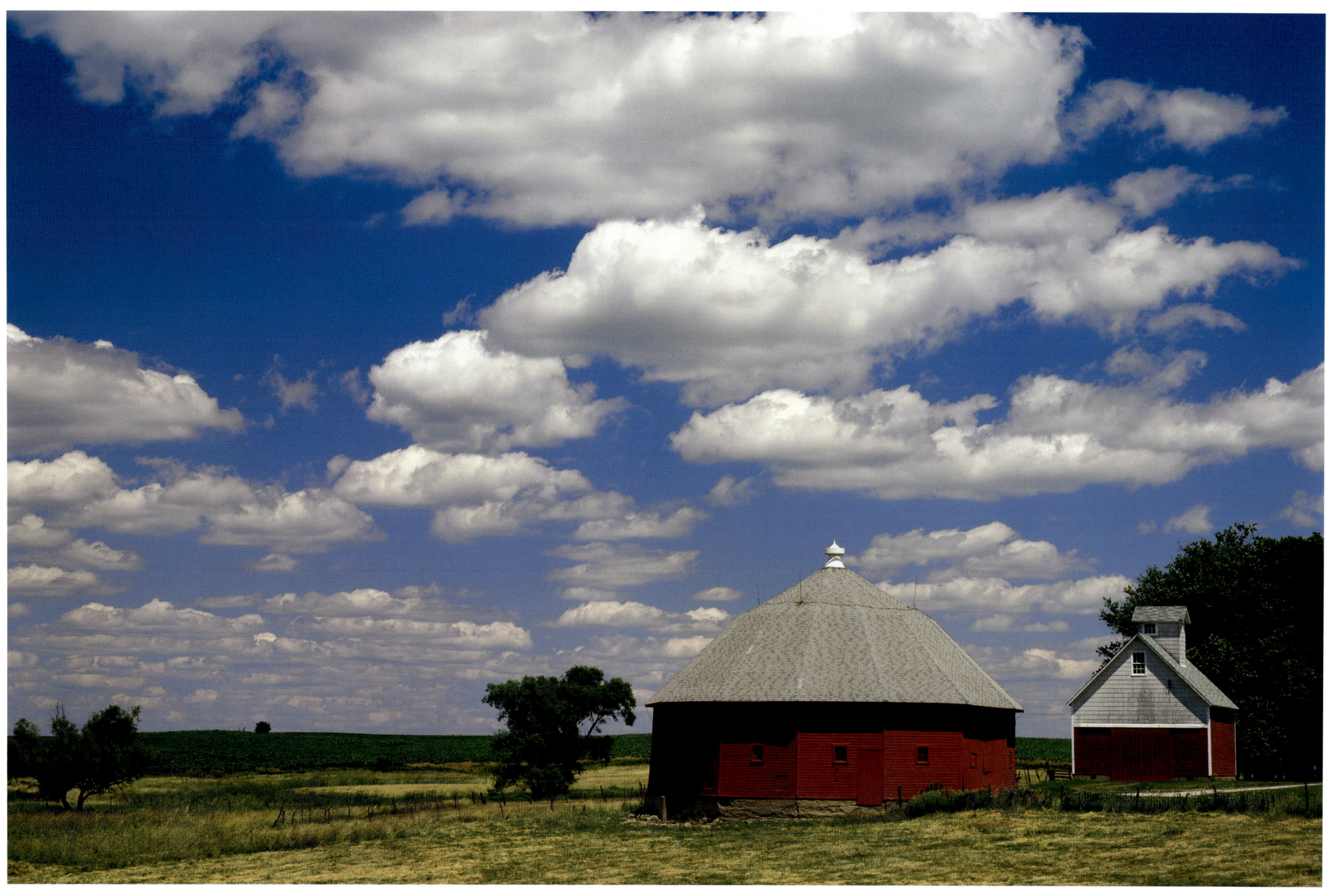

Polygonal barn and carriage house under summer clouds: La Salle County
(Bloomington Ridged Plain, Till Plains Section, Central Lowland Province)
June 1987

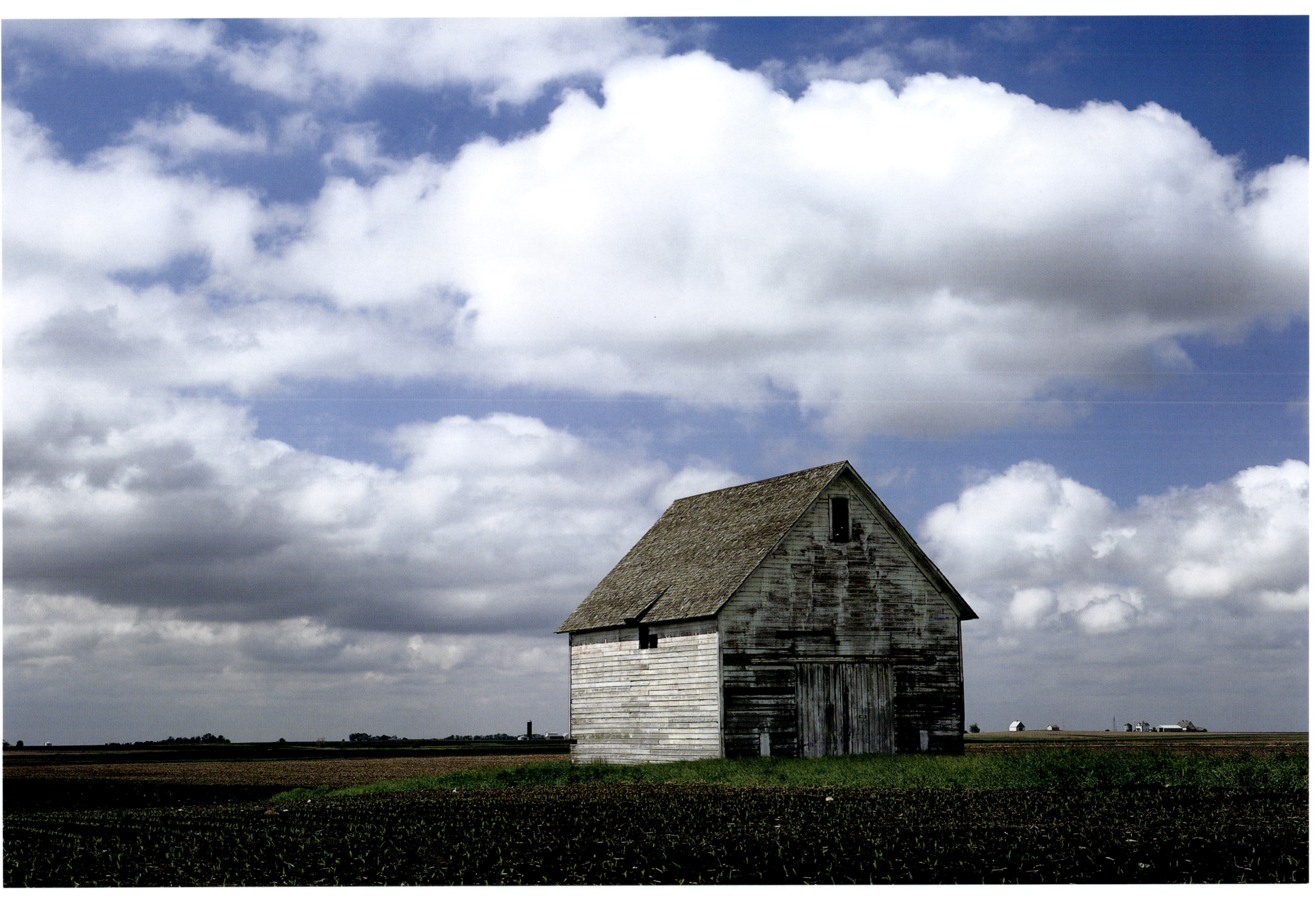

THIS PAGE:

Farm with freshly germinated corn plants: La Salle County *(Bloomington Ridged Plain, Till Plains Section, Central Lowland Province)*
May 1993

PAGES 86-87:

Farm: La Salle County *(Bloomington Ridged Plain, Till Plains Section, Central Lowland Province)*
Black storm clouds build over a farm. Spring storms bring moisture needed by young plants but sometimes destructive violence and tornadoes, too. This storm produced lightning and heavy rainfall. *May 1999*

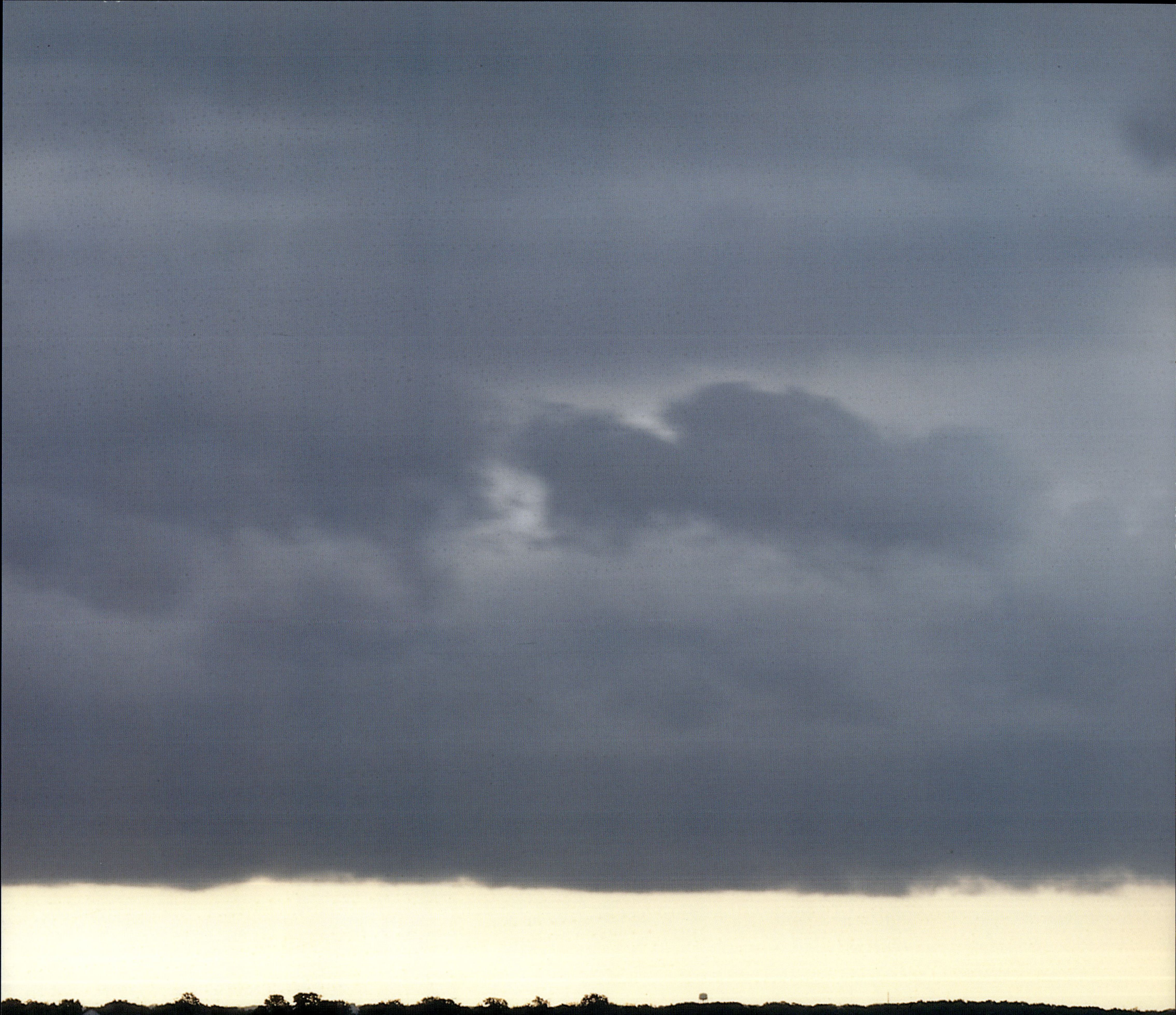

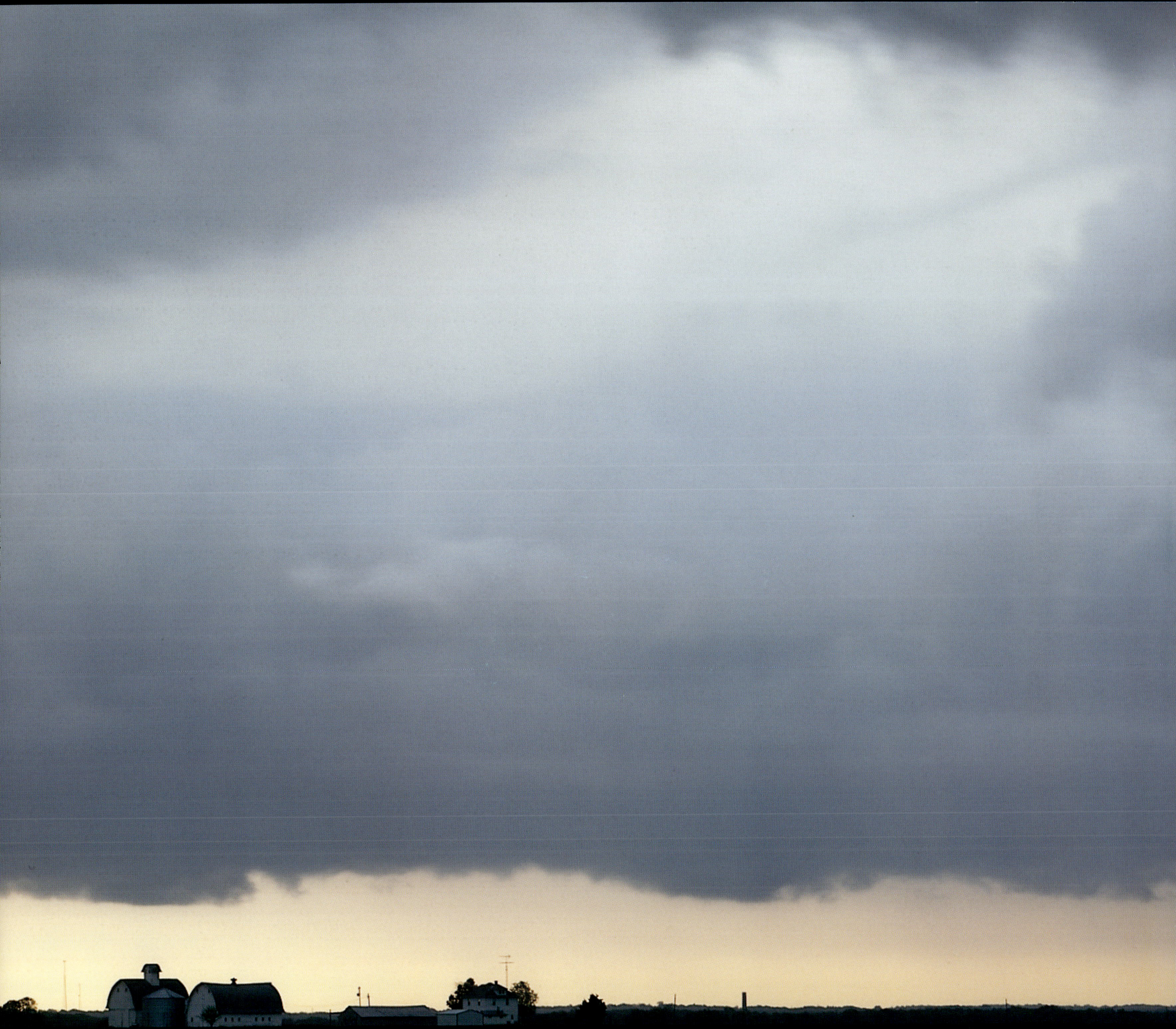

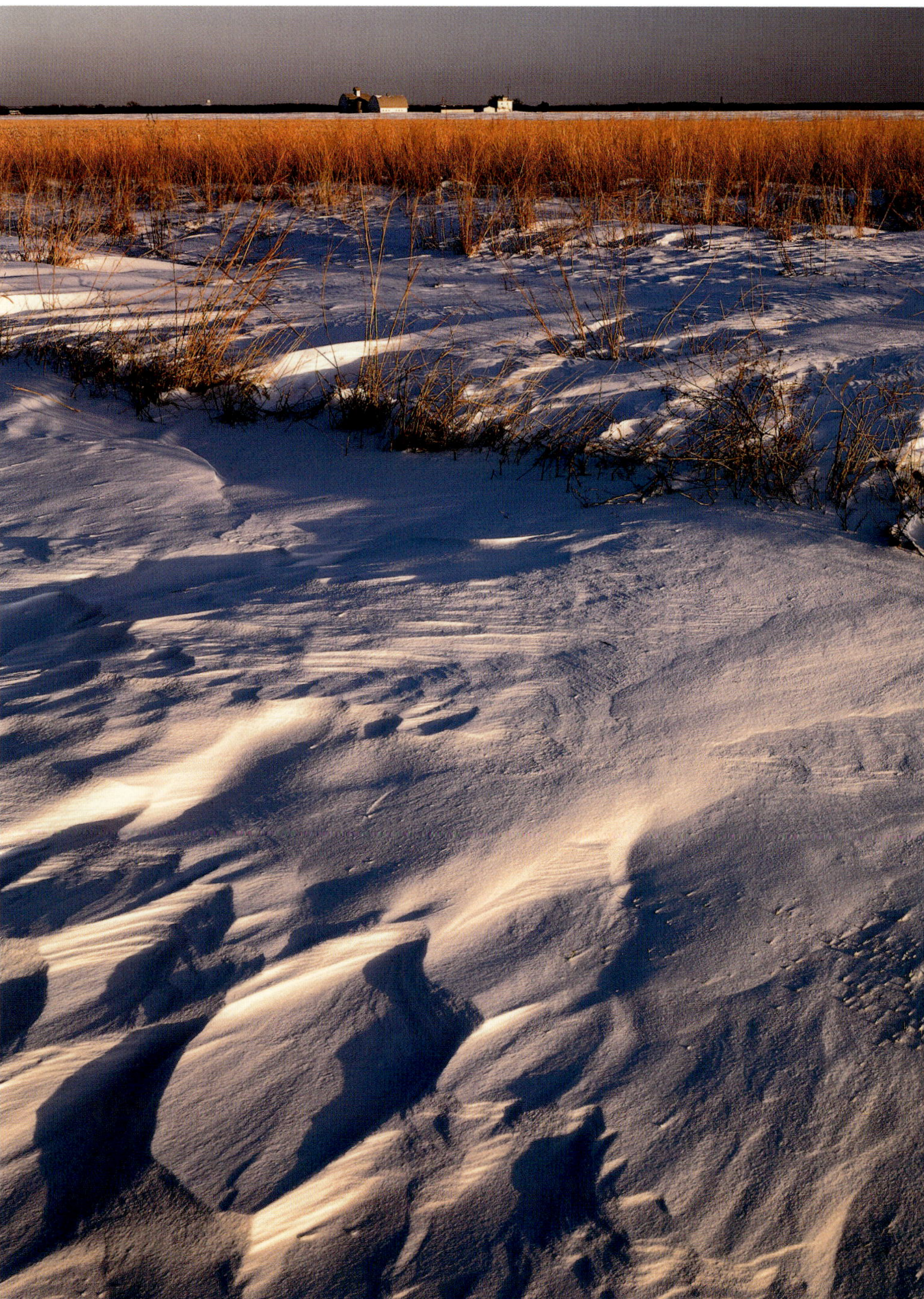

THIS PAGE LEFT:

Prairie: La Salle County *(Bloomington Ridged Plain, Till Plains Section, Central Lowland Province)*
February 1994

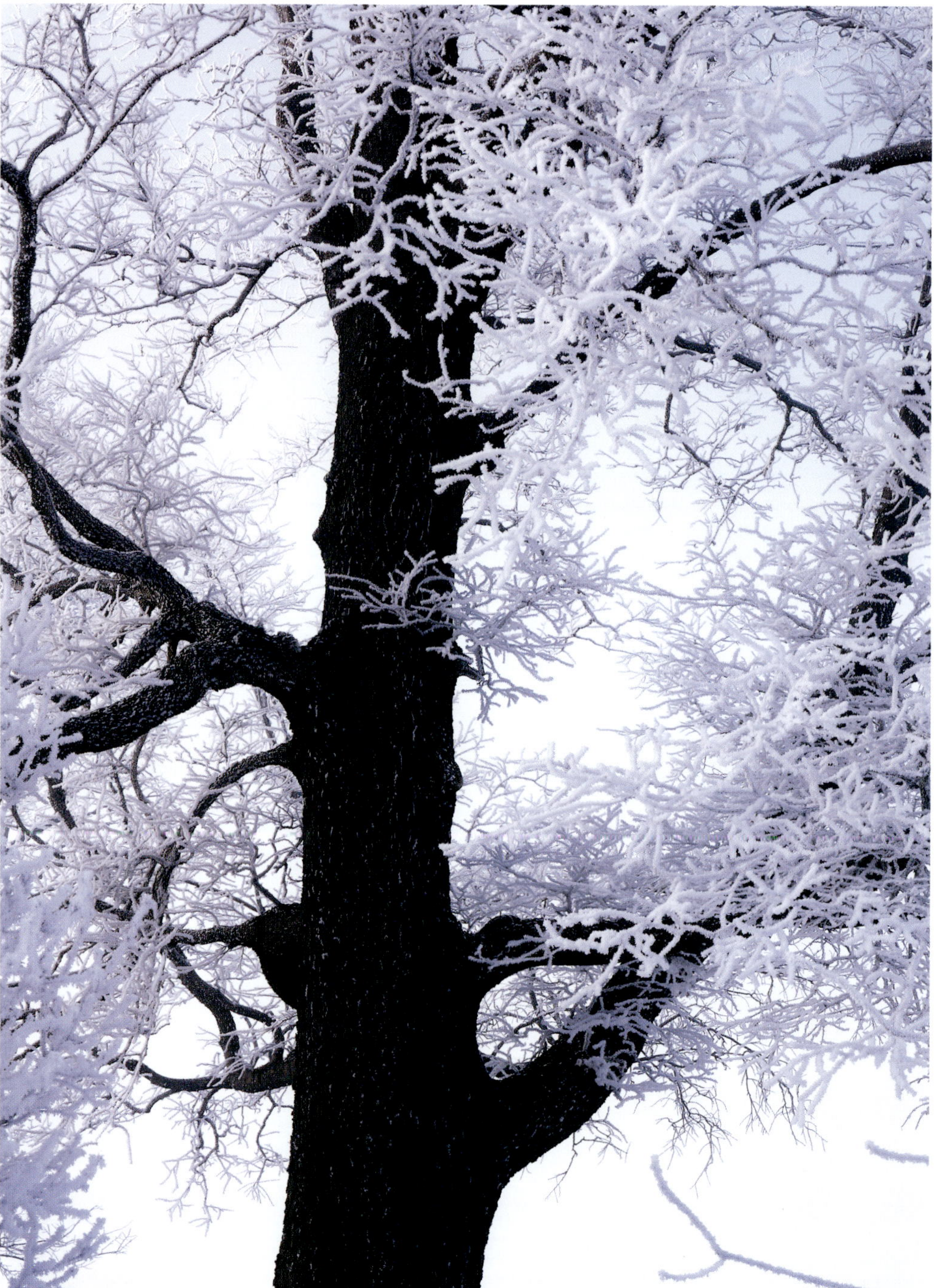

THIS PAGE RIGHT:

Hoarfrosted tree: La Salle County *(Bloomington Ridged Plain, Till Plains Section, Central Lowland Province)*
On foggy winter nights, hoarfrost often congeals on vegetation, but is melted away by the rays of the morning sun. *February 2000*

OPPOSITE PAGE:

Hoarfrost on prairie in foggy sunrise: La Salle County *(Bloomington Ridged Plain, Till Plains Section, Central Lowland Province)*
December 1994

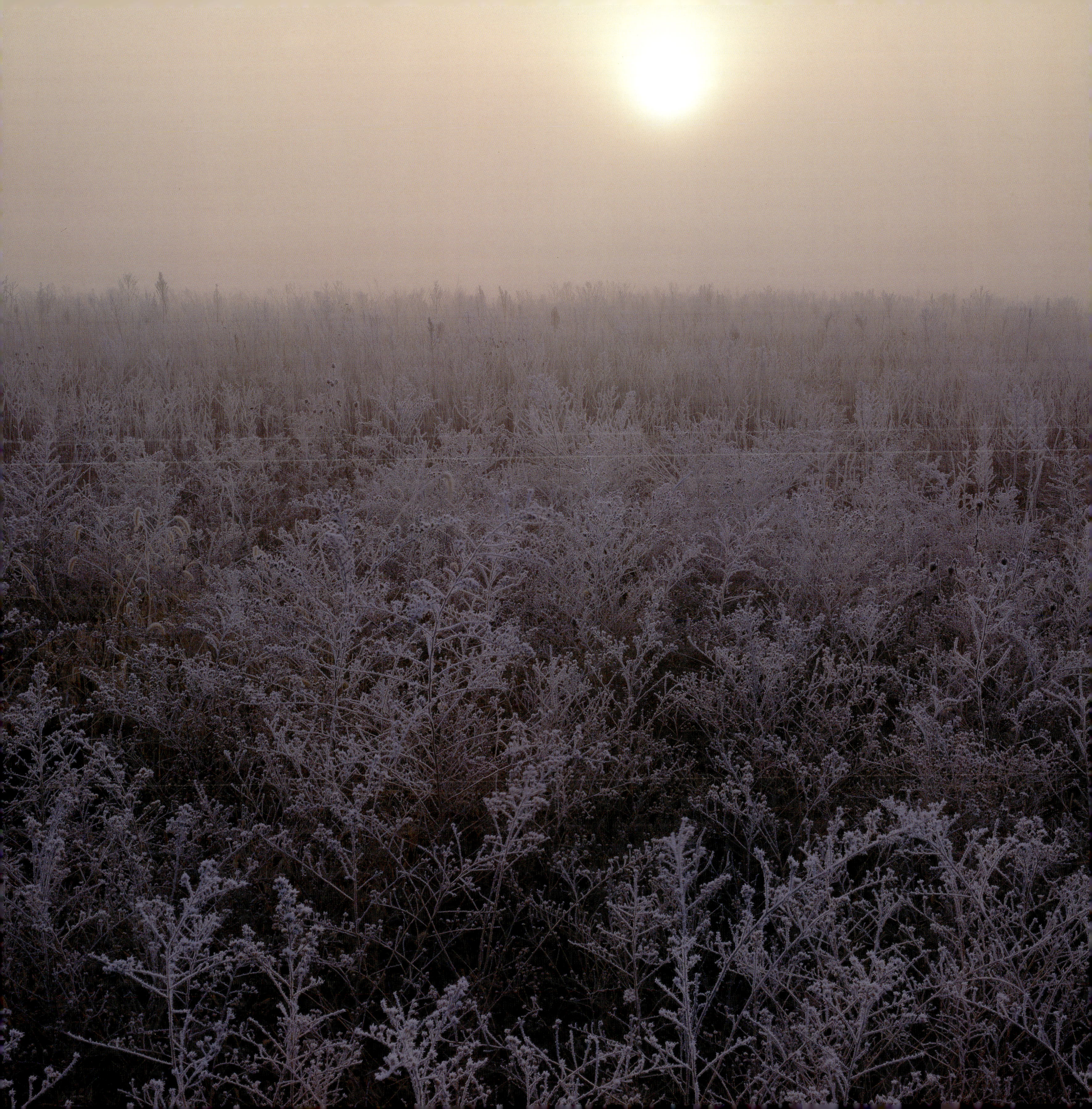

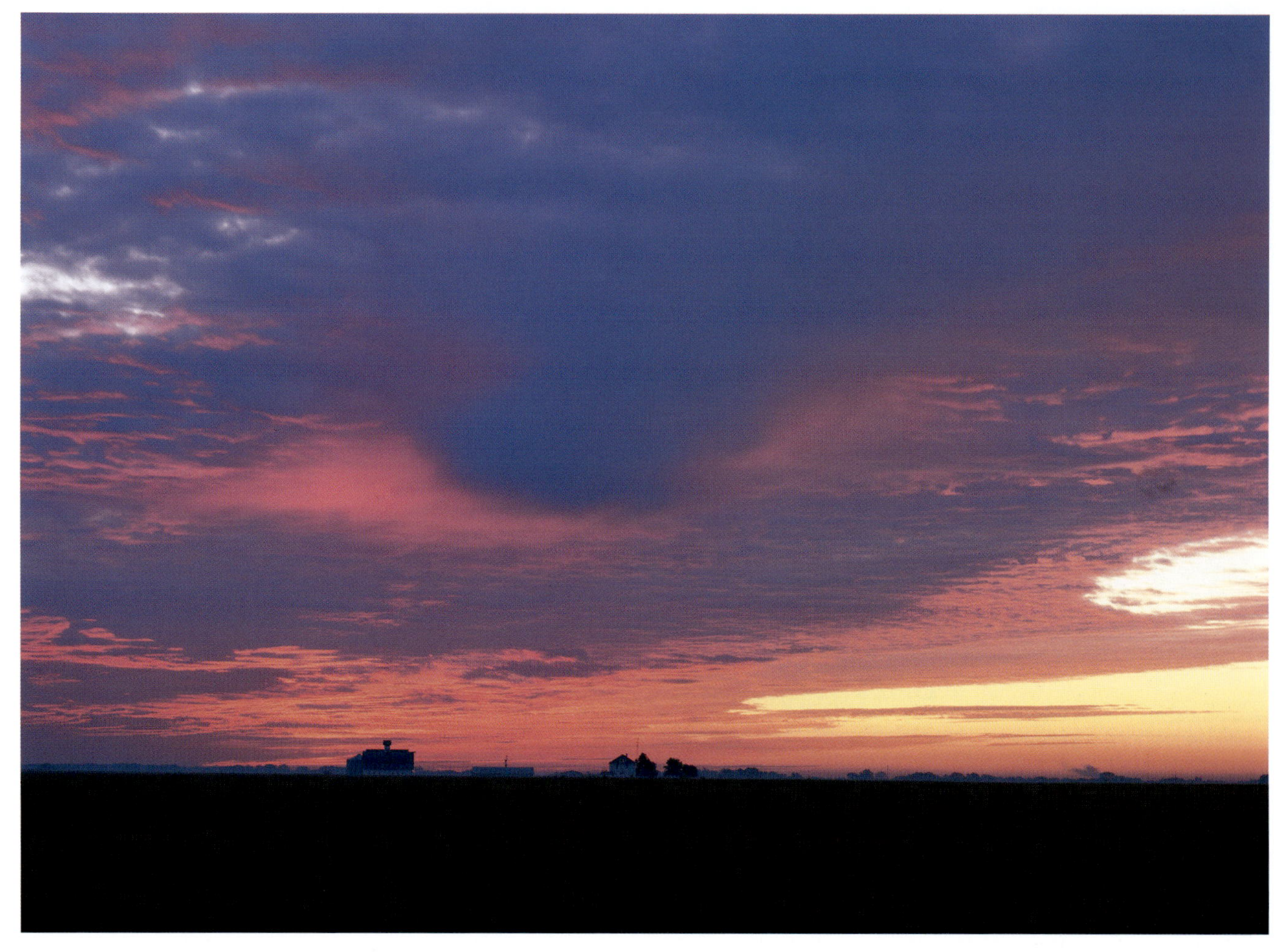

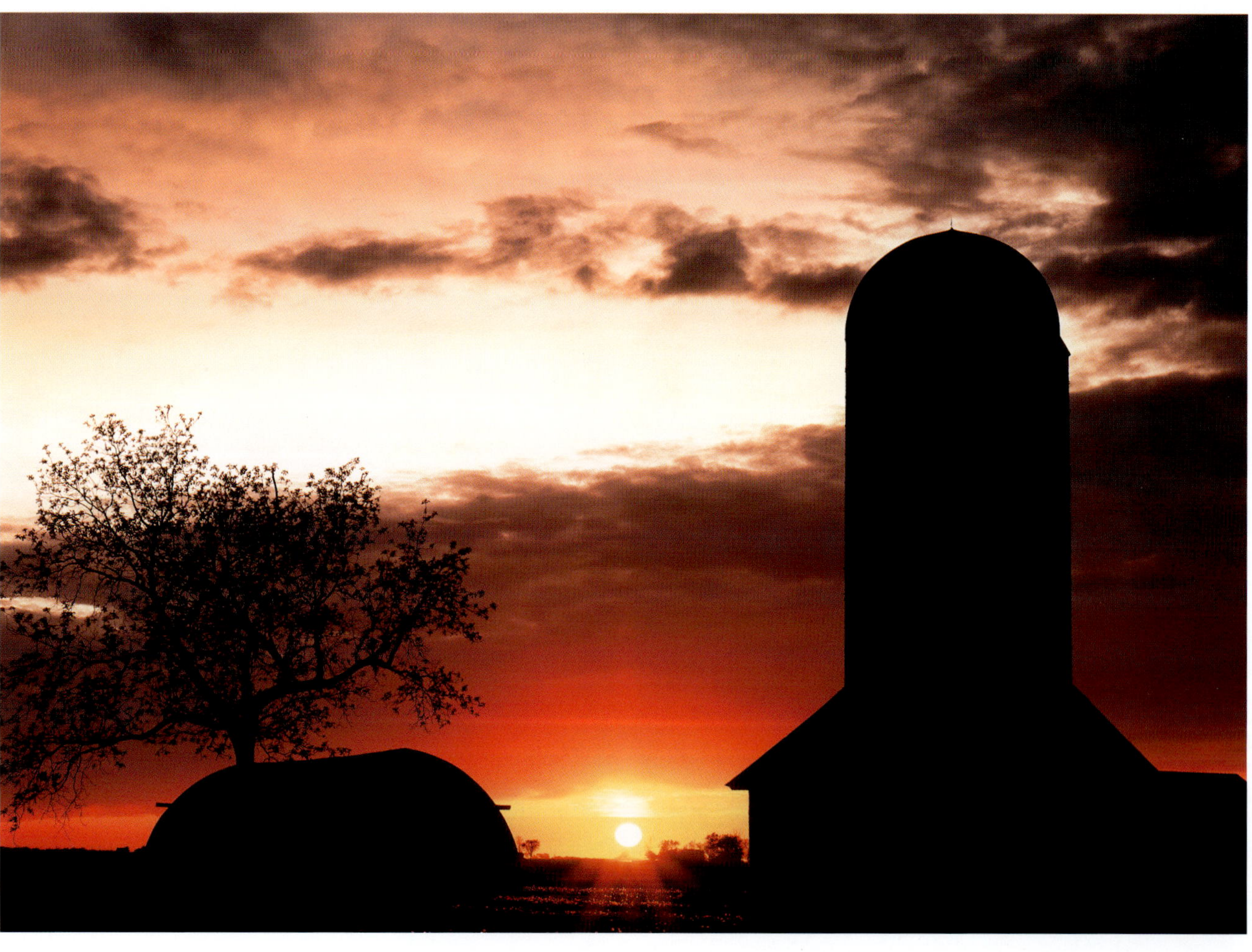

THIS PAGE TOP:

Sunrise over soybean field and farm: La Salle County *(Bloomington Ridged Plain, Till Plains Section, Central Lowland Province)* *September 1995*

THIS PAGE BOTTOM:

Sunset over farm: La Salle County *(Bloomington Ridged Plain, Till Plains Section, Central Lowland Province)*
The sun's rays can usually be captured by on film if some solid body (such as the horizon or a tree) is "touching" the sun in the frame and the camera lens is set for a small aperture. *May 1995*

OPPOSITE PAGE:

Bouncing Bet *(Saponaria officinalis)*: Sunbury Railroad Prairie, Livingston County *(Bloomington Ridged Plain, Till Plains Section, Central Lowland Province)*
Sunbury Railroad Prairie is a remnant of the Grand Prairie located on the Ransom Moraine of the Marseilles Morainal System, which formed during the Wisconsinan glaciation. Its twelve acres are on a gently rolling prairie land. Grassland birds frequenting the area include dickcissel and vesper sparrows. *July 1995*

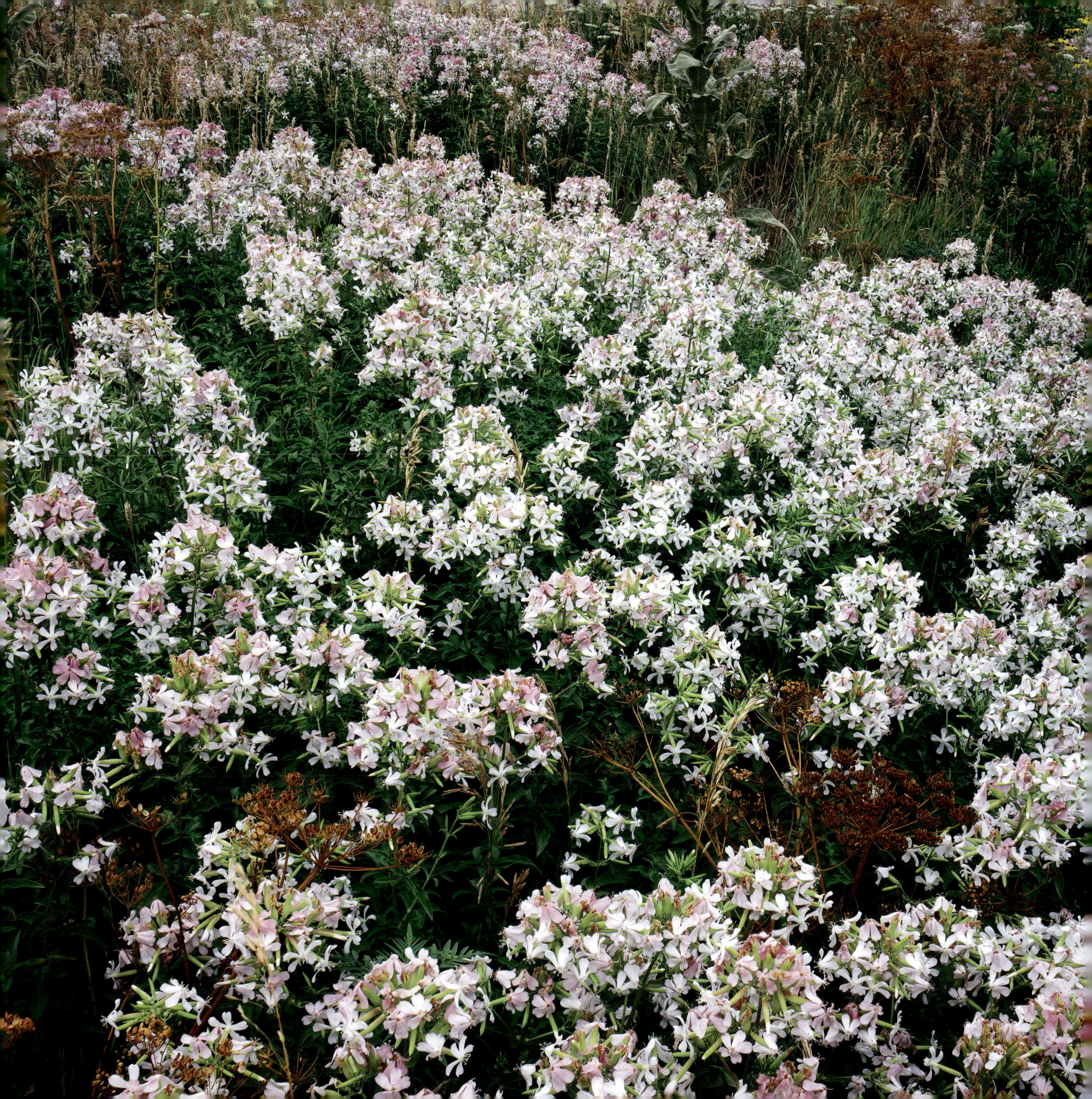

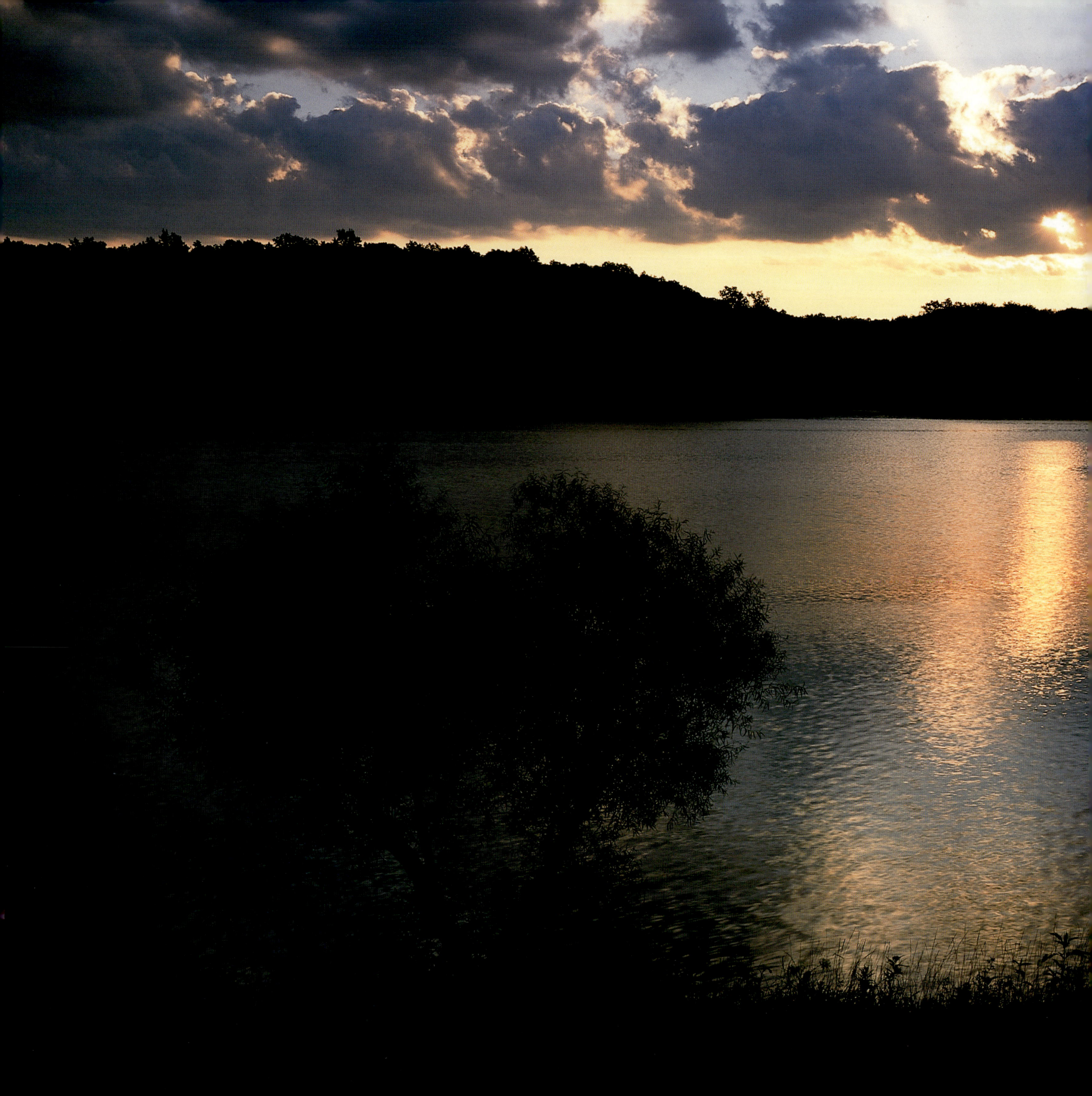

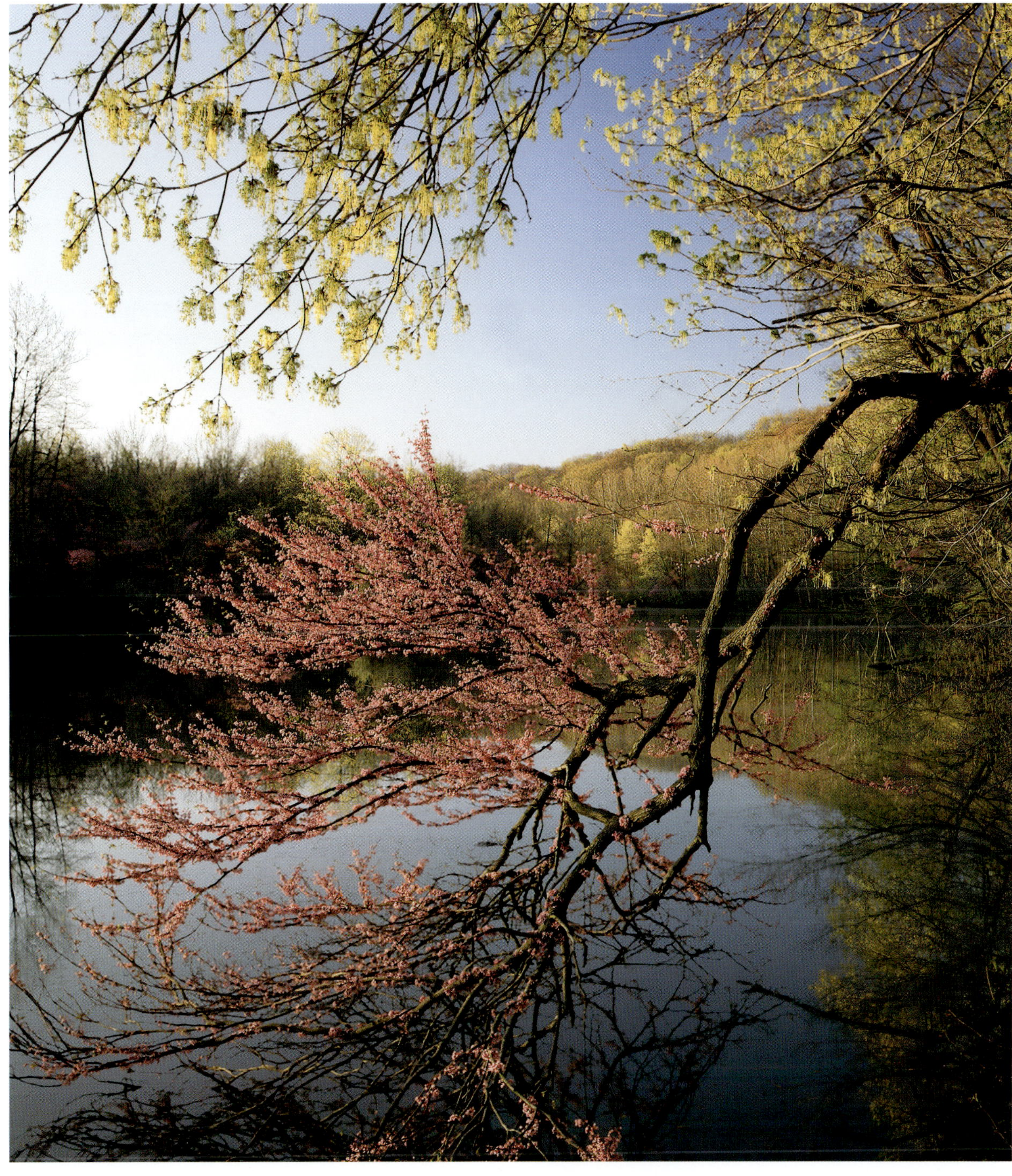

THIS PAGE ABOVE:

Redbud and maple trees lean over Lake 6: Kickapoo State Recreation Area, Vermilion County *(Bloomington Ridged Plain, Till Plains Section, Central Lowland Province)*

Kickapoo State Recreation Area was the first park in the nation built on strip-mined land, purchased from a coal company in 1939 and now largely regenerated. The park's 2,842 acres include lushly forested uplands and bottomlands along the Middle Fork of the Vermilion River. *April 1995*

OPPOSITE PAGE:

Lake Dawson, sunset: Moraine View State Recreation Area, McLean County *(Bloomington Ridged Plain, Till Plains Section, Central Lowland Province)*

The 1,687 acres of Moraine View State Recreation Area are underlain by the midsection of the Bloomington Moraine, which loops across the state from Elgin to Peoria to Saybrook. *August 2001*

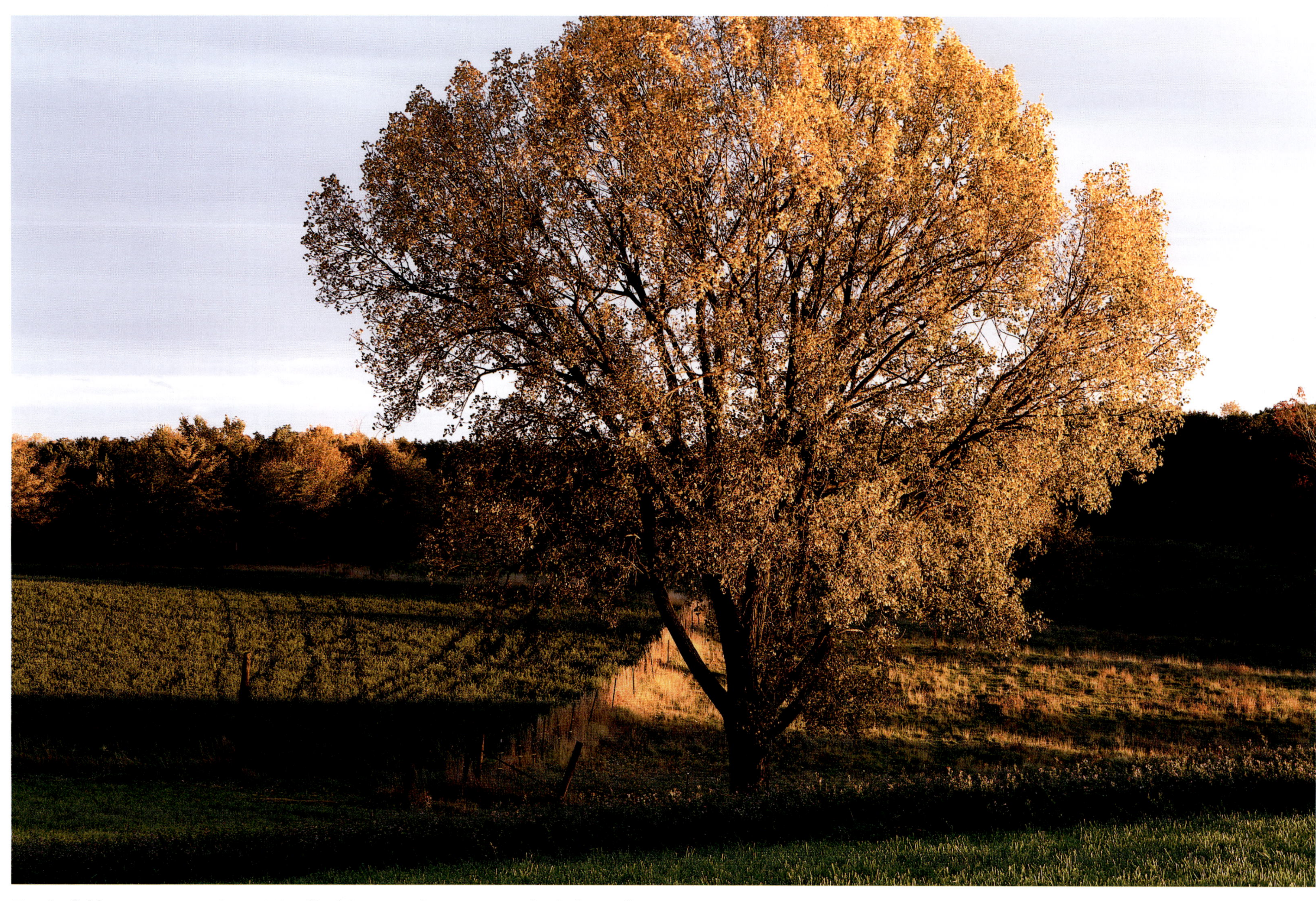

Tree in field at sunset: near Secor, Woodford County *(Bloomington Ridged Plain, Till Plains Section, Central Lowland Province)*
The setting sun broke through a crack in a cloudbank, illuminated the scene for two minutes, and then dropped over the horizon. *October 2001*

ROCK RIVER HILL COUNTRY

TILL PLAINS SECTION OF CENTRAL LOWLAND PROVINCE

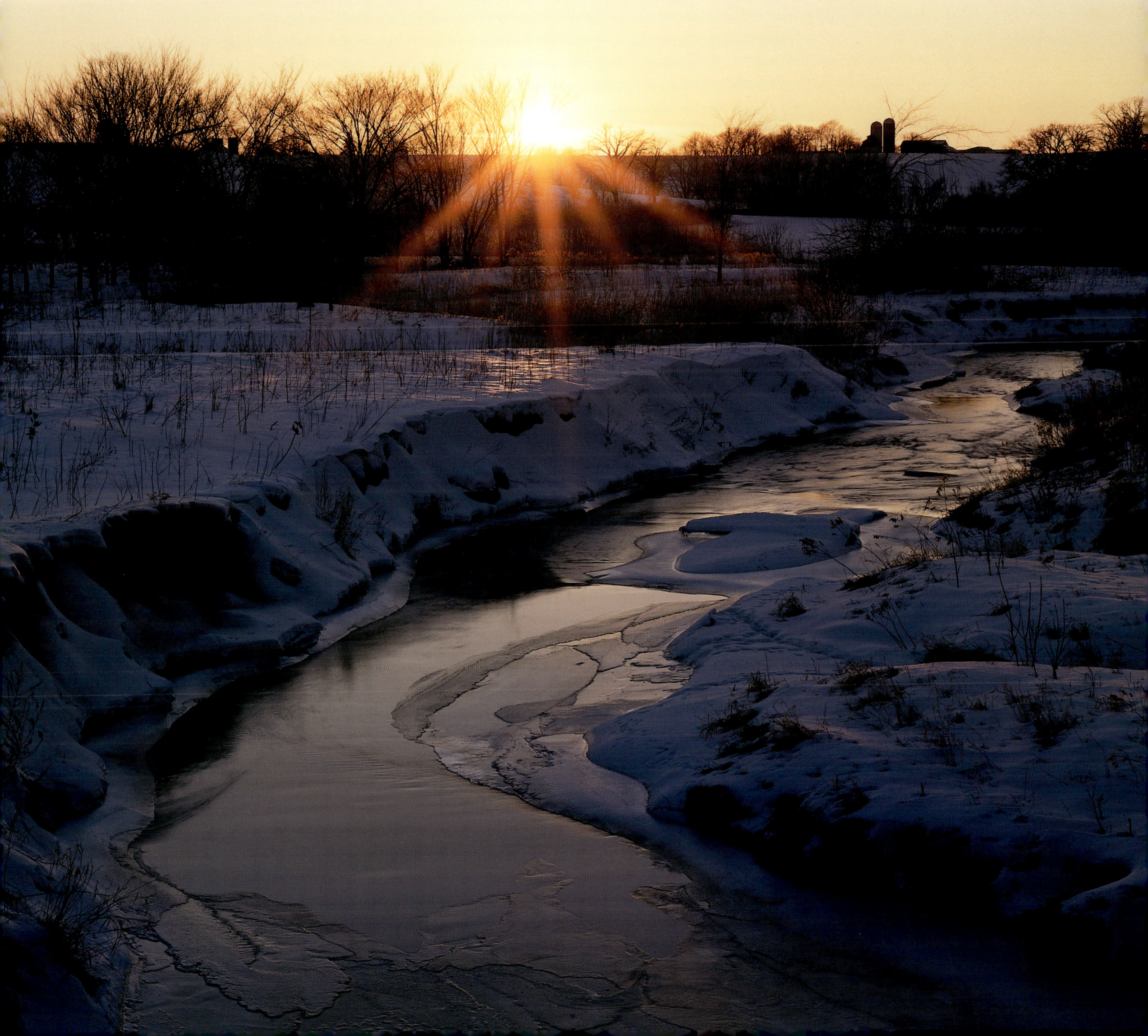

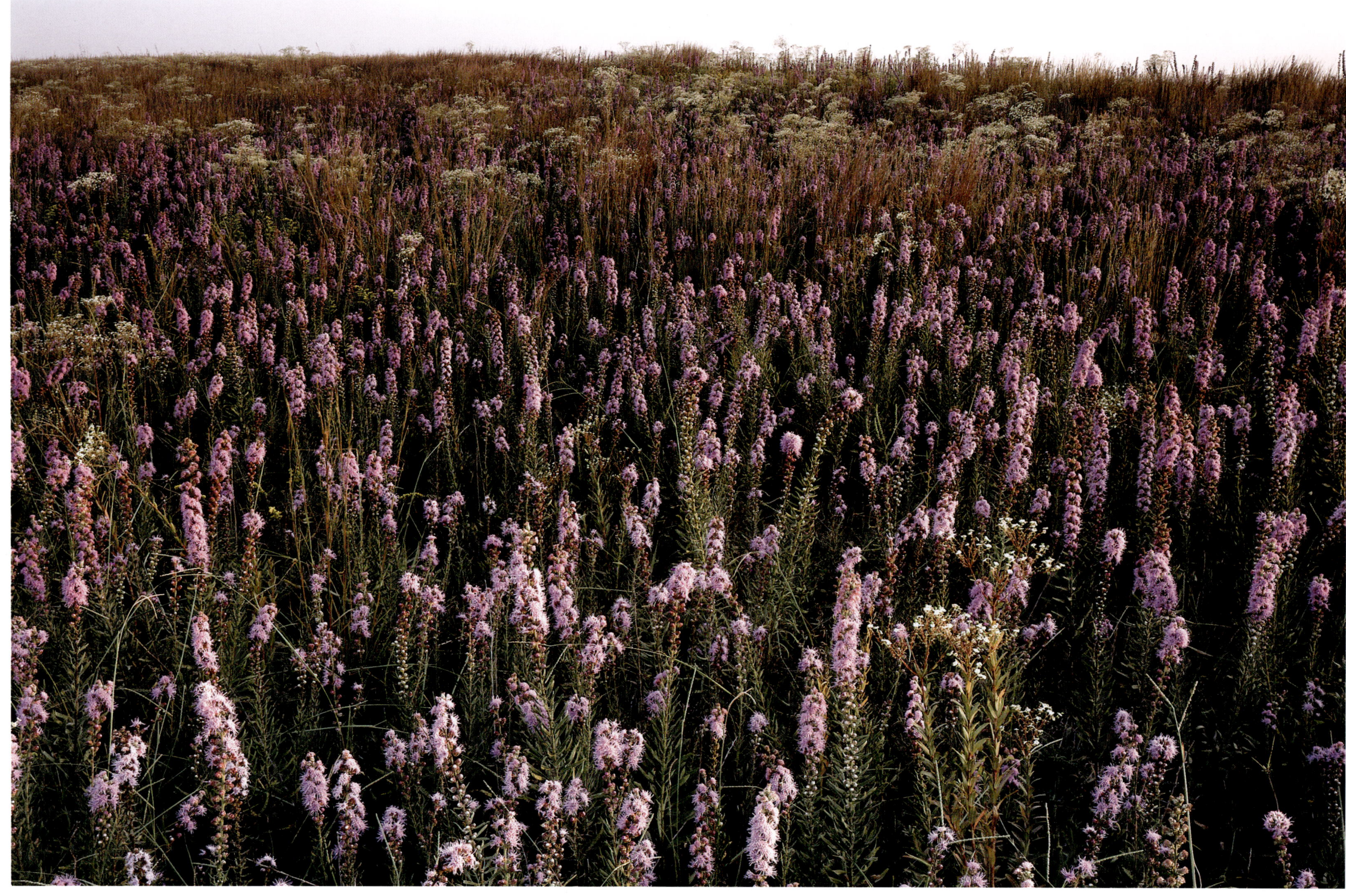

PAGE 95:

Sunset over Franklin Creek: Franklin Creek State Natural Area, Lee County *(Rock River Hill Country, Till Plains Section, Central Lowland Province)*

Franklin Creek State Natural Area encompasses 664 acres near Franklin Grove of hardwood forest, dolomite and sandstone outcrops, and mineral springs. The gorge of Franklin Creek exposes three Ordovician rock formations. At the bottom is the oldest rock formation in the state of Illinois, the New Richmond Sandstone, laid down in the Lower Ordovician, half-a-billion years ago. Above it lie the Shakopee Formation, a sandy dolomite, and the St. Peter Sandstone, laid down in the Middle Ordovician, 460 million years old. Away from these outcrops in the gorge, the bedrock is deeply mantled with till and loess of the Wisconsin glacial episode. *January 1991*

THIS PAGE:

Tall gayfeather *(Liatris pycnostachya)*: Nachusa Grasslands, Lee County *(Rock River Hill Country, Till Plains Section, Central Lowland Province)*

In 1986, the Illinois Nature Conservancy acquired the Nachusa Grasslands, a rolling 2,000-acre tract near Franklin Grove that is a mosaic of eleven floral communities and the third largest prairie remnant in Illinois. Steep sandstone outcrops descending into rocky meadows made the Nachusa Grasslands difficult to plow and so spared it from destruction. *September 1995*

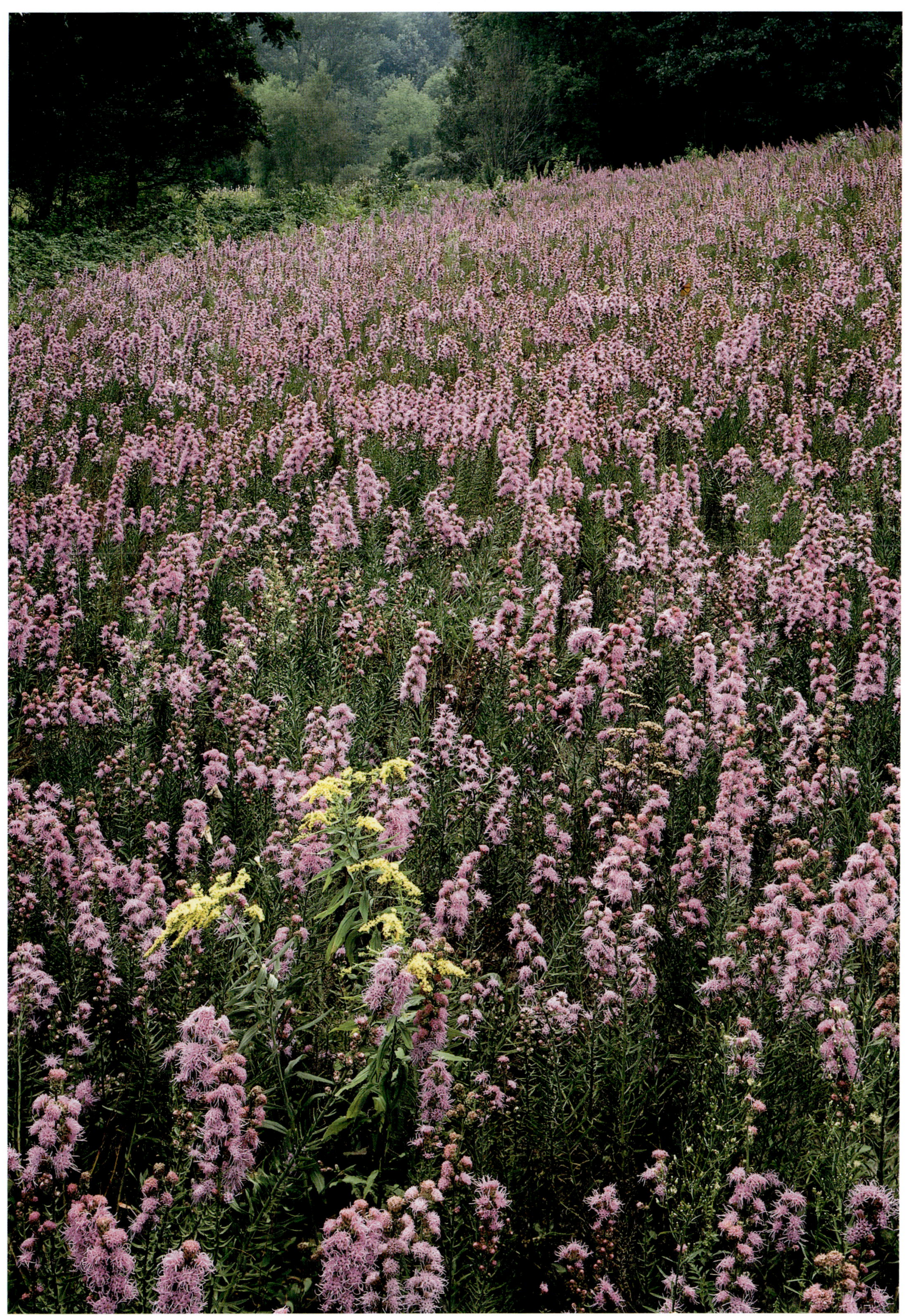

OPPOSITE PAGE:

Blazing star *(Liatris aspera)*: Nachusa Grasslands, Lee County *(Rock River Hill Country, Till Plains Section, Central Lowland Province)*

In 1989, this hillside in the Nachusa Grasslands bloomed with a profusion of blazing star that this photographer has not seen since in that location. What combination of conditions triggered this event in 1989 is not understood. *September 1989*

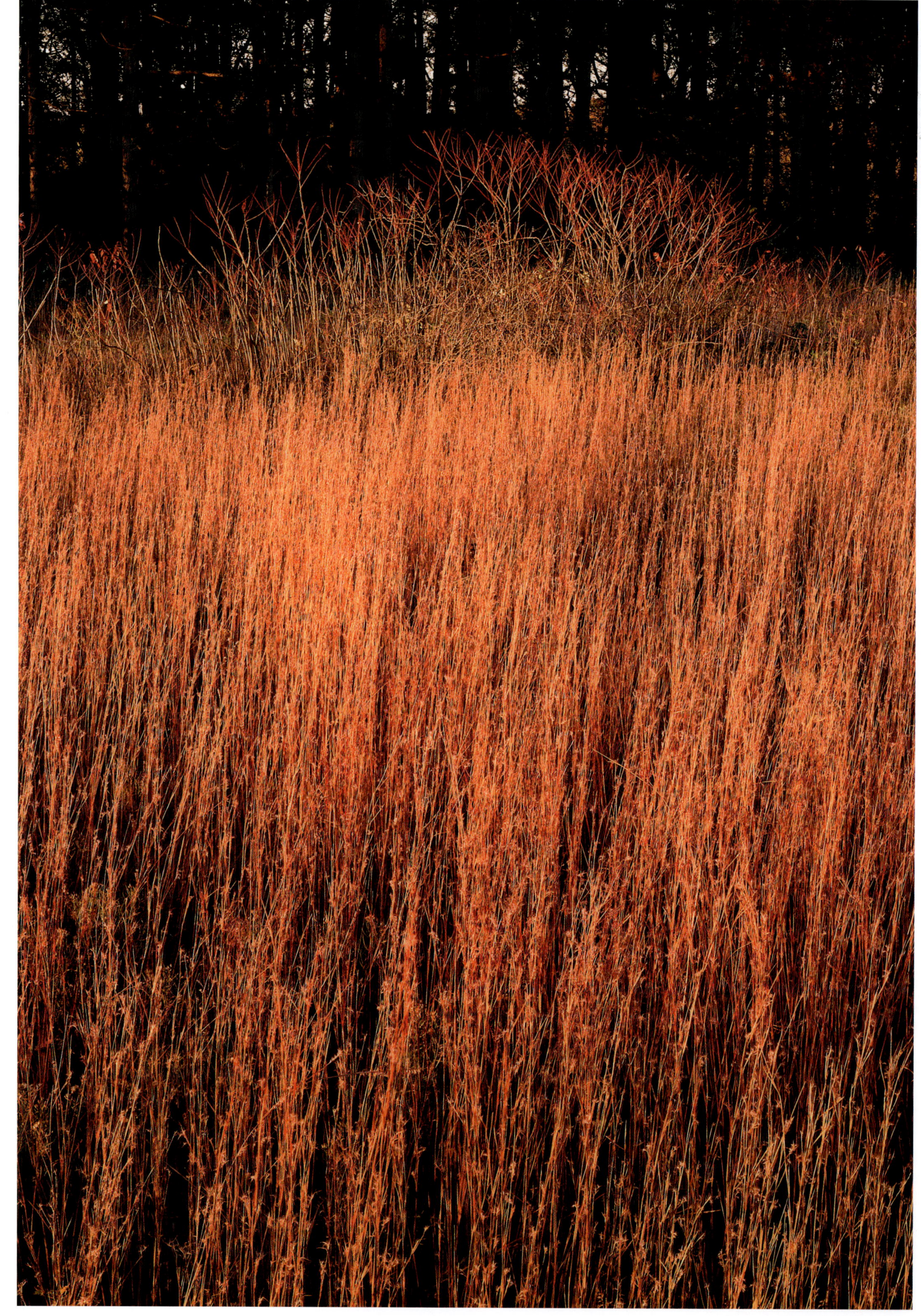

THIS PAGE:

Little bluestem (*Schizachyrium scoparium*) and sumacs: Nachusa Grasslands, Lee County *(Rock River Hill Country, Till Plains Section, Central Lowland Province)*

The Nachusa Grasslands are a fertile environment for prairie grasses, especially little bluestem, which is found in virtually all natural grasslands in the United States. In a state that has lost the vast majority of its natural prairies, Nachusa Grasslands is a rich source of little bluestem seed, harvested for propagation projects after the grass turns golden color in the fall. *October 1996*

OPPOSITE PAGE:

Gable end of red barn and silo: Lee County *(Rock River Hill Country, Till Plains Section, Central Lowland Province)*

January 1991

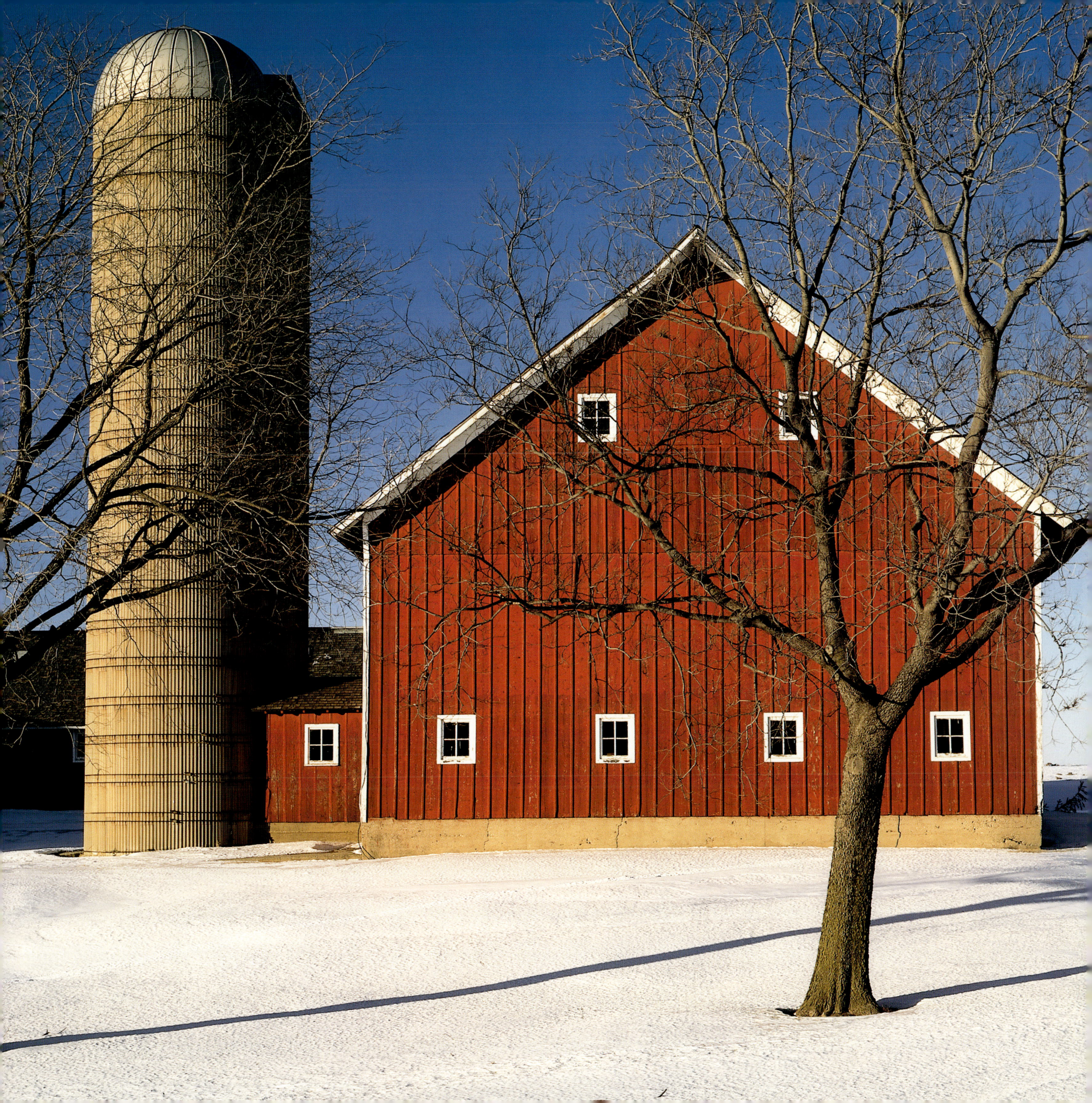

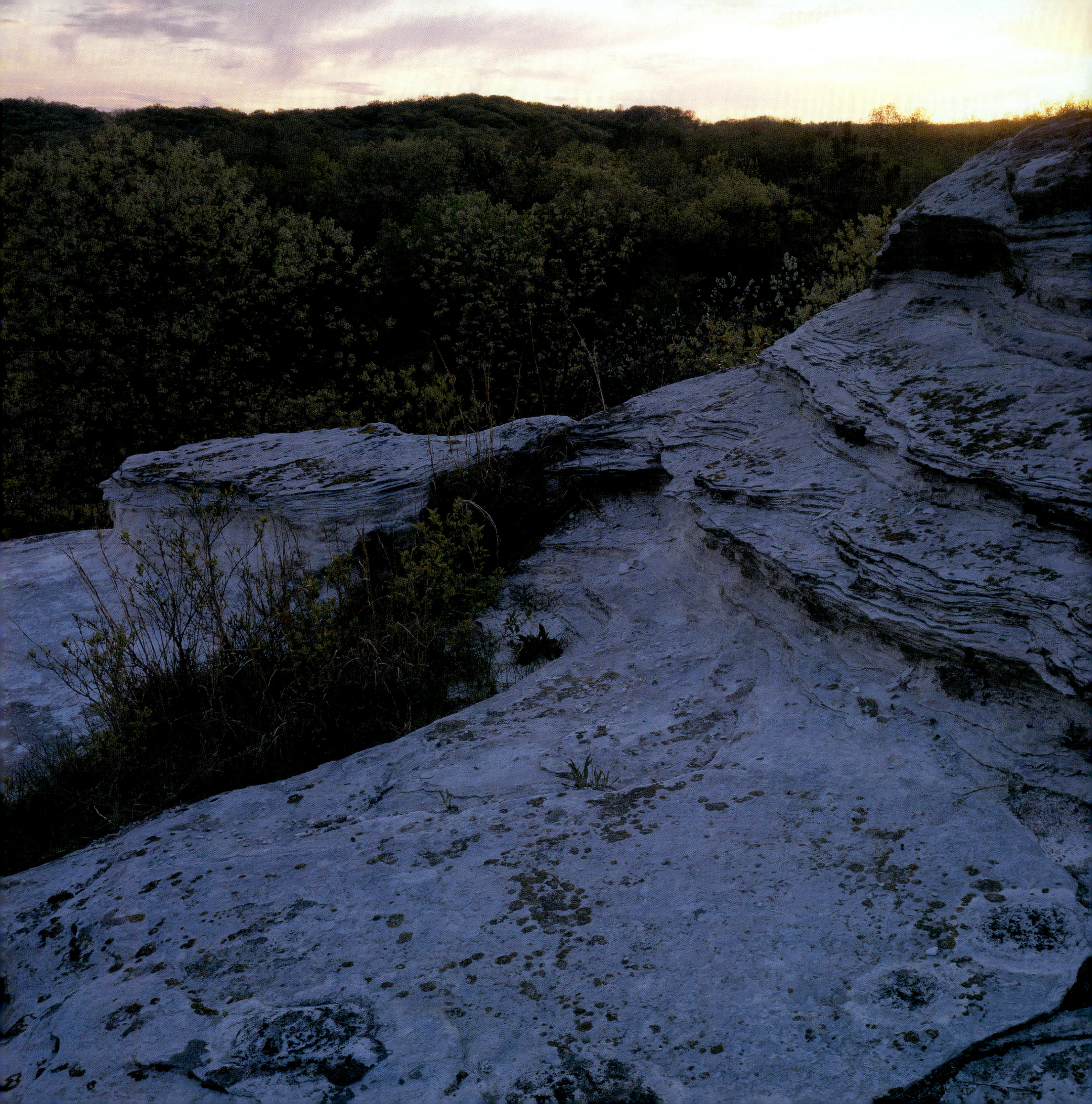

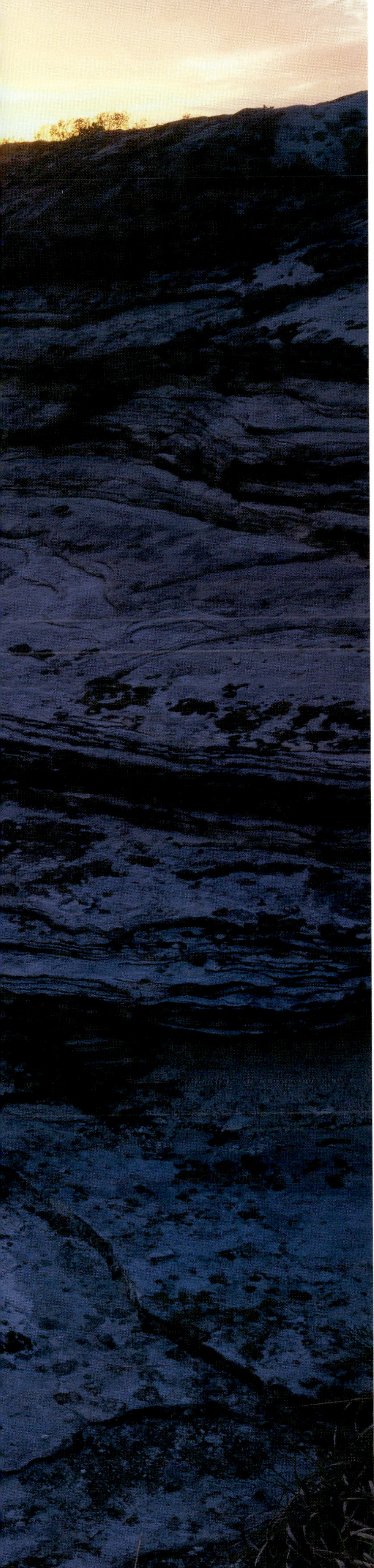

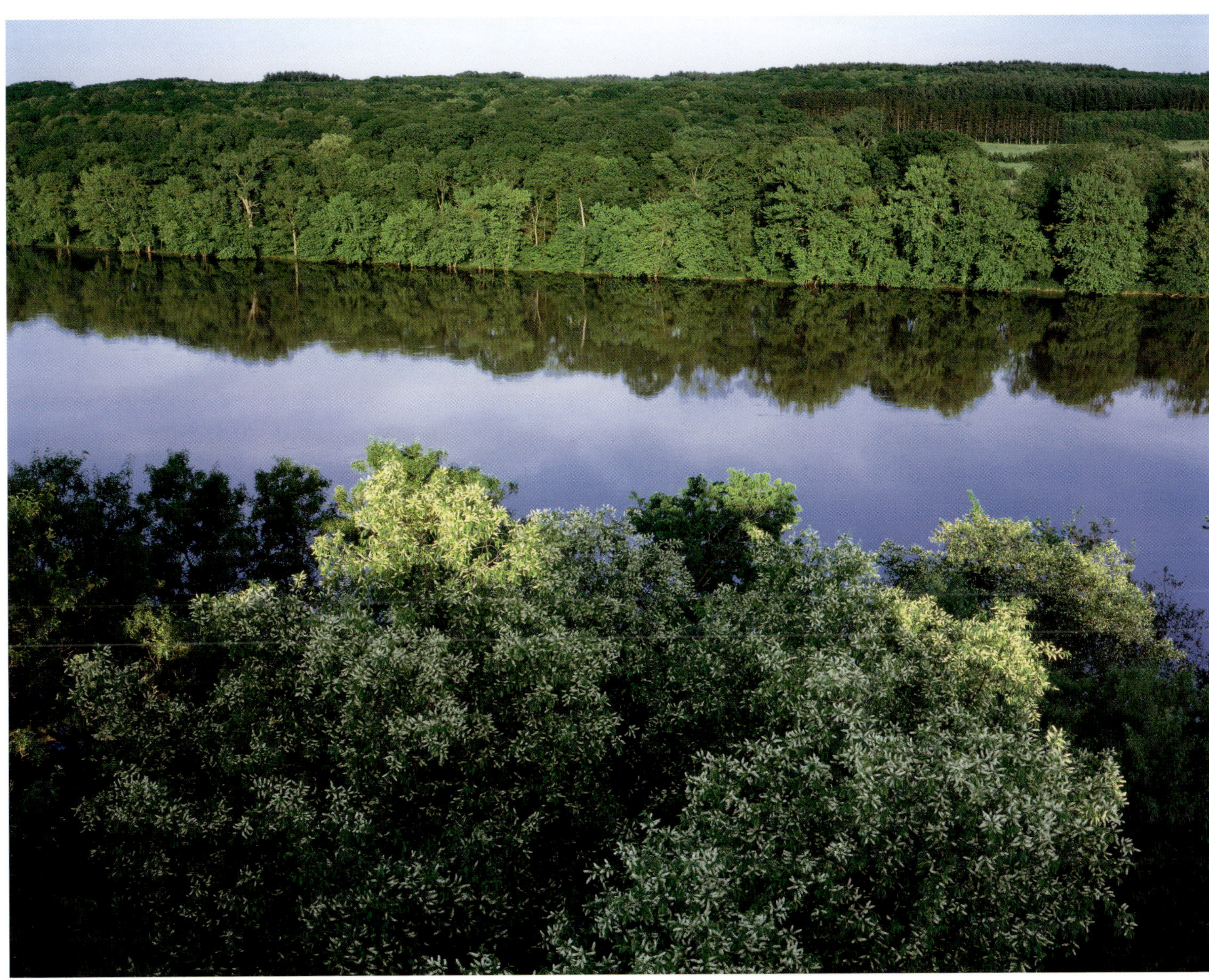

THIS PAGE ABOVE:

Rock River vista from Castle Rock at sunset: Castle Rock State Park, Ogle County *(Rock River Hill Country, Till Plains Section, Central Lowland Province)*
Castle Rock State Park exemplifies the features characteristic of the Rock River Hill Country, including bedrock exposures, ravines, a thin layer of glacial till, and northern plant associations. In one valley, 27 different types of ferns have been identified. *May 1999*

OPPOSITE PAGE:

Castle Rock sandstone bluff at sunset: Castle Rock State Park, Ogle County *(Rock River Hill Country, Till Plains Section, Central Lowland Province)*
The two thousand rolling acres on the west bank of the Rock River a few miles south of Oregon were dedicated Castle Rock State Park in 1978. The park's name derives from the prominent butte of that name, which overlooks the Rock River and is made of St. Peter Sandstone, laid down in the Middle Ordovician 460 million years ago. *May 1995*

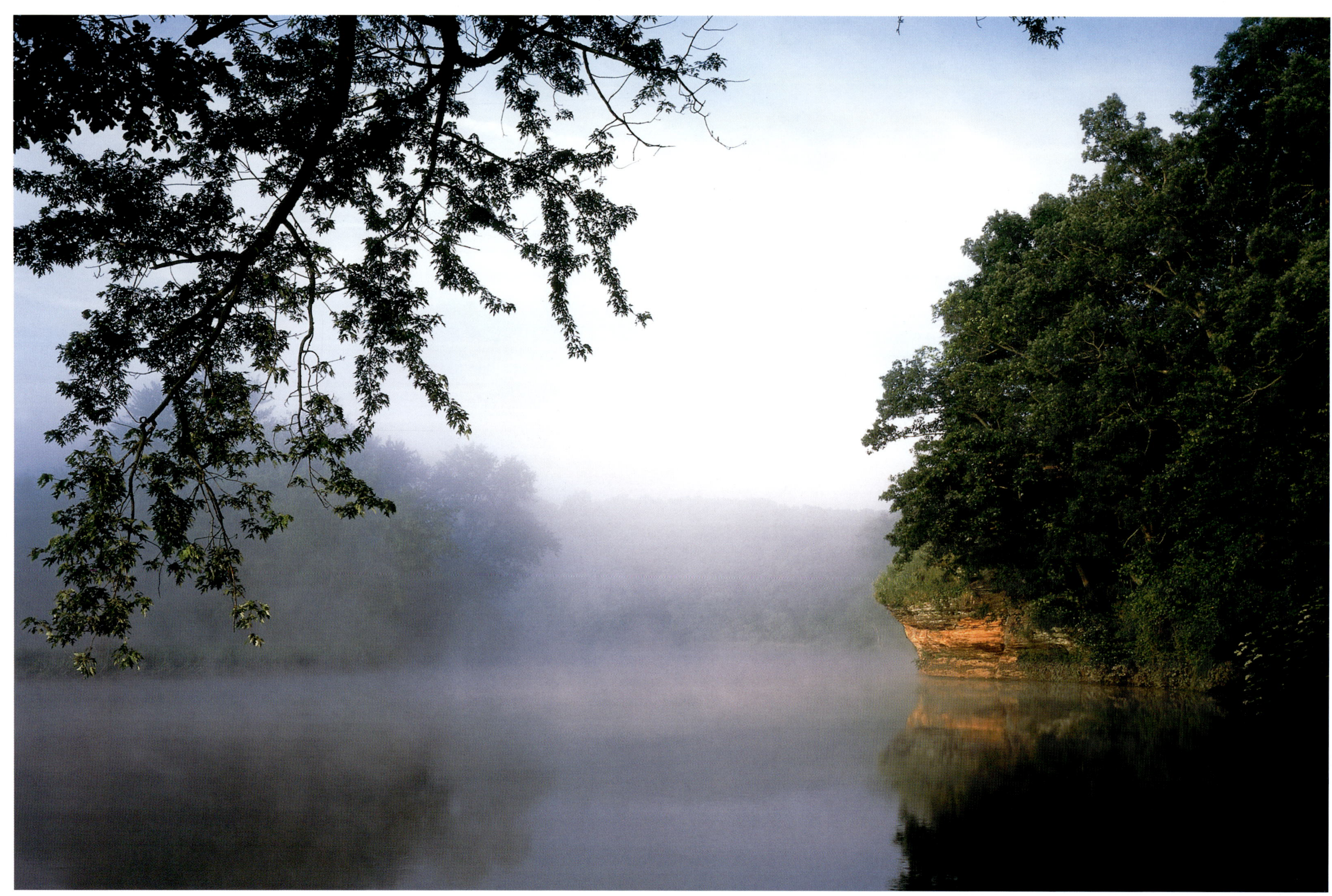

Foggy sunrise vista of Rock River from Castle Rock: Castle Rock State Park, Ogle County *(Rock River Hill Country, Till Plains Section, Central Lowland Province)*
June 1999

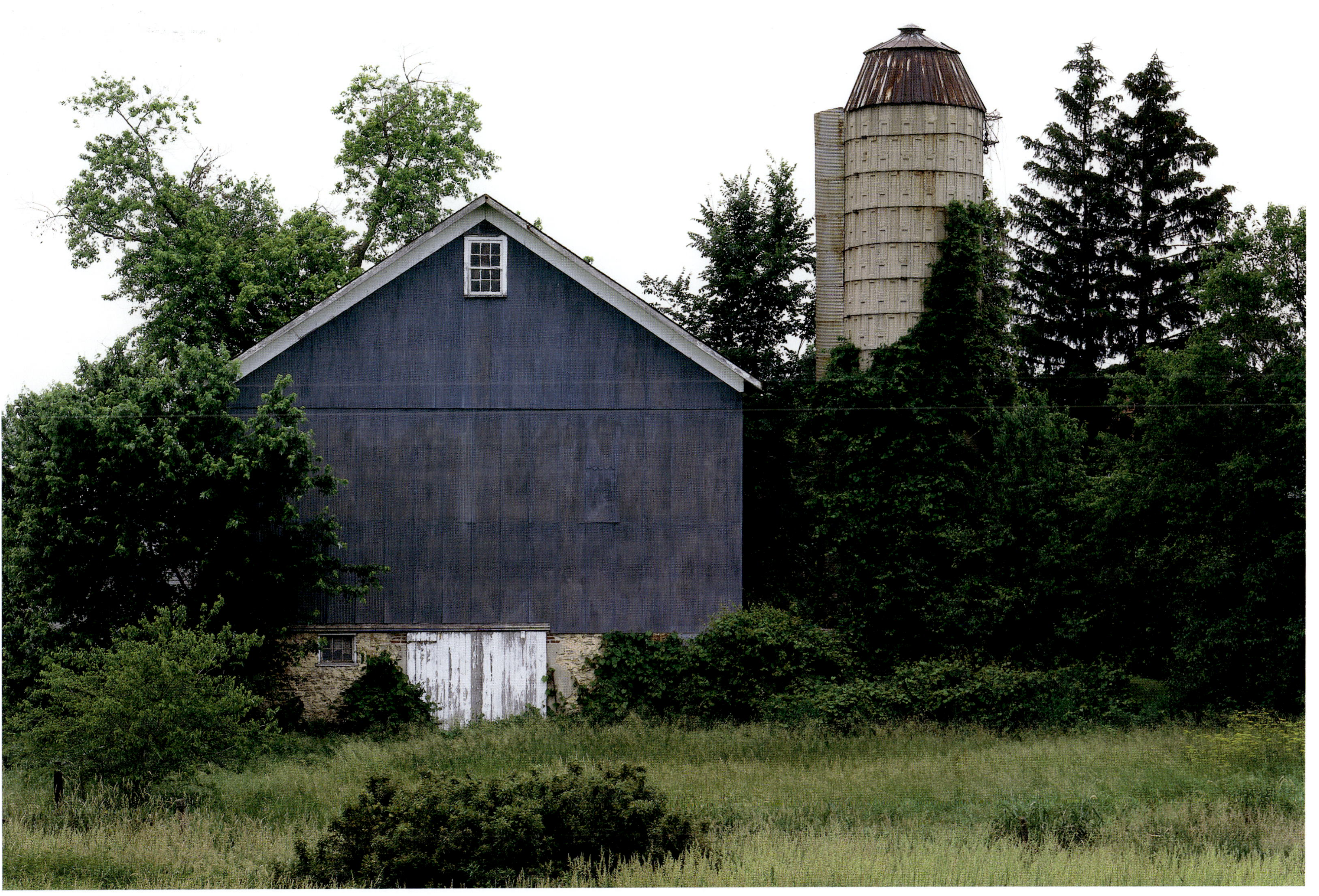

THIS PAGE:

Disused barn and concrete silo: near Dakota, Stephenson County *(Rock River Hill Country, Till Plains Section, Central Lowland Province)*
June 1999

PAGES 104-105:

Farm and contoured seedlings in evening: Stephenson County *(Rock River Hill Country, Till Plains Section, Central Lowland Province)*
The northern Illinois counties on the Wisconsin border contain some of the most picturesque farm scenes in the state. The pastoral tableaux of rolling topography, neat buildings, and geometric plantings attract many painters and photographers. *June 1999*

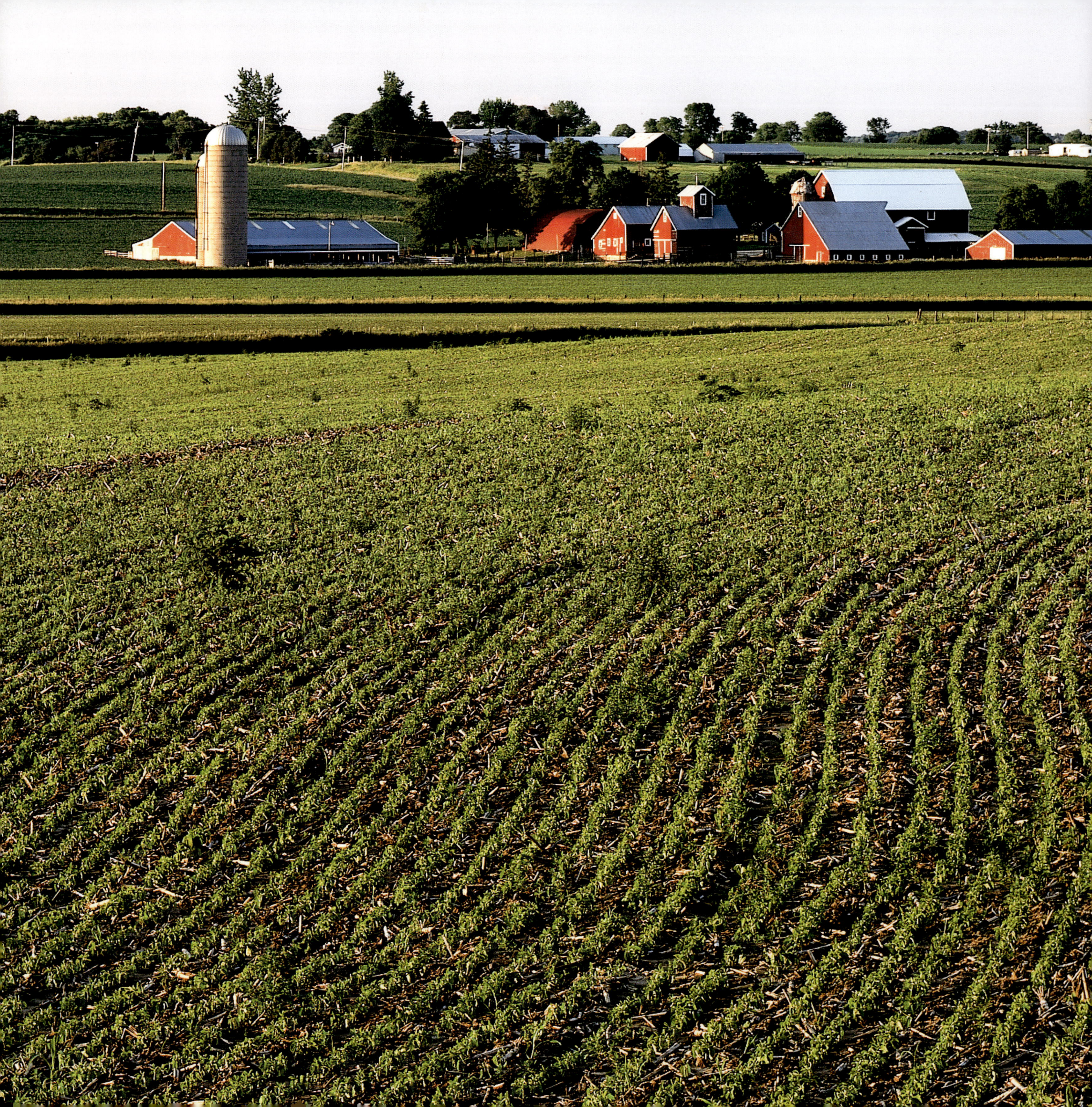

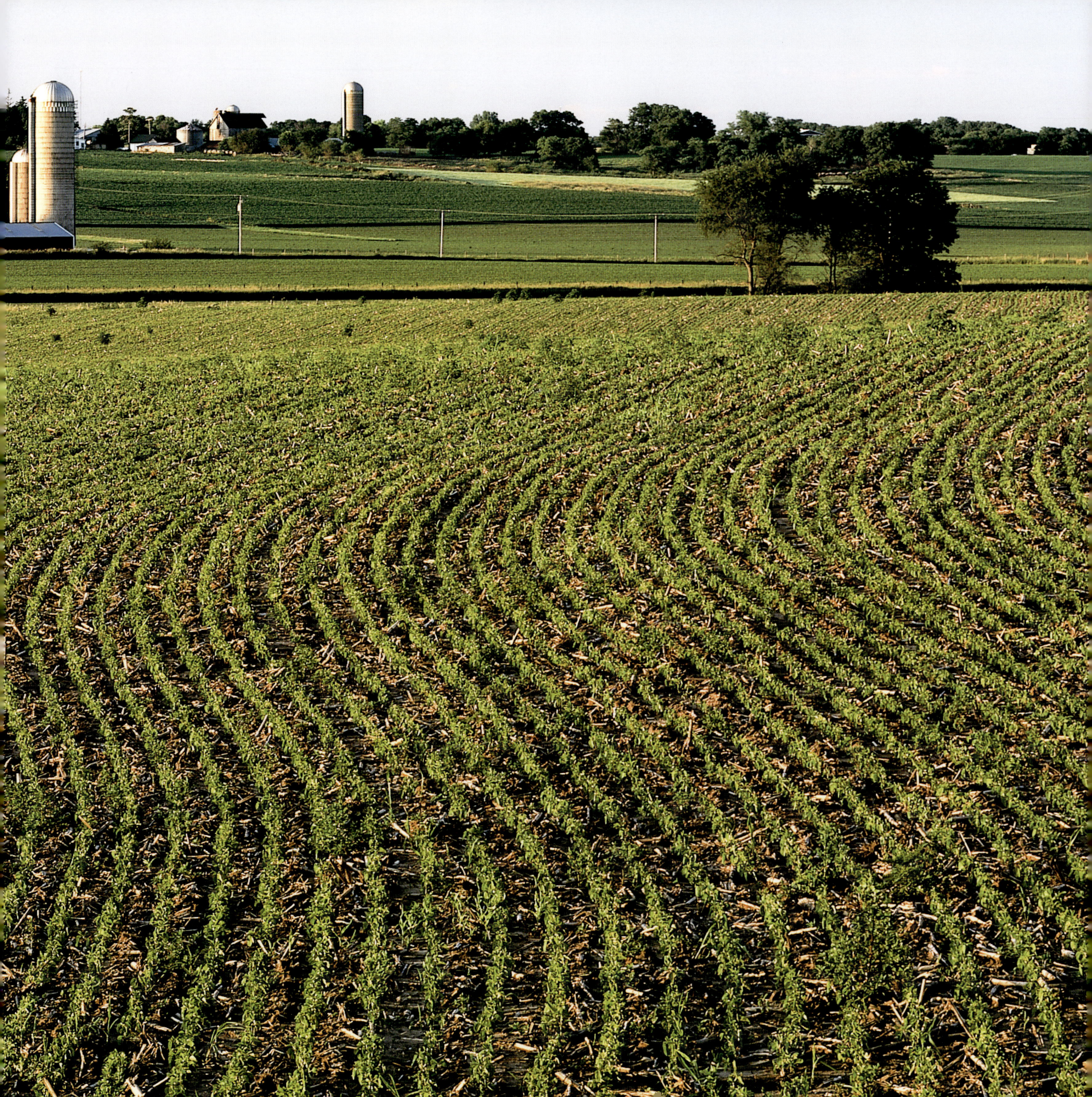

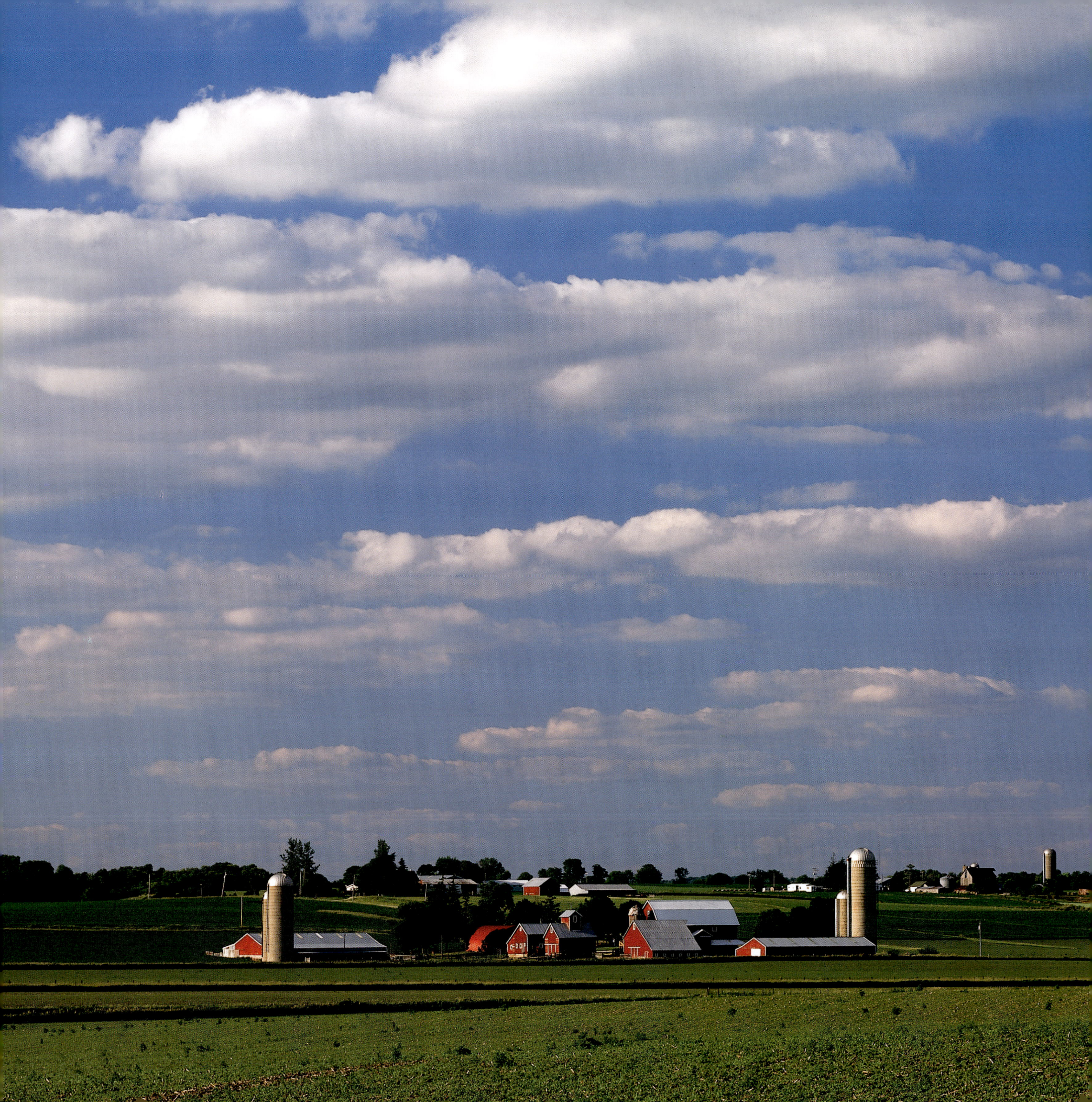

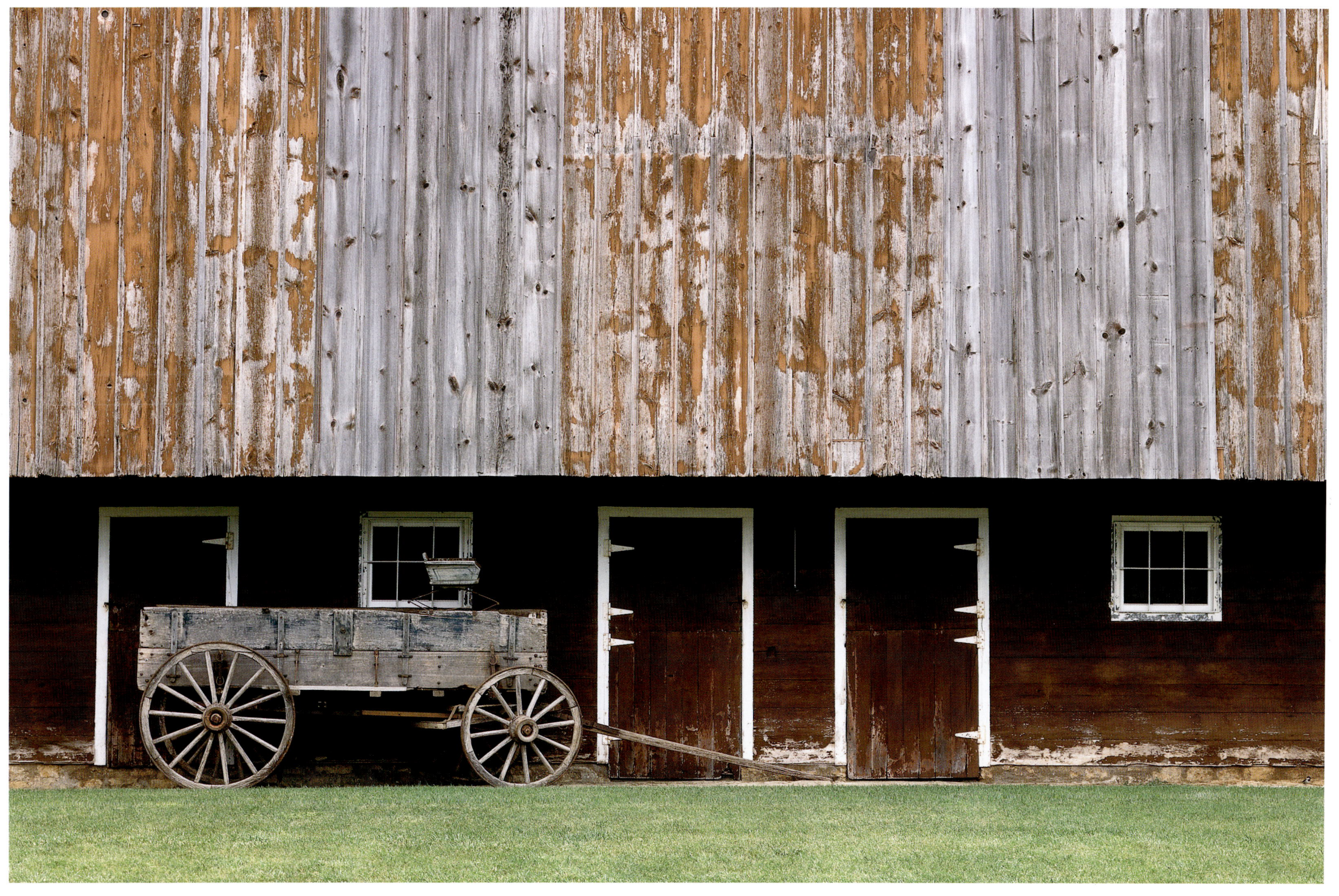

THIS PAGE:

Detail of old barn: near Cedarville, Stephenson County *(Rock River Hill Country, Till Plains Section, Central Lowland Province)*
John Kratzer built this barn in the mid-nineteenth century. *June 1999*

OPPOSITE PAGE:

Farm and contoured seedlings in evening: Stephenson County *(Rock River Hill Country, Till Plains Section, Central Lowland Province)*
June 1999

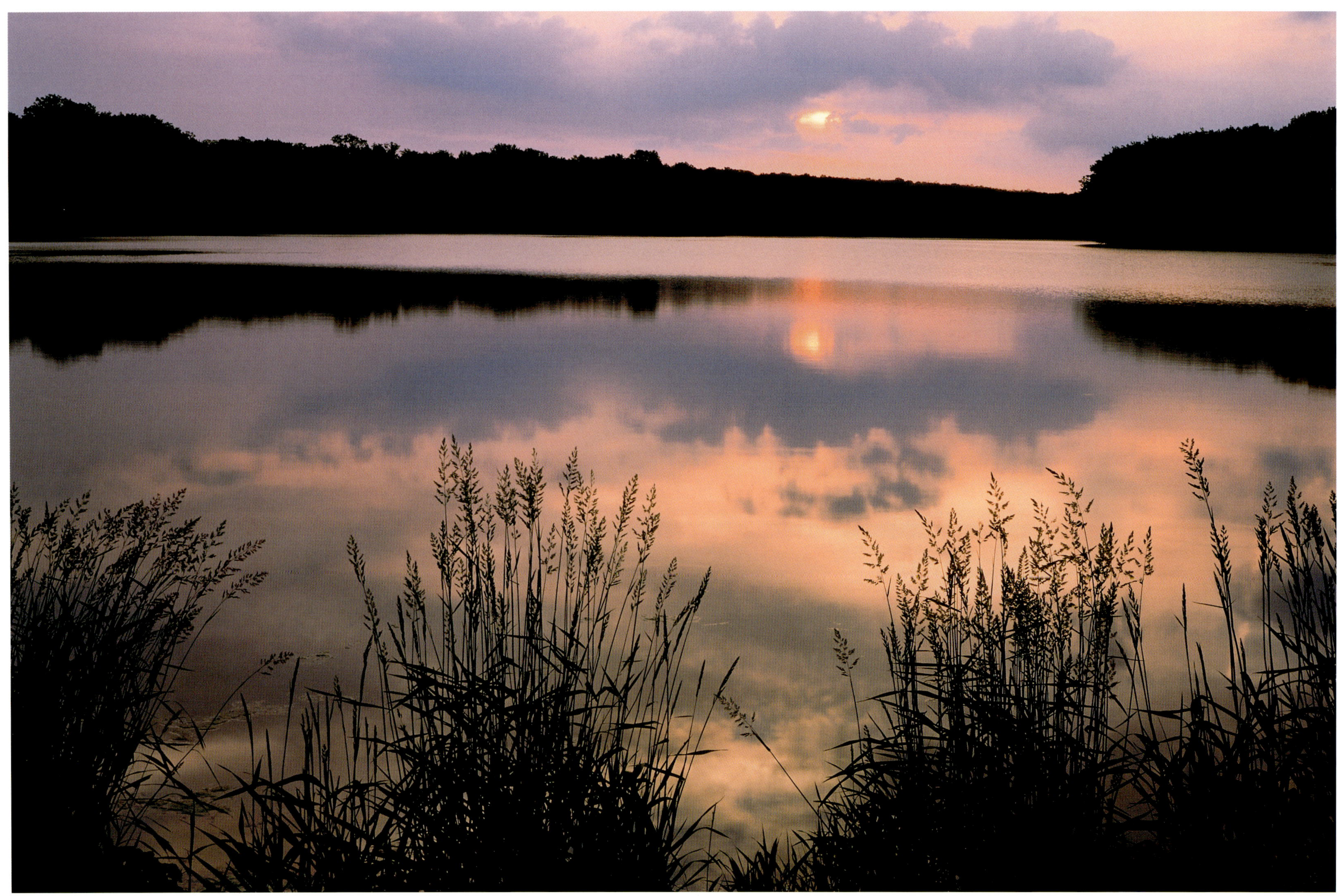

Sunset on Lake Le-Aqua-Na: Lake Le-Aqua-Na State Recreation Area, Stephenson County *(Rock River Hill Country, Till Plains Section, Central Lowland Province)*
The sun breaks through clearing storm clouds at sunset over 40-acre Lake Le-Aqua-Na, six miles from the Wisconsin border. For many years, Lake Le-Aqua-Na State Recreation Area was a border haven for fugitive badgers from Wisconsin. Lake Le-Aqua-Na's fractured name was the winning entry in a contest to name the new artificial lake in 1956. "Le-Aqua-Na"—derived by squirting the word "aqua" between the constituent syllables of the name of nearby town of Lena—is said by old-timers to have beaten out "Aq-Lena-Ua" by a whisker. The name of the lake is kept well mixed by the same axial-flow destratifier that is used to keep the lake well mixed. *June 1999*

OPPOSITE PAGE:

Blazing star *(Liatris pycnostrachya)* and goldenrod *(Solidago rigida)*: Searls Park Prairie Nature Preserve, Rockford, Winnebago County *(Rock River Hill Country, Till Plains Section, Central Lowland Province)*
Located within the city of Rockford, Searls Park Prairie Nature Preserve is a 66-acre black-soil prairie typical of the Rock River Hill Country, consisting of both mesic prairie (dominated by prairie dropseed, Indian grass, and little bluestem) and wet prairie (dominated by tussock sedge, blue-joint grass, and cord grass). *July 1987*

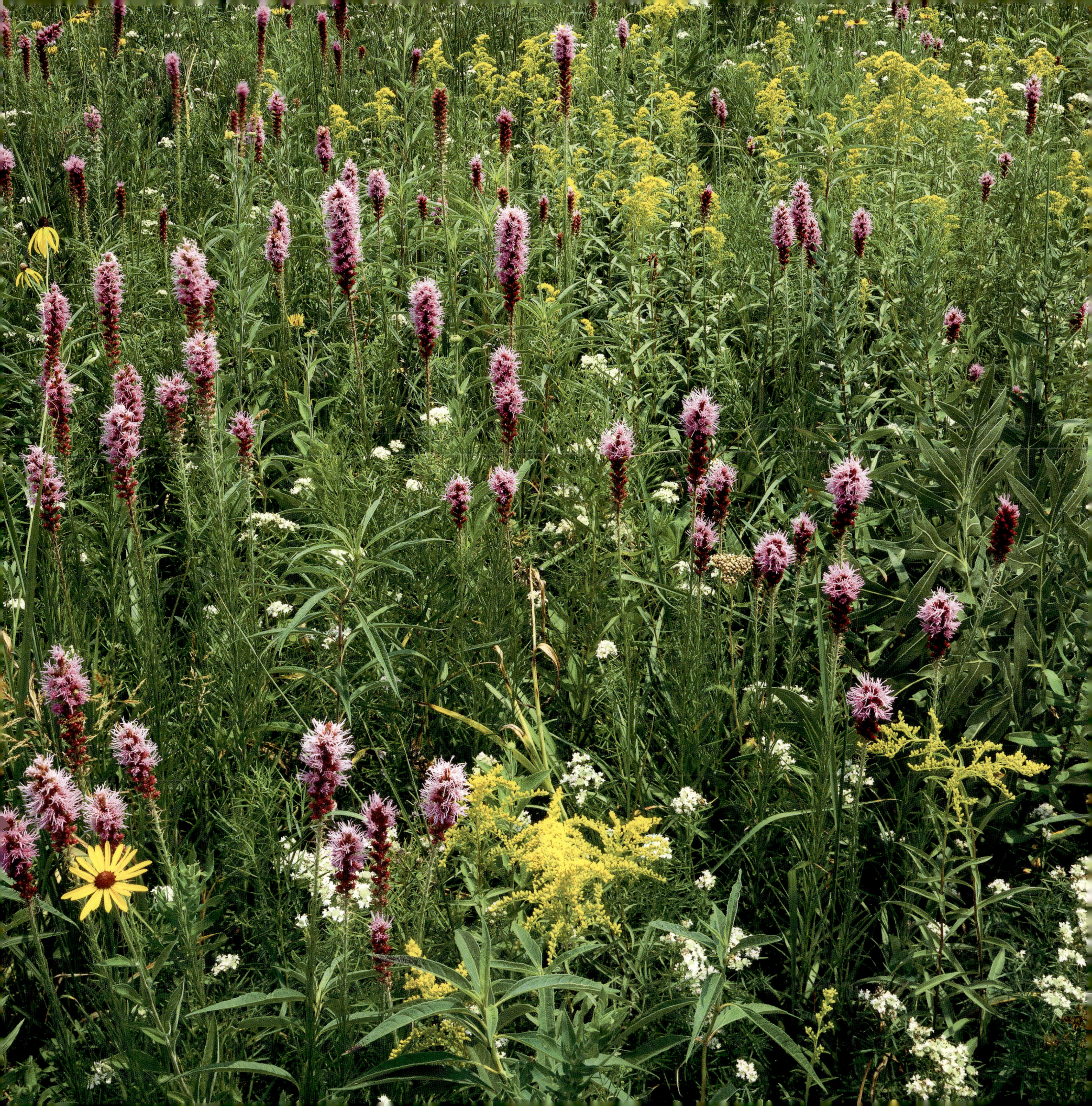

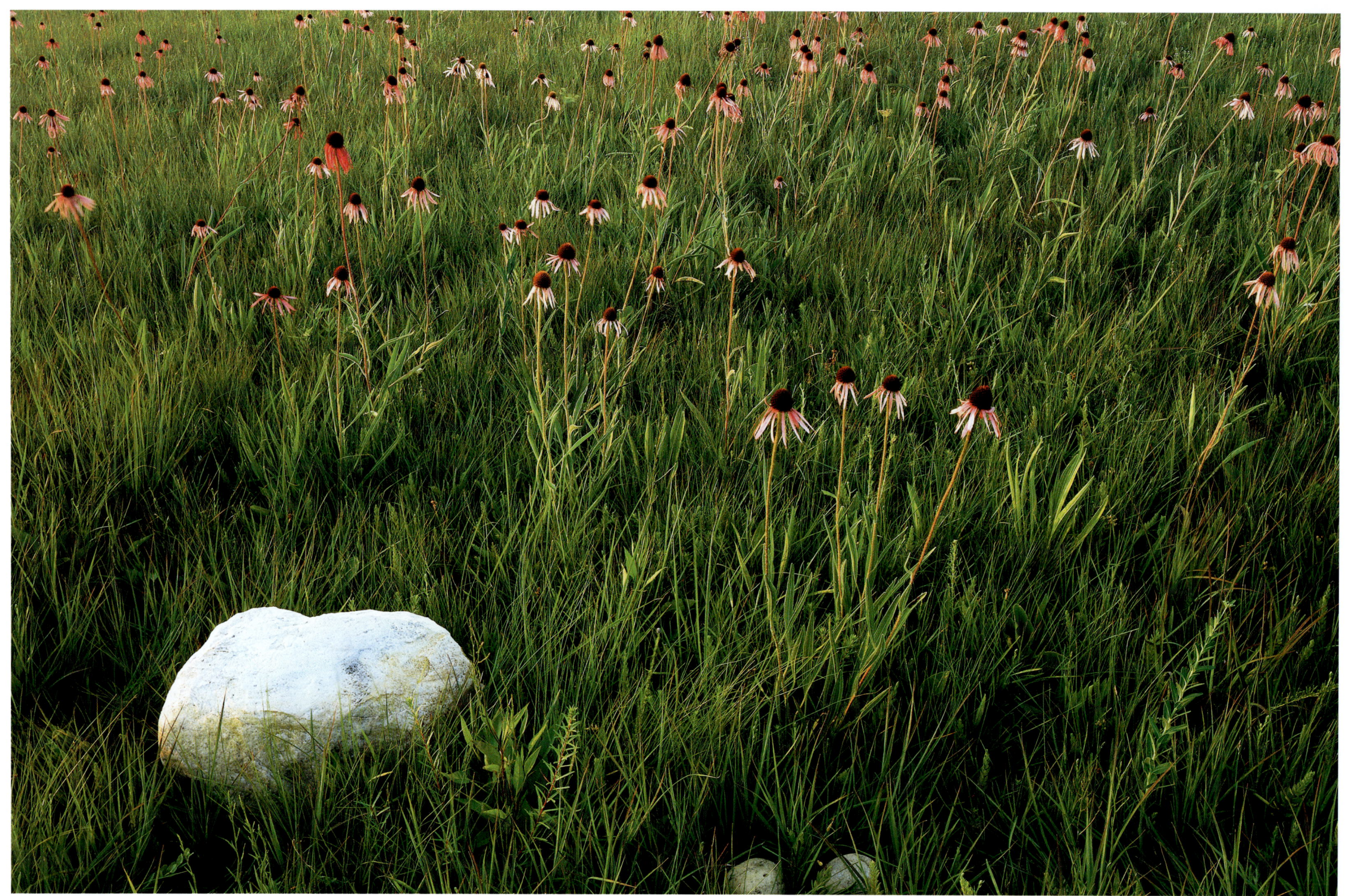

Pale prairie coneflower: Harlem Hills Prairie Preserve, Winnebago County *(Rock River Hill Country, Till Plains Section, Central Lowland Province)*

As the terrain that favored the prairies that once covered nearly three-fifths of Illinois also favors housing development, efforts to preserve prairie vestiges in residential areas have become critical. Harlem Hills Prairie Preserve, located within a residential development in Rockford, is Illinois's largest and finest surviving example of a gravel hill prairie. There are a large number of wildflowers, especially the pale prairie coneflower *(Echinacea pallida)*. In the spring, pasque flowers appear. Rare plants include pink milkwort, downy yellow painted cup, Hill's thistle, and prairie buttercup. *July 1995*

OPPOSITE PAGE:

Sunset over flat farmland: Bureau County *(Green River Lowland, Till Plains Section, Central Lowland Province)*

In a natural analogue of a Chuck Close grid, the geometry of bare boughs divides up the cloud formations of a Midwestern sunset sky for closer study. *January 1991*

GREEN RIVER LOWLAND

TILL PLAINS SECTION OF CENTRAL LOWLAND PROVINCE

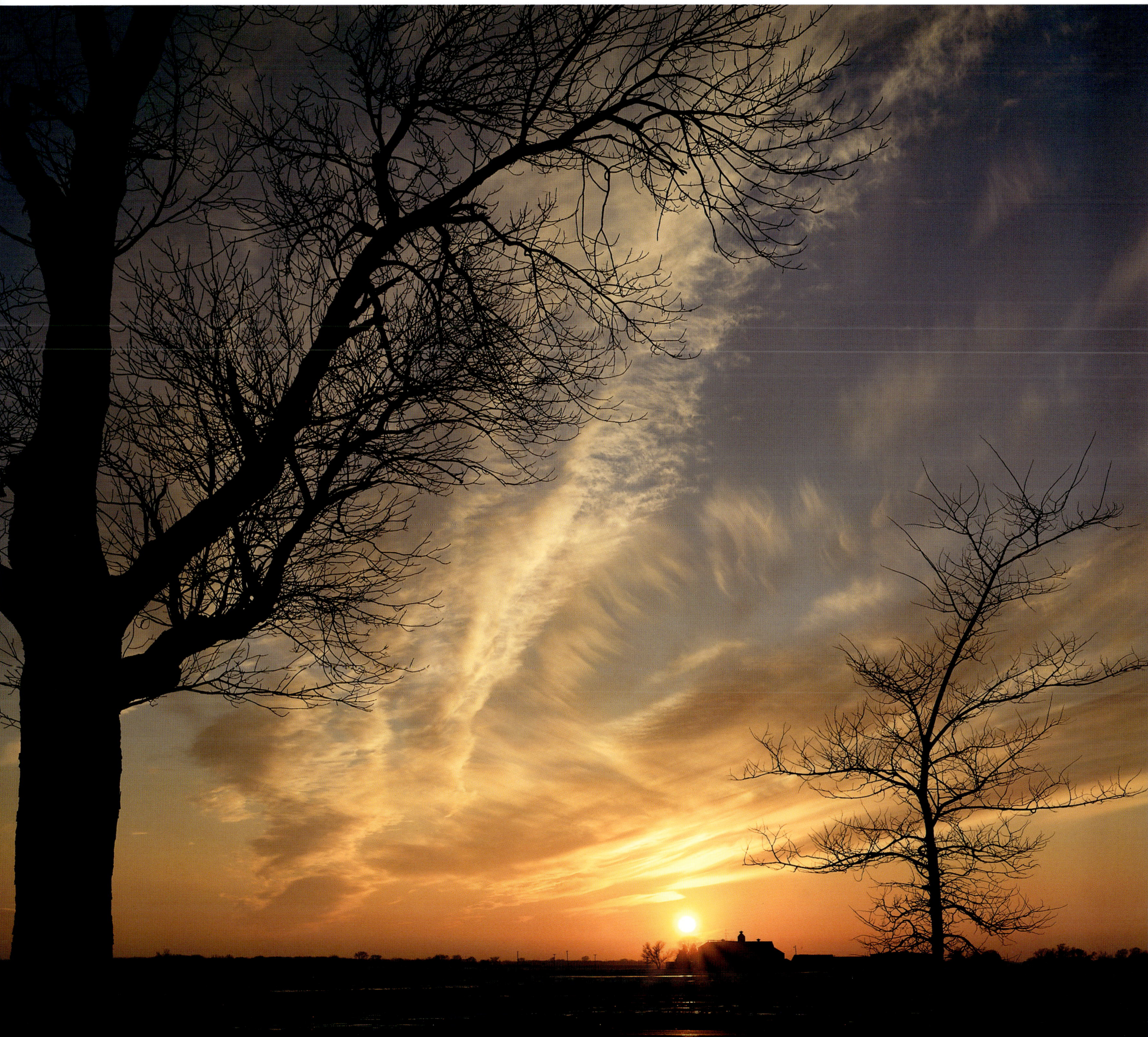

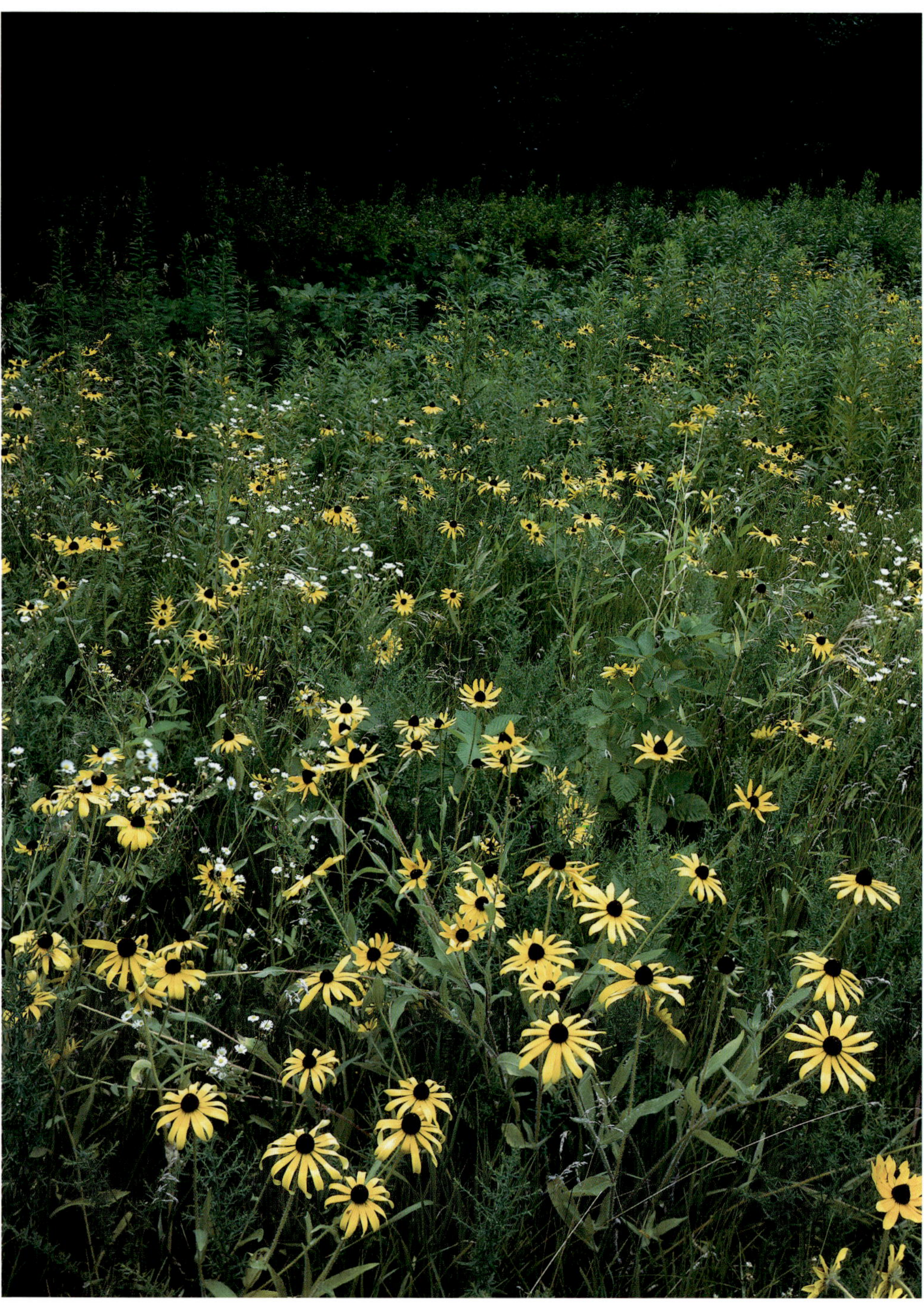

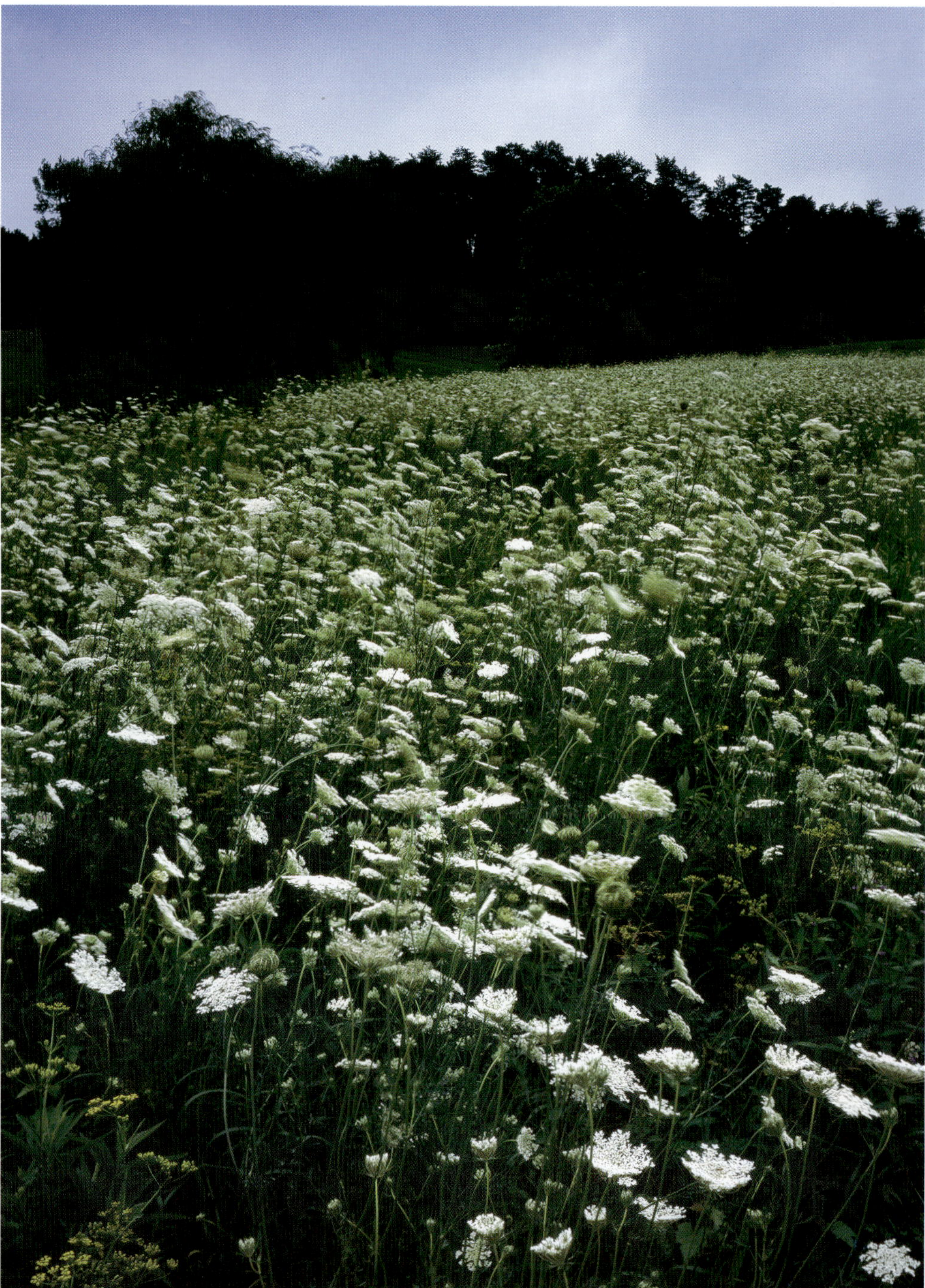

THIS PAGE LEFT:

Field of black-eyed Susans on the edge of forest: Johnson-Sauk Trail State Park, Henry County *(Green River Lowland, Till Plains Section, Central Lowland Province)*
No flower is more characteristic of the Midwest summer than the ubiquitous black-eyed Susan *(Rudbeckia hirta)*. The glacial moraine that underlies the rolling hills of 1,365-acre Johnson-Sauk Trail State Park supports wildflowers and hardwood/pine forests. *July 2001*

THIS PAGE RIGHT:

Field of Queen Anne's lace on the edge of forest: rainy day: Johnson-Sauk Trail State Park, Henry County *(Green River Lowland, Till Plains Section, Central Lowland Province)*
Common throughout the state, Queen Anne's lace *(Daucus carota)* is a wild form of the domesticated carrot that flowers in profusion along roadsides and on glacial moraine hills. Legend has it that the tiny dark red flower in the center of the inflorescence commemorates blood shed during Queen Anne's War (1701-1713). This introduced biennial forb is an ecologically invasive species. *July 2001*

GALESBURG PLAIN

TILL PLAINS SECTION OF CENTRAL LOWLAND PROVINCE

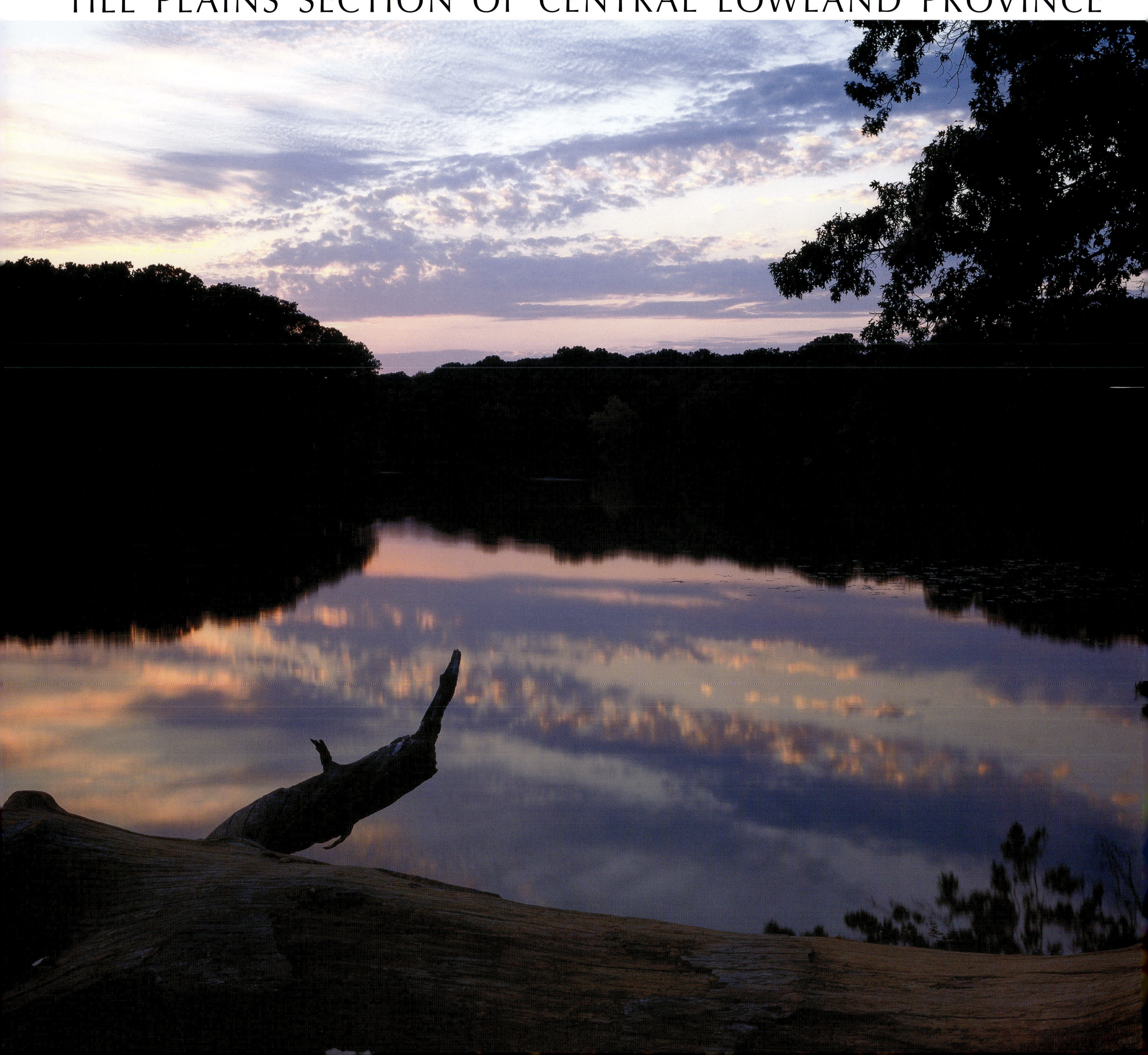

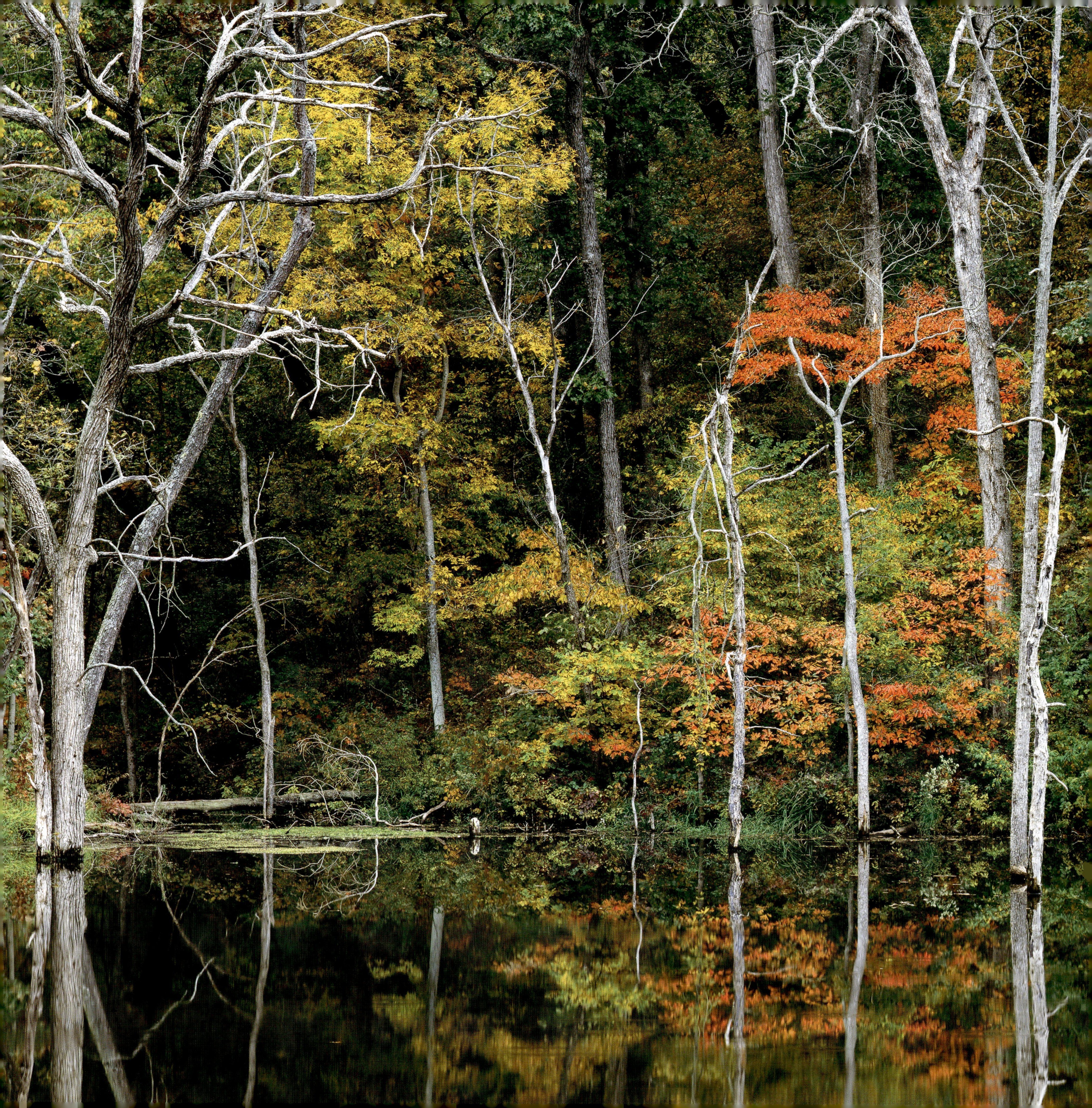

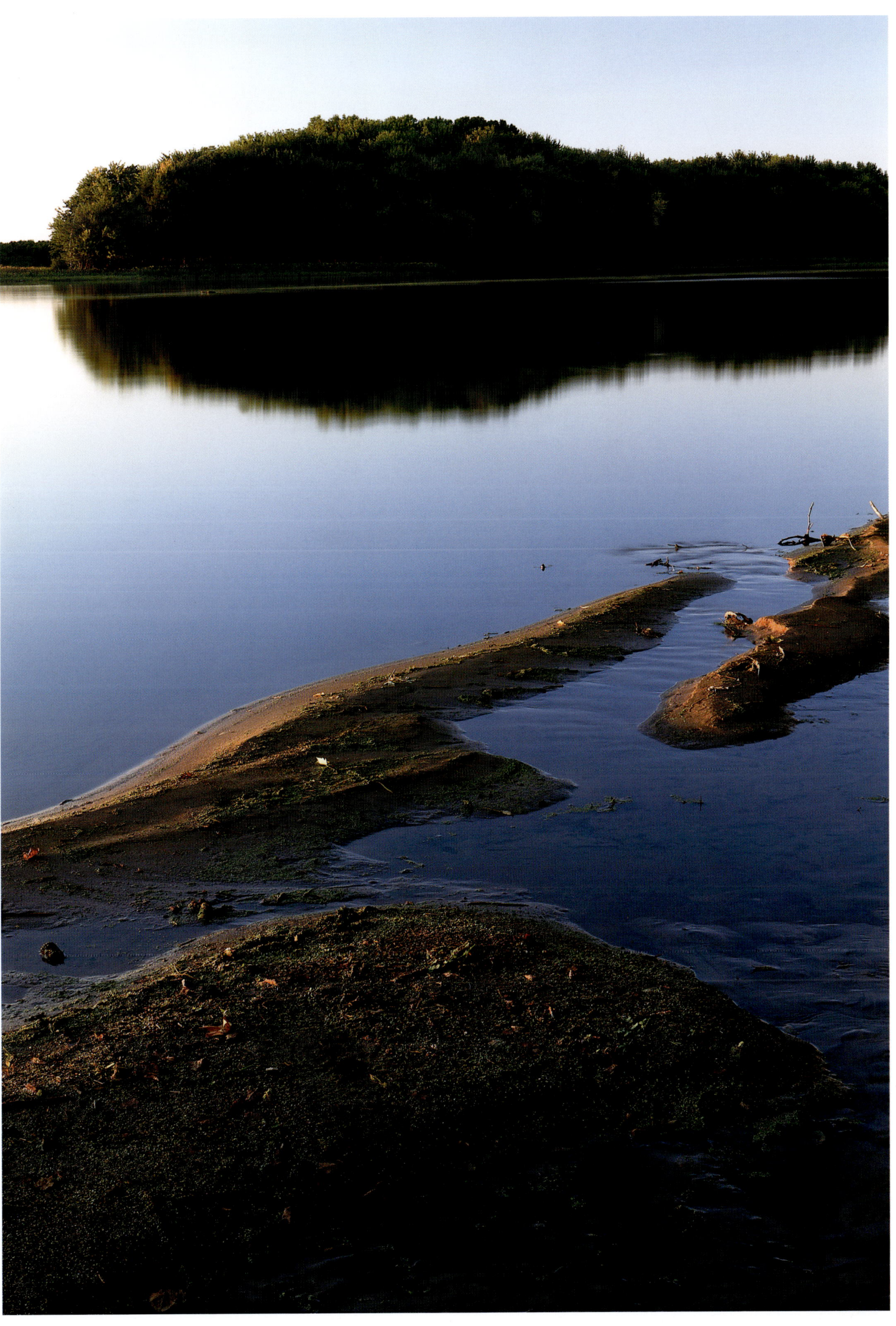

PAGE 113:

Purpureal sunset reflections on Crabapple Lake: Siloam Springs State Park, Adams County *(Galesburg Plain, Till Plains Section, Central Lowland Province)*

Beneath the rainbow colors of its surface, Crabapple Lake teems with rainbow trout, bluegill, redear, green sunfish, and largemouth bass. The 59-acre lake was created in 1955, when an earthen dam was thrown across a tributary of McKee Creek in preparation for the dedication the next year of 3,323-acre Siloam Springs State Park. *October 2001*

OPPOSITE PAGE:

Riparian trees on the banks of Cattail Cove: Siloam Springs State Park, Adams County *(Galesburg Plain, Till Plains Section, Central Lowland Province)*

Cattail Cove is a pond in Siloam Springs State Park, whose name recalls its once famous underground water resources. After the Reverend Reuben K. McCoy discovered and named Siloam Springs in the mid-nineteenth century, he imputed to the waters curative properties against an extraordinary variety of ailments, including alcohol and drug addiction. Hence, the name Siloam, from the pool in Jerusalem to which Jesus sent the blind man to wash the clay from his eyes and see. The spa erected over the springs remained fashionable until the turn of the nineteenth century. *October 2001*

THIS PAGE:

Bank of Mississippi River: Delabar State Park, Henderson County *(Galesburg Plain, Till Plains Section, Central Lowland Province)*

Light from the sun setting softly lights up the muddy shore of the Mississippi River in Delabar State, near Oquawka. The 89-acre park is a mecca for river fishing on the Mississippi and winter ice fishing on the backwaters of the great river. *September 2001*

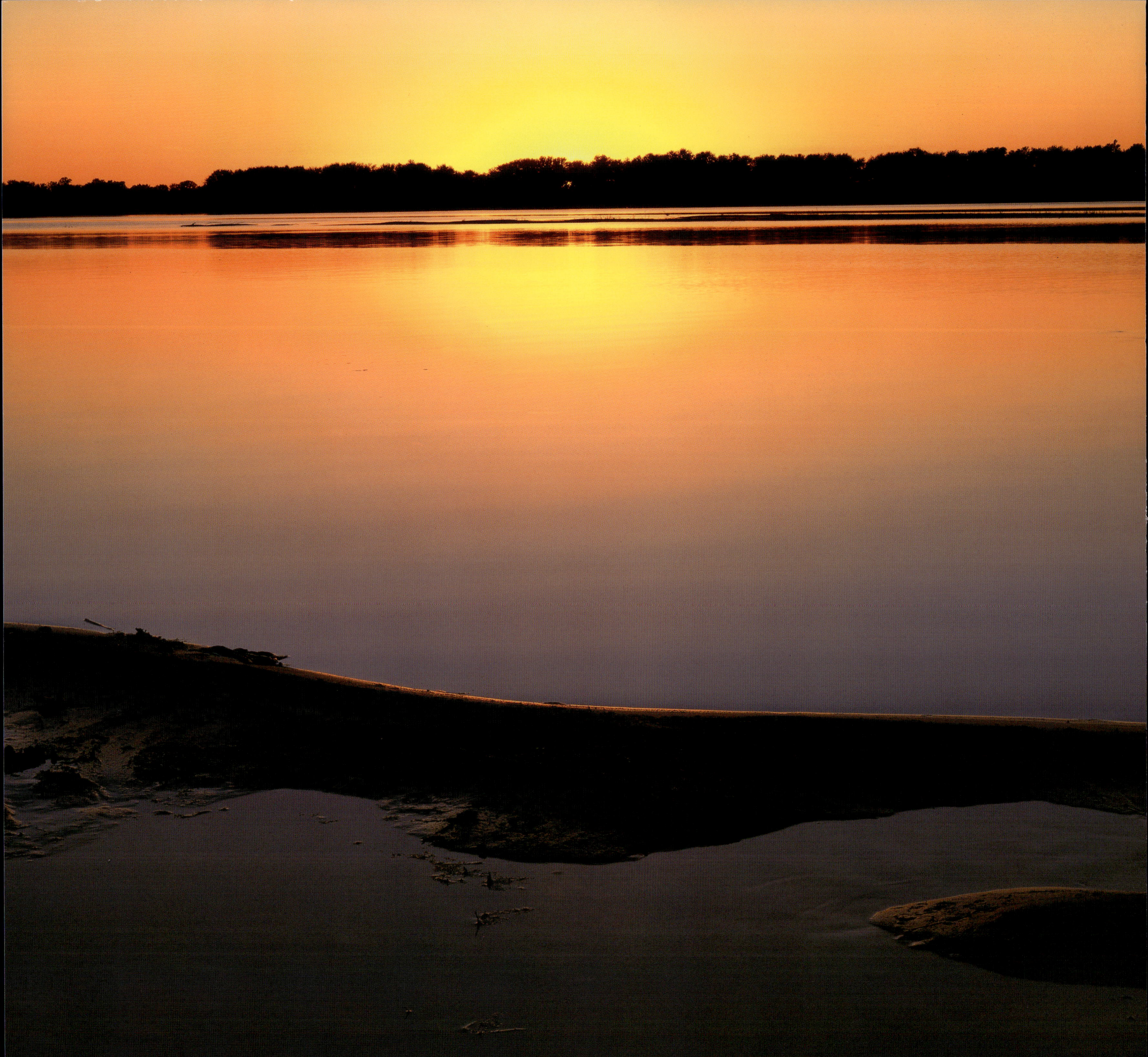

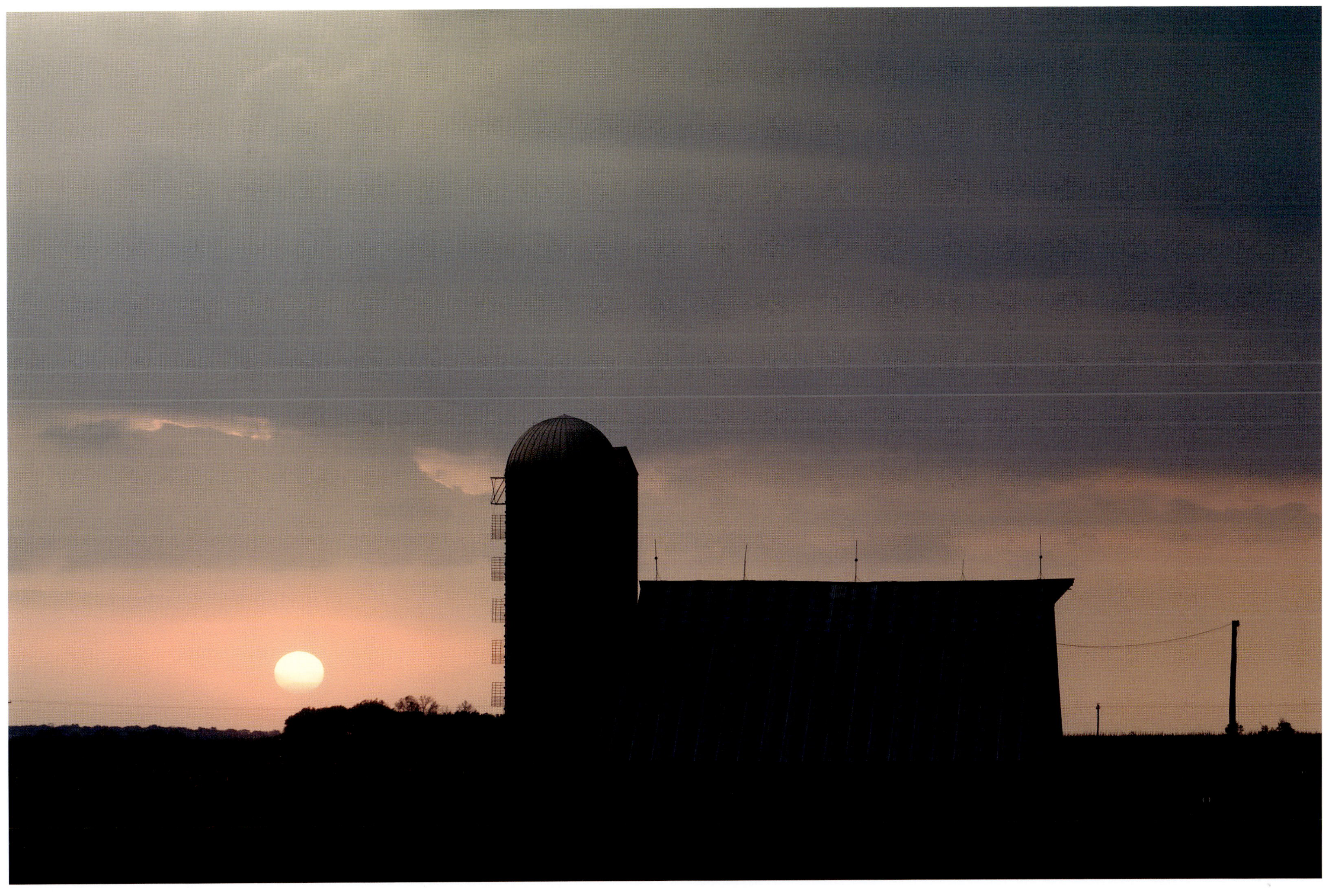

THIS PAGE:

Sunset over barn and silo: Henry County *(Galesburg Plain, Till Plains Section, Central Lowland Province)*

A clearing storm in the fall silhouettes a barn and silo. *October 1986*

OPPOSITE PAGE:

Bank of Mississippi River: Delabar State Park, Henderson County *(Galesburg Plain, Till Plains Section, Central Lowland Province)*

From Delabar State Park provides a superb vantage point for witnessing the sunset colors over the expanse of the Mississippi River. The park offers more intimate views along two miles of trails through 89 acres of oak-birch-hickory forest, frequented by over fifty species of birds. *September 2001*

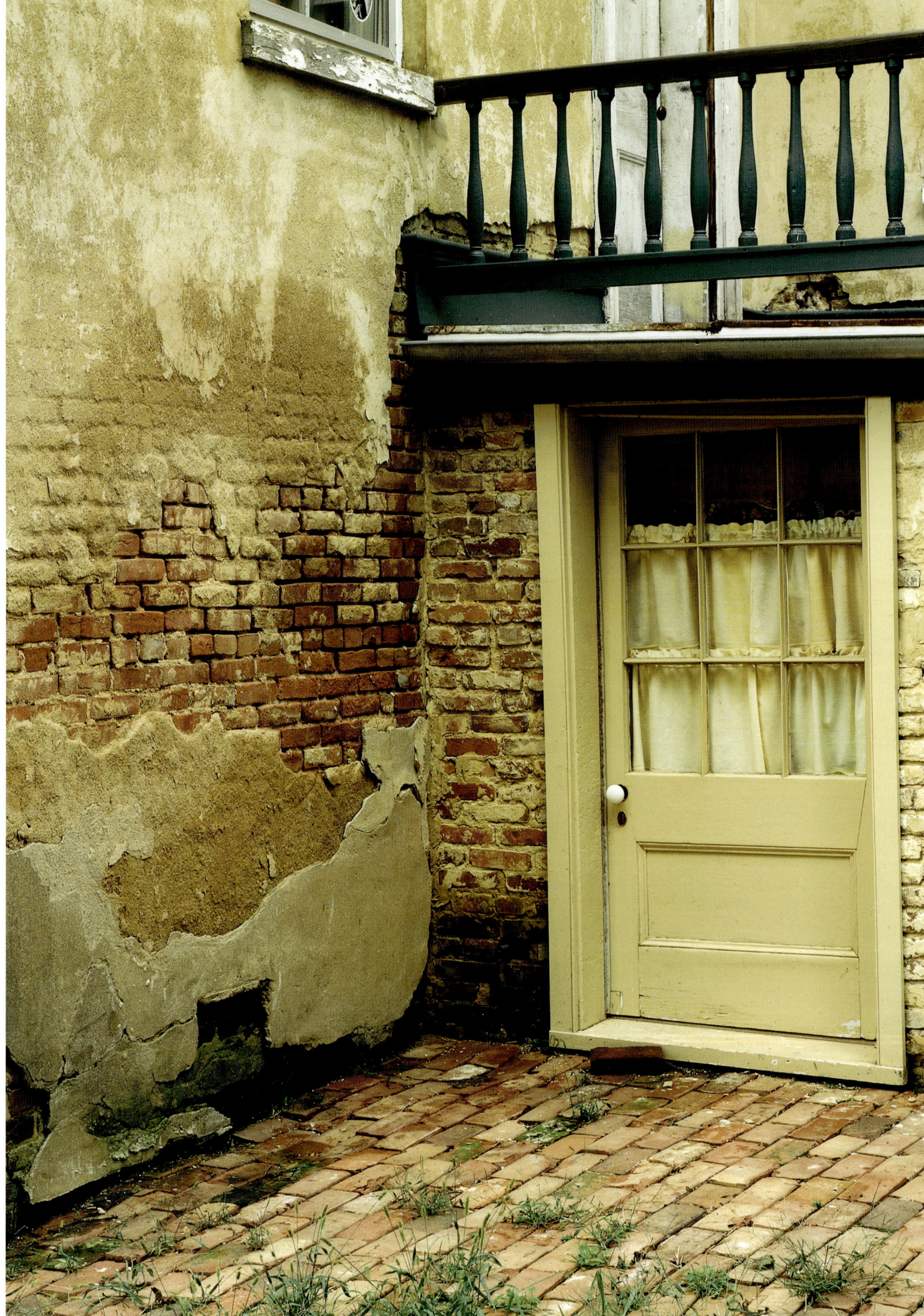

THIS PAGE:

Balcony railing and door of Colony Administration Building: Bishop Hill National Historic Site: Henry County *(Galesburg Plain, Till Plains Section, Central Lowland Province)*

Bishop Hill State Historic Site, eight miles west of Kewanee, preserves many of the communal buildings of the Bishop Hill Colony, a utopian commune that was founded in 1846 by a group of Swedish religious dissidents and persisted for fifteen years, despite the murder of its charismatic leader, Erik Jansson, in 1850. The colonists built twenty large commercial buildings, including the Colony Administration Building built in 1856, and put 12,000 acres of land into production. From 1848 to 1861, Bishop Hill Colony was the major commercial center between Rock Island and Peoria. The colony produced almost everything that the colonists needed and marketed fine linen, furniture, wagons, brooms, and farm products. In 1861, the commune was dissolved and its property was divided among its members. The village of the Bishop Hill State Historic Site was designated a National Historic Landmark in 1984. *October 1986*

OPPOSITE PAGE:

Evening reflections of trees bordering mud-shoal on Argyle Lake: Argyle Lake State Park, McDonough County *(Galesburg Plain, Till Plains Section, Central Lowland Province)*

Seventeen-thousand-acre Argyle Lake State Park is a fisherman's delight. The park's five miles of forested hiking trails disclose many such scenes as this one, in which the setting sun catches the flame of a maple tree reflected in the backwater of Argyle Lake. *September 2001*

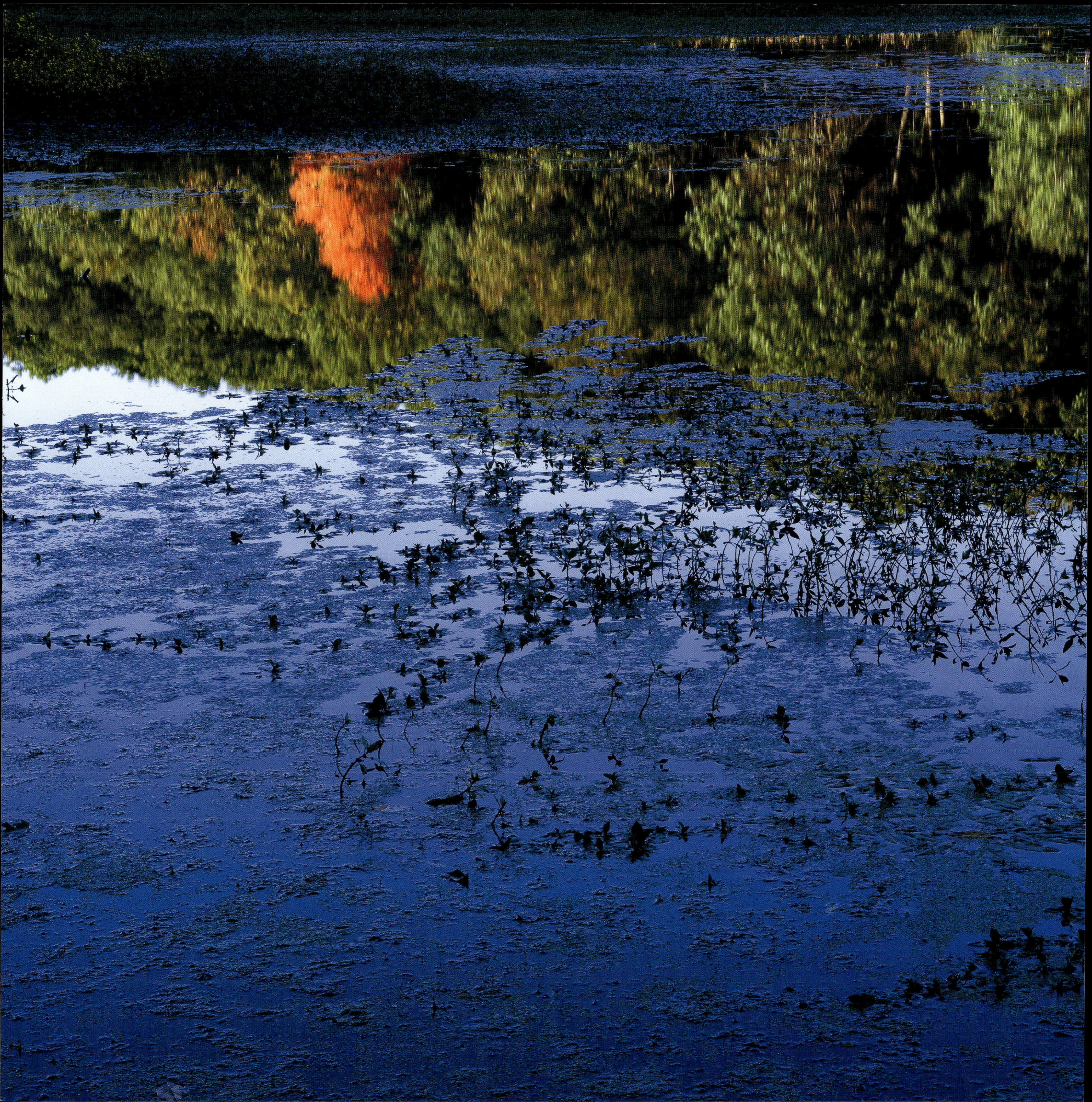

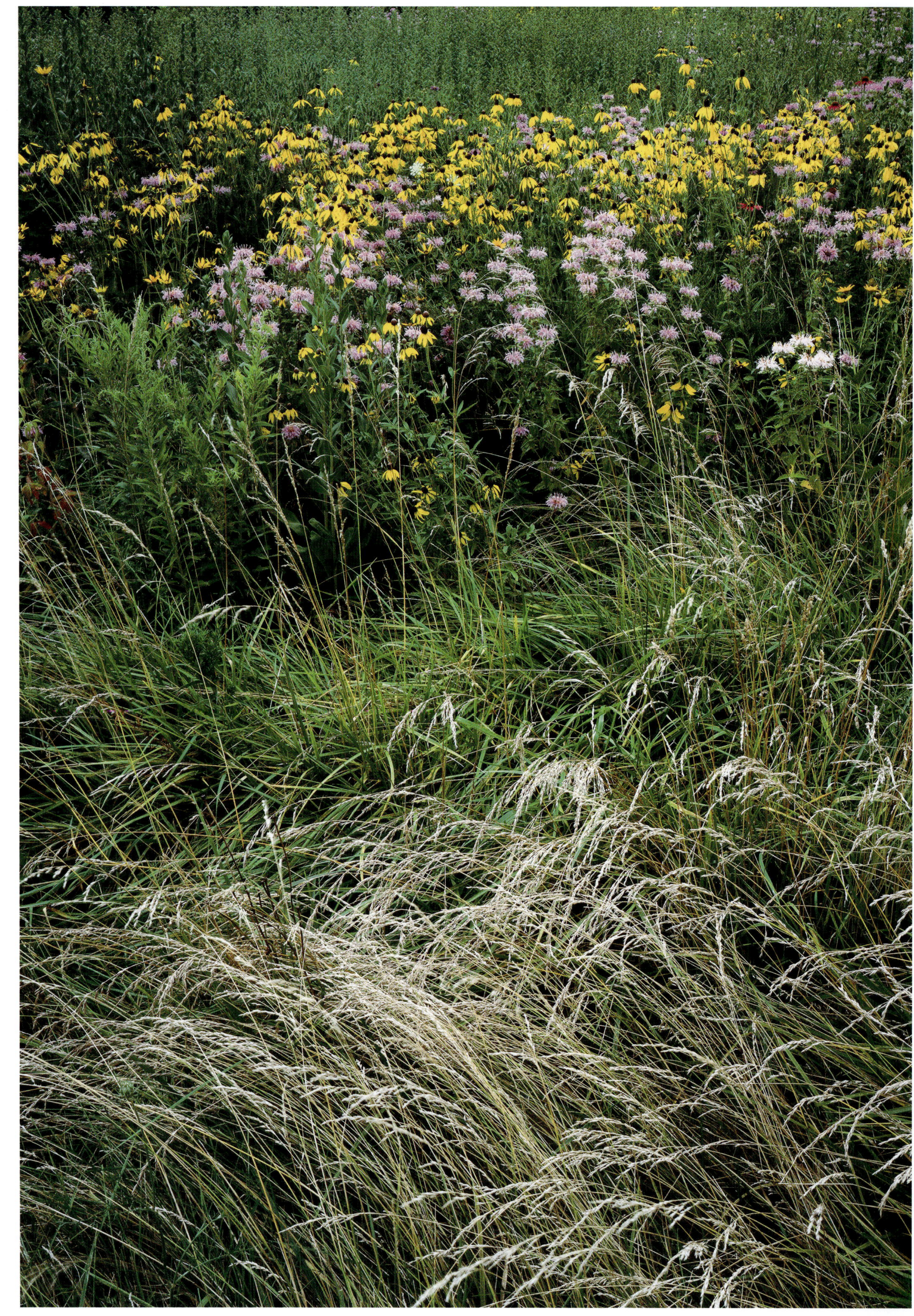

Drooping coneflower, bergamot, and prairie grasses: Rock Island Trail State Park, Stark County *(Galesburg Plain, Till Plains Section, Central Lowland Province)*

Rock Island Trail State Park jogs 26 miles from Alta, Peoria County, to Toulon, Stark County. The well-maintained trail passes through prairie remnants where, amid the grasses, wildflowers such as drooping coneflower and bergamot flower in mid-summer. *July 2001*

SPRINGFIELD PLAIN

TILL PLAINS SECTION OF CENTRAL LOWLAND PROVINCE

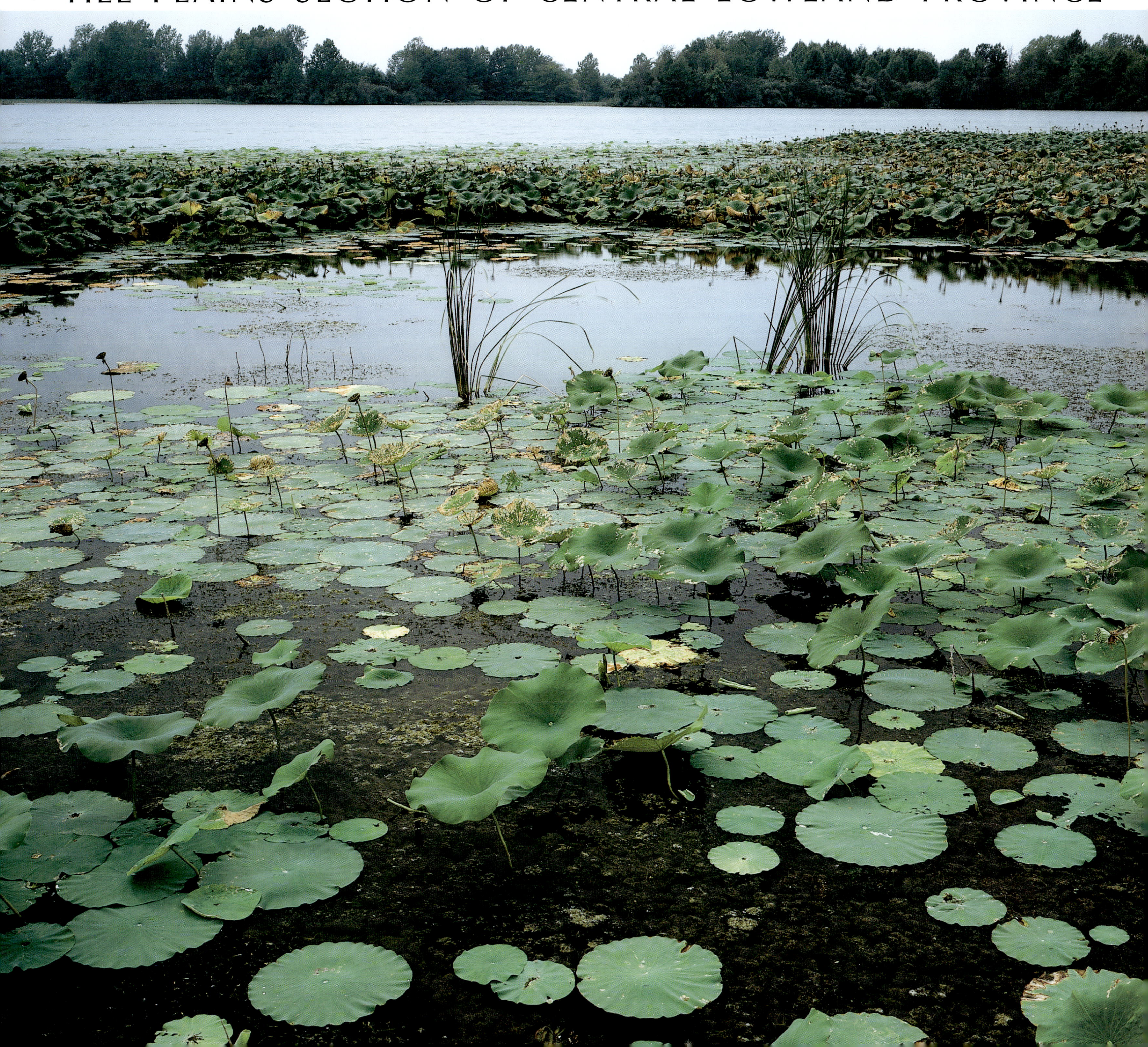

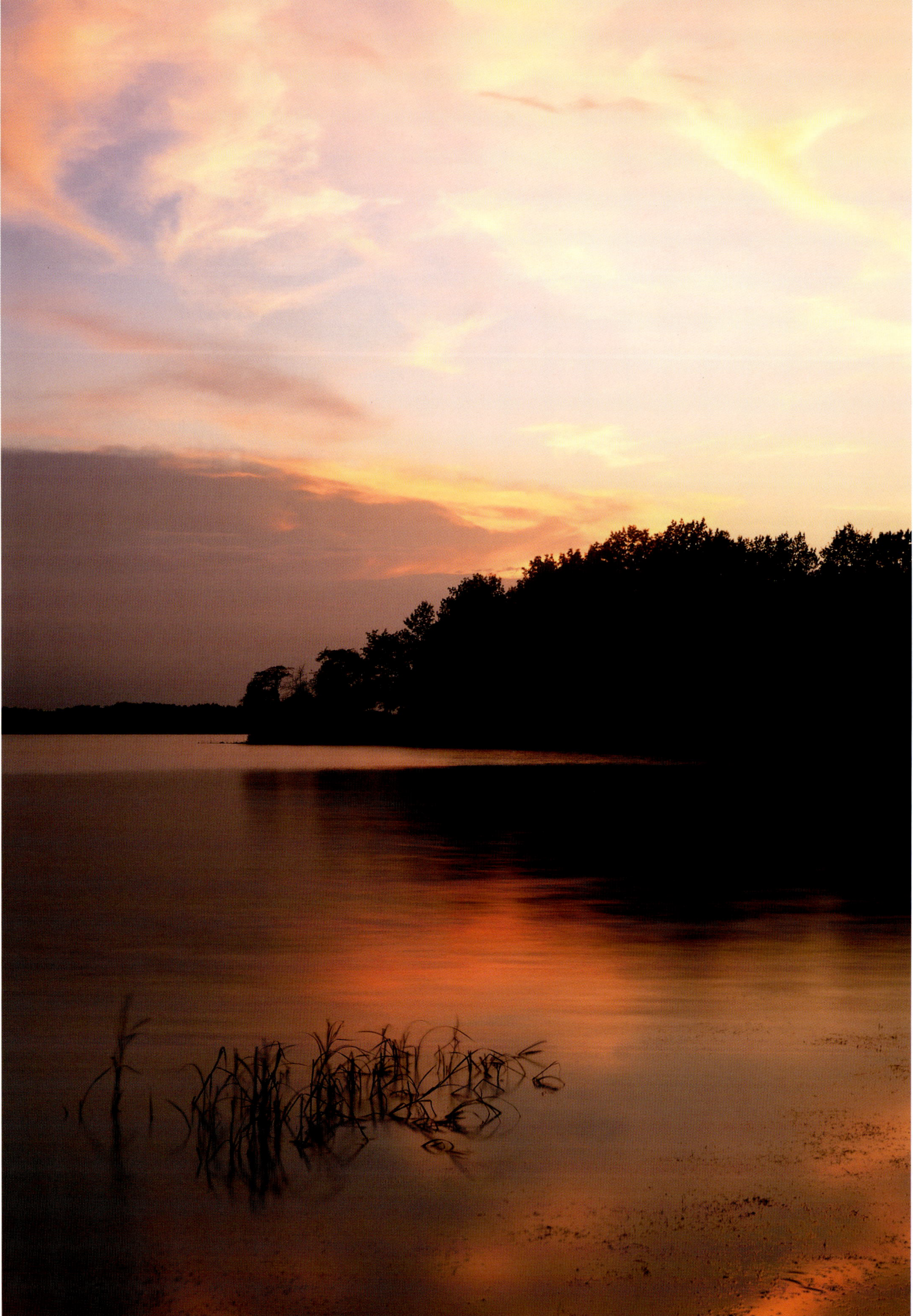

PAGE 121:

Fragrant water lily *(Nymphaea odorata)* on Sangchris Lake: Sangchris Lake State Fish and Wildlife Area, Christian County *(Springfield Plain, Till Plains Section, Central Lowland Province)*
Fragrant water lily covers Sangchris Lake in the summer. The fragrant water lily's flowers, with their yellow centers (both the male and female reproductive parts) surrounded by no less than 25 white petals, float on the water throughout the summer. Each individual blossom, however, lasts no more than five days, opening each morning and closing each afternoon. Pollination is done by beetles. After a flower has closed for the last time, its stalk forms a spiral and draws the fruit under the water. The plant senesces in the fall and overwinters as the underwater rhizome. Native to eastern North America, Nymphaea odorata is regarded in many parts of the country as a showy but aggressive lake invasive. *September 2001*

THIS PAGE:

Sangchris Lake at sunset: Sangchris Lake State Fish and Wildlife Area, Christian County *(Springfield Plain, Till Plains Section, Central Lowland Province)*
One of central Illinois's most popular fishing destinations, Sangchris Lake is well-known for its striped bass, the biggest in the state. *September 2001*

OPPOSITE PAGE:

Sunset over the Peppenhorst Branch of Carlyle Lake: Eldon Hazlet State Recreation Area, Clinton County *(Springfield Plain, Till Plains Section, Central Lowland Province)*
Eldon Hazlet State Recreation Area is attached to the western shore of Carlyle Lake, a 26,000-acre lake created by the Army Corps of Engineers by impounding the Kaskaskia River. The 3,000 acres of the recreation area host almost a million visitors a year. *September 2001*

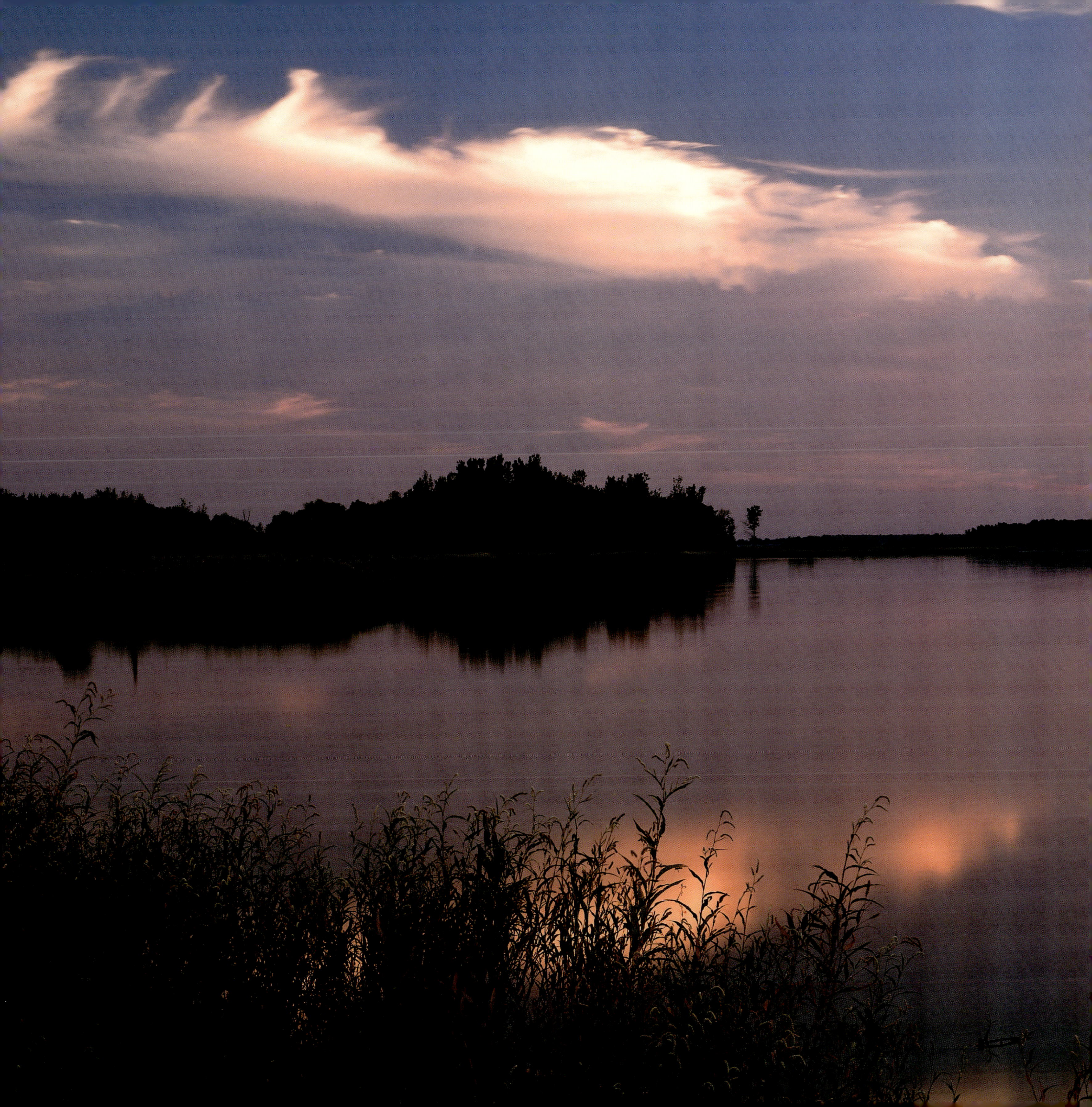

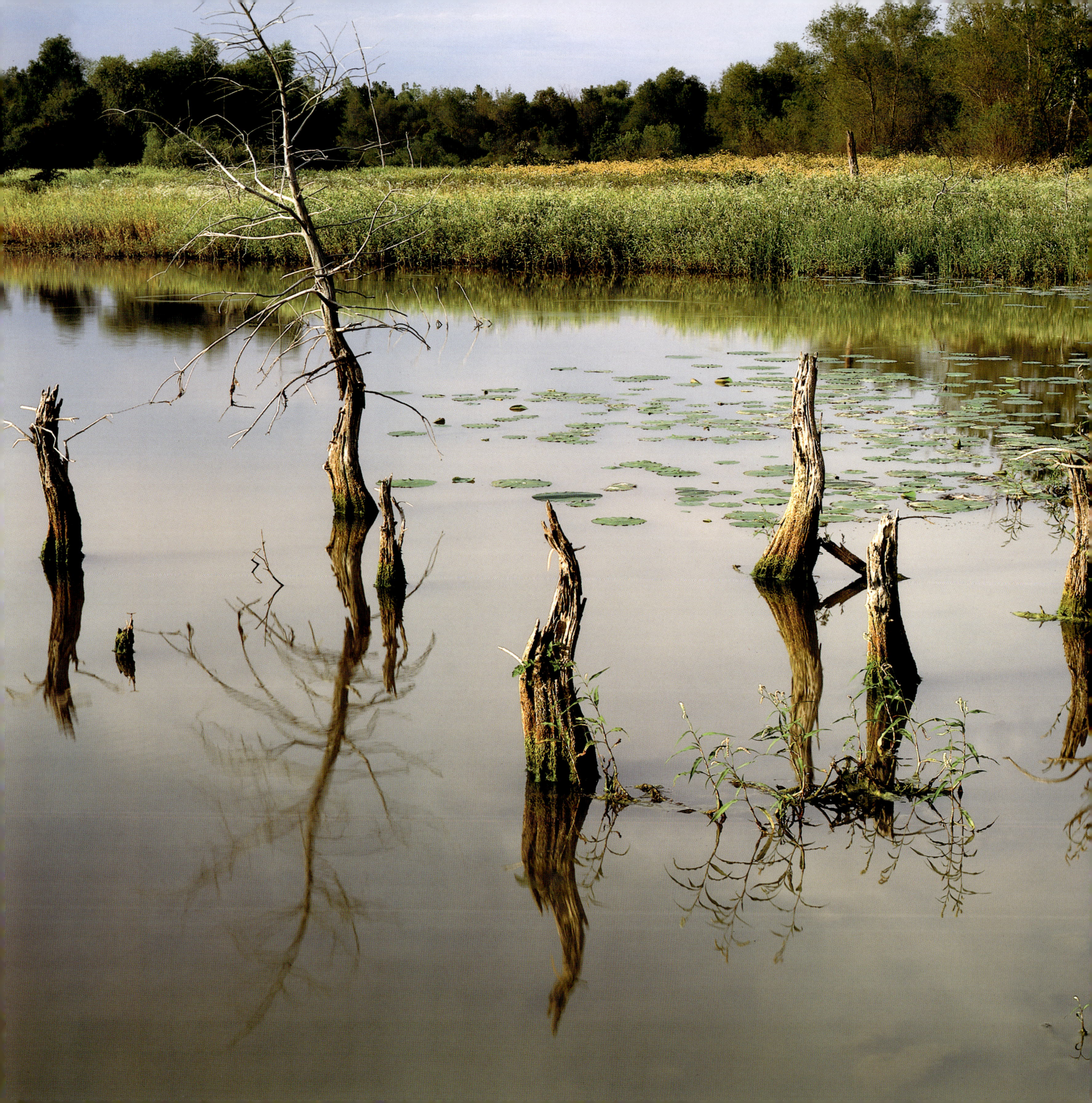

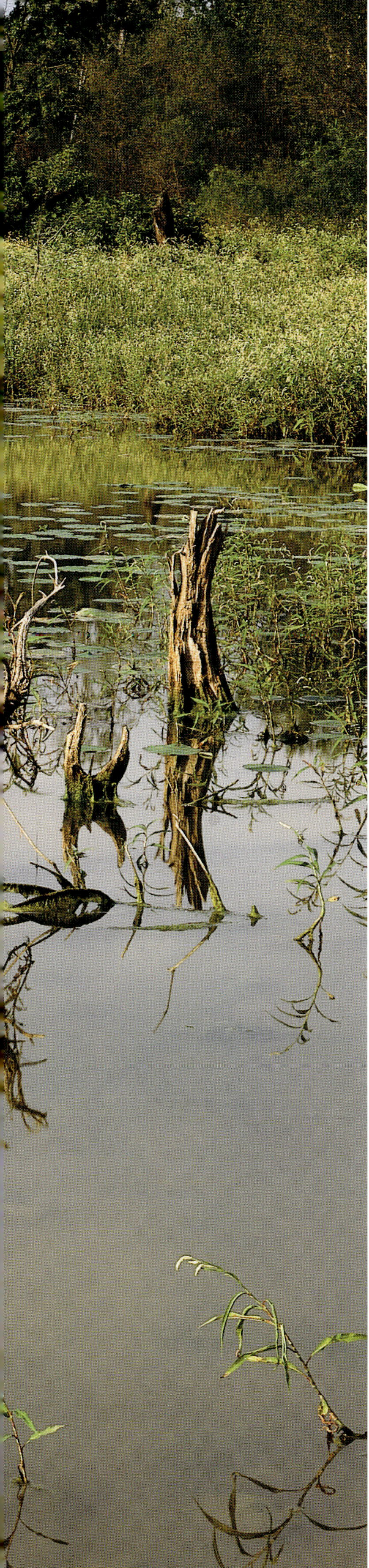

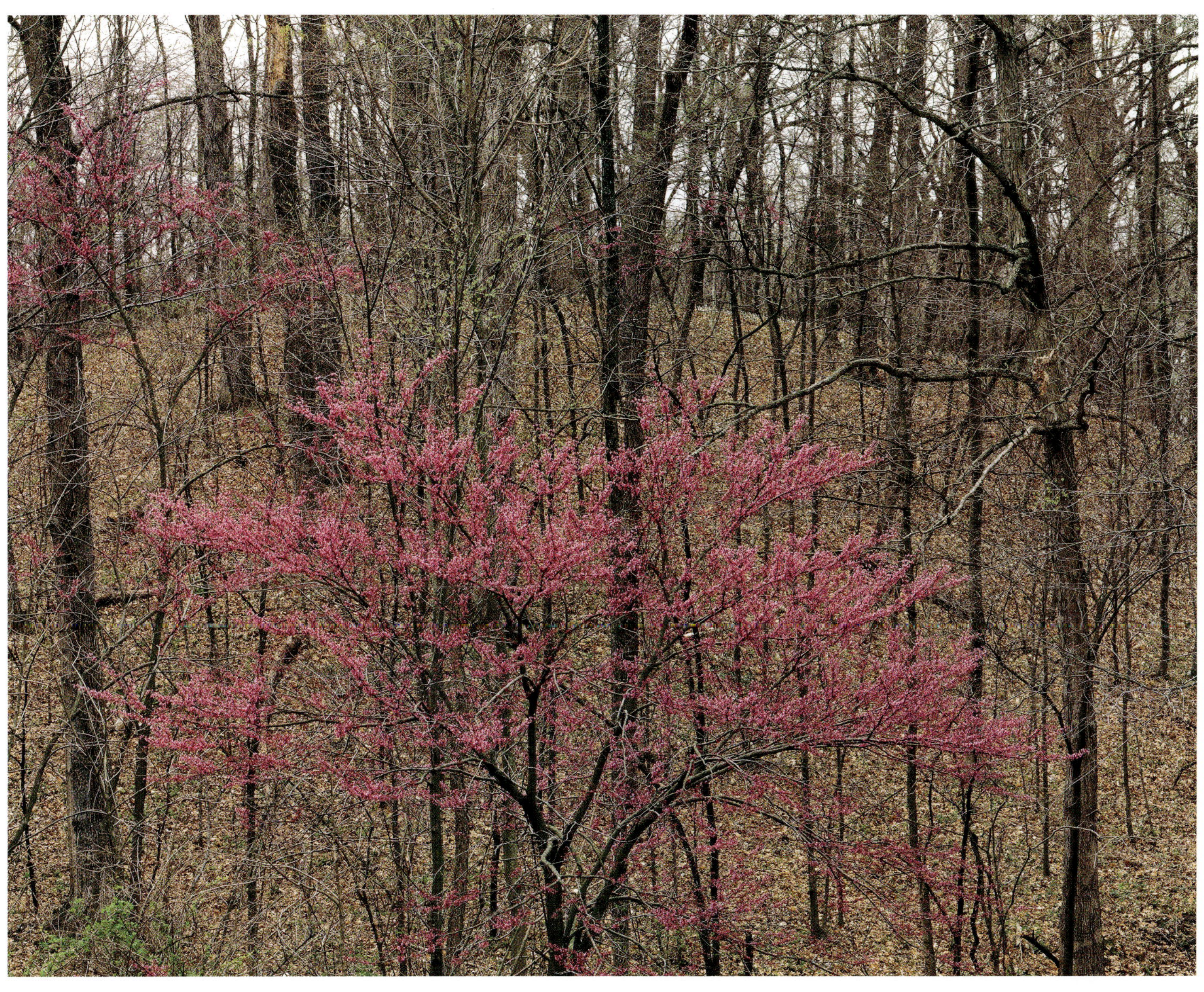

THIS PAGE ABOVE:

Redbud tree in flower: Ramsey Lake State Park, Fayette County *(Springfield Plain, Till Plains Section, Central Lowland Province)*

The 1,980 rolling acres of Ramsey Lake State Park Known used to be known as the "Old Fox Chase Grounds" on account of its popularity with fox and coon hunters. Today, visitors come to savor the beauties of Ramsey Lake and the park's many redbud trees, whose bids are welcome harbingers of spring. *April 1995*

OPPOSITE PAGE:

Still water and banks of the Peppenhorst Branch of Carlyle Lake: Eldon Hazlet State Recreation Area, Clinton County *(Springfield Plain, Till Plains Section, Central Lowland Province)*

One of Illinois's largest recreational reservoirs, Carlyle Lake is a boaters' paradise and home to an annual sailboat regatta. The lake also caters to those seeking contemplative quiet, as might be enjoyed in this backwater of the Peppenhorst Branch. *September 2001*

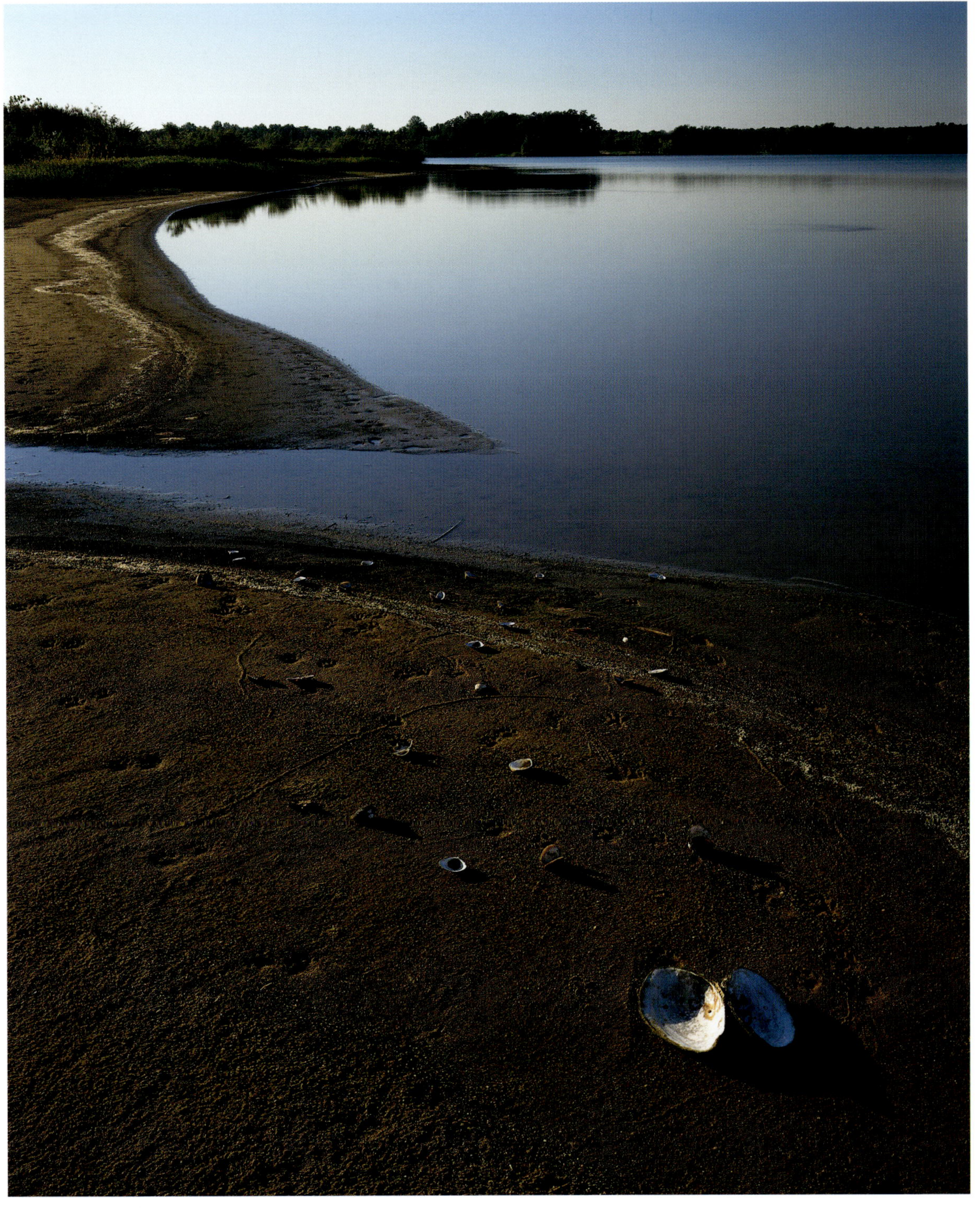

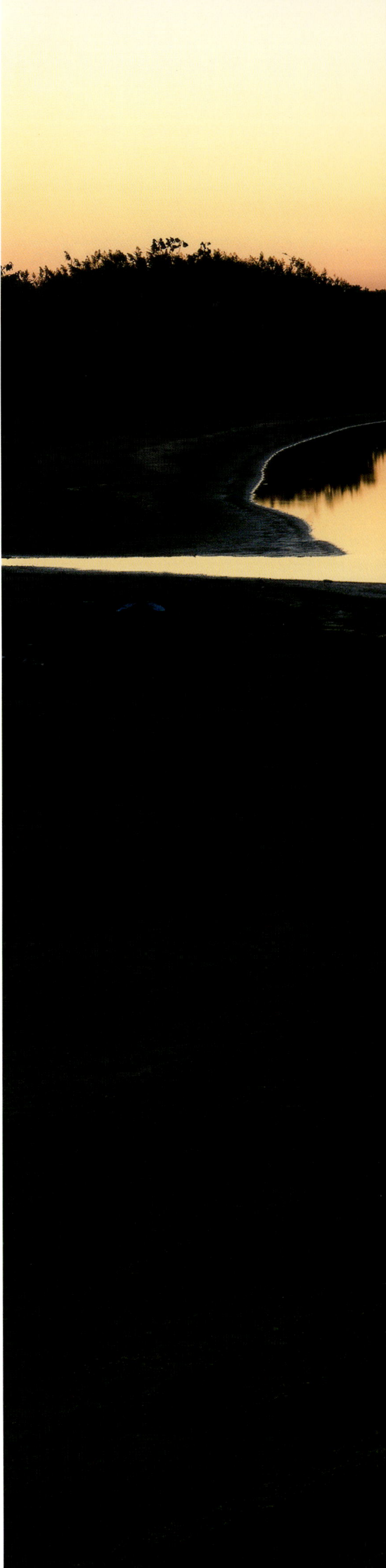

THIS PAGE ABOVE:

Clam shells and raccoon tracks on Newton Lake beach in evening light: Newton Lake State Fish and Wildlife Area, Jasper County *(Springfield Plain, Till Plains Section, Central Lowland Province)*

In 1979, the state designated 1,775-acre Newton Lake and 540 acres of its shoreline a conservation area. Newton Lake State Fish & Wildlife Area is home to some of the remaining flocks of prairie chickens, which are on the endangered species list in Illinois. The lake also provides habitat for raccoons, which dig for clams on its shore. *September 2001*

OPPOSITE PAGE:

Newton Lake beach: Newton Lake State Fish and Wildlife Area, Jasper County *(Springfield Plain, Till Plains Section, Central Lowland Province)*

The glow in this photograph comes from the sunset, not from the electric power generating plant that Central Illinois Public Service Company built on the site to provide over a thousand megawatts of power to sixty-five counties. *September 2001*

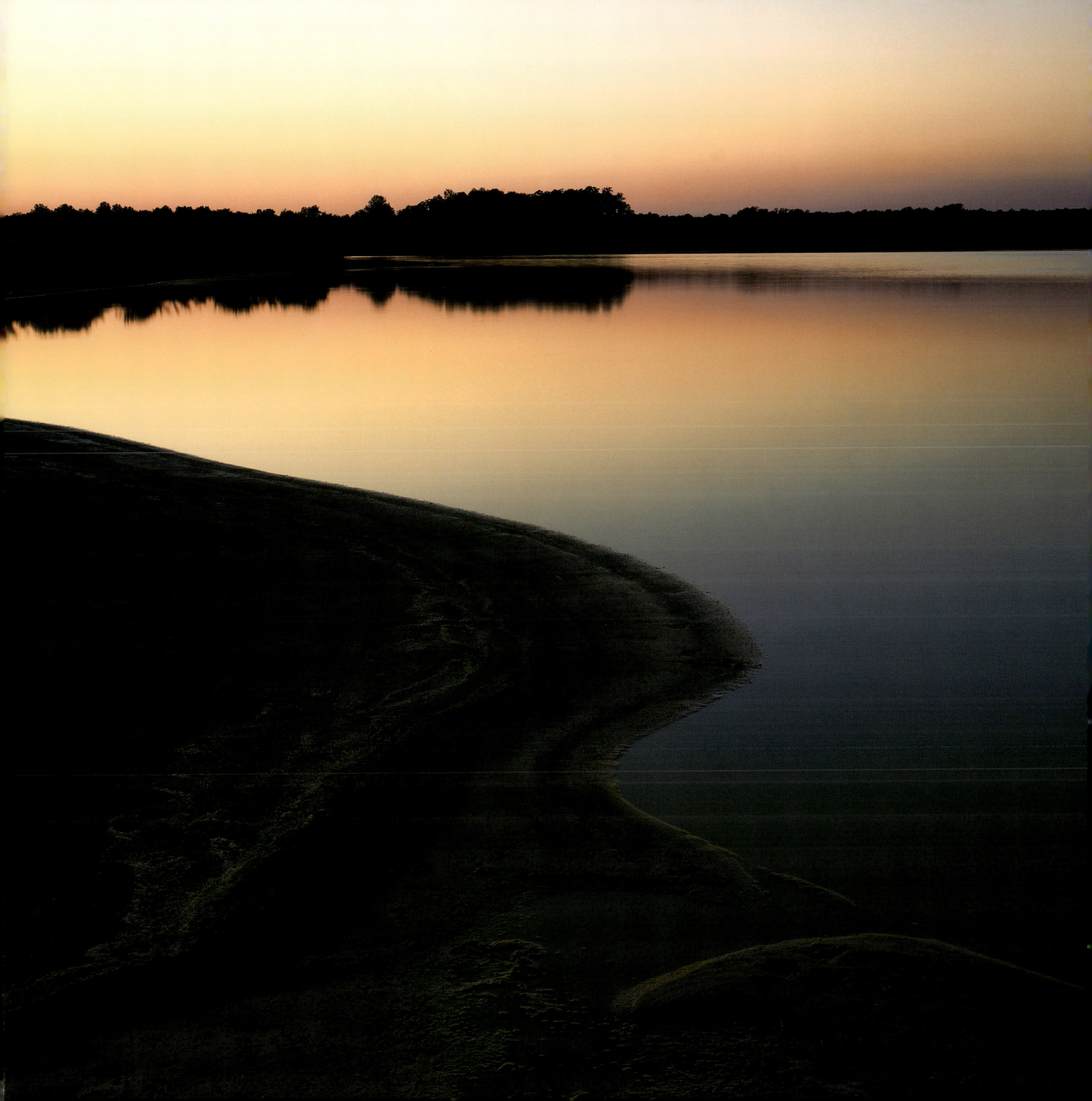

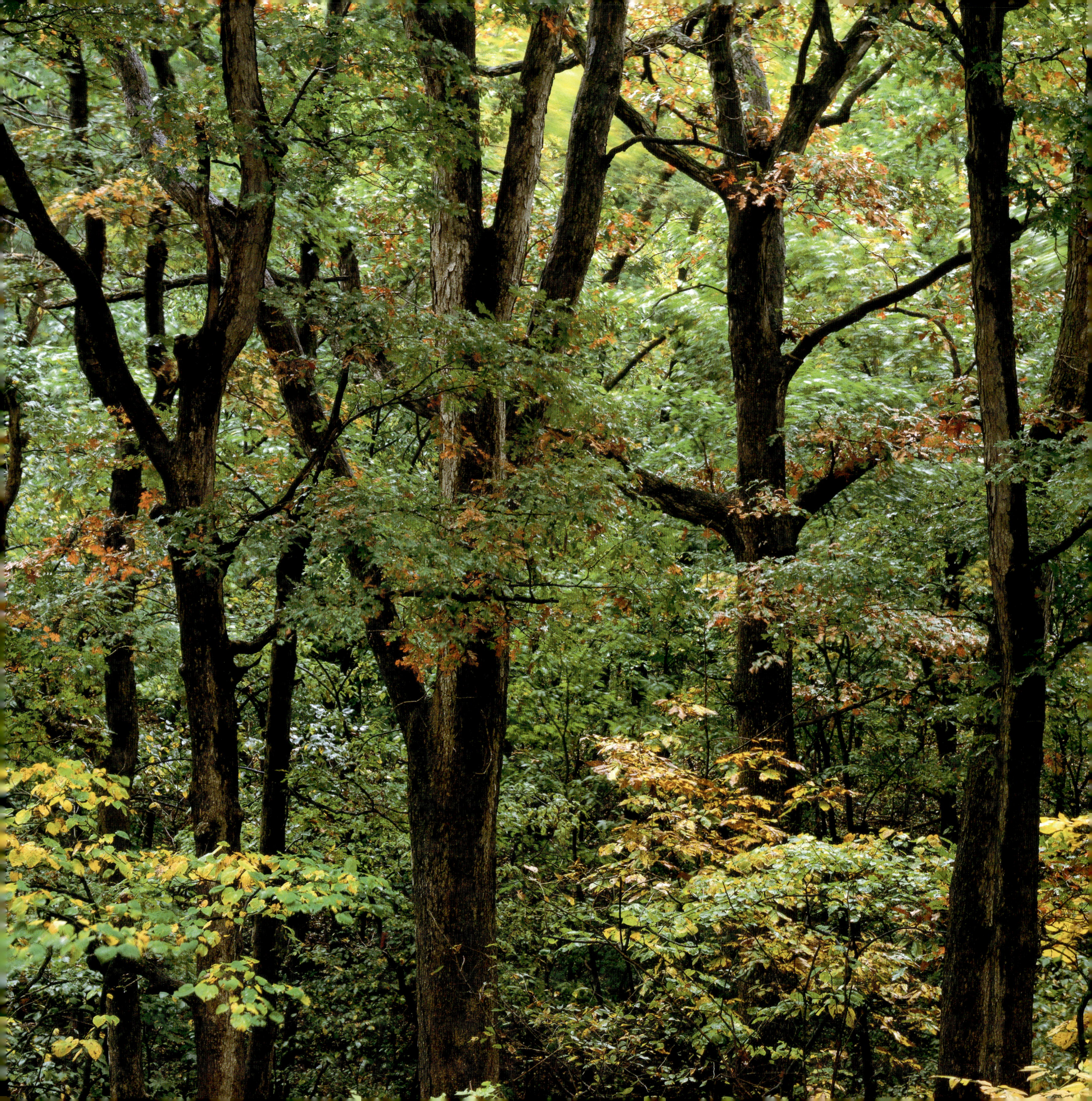

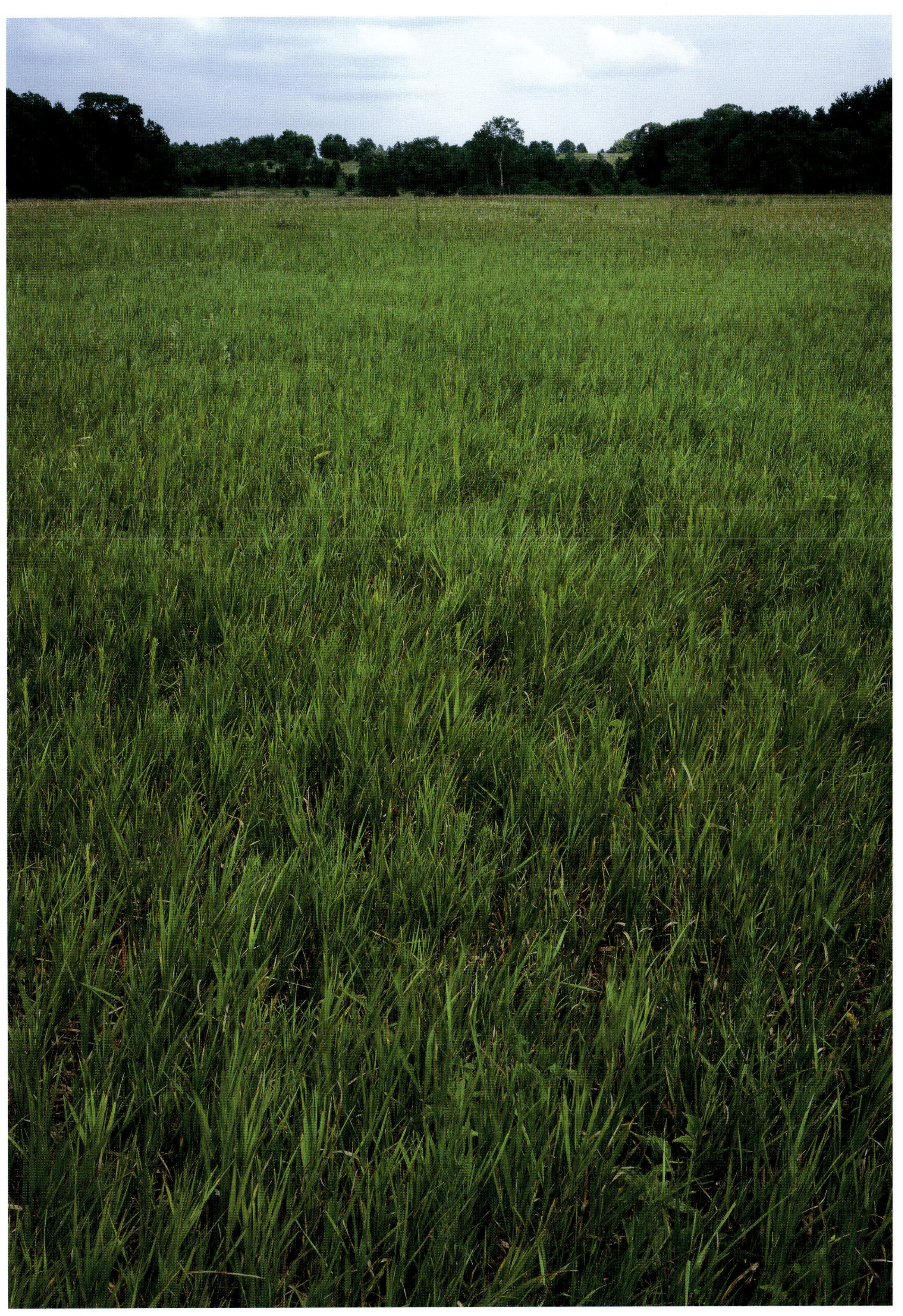

OPPOSITE PAGE:

Forest understory: Beaver Dam State Park, Macoupin County *(Springfield Plain, Till Plains Section, Central Lowland Province)*
Beaver Dam State Park is noted for its dense oak-hickory woodland, home to many animal species, including white squirrels. In the early 1890s, fishermen of Carlinville formed the Beaver Dam Lake Club and deepened 59-acre Beaver Dam Lake with manmade dams. In addition to woodland and lake, the 751-acre park includes bottomland, farmland, open fields, and marsh. *October 2001*

THIS PAGE:

Grass-covered sand dunes fringed by forest: Sand Ridge State Forest, Mason County *(Springfield Plain, Till Plains Section, Central Lowland Province)*
The 7,500 acres of Sand Ridge State Forest near Peoria, named for its well-drained, grass-covered dunes, are home to many arid-zone plant and animal species near the northern limit of their continental range, including prickly-pear cactus, silvery bladderpod, and pocket gophers. *July 2001*

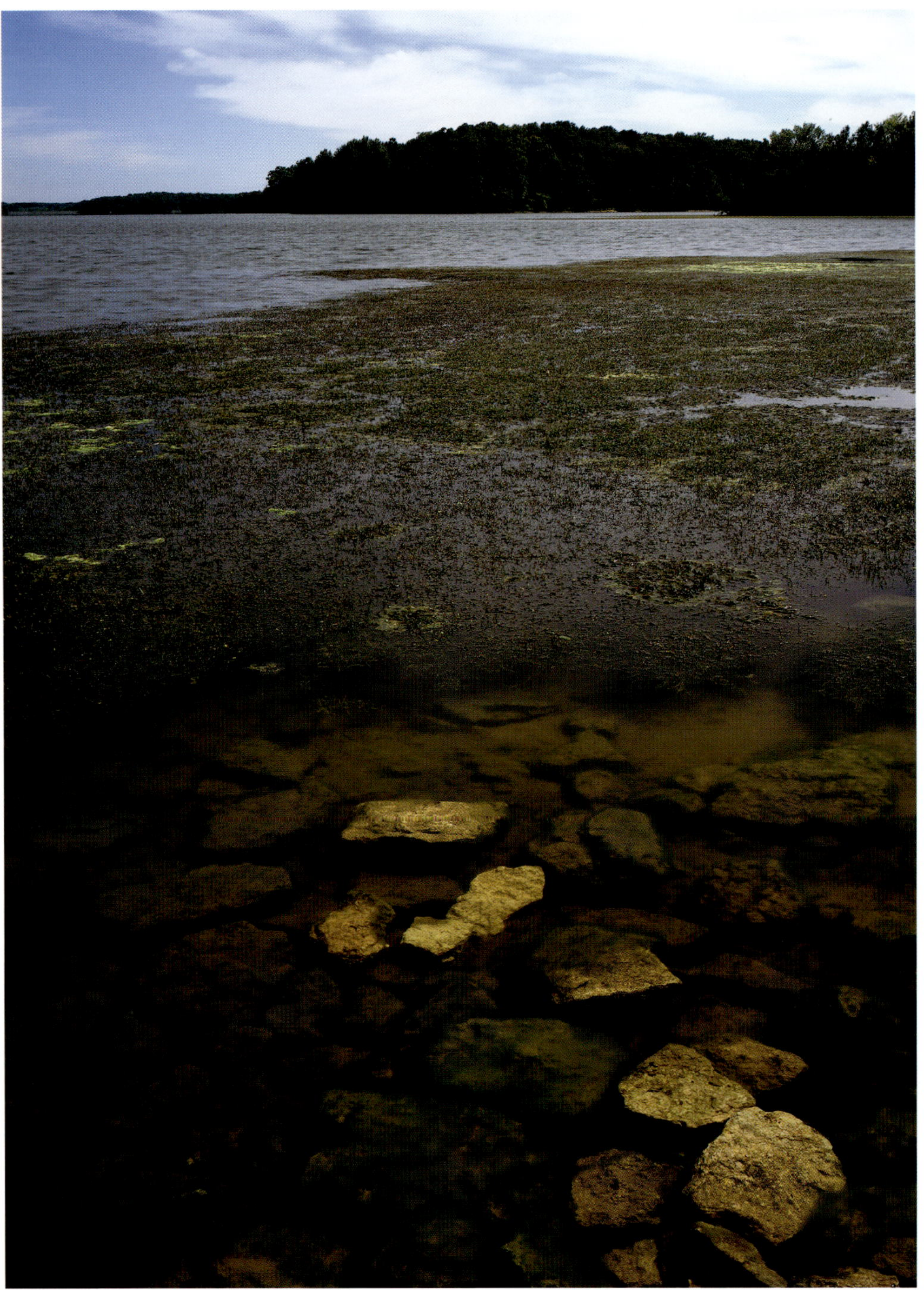

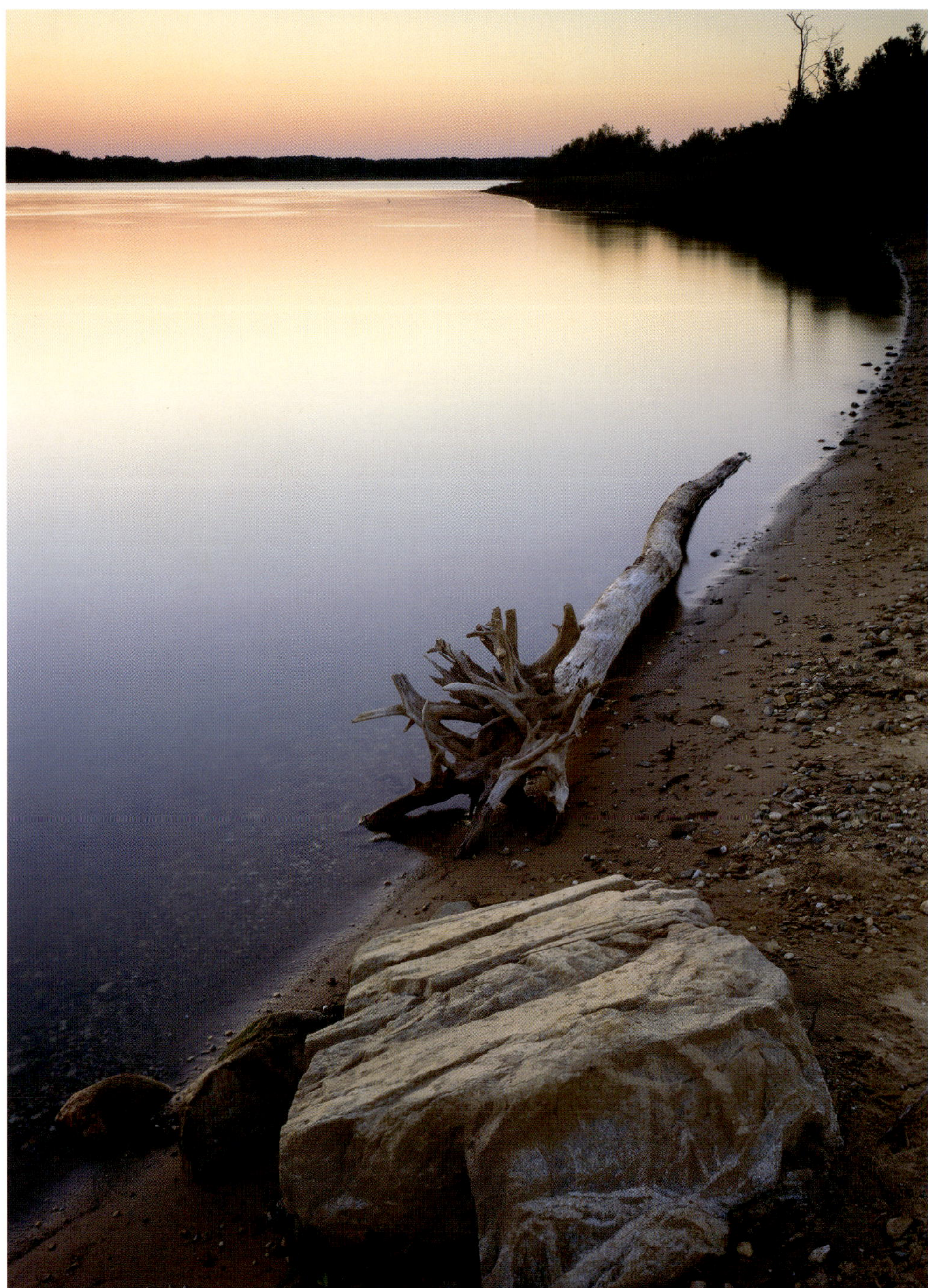

THIS PAGE LEFT:

Coffeen Lake: Coffeen Lake State Fish and Wildlife Area, Montgomery County *(Springfield Plain, Till Plains Section, Central Lowland Province)*
Coffeen Lake State Fish and Wildlife Area is covered by oak/hickory forest. Largemouth bass, crappies, and channel catfish thrive in the 59-foot-deep waters of Coffeen Lake. *September 2001*

THIS PAGE RIGHT:

Lake Shelbyville: Wilborn Creek Recreation Area, Moultrie County *(Springfield Plain, Till Plains Section, Central Lowland Province)*
Lake Shelbyville is impounded behind dams across the Kaskaskia and West Okaw Rivers near Sullivan. This sunset view of Lake Shelbyville is within the Wilborn Creek Recreation Area, a component of the 34,000-acre Shelbyville Fish and Wildlife Area. *September 2001*

OPPOSITE PAGE:

Lake Shelbyville: Wolf Creek State Park, Shelby County *(Springfield Plain, Till Plains Section, Central Lowland Province)*
Lake Shelbyville project extends from Moultie County south into Shelby County. The lake is 11,000 acres in extent and averages 16 feet in depth. Some of Lake Shelbyville's many islands, peninsulas, and coves are seen in this stormy sunset view of a cove in Wolf Creek State Park, on the eastern shore. *September 2001*

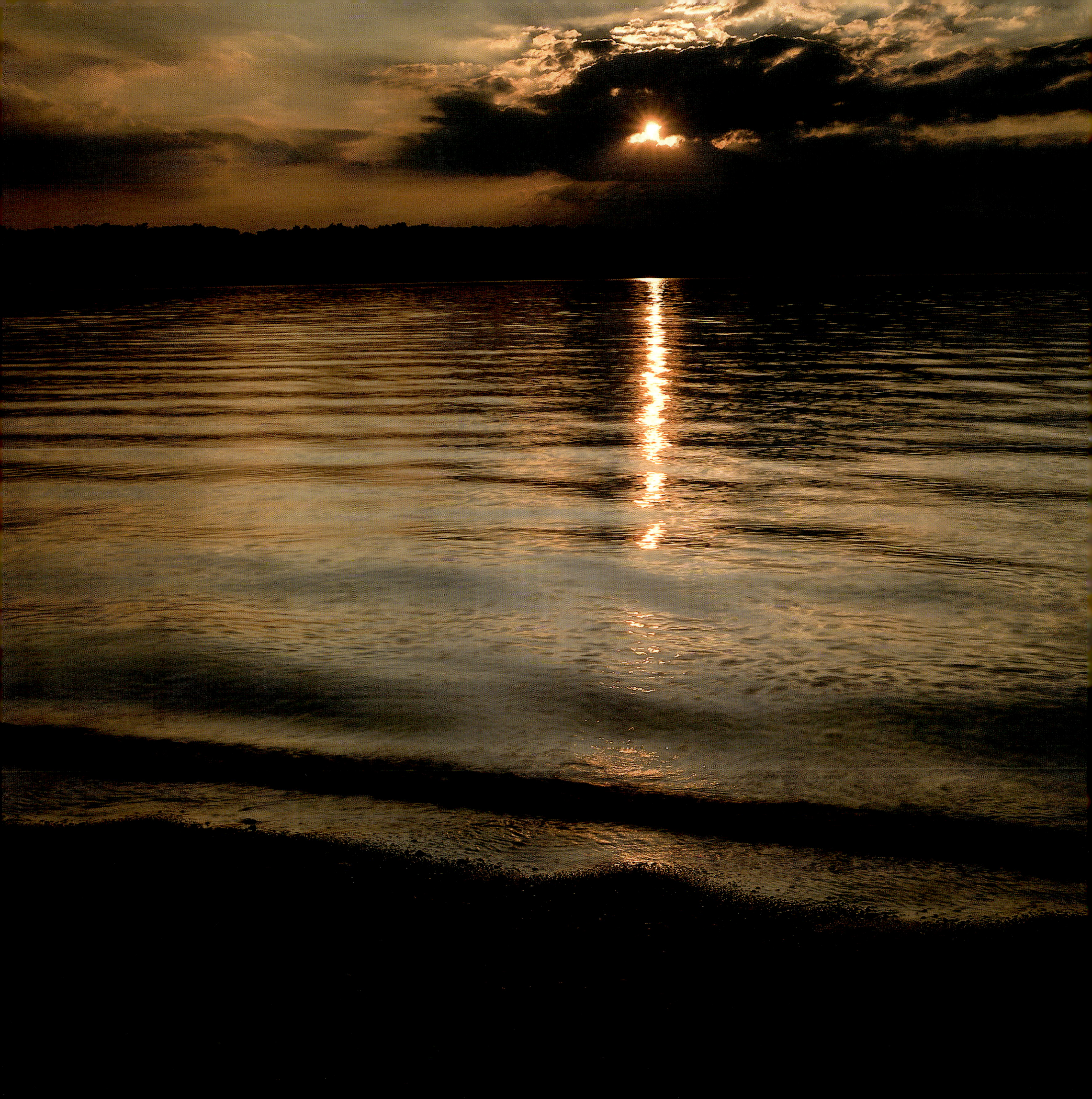

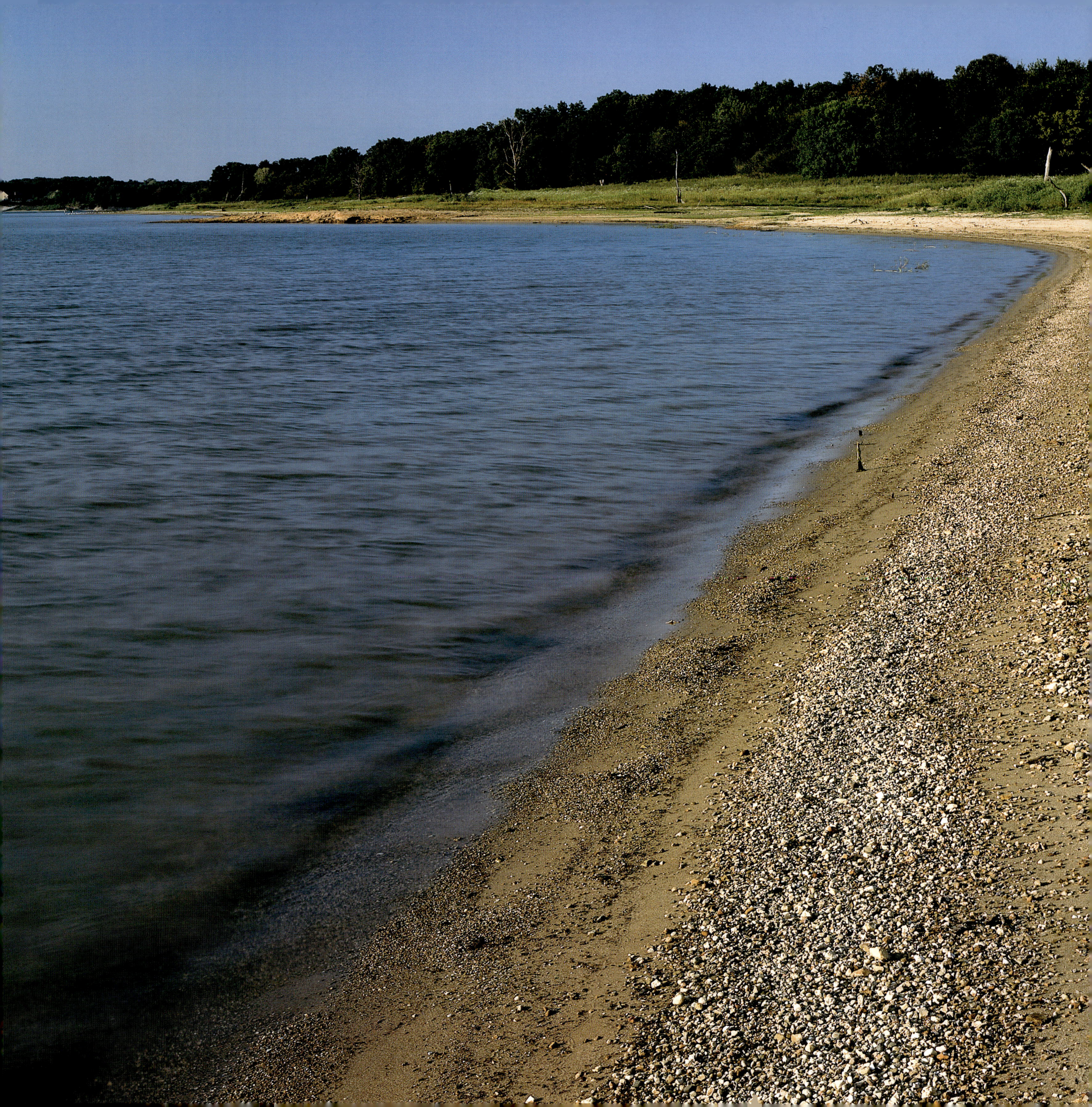

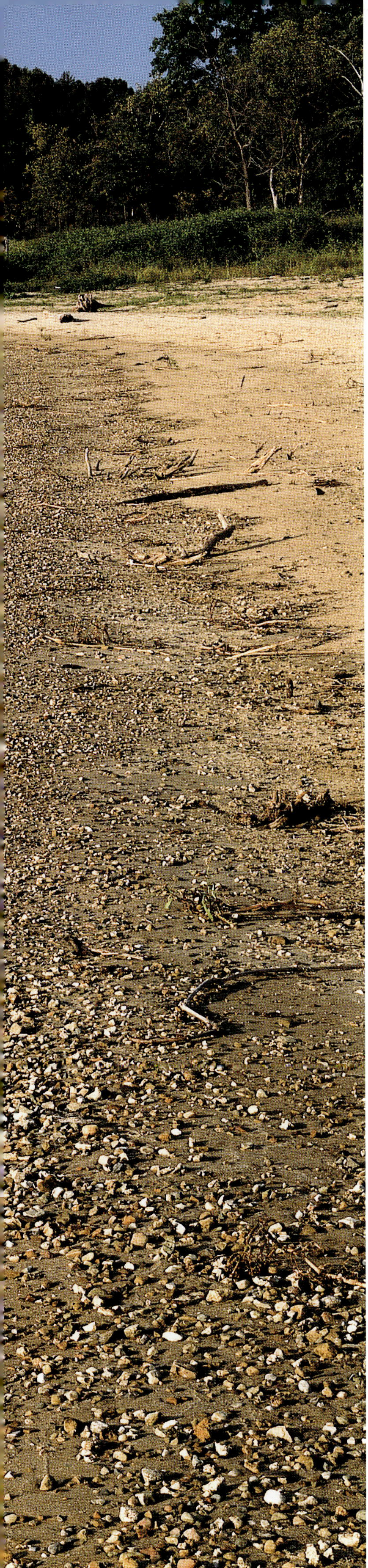

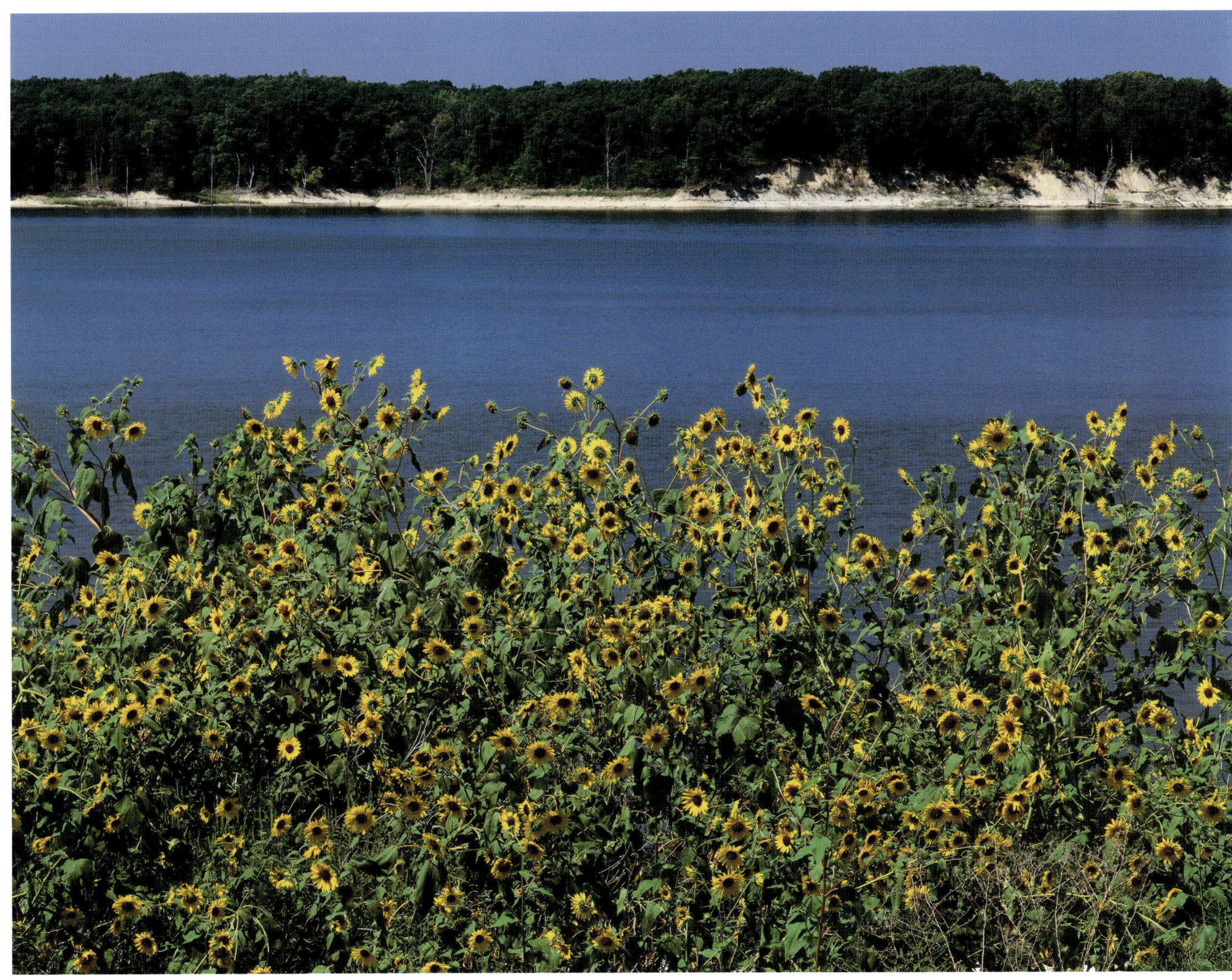

THIS PAGE ABOVE:

Sunflowers on the shore of Lake Shelbyville: "Bo" Woods Recreation Area, Shelby County *(Springfield Plain, Till Plains Section, Central Lowland Province)*
A stand of sunflowers adorns the shore of Lake Shelbyville in "Bo" Woods Recreation Area. This recreation area, part of the Lake Shelbyville Fish and Wildlife Management Area, supports a diverse flora, including oak, hickory, maple, cottonwood, sycamore, and showy flowers. *September 2001*

OPPOSITE PAGE:

Lake Shelbyville: Wolf Creek State Park, Shelby County *(Springfield Plain, Till Plains Section, Central Lowland Province)*
Wolf Creek State Park includes forests, prairies, restored grasslands, and wetlands. *September 2001*

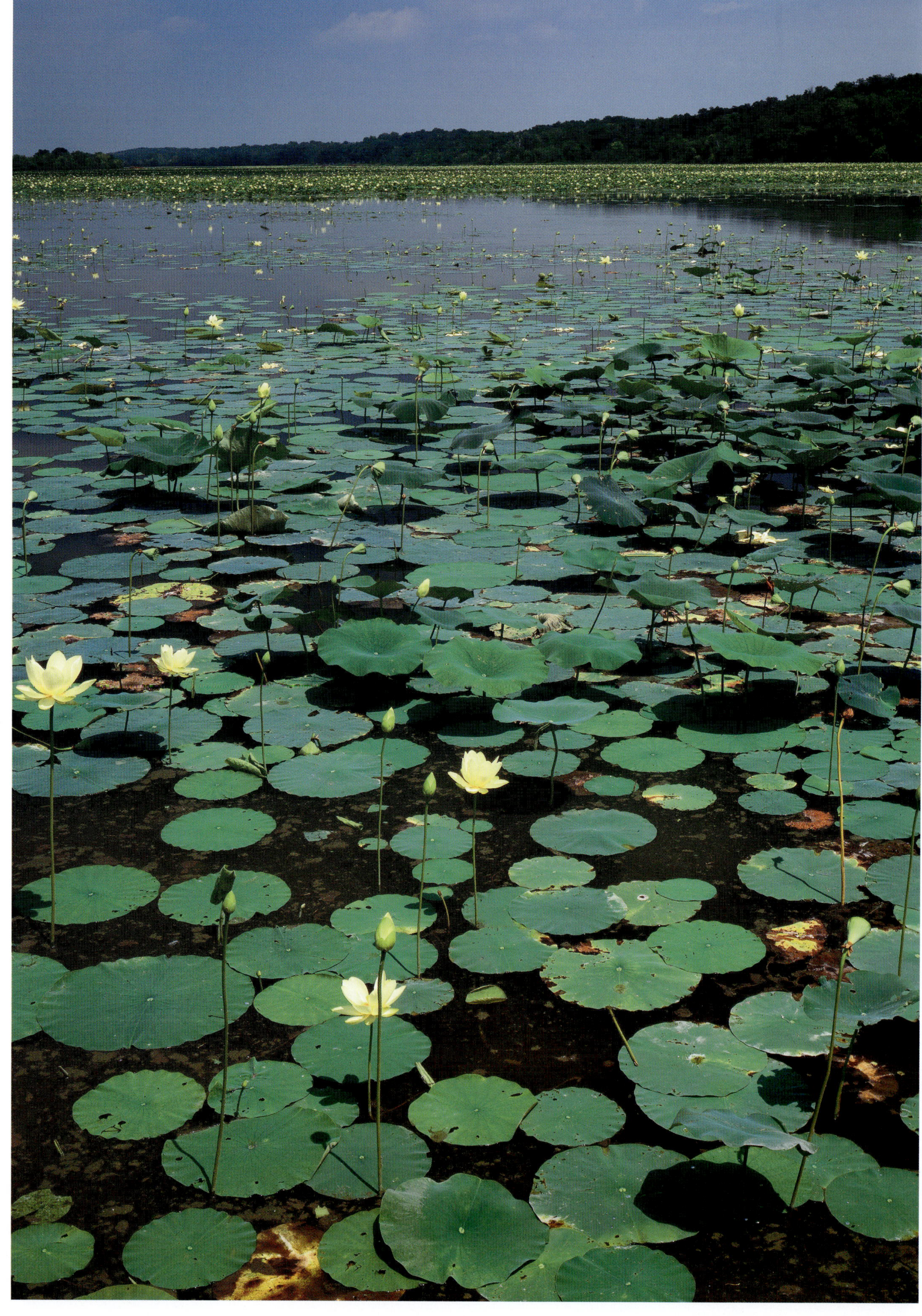

THIS PAGE:

American lotus on Spring Lake: Spring Lake State Fish and Wildlife Area, Tazewell County *(Springfield Plain, Till Plains Section, Central Lowland Province)*
Spring Lake, a long, narrow lake with 18 miles of shoreline, was created by damming the Illinois River. In summer, its surface brightens with the bloom of American lotus *(Nelumbo lutea)*. *August 2001*

OPPOSITE PAGE:

Washington County Lake: Washington County Conservation Area, Washington County *(Mount Vernon Hill Country, Till Plains Section, Central Lowland Province)*
Quail, woodcock, and pheasant abound in 1,440-acre Washington County State Recreation Area, near Nashville. The park is also home to 248-acre Washington County Lake, seen here at sunset. *October 2001*

MOUNT VERNON HILL COUNTRY

TILL PLAINS SECTION OF CENTRAL LOWLAND PROVINCE

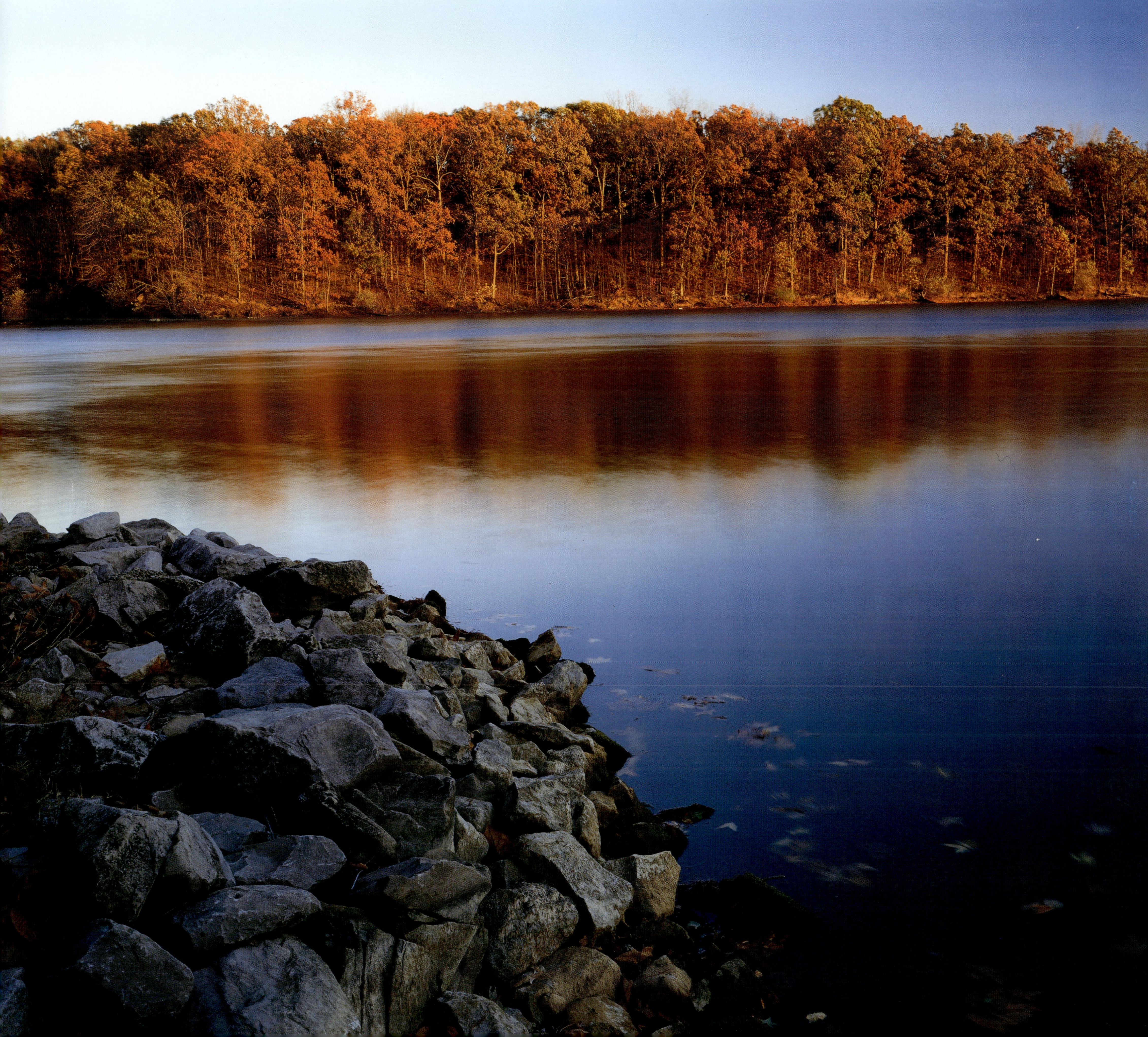

OPPOSITE PAGE:

Sunset over the Upper Mississippi River National Wildlife and Fish Refuge: viewed from Lookout Point in Mississippi Palisades State Park, Carroll County *(Wisconsin Driftless Section, Central Lowland Province)*

Taken from Lookout Point atop the Mississippi Palisades, a two-mile long escarpment of cave-pocked dolomite cliffs north of Savanna ranging between 50 and 110 feet high, this photograph surveys the midpoint of Navigation Pool 13, the reach of the Upper Mississippi River impounded by Lock and Dam 13 near Clinton, Iowa, and backed upstream to Lock and Dam 12 near Bellevue, Iowa. The Upper Mississippi River National Wildlife and Fish Refuge is the longest wildlife refuge in the lower 48 states. The 194,000-acre refuge was established in 1924 to protect bottomland habitat for migratory birds (notably tundra swans, canvasbacks, and neotropical songbirds) and fish (catfish, carp, bluegill, crappie, bass, walleye, and northern pike). The refuge extends 261 miles along the Mississippi River from the Chippewa River in Wisconsin down to Cordova, Illinois. *October 1995*

WISCONSIN DRIFTLESS SECTION OF CENTRAL LOWLAND PROVINCE

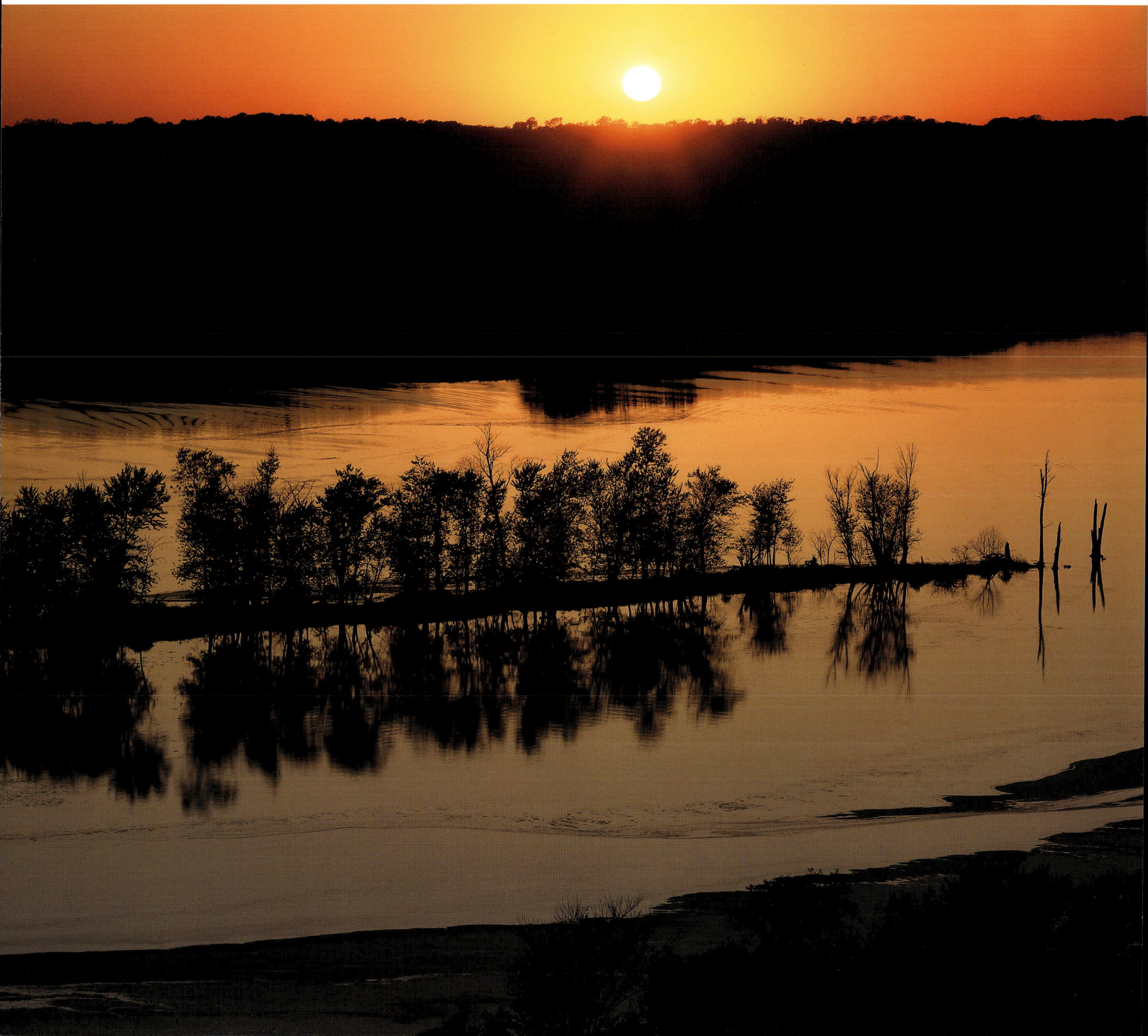

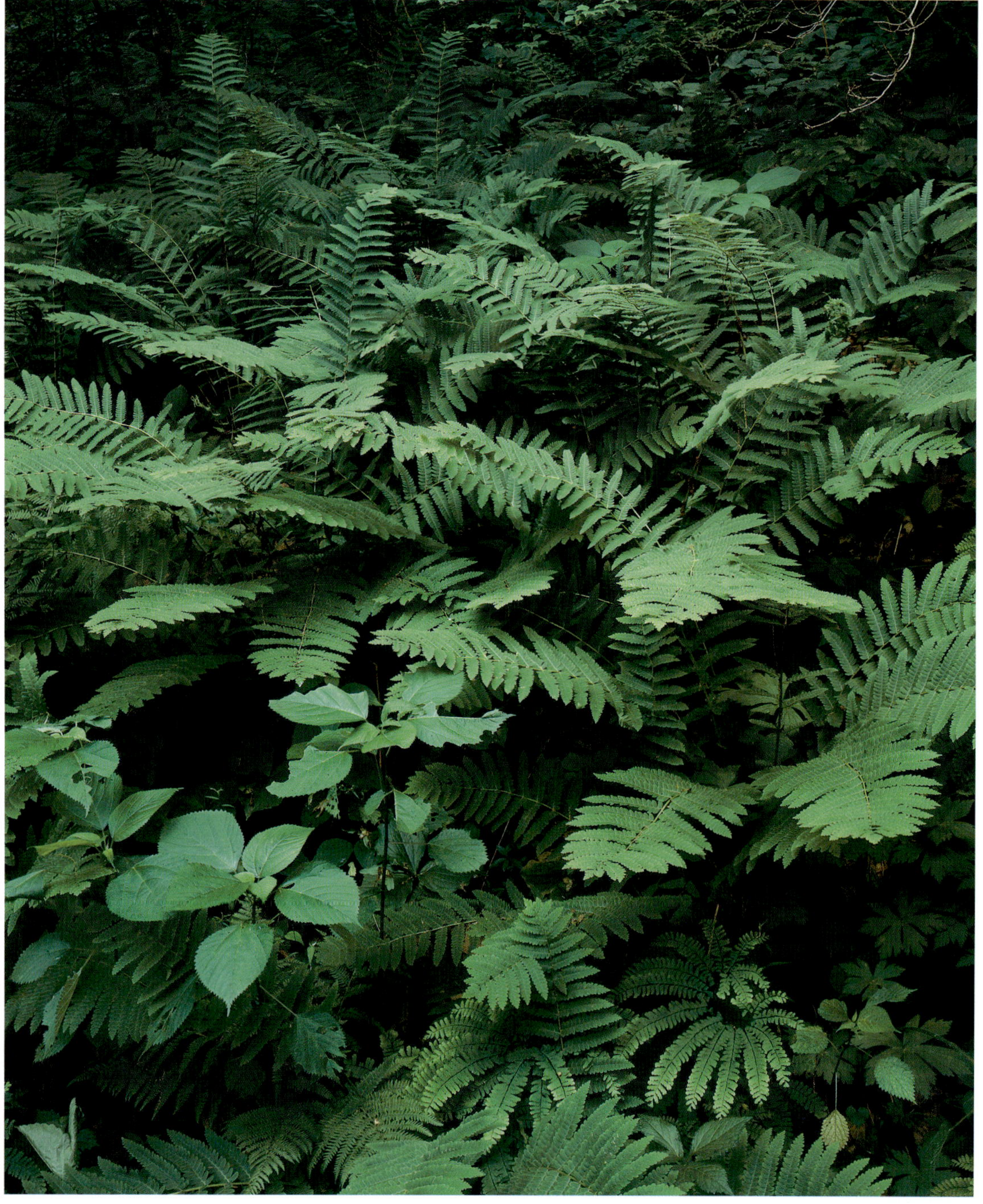

THIS PAGE ABOVE:

Ferns: Mississippi Palisades State Park, Carroll County *(Wisconsin Driftless Section, Central Lowland Province)*
The 2,500-acre area of Mississippi Palisades State Park encompasses not only the Mississippi Palisades but also many deep wooded ravines dissecting unglaciated terrain, at the southern pinch-out of the interlobate enclave known as the Wisconsin Driftless Section, bypassed by the succession of glaciers that rode over most of the rest of Illinois. Ferns dot the steep, shaded ravines. *June 1999*

OPPOSITE PAGE:

Upper Mississippi River National Wildlife and Fish Refuge and bluffs north of Savanna: viewed from Mississippi Palisades State Park, Carroll County *(Wisconsin Driftless Section, Central Lowland Province)*
This southward view also takes in the Savanna-Sabula Bridge, which—not surprisingly—spans the Mississippi River between Sabula, Iowa, and Savanna, Illinois. This steel truss bridge was completed in 1932. *June 1999*

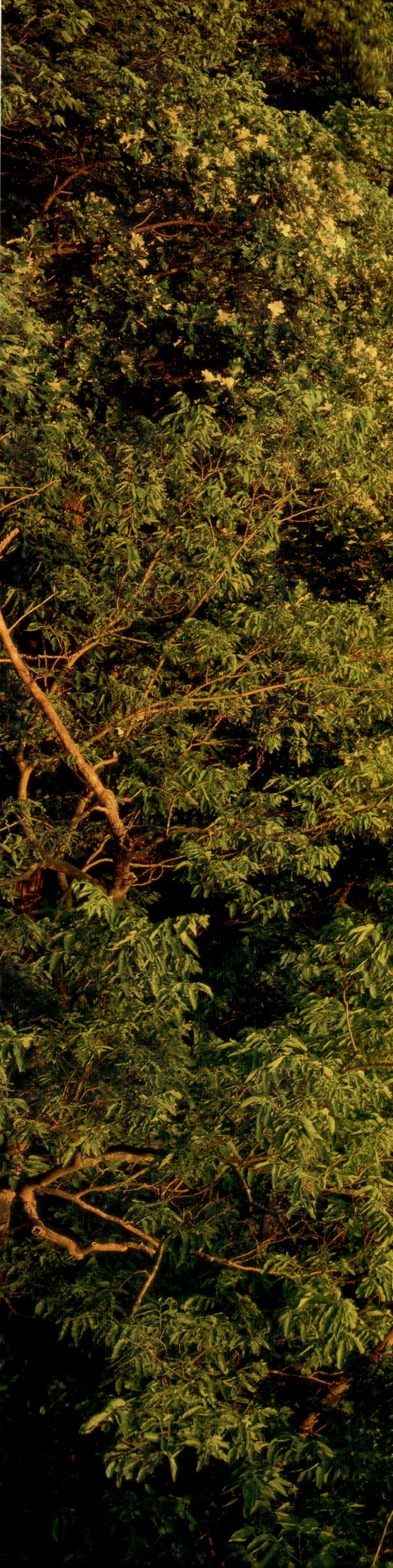

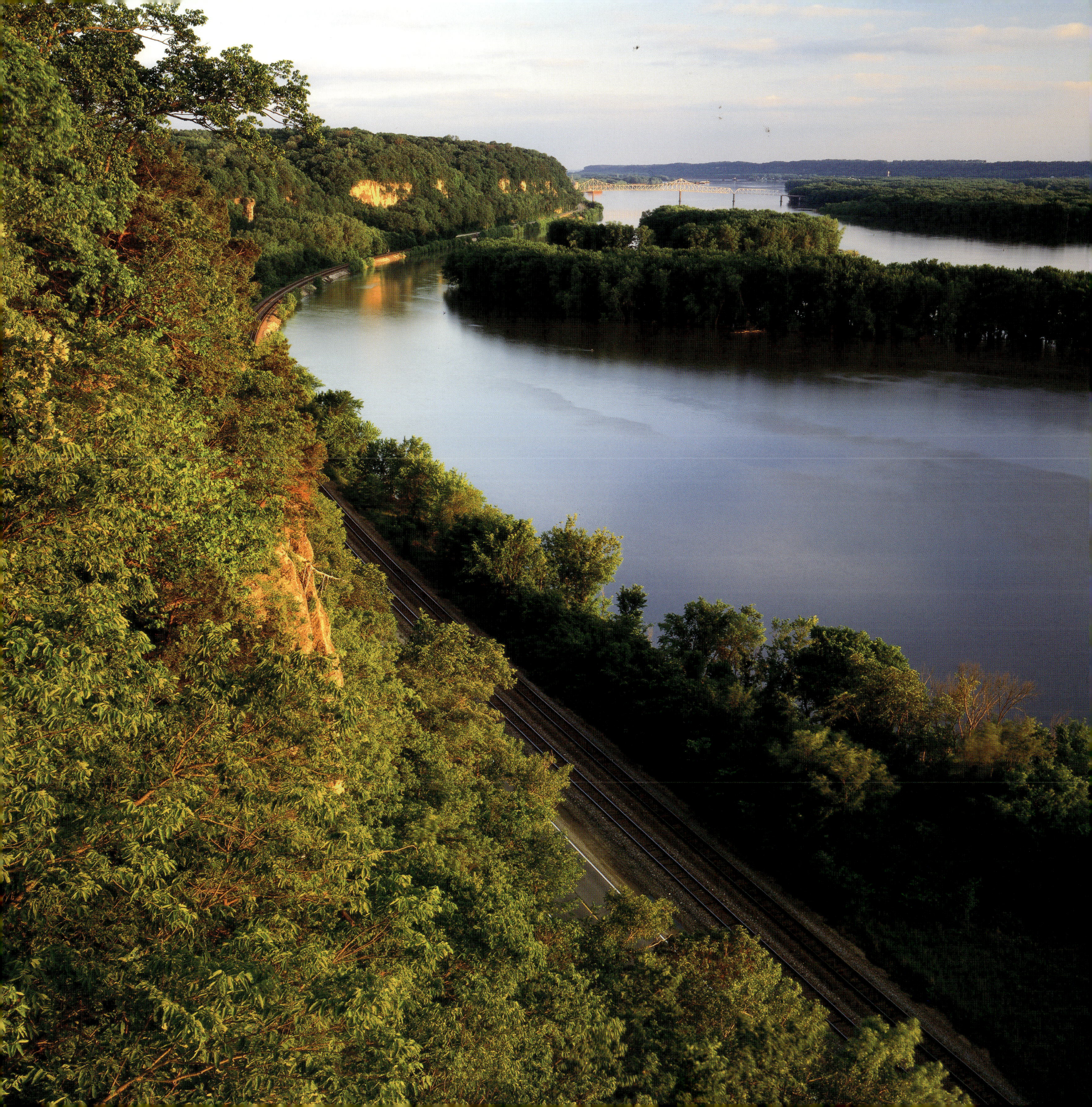

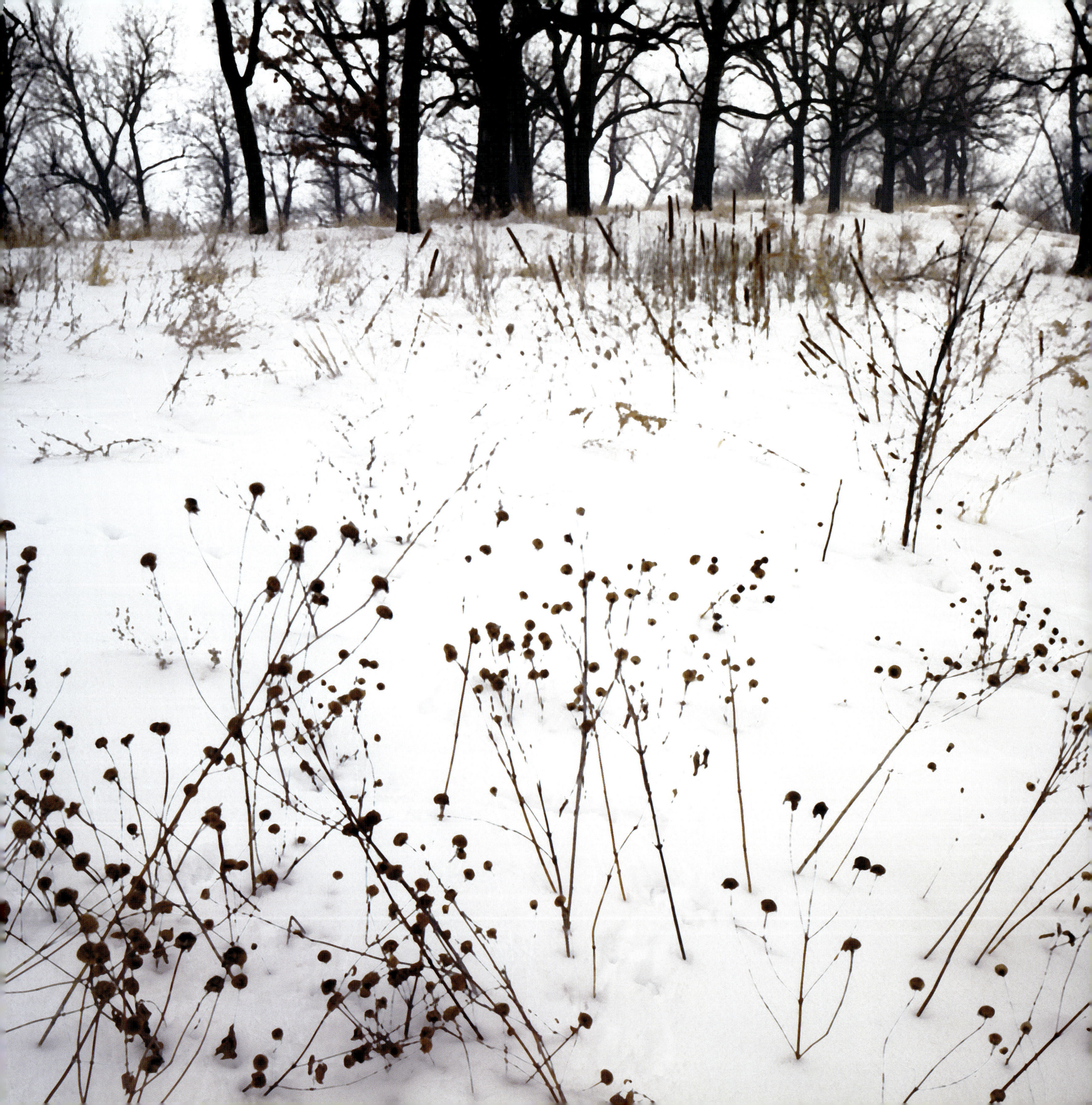

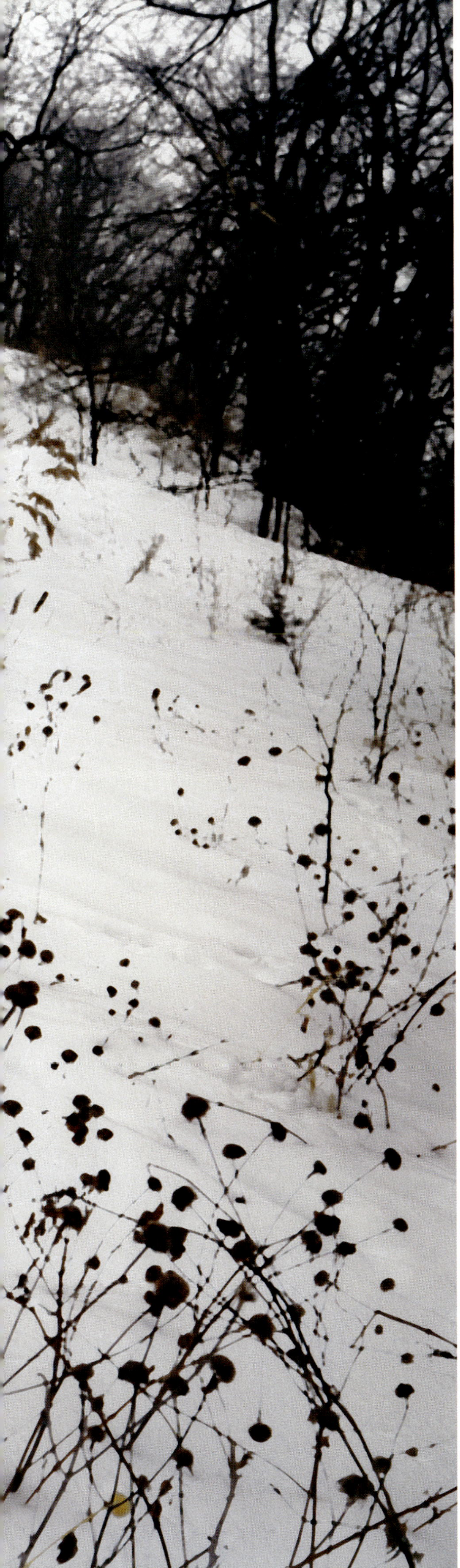

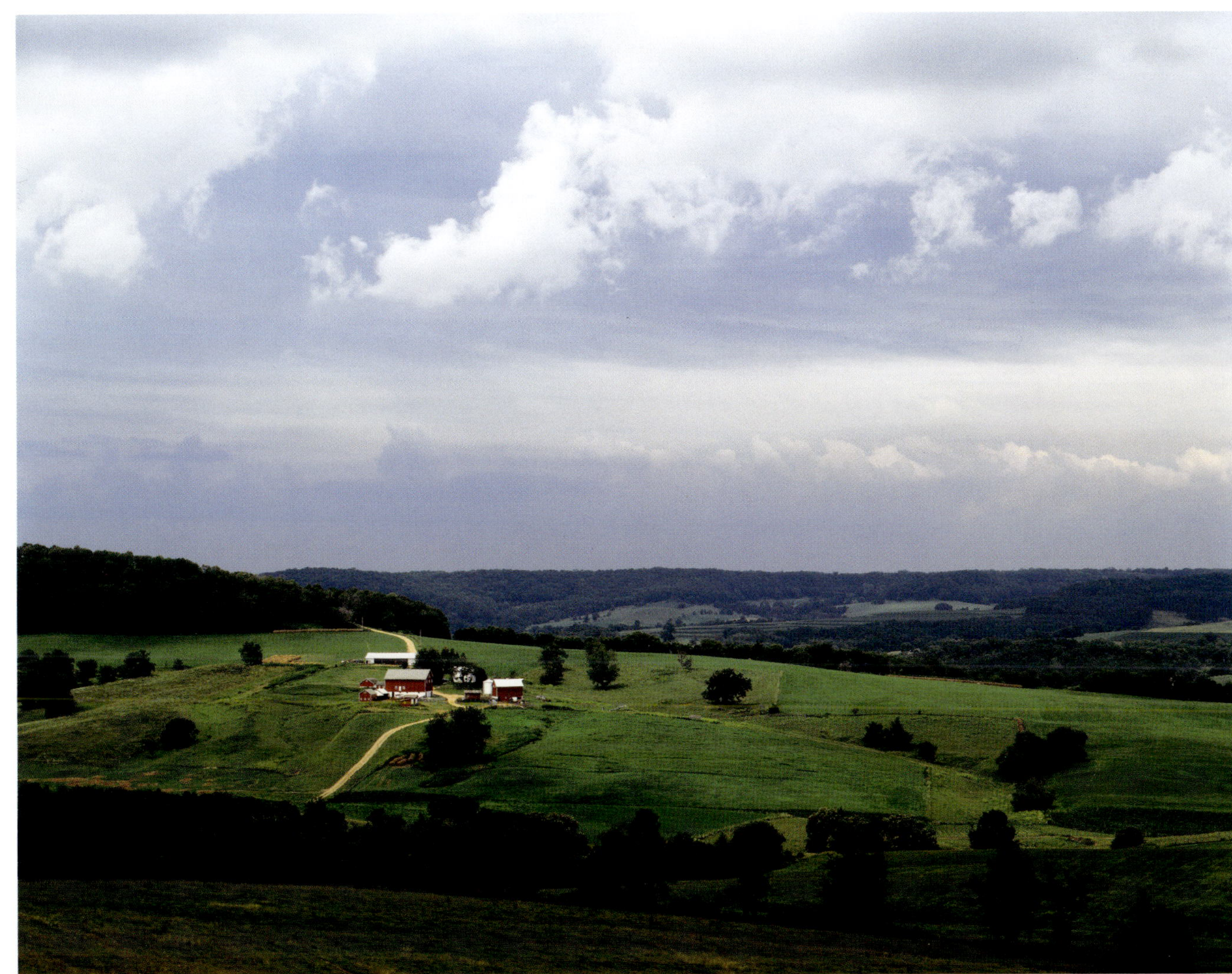

THIS PAGE ABOVE:

Storm clouds over dissected dairy farmland: near Galena, Jo Daviess County *(Wisconsin Driftless Section, Central Lowland Province)*

In a state known for endless miles of flat agricultural land, the farms in the rolling hills of Jo Daviess County have attracted many painters with brush and canvas, as well as tourists who enjoy the pastoral setting surrounding the history-rich town of Galena. *July 1987*

OPPOSITE PAGE:

Field: near Galena, Jo Daviess County *(Wisconsin Driftless Section, Central Lowland Province)*

Plants in a field along the forest edge survive the harsh winter in Jo Daviess County. With temperatures that may drop well below freezing, the next season's seed supply is well protected in the dried flowering heads or buried under a blanket of insulating snow. *January 1999*

OPPOSITE PAGE:

Sunrise on hill overlooking Illinois River: Pere Marquette State Park, Jersey County *(Lincoln Hills Section, Ozark Plateaus Province)*

Named for the Jesuit missionary, Père Jacques Marquette, who accompanied Louis Joliet down the Illinois and Mississippi Rivers in 1673, the 8,000-acre Pere Marquette State Park, on the eastern bank of the Illinois River on its final stretch before merging with the Mississippi River five miles west of Grafton, is one of Illinois's largest parks. The park lies just outside the limit of glaciation, but within the radius of periglacial outwash and loess deposition. Loess, which is fine dust that was comminuted by glaciers and transported by glacial winds, covers all the ridges in the park and is well exposed in the yellow banks along the road to the bluff-tops. *October 1991*

2

OZARK PLATEAUS PROVINCE

LINCOLN HILLS SECTION

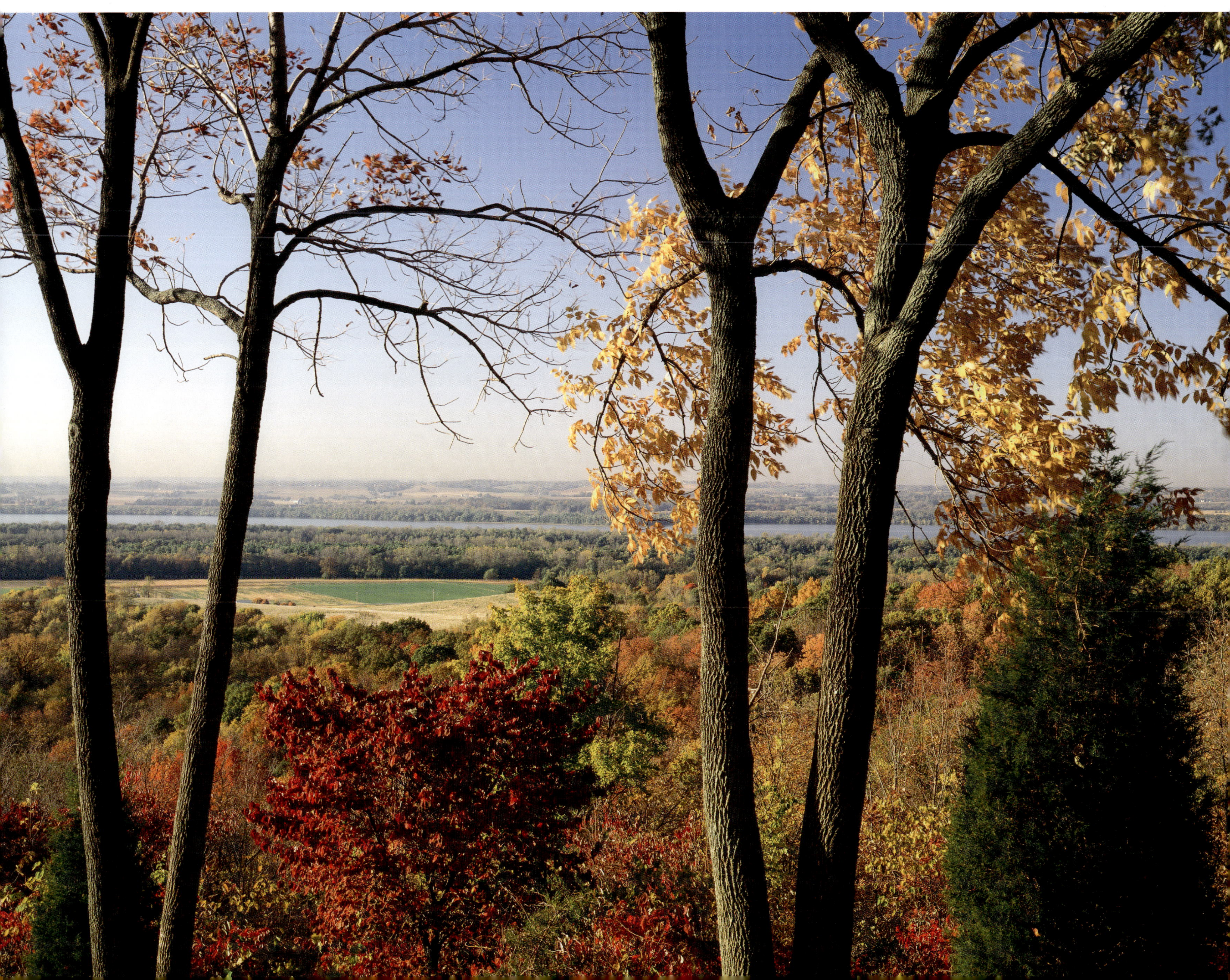

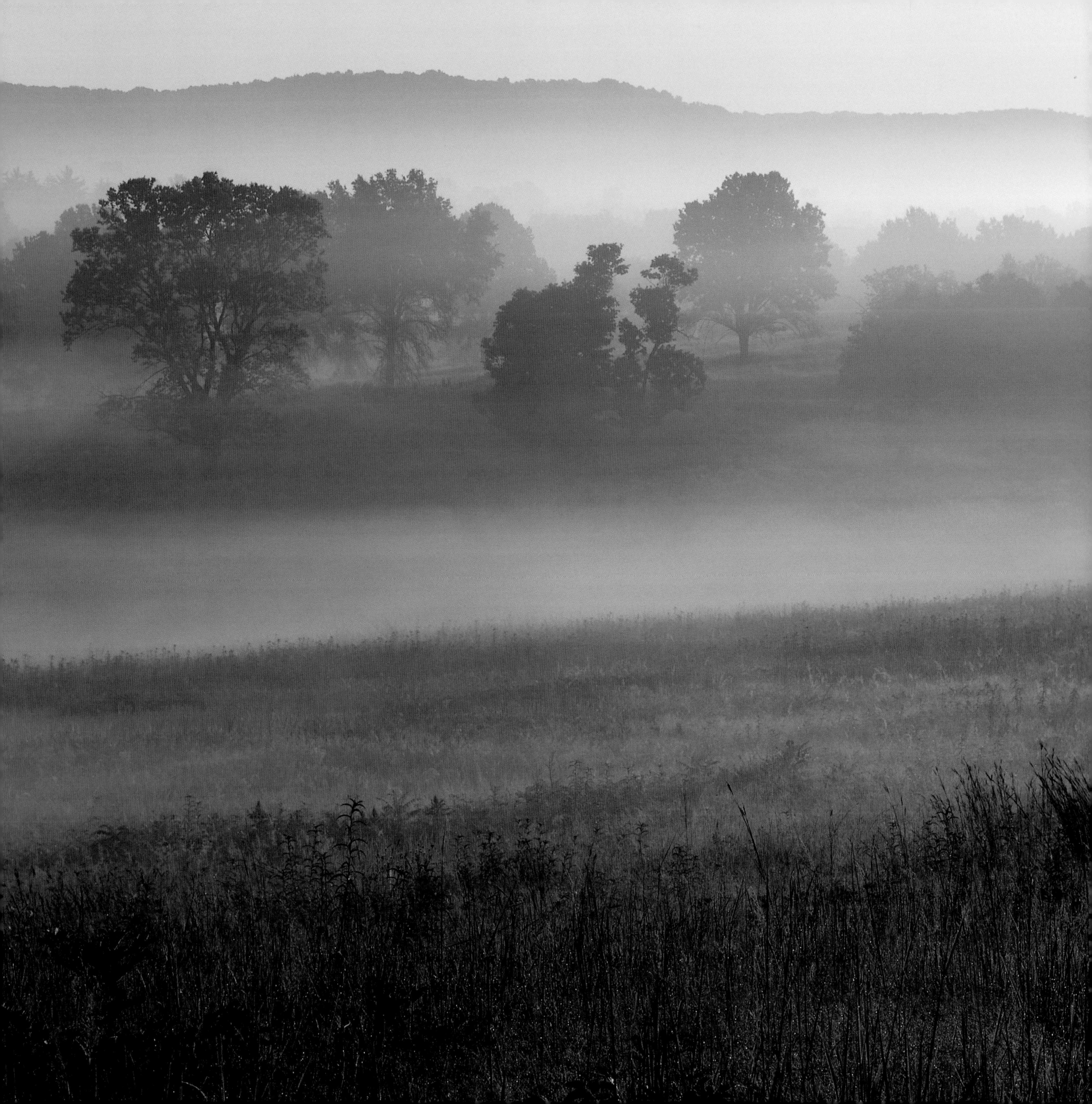

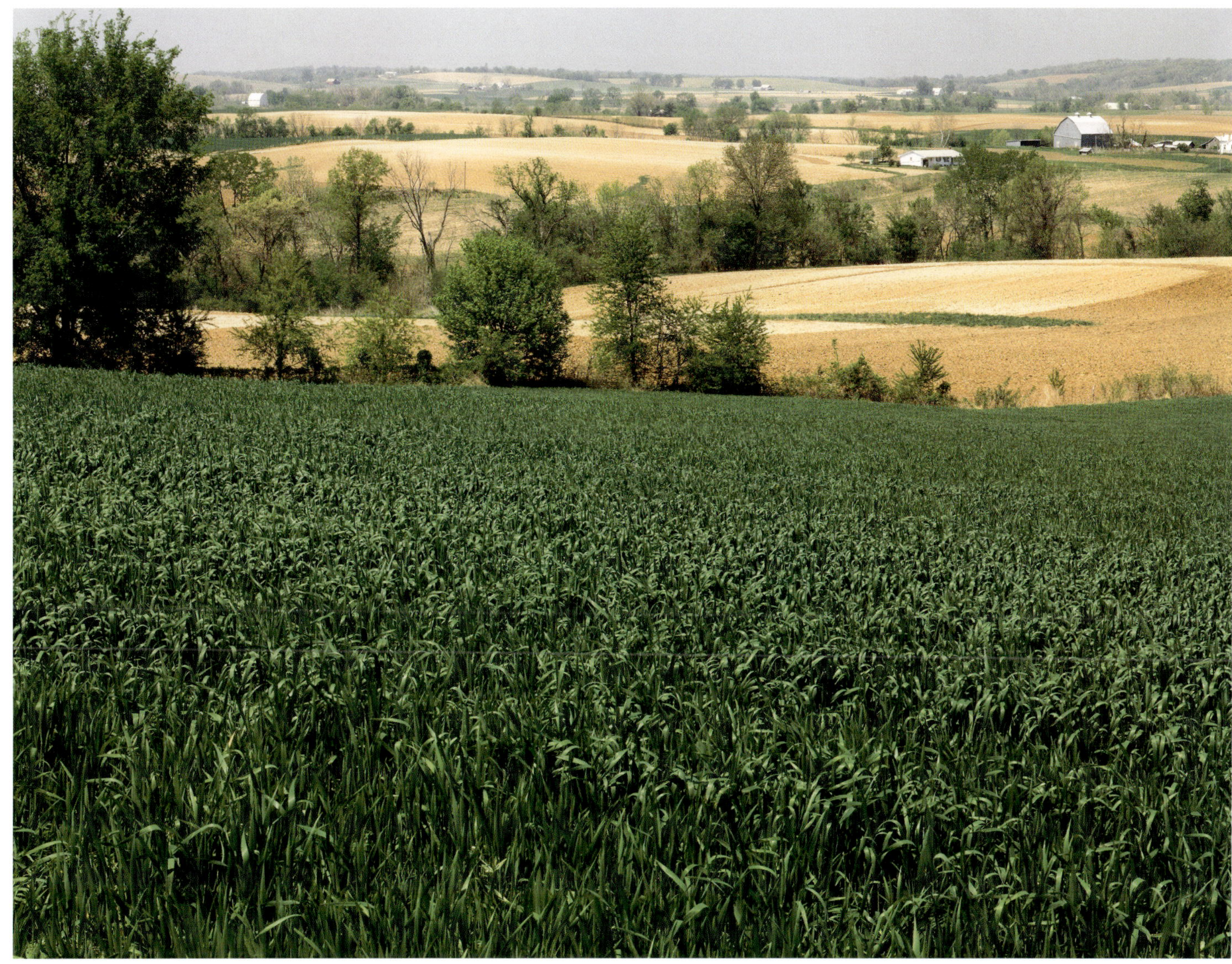

THIS PAGE ABOVE:

Oat field in rolling farmland: Calhoun County *(Lincoln Hills Section, Ozark Plateaus Province)*
The rolling agricultural landscapes in the Lincoln Hills section are similar in appearance to those in the Wisconsin Driftless section, two hundred miles to the north. *April 1987*

OPPOSITE PAGE:

Foggy sunrise on meadow overlooked by hill: Jersey County *(Lincoln Hills Section, Ozark Plateaus Province)*
Rolling wooded hillsides provide picturesque pastoral views along the Illinois and Mississippi River Roads in the western Calhoun, Pike, Jersey, and Greene Counties. A foggy sunrise enshrouding the woodlands is typical of the scenery along the great rivers. *August 1999*

OPPOSITE PAGE:

Banded sandstone: Garden of the Gods Recreation Area, Shawnee National Forest, Hardin County *(Shawnee Hills Section, Interior Low Plateaus Province)*

The rock formations and cliffs at the Garden of the Gods are eroded in the Pounds Sandstone of the Caseyville Formation, laid down 320 million years ago in the Pennsylvanian age. The Pounds Sandstone, which in this area has a thickness of about a hundred feet of fairly pure quartz sandstone bearing numerous white quartz pebbles, is highly resistant to erosion and hence a cliff-former. The Pounds Sandstone commonly shows iron oxide-rich banding, attributed to the Liesegang phenomenon, which involves rhythmic precipitation from colloidal suspensions in the interstitial fluids in porous sandstone. *April 1995*

3
INTERIOR LOW PLATEAUS PROVINCE
SHAWNEE HILLS SECTION

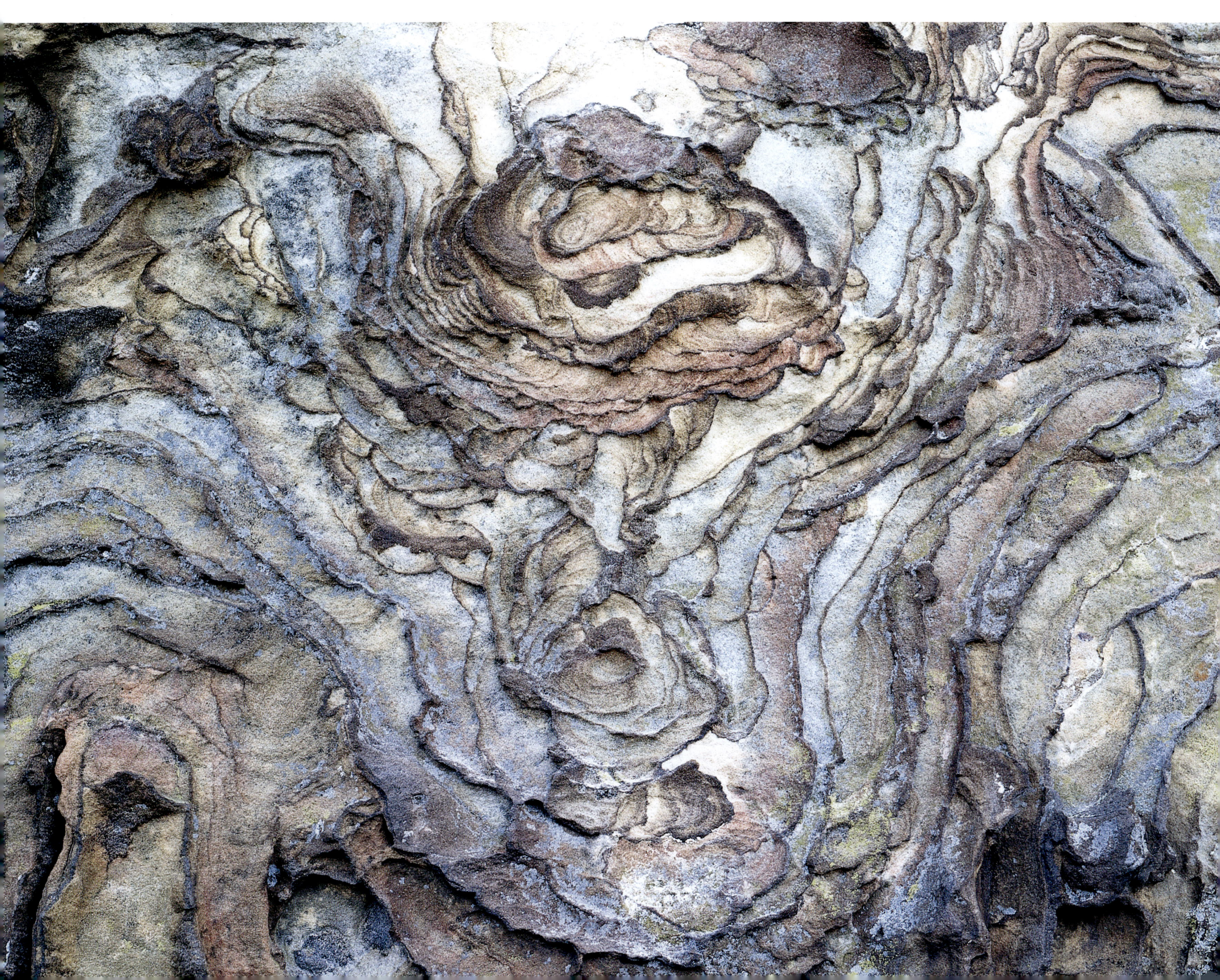

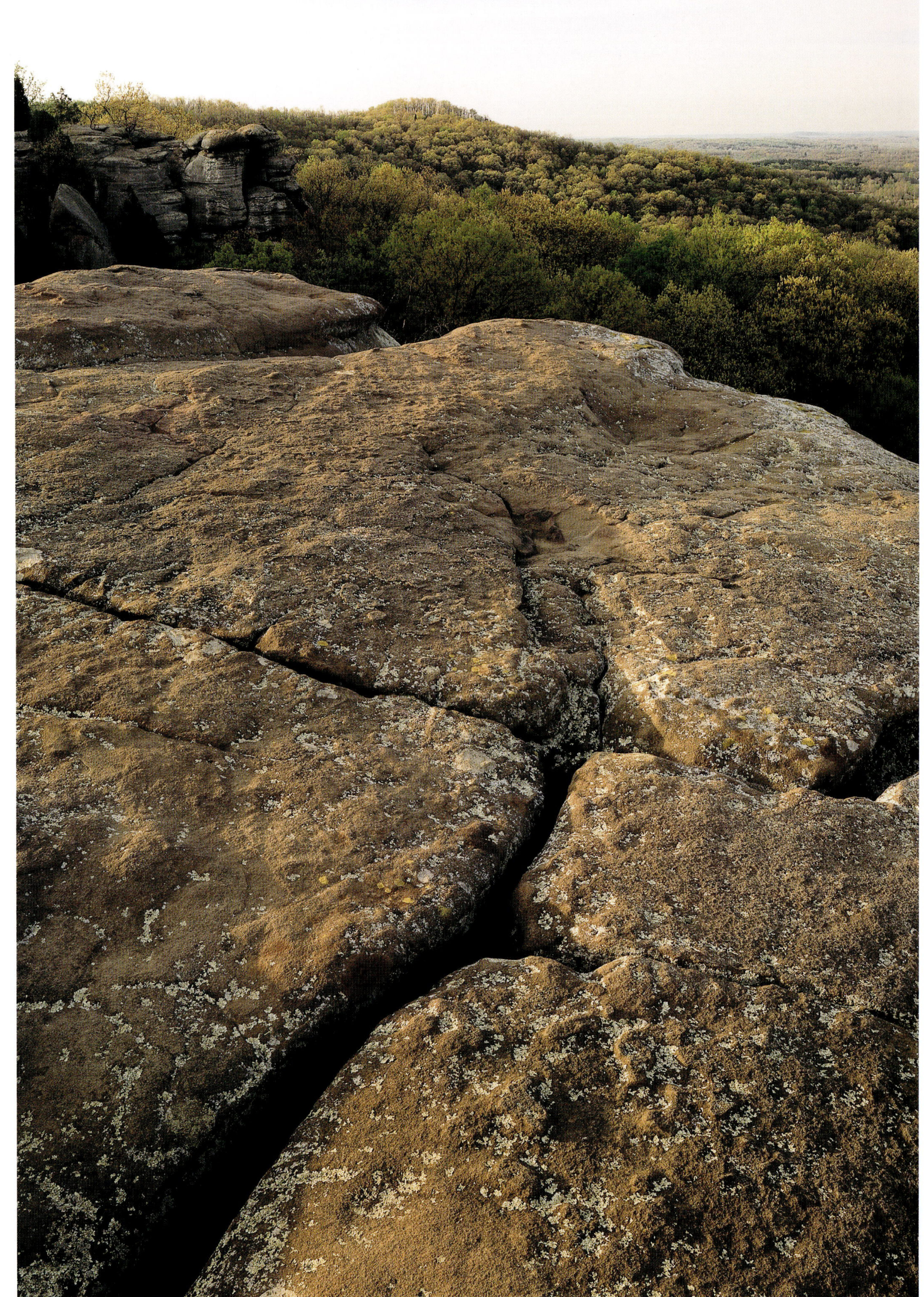

Sandstone bluffs: Garden of the Gods, Shawnee National Forest, Hardin County *(Shawnee Hills Section, Interior Low Plateaus Province)*
The Pounds Sandstone in the Garden of the Gods was laid down as river channel sands debouched 320 million years ago onto a delta in a shallow continental sea that covered most of Illinois, western Indiana, and western Kentucky. The Pounds Sandstone overlies several miles of older sediments and was once buried under another mile of younger sediments, since eroded away. The Pound Sandstone contains high-energy near-shore sedimentary structures such as crossbedding, bimodal sorting, and ripple marks. *April 1995*

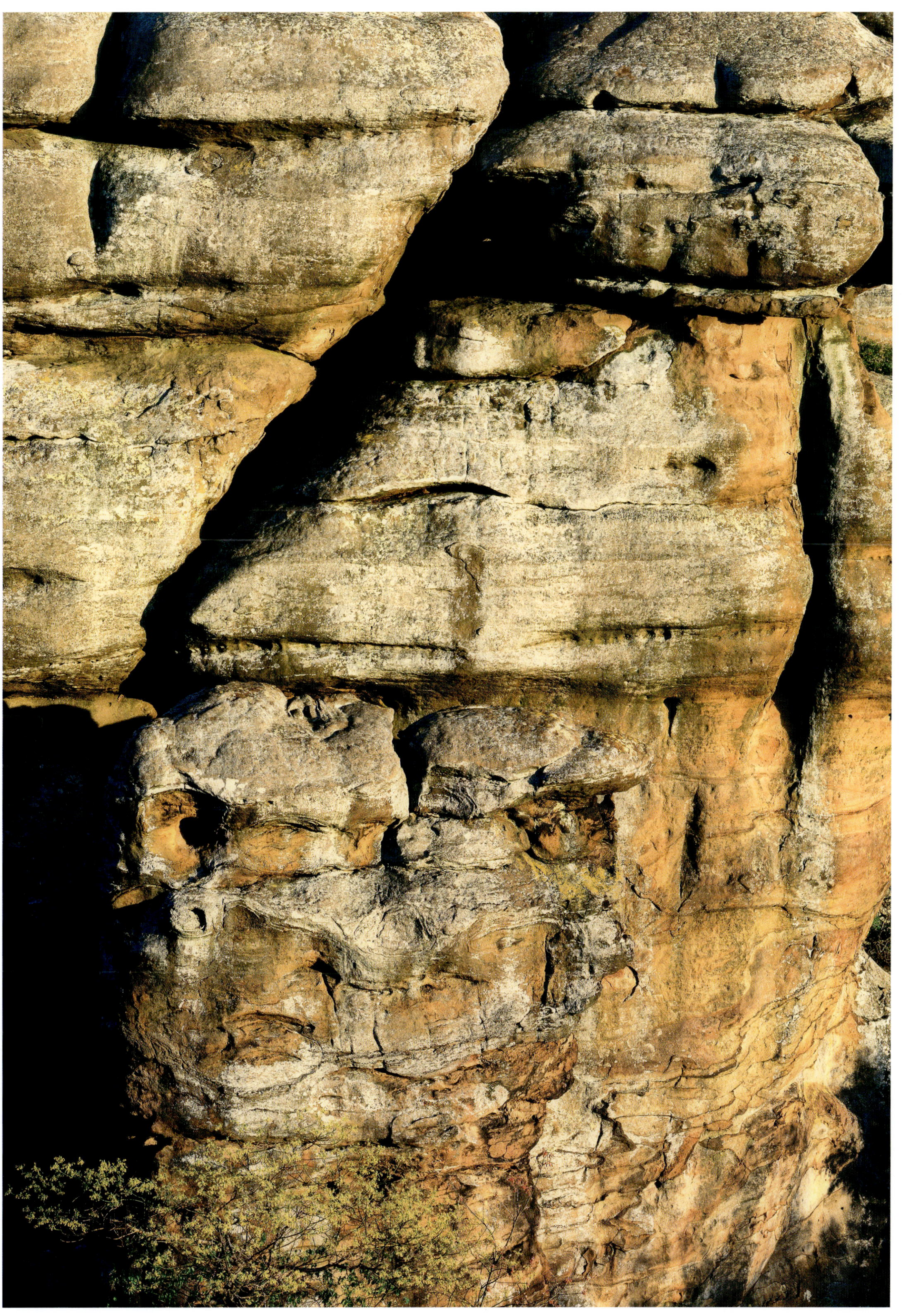

Sandstone bluffs: Garden of the Gods, Shawnee National Forest, Hardin County *(Shawnee Hills Section, Interior Low Plateaus Province)*
The Garden of the Gods is located on the Eagle Valley Syncline's uplifted southern limb, whose north-dipping slopes and high knobs and ridges of Pounds Sandstone have all been deeply dissected by erosion. The east-west-trending Eagle Valley Syncline within the Shawnee Hills section is separated from the Illinois basin to the north by a major fault system that extends east into Kentucky. The southern limit of Pleistocene glaciation lies fifteen miles north of the Garden of the Gods. The bluffs of the Garden of the Gods offer outstanding vistas of the portion of the Shawnee Hills protected by the 3,300-acre of the Garden of the Gods Wilderness Area.
April 1995

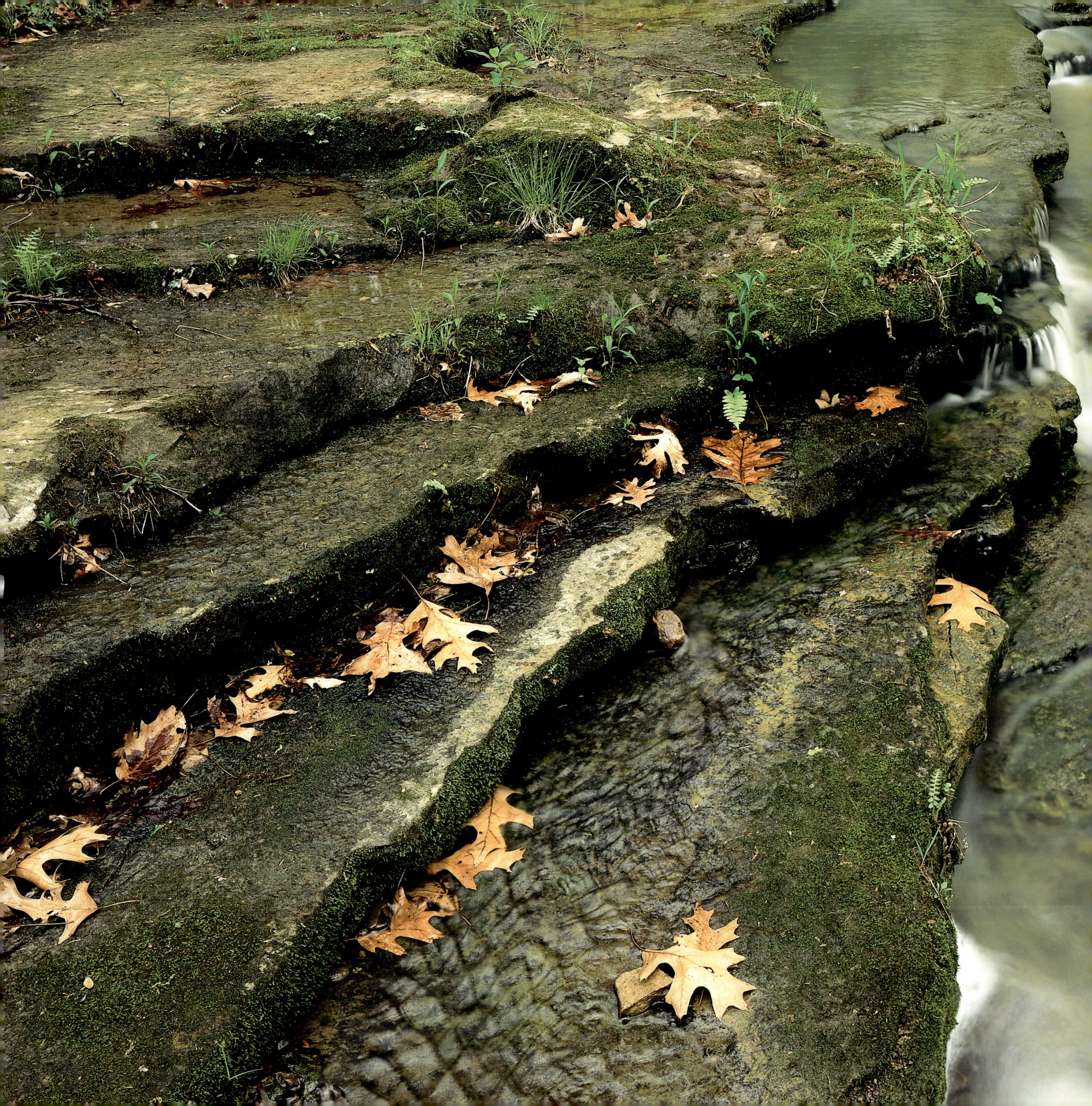

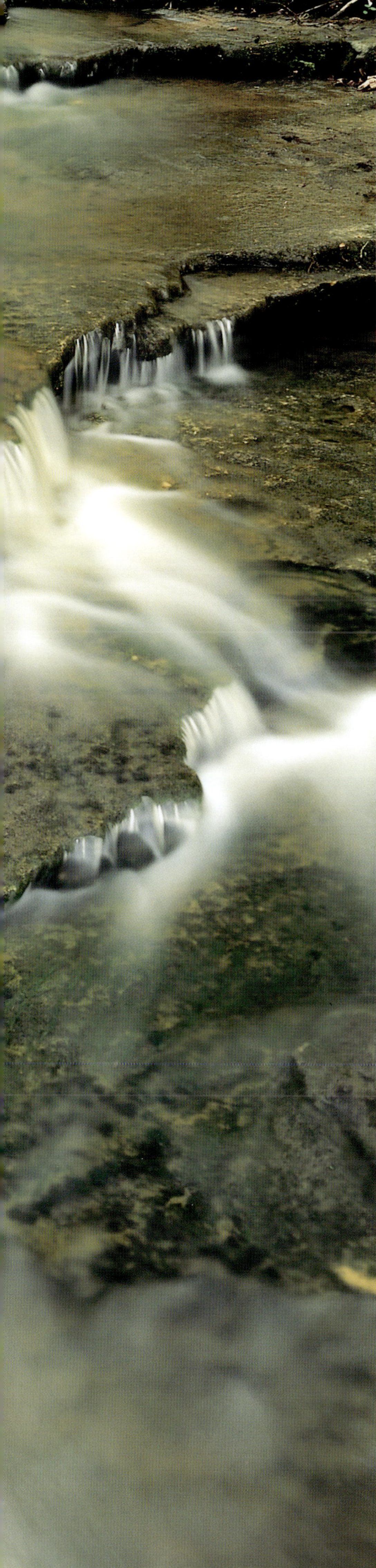

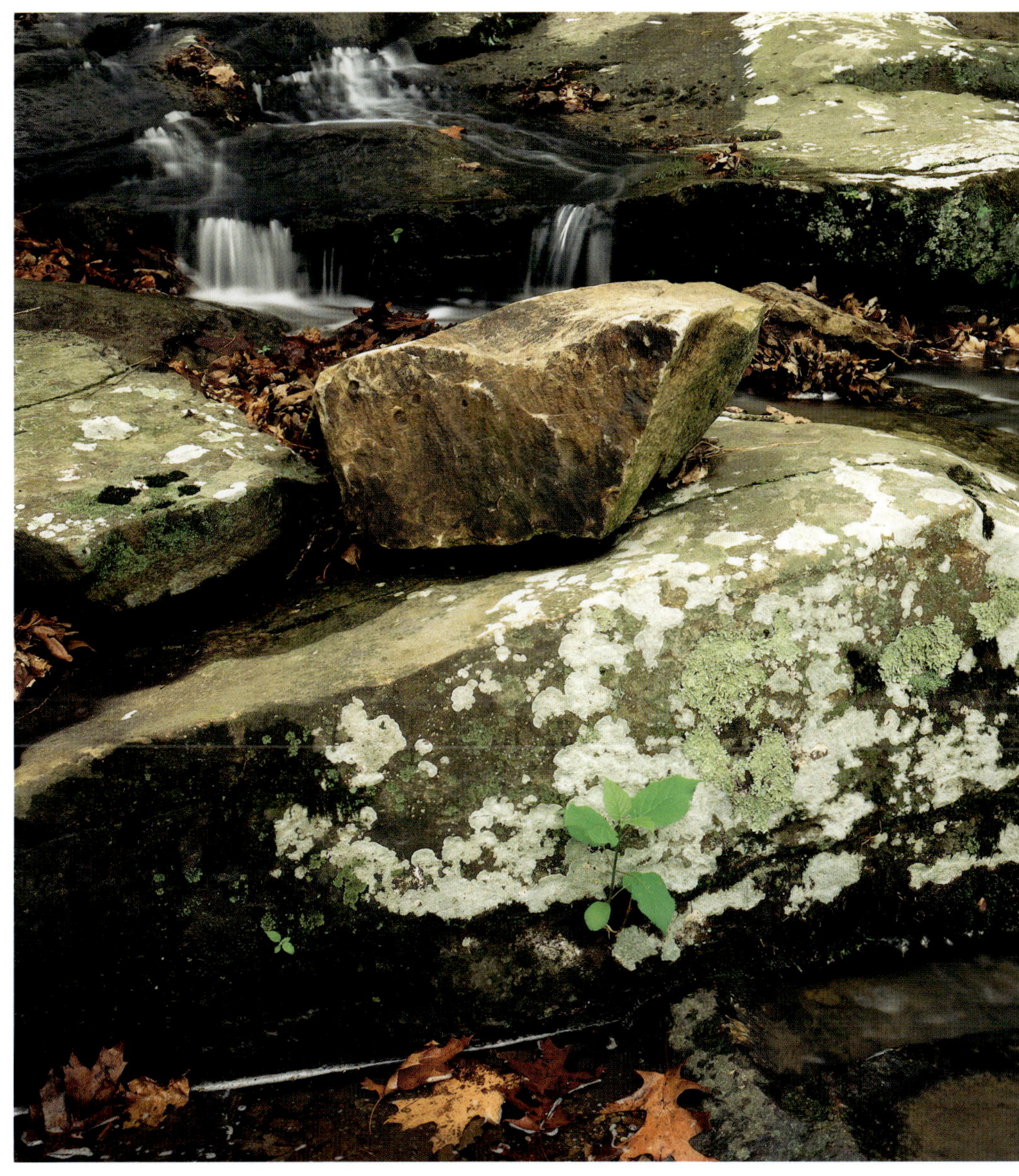

THIS PAGE ABOVE:

Sandstone stream bed beside Stonefort Trail: Giant City State Park, Shawnee National Forest, Jackson County *(Shawnee Hills Section, Interior Low Plateaus Province)*

The sandstone in Giant City State Park belongs to the same member of the Pennsylvanian-age Caseyville Formation as the sandstone in the Garden of the Gods: the Pounds Sandstone, laid down on the margin of an inland sea 320 million years ago, when Illinois was about fifteen degrees north of the paleoequator. *April 1995*

OPPOSITE PAGE:

Sandstone ledges: Giant City State Park, Shawnee National Forest, Jackson County *(Shawnee Hills Section, Interior Low Plateaus Province)*

Giant City State Park, near Carbondale, encompasses 3,694 acres of woods and sandstone outcrops straddling Jackson and Union Counties. The park's name derives from the cyclopean geometry of huge slabs separated from the park's imposing sandstone bluffs. *April 1995*

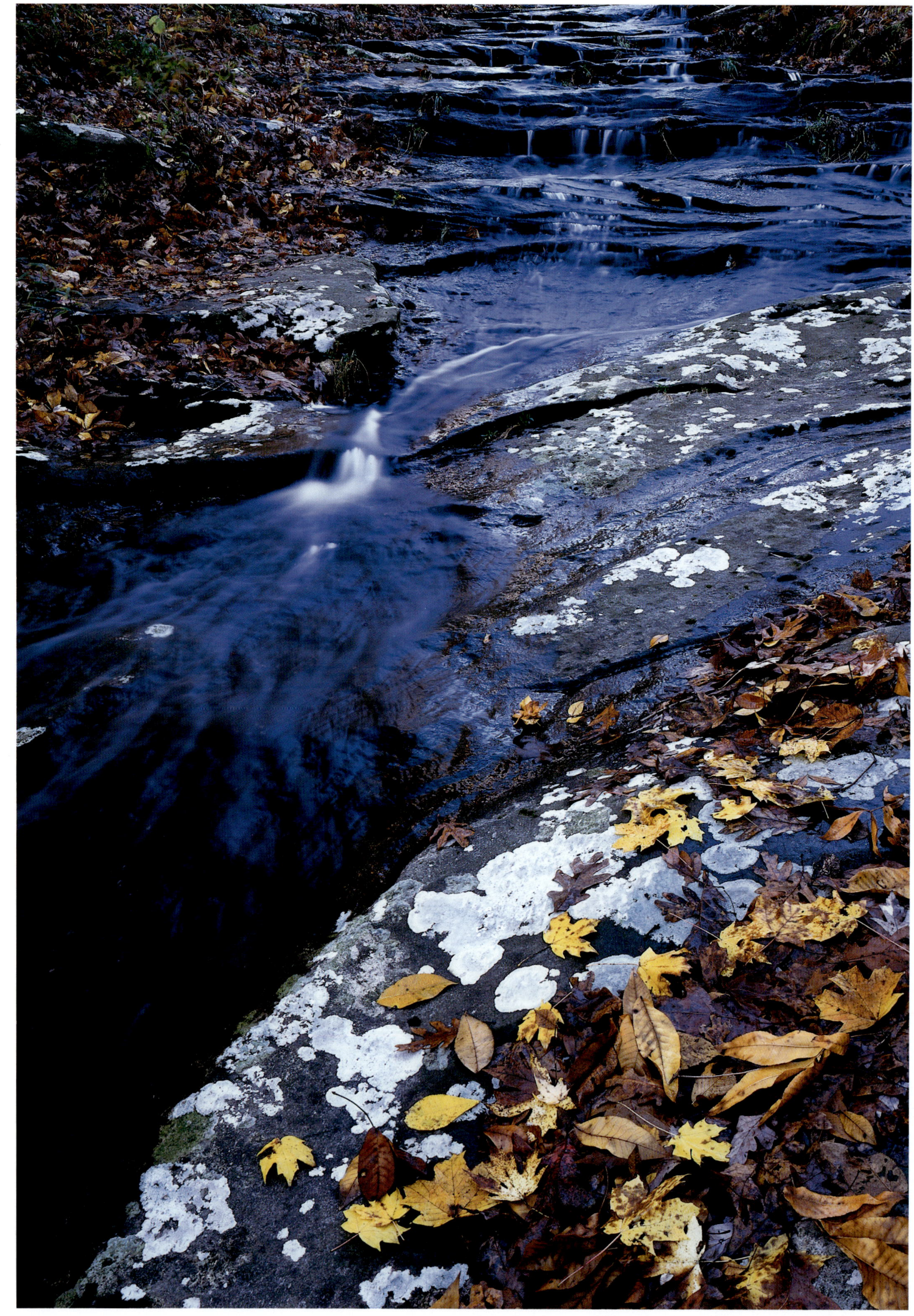

Stream ripples beside Stonefort Trail: Giant City State Park, Shawnee National Forest, Jackson County *(Shawnee Hills Section, Interior Low Plateaus Province)*

The Stonefort is a major archeological site within Giant City State Park, consisting of 370 tons of sandstone blocks piled in a half-acre circle, together with many pit features and a large amount of habitation debris, especially lithics such as projectile points. Radiocarbon dating indicates Lewis-phase occupation, AD 600-1000. The nine other stoneforts known in southern Illinois all appear to be Lewis phase, as well. *October 2001*

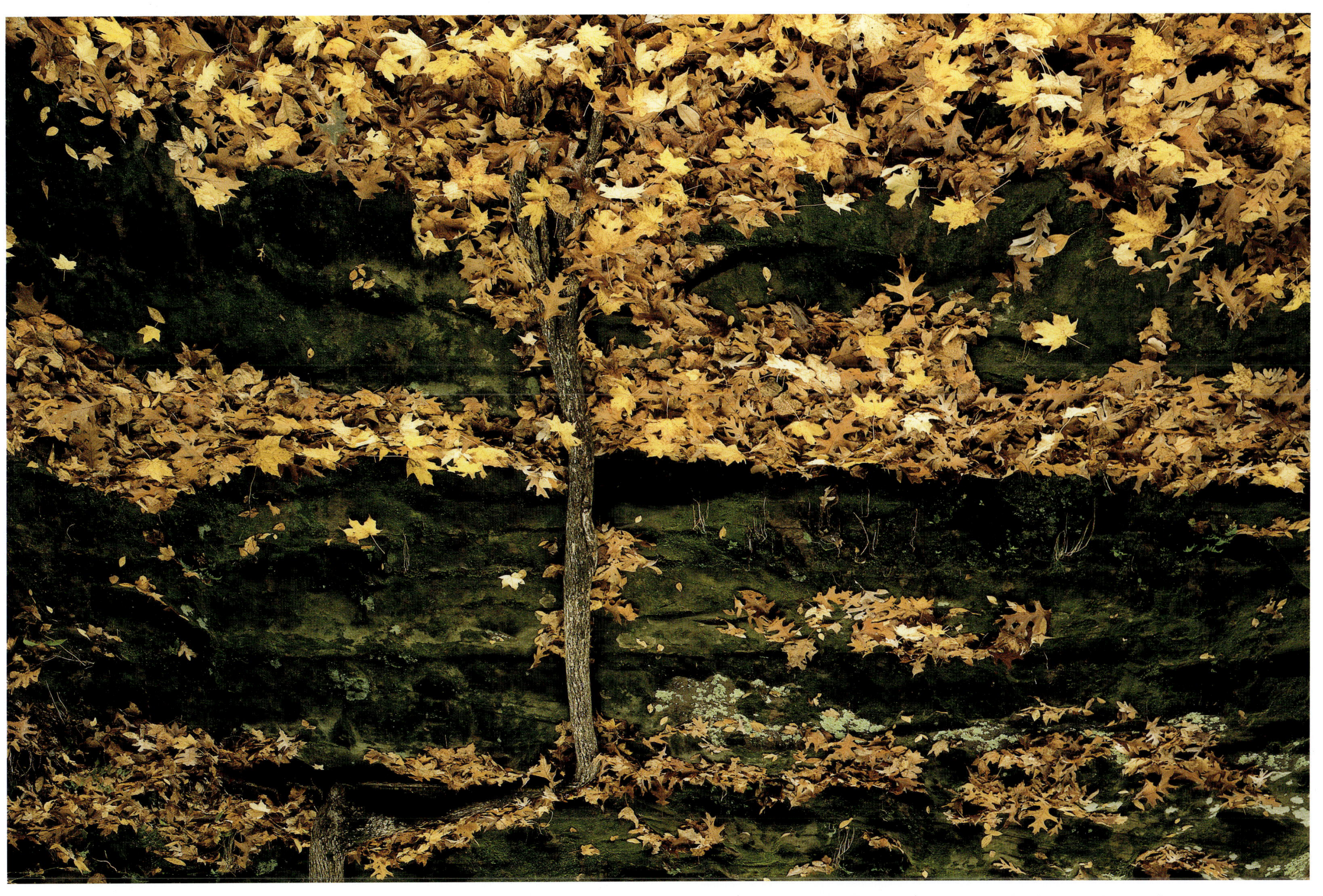

Giant City Nature Trail: Giant City State Park, Shawnee National Forest, Union County *(Shawnee Hills Section, Interior Low Plateaus Province)*
The Giant City Nature Trail traverses the Giant City Streets, as the moss-covered sandstone bluffs are called on account of the fancied resemblance of their rectangular-jointed faces to the handiwork of Brobdingnagian urban planners. *November 1986*

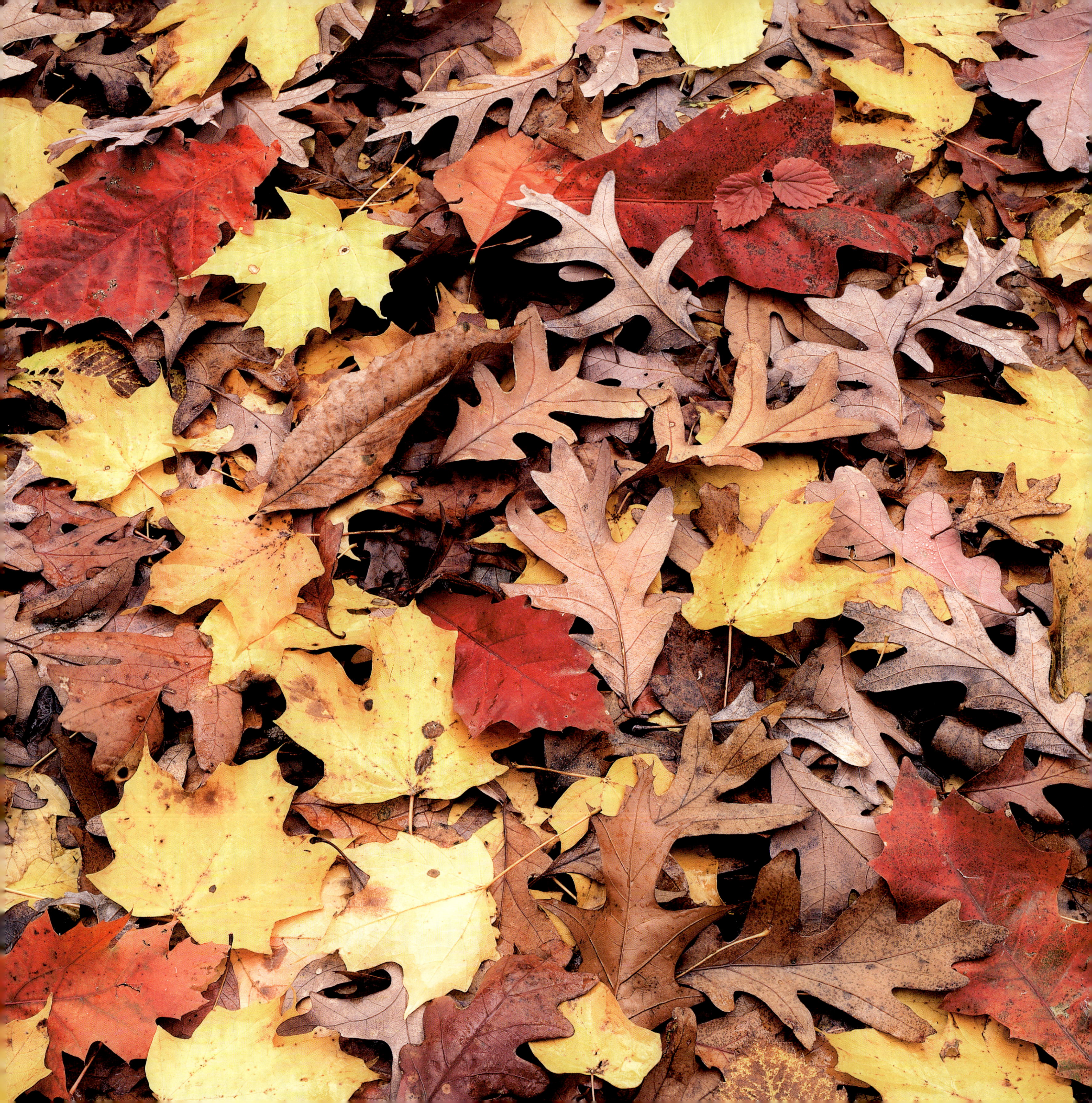

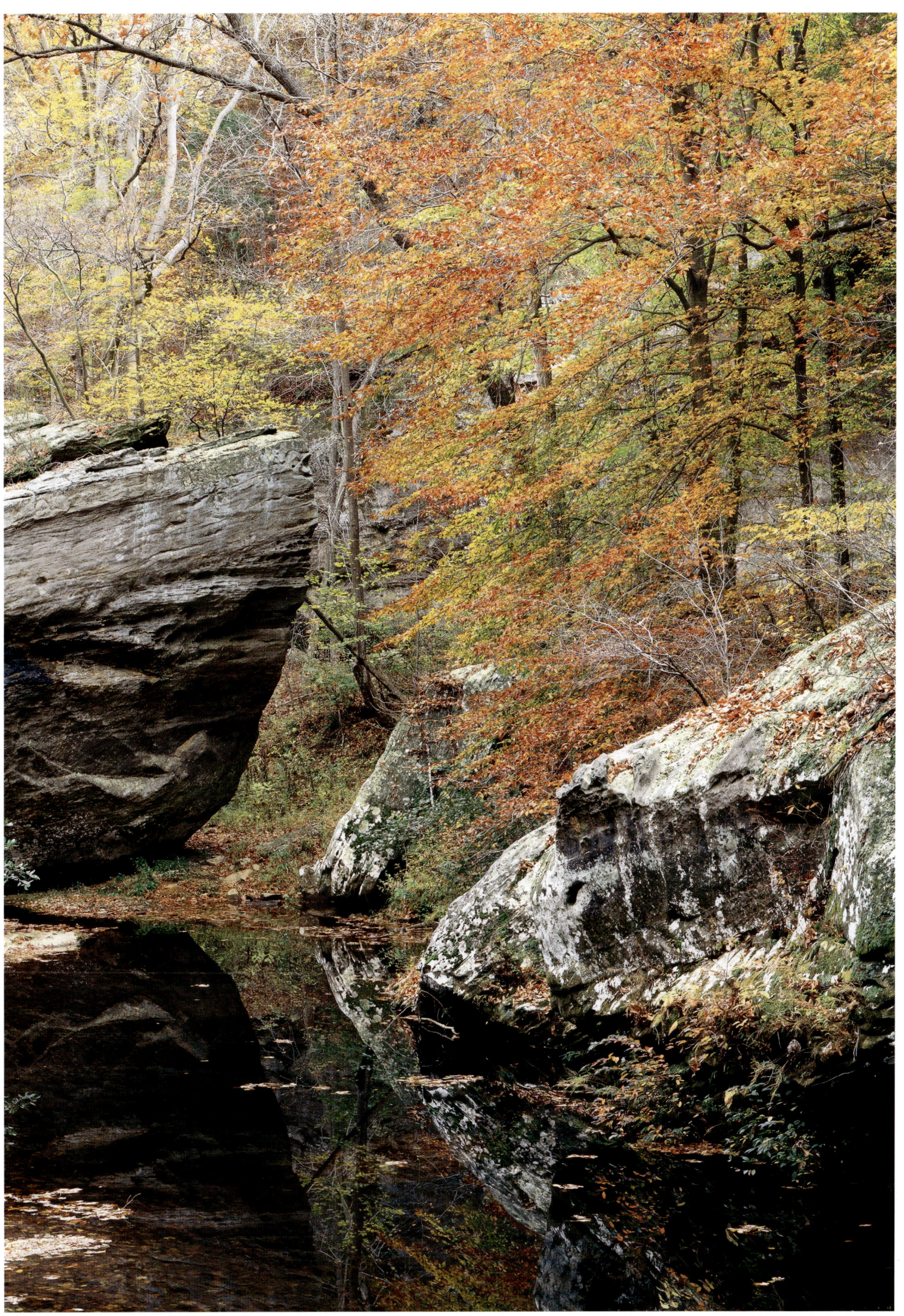

OPPOSITE PAGE:

Dead leaves: Shawnee National Forest, Pope County *(Shawnee Hills Section, Interior Low Plateaus Province)*
November 1995

THIS PAGE:

Fox Gap: Bell Smith Springs Recreation Area, Shawnee National Forest, Pope County *(Shawnee Hills Section, Interior Low Plateaus Province)*
Bell Smith Springs Recreation Area is the fragile jewel of the Shawnee Hills, containing unparalleled examples of ecosystems that adapt to sharply dissected sandstone substrates. Bell Smith Springs has been designated a national natural landmark, a state natural area, and a national recreation area. It is also listed on the National Register of Historic Places, for its cold water springs and large natural bridge have long made Bell Smith Springs a magnet for excursionists. *October 1996*

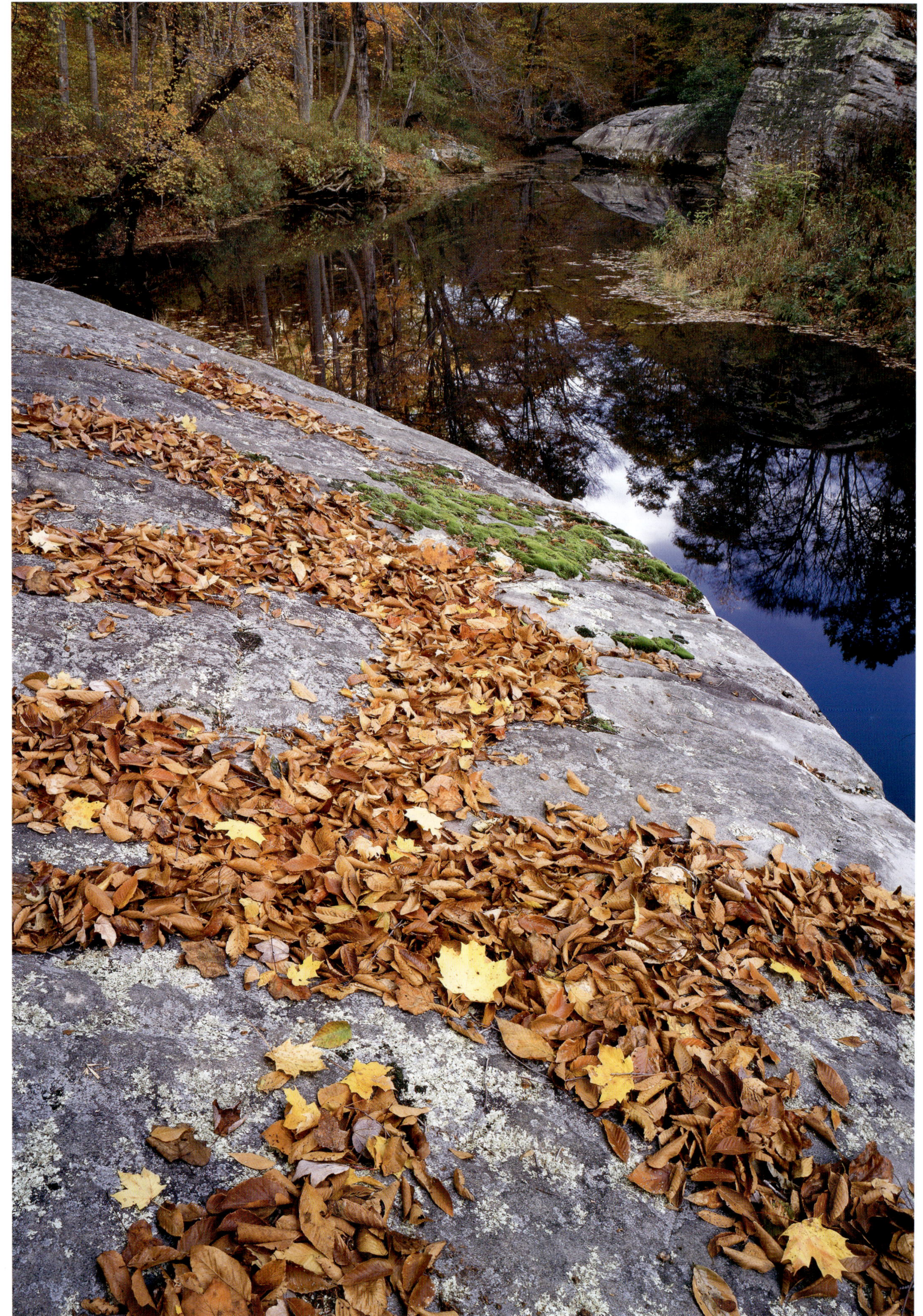

Stream through Fox Gap, viewed from top of sandstone boulder: Bell Smith Springs Recreation Area, Shawnee National Forest, Pope County *(Shawnee Hills Section, Interior Low Plateaus Province)*
Bell Smith Springs Recreation Area is riddled with canyons, at the foot of whose sheer sandstone cliffs huge boulders lie in tumbles. Four creeks come together in the main canyon. Even when these creeks dry up, a dozen cold spring pools continue to fill. The unique hydrology of the canyon contributes to its vegetative diversity: there are over seven hundred plants species at Bell Smith Springs. *October 1996*

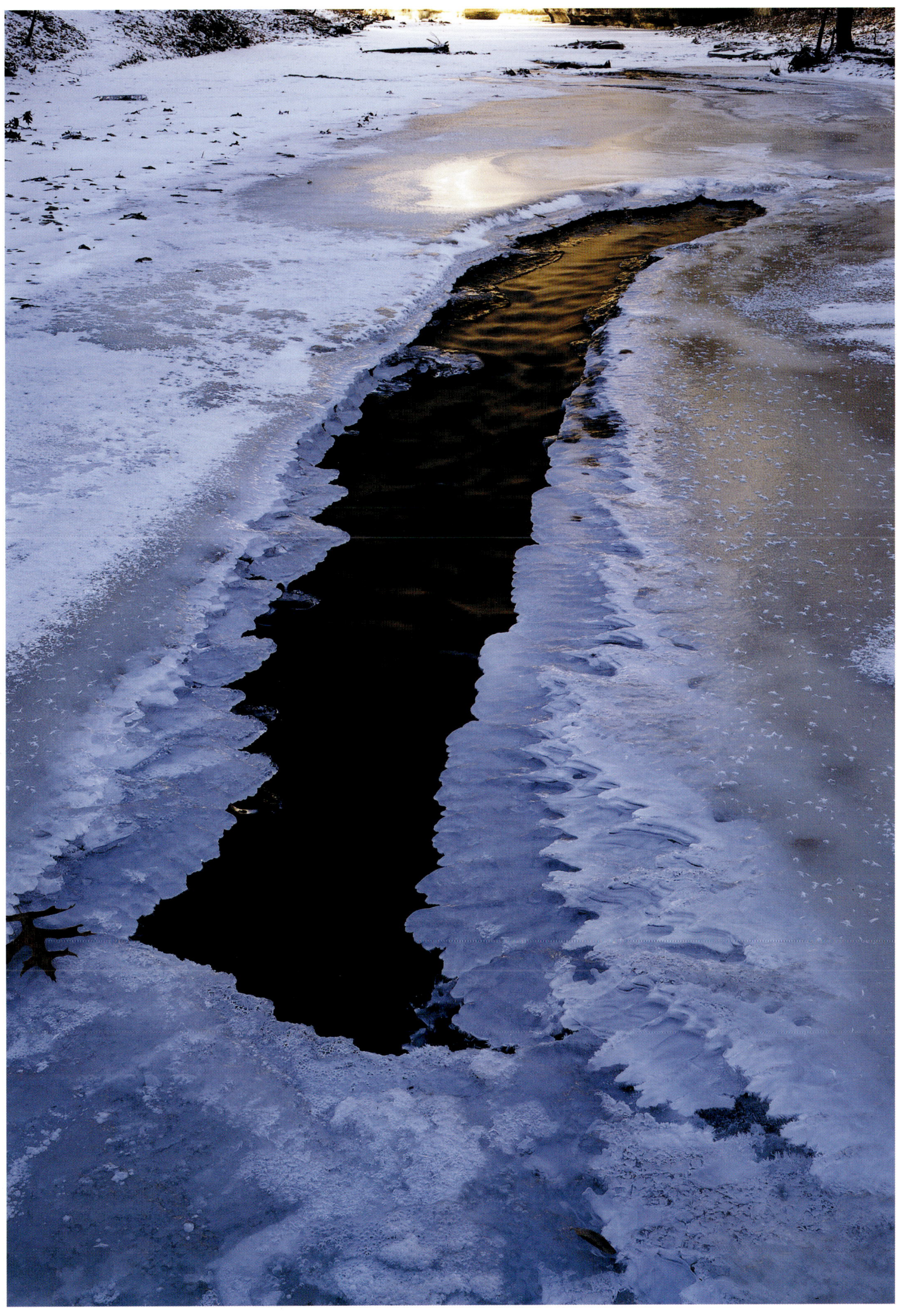

Frozen pond at canyon bottom: Bell Smith Springs Recreation Area, Shawnee National Forest, Pope County *(Shawnee Hills Section, Interior Low Plateaus Province)*
January 1991

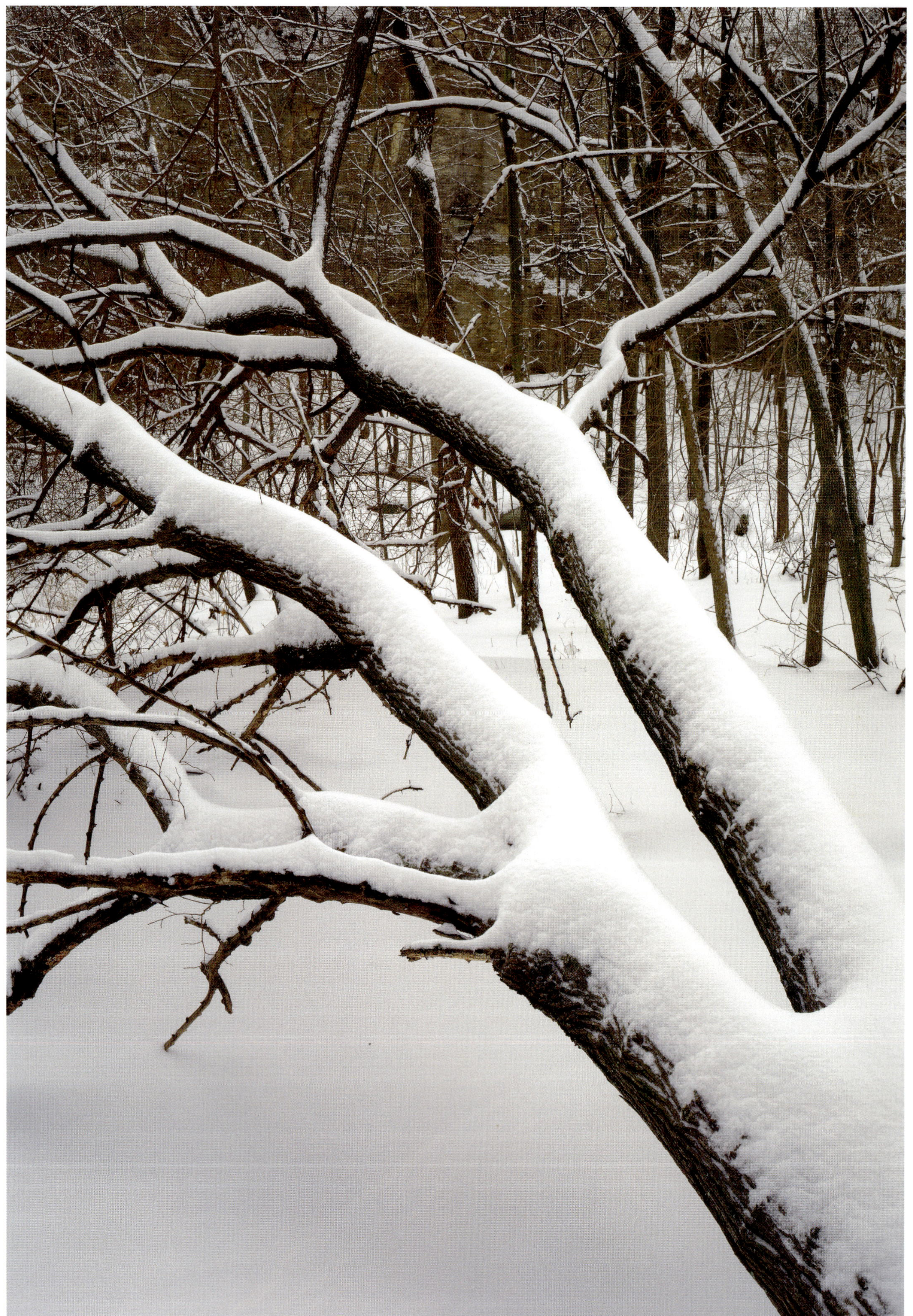

THIS PAGE:

Deciduous trees in snow: Bell Smith Springs Recreation Area, Shawnee National Forest, Pope County *(Shawnee Hills Section, Interior Low Plateaus Province)*

A gentle, damp snow with little accompanying wind can accumulate on bare branches. *January 1991*

OPPOSITE PAGE:

Leaves floating on pond beneath overarching beech: Dixon Springs State Park, Pope County *(Shawnee Hills Section, Interior Low Plateaus Province)*

In the nineteenth century, Dixon Springs was a spa centered on its seven springs of mineral water. The springs exploit a fault that extends through the 800-acre park, ten miles west of Golconda. *October 2001*

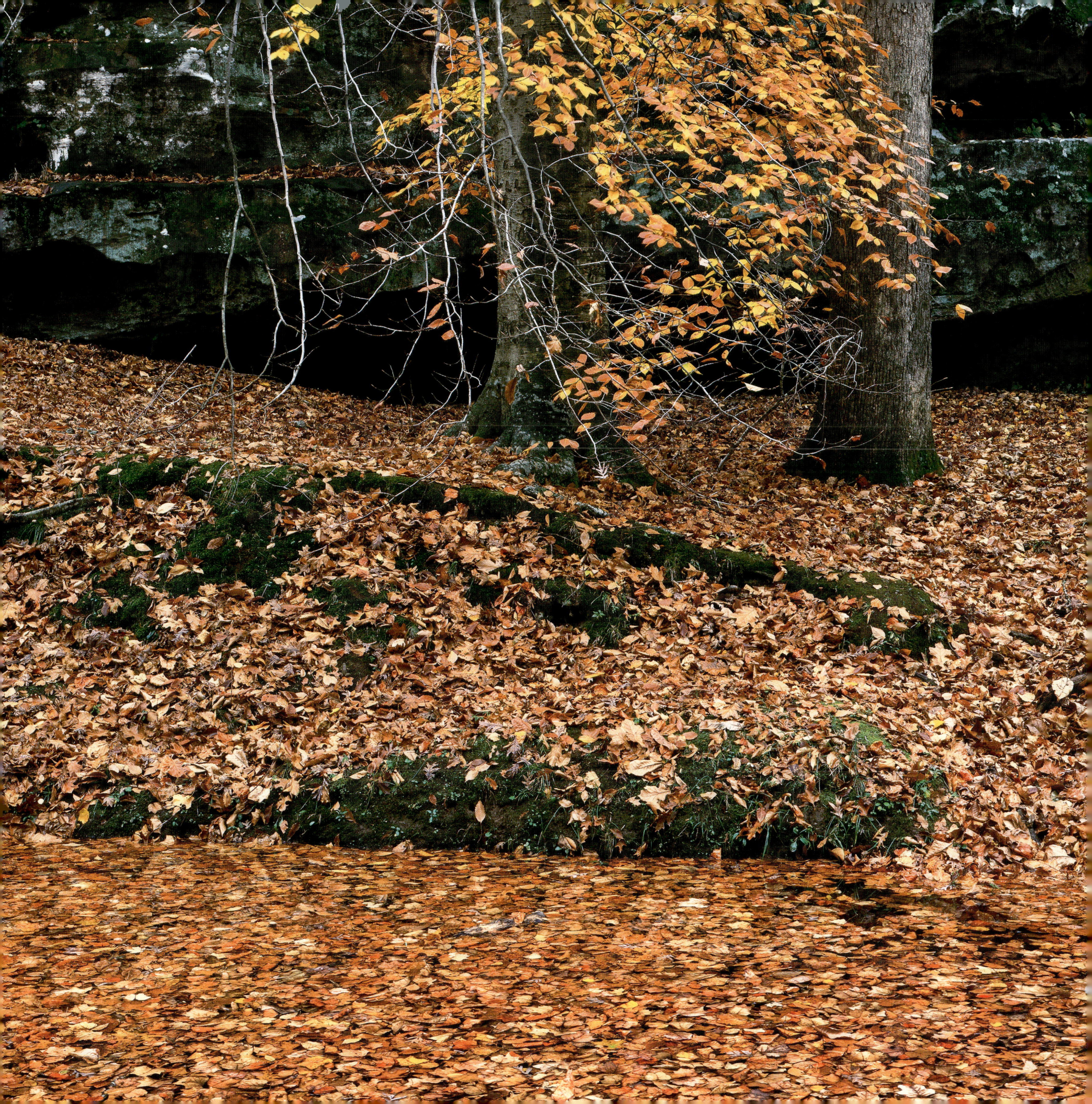

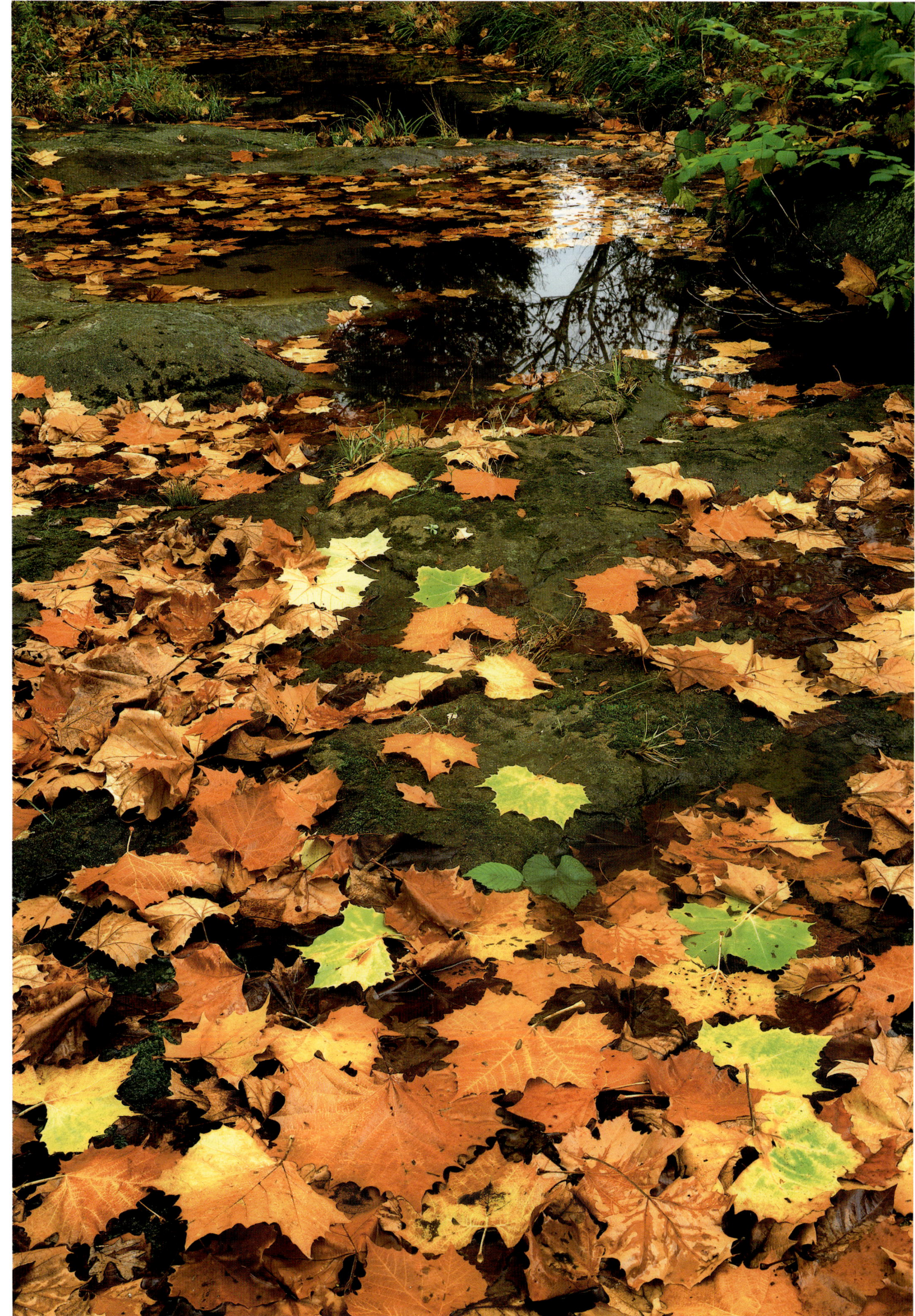

THIS PAGE:

Leaves floating on pond: Dixon Springs State Park, Pope County *(Shawnee Hills Section, Interior Low Plateaus Province)*
October 2001

OPPOSITE PAGE:

Dwarf larkspur *(Delphinium tricorne)*: LaRue Pine Hills Ecological Area, Union County *(Shawnee Hills Section, Interior Low Plateaus Province)*
The 2,500-acre LaRue-Pine Hills Ecological Area located in Union and Jackson Counties southeast of the Big Muddy Rievr is a national natural landmark on account of its floral and faunal richness. The limestone substrate supports over a thousand plant species, forty of which are rare, such as the dwarf larkspur. Habitats include steep bluffs, mesic and dry forests, hilltop prairies, bottomland swamp forests, and open ponds. Limestone cliffs rise up hundreds of feet from the bottomland swamp forests that border the Mississippi River. These cliffs provide over-wintering habitat for the region's venomous snake fauna, including the cottonmouth and timber rattlesnake. *April 1995*

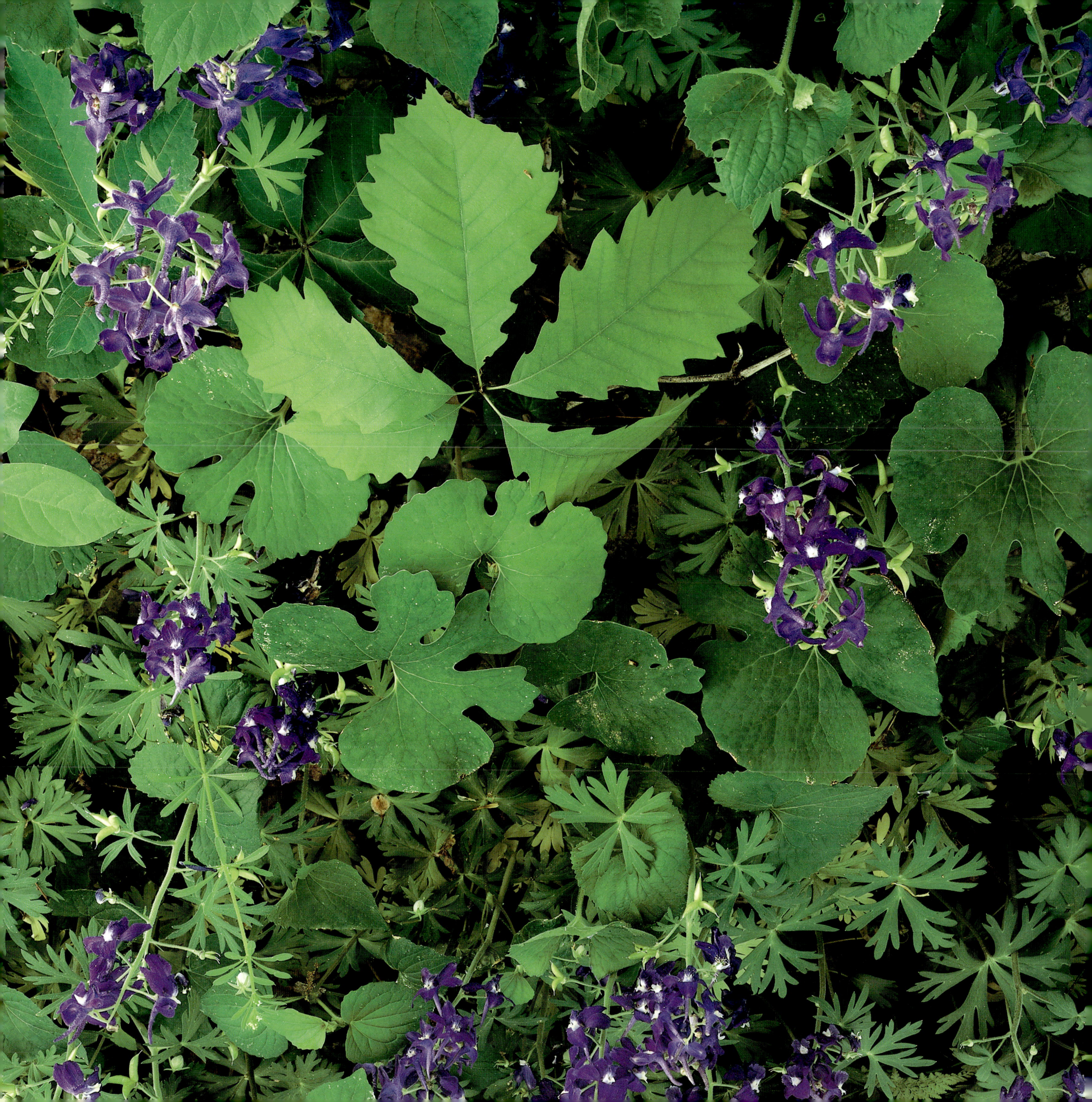

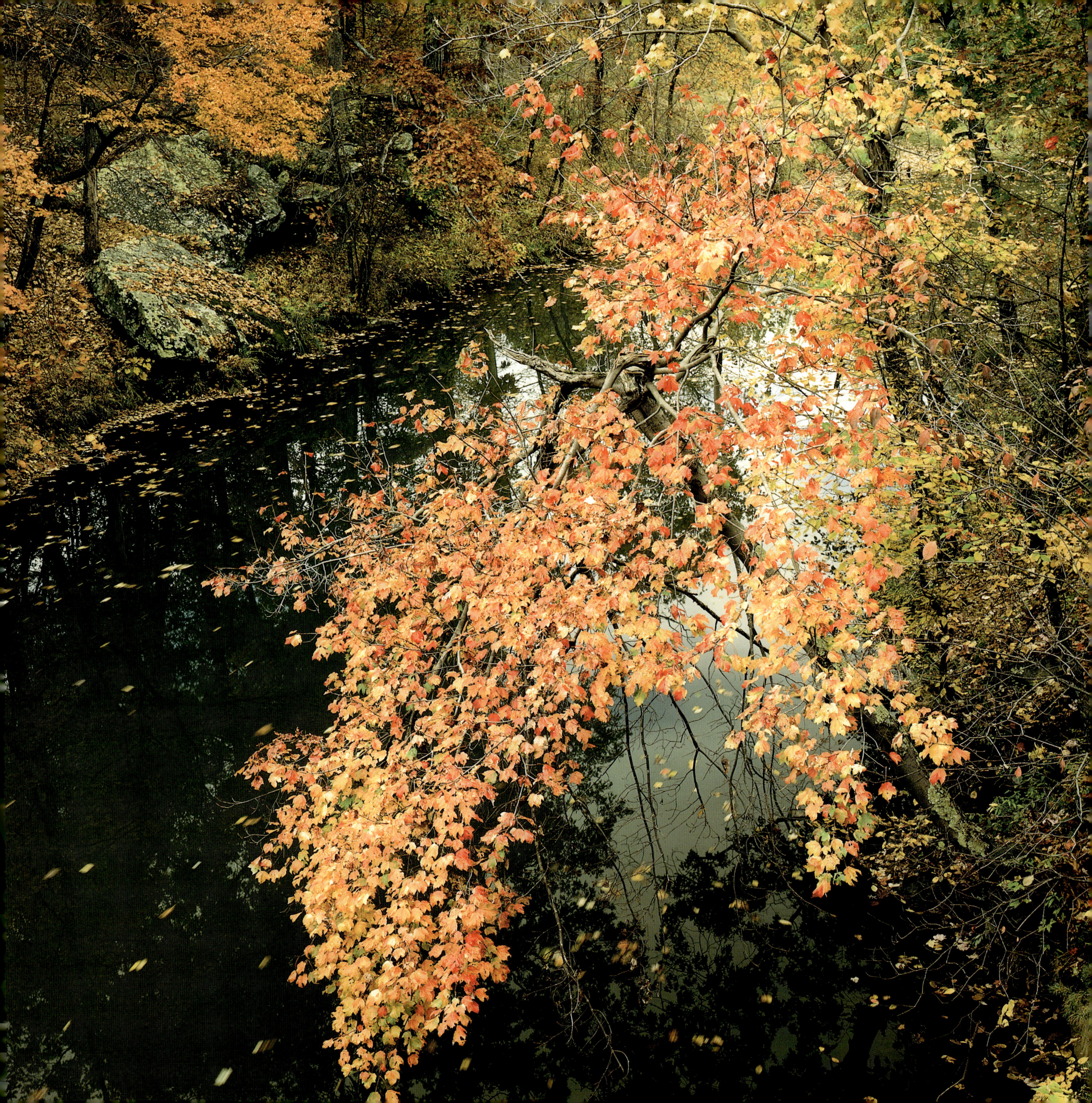

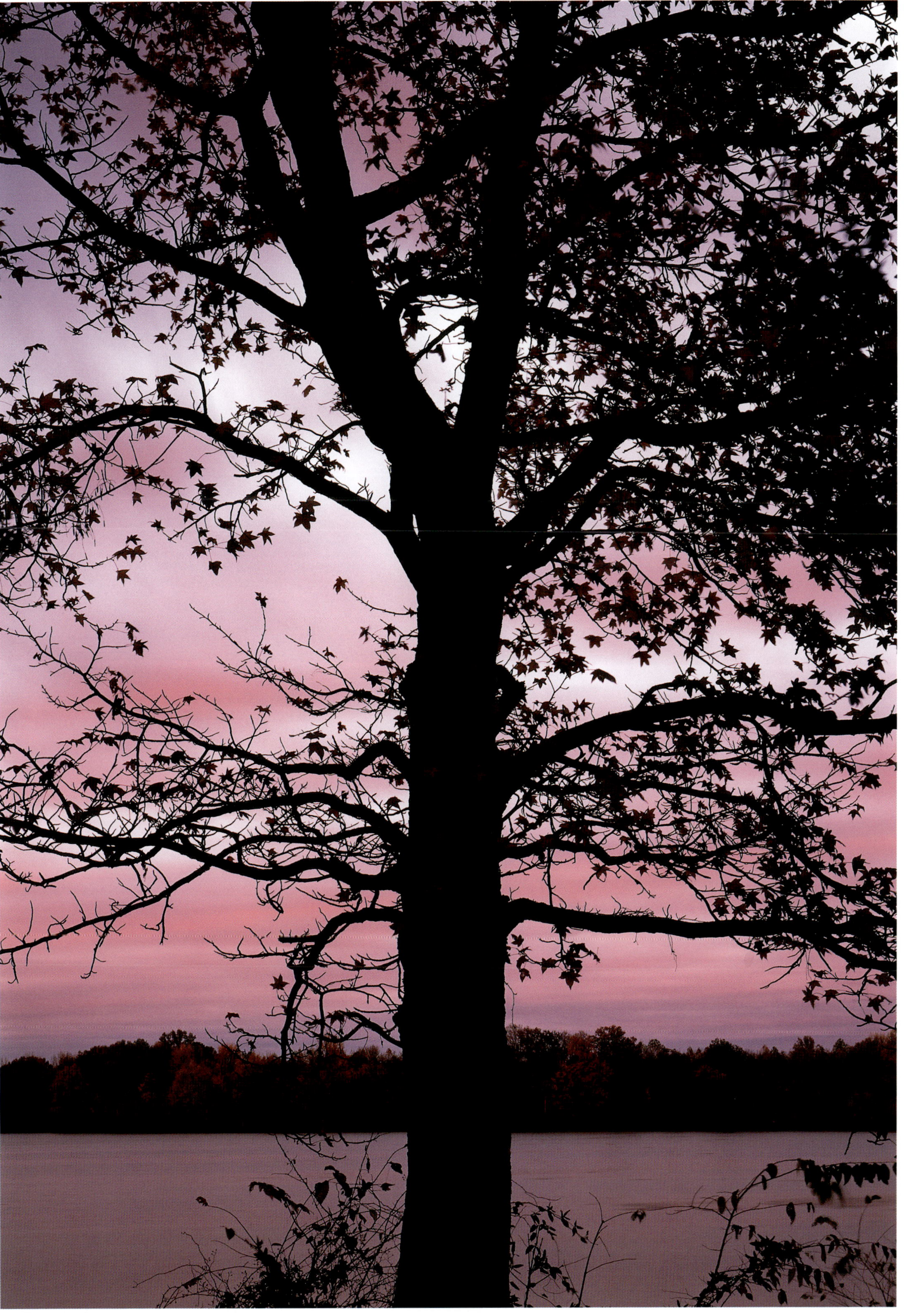

OPPOSITE PAGE:

Maple tree in fall foliage beside pond by Devils Kitchen Lake: Crab Orchard National Wildlife Refuge, Williamson County *(Shawnee Hills Section, Interior Low Plateaus Province)*
Crab Orchard National Wildlife Refuge is unique among national refuges in hosting industrial operations. The refuge's 43,878 acres were transferred to the public in 1947 on that stipulation by the War Department, which had operated the Illinois Ordnance Plant there during the war. The other mandates of the wildlife refuge are more typical of national lands: recreational use, agricultural development, and wildlife conservation. The generally flat terrain yields to forested hills in the south. Half of the refuge is a wildlife sanctuary and provides a major waterfowl stop along the Mississippi Flyway. Five thousand acres are cropland. Three manmade lakes—Crab Orchard, Devils Kitchen, and Little Grassy Lakes—total 8,700 acres in area and teem with fish. Devils Kitchen Lake has some of the best-quality water in Illinois, which reaches a depth of ninety feet. On a clear day, one can see to twenty feet. Thanks to the clarity of the water, sunlight is able support photosynthesis at cool depths in the lake, thereby providing adequate oxygen levels for rainbow trout. Devils Kitchen Lake is one of Illinois's few lakes with rainbow trout. *October 1986*

THIS PAGE:

Sweetgum along Crab Orchard Lake: Crab Orchard National Wildlife Refuge, Williamson County *(Shawnee Hills Section, Interior Low Plateaus Province)*
With 7,000 acres and a 127-mile shoreline, Crab Orchard Lake is easily the biggest of the three manmade lakes in Crab Orchard National Wildlife Refuge. Crab Orchard Lake attracts motor-boaters, sailors, water-skiers, swimmers, and anglers. Crab Orchard Lake is noted for its superior stock of largemouth and white bass. The lake also contains the standard regional fare—crappie, flathead and channel catfish, and bluegill. *October 2001*

OPPOSITE PAGE:

Bald cypress, Horseshoe Lake: Horseshoe Lake Conservation Area, Alexander County *(Coastal Plain Province)*

Horseshoe Lake is an oxbow lake, a relict meander of the Mississippi River whose neck was cut off in the west. The lake is subject to periodic flooding and silt deposition by both the Mississippi and Cache Rivers, reduced since 1929 by a spillway. Backwater from the flooding Mississippi River has contributed to natural restocking of the lake's fish populations, which include bluegill, crappie, channel catfish, largemouth bass, carp, buffalo, gar, and bowfin. Horseshoe Lake anglers developed a fishing technique called "bucktailing" to offset the water depth. Canada geese have wintered at Horseshoe Like since 1928 when the first thousand birds arrived. Sixty years later, populations rose to 300,000 geese. Lately, however, changes in land-use patterns and wintertime temperatures have reduced the count to 75,000 birds. *October 1986*

4 COASTAL PLAIN PROVINCE

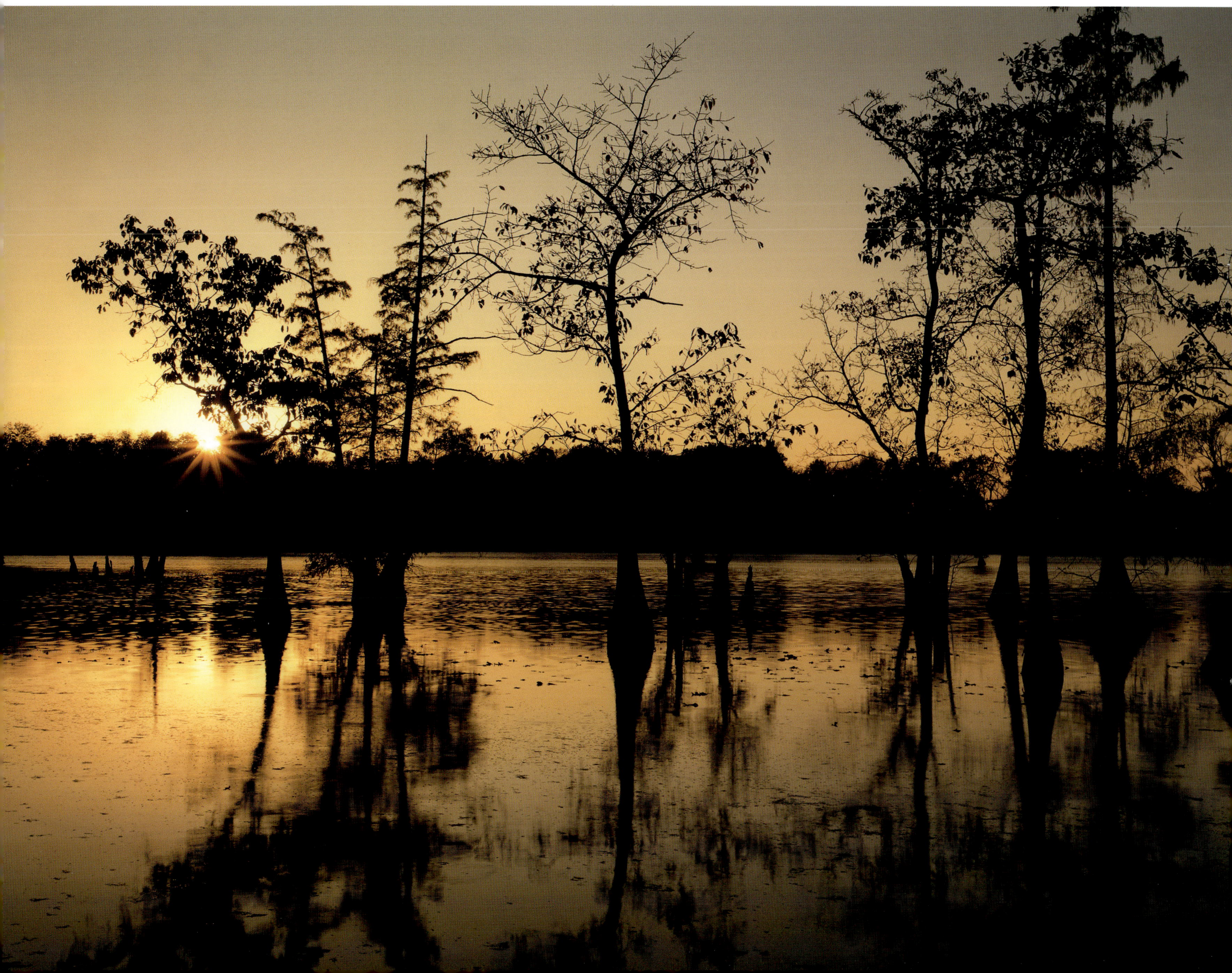

4
COASTAL PLAIN PROVINCE

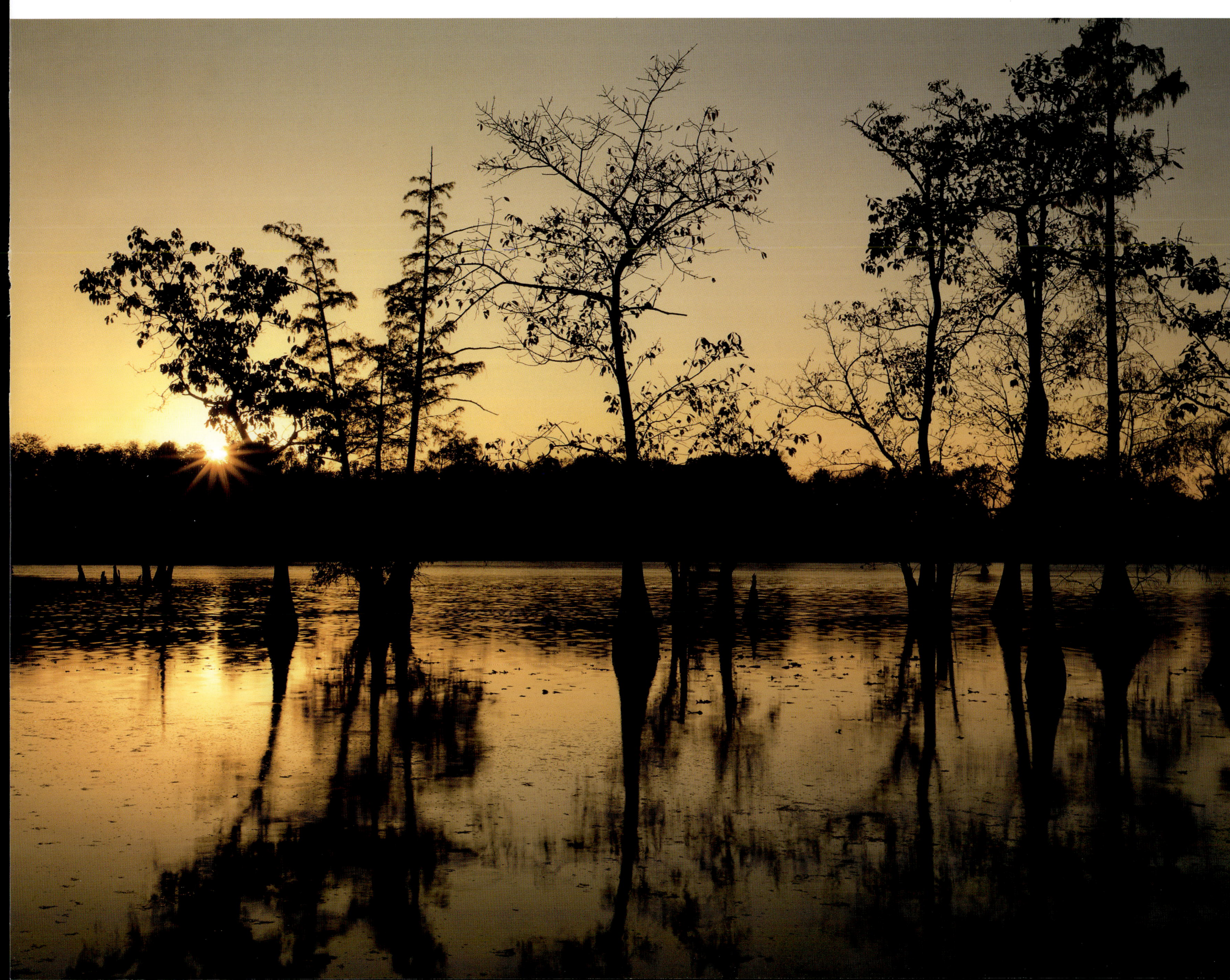

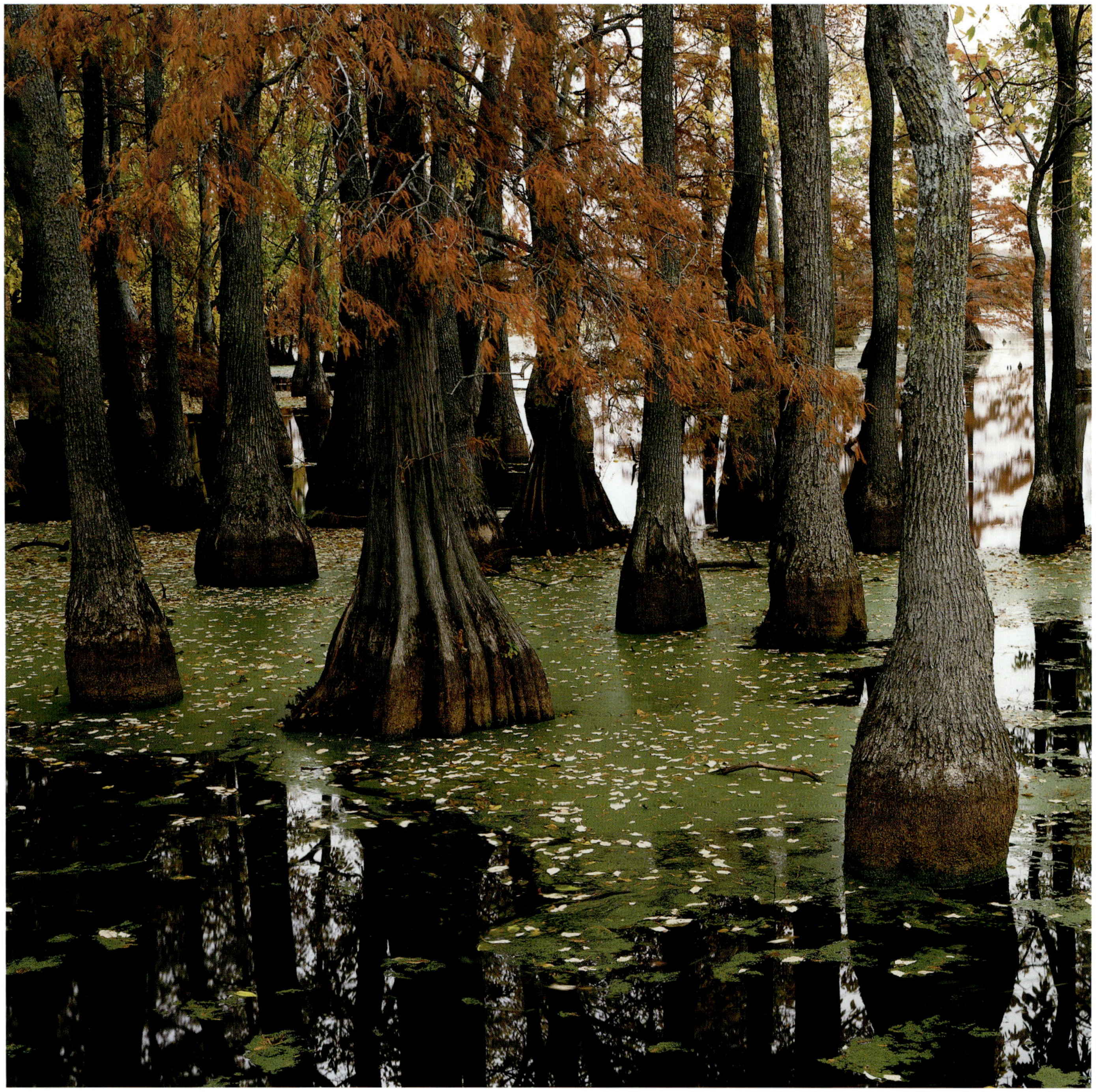

THIS PAGE ABOVE:

Tupelo gum, Horseshoe Lake: Horseshoe Lake Conservation Area, Alexander County *(Coastal Plain Province)*

Tupelo gum is at the northern limit of its range at the southern tip of Illinois. Tupelo gum grows in cypress swamps along the Atlantic coastal plain from Virginia to Texas, including the plain's Mississippi embayment which projects northward as far as Illinois's Little Egypt. Like the bald cypress and other aquatic trees, tupelo gum has a flaring buttressed base and wide-spreading roots. Attaining 100 feet in height and 4 feet in diameter, it has a long clear bole topped by a narrow crown of short spreading branches and large oval leaves. The exceptionally light wood of its swollen butts is used as floats for fish nets. *October 1987*

OPPOSITE PAGE:

Bald cypress and duckweed, Heron Pond: Little Black Slough Unit, Cache River State Natural Area, Johnson County *(Coastal Plain Province)*

Little Black Slough is an administrative unit of the Cache River State Natural Area. Overlooked on the north by the low ridges of the Lesser Shawnee Hills, the Little Black Slough Unit straddles the Upper Cache River across the floodplain of the ancestral Ohio River, which was formed prior to the diversion of the modern Ohio River southward across the topographic divide at Bay City in southern Pope County. Massive old cypress trees, some exceeding forty feet in buttress diameter and a thousand years in age, are found in abundance in the 12,956-acre Cache River State Natural Area. Nestled deep within the shadowy bottomland forests of the Little Black Slough Unit is Heron Pond, a national natural landmark. A boardwalk affords the visitor admission into the seclusion of this primeval cypress swamp, disturbed only by the bird-like voices of tree frogs perched high above in the cypress branches. During the growing season, the cypress trunks rise like cathedral pillars from a floating carpet of brilliant emerald duckweed. *May 1992*

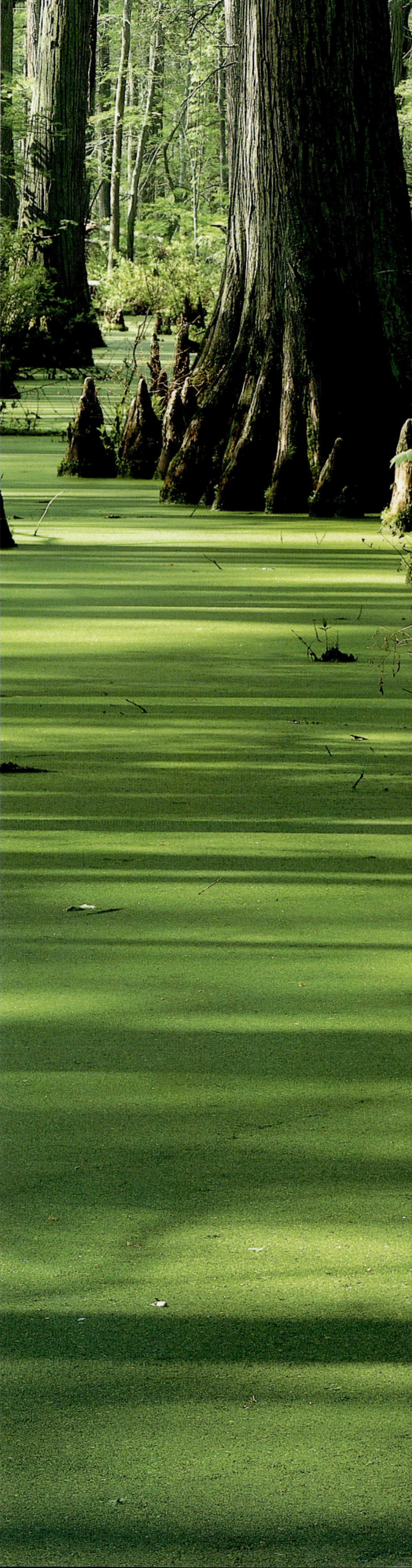

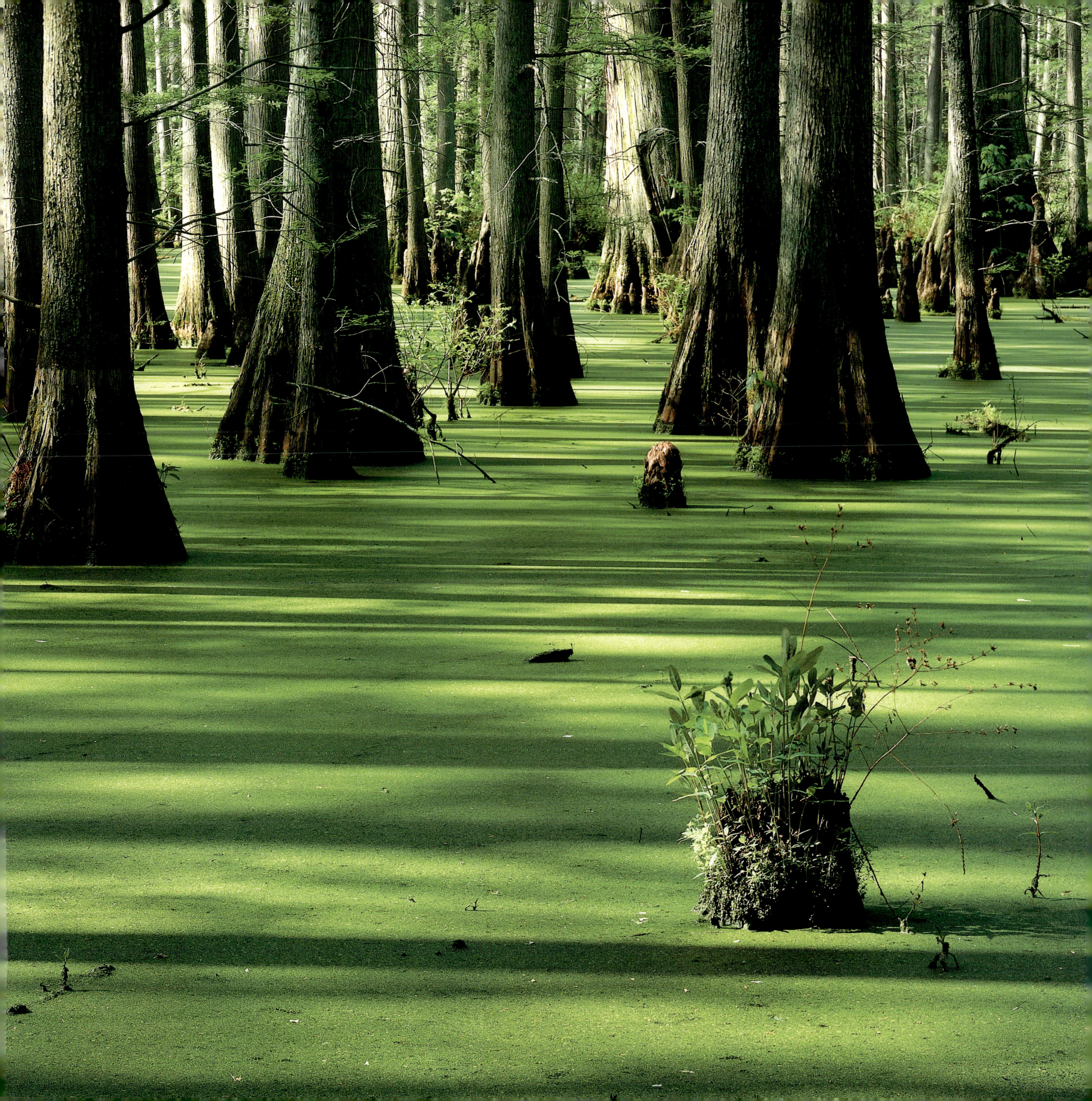